The Life OF THE *Prophet Muḥammad*

VOLUME I

The Center for Muslim Contribution to Civilization

The Life OF THE *Prophet Muḥammad*

VOLUME I

Al-Sīra al-Nabawiyya

Ibn Kathīr

Translated by Professor Trevor Le Gassick

Reviewed by Dr Ahmed Fareed

Garnet
PUBLISHING

The Life of the Prophet Muḥammad
Volume I

Published by
Garnet Publishing Limited
8 Southern Court
South Street
Reading
RG1 4QS
UK

ISBN 1 85964 142 3

First Edition 2000
Reprinted 2002

British Library Cataloguing-in-Publication Data
A catalogue record for this book is available from the British Library

Printed in Lebanon

CONTENTS

In the Name of God, the Beneficent, the Merciful

FOREWORD

THE interrelationship and interaction of human cultures and civilizations has made the contributions of each the common heritage of men in all ages and all places. Early Muslim scholars were able to communicate with their Western counterparts through contacts made during the Crusades; at Muslim universities and centres of learning in Muslim Spain (al-Andalus, or Andalusia) and Sicily to which many European students went for education; and at the universities and centres of learning in Europe itself (such as Salerno, Padua, Montpellier, Paris, and Oxford), where Islamic works were taught in Latin translations. Among the Muslim scholars well-known in the centres of learning throughout the world were al-Rāzī (Rhazes), Ibn Sīnā (Avicenna), Ibn Rushd (Averroes), al Khwārizmī and Ibn Khaldūn. Muslim scholars such as these and others produced original works in many fields. Many of them possessed encyclopaedic knowledge and distinguished themselves in many disparate fields of knowledge.

In view of this, the Center for Muslim Contribution to Civilization was established in order to acquaint non-Muslims with the contributions Islam has given to human civilization as a whole. The Great Books of Islamic Civilization Project attempts to cover the first 800 years of Islam, or what may be called Islam's Classical Period. This project aims at making available in English a wide selection of works representative of Islamic civilization in all its diversity. It is made up of translations of original Arabic works that were produced in the formative centuries of Islam, and is meant to serve the needs of a potentially large readership. Not only the specialist and scholar, but the non-specialist with an interest in Islam and its cultural heritage will be able to benefit from the series. Together, the works should serve as a rich source for the study of the early periods of Islamic thought.

In selecting the books for the series, the Center took into account all major areas of Islamic intellectual pursuit that could be represented. Thus the series includes works not only on better-known subjects such as law, theology, jurisprudence, history and politics, but also on subjects such as literature, medicine, astronomy, optics and geography. The specific criteria used to select individual books were these: that a book should give a faithful and comprehensive account of its field; and that it should be an authoritative source. The reader thus has at his disposal virtually a whole library of informative and enlightening works.

Each book in the series has been translated by a qualified scholar and reviewed by another expert. While the style of one translation will naturally differ from another, the translators have endeavoured, to the extent it was possible, to make the works accessible to the common reader. As a rule, the use of footnotes has been kept to a minimum, though a more extensive use of them was necessitated in some cases.

This series is presented in the hope that it will contribute to a greater understanding in the West of the cultural and intellectual heritage of Islam and will therefore provide an important means towards greater understanding of today's world.

May God Help Us!

Muhammad bin Hamad Al-Thani
Chairman of the Board of Trustees

ABOUT THIS SERIES

THIS series of Arabic works, made available in English translation, represents an outstanding selection of important Islamic studies in a variety of fields of knowledge. The works selected for inclusion in this series meet specific criteria. They are recognized by Muslim scholars as being early and important in their fields, as works whose importance is broadly recognized by international scholars, and as having had a genuinely significant impact on the development of human culture.

Readers will therefore see that this series includes a variety of works in the purely Islamic sciences, such as Qurʾān, *ḥadīth*, theology, prophetic traditions (*sunna*), and jurisprudence (*fiqh*). Also represented will be books by Muslim scientists on medicine, astronomy, geography, physics, chemistry, horticulture, and other fields.

The work of translating these texts has been entrusted to a group of professors in the Islamic and Western worlds who are recognized authorities in their fields. It has been deemed appropriate, in order to ensure accuracy and fluency, that two persons, one with Arabic as his mother tongue and another with English as his mother tongue, should participate together in the translation and revision of each text.

This series is distinguished from other similar intercultural projects by its distinctive objectives and methodology. These works will fill a genuine gap in the library of human thought. They will prove extremely useful to all those with an interest in Islamic culture, its interaction with Western thought, and its impact on culture throughout the world. They will, it is hoped, fulfil an important rôle in enhancing world understanding at a time when there is such evident and urgent need for the development of peaceful coexistence.

This series is published by the Center for Muslim Contribution to Civilization, which serves as a research centre under the patronage of H.H. Sheikh Hamad bin Khalifa al-Thani, Amir of Qatar. It is directed by a Board of Trustees chaired by H.E. Sheikh Muhammad bin Hamad al-Thani, the former Minister of Education of Qatar. The Board is comprised of a group of prominent scholars. These include H.E. Dr Abul-Wafa al-Taftazani*, Deputy Rector of Cairo University, and Dr Yusuf al-Qaradhawi, Director of the Sira and Sunna Research Center. At its inception the Center was directed by the late Dr Mohammad Ibrahim Kazim, former Rector of Qatar University, who established its initial objectives.

The Center was until recently directed by Dr Kamal Nagi, the Foreign Cultural Relations Advisor of the Ministry of Education of Qatar. He was assisted by a

* Died 1994, may Allāh have mercy on him.

Board comprising a number of academicians of Qatar University, in addition to a consultative committee chaired by Dr Ezzeddin Ibrahim, former Rector of the University of the United Arab Emirates. A further committee acting on behalf of the Center has been the prominent university professors who act under the chairmanship of Dr Raji Rammuny, Professor of Arabic at the University of Michigan. This committee is charged with making known, in Europe and in America, the books selected for translation, and in selecting and enlisting properly qualified university professors, orientalists and students of Islamic studies to undertake the work of translation and revision, as well as overseeing the publication process.

CENTER FOR MUSLIM CONTRIBUTION TO CIVILIZATION

INTRODUCTION

THE work at hand in its original Arabic is, in a sense, the product of two minds: the author himself, Abū al-Fidā' ʿImād al-Dīn Ismāʿīl b. ʿUmar b. Kathīr,[1] and, to a lesser extent, its editor, Muṣṭafā ʿAbd al-Wāḥid. In his introduction to the Arabic, ʿAbd al-Wāḥid points out that this work is in fact the culmination of a search for a biography of the Prophet Muḥammad to which Ibn Kathīr makes reference in his celebrated exegesis of the Qur'ān. There is, however, no extant copy of any such independent biographical study traceable to Ibn Kathīr. That such a study did exist is questionable, notwithstanding Ibn Kathīr's own allusion thereto. Given the unavailability of this particular work, ʿAbd al-Wāḥid offers the theory that the biography in question is none other than that which appears in Ibn Kathīr's chief work, his opus on history, the *al-Bidāya wa al-Nihāya*.[2] He argues that the *sīra* section of the latter work is so comprehensive in its analysis of the life and times of the Prophet Muḥammad as to almost obviate the need for any independent study of the same topic. The biography at hand, therefore, is the same as found in the *al-Bidāya*. Nevertheless, ʿAbd al-Wāḥid must be commended for the not inconsiderable task of editing and publishing this particular section as an independent unit, and appropriately titling it *al-Sīra al-Nabawiyya li Ibn Kathīr*.

Ibn Kathīr, whose ancestors are said to have been from Iraq, was himself born around the year 1313 CE/700 AH in the Boesra district of eastern Damascus. He died 74 years later, shortly after suffering a total loss of vision. He counts as his tutors such illustrious personages as the eminent historian Shams al-Dīn al-Dhahabī, the Mālikī jurist Abū Mūsā al-Qarāfī, and the celebrated Damascene polemicist and jurist Ibn Taymiyya al-Ḥarrānī.

Ibn Kathīr's was an era of the great political and social upheavals that posed many challenges to the Muslim world at large, and in particular, to its scholars. What with the scourge of the Tartars threatening the very existence of Islam as a socio-political entity from the outside and the sectarian and ethnic strife created by the Mamluk revolution doing much the same from within, Ibn Kathīr and his

1. According to R. Y. Curtis, *Authoritative Interpretation of Classical Islamic Tafsīr: Critical Analysis of Ibn Kathīr's Tafsīr al-Qur'ān al-ʿAẓīm* (unpublished dissertation, Ann Arbor: University of Michigan, 1989) (21), classical bibliographers have cited Ibn Kathīr's name in more than one way. Al-Dhahabī for instance, in the supplement to his bibliography, *Dhayl Tadhkirat al-Ḥuffāẓ*, gives Ibn Kathīr's name as Ismāʿīl b. ʿUmar b. Kathīr b. Ḍaw b. Kathīr b. Zarʿ. Other versions have been given, however, such as appear in al-Ziriklī's *al-Aʿlām* (1: 320) and ʿUmar Riḍā Kahhāla's *Muʿjam al-Mu'allifīn* (1: 28).

2. According to C. Brockelman in his *Geschichte der Arabischen Literatur* ii. 49, this historical work of Ibn Kathīr is itself based on al-Birzālī's chronicle. For more information see also, Ibn Ḥadjar al-Asqalānī, *al-Durar al-Kāmina* (Cod. Vienna, no. 1172).

colleagues, no doubt, had huge challenges with which to contend. In addition, the unrelenting pestilence and drought that had plagued the Levant and areas east thereof, made their burden all the more unwieldy. He died in 1387 CE/775 AH and lies buried in Damascus next to his master, Ibn Taymiyyah. He was mourned by his wife Zaynab, the daughter of his teacher, al-Mizzī, who, according to some reports, was an accomplished scholar in her own right. She bore him four sons, one of whom succeeded his father to the post of principal of the teaching academy al-Madrasa al-Ṣāliḥiyya.[3]

Ibn Kathīr, true to the pre-eminent tendencies of the academic milieu within which he functioned, brings to his study of the Prophet of Islam the method of the *muḥaddith*, the scholar of *ḥadīth* traditions, more assiduously than he does that of the traditional historian. In doing so, however, he has, I believe, substantially succeeded in combining two of the three sources available for the pursuit of the historical Muḥammad: the *ḥadīth* literature and the *sīra*; the Qurʾān, being the third such source, features less prominently, if not altogether rarely, in his study. Given the very extensive usage of *ḥadīth* material in this particular work, a word about the classical nature of such material and its contemporaneous validity would be appropriate at this point.

Early historical studies of Muslim society and culture, as A. A. Duri points out, "followed broadly two lines that were distinct from each other – that of *ḥadīth*, and that of the tribes (i.e. the *ayyām* anecdotes as narrated by the *akhbārīs* and the *ruwāt*), which is in a sense a continuation of pre-Islamic activities. "These two lines", he explains, "reflect the two major currents in early Islamic society – the Islamic and the tribal lines which influenced all aspects of life."[4] According to Muslim tradition, the learning and transmission of the sayings and actions of Muḥammad, his tacit approvals and disapprovals of the actions of others, and his general behaviour had religious significance second only to that of the Qurʾān. To that end Muslim scholars began the collection of such data as was related to the Prophet and his era even while he was still alive. At first, the system of oral retention was popular, but by the middle of the first century of the Muslim era, written compilations of *ḥadīth* traditions began to appear. By the end of the third quarter of that century, "a pattern was fixed for the learning and teaching of the *ḥadīth* which flourished in the second and third centuries."[5] A system of sorts for verifying the authenticity of such prophetic traditions was allegedly extant from the earliest of times – albeit in a

3. Curtis, 23.

4. Professor Duri's article is in large measure an elucidation of what he calls "the tribal type of history". See in this regard 'The Iraq School of History to the Ninth Century', in *Historians of the Middle East*, ed. B. Lewis and P. M. Holt (Oxford University Press, 1962).

5. M. M. Azami, *Studies in Early Hadith Literature* (Indianapolis: American Trust Publications, 1983), 186,

rather rudimentary manner. That system, however, was neither systematized nor rigorously applied until the advent of the civil wars (*fitna*), whereupon sources were no longer regarded, prima facie, as trustworthy, but were instead increasingly scrutinized to establish authenticity. Thus evolved the elaborate *isnād* system where every *ḥadīth* was scrutinized from two perspectives: the text (*matn*) containing the information transmitted as such, and the chain of transmitters (*sanad*) giving the names of all those responsible for transmitting such information from the Prophet himself.

As indicated earlier, Ibn Kathīr's method in this particular work is more that of the *ḥadīth* scholars than it is of the historian; al-Bukhārī, Muslim and more so, al-Baihaqī, Aḥmad b. Ḥanbal, and Abū Nuʿaim thus feature more prominently as sources for his biography than do historians such as Ibn Isḥāq, Ibn Hishām or Tabarī. But, as ʿAbd al-Wāḥid rightly points out, Ibn Kathīr, on occasion, is not averse to using some rather obscure historical works, some even that are no longer extant: the rare historical tractate of Mūsā b. Uqba, and the *al-Rawḍ al-Anf* of al-Suhaylī are examples thereof.

True to tradition, if not quite on the same scale as, for instance, Ibn Hishām, are Ibn Kathīr's copious citations of poetry, almost all of which seem to have been taken from Muḥammad b. Ishaq's biography of the Prophet. The poems deal with a variety of themes and styles: there is, for instance, the unmistakable sarcasm of Kaʿab b. Zuhayr as reflected in his lampooning of the Prophet, followed by his subsequent retraction and apology as in the much celebrated poem, *Bānut Suʿād*; there is also the occasional celebration of pre-Islamic Arabian chivalry, as in the haunting ode of Abū al-Bakhtarī b. Hishām, when he speaks so movingly of his virtual self-immolation for the love of a friend. Then, of course, there are the evocative panegyrics of Ḥassān b. Thābit in defence of Islam, its Prophet, and his Companions.

Ibn Kathīr, oddly enough for someone who has plumbed the depths of *ḥadīth* methodology, frequently paraphrases, not just the many references to scholars such as Ibn Ishāq, but also, at times, the very *ḥadīth* material he so often quotes. He thus takes almost the same liberties with such material as he does with works on history, and the reader, particularly of the Arabic text, sometimes searches in vain for all but the gist of the traditions that he ascribes to, say, the *saḥīḥ* of Bukhārī or that of Muslim. ʿAbd al-Wāḥid offers two possible reasons for this anomaly; the one I believe to be somewhat more plausible than the other. It may well be, he suggests, that Ibn Kathīr was simply quoting from memory, seeing no need for any further textual verification, or it may also be that he is, in fact, using sources unavailable to us today. This latter hypothesis is, I believe, somewhat disingenuous for it requires, amongst other things, that Ibn Kathīr possessed not one, but an entire set of *ḥadīth* works unique to his library alone!

The text itself suffers from a singular lack of the literary cadence that makes the historical works of al-Ṭabarī, for instance, more of a pleasure to read. This seems to result from Ibn Kathīr's efforts to present an authentic description of the life and times of the Prophet of Islam, and to submit such data as is found in the popular biographical works to the scrutiny of *ḥadīth* literature. The flow of his text is, without question, a casualty of this exercise. But, as has been pointed out by a scholar of the Bible, "If we read biblical narrative (or in this case the *sīra* material) as a story, we abandon its historical truth. If we read it as literature, we will often find literary art in it, but this art takes us further from truth."[6] Not that the method of Ibn Kathīr is altogether without its redeeming features: it certainly provides useful information to scholars, particularly those of the traditional schools, who would prefer to have the classical sources for *sīra* studies close at hand.

The contents of works such as Ibn Kathīr's *sīra* are today regarded by many scholars of Islam as largely proto-historical, focusing, that is, on an era whose source documentation falls short of contemporary historiographical standards. It is, some say, the stuff of myth and legend, entwined in places with real historical data. For modern historians of Islam and the Middle East such as Maxime Rodinson, Patricia Crone et al., *sīra* material contains, in the first instance, virtually "nothing of which we can say for certain that it incontestably dates back to the time of the Prophet".[7] And so, "when doing research about the life and work of the Prophet Muḥammad", Rudi Paret warns, "we on principle distrust the traditional statement and explanation of facts given by later generations, in so far as they cannot be verified by internal evidence or in some other way."[8]

In addition, the work at hand may be seen by some to be no more than the product of one who had a variety of interests in the topic: one who was, at one and the same time, a historian, a scribe of "sacred biography", and also a devotee; the results of an endeavour such as Ibn Kathīr's, therefore, risk being perceived as less than the product of dispassionate scholarship.[9]

This critical approach to Islamic historiography emerged gradually in the 18th and 19th centuries. It was, understandably, only a matter of time before Albert Schweitzer's "quest of the historical Christ" would be appropriated by

6. See Robin L. Fox, *The Unauthorized Version: Truth and Fiction in the Bible* (New York: Alfred A. Knopf, 1992).

7. This particular statement appears in the introduction to Maxime Rodinson's own biography of the Prophet. See Maxime Rodinson, *Mohammed*. Trans. Anne Carter (London, 1971).

8. For the full text of this article see R. Paret, "Recent European Research on the Life and Work of Prophet Muhammad", *Journal of the Pakistan Historical Society*, Karachi, 1958.

9. See in this regard G. D. Newby, *The Making of the Last Prophet: A Reconstruction of the Earliest Biography of Muhammad* (Columbia: University of Southern California Press, 1989).

scholars of Islamic history in their search of the demythologized Muḥammad; after all, this kind of appropriation of the analytical tools indigenous to studies of Christianity for the unravelling of the Islamic historical experience has become almost a convention in Islamic and Middle Eastern studies. Yet the entire process is, I believe, fraught with questionable hypotheses, broad generalizations and a certain disregard for the spatio-temporal factors that shape ostensibly similar events. The application of New Testament heuristic tools such as Form and Redaction criticism to the corpus of information pertaining to the *sīra* seems to betray a casual disregard for the *Sitz im Leben* of that very corpus. The life and work of Jesus is clearly different from that of Muḥammad; the former's mission – if it can be described as such – is, for example, singularly devoid of the political and socio-economic objectives that informed that of the latter. It is, therefore, hardly surprising, as F. E. Peters in his recent article "The Quest of the Historical Muhammad" points out, that "even though a great deal of effort has been invested in research into the life and times of Muḥammad, the results do not seem at all comparable to those achieved in research on Jesus, and the reasons are not at all clear."[10]

Ever since Gustav Weil presented his *Mohammad der Prophet, sein Leben und seine Lehre* in 1843, scholars have endeavoured to unravel the historical Muḥammad using a variety of tools and strategems. Initially the material offered by Muslim historians such as Ibn Ishāq, Ibn Hishām and more importantly, al-Ṭabarī was used almost unquestioningly by Christian scholars who, as Holt characterizes them, belonged mainly to "holy orders".[11] Their primary purpose, it would seem, was to provide a spirited defence of Christian theology and dogma against the claims of Islam and its adherents. The polemics that ensued were, in the main, reflective of the attitude that there was "not any rational inducement in all (that Muslims) believe or practice; insomuch that common sense must be discarded in order to embrace their system."[12] As for Muḥammad, he was for many in that era "so coarse and barbarous an imposter, that there is not a man, who does not or cannot perceive plainly his cheat and corruption."[13] Humphrey Prideaux, the 17th-century lecturer in Hebrew at Oxford, captured rather succinctly the disposition of scholars *vis-à-vis* the study of Muḥammad, in the rather long-winded title of his work, *The true nature of imposture fully display'd in the life of Mahomet. With a discourse annex'd*

10. F. E. Peters, "The Quest of the Historical Muhammad", in *International Journal of Middle East Studies* 23 (19912), 291–315.

11. See P. M. Holt, "The Treatment of Arab Historians by Prideaux, Ockley, and Sale", in *Historians of the Middle East*, ed. B. Lewis and P. M. Holt (Oxford University Press, 1962), 290–302.

12. Ibid., 300.

13. Ibid., 300.

for the vindication of Christianity from this charge. Offered to the consideration of the Deists of the present age.[14] Later Simon Ockley, the somewhat less acerbic and brusque vicar of Swavesey in Cambridgeshire, authored *The History of the Saracens*, a "much more solid contribution to historical knowledge" as Holt puts it, but one that none the less did "not fail to follow common form by stigmatizing Muḥammad in his first line, as 'the great Imposter' and then describing the Arab conquests as 'that grievous calamity'."[15] The liberalism that swept across Europe in the 18th century helped create a relatively less hostile attitude among European scholars towards Islam and its leader. We thus find during that era scholars such as Henri de Boulainvillier emerging. Boulainvillier, his theological affinities notwithstanding, assumed a decidedly more conciliatory tone in his biography of Muḥammad, *La vie de Mahomet*. For him, Christianity is undoubtedly superior to Islam but he is, none the less, quite charitable in his evaluation of his subject, and says: "With respect to the essential doctrines of religion, all that (Muḥammad) has laid down is true; but he has not laid down all that is true; and that is the whole difference between our religion and his."[16]

The quest itself began in earnest in the writings of the Belgian Jesuit, Henri Lammens. Whereas Theodor Noeldeke, prior to him, had largely failed in his attempts to unravel "the historical person of Muhammad", Lammens plodded on, and succeeded to some extent, in demonstrating "the possibility of the critical analysis of the *sīra*". Lammens' efforts, however, were directed, not at a biographical study of Muḥammad *per se*, but rather on the search for the secret of his personal appeal and the rapid expansion of his message. "Muhammad to him, was a historical problem as well as a symbol of Islam's obstinacy and insensitiveness to the missionary influence."[17]

Lammens also happened to be among the first to argue, with some conviction, that the *ḥadīth* traditions as well as the *sīra* material on the Prophet are, on the whole, fictitious. This inaugurated a new perspective on Islamic history: the emphasis shifted from a critique of the actors in that history to the questioning of the source material itself.

In the 19th century, the Hungarian scholar Ignaz Goldziher concluded that much of the *ḥadīth* material was but a "pious fraud . . . invoked by every group (in early Islam) for every idea it evolved; . . . through solid chains (*isnad*) of tradition, all such matters acquired an unbroken tie to the 'Companions' who had heard those pronouncements and statutes from the Prophet or had seen him act

14. Ibid., 291.

15. Ibid., 311.

16. P. M. Holt, *The Treatment of Arab History*, 300.

17. K. S. Salibi, "Islam and Syria in the Writings of Henri Lammens", in *Historians of the Middle East*, ed. B. Lewis and P. M. Holt (Oxford University Press, 1962), 330–342.

in pertinent ways."[18] Later Professor J. Schacht further explored the foregoing hypotheses by subjecting the *isnād* of a few legal traditions to an exhaustive scrutiny. He concluded that "hardly any of these traditions, as far as matters of religious law are concerned, can be considered authentic; they were put into circulation . . . from the first half of the second century onwards."[19] From this others were quick to extrapolate that even the biographical material is fraudulent. Crone thus states: "that the bulk of the *sīra* . . . consists of second century *ḥadīths* has not been disputed by any historian, and this point may be taken as conceded."[20]

Not all Western scholars, however were as eager to jettison the classical material. W. M. Watt, writing in his *Muhammad at Mecca*, is clearly more reluctant than Crone, for example, to reject out of hand all such material, simply on the strength of Schacht's conclusion. He thus maintains that "In the legal sphere there may have been some sheer invention of traditions, it would seem. But in the historical sphere, in so far as the two may be separated, and apart from some exceptional cases, the nearest to such invention in the best early historians appears to be a 'tendential shaping' of the material . . ."[21]

It must be remembered, however, that traditional Muslim scholars display little awareness of the foregoing conundrum. The classical methodology of *ḥadīth* criticism as practised by early Muslim scholars, with its close scrutiny of the *isnād* and the *mutūn* of prophetic traditions, has, in the main, not been discredited, or even questioned, by Muslim scholars. If anything, that methodology has today been given a new lease of life by scholars such as Nāsir al-Dīn al-Albānī, who, for example, regard the re-evaluation of the early sources as integral to what they call the Islamic renaissance (*al-Nahḍa al-Islamiyya*). Such a renaissance, Albānī argues, will fall far short of its goals, without a thoroughgoing purge of what remains of the spurious material that had crept into *ḥadīth* and *sīra* works during the turbulent epoch of early Islamic history.[22] He thus set himself the task of appraising scholars and the Muslim laity alike to those traditions that were deemed spurious by the regimen of classical *ḥadīth* studies. His findings, which were first published under the title "al-Ahādīth al-Daʾīfah wa al-Maudūʿah" in a weekly column in the magazine *al-Tamaddun al-Islamī*, now comprise a multi-volume work, appropriately titled *Silsilah al-Ahādīth al-Daʾīfah wa al-Maudūʿah*.[23]

18. See Goldziher's chapter on the development of the law in Islam in *Introduction to Islamic Law and Theology* (Princeton: Princeton University Press, 1981).

19. J. Schacht, *The Origins of Muhammadan Jurisprudence* (Oxford University Press, 1959).

20. Crone, *Slaves on Horses*, 14–15.

21. W. G. Watt, *Muhammad at Mecca* (Oxford University Press, 1953), xiii.

22. M. N. Al-Albani, *Silsilah al-Ahādīth al-Daʾīfah wa al-Maudūʿah*. Vol. i. Damascus?: Manshurāt al-Maktab al-Islami, 1376 h.

23. Ibid., 6.

Clearly not all contemporary scholars are as eager as Schacht et al. to ring the death knell on *ḥadīth* literature as a tool for unravelling early Islamic history. Azami for one, in his studies on early *ḥadīth* literature has attempted to show that *ḥadīth* literature is indeed the richest source for the investigation of that era, for it provides, among other things, material for the understanding of the legal, cultural and religious ideas of those early centuries. He maintains that the theories of Margoliouth, Goldziher and more recently, Schacht can no longer be incontestably accepted given the recent discoveries of manuscripts or research. According to him

> "In the period referred to, works on the biography of the Prophet and on other historical topics were in a very advanced stage. We find that work on the biography of the Prophet was begun by the Companions. ʿAbd Allāh b. ʿAmr b. al-ʿAs recorded many historical events. It is possible still to trace his work in the *ahadīth* narrated by ʿAmr b. Shuʾaib (d. 118 AH) as he utilized his great grandfather ʿAbd Allāh b. ʿAmr's books. ʿUrwah (d. 93 AH) in his biography of the Prophet names his authority and most probably he had obtained the information in writing. There are works mentioned here and there on a single topic of the Sirah, e.g. *Memorandum on the Servants of the Prophet*, a book on the ambassadors of the Prophet to different rulers and chieftains with their negotiations. There are references to the collections of the Prophet's letters in a very early period."[24]

But it is, in fact, these very sources that Azami cites that have, through the use of contemporary literary and hermeneutical tools, been relegated to no more than "the rubble of early Muslim history". For Patricia Crone therefore, the "inertia" of material such as appears heretofore "comes across very strongly in modern scholarship on the first two centuries of Islam."[25] "The bulk of it", she argues, "has an alarming tendency to degenerate into mere rearrangements of the same old canon – Muslim chronicles in modern languages and graced with modern titles."[26]

Others, such as Juynboll, have strived to arrive at the inevitable *solution intermédiaire*, "a conceivable position that could be taken between the two points of view represented respectively by Muslim and Western scholarship."[27] For him therefore, the *ḥadīth* traditions "taken as a whole" do provide a fairly reliable rendition of early Islamic history, and "a judiciously and cautiously formulated overall view of what all those early reports . . . collectively point to, may in all likelihood be taken to be not very far from the truth of 'what really happened'."[28]

24. Azami, *Early Hadith*, 7–8.

25. See in this regard the introduction to her work, *Slaves on Horses: The Evolution of the Islamic Polity* (Cambridge University Press, 1980).

26. Ibid., 13.

27. See G. H. A. Juynboll, *Muslim Tradition: Studies in Chronology, Provenance and Authorship of Early hadith* (Cambridge University Press, 1983), 1.

28. Ibid., 7.

Finally, the true value of this particular work probably resides outside the context of the foregoing academic debate, for as Gadamer explains in *Truth and Method*,[29] "The meaning of a literary work is never exhausted by the intentions of its author; as the work passes from one cultural or historical context to another, new meanings may be culled from it which were perhaps never anticipated by its author or contemporary audience."[30]

Ahmed Fareed
Reviewer of Volume I

29. H. G. Gadamer, *Truth and Method* (London, 1975).

30. This is in fact an interpretation of Gadamer's thoughts as espoused by T. Eagleton in his study, *Literary Theory: An Introduction* (Minneapolis: University of Minnesota Press, 1983), 71.

TRANSLATOR'S PREFACE

As has often been observed, translation is impossible, since the associations and emotive content of words in one language and culture differ from those of all others. Attempts at translation, therefore, inevitably represent strivings for compromise. While accuracy and precision are prime objectives, the ultimately necessary requirements for clarity and comprehension in the host language may require simplification or even omission from the original text. The dilemmas inherent in these conflicting objectives are at times irreconcilable, and this is particularly true when one is dealing, as here, with languages and cultures so far removed as ancient Arabic and modern English. This translation, composed in everyday, contemporary English, gives no impression of the ubiquitous rarities, oddities and archaisms of vocabulary and syntax that make the original extremely challenging to comprehend. It is hoped, of course, that the innumerable compromises that this translation represents will be accepted as good-faith attempts to convey the spirit and purpose of the original in a form that readers of English will not find impossibly daunting.

In some instances Ibn Kathīr repeats anecdotal *aḥādīth* with differing chains of authority that are almost identical in content; often, as will be seen, the accounts differ in only very few of their words and these are typically vocabulary rarities. While such variations between accounts may seem of scant interest to the Western reader, they have nevertheless been left complete and intact in this translation. Including them in full, as in the original work, gives a strong impression of the care with which these anecdotes have been handed down and the impression of their likely authenticity is therefore enhanced. This seems especially the case where the discrepancies involve vocabulary rarities that are synonymous. It seems that it would be just such words that would have been subjected to dispute, change or loss from memory.

Ibn Kathīr's objective was to appear authoritative and discriminating in his choices of inclusion and discussion of specific *aḥādīth*; to him the listing of all the names of his authorities and his comments on their reputations was an essential component of this lectures. The give-and-take of oral lecturing – of which this work is essentially a record – would have enabled immediate verbal clarification. Our English text, in contrast, has to stand by itself, and to present an inherent and visible logic and clarity; it must also give some impression of the reliability of the Arabic text that is indicated by its complexity, and by the care with which the names of quoted sources are given and at times evaluated.

A perpetual challenge in presenting this text has therefore been to leave the essential narratives clear and succinct while including yet simplifying the lines of authority on which their authenticity is based. The names of authorities quoted have been included in full, since their identities were of prime importance for the initial 'readership' of this work as well as to students and researchers today. However, the exact nature and relative value of the means of transmission from authority to authority and the suggestions implied of Ibn Kathīr's preference for certain sources over others, have not been conveyed with exactitude, since common English vocabulary is unable to convey some of the subtleties of the Arabic technical terms employed for this purpose. The essential completeness of the original text in this translation does, however, enable serious students of early Islamic materials to bring their own differentiation to bear by their knowledge of the reputations of the persons quoted.

Certain words common in this text – such as *Abū* and *sūrat* – change in their form in Arabic to accord with basic grammatical rules. Here, however, to avoid confusion for those readers who do not know Arabic, they have been left in the form in which they are most commonly met. Initial *hamza*, moreover, has been omitted. Since early Arabic manuscripts, like the Arabic printed version of this text, are devoid of quotation marks, the identity of the narrator is sometimes unclear. Similarly, it is occasionally difficult to discern whether comments at the end of an account are those of the transmitting authority or of Ibn Kathīr himself. Footnotes referring to these and similar textual difficulties have been kept to a minimum, while brief parenthetical explanatory comments have sometimes been inserted to aid the general reader.

Discriminating and knowledgeable readers and reviewers will no doubt find discrepancies and perhaps inaccuracies in this lengthy and demanding text, especially in the extensive poems quoted. For these the translator – and his reviewers, text editors and typesetters – apologize. But since this work offers intimate details not elsewhere available in English about Arabian history and the inspiration and leadership of Islam in its earliest formative period, it would seem unsatisfactory to leave it in a language and form accessible only to a small coterie of scholars. The evident religious historical and philosophical interest of this text suggests that all those associated with its production may properly take refuge and find consolation from criticism in the knowledge that 'to err is human'. To attempt the impossible, moreover, while perhaps foolhardy, is surely more laudable than to make no attempt at all.

Trevor Le Gassick
Ann Arbor, 1997

VOLUME I

In the name of God, the most Beneficent, the most Merciful

It has been said that all Arabs trace their origins to Ishmael, the son of Abraham; upon them both be peace, salutation, and homage. However, what is well known to be true is that the *ʿarab al-ʿĀriba* (the original Arabs) came before Ishmael. Among them were the peoples of Ād, Thamūd, Ṭasm, Jadīs, Umaym, Jurhum, and the ʿAmālīq, as well as others known only to God. Also, these peoples both came before and were contemporaries of *al-Khalīl*.[1] Yet the *ʿarab al-mustaʿriba* (the Arabized Arabs), the Arabs of the Ḥijāz, were descendants of Ishmael, son of Abraham; upon both of them be peace.

The Arabs of the Yemen, the Ḥimyar, are well known to have been from Qaḥṭān, whose name was Muhzam, as Ibn Mākūlā said. It has been stated that they were a group of four brothers; Qaḥṭān, Qāḥiṭ, Muqḥiṭ, and Fāligh. Qaḥṭān was the son of Hūd; it is also said that he was Hūd, or that Hūd was his brother or one of his offspring. Qaḥṭān is also said to have descended from Ishmael, as Ibn Isḥāq and others relate it. One authority stated that Qaḥṭān was the son of al-Hamaysaʿ, son of Tayman, son of Qaydhar, son of Nabt, son of Ishmael. And there are other genealogies tracing him back to Ishmael; but God knows best. Al-Bukhārī treats this in his chapter on tracing the ancestry of Yemen back to Ishmael. He states that Musaddad related to him, quoting Yaḥyā, from Yazīd b. Abī ʿUbayd, and also Salama – God be pleased with him – as follows, "The Messenger of God (ṢAAS) went out and confronted a group from Aslam who were fighting one another with swords. He said to one of the two sides, 'Combat, O sons of Ishmael, I am with the so-and-so tribe.' So they stopped fighting. 'What's wrong with you?' he asked. 'But how can we combat if you are with the so-and-so tribe?' they replied. 'Go on, combat,' he insisted, 'I'm with all of you.'"

Al-Bukhārī alone gives this tradition. In one of his versions the tradition goes, "Combat, O sons of Ishmael. Your forebear was a skilled marksman. Combat; I'm with Ibn al-Adraʿ." And when they stopped fighting, he said, "Go on, combat. I'm with all of you."

Al-Bukhārī states, "And Aslam b. Afṣā b. Ḥāritha b. ʿAmr b. ʿĀmir is from the tribe of Khuzāʿa." He means the following: that Khuzāʿa was one group of those who were split off from the tribes of Sabaʾ when God sent on them the flood of al-ʿAram, as will be explained later. And the Aws and the Khazraj tribes

1. *al-Khalīl* is an epithet of Abraham, which literally means in Arabic "the true friend" or "companion". Here this honorific connotes "the true follower of God".

were from Saba᾿ also. The Prophet (ṢAAS) had said to them, "Combat, O sons of Ishmael." By so saying he was pointing out that they were from Ishmael's line of ancestry. Others interpret his words as meaning the entire Arab race, though that interpretation is far-fetched, since it contradicts without proof the apparent meaning. But the overwhelming view is that the Qaḥṭānī Arabs, whether they were from Yemen or somewhere else, were not from the line of Ishmael.

Most consider that all the Arabs are divided into two strains, those of Qaḥṭān and those of ʿAdnān. Those of Qaḥṭān consist of two peoples: Saba᾿ and Ḥaḍramawt. Those of ʿAdnān are also from two peoples: Rabīʿa and Muḍar, the two sons of Nizār b. Maʿad b. ʿAdnān. A fifth people, the Quḍāʿa, are the object of dispute. One theory asserts that they are from ʿAdnān; Ibn ʿAbd al-Barr reports that the majority so believes. This theory is related from Ibn ʿAbbās, Ibn ʿUmar, and Jubayr b. Muṭʿim. It is also preferred by al-Zubayr b. Bakkār, his uncle Muṣʿab al-Zubayrī, and Ibn Hishām. According to Ibn ʿAbd al-Barr and others, the name "Quḍāʿa son of Maʿad" appeared in a *ḥadīth* but this is incorrect.

In addition it is said that Quḍāʿa continued to trace the ancestry back to ʿAdnān, both before and after the coming of Islam. But by the time of Khālid b. Yazīd b. Muʿāwiya, some of them being maternal uncles of his, they were tracing back to Qaḥṭān. In that regard Aʿshā b. Thaʿlaba composed the following verses:

"Inform Quḍāʿa in the letter that but for the vicars of God's people, they would not have been embraced (into Islam).
Qudāʿa has said, 'We are among the fortune blessed.'[2]
And only God knows if they have been honest and spoken true.
They claimed a father who never had their mother;
They may know, but they are fearful (to tell the truth)."

Abū ʿAmr al-Suhaylī has also mentioned unique Arab poetry which reproaches Quḍāʿa for attributing their descent to Yemen. But God knows best.

The second theory is that Quḍāʿa has descended from Qaḥṭān; Ibn Isḥāq, al-Kalbī, and a number of other genealogists subscribe to this view.

Ibn Isḥāq gave his genealogy as being Quḍāʿa b. Mālik, b. Ḥimyar, b. Saba᾿, b. Yashjub, b. Yaʿrub, b. Qaḥṭān.

A certain poet of theirs, ʿAmr b. Murra, a Companion of the Prophet to whom two *ḥadīths* are attributed, composed the verses:

"O caller, summon us and rejoice;
Be of Quḍāʿa, stand not aloof in shame.
We descend from the noble and handsome

2. A play on Yemen, pronounced "yaman" in Arabic, a word meaning "success", "happiness", "luck".

Quḍāʿa, son of Mālik, son of Ḥimyar.
The line is well-known and fault-free,
Engraved in the stone beneath the pulpit."

One genealogist gave the line as follows: Quḍāʿa b. Mālik, b. ʿAmr, b. Murra, b. Zayd, b. Ḥimyar.

Ibn Lahīʿa stated, on the authority of Maʿrūf b. Suwayd from Abū ʿUshāba Muḥammad b. Mūsā, from ʿUqba b. ʿĀmir, that the last-mentioned said, "I asked the Messenger of God (ṢAAS) whether we were descended from Maʿad. He replied that we were not. So I asked who we were. He replied, 'You are descended from Quḍāʿa b. Mālik b. Ḥimyar.'"

Abū ʿUmar b. ʿAbd al-Barr said the following: "People do not dispute that Juhayna b. Zayd b. Aswad b. Aslam b. ʿImrān b. al-Ḥāf b. Quḍāʿa is the tribe of ʿUqba b. ʿĀmir al-Juhanī. Accordingly, Quḍāʿa would be in Yemen in the tribe of Ḥimyar b. Sabaʾ."

Some genealogists combine these ancestries, as in the report of al-Zubayr b. Bakkār and others to the effect that Quḍāʿa was a woman of the Jurhum who was married to Mālik b. Ḥimyar, from whom she gave birth to Quḍāʿa. Then, she married Maʿad b. ʿAdnān, while her son was still small; some even claim that she was pregnant with Quḍāʿa prior to her marriage (to Maʿad). Thus, Quḍāʿa was ascribed descent from his mother's husband, as was frequently the custom in such cases. But God knows best.

Muḥammad b. Sallām of Basra, the skilled genealogist, said, "The Arabs came from three strains: ʿAdnān, Qaḥṭān, and Quḍāʿa." When he was asked who were the more numerous, the descendants of ʿAdnān or those of Qaḥṭān, he replied, "It depends on Quḍāʿa; if they related to Yemen, then Qaḥṭāns are more numerous; if to Aden, then ʿAdnāns are more."

All this points to Quḍāʿa's inconsistency in relating their descent. However, if the aforementioned *ḥadīth* from Ibn Lahīʿa is true, then it proves their being from Qaḥṭān. But God knows best. And God Almighty did state: "O people, we have created you from a male and a female and made you into nations and tribes, that you may know one another. Truly, in God's sight it is the most pious of you who are the most noble" (*sūrat al-Ḥujurāt*, XLIX, v.13).

Genealogists indicate that their taxonomy has the following order: *shuʿūb* (peoples); *qabāʾil* (tribes); *ʿamāʾir* (tribal confederations); *buṭūn* (sub-tribes); *afkhādh* (small divisions of a tribe); *faṣāʾil* (extended kinsfolk); and *ʿashāʾir* (extended families). And the last refers to those closest to a man, and there are no more terms thereafter.

Let us begin with mention of the Qaḥṭān, then the Arabs of the Ḥijāz who are the ʿAdnān, and discussion of the *jāhiliyya* era (before Islam, that is) as a way of leading up to the biography of the Messenger of God (ṢAAS). All this if it be the will of God, in whom there is trust.

Al-Bukhārī stated, in his chapter, *An Account of Qaḥṭān*, as follows: "ʿAbd al-ʿAzīz b. ʿAbd Allāh told us, quoting Sulaymān b. Bilāl, from Thawr b. Zayd, from Abū al-Ghayth, from Abū Hurayra, that the Prophet (ṢAAS) said, 'Judgement Day will not come until a man from the Qaḥṭān goes forth driving the people before him with his stick.' Muslim also relates it in that way, from Qutayba, from al-Darāwardī, from Thawr b. Zayd."

Al-Suhaylī said that Qaḥṭān was the first to whom were spoken the phrases *abayta al-laʿna*[3] (i.e. "you have scorned the malediction") and *anʿim ṣabāḥan* (i.e. "have a happy morning!").

The Imām Aḥmad said, "Abū al-Mughīra related to us, from Jarīr, and Rāshid b. Saʿd al-Muqrāʾī told me, from Abū Hayy, from Dhū Fajar, that the Messenger of God (ṢAAS) said, 'This status once belonged to Ḥimyar, but God withdrew it from them and placed it with Quraysh and *waw, sin, yā, ʿayn, waw, dal, alif ḥamza, lām, yā, hā, mīm.*'" ʿAbd Allāh said, "This was in a document of my father, and as he related it to us he spoke it out directly as meaning the words, *wa sayaʿūdu ilayhim*, meaning 'it will return to them.'"

The Story of Sabaʾ.

God Almighty said, "For Sabaʾ there was indeed a sign in their dwelling-place: two gardens, on the right hand and on the left. 'Eat of the bounty from your Lord, and render Him thanks.' Good was the country, and forgiving the Lord. But they turned away, so We sent down upon them the torrent of al-ʿArim, and changed their gardens into ones of bitter fruit, tamarisks, and a few lote trees. Thus We punished them for their disbelief, and is it not the disbelievers alone whom We punish? And We placed between them and the villages We had blessed other settlements, easily seen, well spaced for journeying, (saying) 'Travel in them in safety by day and night.' They responded, 'O God, extend the distances between our travel stops.' They harmed themselves, and We made of them tales to be told and scattered them asunder. In that there are signs for all who are truly patient and thankful" (*sūrat Sabaʾ*, XXXIV, v.15–19).

The genealogists, including Muḥammad b. Isḥāq, give the name as Sabaʾ ʿAbd Shams b. Yashjub b. Yaʿrub b. Qaḥṭān; they say that he was the first of the Arabs who *sabaʾ*[4] and that that was why he was called Sabaʾ. He was also called *al-Rāʾish* ("the philanthropist"), because he gave to the people from his own wealth.

3. A salutation made to kings in the pre-Islamic era, meaning "your deeds are too impeccable to deserve malediction, O king."

4. The word lends itself to various interpretations. Thus A. Guillaume, in his translation of Ibn Isḥāq's *The Life of Muḥammad* (Oxford, 1955, p4) renders it "to take captives". Dictionaries give other meanings that might also fit this context. For example, in E. W. Lane's *Arabic-English Lexicon* we find *sabaʾ* as "to renege on an oath" or "to imply God's abandonment of a person".

Al-Suhaylī said, "It is related that he was the first person to be crowned." Some stated that he was a Muslim and that he wrote verses predicting the advent of the Messenger of God (ṢAAS). In that poetry are the lines:

"He will control after us a mighty domain,
A prophet who will give not licence to evil.
After him, other kings from among them will hold sway
Ruling all men, with no dishonour nor disgrace.
After them, rulers of ours will control
And our kingdom will be fragmented.
After Qaḥṭān a prophet will rule,
Pious, humble, the very best of mankind.
He will be named Aḥmad, and I wish
I could be given to live a year after his coming
To support him and award him my aid
With all fully-armed warriors and all marksmen.
When he appears, become his helpers and let
Him who meets him pass on my greeting."

Ibn Diḥya related this in his book *al-Tanwīr fī Mawlid al-Bashīr al-Nadhīr* (*Illuminating the Birth of the Messenger, the Herald*).

Imām Aḥmad stated that Abū ʿAbd al-Raḥmān related to him, quoting ʿAbd Allāh b. Lahīʿa, on the authority of ʿAbd Allāh b. Hubayra al-Sabaʾī, from ʿAbd al-Raḥmān b. Waʿla, that the last-named said that he heard ʿAbd Allāh b. ʿAbbās say that a man once asked the Prophet (ṢAAS) who or what Sabaʾ might signify, whether a man, a woman, or a territory. He replied, "Certainly he was a man who gave birth to ten children. Six of them dwelled in Yemen and four in Syria. Those in Yemen were Madhḥij, Kinda, al-Azd, the Ashʿarīs, Anmār, and Ḥimyar, all Arabs; in Syria they were Lakhm, Judhām, ʿĀmila, and Ghassān."

We related in our *Tafsīr* (*Exegesis*) that it was Farwa b. Musayk al-Ghuṭayfī who asked about that; also therein we analysed the lines of transmission and the phraseology of this tradition. And all praise be to God!

What is meant here is that Sabaʾ encompasses all these tribes. Among them there used to be [kings] in the lands of Yemen called the *tabābiʿa; tubbaʿ* in the singular. Their kings would wear crowns during their reign, as also did the Chosroes, the kings of the Persians. The Arabs used to apply the word *tubbaʿ* to each king who rules Yemen, along with al-Shahr and Ḥaḍramawt, just as they applied *qayṣar* to kings ruling Syria and the peninsula, *kisrā* to those ruling Persia, *farʿūn* to Egypt's rulers, *al-najāshī* to those over Abyssinia, and *baṭlaymūs* to India's kings. Balqīs[5] was one of the Ḥimyarite rulers of Yemen. They used to be in a state of great felicity, with abundant prosperity and a plenitude of local fruits and pro-

5. Balqīs is identified as the Queen of Sheba who married King Solomon.

duce. However, they lived in rectitude, propriety, and right guidance. But when they replaced God's blessings by disbelief, these kings brought their people to ruin.

Muḥammad b. Isḥāq stated from Wahb b. Munabbih, "God sent to them 13 prophets." And al-Suddī claimed that he sent 12,000 prophets to them! But God knows best.

What is implied here is that they deviated from the true guidance into error and bowed down to the sun apart from God. That was so in the time of Balqīs and beforehand as well, continuing up to when God sent the flood of al-ʿArim upon them. As the Almighty said, "But they turned away, so We sent down upon them the torrent of al-ʿArim, and changed their gardens into ones of bitter fruit, tamarisks, and a few lote trees. Thus We punished them for their disbelief, and is it not the disbelievers alone whom We punish?" (*sūrat Sabaʾ*, XXXIV, v.16–17).

A number of former and contemporary scholars on the Qurʾān commentaries and others have related that the Maʾrib dam was constructed where waters flowed between two mountains; in ancient times they built an extremely strong dam there so that the water-level reached these mountain tops. On those mountains they planted many fields and orchards with elegant and highly productive trees. It is said that Sabaʾ b. Yaʿrib built it and that it was fed by 70 valleys with 30 outlets for the water from it. But he died before it was completed and so Ḥimyar finished it after him. It was one *farsakh*[6] long and one *farsakh* wide. People lived there in great felicity, prosperity, and ease. So much so, that Qatāda and others related that the orchards gave fruit of such quantity and ripeness that a woman could fill a large basket on her head from the fruit dropping in it as she passed below. It is said that there were no fleas or dangerous beasts there; the climate being wholesome and the land excellent, as the Almighty stated, "For Sabaʾ there was indeed a sign in their dwelling-place; two gardens, one on the right hand and one on the left. 'Eat from the bounty of your Lord, and render Him thanks – a fair land and a much-forgiving Lord'" (*sūrat Sabaʾ*, XXXIV, v.15). And He also stated, "And so your Lord proclaimed: 'If you give thanks, I give you increase thereof; but if you show ingratitude, then is my punishment severe indeed'" (*sūrat Ibrāhīm*, XIV, v.7).

Then they worshipped other than God and were discontent with His bounty; after He had made their travel stages close together, made good their orchards, and secured their roads, they asked Him to extend their travel stages, to make their journeys difficult and tiresome, and to replace good by evil. They did just like the Israelites when they requested that He exchange manna and quails for vegetables, cucumbers, garlic, lentils, and onions. And so they nullified that great blessing and common good by despoiling the land and scattering the people, then, as the Almighty said, "they turned away and so We sent down upon them the torrent of al-ʿArim" (*sūrat Sabaʾ*, XXXIV, v.16).

6. Parasang, an ancient Persian measure of length, equal to about $3\frac{1}{2}$ miles.

More than one source related that God dispatched rodents against the base of the dam, that is, large rats, or, it is said, moles; and when people knew of this, they set up nets. But, it having been so decreed, these efforts did no good and their precautions were useless. When the destruction at the base was well advanced, the dam fell and collapsed and the water flowed out. Thus the streams and rivers were cut off; all those fruits were lost and all the produce and trees perished. Afterwards they were replaced with inferior trees and fruits, as All-powerful and Almighty God has stated, "and we changed their gardens into ones of *khāmṭ* and *athl* (bitter fruit and tamarisks)" (*sūrat Sabaʾ*, XXXIV, v.16).

Ibn ʿAbbās, Mujāhid, and others stated that *khāmṭ* is the *arāk* tree which gives a fruit known as the *barīr*, whereas the *athl* is the *ṭarfāʾ*, the tamarisk, or some such similar tree that produces wood without fruit. The Qurʾān verse continues, "and a few lote-trees". This refers to the fact that when the *nabaq*, the "Christ's thorn" tree, gives fruit it does so in very small quantity despite the profuseness of its thorns. The proportion of its fruit is similar, then, to what the proverb implies, "like the meat of a scrawny camel high on a rock-strewn mountain", not an easy path to be climbed, nor a nice fat meal to be attained. This, then, is why the Almighty states, "Thus We punished them for their disbelief, and is it not the disbelievers alone whom We punish?"

That is, He only metes out such severe punishment to those who disbelieve in Him, give the lie to His messengers, disobey His commands, and defile His sanctuaries.

The Almighty also said, "We made of them tales to be told and scattered them asunder." In fact, when their wealth was gone and their lands were in ruin, they were forced to depart. So they scattered into the lower areas and into the higher reaches of the country, in all directions, *aydī Sabaʾ* (in disarray that is) as the common idiom goes. Some of them settled in Ḥijāz, the Khuzāʿa tribe among them; they migrated to the suburbs of Mecca, with the consequences that we will relate later. Others went to what is now Medina, being the first to settle there. They were later joined by three tribes of Jews: Banū Qaynuqāʿ, Banū Qurayẓa, and Banū al-Naḍīr. These made a pact with the tribes of Aws and Khazraj and stayed with them, as we will relate. Other groups from Sabaʾ moved to Syria and it was later they who became Christian; these were the Ghassān, ʿĀmila, Bahrāʾ, Lakhm, Judhām, Tanūkh, Taghlib, and others.

Muḥammad b. Isḥāq stated that Abū ʿUbayda told him that al-Aʿshā b. Qays b. Thaʿlaba, also known as Maymūn b. Qays, spoke the verses:

"In that there is a moral for those who seek morals,
Maʾrib was wiped out by the torrent of al-ʿArim,
Marble, built for them by Ḥimyar,
Which did not budge when the raging billows came.

Its water irrigated the crops and the vines
Far and wide, since it was decreed
Then they were scattered and could not
Give drink to a child when just weaned."

Muḥammad b. Isḥāq, in his biography of the Prophet (ṢAAS), indicated that the first man to leave Yemen before the flooding of al-ʿArim was ʿAmr b. ʿĀmir of the Lakhm tribe. Lakhm was the son of ʿAdī b. al-Ḥārith b. Murra b. Udad b. Zayd b. Hamaysaʿ b. ʿAmr b. ʿArīb b. Yashjub b. Zayd b. Kahlān b. Sabaʾ. Lakhm's genealogy has also been given as Lakhm b. ʿAdī b. ʿAmr b. Sabaʾ, as Ibn Hishām states.

According to Ibn Isḥāq, "The reason for his departure from Yemen was, as Abū Zayd *al-anṣārī* related to me, that he saw rodents burrowing into the Maʾrib dam which held back the water which they distributed over their land as they pleased. He realized that the dam would not last, and so he decided to emigrate from Yemen. So he tricked his people, as follows. He ordered his youngest son to stand up to him and strike him back if he should berate and strike him. His son did as he was told and ʿAmr then said, 'I will not remain in a land where my youngest son has slapped my face.' So some of Yemen's tribal leaders said, 'Let's take advantage of ʿAmr's anger and buy up his properties.' Then ʿAmr moved with his sons and grandsons. The Azd tribe then stated that they would not remain behind after ʿAmr; so they sold their properties and left with him. They journeyed until they reached the land of ʿAkk, crossing to and fro across their territory. So ʿAkk attacked them, their battles favouring first one side, then the other. On this fighting, ʿAbbās b. Mirdās spoke the following verses:

'And ʿAkk b. ʿAdnān were those who toyed with
Ghassān until they were completely expelled.'

" ʿAmr's people therefore disengaged from them and dispersed in different directions. The family of Jafna b. ʿAmr b. ʿĀmir went to Syria, while the Aws and the Khazraj settled in Yathrib and Khuzāʿa went to Marra.[7] The Azd al-Sarāt went to al-Sarāt, the Azd ʿUmān to ʿUmān. Then God dispatched the torrent down upon the dam and destroyed it, concerning which event God revealed these verses in the Qurʾān." Something close to this account was also related from al-Saddī.

According to Muḥammad b. Isḥāq in this account, ʿAmr b. ʿĀmir was a soothsayer. Others say that his wife, Ṭarīfa daughter of al-Khayr, the Ḥimyarite woman, was a soothsayer and that she told him of the imminent doom of their country. Apparently they saw proof of that in the rats being given control over their dam, and that was why they acted as they did. God alone knows best.

7. Known as *marr al-Zahrān*, on the road to Mecca.

I have given a lengthy account of ʿAmr's story, from ʿIkrima, as related by Ibn Abī Ḥātim, in my *Tafsīr* (*Exegesis*).

DIVISION

Not all of Sabaʾ left Yemen when they were afflicted with the torrent of al-ʿArim; the majority of them remained. The people of Maʾrib, who had the dam, moved into different parts of the country. That is the gist of the previously mentioned *ḥadīth* coming down from Ibn ʿAbbās to the effect that all the tribes of Sabaʾ did not leave Yemen, but four went to Syria while six remained. These were Madhḥij, Kinda, Anmār, and the Ashʿarīs. Anmār was the father of Khathʿam, Bajīla, and Ḥimyar; so these were the six tribes from Sabaʾ who remained in Yemen. They continued retaining the rights of power and the *tabābiʿa* kingship until the king of Abyssinia took that position from them through the army he sent under his two generals Abraha and Aryāṭ. The Abyssinian rule lasted some 70 years until Sayf b. Dhū Yazan the Ḥimyarite regained control, and that was a short time before the birth of the Messenger of God (ṢAAS). This we will recount in detail shortly, God willing, and upon Him is all trust and dependence.

Later the Messenger of God (ṢAAS) sent ʿAlī and Khālid b. al-Walīd to the people of Yemen, then he sent Abū Mūsā al-Ashʿarī and Muʿādh b. Jabal. They were calling people to worship God and making clear to them matters of doctrine. After that al-Aswad al-ʿAnsī gained control over Yemen and he expelled the deputies of the Messenger of God (ṢAAS). When al-Aswad was killed, the power of Islam became firmly established over Yemen, during the rule of Abū Bakr "the trusting", God be pleased with him.

The Story of Rabīʿa b. Naṣr b. Abū Ḥāritha b. ʿAmr b. ʿĀmir.

The man referred to in the above heading was of the Lakhm tribe; this is what Ibn Isḥāq related. Al-Suhaylī stated that the genealogists of Yemen give his name as Naṣr b. Rabīʿa; but he was really Rabīʿa b. Naṣr b. al-Ḥārith b. Namāra b. Lakhm. Al-Zubayr b. Bakkār gave his genealogy as Rabīʿa b. Naṣr b. Mālik b. Shaʿwadh b. Mālik b. ʿAjam b. ʿAmr b. Namāra b. Lakhm. Lakhm was the brother of Judhām; he was named Lakhm because he had *lakhm*ed his brother on the cheek, i.e. he had struck him there. The brother bit his hand in return so *jadham*ing it; hence he was called Judhām.

Rabīʿa was one of the *tubbaʿ* kings of Ḥimyar, and about him is told the tale of his contacts with the two soothsayers Shiqq and Saṭīḥ, and how they warned him of the coming of the Messenger of God (ṢAAS).

Saṭīḥ was named Rabīʿ b. Rabīʿa b. Masʿūd b. Māzin b. Dhi'b b. ʿAdī b. Māzin Ghassān. Shiqq was the son of Ṣaʿb b. Yashkur b. Ruhm b. Afrak b. Qays b.

ʿAbqar b. Anmār b. Nizār. Some say that Anmār was the son of Irāsh b. Liḥyān b. ʿAmr b. al-Ghawth b. Nābit b. Mālik b. Zayd b. Kahlān b. Sabaʾ. It is said that Saṭīḥ had no limbs but was like a waterskin, with his face in his chest. When he got angry he would puff up and sit. Shiqq was one-half a man. And it is said that Khālid b. ʿAbd Allāh al-Qasrī was of his progeny. According to al-Suhaylī both Shiqq and Saṭīḥ were born on the same day when Ṭarīfa, daughter of al-Khayr, the Ḥimyarite woman, died. It is said that she spat into the mouth of each of them, each therefore inheriting the gift of divination from her. She was the wife of ʿAmr b. ʿĀmir, previously mentioned. But God knows best.

Muḥammad Ibn Isḥāq said that Rabīʿa b. Naṣr was king of Yemen and of the true line of the *tubbaʿ* kings. He saw a vision that awed and terrified him. So he gathered every single soothsayer, magician, bird prognosticator, and star foreteller in his kingdom and told them, "I have seen visions that amazed and scared me. Tell me what they were and how to interpret them." They replied, "Relate them to us and we will interpret them." He responded, "If I do tell you what they were I won't feel secure with your explanation; the only one capable of interpreting them will be someone who knows what they were before I tell them."

One of the wise men then suggested, "If that is what the king wants, then he should send for Shiqq and Saṭīḥ. No one is more knowledgeable than they; they will tell him what he asked for."

So the king sent for them, and Ṣatīḥ arrived before Shiqq. Their conversation went as follows:

The king: "I have seen visions that amazed and scared me; tell me what they were, and if you are right you will interpret them correctly."

Saṭīḥ: "I will do so. You saw fire emerge from the darkness, fall on low ground, and consume every living being with a skull."

The king: "You've not made a single error, Saṭīḥ. So how do you interpret them?"

Saṭīḥ: "I swear by all the snakes between the two stony plains, that the Abyssinians will descend upon your land and will surely reign over all between Abyan and Jurash."

The king: "That, Saṭīḥ, angers and hurts me greatly; will that occur in my time or later?"

Saṭīḥ: "Later, by your father I swear, some time later, after more than 60 or 70 years have passed."

The king: "And will their dominion endure or be cut short?"

Saṭīḥ: "It will be cut down to some 70 years, and then they will be killed and expelled in flight."

The king: "Who will then follow, after their killing and expulsion?"

Saṭīḥ: "Iram Dhū Yazan will follow, emerging from Aden to fight them, and he will not leave one of them in Yemen."

The king: "And will his era endure or be cut short?"

Saṭīḥ: "It will be cut short."

The king: "Who will do this?"

Saṭīḥ: "A prophet, pure, to whom revelation comes from the All-high."

The king: "And from where will this prophet come?"

Saṭīḥ: "He will descend from Ghālib b. Fihr b. Mālik b. al-Naḍr. And the rule will be with his people till the end of time."

The king: "Does time end?"

Saṭīḥ: "Yes, on that day when the first and the last shall all be assembled and the good will be happy, the evil mortified."

The king: "Is this really true, what you're telling me?"

Saṭīḥ: "Yes, by the twilight, the dark of night, and the spreading dawn, what I told you really is the truth."

Then Shiqq arrived and the king spoke to him as he had to Saṭīḥ but hid from him what he had foreseen to establish whether they would be in agreement or not. Shiqq told him, "You saw fire emerge from the dark, fall down between a meadow and a hillock, and eat up every breathing creature there."

When Shiqq said this, the king knew that they were in agreement and saying one and the same thing, except for Saṭīḥ's words being "fall on low ground and consume every living being with a skull", while Shiqq's were "between a meadow and a hillock and eat up every breathing creature there". So the king told him he had it right and asked his interpretation.

Shiqq: "I swear by all the men who live between two stony plains that the blacks will descend upon your land, oppress all your young, and reign over all between Abyan and Najran."

The king: "By your father, Shiqq, that angers and hurts me greatly; will that occur during or after my reign?"

Shiqq: "No, it will be in a later period. And then a great man will emerge to save your people and inflict on your enemies all disgrace."

The king: "And who will this great saviour be?"

Shiqq: "A young man who is guilt-free and faultless and will emerge from the line of Dhū Yazan."

The king: "And will his reign last long?"

Shiqq: "No, it will be brought short by a messenger dispatched, who will bring truth and justice, and come from a people of religion and virtue in whom power shall reside until the Day of Separation."

The king: "What is the Day of Separation?"

Shiqq: "A day when the pious shall be rewarded, when calls shall be made from the heavens that the living and the dead shall hear, and men shall be gathered to the appointed place. Then the pious shall receive victory and rewards."

The king: "Is it really true what you predict?"

Shiqq: "Yes, by the Lord of the heavens and the earth and of all high and low between them both, what I have informed you is all true and doubt-free."

Ibn Isḥāq stated that the soothsayers' prediction had great impact on Rabīʿa b. Naṣr and so he provisioned all his family and relatives for departure to Iraq. He wrote for them to a Persian king called Sābūr b. Khurzādh who settled them in al-Ḥīra. According to Ibn Isḥāq, the progeny of Rabīʿa b. Naṣr included al-Nuʿmān b. al-Mundhir, son of al-Nuʿmān b. al-Mundhir b. ʿAmr b. ʿAdī b. Rabīʿa b. Naṣr. This al-Nuʿmān was viceroy over al-Ḥīra for the Persian kings; and the Arabs used to send delegations to him and gave him praise. This, then, is what Muḥammad b. Isḥāq said about al-Nuʿmān b. al-Mundhir being of the line of Rabīʿa b. Naṣr, according to most people. Ibn Isḥāq related that when the sword of al-Nuʿmān b. al-Mundhir was brought to the Commander of the Faithful, ʿUmar b. al-Khaṭṭāb, he asked Jubayr b. Muṭʿim from whom it had come. He replied, "From the remains of Qanaṣ b. Maʿad b. ʿAdnān." Ibn Isḥāq commented that it was unclear who that person was.

The Story of Tubbaʿ Abū Karib Tubbān Asʿad, king of Yemen, with the people of Medina; how he wished to raid the Holy Sanctuary at Mecca. Then he dignified and venerated it and covered it with cloth; thus he was the first to do so.

Ibn Ishāq stated that when Rabīʿa b. Naṣr died all kingship in Yemen reverted to Ḥassān b. Tubbān Asʿad Abū Karib. Tubbān Asʿad was the last *tubbaʿ*; he was the son of Kulkī Karib b. Zayd. Zayd, the first *tubbaʿ*, was the son of ʿAmr Dhū al-Adhʿār b. Abraha Dhū al-Manār b. al-Rāʾish b. ʿAdī b. Ṣayfī b. Sabaʾ al-Aṣghar b. Kaʿb Kahf al-Ẓulum b. Zayd b. Sahl b. ʿAmr b. Qays b. Muʿāwiya b. Jusham b. ʿAbd Shams b. Wāʾil b. al-Ghawth b. Qaṭan b. ʿArīb b. Zuhayr b. Ayman b. al-Hamaysaʿ b. al-ʿAranjaj. The latter was Ḥimyar b. Sabaʾ al-Akbar b. Yaʿrub b. Yashjub b. Qaḥṭān. ʿAbd al-Mālik b. Hishām gave Sabaʾ's line as being son of Yashjub b. Yaʿrub b. Qaḥṭān.

According to Ibn Isḥāq, Tubbān Asʿad Abū Karib was he who went to Medina and led two Jewish rabbis to Yemen and refurbished and covered with cloth the holy sanctuary. His reign preceded that of Rabīʿa b. Naṣr. He had routed his return journey from a campaign in the east through Medina. First he had passed there without bothering its inhabitants and left among them a son of his who was treacherously killed. He advanced against it, determined to destroy it, wipe out its people, and cut down its date-palms. So this clan of the *anṣār*[8]

8. The Medinan followers of the Prophet Muḥammad who granted him refuge after his emigration from Mecca.

joined up against him, their leader being ʿAmr b. Ṭalla, the brother of Banū al-Najjār and also one of Banū ʿAmr b. Mabdhūl. Mabdhūl's name was ʿĀmir b. Mālik b. al-Najjār, and al-Najjār's name was Taym Allāh b. Thaʿlaba b. ʿAmr b. al-Khazraj b. Ḥārith b. Thaʿlaba b. ʿAmr b. ʿĀmir.

Ibn Hishām stated that ʿAmr b. Ṭalla was ʿAmr b. Muʿāwiya b. ʿAmr b. ʿĀmir b. Mālik b. al-Najjār, that Ṭalla was his mother and that she was the daughter of ʿĀmir b. Zurayq al-Khazrajiyya.

Ibn Isḥāq's account proceeds: "A certain man of Banū ʿAdī b. al-Najjār, called Aḥmar, attacked and killed one of the followers of Tubbaʿ whom he found cutting down date clusters off one of his date-loaded palm trees, saying, 'Dates belong only to those who pollinate them.' This added to Tubbaʿ's animosity towards them and fighting broke out.

"The *anṣār* claimed that they would fight against him by day and host him by night; their saying this surprised Tubbaʿ who would say, 'Our people, by God, are certainly generous!'"

Ibn Isḥāq related about the *anṣār* that Tubbaʿ's anger was directed only against the Jews and that they, the *anṣār*, protected them from him. Al-Suhaylī stated that Tubbaʿ only came to give victory to the *anṣār*, his cousins, against the Jews who had taken up residence with them in Medina on certain conditions that they had not kept, and because they were behaving arrogantly. God knows best.

Ibn Isḥāq's account relates that while Tubbaʿ was engaged in this fighting against them, two Jewish rabbis came to him; they were both deeply learned men from Banū Qurayẓa. When they heard how he intended to destroy the city and its inhabitants, they told him, "O king, do not do this. Unless you adopt a different course from that you intend, you will be prevented from accomplishing it, and we will not be able to save you from swift retribution." Tubbaʿ asked why this was so, and they replied, "This is where a prophet will migrate; he will go forth from this holy sanctuary from Quraysh in times to come and this shall be his home and his abode."

So Tubbaʿ changed his plan; he recognized the learning they had and was intrigued by what he had heard from them. He therefore departed from Medina and adopted the rabbis' religion. According to Ibn Isḥāq, Tubbaʿ and his people had idols whom they worshipped.

Tubbaʿ then set off towards Mecca on his way to Yemen. When he arrived between ʿUsfān and Amaj he was approached by some men of the tribe of Hudhayl b. Mudrika b. Ilyās b. Muḍar b. Nizār b. Maʿad b. ʿAdnān. They asked him, "O king, may we lead you to an ancient treasury overlooked by kings before yourself, in which there are pearls, chrysolite, sapphires, gold, and silver?" "Certainly you may," he replied. They said, "It is a building in Mecca whose people worship it and offer prayers there."

Actually the Hudhaylīs sought to destroy him by this, since they knew that any king wanting this or being disrespectful there would perish.

After agreeing to their suggestion Tubbaᶜ sent word to the two rabbis asking their advice. They replied, "Those people wished only your death and the destruction of your army. We know of no other building than that in the land that God Almighty and Glorious has taken for Himself. If you do as they suggest, you will perish, as will all those with you."

Tubbaᶜ asked what he should do when he approached the building and they said he should do the same as those who lived there, that he should circumambulate it and venerate and honour it, shaving his head and acting with humility before it until he left it.

The king then asked, "What is it that prevents you both from doing the same?" They replied, "It certainly is the house of our father Abraham, on whom be peace, and it is as we told you, but the people there have created a barrier between us and it by the idols they have set up about it and the blood they shed there. They are unclean and polytheists." This was the gist of their words.

Tubbaᶜ saw the good of their advice and the truth of their words and so he summoned the men from Hudhayl, cut off their hands and feet, and continued to Mecca. There he performed the circumambulation of the building, made sacrifice, and shaved his head. He remained in Mecca for six days, so they say, providing sacrificial feasts for its people and giving them honey to drink. In a dream he was shown that he should cover the building, so he clothed it with palm fronds. Then, in another dream, he was shown that he should clothe it in something better, so he dressed it with a Yemeni tribal fabric. Again he had a vision that he should clothe it even better, so he covered it with fine sheets and striped cloth. People claim that Tubbaᶜ was thus the first to clothe the building. He ordered its guardians from the Jurhum tribe to clean it thoroughly and to prevent any blood, dead bodies, or menstruating women from coming close to it. He also made for it a door and a key.

On this subject Subayᶜa, daughter of al-Aḥabb, spoke the following verses for her son Khālid b. ᶜAbd Manāf b. Kaᶜb b. Saᶜd b. Taym b. Murra b. Kaᶜb b. Lu'ayy b. Ghālib, telling him to avoid sinning in Mecca and reminding him what Tubbaᶜ had done there:

"O my son, in Mecca neither do wrong to the young nor to the old.
Preserve its sanctity, my son, and let not conceit confuse you.
Whoever sins in Mecca, my son, meets extreme disaster.
His face, my son, shall be beaten, his cheeks consumed by fire.
I have tested this there, my son, and found those harming it perish.
God made it secure, though no towers are built in its courtyards.
God made its birds inviolate and also the white-footed crows on Mt. Thabīr.
Tubbaᶜ raided it, but dressed its buildings with new, smooth cloth.

My God humbled his power there, so he made proper sacrifice,
Walking barefoot towards it, in its courtyard,
And offering two thousand camels,
Well-feeding its people the flesh of Mahry camels and cattle,
Giving them strained honey and barley-water to drink.
And God destroyed the army of the elephants, casting rocks amongst them,
Ending their rule in far distant lands, in Persia and Khazīr.
So hear when this is told, and understand how things ended."

Ibn Isḥāq continued: "Thereafter Tubbaʿ left for Yemen, taking his armed men and the two rabbis with him. On his arrival he asked his people to adopt the religion he had embraced, but they refused until it should be put to the test of fire as was the custom in Yemen."

He went on: "I was told by Abū Mālik b. Thaʿlaba b. Abū Mālik al-Quraẓī that he heard Ibrāhīm b. Muḥammad b. Ṭalḥa b. ʿUbayd Allāh say that when Tubbaʿ reached the outskirts of Yemen, Ḥimyar intercepted him and denied him entry. They told him, 'You shall not enter our land; you have abandoned our faith.' So Tubbaʿ called on them to embrace his new religion, proclaiming it to be better than theirs. They asked whether he would agree to put the issue between them to the test of the fire, and he agreed."

He continued: "There was in Yemen, as Yemenis assert, a fire they would employ to adjudicate differences; it would consume wrongdoers but not harm the innocent. And so Tubbaʿ's people and the two rabbis walked to the fire site. His people took their idols and carried their sacrificial offerings, while the rabbis wore their sacred books around their necks. They all sat near the spot from which the fire would emerge. When it raged towards them they drew away and avoided it. The onlookers berated them and ordered them to endure it, and they did so until it enveloped them and consumed their idols and sacred objects and those men of Ḥimyar who carried them. But the two rabbis emerged safe, with their holy books around their necks, unharmed though their foreheads were sweating. Thereupon the Ḥimyarites adopted their religion; and this was how Judaism began in Yemen."

Ibn Isḥāq continued to report that one authority told him that the two rabbis and the men of Ḥimyar approached the fire only seeking to force it back, for it was said that truth lay with him who could do this. The Ḥimyarites approached the fire bearing their idols to force it back, but it closed on them seeking to consume them. So they drew away and were not able to force it back. Later the two rabbis approached it and began reciting the Torah. The fire withdrew from them and so they forced it back to where it emerged. Thereupon the Ḥimyarites adopted their religion. But God knows best which report is true.

Ibn Isḥāq went on: " They had a temple called Riʾām which they venerated and where they made sacrifice; there they received oracular messages while engaged in their polytheistic practices. The two rabbis told Tubbaʿ, 'It is just a devil who is deceiving the people that way; let us deal with him.' Tubbaʿ agreed and the rabbis, so the Yemenis say, forced out from it a black dog which they killed. Then they destroyed that temple; and its ruins – so I have been told – still to this day bear traces of the blood shed on it."

In our new *Tafsīr* (*Exegesis*) of the Qurʾān we have told of the tradition coming from the Prophet (ṢAAS) wherein he said, "Do not curse Tubbaʿ; he had become a Muslim."

Al-Suhayli stated that Muʿammar related from Humām b. Munabbih from Abū Hurayra that the Messenger of God (ṢAAS) said, "Do not curse Asʿad the Ḥimyarite; it was he who first clothed the *kaʿba*." According to al-Suhaylī, Tubbaʿ spoke the following verses when the two rabbis told him about the Messenger of God (ṢAAS):

> "I do testify that Aḥmad is a messenger from God, guiltless his soul,
> If only my life were extended up to his, I would have been a helper, a cousin to him,
> I would have fought his enemies with the sword and cleared all cares from his breast."

These verses continued to be handed down and memorised among the *anṣar*; they were with Abū Ayyūb *al-anṣārī*, may God be pleased with him and bless him. Al-Suhaylī stated that Ibn Abū al-Dunyā indicated in his *Kitāb al-Qubūr* (*Book of Graves*) that a grave was dug up at Ṣanʿā in which two females were found and along with them a silver tablet on which was written in gold, "This is the grave of Lamīs and Ḥubbā, two daughters of Tubbaʿ, who died declaring, 'There is no God but God alone and without peer,' and before them the righteous had died saying the same."

Later, rule passed to Ḥassān b. Tubbān Asʿad, and he was the brother of al-Yamāma al-Zarqāʾ who was crucified on the gate of the city of Jaw, which from that day on was named al-Yamāma.

Ibn Isḥāq continued that when Tubbaʿ's son Ḥassān b. Abī Karib Tubbān Asʿad became king, he set out with the people of Yemen, wishing to subdue the lands of the Arabs and the Persians. But by the time they were somewhere in Iraq, the Ḥimyarites and the Yemenites disliked going further with him and wanted to return to their own countries and families. So they spoke to a brother of Ḥassān named ʿAmr, who was there with him in the army, as follows: "Kill your brother Ḥassān and we will make you king over us and you can take us back home." He said he would, and there was agreement about this except in the case of Dhū Ruʿayn the Ḥimyarite. He urged ʿAmr against this, but ʿAmr disagreed. So Dhū Ruʿayn composed a poem containing the following two verses:

"Whoever would exchange insomnia for sleep? Happy he who sleeps in peace.
Though Ḥimyar has betrayed in treachery, Dhū Ruʿayn has God's forgiveness."

This poem he then entrusted to ʿAmr. When the latter did kill his brother Ḥassān and returned to Yemen, he was deprived of sleep and suffered insomnia. When he asked physicians, astrologists, soothsayers, and diviners what was wrong, they told him, "No one has ever killed his brother or relative unjustly without losing his sleep and suffering insomnia." Thereupon he set about killing all those who had encouraged him to murder his brother. Finally, he came to Dhū Ruʿayn who told him, "I have cause for you to spare me." When ʿAmr asked why, he drew attention to the document he had entrusted to him. ʿAmr then took out the verses, read them and realized that Dhū Ruʿayn had advised him well. ʿAmr perished and Ḥimyar's state fell into disorder and disarray.

USURPATION OF THE THRONE OF YEMEN BY LAKHNĪʿA DHŪ SHANĀTIR.

He ruled there for 27 years.

Ibn Isḥāq continued that a Ḥimyarite not of the royal lines then took control of Yemen, a man called Lakhnīʿa Yanūf Dhū Shanātir. He murdered the most prominent Yemenites and abused the country's royal families. He was, moreover, a most depraved man, behaving as had the people of Lot. He would send for a royal prince and attack him in an upper chamber he had constructed for that purpose; this was to prevent the prince from ruling after him. Eventually he would look down from his high chamber to his guards and soldiers below and place a tooth-cleaning stick in his mouth to show them that he had finished with the prince.

One day he sent for Zurʿa Dhū Nuwās b. Tubbān Asʿad, the brother of Ḥassān, who had been a small boy when Ḥassān was murdered. He had grown up to be a fine, intelligent, and handsome young man. When a messenger came to fetch him he realized what was in store for him, so he hid a thin metal blade between his foot and sandal. When they were alone and Lakhnīʿa attacked him, Dhū Nuwās fought back and stabbed and killed him. Then he cut off his head and placed it in the window out of which Lakhnīʿa had looked below. Having placed a tooth-cleaning stick in his mouth he then went outside. The guards called to him, "Hey there, Dhū Nuwās, fresh and moist, or all dried out?" He told them in reply to ask the head of "Hell-bent" there in the window, and they saw that Lakhnīʿa's head had been cut off. They then caught up with Dhū Nuwās and implored him to be their king now that he had spared them from the evil tyrant.

So they made him king, and Ḥimyar and the tribes of Yemen united under him. He was the last of the kings of Ḥimyar. He took the name Yūsuf and ruled for an extended period.

In Najrān there were still some remnants of followers of the religion of Jesus, son of Mary, on whom be peace. They were people of goodness and virtue and their leader's name was ʿAbd Allāh b. al-Thāmir.

Ibn Isḥāq then related how the people of Najrān adopted Christianity due to the influence of a man named Faymiyūn, a Christian from Syria. He was a man whose prayers were answered and was accompanied by a man named Ṣāliḥ. They spent each Sunday in prayer, while Faymiyūn worked the rest of the week as a builder. He said prayers for the sick, the crippled, and the disabled, and their ills would be cured. Eventually he and his friend were taken prisoner by bedouins and were sold in Najrān. The man who bought Faymiyūn was astonished to see that when he began his prayers in the house at night it would fill with light.

The people of Najrān worshipped a tall palm tree, bowing down before it and festooning it with their wives' jewellery. Faymiyūn said to his master, "If I were to say a prayer to God against this tree and it were destroyed, would you recognize that your religion is false?" His master agreed that he would, and gathered all the people from Najrān together. Faymiyūn then went into his prayer-room and asked God to destroy the tree. So God sent a storm that tore it up by the roots and threw it flat on the ground. Thereupon the people of Najrān adopted Christianity and he encouraged them to follow the Gospel until they were overtaken by the same events that affected the Christians all over the world.

That was how Christianity came to Najrān in the Arab lands.

Then Ibn Isḥāq related the story of ʿAbd Allāh b. al-Thāmir when he adopted Christianity at the hands of Faymiyūn and how Dhū Nuwās killed him and his companions and dug the *ukhdūd*, the trench, for them. According to Ibn Hishām that *ukhdūd* was a long trench in the ground like a ditch. Dhū Nuwās kindled fires in it and burned these people with them; he also killed many others, to the total of almost 20,000, as is examined at length in the study of *sūrat al-Burūj* (LXXXV) in our *Tafsīr* (*Exegesis*) of the Qurʾān.[9] And all praise be to God!

An Account of how rule in Yemen passed from Ḥimyar and was transferred to the black Abyssinians.

The aforementioned events support the predictions of the two soothsayers, Shiqq and Saṭīḥ. Only one of the people of Najrān survived; his name was Daws Dhū Thaʿlabān and he escaped on his horse in the desert and could not be caught. He continued travelling until he reached Caesar, the emperor of Byzantium. Since the emperor was also a Christian, as he was, he told him what Dhū Nuwās and his troops had done and asked his aid. The emperor replied

9. Ibn Kathīr, *Tafsīr . . .*, Vol. 4, pp491–7.

that Daws' land was very far, but that he would write a message to the king of Abyssinia who was also of the same religion and whose country was closer at hand. The emperor then wrote such a message asking him to provide help and to seek revenge for Daws.

So Daws took Caesar's letter to the Negus[10] who dispatched 70,000 troops from Abyssinia under the leadership of one of his officers named Aryāṭ, along with another named Abraha al-Ashram. Aryāṭ crossed over the sea and reached the shores of Yemen, accompanied by Daws. Dhū Nuwās came out to meet him with his forces made up from Ḥimyar and the Yemeni tribes under his control. When they engaged, Dhū Nuwās and his men were defeated. When he realized that disaster had befallen himself and his people, Dhū Nuwās turned his horse to the sea and beat it until it entered the water and took him through the shallows and out to the depths of the sea where he perished. Aryāṭ entered Yemen and took control there. At this point Ibn Isḥāq records several poems by the Arabs detailing these strange events. These poems are in fine, eloquent, vivid, and elegant language, but we omit them here to avoid boring or wearying the reader. And God is our helper.

An Account of how Abraha al-Ashram rebelled against, fought, and killed Aryāṭ, and so assumed power over Yemen.

Ibn Isḥāq stated: "Aryāṭ remained in control over Yemen for some years but eventually Abraha challenged him and the Abyssinian forces split into two sides. One side moved to attack the other, but when the armies approached for battle, Abraha sent a message to Aryāṭ suggesting that he was wrong to pit the Abyssinians against one another to the ultimate damage of all, and that they should meet alone in battle, all forces then combining under the authority of the one victorious. To this Aryāṭ responded with agreement.

"Abraha, a short, stocky man and a devout Christian, then went out to fight Aryāṭ who was tall, handsome, powerfully built, and bore a javelin. Behind Abraha was a slave named ʿAtwada protecting his rear. Aryāṭ struck out, aiming at the top of Abraha's head, but his javelin hit him on the forehead and slit his eyebrow, eye, nose, and lip; that was why he was known as *al-Ashram*, i.e. the cleft-face. Then ʿAtwada advanced from behind Abraha and attacked and killed Aryāṭ. The forces of Aryāṭ went over to Abraha and all Abyssinians in Yemen united under him. Abraha then paid over the blood price for Aryāṭ's death.

"When this news reached the Negus, who had dispatched them both to Yemen, he was furious at Abraha, for he had attacked and killed his commander without orders from himself. Then the Negus swore an oath that he would give

10. The title given to the ruler of Abyssinia (now Ethiopia).

Abraha no respite until he had trodden his land and cut off his locks. So Abraha shaved his head and filled a leather bag with Yemeni soil which he sent to the Negus with a message saying, 'O king, Aryāṭ was merely your slave as I am. We differed about your command; everyone owes you obedience. But I was stronger, more effective, and more skilful than he was in managing Abyssinian affairs. I shaved my head completely when I heard of the king's oath and have sent to him a bag of my country's soil so that he may tread it underfoot and so keep his oath.' This message pleased the Negus when he received it, and he sent him a message that Abraha should remain in Yemen until further orders. And so it was that Abraha did remain in Yemen."

An Account of why Abraha attacked Mecca with elephants to put the kaʿba *to waste and how God quickly destroyed him.*

As God Almighty stated in the Qurʾān, "Have you not seen how God dealt with those who had elephants? Did he not defeat their scheme, sending flocks of birds which cast upon them stones of baked clay, rendering them like digested chaff?" (*sūrat al-Fīl*, CV, v.1–5).

It was said, according to al-Ṭabarī, that the first person to tame an elephant was Ifrīdūn b. Athfiyān, who killed al-Daḥḥāk. It was also he who first saddled horses. The first person to domesticate and ride a horse, though, was Faṭhamūrath, who was the third of the world's kings. It was also said that Ishmael, son of Abraham, upon both of whom be peace, was the first to ride a horse, and it is likely that he was the first Arab to ride. But God knows best.

Some say that, in spite of their size, elephants are scared of cats. Some army commanders brought cats into the pitch of battle when fighting the Indians, and so the elephants ran away.

Ibn Isḥāq continued: "Later Abraha built al-Qullays church in Ṣanʿāʾ, the like of which had never at that time been seen on earth before. He wrote to the Negus saying, 'I built a church for you the like of which was never built for any king before you, and I will not cease striving until I divert to it the Arabs' pilgrimage.'"

Al-Suhaylī stated that Abraha sought to humiliate the people of Yemen by building this ugly church, humbling them in a variety of ways. He invariably amputated the hand of any labourer who arrived for work after dawn. He began to transfer to it, from the Balqīs palace, marble, stone, and splendid furnishings. In it he erected crosses of gold and silver and pulpits made of ivory and ebony. Al-Qullays was built very tall indeed and its spaciousness was amazing. When eventually Abraha died and the Abyssinians dispersed, spirits would inflict evil on anyone daring to take any of its building materials or furnishings. This was because the building was undertaken in the name of two idols, Kuʿayb and his wife. The height of each of these was 60 cubits. Consequently the Yemenis left the church alone. It remained just as it had been up till the time of al-Saffāḥ, the first of the ʿAbbāsid caliphs. He sent there a group of men of determination, judgement, and knowledge who demolished it stone by stone; and today its remains are completely effaced.

Ibn Isḥāq continued: "When the Arabs learned of and talked about Abraha's message to the Negus, a certain intercalator of the Kināna tribe became enraged; the intercalators were the ones who would postpone a sacred month in Mecca, during which warfare would have been forbidden, when they wanted to make war. This is referred to in the Qurʾān: 'The practice of postponing (the sacred month) is merely further disbelief'" (*sūrat al-Barāʾa*, IX, v.37).

Ibn Isḥāq went on: "This Kinanite then travelled to the al-Qullays church and squatted down there, that is he defecated without anyone seeing, then left and returned home. When Abraha was informed of this he demanded to know who had done such a thing. He was told: 'It was one of the people of that *bayt* (building) in Mecca to which the Arabs made pilgrimage. When he heard of what you said of your intention to change the Arabs' pilgrimage to this church of yours, he became angry and so defiled it, thereby indicating that it was unworthy of being a place of pilgrimage.'

"Abraha was enraged at this and he swore that he would go to the *kaʿba* and destroy it. And so he ordered his Abyssinian troops to equip themselves and make ready, and then he set forth with his elephant. The Arabs were highly anxious and alarmed when they heard of this and considered it their duty to do battle with him, when they learned he wanted to destroy the *kaʿba*, God's sacred edifice. A member of the Yemeni nobility named Dhū Nafr summoned his people and those Arabs who would support him to do battle with Abraha and prevent his destruction of the *kaʿba*. Some did respond and they engaged in battle. Dhū Nafr and his supporters were vanquished and he himself was taken prisoner and brought before Abraha. When about to be killed, Dhū Nafr suggested to Abraha that he might well be more useful to him alive than dead. So Abraha kept him prisoner, in chains; he was a clement person.

"Abraha continued ahead to meet further adversaries and in the area of Khathʿam came up against Nufayl b. Ḥabīb al-Khathʿamī with his two allied tribes of Shahrān and Nāhis, along with other Arab supporting tribes. They did battle, Abraha won, and took Nufayl prisoner. When Abraha was about to execute him, Nufayl pleaded for his life and offered to be his guide in the Arab territory, guaranteeing that the tribes under him would be obedient to Abraha. So Abraha released him and went on ahead, with Nufayl acting as guide.

"Reaching Ṭāʾif, Abraha was met by Masʿūd b. Muʿattib b. Mālik b. Kaʿb b. ʿAmr b. Saʿd b. ʿAwf b. Thaqīf along with the warriors of Thaqīf. They addressed Abraha, saying, 'O king, we are your slaves, fully obedient to you; we have no dispute with you and this temple of ours is not the one you want.' By this they meant the temple devoted to the goddess al-Lāt. 'What you want is the building in Mecca; we will send guides to take you there.' So Abraha passed them by unmolested."

Ibn Isḥāq went on, "The temple of al-Lāt was one they had there in al-Ṭā'if that they venerated almost as was the *kaʿba*.

"So Thaqīf sent with Abraha Abū Righāl as guide to Mecca. They travelled as far as al-Mughammis where they made a stop. It was there that Abū Righāl died and thereafter the Arabs stoned his grave; his grave is the one at al-Mughammis that people still stone. In the story of Thamūd, Abū Righāl was one of their men who would seek refuge at the sanctuary but was struck and killed by a stone as he left it. Once the Messenger of God (ṢAAS) said to his Companions, 'And the proof is that he was buried with two branches of gold.' When his grave was disinterred, they did find them. He was said to be known as Abū Thaqīf."

The connection between this and Ibn Isḥāq's account is that the name of this latter Abū Righāl was the same as that of his ancestor and that the people stoned his grave just as they did that of the former. But God knows best. Jarīr spoke the verse: "When al-Farazdaq dies, then may people stone his grave like they stoned Abū Righāl's."[11]

It seems evident that he was the second.

Ibn Isḥāq continued: "When Abraha made a halt at al-Mughammis he sent on ahead to Mecca one of his Abyssinian men named al-Aswad b. Maqṣūd with some cavalry. He brought to him the possessions of the people of Tihāma, from Quraysh and others; this included 200 camels belonging to ʿAbd al-Muṭṭalib b. Hāshim who was at that time the leader and elder of Quraysh. As a result, Quraysh, Kināna, and Hudhayl, and all those venerating the *kaʿba* decided to do battle with Abraha but abandoned this idea when they learned they had insufficient power to match him."

Abraha then sent Ḥunāṭa the Ḥimyarite to Mecca with the following order: "Find the leader and the most noble of these people. Then tell him that the king says, 'I have not come to war upon you, but only to destroy that building (the *kaʿba*). If you do not engage in warfare to prevent our access to it, then I shall have no need for your blood.' If he does not want war, bring him to me with you."

When Ḥunāṭa entered Mecca he asked after the leader of Quraysh. He was directed to ʿAbd al-Muṭṭalib b. Hāshim and so passed on Abraha's message to him. ʿAbd al-Muṭṭalib replied, "By God, we do not want war with him and have not the power for it; this house is God's sacred house and that of His true follower Abraham, upon whom be peace." He was saying in effect, "If God does

11. Jarīr and al-Farazdaq, who lived during the seventh to eighth centuries AD, are remembered chiefly for their satiric verses aimed at one another.

protect it from Abraha, then it is because it is His holy sanctuary and His house. If he abandons it to him, then, by God, there's no way for us to defend it."

Ḥunāṭa then told ʿAbd al-Muṭṭalib that he must accompany him to Abraha in accord with his orders.

So ʿAbd al-Muṭṭalib set off along with some of his sons. Arriving at Abraha's encampment, he asked to see Dhū Nafr, who was a friend of his. When he met Dhū Nafr, still in confinement, he asked him whether he had any solution to their predicament. Dhū Nafr replied, "How can a man have a solution when he is a king's prisoner and is expecting to be killed at any time? I have no advice to give you, except to say that Unays, the elephant keeper, is a friend of mine. I will send him a message strongly commending you and ask him to seek permission for you to address the king. Speak to him as you see fit, and Unays will intercede on your behalf as well as he can."

ʿAbd al-Muṭṭalib agreed and Dhū Nafr sent Unays the following message: "ʿAbd al-Muṭṭalib is lord of Quraysh and custodian of the well[12] of Mecca; he feeds both men in the plains and wild animals on the mountains. The king seized 200 of his camels. So seek permission for him to see the king and intercede for him as best you can." Unays responded that he would.

Unays then spoke to Abraha, saying, "O king, here at your door seeking audience is the lord of Quraysh and keeper of the well of Mecca; he feeds both men in the plains and the wild beasts in the mountains. Allow him in to see you to discuss a matter with you." Abraha let him in.

ʿAbd al-Muṭṭalib was the most dignified, handsome, and impressive of men. When Abraha saw him, he wanted to honour him by not making him sit below himself. But he did not want the Abyssinians to see him sitting next to himself on the throne. So Abraha descended, sat down on a carpet, and had ʿAbd al-Muṭṭalib take his place beside him. He then told his interpreter to ask why he had come and he did so. ʿAbd al-Muṭṭalib replied, "What I want is for the king to return the 200 camels he took from me as compensation."

Hearing this, the king told his translator to reply as follows: "You impressed me when I saw you, but you displeased me when you spoke. You want to talk to me about 200 camels I took from you in compensation, but not about the building which is your religion and your ancestors' religion that I have come to destroy?"

ʿAbd al-Muṭṭalib replied, "I am the owner of the camels; the building has its own master who will protect it."

Abraha replied, "He won't protect it from me."

"Then it's between you and Him," ʿAbd al-Muṭṭalib said.

And so Abraha returned his camels to ʿAbd al-Muṭṭalib.

12. The reference is to *zamzam*, the holy well in Mecca.

Ibn Isḥāq stated that when he went in to see Abraha, ʿAbd al-Muṭṭalib was accompanied by Yaʿmur b. Nafātha b. ʿAdī b. al-Dīl b. Bakr b. ʿAbd Manāt b. Kināna, leader of Banū Bakr tribe, and Khuwaylid b. Wāʾila, leader of Hudhayl.

These men offered Abraha one-third of the produce of Tihāma if he would withdraw and not destroy the building. But Abraha refused their offer. And God alone knows whether or not that happened.

When they left Abraha, ʿAbd al-Muṭṭalib went to report to Quraysh and told them to retreat from Mecca to defensive positions in the mountains. Then ʿAbd al-Muṭṭalib took hold of the metal door knocker of the *kaʿba* and stood there with a group of men from Quraysh praying to God and asking His help against Abraha and his troops. As he stood holding the *kaʿba* door knocker, ʿAbd al-Muṭṭalib recited the verses:

> "O God, Your worshippers protect their homes, so protect Your building,
> Let not their cross and their power vanquish Yours tomorrow
> If You should leave them free with our *qibla*,[13] then that is what You will."

Ibn Hishām said that these were what he found to be the authentic verses of this poem.

Ibn Isḥāq reported that ʿAbd al-Muṭṭalib then released the *kaʿba* door-knocker and went off, along with his men of Quraysh, to the mountain peaks, taking up defensive positions and waiting for whatever Abraha might do.

Next morning Abraha prepared to enter Mecca, readying his elephant and equipping his troops. The elephant's name was Maḥmūd. When they directed the elephant towards Mecca, Nufayl b. Ḥabīb came close to it, took its ear and told it, "Kneel down, then go back to where you came from. Here you are in God's holy land." Then he released the elephant's ear and it knelt.

According to al-Suhaylī this means that the elephant fell to the ground, since it is not in the nature of elephants to kneel; although it has been said that some elephants do kneel like camels. God knows best.

Nufayl b. Ḥabīb hurried off into the mountains. Abraha's troops beat the elephant to make it stand up, struck its head with axes, and stuck hooks into its hide until it bled. But it refused to stand. Then they turned it to face towards Yemen, and it got up and moved in a hurry. When they directed it towards Syria and then towards the east it did the same. But when they turned it towards Mecca it knelt again.

Then God sent against them birds from the sea like swifts and crows, each one of which carried three stones, one in its beak and one in each claw. The stones were like chickpeas and lentils. Every soldier hit died, but not all were struck.

13. The *qibla* is the direction, usually indicated by a decorated niche in the wall of a mosque, to which Muslims turn in prayer, towards the *kaʿba*, that is.

So they retreated in haste along the road by which they had come, calling out for Nufayl b. Ḥabīb to lead them on the way back to Yemen. About this situation Nufayl spoke these verses:

> "Greetings to you from us, O Rudayna. How much we have gladdened our eyes this morning!
> Rudayna, had but you seen, but may you see not, what we saw at Mt. Muḥaṣṣab.
> Then you would have forgiven and praised me, and not felt ill will at what passed between us.
> I praised God to see the birds, and feared that a stone be cast upon me.
> While all called out for Nufayl, as though I owed the Abyssinians some debt."

Ibn Isḥāq continued, "So down they scrambled by any path, dying randomly where they went. Abraha was struck on his body and they carried him away as his fingers dropped off one by one. As they fell pus and blood emerged. When they got him to Ṣanʿā he was like a baby bird. He finally died when his heart burst from his chest. Or so they say."

Ibn Isḥāq went on to relate that Yaʿqūb b.ʿUtba told him that it was reported that measles and smallpox were seen for the first time in Arab lands that year. Also that that was the first year bitter plants were observed there: the African rue, the colocynth, and the *Asclepias gigantea*.

Ibn Isḥāq commented that when God sent Muḥammad (ṢAAS) one of the actions he enumerated as God's grace and bounties upon Quraysh was His having repelled the Abyssinians and saved Quraysh for posterity. And so God spoke in the Qurʾān, "Have you not seen how God dealt with those who had elephants? Did he not defeat their scheme, sending flocks of birds which cast upon them hard stones of baked clay, rendering them like digested chaff?" (*sūrat al-Fīl*, CV, v.1–5).

At this point both Ibn Isḥāq and Ibn Hishām go into interpretations of this chapter and the one that follows it. I have dealt with this in my *Tafsīr* (*Exegesis*)[14] in all sufficiency, God be willing, and to Him is due all praise and credit.

Ibn Hishām stated that the word *al-abābīl*, flocks, means groups; the Arabs used no singular form for this noun that we know. He also stated that regarding the word *al-sijjil*, i.e. "hard", Yūnus the grammarian and Abū ʿUbayda told him that the Arabs used it to mean "very solid". Some commentators claim that the latter is really two Persian words made into one by the Arabs, they being *sanj* and *jill*. The first of these means "stone", the second "clay", so the combination word would indicate something made of both of these. The word *ʿaṣaf* in the Qurʾān passage quoted above means vegetation foliage that has not been chewed. Al-Kisāʾī said that he had heard from a grammarian that the singular of the word *al-abābīl* is *ibbīl*.

14. Ibn Kathīr, *Tafsīr* . . . , Vol. 4, pp548–53.

Many early authorities interpreted this word *al-abābīl* to mean birds that follow one another hither and thither in groups.

According to Ibn ʿAbbās they had beaks like those of birds but paws like those of dogs.

ʿIkrima said that their heads were like those of lions which emerged at them from the sea and that these were green.

ʿUbayd b. ʿUmayr said that they were black sea-birds bearing stones in their beaks and claws.

According to Ibn ʿAbbās they were similar in form to the griffins of North Africa. He also maintained that the smallest stones they had were like human heads, some as big as camels. That is what Yūnus b. Bukayr said on the authority of Ibn Isḥāq. It is also said they were small – but God knows best.

Ibn Abī Ḥātim said that he was told, by Abū Zurʿa, Muḥammad b. ʿAbd Allāh b. Abū Shayba, and Abū Muʿāwiya, from al-Aʿmash, Abū Sufyān, and ʿUbayd b. ʿUmayr, that when God wished to destroy those with the elephant He sent upon them birds like swifts that were raised up from the sea. Each bird carried three stones, two in its claws and one in its beak. He said the birds came, lined up over their heads, screeched, and dropped what was in their claws and beaks. Each stone that fell on a man's head exited through his behind and each stone that fell on one side of a man exited from the other. God also sent a fierce gale which struck the stones and increased their velocity. And so they were all killed.

But, as Ibn Isḥāq has stated above, not all were struck by the stones. Some did return to Yemen to tell their people of the disaster that befell them. And it was also said that Abraha, God curse him, went back, his fingers dropping off one by one, and that when he reached Yemen his chest burst open and he died.

Ibn Isḥāq related that ʿAbd Allāh b. Abū Bakr told him, on the authority of ʿAmra, that ʿĀʾisha[15] said, "I saw the elephant's keeper and guide in Mecca, both blind and crippled, begging for food." As mentioned above, the keeper's name was Unays, though no name was given for its guide. But God knows best.

Al-Naqqāsh stated in his Qurʾān exegesis that a torrent bore away their bodies into the sea. Al-Suhaylī said that the events of the elephant occurred on the first day of Muḥarram, year 886 of the era of Dhū al-Qarnayn (Alexander the Great).

And I add that it was the same year that the Messenger of God (ṢAAS) was born, as is generally known. It is also said, however, that these events preceded his birth by some years, as we will report, God willing, and in Him we trust.

Here Ibn Isḥāq mentions the poetry recited by the Arabs on this great occasion on which God rendered His sacred house victorious, wishing it to be honoured, respected, purified, and dignified through the mission of Muḥammad (ṢAAS) and through the true religion He legislated to him. One of the elements of this

15. ʿĀʾisha was the daughter of Abū Bakr and became the wife of the Prophet.

religion, indeed one of its pillars, is prayer, the direction of which would be towards this sanctified *kaʿba*. What God did then to the elephant's army was not a victory for Quraysh over the Abyssinian Christians; the Abyssinians were at that time closer to it (i.e. to victory from God) than the polytheist Quraysh. The victory belonged to the sacred house and served to set the foundation and pave the way for the mission of Muḥammad (ṢAAS).

Included in this poetry are the verses of ʿAbd Allāh b. al-Zibaʿrā al-Sahmī:

"They fled in terror from Mecca's interior, its sanctuary undisturbed for ages past;
Sirius had created no nights inviolate since not even one of the mightiest of men could ever aspire to attack it.
Ask the Abyssinian prince what he saw of it; he who has knowledge of it shall inform the ignorant.
Sixty thousand men did not return to their land, even their sick did not live after their homecoming.
ʿĀd and Jurhum were there before them, but God held it high above all men."

Abū Qays b. al-Aslat *al-anṣārī* al-Madanī also spoke verses on the subject:

"God's work it was the day of the Abyssinians' elephant; many times did they urge it on, but it didn't budge;
Their hooks were under its sides and they slashed its trunk until it tore.
They used a knife instead of a whip; when they aimed it at its back it was badly wounded.
So it turned and ran away, and those there did fail for their evil.
God sent a gale down upon them, overwhelming them as if they were dwarves.
Their priests urged fortitude but they screamed like bleating sheep."

Abū al-Ṣalt Rabīʿa b. Abū Rabīʿa Wahb b. ʿAllāj al-Thaqafī spoke the following verses, though Ibn Hishām attributed them to Umayya b. Abū al-Ṣalt:

"Our Lord's signs are manifestly clear, only disbelievers doubting them.
He created night and day and all clear, its reckoning determined.
Then a merciful Lord makes clear the day with a sun of spreading rays.
He kept the elephant at al-Mughammis until it crawled as though hamstrung.
Kneeling down like a camel, and still, as if it were carved out of a rock from the mountain.
Around it heroes from among the kings of Kinda, eagle-like lords in wars
They left it, then all fled in fright, each with a broken leg.
All religions except Abraham's *al-Ḥanīfa* are null in God's sight on Judgement Day."

Abū Qays b. al-Aslat said also:

"Arise and pray to your God, cleansing yourself at the pillars of His house between the rugged mountains.
From it you had a certain calamity on the day of Abū Yaksūm [Abraha, tr.], leader of the phalanges:

His élite walks on the plain, his troops on their camels at the mountain heights.
When you received victory from the Owner of the Throne, hosts of angels repelled them, casting soil and stones.
Quickly they turned in flight; and of the Abyssinians all who returned were injured."

Also among such verses is the one of ʿUbayd Allāh b. Qays al-Ruqayyāt extolling the greatness of the *kaʿba* and its protection through the destruction of those wishing it harm:

"Split-face (Abraha) attacked it, coming with his elephant, but his army turned back, defeated.
Birds rained stones down upon them until he was like a man being stoned.
Whoever attacks that place returns with his armies defeated, humiliated."

Ibn Isḥāq and others related that upon the demise of Abraha, his son Yaksūm assumed power, followed by the latter's brother Masrūq b. Abraha. He was the last of their kings and it was from him that Sayf b. Dhū Yazan of Ḥimyar wrested the kingship with the aid of troops he brought from Chosroe Anūshirwān, as we shall relate. The events with the elephant occurred in the month of Muḥarram, in the year 886 in the era of Dhū al-Qarnayn, Alexander son of Phillip, the Macedonian, after whom the Greeks count their calendar.

Abraha and his two sons having died and Abyssinian rule over Yemen having ended, al-Qullays, the temple Abraha had built, in his ignorance and stupidity, as a substitute for the Arab pilgrimage, was abandoned and left unattended. He had constructed over it two wooden idols, Kuʿayb and his wife, each one 60 cubits high. These idols were invested by spirits, and consequently anyone chancing to take anything from the temple building or its furnishings would come to harm. This continued to be the case until the time of al-Saffāḥ, the first of the ʿAbbāsid caliphs. When he was told about it and all its marble and furnishings that Abraha had brought from the Balqīs castle in Yemen, he sent people to disassemble it stone by stone and to take away all its contents. That is how al-Suhaylī related it; God knows best.

An Account of the reversion of the kingship from the Abyssinians to Sayf b. Dhū Yazan the Ḥimyarite, just as the two soothsayers had predicted to Rabīʿa b. Naṣr, the Lakhmite.

Muḥammad b. Isḥāq, God have mercy on him, said that when Abraha died, his son Yaksūm b. Abraha became king over the Abyssinians. Abraha's agnomen was Abū Yaksūm, i.e. the father of Yaksūm. Then, when Yaksūm died his brother Masrūq b. Abraha became the Abyssinian king over Yemen.

Ultimately, the people of Yemen having so long suffered in misery, Sayf b. Dhū Yazan, the Ḥimyarite, became rebellious. His genealogy was Sayf b. Dhū Yazan b. Dhū Aṣbaḥ b. Mālik b. Zayd b. Sahl b.ʿAmr b. Qays b. Muʿāwiya b. Jashm b. ʿAbd Shams b. Wāʾil b. al-Ghawth b. Quṭun b. ʿArīb b. Zuhayr b. Ayman b. al-Hamaysaʿ b. al-ʿAranjaj, the last being Ḥimyar b. Sabaʾ. Sayf was also known as Abū Murra.

He made his way to the Byzantine emperor and complained to him of the state of affairs in Yemen, asking him to oust the Abyssinians and appoint him governor there. He suggested the emperor send from Byzantium whatever troops he thought necessary for this purpose and so himself would become king of Yemen. The emperor declined.

So Sayf went to al-Nuʿmān b. al-Mundhir, who was Chosroe's vice-regent over al-Ḥīra and the neighbouring territories in Iraq, and complained to him about the Abyssinians. Al-Nuʿmān responded that every year he sent an official delegation to Chosroe, and invited Sayf to stay with him until then. Sayf agreed.

Sayf later did accompany al-Nuʿmān, who took him in to see Chosroe, seated in the chamber where his crown was kept. His crown was like a large grain bucket and was, so they say, set with rubies, chrysolites, pearls, gold, and silver, suspended by a gold chain from the dome of his audience chamber. His neck did not bear the crown; he was kept hidden by a cloth until he sat down there. Then he would put his head into his crown. When he was thus positioned on his throne, the cloth would be removed. All who saw him for the first time would kneel down in awe of him.

When Sayf entered he bowed his head down low, and the king commented, "It is really stupid to come in through such a tall doorway and bow one's head down so low!"

When this remark was transmitted to Sayf, he responded that he had only done this out of his preoccupying distress that overwhelmed all else. He then went on to say, "O king, crows have taken charge of our country!"

"What crows?" Chosroe asked, "the ones from Abyssinia or from Sind?"

"From Abyssinia. I've come to ask your help; and you shall have kingship over all our land."

Chosroe replied, "Your country is far away, and its riches meagre. I'm not going to embroil an army from Persia in Arabia. I don't need that."

He then presented Sayf with 10,000 pure-minted dirhams and a robe of honour. Having received these, Sayf went outside and began distributing the money to people. When the emperor heard of this he wondered why, and so sent for him and asked him why he was throwing away a king's gift to people.

Sayf replied, "What else am I to do with your gift? Are not the mountains of my country made of gold and silver?"

He said this to arouse Chosroe's interest. So Chosroe then assembled his advisers and asked their counsel about Sayf and his mission. They reminded him of the presence in his gaols of prisoners he had condemned to death and suggested he send them with Sayf. For if they were killed that was what Chosroe had intended for them anyway, and if they triumphed his own domain would be expanded.

Chosroe therefore sent off with Sayf eight hundred men from his prisons and placed them under the command of a man named Wahriz, an elder of the highest repute and ancestry. They set sail in eight ships, of which two sank; so six ships eventually arrived on the coast of Aden.

Sayf gathered together all his own men he could to help Wahriz, saying, "My leg is with yours till we all die or all triumph." Wahriz replied that that was fair.

Masrūq b. Abraha then came out with his troops to meet them in battle. Wahriz sent his own son out to do combat and test their mettle. Wahriz's son was slain; this increased the anger and hatred the father had for them.

When the enemy troops were positioned on the battlefield, Wahriz asked his men to indicate which was their king. They pointed to a man on an elephant with a crown and wearing a ruby between his eyes. He saw him and told them not to attack him.

For some time nothing was done. Then Wahriz asked what the Abyssinian leader was doing now. They told him he was now on a horse. Again Wahriz told them not to attack him, and for long they waited. Eventually Wahriz asked after the king and was told he was now on a mule. "So", Wahriz commented, "on an ass's filly, is he? He has humbled himself and his domain. I'll take a shot at him. If you see his companions not moving, then stay still till I give you further orders, for I will have missed the man. But if you see his people crowding around him and not advancing, I shall have hit him. In that case, you advance at them."

With that he braced his bowstring; they say his bow was so stiff only he could brace it. He then had his eyebrows tied back and let the arrow fly. He split the ruby between the king's eyes and the arrow pierced right through his head and emerged from its back. He was knocked off his mount, and the Abyssinians milled around him in confusion. The Persians charged and the Abyssinians were defeated, being killed or fleeing in all directions.

Wahriz advanced to enter Ṣanʿāʾ. When he reached its gateway he insisted that his banner could never enter in a lowered position, and that they should therefore demolish the gate. This was done and he went inside with his banner held high. Sayf b. Dhū Yazan then said:

> "People thought the two kingdoms had united.
> If some had really believed it, then the matter would be serious and grave.
> We killed the general Masrūq and spilt blood on the sandhills.

The new general, Wahriz, the people's general, swore an oath
Not to drink wine before taking prisoners and booty."

Arabs from Ḥijāz and elsewhere came in delegations to Sayf, praising him and congratulating him that the kingship had gone to him. Quraysh sent such a delegation and its number included ʿAbd al-Muṭṭalib b. Hāshim. Sayf gave him the glad tidings of the coming of the Messenger of God (ṢAAS) and informed him of what he knew about him. Details of this will be given hereafter in the chapter related to the predictions of his coming.

According to Ibn Isḥāq, Abū al-Ṣalt b. Rabīʿa al-Thaqafī spoke the following verses. However, Ibn Hishām attributed them to Umayya b. Abū al-Ṣalt.

"Let vengeance seekers be like Ibn Dhū Yazan, who took to the sea and for ages sought a way to his enemies,
Going to Caesar when his journey seemed right, but finding there none of what he sought.
Then he turned after ten years to Chosroe, disregarding his life and the cost
Until he came bringing a band of free men; how quickly you sped!
What a fine group of men; I never saw their like before.
Persian braves, mighty warriors, archers, like lions raising their cubs in the forests,
Their bows shooting arrows like *howdah* poles, swiftly dispatching their enemies.
You sent lions against black dogs, their prey defeated and lost in the land
So drink up, enjoy your crown, and settle at the top of Ghumdān's palace as your permanent home.
Those were fine deeds. They were not two pails of milk mixed with water and later turning to urine!"

It is said that *Ghumdān* mentioned here was a palace in Yemen built by Yaʿrub b. Qaḥṭān; it was owned after him by Wāʾila b. Ḥimyar b. Sabaʾ. It was reputed to be 20 storeys high. God knows best.

Ibn Isḥāq relates that ʿAdī b. Zayd al-Ḥīrī, of the Banū Tamīm, spoke these verses,

"What after Ṣanʿāʾ? There lived governors of abundant gifts.
Its builders raised it high to the scattering clouds, its chambers musk-scented.
Guarded by the mountains against the enemy hordes, its heights unscalable.
The hooting of owls pleasingly answered at night by the flute players.
Fate led there the army of free men, their knights in procession,
Crossing the desert on mules bearing death, accompanied by their foals,
Until the princes saw them from the castle heights, their divisions armour-clad,
The day they shouted at the barbarians and al-Yaksūm, 'Damn all who flee!'
A day long remembered, when a prosperous way of life ended which had been secure,
A day when the one was replaced by the many, so times change, many the marvels,
After the Tubbaʿ kings came noblemen whose satraps held quiet sway there."

According to Ibn Hishām this is what Saṭīḥ meant when he said, "Iram Dhū Yazan will follow, emerging from Aden to fight them, and he will leave not one of them in Yemen." This is also what Shiqq meant by saying, "a young man, guilt-free and faultless, who will emerge from the line of Dhū Yazan."

Ibn Isḥāq's account states, "So Wahriz and the Persians stayed in Yemen. And the *abnā'*[16] who live in Yemen today are descendants of these Persian troops."

The rule of the Abyssinians in Yemen, lasting between Aryāṭ's arrival and the death of Masrūq b. Abraha at the hands of the Persians and the removal of the Abyssinians, was 72 years. Their dominion was passed through four rulers, Aryāṭ, then Abraha, then Yaksūm b. Abraha, and finally Masrūq b. Abraha.

An Account of how Persian rule in Yemen ended.

Ibn Hishām's account states that eventually Wahriz died and Chosroe appointed his son al-Marzubān b. Wahriz over Yemen; when he died, Chosroe appointed the latter's son al-Taynujān. Later Chosroe exiled al-Taynujān from Yemen and appointed Bādhān to the rule; it was during his reign that the Messenger of God (ṢAAS) was appointed to his mission.

Ibn Hishām also relates that he was informed, on the authority of al-Zuhrī, that the latter said that Chosroe wrote the following to Bādhān, "I am told that a man from Quraysh has appeared in Mecca claiming to be a prophet. Travel to him and seek his repentance. If he repents, well and good. If he does not, send me his head!"

Bādhān sent Chosroe's message to the Messenger of God (ṢAAS) who replied, "God has promised me that Chosroe will be killed on such and such a day and month." When this response was brought to Bādhān he came to a halt and waited, saying, "If indeed he be a Prophet, it will occur as he said." And God did kill Chosroe on the day foreseen by the Messenger of God (ṢAAS).

According to Ibn Hishām he died at the hands of his son Shīrawayh. Others state that his sons joined forces to kill him.

This Chosroe was by name Abrawīz b. Hurmuz b. Anushirwān b. Qabbādh. It was he who defeated the Byzantines, as referred to in the Almighty's words in the Qur'ān, "A.L.M. The Romans have been defeated in the closest land" (*sūrat al-Rūm*, XXX, v.1–3). This will be explained later.

According to al-Suhaylī his death occurred the night of Tuesday, the tenth of Jumādā al-Ūlā, of the year 9 AH. What happened, it is thought, though God

16. The word in Arabic means "sons". Originally it was used in this context to refer to the offspring of the Persians who accompanied Sayf b. Dhū Yazan to Yemen. Then the term became more loosely used to refer to those whose mothers were not from the same race as their fathers.

alone knows, is that when the Messenger of God (ṢAAS) wrote to Chosroe inviting him to accept Islam, he became enraged, tore up the letter and then wrote his own instructions to his governor in Yemen.

Some accounts report that the Messenger of God (ṢAAS) replied to Bādhān's emissary with the words, "This night my Lord has killed your lord." And it was as he said, Chosroe being killed that very same night by his sons as a result of his having changed from justice to tyranny. Having deposed him they appointed his son Shīrawayh in his place. But he only lived on for six months or less after he had murdered his father.

Khālid b. Ḥiqq al-Shaybānī spoke the following verses on this:

> "And there was Chosroe, sliced up by his sons with swords as if he were meat.
> One day fate did bring him to term; is there not a term for every pregnant mother?"

Al-Zuhrī added that when news of Chosroe's death reached Bādhān, he sent word to the Messenger of God (ṢAAS) of the acceptance of Islam by himself and the Persians along with him. His Persian envoys asked, "To whom do we belong, Messenger of God?" He replied, "You are from us and to us, the people of the House." According to al-Zuhrī, that was why the Messenger of God (ṢAAS) spoke the words, "Salmān is of us, the people of the House."

It seems that this was after the emigration of the Messenger of God (ṢAAS) to Medina. He therefore sent his commanders to Yemen to inform people of what was good and to call upon them to believe in God, the Almighty and Glorious. First he dispatched Khālid b. al-Walīd and 'Alī b. Abū Ṭālib; later Abū Mūsā al-Ash'arī and Mu'ādh b. Jabal followed them, and Yemen and its people accepted Islam.

Bādhān died and his son Shahr b. Bādhān ruled after him. It was he whom al-Aswad al-'Ansī killed after al-Aswad had pretended prophecy and taken Shahr's wife, as we will report, and expelled from Yemen the deputies of the Messenger of God (ṢAAS). When al-Aswad was killed the authority of Islam returned.

Ibn Hishām stated that it was he whom Saṭīḥ had meant by his words, "A Prophet pure to whom revelation comes from the All-high." He was also meant by Shiqq when he said that Persian rule would be "brought short by a messenger dispatched, who will bring forth truth and justice among a people of religion and virtue, in whom power shall reside until the Day of Separation."

Ibn Isḥāq states also that there was, so they claim, a stone inscription in Yemen, from the Book of Psalms, dating from ancient times which read, "Who rules Dhamār? Ḥimyar the Good. Who rules Dhamār? The evil Abyssinians. Who rules Dhamār? The free Persians. Who rules Dhamār? Quraysh the merchants."

A poet's words on this subject are recorded by al-Masʿūdī as follows, "When Dhamār was named, it was asked, 'To whom do you belong?' 'To Ḥimyar the good', came the reply. Asked to whom next, the reply came, 'To the Abyssinians most vile.' 'To whom next?' it was asked, and 'To the free Persians' came the reply. 'To whom next?' it was asked, and 'To the merchants of Quraysh,' came the reply."

It is said that these verses quoted by Muḥammad b. Isḥāq were found inscribed at the grave of Hūd, upon whom be peace, when the wind exposed his tomb in Yemen. That was shortly before the time of Balqīs, in the days of Mālik b. Dhū al-Manār, brother of ʿAmr Dhū al-Adhʿār b. Dhū al-Manār. It is said also that it was inscribed on Hūd's tomb and that those were his own words.

It is al-Suhaylī who related this; God knows best.

The Story of al-Sāṭirūn, King of al-Ḥaḍr

His story was related at this point by ʿAbd al-Mālik b. Hishām because of what certain scholars of genealogy had stated in connection with al-Nuʿmān b. al-Mundhir, mentioned above. They related that when Sayf b. Dhū Yazan went to al-Nuʿmān and asked him for help in regaining control over Yemen, it was stated that al-Nuʿmān had descended from al-Sāṭirūn, king of al-Ḥaḍr.

We earlier stated from Ibn Isḥāq that al-Nuʿmān b. al-Mundhir was of the line of Rabīʿa b. Naṣr, and that it was reported from Jubayr b. Muṭʿim that he was a descendant of Qanaṣ b. Maʿad b. ʿAdnān. These are, then, three statements on his genealogy, and Ibn Hishām went on to tell about the king of al-Ḥaḍr.

Al-Ḥaḍr was a great fortress built by that king, whose name was al-Sāṭirūn, on the banks of the Euphrates. It was positioned high up and built tall and very spacious, its accommodations being like those of a large town. It was extremely well fortified and decorated in the utmost luxury, splendour, and good taste; it received taxes from all the surrounding areas.

The genealogy of al-Sāṭirūn, as given by Ibn al-Kalbī, was al-Dayzin b. Muʿāwiya b. ʿUbayd b. Ajram, from the tribe of Sulayḥ b. Ḥulwān b. al-Ḥāf b. Quḍāʿa.

Others said that he was of the al-Jarāmiqa, one of the Ṭawāʾif kings whom he used to lead when they gathered to make war against one of their enemies. His fortress was between the Tigris and the Euphrates.

Ibn Hishām went on to state that Chosroe Sābūr Dhū al-Aktāf attacked al-Sāṭirūn, king of al-Ḥaḍr.

Someone other than Ibn Hishām stated that the one who attacked the king of al-Ḥaḍr was Sābūr b. Ardashīr b. Bābik, the first of the Sassanian kings, who humiliated the Ṭawāʾif kings and returned control to the Chosroes. Sābūr Dhū al-Aktāf, this authority claims, came a long time afterwards. God knows best. That information comes from al-Suhaylī.

Ibn Hishām's account continues, "And Sābūr besieged al-Ḥaḍr for two years." Others say four years.

His reason for doing this was that al-Sāṭirūn had attacked Sābūr's territory during the latter's absence in Iraq. The daughter of al-Sāṭirūn, whose name was al-Naḍīra, looked down and saw Sābūr dressed in silk garments and wearing a gold crown studded with topaz, emeralds and pearls; and he was handsome. So she secretly sent him a message asking if he would marry her if she opened the fortress gate for him. He replied that he would.

That evening al-Sāṭirūn drank wine till he was drunk; he was always drunk when he went to bed. Then she took the fortress keys from beneath his head and gave them to a servant of hers who opened the gates. Another account states that she directed Sābūr's people to a wide water channel through which they entered al-Ḥaḍr. Yet another version has her telling them of a spell over the fortress; they knew it would not be conquered until a grey pigeon was taken, its feet dyed with the menstrual fluid of a blue-eyed virgin, and then released. If it dropped on the walls of the fortress the spell would be removed and the gates would open. Sābūr did this, and the gates did come open.

So Sābūr went inside, killed al-Sāṭirūn, confiscated al-Ḥaḍr and then destroyed it. Then he took al-Naḍīra away with him and married her. While sleeping at night in bed, she began tossing and turning and could not sleep. Sābūr had candles brought and they searched her bed, in which they discovered one myrtle leaf. Sābūr asked her if that was what had kept her awake, and she replied that it was.

Sābūr asked her how her father had treated her. She answered, "He furnished me with silk brocade, dressed me in silk, gave me the choicest food[17] to eat and wine to drink."

Sābūr commented, "And then you treated him the way you did! You'd do the same to me quicker!"

Then he tied her tresses to the tail of a horse and it galloped away until she was killed.

Aʿshā Banī Qays b. Thaʿlaba composed these verses about this:

"Consider al-Ḥaḍr and its people's ease; but do blessings last forever?
Shāhbūr kept his troops there two years, striking it with their adzes.
And when he gave prayer to his Lord, and repented, He took no revenge.
Did his Lord provide him extra power, and was there ever the like of his castle?

17. In the original the text reads, "gave me brain as food to eat". Cooked brain was considered a delicacy.

He had appealed to his people, 'Come to your task; it is set;
Die nobly with your swords; I see death is ordained for those so fated.' "

Also ʿAdī b. Zayd spoke the following verses in this regard,

"Al-Ḥaḍr was afflicted from above by a dreadful, terrible, huge calamity
Due to a maiden who did not protect her father when he was delirious and off his guard;
She gave him much evening wine, undiluted, which he drank abundantly. And wine deludes, its imbiber never quenched.
That night she surrendered her people, believing the (enemy's) chief would marry her,
But next morning the bride's reward was blood running in streams,
Al-Ḥaḍr was ruined and confiscated; her chamber was fired and its contents burned."

ʿAdī b. Zayd also recited the verses,

"O malicious blamer of fate, are you guilt-free and perfect?
Or has time promised you a solid pledge to be ever safe? Indeed you are stupid and conceited.
Or whom did you see fate made immortal, and who had a watchful guard lest he be harmed?
Where now is Caesar Anūshirwān, the king of kings, or where Sābūr before him?
The noble Banū Aṣfar, kings of Byzantium, not one of them remains remembered.
And al-Ḥaḍr's lord, built by him, with both the Tigris and the al-Khābūr rivers made to flow to it,
Of marble built and plaster adorned, with birds nesting in its heights,
Unsuspecting of misfortune, yet all state now gone, its gates deserted.
Remember the lord of al-Khawarnaq,[18] who set forth one day, though right guidance requires thought.
His wealth and properties delighted him, the sea was his command, and his palace al-Sadīr,
Yet his heart was converted and he said, 'What joy for the living to death progressing,
Then becoming like leaves dried and tossed by the wind and breezes?' "

The man referred to in the verses above as the 'lord of al-Khawarnaq' was a king of by-gone days who had been warned by a learned man of his time about his conduct and practices. The king had exceeded his bounds, become arrogant and self-willed, and followed his own instincts unbridled. The learned man warned him by reference to the kings and states that had preceded him, how

18. He is referring to al-Nuʿmān, king of al-Ḥīra, who owned the two palaces of al-Khawarnaq and al-Sadīr. He is mentioned frequently in the poetry of the pre-Islamic era.

they had gone without a trace, and that nothing he took from others would not be transmitted from him in turn to those following him. This advice had impact and influence on him, and he was converted, giving thought to both his present and past and to the constraints of the grave. So he repented, returned to the faith and changed his ways. He abdicated, dressed himself as a mendicant, went off into the wilderness and the desert, and enjoyed solitude, shunning that pursuit of the senses and disobedience to the Lord of the Heavens followed by most people.

His story was told in extensive detail by the Sheikh and Imām Muwaffaq b. Qudāma al-Maqdisī, may the Almighty have mercy on him, in his book *Al-Tawwābūn* (*The Repentants*). Similarly, the *ḥafiẓ* Abū al-Qāsim al-Suhaylī reported it, thoroughly documented, in his book *Al-Rawḍ al-Unuf* (*The Virgin Meadows*) which is clearly written and well organized.

An Account of the Ṭawāʾif *kings.*

Regarding the ruler of al-Ḥaḍr, Sāṭirūn, he was, as previously explained, considered a precursor to the rest of the *Ṭawāʾif* ('factions') kings. He lived at the time of Alexander, son of Phillip of Macedonia, the Greek. This came about when Alexander defeated the king of the Persians, Darius son of Darius. Alexander subjugated Darius's kingdom, destroyed his land, arrested the best of his people, expropriated his produce, scattered the Persians to the winds, and determined that they should never thereafter join together and unite their forces.

So he began appointing a separate king over each group of people in any given area, Arabs and non-Arabs alike. Thereafter each of these kings would protect his own area, preserve his own allotment, and exploit his own region. When one king died, he would be succeeded by his son or by some other one of his people. This system prevailed for about 500 years.

Eventually, in the time of Ardashīr b. Bābik of Banū Sāsān b. Bahman b. Asfandiyār b. Yashtāsib b. Lahrāsib, their kingdom returned to its former condition. Ardashīr took over, rejoined the petty kingdoms altogether in one, and ended the rule of the *Ṭawāʾif* kings; so not a trace of them remained.

Ardashīr delayed besieging the oldest-established, greatest, and most powerful of these kinglets, the ruler of al-Ḥaḍr, since he was their leader and precursor. When Ardashīr died, his son Sābūr turned his attention to al-Ḥaḍr and besieged it until he conquered it, as told above. And God, all Glorious and Almighty, knows best.

An Account of the sons of Ishmael who were the Arabs of Ḥijāz, and of events of the jāhiliyya *period up to the time of the Mission.*

We have already, in a previous work,[19] given an account of Ishmael, upon whom be peace, along with the Prophets. It tells of how his father Abraham, upon whom be blessings and peace, bore him away with his wife Hājar and made them to dwell in the Mecca valley between the mountains of Fārān, an unpleasant and desolate place. Ishmael was still unweaned at the time. Then Abraham went away and left them there, God having commanded him to do so. Ishmael's mother had nothing except a leather bag containing dates and a skin-bottle with water in it. When that was exhausted, God made the well *zamzam* flow for Hājar, it being a tasty sustenance for the hungry and a cure for the sick, as is related in the long *ḥadīth* of Ibn ʿAbbās recorded by al-Bukhārī, God have mercy on him.

Later, Jurhum, who were a group of the original Arabs who were descended from the ancient Arab tribes, settled near Hājar in Mecca, with no right to the water except for their own drinking and use. Hājar felt comfortable and secure with them.

Abraham, peace be upon him, kept an eye on them all the time; it is said he would ride his horse, al-Burāq, on his journeys to and from Jerusalem.

Later, when the boy became a youth and he would busy himself with his father, the issue of making sacrifice arose, the sacrifice being in reality Ishmael.

When Ishmael grew up, he married a woman from Jurhum, then left her and married another, the daughter of Muḍāḍ b. ʿAmr al-Jurhumī. She bore him 12 sons whose names have been mentioned before. These were: Nābit, Qaydhar, Adhbul, Misha, Mismaʿ, Mashī, Dimmā, Adhar, Yaṭūr, Nabsh, Ṭīmā, and Qaydhumā. These are as given by Muḥammad b. Isḥāq and others using written sources. He also had one daughter whose name was Nasma; it was she he married to his nephew al-ʿĪṣū b. Isḥāq b. Abraham. From her were born to him al-Rūm and Fāris, and also al-Ashbān, in one of the two accounts.

The Arabs of Ḥijāz, with all their different tribes, are traced in their genealogy to Ishmael's two sons Nābit and Qaydhar. After Ishmael, the governor and ruler-in-chief of Mecca and the custodian of the temple and of the well *zamzam* was Nābit, cousin through his mother to the Jurhumites.

Later the Jurhumites gained control over *al-bayt* (the *kaʿba*), being jealous of their relatives, and ruled in Mecca and the areas around it for a long time in place of Ishmael's line. The first to gain control after Nābit was Muḍāḍ b. ʿAmr b. Saʿd b. al-Raqīb b.ʿAybar b. Nabt b. Jurhum.

19. Ibn Kathīr, *al-Bidāya wa al-Nihāya* (*The Beginning and the End*), Vol. 1.

Jurhum was the son of Qaḥṭān. His line was also given as Jurhum b. Yaqṭun b. ʿAybar b. Shālikh b. Arafkhshud b. Sām b. Nūḥ al-Jurhumī. The Jurhumites settled in the heights of Mecca, at al-Quʿayqiʿān.

Al-Samaydaʿ, leader of Qaṭūrāʾ had settled with his people in the lower part of Mecca. The Jurhumites and Qaṭūrāʾ, charged a tax on all who passed by them on their ways to Mecca.

Ultimately warfare broke out between the tribes of Jurhum and Qaṭūrāʾ. Al-Samaydaʿ was killed, and full power over Mecca and *al-bayt* thus were gained by Muḍāḍ. The descendants of Ishmael did not contend with him despite their large numbers, respected position, and the diversity of their locations throughout Mecca and its surroundings; this was due to their family ties to them and to the majesty of the sacred *bayt*.

After Muḍāḍ, power went to his son al-Ḥārith and then to his son, ʿAmr.

Later Jurhum acted wrongfully in Mecca and corruption there spread. People came to disrespect the sacred mosque. It is even said that one of their men, named Isāf b. Baghī, and a woman named Nāʾila, daughter of Waʾil, met inside the *kaʿba* and that he committed fornication with her. And so God turned them into two rocks which the people set up near the temple as a warning to others. After a great deal of time had passed, these two rocks became the object of worship aside from God, during the period of Khuzāʿa. This will be further explained later. These became two idols set on high and named Isāf and Nāʾila.

When the misdeeds of Jurhum in the sacred land grew worse, Khuzāʿa, who had settled near the sanctuary, arose against them. They, Khuzāʿa, were of the line of ʿAmr b. ʿĀmir who had left Yemen because of what he expected would occur with the ʿArim torrent, as we have related above. It is also said that Khuzāʿa traced their descent to Ishmael's sons. God knows best.

Anyway, Khuzāʿa did join together to fight Jurhum and they engaged in battle; the descendants of Ishmael sided with neither party.

Khuzāʿa, being the tribe of Bakr b. ʿAbd Manāt and Ghubshān, gained victory and ousted them from the *kaʿba*.

ʿAmr b. al-Hārith b. Muḍāḍ al-Jurhumī, their leader, made off with the *kaʿba*'s two gazelles, made of gold, the cornerstone, the 'black stone' that is, as well as decorated swords and other items, and buried them all in the well *zamzam*, which he filled with earth. Then he and his people moved out, back to Yemen.

On this subject ʿAmr b. al-Ḥārith b. Muḍāḍ composed the following:

> "Her tears flowing and her eyes red and sore, in grief she said
> 'It's as though between al-Ḥajūn and al-Ṣafā there has never been a friend, and no evening pleasure in Mecca.'
> So I told her, my heart made to flutter as though by a bird between my ribs:

'Yes indeed; we were its people but changing times and evil misfortunes destroyed us,
We were custodians of the *kaʿba* after Nābit, circling it around, our fine state clear.
We took charge of the temple after Nābit with dignity, the wealthy gaining no favour with us.
We had power and prestige, so be proud of our reign, no tribe there more proud than us.
Did you not marry a woman to Ishmael, the finest man I knew, so his descendants are from us, and we are his relatives.'
So what if the world turn against us? Life has its turns and tribulations
It was the king, the almighty ruler, who used his power to oust us; thus, O people, do the fates decree.
If the carefree sleep and I not rest, then I say, 'O enthroned one, why did Suhayl and ʿĀmir die?'
In exchange for them I got faces I dislike, tribes including Ḥimyar and Yuḥābir.
We were despised, after having been in delight, passing years thus biting us.
Tears flowed from eyes weeping for a land with a secure and sacred place and shrines,
Weeping for a place whose pigeons are left unharmed, living safe there, and sparrows too.
In it wild animals are safe and may leave it without fear – they would never be attacked."

According to Ibn Isḥāq, ʿAmr b. al-Ḥārith b. Muḍāḍ also spoke as follows addressing Banū Bakr and Ghubshān who came to power after themselves in Mecca:

"O people, move along; your end is that one day you will not be able to move.
Urge on your mounts, release their reins before your death, and do with us what you will do.
We were people as you were; fate changed us; you will become as we became."

Ibn Hishām stated that these verses were the ones he found to be genuine. And a certain authority on poetry told me that these verses are the first poems spoken by the Arabs and that they were discovered inscribed on rocks in Yemen, their author's name not being given.

Al-Suhaylī recorded companion verses to this poetry, telling along with them a strange tale and peculiar chants. He said that Abū al-Walīd al-Azraqī, in his book *Faḍāʾil Mecca* (*The Virtues of Mecca*), added to the above-mentioned verses by ʿAmr b. al-Ḥārith b. Muḍāḍ the following:

"Fate has turned against us and destroyed us through injustice there, our people plundering others.
Ask about the deeds of others before you, so that the path of disgrace be made clear.
Once before you we were kings over people, living resident in God's sanctuary."

The Story of Khuzā'a and an account of 'Amr b. Luḥayy and the worship of idols in Arab lands.

According to Ibn Isḥāq, Ghubshān of Khuzā'a governed the *ka'ba* instead of Banū Bakr b. 'Abd Manāt; the first of these new rulers was 'Amr b. al-Ḥārith the Ghubshānī. At that time Quraysh were migrants, living in small settlements and little encampments scattered about among their people, Banū Kināna.

Khuzā'a were so-named because they *takhazza'ū*, separated, from the men of 'Amr b. 'Āmir when they came from Yemen on their way to Syria. Khuzā'a stopped in Marr al-Dhahrān and settled there.

On this subject 'Awn b. Ayyūb al-Anṣārī and thereafter al-Khazrajī spoke the following verses:

> "When we went down into the vale of Marr Khuzā'a 'separated' from us into small groups of people;
> They occupied every valley of Tihāma, seeking protection by their solid spears and sharp-pointed swords."

Abū al-Mutahhir Ismā'īl b. Rāfi' al-Anṣārī al-Awsī said:

> "When we went down to the vale of Mecca Khuzā'a gave praise to the house of the intolerant eater
> Taking residence in small villages and riding off in separate groups to all settlements in high land and low.
> They ousted Jurhum from the vale of Mecca, wrapping themselves in strong-backed Khuzā'a pride."

So Khuzā'a took control of the *ka'ba*, inheriting that rule by primogeniture until the last of them, Ḥulayl b. Ḥubshiyya b. Salūl b. Ka'b b. 'Amr b. Rabī'a al-Khuza'ī. It was his daughter Ḥubbā who got married to Quṣayy b. Kilāb; to him were born his four sons 'Abd al-Dār, 'Abd Manāf, 'Abd al-'Uzzā, and 'Abd. Eventually he gained control over the *ka'ba*, as I will later explain in detail if God Almighty wills it, and in Him is all trust.

Khuzā'a continued controlling the temple some 300 years; some say 500, and God knows best. Their period of rule was damned, because it was during their period that idols were first worshipped in Ḥijāz.

This came about because of their leader 'Amr b. Luḥayy, God curse him; it was he who first influenced them towards idol worship. He was a man of enormous wealth. They say he gouged out the eyes of 20 camels to show that he owned 20,000 of them.

It was a custom among the Arabs that anyone who came to own 1,000 camels should gouge out the eyes of one of them. By doing this he would avert the evil eye of malicious envy from them. Al-Azraqī was one of those who related this practice.

According to al-Suhaylī, in the time of *al-ḥajj*, the pilgrimage, he probably sacrificed 10,000 animals and awarded 10,000 sacerdotal garments per year. He would feed the Arabs, preparing for them food of dates mixed with butter and honey, and give them barley wine to drink. They say that his word and deed were like law among them, due to his generosity, and to the high regard and deep respect they held for him.

Ibn Hishām states that a learned man told him that ʿAmr b. Luḥayy once left Mecca for Syria on business and reached Maʾāb in the Balqāʿ region. There at that time lived the ʿAmālīq, the sons of ʿImlāq or, as some say,ʿImlīq b. Lāwadh b. Sām b. Nūḥ. ʿAmr witnessed them worshipping idols, so he asked them why. They replied that if they asked the idols for rain it came, or for victory they won it.

ʿAmr then asked them to give him an idol he could take to Arab lands where it could be worshipped, and they gave him one named Hubal. This he brought to Mecca and set on a pedestal and ordered the people to worship and venerate it.

According to Ibn Isḥāq, people claimed that the first to worship idols were of the tribe of Ishmael. They did so because as they started to travel outside Mecca, having felt constrained and overcrowded there and seeking living-space elsewhere, they would always carry with them a stone from the sanctuary to venerate the shrine. Wherever they settled they would put down the stone and circumambulate it as they would the *kaʿba*. Eventually they took to worshipping any stone that pleased or inspired them, thus reverting to pagan ways and neglecting the religion they had followed.

In the *ṣaḥīḥ* collection we find a statement from Abu Rajāʾ al-ʿUṭāridī as follows: "In the pre-Islamic period, if we found no rock then we would gather up a pile of dirt, bring a goat, milk it on to the pile, and then circumambulate it."

Ibn Isḥāq's narration goes on: "And they substituted another religion for that of Abraham and Ishmael, upon both of whom be peace, worshipping idols and following the false ways of the people before them."

Nevertheless they did maintain some of the practices of the era of Abraham, upon whom be peace. These included venerating the *kaʿba*, circumambulating it, going there for pilgrimage and visitation, mounting the hills of ʿArafāt and Muzdalifa, making sacrifice and invoking God's name at both pilgrimage and visitation and at the same time introducing innovations.

The tribes of Kināna and Quraysh would make the cry, "*Labbayka, Allāhumma, labbayka*! At your service, O God, at your service! At your service; you have no partner except one who is yours. You rule him, he rules not."

They would affirm His unity in their invocation and then include reference to their idols as well while asserting that He had power over them. God Almighty stated to Muḥammad (ṢAAS), "Most of them do not believe in God without associating others" (*sūrat Yūsuf*, XII, v.106). This meant, "they do not state My unity out of knowledge of My right unless they also ascribe to me some associate of My own creation."

Al-Suhaylī and others state that the first to utter this prayer was ʿAmr b. Luḥayy and that Satan appeared before him as an old man and taught him that. ʿAmr would listen as he recited it, then say as he had. And the Arabs followed his lead in so reciting.

And it is established in al-Bukhārī's *ṣaḥīḥ* collection that the Messenger of God (ṢAAS) would say "*Qadi. Qadi*", when he heard people recite the words, "At your service, O God, you have no partner." That meant: "Enough right there!"

Al-Bukhārī stated that Isḥāq b. Ibrāhīm related to him, quoting Yaḥyā b. Ādam, quoting Isrāʾīl, from Abū Ḥafs, from Abū Hurayra, that the Prophet (ṢAAS) said, "The first person to set slaves free and also to worship idols was Abū Khuzāʿa ʿAmr b. ʿAmir and I have seen him dragging his intestines in hell-fire." Aḥmad (*sic*) is unique in giving the account thus.

This account necessitates that ʿAmr b. Luḥayy was Abū Khuzāʿa, all the tribe being traced back to him, as some genealogists maintain, according to Ibn Isḥāq and others. Had we been left with only that one account, then it would be plain as it stands, even to be considered documentary. But other accounts exist which contradict it in some ways.

Al-Bukhārī stated that Abū al-Yamān told him that Shuʿayb told him from al-Zuhrī that the latter heard al-Musayyab say, "*Al-baḥīra* is the camel that is not milked by anyone, since its milk is left for the idols; and *al-sāʾiba* is the camel that does not carry anything since it is set aside for their gods."

Abū Hurayra stated that the Prophet (ṢAAS) said, "I saw ʿAmr b. ʿĀmir al-Khuzāʿī dragging his insides in hell-fire; he was the first person who set loose the *al-sāʾiba* camels."

Al-Bukhārī also relates it thus, and Muslim too, from a tradition from Ṣāliḥ b. Kīsān, from al-Zuhrī, from Saʿīd and back to Abū Hurayra.

Then al-Bukhārī states that Ibn al-Hād passed it on from al-Zuhrī.

According to al-Ḥākim, al-Bukhārī meant that Ibn al-Hādd recounted it from ʿAbd al-Wahhab b. Bukht from al-Zuhrī. That is what he stated.

Aḥmad related it from ʿAmr b. Salama al-Khuzāʿī, from al-Layth b. Saʿd, from Yazīd b. al-Hād, from al-Zuhrī, from Saʿīd back to Abū Hurayra, who said that he heard the Messenger of God (ṢAAS) state: "I saw ʿAmr b. ʿĀmir dragging his insides in hell-fire; it was he who first let loose the *sawāʾib* (pl. of *sāʾiba*) and who *baḥara*, set aside the milk of, the *baḥīra* camels."

ʿAbd al-Wahhāb b. Bukht was mentioned by neither of these authorities, though he was by al-Ḥākim. God knows best.

Aḥmad also said that ʿAbd al-Razzāq related to him, quoting Maʿmar, from al-Zuhrī, from Abū Hurayra who said that the Messenger of God (ṢAAS) said:

"I saw ʿAmr b. ʿĀmir al-Khuzāʿī dragging his insides in hell-fire, and it was he who first let loose the *sawā'ib*."

This tradition, as given, is missing a link of transmission. The correct chain would be to include al-Zuhrī as having received it from Saʿīd, as above.

Use in this tradition and the previous one of the term *al-Khuzāʿī* in the name indicates that he was not the founder of the tribe but rather named after it. Also the use in the narration of the term *Abū Khuzāʿa*, the father of Khuzāʿa, as further above, is a slip of the pen by the traditionalist for *Akhū Khuzāʿa*, brother of Khuzāʿa, or an indication that he was given the nickname Abū Khuzāʿa. Use of this last term could not be intended as informing us that he was father of the whole Khuzāʿa tribe; God knows best.

Muḥammad b. Isḥāq said that Muḥammad b. Ibrāhīm b. al-Ḥārith al-Taymī related to him that Abū Ṣāliḥ al-Sammān told him that he heard Abū Hurayra say that he heard the Messenger of God (ṢAAS) say to Aktham b. al-Jawn al-Khuzāʿī: "O Aktham, I saw ʿAmr b. Luḥayy b. Qamaʿa b. Khindif dragging his insides in hell-fire and I never saw two men more alike than you and he." Aktham replied, "Maybe this resemblance to him is harmful to me, O Messenger of God?" He answered, "No; you are a believer while he is a disbeliever. It was he who first changed the religion of Ishmael, who set up idols, who set aside *al-baḥīra* camels' milk for the idols, established certain animals as free from burden-bearing, disallowed sacrifice of the male of twin goats, or considered certain stallion camels free from work."[20] There are no traditions to this effect in the "books," i.e. the canon.[21]

Ibn Jarīr related this same tradition in similar words from Hannād b. ʿAbda, from Muḥammad b. ʿAmr, from Abū Salama, from Abū Hurayra, back to the Prophet (ṢAAS). And this tradition too is not in the "books".

Al-Bukhārī said that Muḥammad b. Abū Yaʿqub Abū ʿAbd Allāh al-Kirmānī related to him that Ḥassān b. Ibrāhīm told him, quoting Yūnus from al-Zuhrī, from ʿUrwa that ʿĀ'isha said that the Messenger of God (ṢAAS) said, "I saw hell with its denizens beating one another and I saw ʿAmr dragging along his insides; it was he who first set loose the *al-sā'iba* camels." Al-Bukhārī alone reported this *ḥadīth*.

What is meant here is that ʿAmr b. Luḥayy, God curse him, introduced certain innovations into the religion by which he changed the religion of Abraham. The Arabs imitated him in adopting these and thus strayed far off, in ways that were deplorable and atrocious.

Almighty God had expressed disapproval of these things in various verses of His unassailable Qur'ān. The Almighty stated: "And do not speak lies with what

20. See *sūrat al-Mā'ida*, V, v.103.

21. He is referring to the canonical sources of law based on authenticated traditions.

your tongues describe, saying: 'This is lawful', and, 'this is unlawful', thus falsely attributing lies to God" (*sūrat al-Naḥl*, XVI, v.116). The Almighty also said, "God has not ordained the *baḥīra*, the *sāʾiba*, the *waṣīla*, or the *hāmī*. But it is those who disbelieve who falsely attribute lies to God. Yet most of them do not understand" (*sūrat al-Māʾida*, V, v.103).

I have elsewhere elaborated on all this and shown how the earlier authorities differed among themselves in explaining that. Those who wish may find it there;[22] and to God all praise and goodwill.

The Almighty also said, "And they put aside for what they know not a portion of what We have provided for them. By God, you will surely be questioned about what you have been falsely attributing" (*sūrat al-Naḥl*, XVI, v.56).

The Almighty stated as well, "And they set aside for God a portion of the crops and livestock He bestowed on them and said, 'This is for God!' by their assertion, and, 'This is for our associate gods!' So that which is for their associates does not reach God, while what was God's does reach their associates! Evil is what they judge. Likewise, these associates have deemed appropriate for many of the polytheists the killing of their children; this is to destroy them and distort their religion. Had God not wished, they would not have done so. So ignore them and what they invent. They said: 'These are animals and produce that are sacrosanct. None but whom we say shall taste them.' This they claim, and, 'These are animals whose backs are sacrosanct.' And, 'These are animals over whom God's name shall not be invoked.' These are falsehoods attributed to God and He will punish them for their inventions. And they said, 'What is within the wombs of these animals is specifically for our menfolk and forbidden for our wives', whereas if it be stillborn then they are all partners in it. God will punish them for their characterizations. He is wise, all-knowing. Lost are those who killed their children foolishly and without knowledge, and who proscribed what God has endowed them with, attributing falsehood to God. They had gone astray, and they were not rightly guided" (*sūrat al-Anʿām*, VI, v.136–40).

In his *ṣaḥiḥ* collection, al-Bukhārī stated, in his chapter entitled: "The Arabs before Islam" that Abū al-Nuʿmān and Abū ʿAwāna both related to him on the authority of Abū Bishr, from Saʿīd b. Jubayr, from Ibn ʿAbbās who said: "If it please you to know the ignorance of the Arabs before Islam, then read those verses coming after verse 130 in *sūrat al-Anʿām*: 'Lost are those who killed their children foolishly and without knowledge and who proscribed what God has endowed them with, attributing falsehood to God. They had gone astray, and they were not rightly guided'" (VI, v.140).

We have given explanation for this verse and how they used to innovate with foolish and immoral laws, which their leader ʿAmr b. Luḥayy, God damn him,

22. Ibn Kathīr, *Tafsīr* . . . Vol. 2, pp107–9.

had thought gave some benefit and kindness to animals. In this he was a liar and a cheat.

Yet despite this folly and error, those silly and ignorant people did follow his lead. In fact they followed him into errors even more grievous and serious than these, namely in worshipping idols along with God the Almighty and Glorious.

They thus brought changes into the true religion and straight path God had sent down to Abraham, His true companion, which is worship of God alone without associate, and proscription of polytheism.

They changed the ceremonies of the pilgrimage and the tenets of the religion without knowledge or proof or directives either strong or weak. In this they behaved similarly to those of the polytheist peoples who had preceded them.

They were like the people of Noah. These were those who first associated others with God and who worshipped idols. For this reason God sent Noah to them. He was the first messenger sent to turn people from worship of idols, as we learn from Noah's story in the Qurʾān: "And they said: 'Do not abandon your gods; do not forsake Wadd, Suwāʿ, Yaghūth, Yaʿūq, and Nasr'; many did they lead astray. Give evil-doers increase of nothing but their error!" (*sūrat Nūḥ*, LXXI, v.23–4).

Ibn ʿAbbās said that these were persons of virtue from among Noah's people; when they died people would attend their graves and eventually came to worship them. We have previously given enough information about their worship practices[23] to obviate need for its repetition here.

According to Ibn Isḥāq and others, having made these changes to the religion of Ishmael, the Arabs continued having idols. Banū Kalb b. Wabra b. Taghlib b. Ḥulwān b. ʿImrān b. al-Ḥāf b. Qudāʿa had an idol named Wadd. It was set up in Dūmat al-Jandal. At a place called Ruhāṭ there was Suwāʿ, idol of the Banū Hudhayl b. Ilyās b. Mudrika b. Maḍar. Yaghūth was the idol for Banū Anʿam from Ṭayyiʾ, and for the people of Jurash from Madhḥij. It was set up at Jurash. Also there was Yaʿūq in the land of Hamdān in Yemen, used by Banū Khaywān, a tribe of Hamdān. In the land of Ḥimyar was Naṣr, belonging to a tribe called Dhū al-Kulāʿ.

Ibn Isḥāq goes on to report that Khawlān had in their land an idol called ʿAmm Anas. They would, it is said, set aside part of their crops and livestock for division between it and God. Whatever of God's portion came into the share of ʿAmm Anas they would leave for the latter, while if any set aside for ʿAmm Anas went into the portion set aside for God, they would retrieve it for ʿAmm Anas. It was about them that God revealed, "And they set aside for God a portion of the crops and livestock which He had bestowed upon them" (*sūrat al-Anʿām*, VI, v.136).

23. Ibn Kathīr, *Tafsīr* . . . , Vol. 4, pp426, 427.

Banū Milkān b. Kināna b. Khuzayma b. Mudrika had an idol named Sa‘d, a tall rock in open desert in their territory. One of their men took a herd of his camels to stand near by there to receive the idol's blessing, so they say. But when the camels, which were for meat and not riding, saw the idol stained with the blood of sacrifices, they shied away and scattered in all directions. Their owner became enraged and picked up a rock and threw it at the idol, saying, "May God not bless you; you caused my camels to flee from me!" Then he went off to find them and round them up. When he had done so, he spoke the verses:

> "We came to Sa‘d for him to put us all together, but Sa‘d scattered us; so we are not of Sa‘d.
> Is Sa‘d anything but a stone in the desert offering no prayer for anyone, whether misled or rightly guided."

Ibn Isḥāq went on to report that Daws had an idol belonging to ‘Amr b. Ḥumama al-Dawsī. Moreover Quraysh had emplaced an idol over a well inside the *ka‘ba* whose name was Hubal. As previously stated, Ibn Hishām reported it to have been the first idol set up by ‘Amr b. Luḥayy, God curse him.

Ibn Isḥāq goes on to state that they adopted Isāf and Nā᾿ila as gods, emplaced near *zamzam*, where they would make sacrifice to them. He reports that they were a man and a woman who had sexual intercourse in the *ka‘ba*, and so God transformed them into two rocks.

Ibn Isḥāq went on to state that ‘Abd Allāh b. Abū Bakr b. Muḥammad b. ‘Amr b. Ḥazm reported that ‘Amra quoted ‘Ā᾿isha as saying, "We always heard that Isāf and Nā᾿ila were a man and a woman of Jurhum who fornicated in the *ka‘ba*, so God, Almighty and Glorious, turned them both into stone." God knows best.

And it has also been said that God did not postpone their punishment until they had fornicated there, but that He transformed them before the deed and that thereafter they were set up on the mountains of al-Ṣafā and al-Marwa. When it was the time of ‘Amr b. Luḥayy, he placed them both at *zamzam* and people began circumambulating them.

On this subject Abū Ṭālib spoke the verse:

> "Where the Ash‘arūn kneel their mounts, where the streams flow from Isāf and Nā᾿il."

Al-Wāqidī reported that when the Messenger of God (ṢAAS) ordered the destruction of Nā᾿ila, the day he conquered Mecca, there emerged from it a black woman with grey hair tearing at her face, lamenting and wailing loudly.

Al-Suhaylī has said that Ajā and Sulmā, which are two mountains in Hijāz, were in fact named after a man named Ajā b.‘Abd al-Ḥayy who fornicated with Sulmā, daughter of Ḥām, and that they were both turned into idols in these mountains that were named after them. He also said that between Ajā and Sulmā Ṭayyiʾ had an idol named Qals.

Ibn Isḥāq's account goes on to say that the people of each house had an idol they would worship there and that if a man were to journey he would touch the idol before mounting. This was also what he would begin by doing upon his return before he went inside to his family. When God sent Muḥammad (ṢAAS) with the message of the unity of God, Quraysh said, "He has made the gods into one god! How very strange!"

Ibn Isḥāq went on to relate that along with the *kaʿba* the Arabs venerated *tawāghīt*. These were buildings they honoured in much the same way as they did the *kaʿba*. They had custodians and priests, and offerings would be made to them just as to the *kaʿba*, along with the rituals of circumambulation and blood sacrifice. But they still recognized the precedence of the *kaʿba* over them because it was the building and mosque of Abraham, God's true companion, peace be upon him.

Quraysh and the Banū Kināna had an idol named al-ʿUzzā at Nakhla and Banū Shaybān of Sulaym were its custodians and priests; they were allies of Banū Hāshim. Khālid b. al-Walīd destroyed it when he conquered them, as we shall relate.

Al-Lāt was the idol for Thaqīf at al-Ṭāʾif and its custodians and priests were Banū Muʿattib from Thaqīf. Abū Sufyān and al-Mughīra b. Shuʿba destroyed it after the people of al-Ṭāʾif accepted Islam, as we shall relate later.

Manāt was the idol of the tribes of al-Aws and al-Khazraj and the people of Medina who shared their religion in the coastal region, towards al-Mushallal in Qudayd. Abū Sufyān destroyed it also. Some say it was ʿAlī b. Abū Ṭālib who did it, as we will relate.

Dhū al-Khalaṣa was an idol of Daws, Khathʿam, and Bajīla and the Arabs in their territory of Tabāla. It was called "the southern (Yemeni) *kaʿba*", while the one in Mecca was known as the "northern (Syria, Shāmī) *kaʿba*". Jarīr b. ʿAbd Allāh al-Bajlī destroyed it, as we will explain.

Qals was an idol of Ṭayyiʾ and those two nearby mountains, meaning Ajā and Sulmā, famous mountains referred to above.

Riʾām was a temple of Ḥimyar and the people of Yemen, as above related in the story of Tubbaʿ, one of the kings of Ḥimyar, and the story of the two rabbis when they destroyed it and killed a black dog that came from it.

Ruḍāʾ was a temple of Banū Rabīʿa b. Kaʿb b. Saʿd Ibn Zayd Manāt b. Tamīm. About it al-Mustawghir Kaʿb b. Rabīʿa b. Kaʿb spoke the verse:

> "I struck Ruḍāʾ so violently I left it a ruin in a black plain.
> And ʿAbd Allāh helped in destroying it, and with the like of ʿAbd Allāh sins are obliterated."

It is said that this al-Mustawghir lived for 330 years, he being the longest-lived of all Muḍar. It was he who spoke the lines:

"I have wearied of life and its length; I have lived for years in their hundreds;
One century was followed by two more, adding up the years from all the many months.
Is what is left anything but like what we spent? Days and nights pass and urge us on."

According to Ibn Hishām these lines should be attributed to Zuhayr b. Janāb b. Hubal.

Al-Suhaylī stated that the persons who lived longer than two or three hundred years include this Zuhayr, ʿUbayd b. Shariyya, Daghfal b. Ḥanẓala al-Nassāba, al-Rabīʿ b. Ḍabaʿ al-Fuzārī, Dhū al-Isbaʿ al-ʿAdwānī and Naṣr b. Dihmān b. Ashjaʿ b. Rayth b. Ghaṭfān. The hair of this last-mentioned blackened after it had turned white, and his back became straight after having been crooked.

Ibn Isḥāq's account continues, indicating that Dhū al-Kaʿbāt was an idol of Bakr and Taghlib, the two sons of Wāʾil, and Iyād at Sandād. Concerning it Aʿshā of Banū Qays b. Thaʿlaba spoke the verse:

"Between al-Khawarnaq, al-Sadīr, Bāriq, and the temple with battlements at Sandād."

The first part of this poem is as follows:

"I have learned, even if I lived longer, that one's path is that followed by the ancients.
What can I hope after the Āl Muḥarriq have left their homes and after Iyād too?
They settled at Anqara, where Tigris water flowed to them, coming from the lofty mountains,
The land of al-Khawarnaq, al-Sadīr, and Bāriq, and the house of temples of Sindād.
The winds stormed over the sites of their dwellings, as though their time were predestined,
And I see that pleasure and all things enjoyed turn to decay and end."

According to al-Suhaylī, al-Khawarnaq was a palace built by al-Nuʿmān the Elder for Sābūr so that he could have his children there in it with him. It was designed by a man named Sinammār over 20 years. No finer building than it had ever been seen. Al-Nuʿmān feared that Sinammār might build a similar one for others, so he cast him down from its heights and killed him. A poet therefore spoke the following lines about him:

"He recompensed me, may God give him His worst punishment, as Sinnamār was recompensed, and he was guiltless.

Except his striving on the building for twenty years with the best bricks, saffron and ceramics.

And when the building was complete and it towered like a mountain or a difficult height

He threw down Sinammār on to the top of his head; that being, by God, one of the most ignominious acts ever done."

Al-Suhaylī stated that al-Jāḥiẓ recited it in his *Kitāb al-Ḥayawān* (*Book of Animals*). The word *al-Sinammār* is one of the names of the moon. What is implied here is that all such houses were destroyed when Islam came. The Messenger of God (ṢAAS) dispatched troops of his men to each of these palaces to destroy them, and he sent to those idols men who broke them to pieces. Ultimately nothing remained to rival the *kaʿba*, and God was worshipped alone and without associate. All this will be explained in detail in its place, if God Almighty wills it, and in Him there is trust.

An Account of ʿAdnān, Forebear of the Arabs of the Ḥijāz from whom the line goes down to the Prophet (ṢAAS).

There is no question of ʿAdnān being of the line of Ishmael, son of Abraham, upon both of whom be peace. What dispute there is relates to the number of forebears there were from ʿAdnān to Ishmael according to the various sources.

At one end of the spectrum, there is the extreme view that considers there to have been forty; this is the view of Christians and Jews who adopted it from the writings of Rakhiyā, the clerk of Armiyā (Jeremy) b. Ḥalqiyā, as we will relate.

Some authorities maintain there were thirty, others twenty, yet more fifteen, ten, nine, or seven.

It has been said that the lowest estimate given is for four, according to the account given by Mūsā b. Yaʿqūb, on the authority of ʿAbd Allāh b. Wahb b. Zumʿa al-Zumaʿī from his aunt, and then from Umm Salama who stated that the Prophet (ṢAAS) said that the line was: "Maʿad b. ʿAdnān b. Adad b. Zand b. al-Yarā b. Aʿrāq al-Tharā".

According to Umm Salama this Zanad was al-Hamaysaʿ, al-Yarā was Nābit, while Aʿrāq al-Tharā was Ishmael. This was implied because he was Abraham's son; for Abraham was not consumed by hell-fire, since fire does not consume moist earth, the meaning of *al-tharā*.

Al-Dārqaṭnī stated that he knew of no "Zand" except the one in this tradition, and Zand b. al-Jawn, who was Abū Dalāma the poet.

Abū al-Qāsim al-Suhaylī and other Imāms stated that the time lapse between ʿAdnān and Ishmael was too great for there to have been only four, ten, or even twenty generations between them. That, they said, was because the age of Maʿad son of ʿAdnān was twelve at the time of Bukhtunaṣṣar (Nebuchadnezzar).

Abū Jaʿfar al-Ṭabarī and others related that Almighty God sent a revelation at that time to Armiyāʾ b. Ḥalqiyā' telling him to go to Bukhtunaṣṣar to inform him that God had given him rule over the Arabs. And God commanded Armiyāʾ to carry with him Maʿad b. ʿAdnān on the horse al-Burāq so that they would not bear him any rancour saying, "For I shall draw forth from his loins a noble Prophet by whom I shall seal the prophets."

Armiyāʾ did that, bearing Maʿad on al-Burāq to the land of Syria where he grew up among the Jews who remained there following the destruction of the temple at Jerusalem. There he married a woman named Maʿāna, daughter of Jawshin of Banū Dibb b. Jurhum, before returning to his own land. He returned after unrest had quietened down and accord prevailed in the Arabian peninsula. Rakhiyā, Armiyāʾ's scribe, wrote his master's genealogy down in a document he had there which was to go into Armiyāʾ's library; and he similarly preserved the genealogy of Maʿad. But God knows best.

And this is why Mālik, God bless him, did not enthuse over the attempt at tracing genealogy back to before ʿAdnān.

Al-Suhaylī commented further, "We have merely discussed tracing back these lines to accord with the school of thought of those scholars who favour and do not disapprove of it, men such as Ibn Isḥāq, al-Bukhārī, al-Zubayr b. Bakkār, al-Ṭabarī, and others."

As for Mālik, God have mercy on him, he expressed disapproval when asked about someone tracing his descent back to Adam and commented: "Whence comes to him knowledge of that?" When he was asked about tracing back to Ishmael, he expressed similar disapproval, asking, "Who could provide such information?" Mālik also disliked tracing the genealogy of the prophets, such as saying, "Abraham son of so-and-so". Al-Muʿayṭī stated this in his book.

Al-Suhaylī commented also that Mālik's viewpoint was analogous to what was related of ʿUrwa b. al-Zubayr who is reported to have said, "We have found no one who knows the line between ʿAdnān and Ishmael."

It is reported that Ibn ʿAbbās said, "Between ʿAdnan and Ishmael there were 30 ancestors who are unknown."

Ibn ʿAbbās is also reputed to have said when he traced back lines of descent as far as ʿAdnān: "The genealogists have lied. Twice or thrice." And that (scepticism)[24] is even more characteristic of Ibn Masʿūd, whose (attitude) was like that of Ibn ʿAbbās.

ʿUmar b. al-Khaṭṭāb stated, "We carry back the genealogy only as far as ʿAdnān."

24. Translator's interpretation.

Abū ʿUmar b. ʿAbd al-Barr stated in his book *Al-Anbaʾ fī Maʿrifat Qabāʾil al-Ruwāh* (*Facts Concerning Knowledge of the Tribes of the Transmitters*) that Ibn Lahīʿa related from Abū al-Aswad that he heard ʿUrwa b. al-Zubayr say, "We never found anyone who knew genealogy back past ʿAdnān, nor past Qaḥṭān, unless they were using conjecture."

Abū al-Aswad stated that he had heard Abū Bakr Sulaymān b. Abū Khaythama, one of the very most knowledgeable men of the poetry and the genealogy of Quraysh, say, "We never knew anyone with information going back beyond Maʿad b. ʿAdnān, whether relating to poetry or other knowledge."

Abū ʿUmar said that there was a group of the predecessors including ʿAbd Allāh b. Masʿūd, ʿAmr b. Maymūn al-Azdī, and Muḥammad b. Kaʿb al-Quradhī who, when they recited the verse from the Qurʾān "and those after them whom no one but God knows" (*sūrat Ibrāhīm*, XIV, v.9) would comment, "The genealogists lied."

Abū ʿUmar, God have mercy on him, stated, "We hold the meaning of this to differ from their interpretation. What is implied is that regarding those who claim to enumerate Adam's descendants, no one knows them except God who created them. But as for the lines of descent of the Arabs, the scholars conversant with their history and genealogy were aware of and learned by heart about the people and the major tribes, differing in some details of that."

Abū ʿUmar continued to state that the leading scholars regarding the genealogy of ʿAdnān gave his descent as: "ʿAdnān b. Udad b. Muqawwim b. Nāḥūr b. Tayraḥ b. Yaʿrub b. Yashjub b. Nābit b. Ishmael b. Abraham, peace be upon the latter two mentioned." And this is how Muḥammad b. Isḥāq b. Yasār gave it in the Prophet's biography.

Ibn Hishām stated, "ʿAdnān is said to be the son of Udd", meaning that he was ʿAdnān b. Udd b. Udad.

Thereafter Abū ʿUmar listed the remainder of the lineage back to Adam.

As for the genealogies of the other Arab tribes back to ʿAdnān, these are preserved and well known and no two people conflict about them.

The genealogy of the Prophet (ṢAAS) back to ʿAdnān is incontestably clear, as evident as the break of day. A verbatim *ḥadīth marfūʿ*[25] has been reported to support that. We will give it in the appropriate place, after discussion of the Arab tribes and reporting their genealogies and how these were accurately arranged into the lines of lofty and noble descent. All this, if God Almighty wills it, and in Him we trust and depend; there is no power and no strength except in God the Powerful, the Wise.

25. This term denotes a tradition that is traceable in ascending order of authorities back to the Prophet Muḥammad. See Glossary.

Nothing could be finer than the verses stating the Prophet's genealogy by Imām Abū al-ʿAbbās ʿAbd Allāh b. Muḥammad al-Nāshīʾ in the famous poem ascribed to him as follows:

"I praised the Messenger of God, seeking by praising him a plenitude of the best of rewards for myself;

I praised a man beyond praise, unique in his qualities, far beyond others far or near,

A Prophet whose light shone high in places east, his gifts apparent to the people of places west.

The prophets brought him to us before his coming, news of him spreading on all sides.

The foretelling divines began calling his name, using it to fend off the impact of misleading ideas.

Idols were given voice declaring to God their innocence of those who told the untruths.

They spoke in clear words to the unbelievers, 'A prophet has come to you from Luʾayy b. Ghālib.'

And evil spirits wanted to eavesdrop but shooting stars scattered them from their seats.

He led us to where we would never have found our way, so lengthy was our blindness to clear philosophies.

He brought evidences showing that they were signs from one Almighty in reward and punishment

One of which was the splitting of the moon in two, mountain tops then being covered as if by a turban by the moonbeams.

And another was the rising of water springs between his fingertips while no wells or pools were near.

By it he quenched the thirst of a large crowd; and the water flowed into rivulets in all directions, down to the plain land.

And a well brimmed over at his arrow's touch, one before too dry for a single drinker's palate.

And the udder flowed to his palm's rub, which before when squeezed for liquid had no teat to respond to a milkman's touch.

And there was eloquent utterance from the hand of a fortune-teller about plans of an enemy bent on attack.

And his being told of matters before their being, and of the after-effects to come when these did arise.

And from those signs there was revelation he brought, one that is expedient, to come with a multitude of wonders.

Thought could not conceive of it,[26] and so the like of which no eloquent man could articulate, nor did it occur to the mind of any preacher.

It encompassed all knowledge, embraced all wisdom, eluding the aim of the scheming and deceitful.

26. The reference is to the revelation of the Qurʾān.

He brought it to us, not through a trickster's tales, a scribe's pages, or an author's description.

Revelation comes to him sometimes to answer a questioner, to respond to a solution seeker, or in the exhortation of someone who is conversing;

For the bringing of proofs, the imposition of laws, the telling of narration, or the interpretation of purpose;

For the quotation of proverbs, the proving of a case, the revealing of some disbeliever, or the suspension of a liar;

In the meeting of some assembly, in the thick of some battle, or as difficult, puzzling problems occur.

So, it came down in different ways, with straight-out meaning and flowing varieties.

Its verses confirm each other, as if their meanings were scrutinized by a watchful eye.

And the inability of man to achieve such as we have described is well known by the many who attempted (to imitate it).

For father he had ʿAbd Allāh, the most noble of fathers, inheriting from him the most noble of qualities.

And from Shayba, be he praised, in whom Quraysh had pride above all others of honour and high station;

He who by whose face clouds were sought to bring rain, and whose views were followed in troubled times.

And from Hāshim, who built his lofty, honourable repute through brave exploits and his gracious generosity.

And ʿAbd Manāf, who taught his people not to exceed the bounds of their ambitions, and how to control their desires.

And Quṣayy, whose nobility of line is at such a level as to be beyond anyone's reach;

Through him God assembled the tribes after they had been split apart by the greed of thieving hands.

And Kilāb attained a fortress in the peaks of glory, beyond the reach of all, near and far alike.

And Murra, whose firmness of resolve was not dissolved by the disgrace of any fool or the evil of any sinner.

And Kaʿb, whose glory was too high for any seeker of fame to follow his footsteps; and who reached the highest rank with the least of efforts.

And Luʾayy who wiped out his enemies; thus he subdued the supercilious, the haughty, and the most victorious.

And in Ghālib was such courage that he refused for his people to be overcome by any mighty one, and repelled from them every violent enemy.

And Fihr had in Quraysh an oratory to rely upon when conflicts erupted.

And Malik was always the best of *maliks* (lords), the most honourable of companions, the most honourable of masters.

And al-Naḍr had such elevation as to outstrip all, right on up to meet the gleaming light of the stars.

By my life, Kināna displayed even before him qualities too fine for any conqueror to attain.

And before him Khuzayma established in his honour an ancient heritage from honoured kin.

And Mudrika, no man ever *yudrik* (achieved) the like of what he had. He was most virtuous and most high, beyond mere base pursuits.

And Ilyās, for him *al-yaʾs* (despair) was dictated for his enemies even before the squadrons met in battle.

And for Muḍar the total glory had always been his whenever mounted warriors had met in battle.

And Nizār achieved among his people a leadership position, so lofty as to outstrip the gaze of anyone staring hard to see.

And Maʿad was an *ʿudda* (instrument) for his allies when they feared the plots of their warring foe.

And ʿAdnān is still, if his virtue be assessed, unique and above all peer or companion.

And for Udd, virtue *taʾadda* (was discharged) emanating from his self-resolve and an inheritance passed down from grand, wise chieftains.

And in Udad there was calm judgement adorned with sagacity, for calm judgement gains from a frowning of eyebrows.[27]

And Hamaysaʿ continued to reach ever-new heights, and follow after the desired far-reaching aspirations.

And Nabt who came from the family tree of glory had built up his lofty refuge on the towering mountains.

And Qaydhār was accorded the generosity of Ḥātim, the wisdom of Luqmān and the determination of Ḥājib.

These were progeny of Ishmael, true to his vows, a man whose level of greatness could never be exceeded by others.

And God's "companion" (Abraham) who was the most noble of men ever to walk or ride upon earth.

And Tāriḥ, whose lasting reputation for generosity had made apparent his laudable deeds.

And Nāḥūr, the *naḥḥār* (butcher) of his enemies had many memorable accomplishments those accounting cannot enumerate.

And Ashraʿ, a forest lion in battle, cutting a person to shreds with his sharp weapons.

And Arghū, a deputy to be trusted in warfare, tenacious against a mean-spirited antagonist.

And Fāligh is not left behind his people in virtue, nor does he pass beneath them in rank.

And Shālikh and Arfakhshidh and Sām, had qualities so great as to protect them from any detractor or accuser.

And Nuḥ (Noah) still retains high regard with God, who counts him among good men, well-chosen.

27. The frowning eyebrows imply deep thought or sagacity.

And Lamk, his father, stood out among the finest, brave against the mailclad warrior.

And before Lamk there was yet Mutawashlikh, who drove away his enemies with tough spears.

And Idrīs the prophet was one with status with God beyond compare with that of any ambition.

And Yārid was a man great among his people's leaders, scornful of the base, clear and precise in his purpose.

And Mihlayīl had understanding of virtues from which all unpleasant defects had been refined away.

And Qaynān of old acquired the glory of his people, gaining the summit of prestige by the stride of his riding camels.

And Anūsh devoted himself to glory and deemed it far above base desires.

And Shīth stuck to principle, a man of virtue and nobility, free of mean faults.

All of these gained from Adam's light and from his stem gathered the fruits of goodness.

And the Messenger of God was the most noble ever born; he emerged from the line of all these fine, distinguished individuals.

His male forebears matched his female ancestors, all clear of any taint of disgrace.

May there be upon him the peace of God on every day that dawn gives us light and at every sunset too."

Thus did Sheikh Abū ʿUmar b. ʿAbd al-Barr present to us this ode, as did also our Sheikh Abū al-Ḥajjāj al-Mizzī, the *ḥāfiẓ*, in his edition of the poetry of Abū al-ʿAbbās ʿAbd Allāh b. Muḥammad al-Nāshiʾ, known as Ibn Sharshīr.

His origins were from al-Anbār. He went to Baghdad and then travelled to Egypt, where he stayed until he died in the year 293 AH. He was a *Muʿtazilī* theologian, and Sheikh Abū al-Ḥasan al-ʿAshʿarī wrote about him in his text *al-Maqālāt*, in his discussion of the *Muʿtazila*.

He was an accomplished poet, to the degree that his mastery was such that he would invent verses that reversed those of others, and composed poetry to challenge other poets, devising oratorical phrases and rhetorical flourishes they could not match. Consequently some accused him of insanity and delirium.

Al-Khaṭīb al-Baghdādī referred to him as having composed an ode in monorhyme that totalled some 4,000 verses. Al-Nājim quoted these and recorded his death, as stated above.

I comment that this ode gives evidence of his virtue, eloquence, knowledge, understanding, fine memory, diction, and masterly poetic skills. These verses on the noble lineage of the Prophet (ṢAAS) are precious jewels from his great repertoire of poetry. God bless him and reward him for all his activities.

An Account of the genealogical origins of the Arabs of Ḥijāz up to ʿAdnān.

These matters are due to ʿAdnān having had two sons, Maʿad and ʿAkk.

According to al-Suhaylī, ʿAdnān also had a son named al-Ḥārith, and another named al-Madhhab. It is also stated that some include al-Daḥḥāk among his sons. However, al-Daḥḥāk is also said to have been a son of Maʿad, not ʿAdnān. It is also believed that ʿAdan, for whom the city of Aden is named, and similarly Abyan, were named after sons of ʿAdnān. That is what al-Ṭabarī related.

ʿAkk married into the Ashʿarī tribe and lived in their territory in Yemen. Their language became unified and some of the people of Yemen claimed them as their own. They give his line as ʿAkk b. ʿAdnān b. ʿAbd Allāh b. al-Azd b. Yaghūth; others give the line as ʿAkk b. ʿAdnān b. al-Dhayb b. ʿAbd Allāh b. al-Asad. Al-Rayth is also given as an alternative to al-Dhayb. What is true is what we have stated, that they are of the line of ʿAdnān. ʿAbbās b. Mirdās spoke the verse:

> "ʿAkk b. ʿAdnān, who toyed with Ghassān until they were totally driven away."

As for Maʿad, he had four sons: Nizār, Quḍāʿa, Qanaṣ, and Iyād. Quḍāʿa was Maʿad's first-born who was commonly known by the surname of Abū Quḍāʿa (father of Qudāʿa). We have earlier given a different genealogy for Quḍāʿa, but it is this one that is considered correct by Ibn Isḥāq and others. And God knows best.

As for Qanaṣ, it is said that his line died out, except that al-Nuʿmān b. al-Mundhir who was Chosroe's governor at al-Ḥīra was one of his descendants, according to a number of past authorities. Another view is that he was from Ḥimyar, as we have indicated earlier. God knows best.

As for Nizār, to him were born Rabīʿa, Muḍar, and Anmār. Ibn Hishām indicated that Iyād was also the son of Nizār, as was spoken in the following verse:

> "[A]nd braves their faces fine, descendants of Iyād b. Nizār b. Maʿad."

He stated that Iyād and Muḍar were full brothers, their mother being Sawda, daughter of ʿAkk b. ʿAdnān. And the mother of Rabīʿa and Anmār was Shuqayqa, daughter of ʿAkk b. ʿAdnān. Her name was also given as Jumʿa, daughter of ʿAkk b. ʿAdnān.

According to Ibn Isḥāq, Anmār was the father of Khathʿam and Bajīla, of the tribe of Jarīr b. ʿAbd Allāh al-Bajalī. He added that they went to Yemen and stayed there.

Ibn Hishām said that the Yemenis state his line to have been Anmār b. Irāsh b. Liḥyān b. ʿAmr b. al-Ghawth b. Nabt b. Mālik b. Zayd b. Kahlān b. Saba'.

I consider that the tradition quoted above relating to Saba' substantiates this. God knows best.

They say that Muḍar was the first to use chants with camels. That is because he had a fine voice and because one day he fell off his mount and dislocated his arm. In pain he shouted, "Wāyadayāh! Wāyadayāh!" ("Oh, my hands, my hands!") and at that the camels stretched out their necks listening.

According to Ibn Isḥāq, Muḍar b. Nizār had two sons, Ilyās and ʿAylān. To Ilyās were born Mudrika, Ṭābikha and Qamaʿa; their mother was Khindif, daughter of ʿImrān b. al-Ḥāf b. Quḍāʿa.

Ibn Isḥāq stated that Mudrika's real name was ʿĀmir, and that of Ṭābikha was ʿAmr. One day they went hunting and while they were cooking their catch, their camels ran off. ʿĀmir chased after them and caught them, while his brother sat cooking. When they returned to their father and related this to him, he commented to ʿĀmir, "You are Mudrika" (the catcher), while to ʿAmr he said, "You are Ṭābikha" (the cook). As for Qamaʿa, the genealogists of Muḍar claim that Khuzāʿa was a son of ʿAmr b. Luḥayy b. Qamaʿa b. Ilyās.

In my view it is obvious that he was a descendant of theirs and not of their father, and that they were of Ḥimyar, previously mentioned. God knows best.

Ibn Isḥāq said that Mudrika gave birth to Khuzayma and Hudhayl, and that their mother was a woman from Quḍāʿa tribe. To Khuzayma were born Kināna, Asad, Asada, and al-Hūn.

Kināna gave birth to al-Naḍr, Mālik, ʿAbd Manāt, and Milkān. Abū Jaʿfar al-Ṭabarī added to these four ʿĀmir, al-Ḥārith, al-Naḍīr, Ghanam, Saʿd, ʿAwf, Jarwal, al-Jarāl, and Ghazwān.

An Account of Quraysh regarding their genealogy, etymology, and merit. They are the tribe of al-Naḍr b. Kināna.

According to Ibn Isḥāq, the mother of al-Naḍr was Barra, daughter of Murr b. Udd b. Ṭābikha (Ibn Hishām adds that Ṭābikha was the son of Ilyās b. Muḍar), while the rest of his sons were of a different mother. Ibn Hishām disagrees with Ibn Isḥāq, having Barra daughter of Murr as the mother of al-Naḍr, Mālik, and Milkān. The mother of ʿAbd Manāt was Hāla, daughter of Suwayd b. al-Ghiṭrīf from Azd of Shanūʾā.

Ibn Hishām stated that al-Naḍar was Quraysh; anyone born in his line is a Qurayshite, anyone not so born is not. He also said that some state that Fihr b. Mālik was Quraysh, those of his line therefore being Qurayshite; those not of his line were non-Qurayshite.

These two statements have been handed down by more than one expert genealogist, such as Sheikh Abū ʿUmar b. ʿAbd al-Barr and al-Zubayr b. Bakkār, Musʿab, and others.

According to Abū ʿUbayd and Ibn ʿAbd al-Barr, the majority's view is that Quraysh derived from al-Naḍr b. Kināna, based on a *ḥadīth* of al-Ashʿath b. Qays. And it is this authority who was an important source for Hishām b. Muḥammad b. al-Sāʾib al-Kalbī and Abū ʿUbayda Maʿmar b. al-Muthannā; he is a prime resource for the doctrine of al-Shāfiʿī, may God bless him.

Abū ʿUmar, moreover, chose Fihr b. Mālik as the originator of Quraysh, insisting that anyone today having descent from Quraysh stems from Fihr b. Mālik. He then related the choice made in his statement to the authority of al-Zubayr b. Bakkār, Muṣʿab al-Zubayrī and ʿAlī b. Kaysān, saying, "They are the source for this, al-Zubayr b. Bakkār having stated, 'The genealogists of Quraysh and others are agreed that Quraysh branched off only from Fihr b. Mālik.' The genealogists of Quraysh whom I have consulted consider those of his line to be Qurayshites, whereas those prior to him in their line are thought not from Quraysh."

Abū ʿUmar then effectively substantiated this view and defended it by pointing out that he and those of similar views were those most knowledgeable of the genealogy and history of their own people.

Al-Bukhārī related from the tradition of Kulayb b. Wāʾil as follows: "I said to the nursemaid (meaning Zaynab, daughter of Abū Salama) of the Prophet (ṢAAS) 'Tell me about the Prophet (ṢAAS). Was he from Muḍar?' She replied, 'From whom else but from Muḍar of Banū al-Naḍr b. Kināna?'"

Al-Ṭabarānī said, "We were told by Ibrāhīm b. Nāʾila al-Aṣbahānī, by Ismāʿīl b. ʿAmr al-Bajalī, and by al-Ḥasan b. Ṣāliḥ from his father, from al-Jashīsh al-Kindī who said, 'A group of people from Kinda tribe came to the Messenger of God (ṢAAS) and told him, "You are from us," claiming kinship with him. But he responded, "No, we're Banū al-Naḍr b. Kināna; we neither contradict our mother nor refute our father."'"

Imām Abū ʿUthmān Saʿīd b. Yaḥyā b. Saʿīd said, "We were told by my father and by al-Kalbī on the authority of Abū Ṣāliḥ from Ibn ʿAbbās that the latter said, 'A man from Kinda, called al-Jashīsh, came to the Prophet (ṢAAS) and said, "O Messenger of God, we claim ʿAbd Manāf as one of us." The Prophet (ṢAAS), turned away from him. The man came back with the same comment and again was ignored. Once more he said the same. Then the Prophet (ṢAAS) stated, "We are from Banū al-Naḍr b. Kināna. We neither contradict our mother nor refute our father."'"

Al-Ashʿath commented (probably to al-Jashīsh, tr.) "Shouldn't you have stayed silent after the first time?"

This response refuted their claim, and from the tongue of his Prophet (ṢAAS). And this is strange also from this viewpoint; al-Kalbī, moreover, is a weak authority. But God knows best.

Imām Aḥmad said that Bahz and ʿAffān related to him as follows: "We were both told by Ḥammād b. Salama that ʿUqayl b. Abū Ṭalḥa said (ʿAffān gave his name as ʿUqayl b. Ṭalḥa al-Salmī) on the authority of Muslim b. al-Hayṣam from al-Ashʿath b. Qays, that the latter said that he came to the Messenger of God (ṢAAS) in a delegation from Kinda. (ʿAffān added the words 'who did not consider me their best man') and said to him, 'O Messenger of God, we claim you to be one of us.' The Messenger of God (ṢAAS) replied, 'We are Banū al-Naḍr b. Kināna; we neither contradict our mother nor refute our father.'"

Al-Ashʿath b. Qays commented, "By God, I never hear anyone denying that Quraysh is from al-Naḍr b. Kināna without whipping him to the limit."

And thus was this related by Ibn Māja along various lines of transmission from Ḥammād b. Salama.

This line of tradition is truly fine and is authoritative in this matter. No attention is due thereafter to any opposing view. But God knows best. All praise and credit belong to God.

Jarīr b. ʿAṭiyya al-Tamīmī spoke the following verses in praising Hishām b. ʿAbd al-Mālik b. Marwān:

> "The mother who gave birth to Quraysh was not one as to cause doubt as to ancestry, nor was she barren;
> And no stud was of more noble stock than your father, nor was there ever an uncle more fine than Tamīm."

Ibn Hishām stated: "Here is meant the mother of al-Naḍr b. Kināna, who was Barra daughter of Murr, sister of Tamīm b. Murr."

The derivation of the word Quraysh is said to come from the word *al-taqarrush*, which means to join together after dispersal. This relates to the period of Quṣayy b. Kilāb when they were dispersed and he brought them together at the holy sanctuary, as we shall explain. Ḥudhāfa b. Ghānim al-ʿAdawī spoke the verse:

> "Your father was Quṣayy, known as 'the gatherer'; through him God gathered together the tribes from Fihr."

Some say that Quṣayy was known as Quraysh. The word meant "gathering together"; *al-taqarrush* meant *al-tajammuʿ* or "joining together", as Abū Khalda al-Yashkurī said: "Brothers who gathered (*qarrashu*) upon us faults, in our recent era and also ancient . . ."

It is also said that Quraysh were so named from *al-taqarrush*, a word meaning business and trading. This was related by Ibn Hishām, God have mercy on him.

Al-Jawharī said, "*al-qarsh* means 'earning' and 'accumulating' and the verbal form is *qarasha* in the past tense, *yaqrushu* in the present tense." Al-Farrāʾ stated that it was from this word that Quraysh was named, they being a tribe and their originator al-Naḍr b. Kināna. All his descendants are Qurayshite back as far as Kināna's son, but not before him.

Some say the word stems from the idea of *al-taftīsh*, i.e. "search". Hishām b. al-Kalbī stated that al-Naḍr b. Kināna was named "Quraysh" because he would "*yaqrish*" for what people lacked or needed, providing that with his own wealth. *Al-taqrīsh* means *al-taftīsh* and his sons would *yaqrishunā*, i.e. "search out" pilgrims in need and donate to them what they needed to return home. And so they were named "Quraysh" because of their engaging in this *qarsh*.

Al-Ḥārith b. Ḥilliza made a verse to the effect that *al-taqarrush* meant *al-taftīsh*:

> "O you who speaks and 'searches' (*al-muqarrish*) for us with ʿAmr, is he allowed to live?"

It was al-Zubayr b. Bakkār who related that verse.

Quraysh was also said to be a diminutive form of *qarsh*, a sea animal. A poet once said:

> "*Quraysh* are those that inhabit the sea; for them the Quraysh were named 'Quraysh'."

Al-Bayhaqī said that Abū Naṣr b. Qatāda informed him that Abū al-Ḥasan ʿAlī b. ʿĪsā al-Mālīnī, quoting Muḥammad b. al-Ḥasan b. al-Khalīl al-Nisawī, related that Abū Kurayb told them from Waqīʿ b. al-Jarrāḥ, on the authority of Hishām b. ʿUrwa on the authority of his father from Abū Rakāna al-ʿĀmirī that Muʿāwiya asked Ibn ʿAbbās, "Why were Quraysh so named?" He replied, "After a sea creature, the biggest of all, that is called *al-qarsh*. It never passes by anything, lean or fat, without eating it." "So recite me some verse about that," Muʿāwiya asked, and Ibn ʿAbbās spoke the verses of al-Jumaḥī as follows:

> "Quraysh are those that inhabit the sea; for them the Quraysh were named Quraysh,
> They eat all, lean or fat, not leaving a feather of any two-winged thing.
> Thus in the land the tribe of Quraysh eats up the land ravenously.
> Theirs is at the end of time a prophet; among them will be plenty of wounded and dead."

It is also said they were named after Quraysh b. al-Ḥārith b. Yakhlud b. al-Naḍr b. Kināna. He was the guide and the storeskeeper of Banū al-Naḍr. The Arabs would say, "The caravan of Quraysh" has come, instead of the "caravan of Banū al-Naḍr". They also say that it was his son Badr b. Quraysh who dug the well attributed to him where the great battle occurred on the day of al-Furqān ("proof", i.e. the battle of Badr) when the two armies met. God knows best.

The relative adjective derived from Quraysh is *qurashī* or *qurayshī*. Al-Jawharī said, "And the latter is the standard."

A poet spoke the verse,

> "Every Qurayshite (*qurayshī*) who is honourable, quick to fill demands for generosity and honour."[28]

Muslim related in his *ṣaḥīḥ* collection from a tradition of Abū ʿAmr and al-Awzaʿī that Shaddād Abū ʿAmmār related to him that Wāthila b. al-Asqaʿ told him that the Messenger of God (ṢAAS) said, "God chose Kināna from among the sons of Ishmael, Quraysh from Kināna, Hāshim from Quraysh and myself from the descendants of Hāshim."

Abū ʿAmr b. ʿAbd al-Barr said, "Banū ʿAbd al-Muṭṭalib are known as the *faṣīla*, the family, of the Messenger of God (ṢAAS); Banū Hāshim was his *fakhdh*, his tribal subsection; Banū ʿAbd Manāf was his *baṭn*, his tribal subdivision; Quraysh was his *ʿimāra*, his mini-tribe; Banū Kināna was his *qabīla*, his tribal confederation; and Muḍar was his *shaʿb*, his people. May God's blessings and peace be upon him always till the Day of Judgement."

Ibn Isḥāq stated, "Al-Naḍar b. Kināna gave birth to Mālik and Yakhlud." To these Ibn Hishām added "al-Ṣalt". The mother of them all was the daughter of Saʿd b. al-Ẓarib al-ʿAdwānī.

Kuthayyir b. ʿAbd al-Raḥmān, who is Kuthayyir ʿAzza, one of the Banū Mulayḥ b. ʿAmr of Khuzāʿa, spoke the verses:

> "Is my father not al-Ṣalt, my brothers not the finest among the noblemen of Banū al-Naḍr?
> You see on us as on them the same kerchiefs of mixed weave and the same Ḥaḍramī waist-wrappers
> So if you are not of Banū al-Naḍr, then leave the green thorn trees at the ends of the high valleys."

Ibn Hishām said that Banū Mulayḥ b. ʿAmr were descendants of al-Ṣalt b. al-Naḍr.

According to Ibn Isḥāq, Mālik b. al-Naḍr fathered Fihr b. Mālik, his mother being Jandala, daughter of al-Hārith b. Muḍāḍ al-Aṣghar. Fihr fathered Ghālib, Muḥārib, al-Ḥārith, and Asad, their mother being Laylā, daughter of Saʿd b. Hudhayl b. Mudrika. Ibn Hishām stated that they had a sister from their father named Jandala, daughter of Fihr.

According to Ibn Isḥāq, Ghālib b. Fihr had sons named Luʾayy b. Ghālib and Taym b. Ghālib who were known as the Banū al-Adram. Their mother was Salmā, daughter of ʿAmr al-Khuzāʿī.

Ibn Hishām states there was another son, Qays b. Ghālib, whose mother was Salmā, daughter of Kaʿb b. ʿAmr al-Khuzāʿī and that she was the mother of Luʾayy and Taym.

28. Several lines of abstruse poetry illustrating Arabic grammatical concepts have been omitted from the English translation.

According to Ibn Isḥāq, Lu'ayy b. Ghālib had four sons: Ka'b, 'Āmir, Sāma, and 'Awf.

Ibn Hishām said he was also reputed to have had another son, al-Ḥārith, and that they made up the Jusham b. al-Ḥārith among Hizzān of Rabī'a. And another son was Sa'd b. Lu'ayy who came to be the *bunāna* among Shaybān b. Tha'laba. *Bunāna* was a nursemaid for them. There was also Khuzayma b. Lu'ayy who formed the 'Ā'idha among Shaybān b. Tha'laba.

Then Ibn Isḥāq gives the story of Sāma b. Lu'ayy and how he went to 'Umān and lived there. That was due to a quarrel between himself and his brother 'Āmir. 'Āmir made him afraid and so he fled to 'Umān, dying there as a stranger. What happened was that while he was grazing his camel a snake bit its lip making it fall on its side. Then the snake bit and killed Sāma. It is said that he wrote these verses with his finger on the ground:

"Eyes, weep for Sāma b. Lu'ayy, the snake has clung to Sāma.
None such as Sāma b. Lu'ayy have I seen, found a dead victim of a camel.
Send a messenger to 'Āmir and Ka'b that my soul yearns for them.
Though my home is in 'Umān I am a Ghālibī who emigrated but not from poverty.
Perhaps the glass you have poured, Ibn Lu'ayy, fearing death, has not really been poured.
You aimed to repel death, O Ibn Lu'ayy, but no one so intending has power over death,
And many a silent, plodding camel you've left prostrate after long, intense exercise."

And Ibn Hishām said that he heard that a son of Sāma went to the Messenger of God (ṢAAS) and introduced himself as descended from Sāma b. Lu'ayy. The Messenger of God (ṢAAS) asked him, "The poet?" One of his Companions then said, "O Messenger of God, you seem to be referring to his line of verse,

'Perhaps the glass you've poured, Ibn Lu'ayy, fearing death, has not really been poured.'

And he answered, "Yes indeed."

Al-Suhaylī recorded from others that Sāma had no children. Al-Zubayr said, "Sāma b. Lu'ayy had Ghālib, al-Nābit, and al-Ḥārith." Others maintained that he had descendants in Iraq who hated 'Alī. Among them was 'Alī b. al-Ja'ad, who used to revile his father for having named him 'Alī. Among the descendants of Sāma b. Lu'ayy was Muḥammad b. 'Ar'ara b. al-Yazīd, who was the sheikh of al-Bukhārī.

Ibn Isḥāq said, "They claim that 'Awf b. Lu'ayy travelled with a caravan from Quraysh and to the territory of Ghaṭafān b. Sa'd b. Qays b. 'Aylān. There he was delayed so the rest of his people left him behind and went off. Then Tha'laba b.

Saʿd, he being his brother by the genealogy of Banū Dhubyān, came along, detained him, arranged his marriage, and treated him like an intimate and a brother. His relationship became widely known among Banū Dhubyān.

They say it was Thaʿlaba who said to ʿAwf the following verse when he was delayed and left behind:

> "O Ibn Luʾayy, tether your camel with me; your people have left you and you ought not to be left."

Ibn Isḥāq continued to indicate that either Muḥammad b. Jaʿfar b. al-Zubayr, or Muḥammad b. ʿAbd al-Raḥmān b. ʿAbd Allāh b. al-Ḥusayn told him that ʿUmar b. al-Khaṭṭāb had said, "If I were to claim an attachment to any Arab tribe or that they had a relationship to us, it would be to Banū Murra b. ʿAwf. We know kindred men among them and also how they treated that man." By this he meant ʿAwf b. Luʾayy.

He went on to relate that a man he did not distrust had told him that ʿUmar b. al-Khaṭṭāb said to some men of Banū Murra: "If you want to trace back your genealogy to your kinfolk, then trace it to ʿAwf."

Ibn Isḥāq added that these people were nobles of Ghaṭafān, their leaders and élite, with good reputation locally and in all of Ghaṭafān and Qays, and that they did maintain their own genealogy. If their ancestry were referred to by others, they would say, "We neither deny nor disown it. That is the ancestry we prefer." Then they would recite their verses recalling their relationship to Luʾayy.

Ibn Isḥāq said that they practised the system of *basl.* This entailed the practice among the Arabs of considering eight months of their year as sacrosanct. The Arabs would recognize that and allow them safe-conduct in those months and they would allow them the same. Rabīʿa and Muḍar, however, to my knowledge only considered four months a year as sacred, these being Dhū al-Qaʿda, Dhū al-Ḥijja, al-Muḥarram; and concerning the fourth, Rajab, they differed. Muḍar considered that it fell between Jumādā and Shaʿbān, while Rabīʿa maintained it came between Shaʿbān and Shawwāl.

It has been established in both of the *ṣaḥīḥ* collections, on the authority of Abū Bakrah, that the Messenger of God (ṢAAS) stated in his *khuṭbat al-wadāʿ*, farewell address, "Time has revolved in its own fashion since the day God created the heavens and the earth, the year consisting of twelve months, four of which are sacred. Three of these are contiguous: Dhū al-Qaʿda, Dhū al-Ḥijja, and al-Muḥarram, and there is also Muḍar's month of Rajab which comes between Jumādā and Shaʿbān." Thus by saying this he expressed preference for the view of Muḍar and not for that of Rabīʿa.

God the Almighty and Glorious stated in the Qurʾān, "With God the months number twelve, so ordained by God, (since) the day he created the heavens and the earth; of these four are sacred" (*sūrat al-Tawba*, IX, v.36).

This constitutes a reply to Banū ʿAwf b. Luʾayy for their considering the sacred months eight in number. In so doing they added to God's decree, introducing therein something which was not part thereof.

His statement in the *ḥadīth* that "three are contiguous [months]" is a disapproval of the attitude of the *al-nasīʾ* people who delayed the sacred month, making it Ṣafar, rather than al-Muḥarram. Also, the phrase therein "Muḍar's month of Rajab" is a refutation of Rabīʿa's view.

Ibn Isḥāq stated that Kaʿb b. Luʾayy had three sons, Murra, ʿAdī and Huṣayṣ. Murra also had three, named Kilāb, Taym and Yaqaza, from three mothers.

Kilāb gave birth to two sons, Quṣayy and Zuhra; the mother of both was Fāṭima, daughter of Saʿd b. Sayal, one of the al-Jadara of Juʿthumat al-Asad from the Yemen, who were allies of Banū al-Dīl b. Bakr b. ʿAbd Manāt b. Kināna. Of her father a poet spoke the verse:

> "We have never seen any person, of all the people we have known, like Saʿd b. Sayal
> A knight who combats with both his right hand and left; if his foe stood down from battle he would dismount
> A knight luring horsemen to destruction like a kestrel with partridges."

According to al-Suhaylī, Sayal's full name was Khayr b. Jamāla and he was the first person who had swords plated with gold and silver.

Ibn Isḥāq stated that they were known as the "al-Jadara" because ʿĀmir b. ʿAmr b. Khuzayma b. Juʿthuma had married the daughter of al-Ḥārith b. Muḍāḍ the Jurhumite. The Jurhum were at that time guardians of the House of God and built a *jidār*, a wall, around the *kaʿba*; ʿĀmir was therefore named al-Jādir and his descendants al-Jadara.

An Account of Quṣayy b. Kilāb and of his part in regaining guardianship over the kaʿba *for Quraysh by taking it from Khuzāʿa. How Quraysh gathered together at the holy place which God secured for the worshippers, after having lived scattered and fragmented in the mountains and hollows.*

What happened was that when his father died, Quṣayy's mother was married to Rabīʿa b. Ḥarām of ʿUdhra and he took her and her son to his own country. Later, when he grew up, Quṣayy came to Mecca and married Ḥubbā, daughter of the chief of Khuzāʿa, Ḥulayl b. Ḥubshiyya.

Regarding Khuzāʿa, they say that Ḥulayl entrusted guardianship over the holy House to Quṣayy because of the large family Quṣayy had with his daughter. Ḥulayl told him, "You have more right to it than I do."

Ibn Isḥāq stated that this account was heard only from Khuzāʿa. He said that others claim that he sought the assistance of his maternal brothers, their leader being Rizāḥ b. Rabīʿa, and of the tribes of Kināna and Qudāʿa and of some men in the Mecca region from Quraysh and others. And so he ousted them (Khuzāʿa) from the House of God and he himself assumed control over it.

This all occurred because the prerogative of the pilgrims' *ijāza*[29] was held by the Sūfa. They were the tribe of al-Ghawth b. Murr b. Udd b. Ṭābikha b. Ilyās b. Muḍar. People did not throw their stones (Jimār) until they (the Sūfa) had done so, nor did they leave Minā before the Sūfa did; these prerogatives remained theirs until they died out.

Then Banū Saʿd b. Zayd Manāt b. Tamīm inherited these rights from them by kinship. The first of them was Ṣafwān b. al-Ḥārith b. Shijna b. ʿUṭārid b. ʿAwf b. Kaʿb. b. Saʿd b. Zayd Manāt b. Tamīm. This power resided in his people until the rise of Islam in the time of the last of them, who was Karib b. Ṣafwān.

The *ijāza*, the descent from al-Muzdalifa,[30] was the prerogative of ʿAdwān until the coming of Islam in the time of the last of them, who was Abū Sayyāra ʿAmīla b. al-Aʿzal. His name was said to have been al-ʿĀṣ, while al-Aʿzal's name was Khālid. He used to give people the permission while seated on a one-eyed ass he had, for 40 years moving forth on it at that station. He was the first person to establish the bloodwit at 100 camels, as well as the first to say the phrase, "Mt. Thabīr shines so that we may ride forth."

That is what al-Suhaylī related.

And there was ʿĀmir b. al-Ẓarib al-ʿAdwānī. In the case of all conflicts arising among the Arabs, they would come to him for adjudication and accept whatever he decided. On one occasion they asked him to resolve the matter of inheritance to a hermaphrodite. He lay awake all night reflecting on how to adjudicate this and when a slave-girl of his, Sukhayla by name, who used to pasture his sheep, saw him thus, she enquired of him, "What is wrong with you, poor thing, that you spend the night awake?" So he told her, in case she might be of help. And she replied, "Judge by where from urination comes." He commented, "Sukhayla, you've shown the way well, by God." And that was how he did decide.

Al-Suhaylī pointed out that reaching a decision by such logic constituted use of *al-istidlāl bi al-amārāt wa al-ʿalāmāt*, "inference from signs and indications", a method with a basis in the law. God stated in the Qurʾān: "And they brought his shirt with false blood upon it" (*sūrat Yūsuf*, XII, v.18) since it bore no signs of a wolf's fangs. God also stated, "If his shirt has been torn from the front, she has

29. The giving of permission to the pilgrims to descend from Mt. ʿArafāt.

30. A station midway between Minā and ʿArafāt where pilgrims spend the night of 9th Dhū al-Ḥijja on their return journey from ʿArafāt.

told the truth and he is a liar, whereas if the shirt has been torn from behind, then she lied and he is truthful" (*sūrat Yūsuf*, XII, v.26–7). And in the *ḥadīth*, there are the words, "Wait for her; if she delivers it (the baby) as comely, light-brown, and with curly locks, then indeed it is (the child) of him whom she was accused of being with."

Ibn Isḥāq went on to state that *al-nasī'*, the postponement of sacred months, was decided by the time of Fuqaym b. ʿAdī b. ʿĀmir b. Thaʿlaba b. al-Ḥārith b. Mālik b. Kināna b. Khuzayma b. Mudrika b. Ilyās b. Muḍar. He reported that the first of the Arabs to intercalate the months was al-Qalammas, who was Ḥudhayfa b. ʿAbd b. Fuqaym b. ʿAdī. After him came his son ʿAbbād, and then Qalaʿ b. ʿAbbād, followed by Umayya b. Qalaʿ and ʿAwf b. Umayya. The last of them was Abū Thumāma Junāda b. ʿAwf b. Qalaʿ b. ʿAbbād b. Ḥudhayfa, the last named being al-Qalammas. Islam arose during Abū Thamāma's time.

When the Arabs had completed the pilgrimage they would gather around him and he would address them, specifying which months were sacred. If he wanted to establish a free period, he would declare al-Muḥarram free and substitute Ṣafar for it to accord with the number of months God had made sacred. He would state, "O God, I have made free the first of the al-Ṣafar months, and postponed the others till next year." And the Arabs would follow him in that. On this matter the following verses were spoken by ʿUmayr b. Qays, one of Banū Firās b. Ghanm b. Mālik b. Kināna; ʿUmayr was also known as Jadhl al-Ṭiʿān:

> "Maʿad have learned that my people are noble, that they have noble forebears.
> Which people have escaped our retribution and which have we not bridled?
> Are we not those who intercalate for Maʿad, deciding which free months shall be made sacred?"

Quṣayy was lord and master over his people, obeyed and revered. Eventually he gathered Quraysh together from their various locations in the Arabian peninsula and gained the help of the Arab tribes that obeyed him in making war on Khuzāʿa, in removing them from the House of God, and in handing over its guardianship to himself. They engaged in many battles with much bloodshed and then agreed upon arbitration. They appointed as arbitrator Yaʿmur b. ʿAwf b. Kaʿb b. ʿĀmir b. Layth b. Bakr b. ʿAbd Manāt b. Kināna who decreed that Quṣayy was more fit for guardianship over the House than Khuzāʿa was. He ruled that all losses inflicted on Quṣayy by Khuzāʿa and Banū Bakr were an issue that should be "crushed underfoot", and that what losses Khuzāʿa and Banū Bakr had received from Quraysh, Kināna, and Quḍāʿa should be compensated by bloodwit payment. His decision meant that Quṣayy should be given free access to Mecca and the *kaʿba*. Thereat Yaʿmur was nicknamed *al-Shadhdhākh*, "the crusher".

Ibn Isḥāq further related that Quṣayy thus gained guardianship over the House and control over Mecca. He brought together to Mecca his people from their dwellings and acted as king over them and over all the Meccans as well; and they treated him as king. However, he confirmed the Arabs in their prior practices, considering that to be a duty incumbent upon himself that he ought not change. He thus confirmed Ṣafwān, ʿAdwān, *al-nasaʾa*, "the intercalators", and Murra b. ʿAwf in their previous practices, until Islam came and God destroyed all of that.

Quṣayy was the first of Banū Kaʿb who took the kingship and was obeyed as such by his people. He had rights of the *ḥijāba*, the *saqāya*, the *rifāda*, the *nadwa*, and the *liwāʾ*.[31] Thus he controlled all of Mecca's honours. He divided up Mecca among his people into quarters and he settled each family of Quraysh into their dwellings there.

And so I say, that thus right was done to those worthy of it, justice returning after having left. Quraysh settled in their dwellings, ended the aims and aspirations of Khuzāʿa, and regained their ancient and venerable house. Nevertheless, they kept what Khuzāʿa had instituted, including the worship of idols, setting them up around the *kaʿba*, making sacrifice to them, praying near them, and beseeching help and fortune from them.

Quṣayy settled the Quraysh tribes in the plains and also in the heights of Mecca and they were henceforth known respectively as the "plains Quraysh" and the "highland Quraysh".

Quṣayy b. Kilāb enjoyed total authority, including being guardian and keeper of the *kaʿba* and the awarder of battle banners. He also constructed a building to prevent violence and resolve disputes; this he named the *dār al-nadwa*, the assembly house. When a conflict became serious the chiefs of each of the tribes would meet, take counsel there, and decide the issue. All contracts and marriage agreements would be made there. And that was also the only place where a girl would first wear the *daraʿ*, the sleeved chemise, when she reached the age to do so.

The door to this building was facing the *masjid al-ḥarām*, the holy mosque. Later it became owned by Ḥakīm b. Ḥizām, after belonging to Banū ʿAbd al-Dār. He sold it, during the reign of Muʿāwiya, for 100,000 dirhams. Muʿāwiya criticized him for having done so, saying, "You've sold your people's honour for 100,000."

But Ḥakīm replied, "But today nobility is measured by one's piety. I bought it, by God, before Islam for a skinful of wine and now here I've sold it for 100,000. And I swear that the money will go to charity in God's cause, so which of us had been cheated?" This was related by al-Dārquṭnī in the *Asmāʾ Rijāl al-Muwaṭṭaʾ* (*Identities of the Men in the Muwaṭṭaʾ*) (of Mālik b. Anas).

31. These terms refer, respectively, to the guardianship of the temple, the provision of water for the pilgrims, the provision of food for them, the presiding over their assemblies, and the issuance of the banners carried by them.

He had the prerogative of providing drink for the pilgrims; they drank only from his cisterns. At that time, in Mecca the holy well, *zamzam*, was obliterated, as it had been since the time of Jurhum. People had forgotten about it because of its great antiquity and they could not locate its whereabouts. According to al-Wāqidī, Quṣayy was the first person to institute lighting a fire at al-Muzdalifa to guide people coming there from ʿArafāt.

The word *al-rifāda* means providing food for the pilgrims during the pilgrimage season until they leave to return to their own countries.

Ibn Isḥāq went on to relate that Quṣayy had imposed this *rifāda* on his people, having said, "O People of Quraysh, you are God's neighbours and the inhabitants of Mecca and of the holy places. The pilgrims are God's guests and visitors to His House. They have full right to hospitality. So provide food and drink for them during the pilgrimage days, until they depart from you." And so they did. Each year they would set aside a portion of their wealth as a tribute they would pay him. He would use it to provide food for the people during the days they were at Minā. This practice was followed at his command during *al-jāhiliyya*, the pre-Islamic period, and it has passed on thereafter up to the present. It is the food the sultan provides for people at Minā each year until the pilgrimage ends.

My own comment is to add that this practice ended after the time of Ibn Isḥāq. It was then ordered that a portion of the *bayt al-māl*, the general treasury, be spent to transport food and drink for wayfarers arriving for the pilgrimage. This was a good policy for reasons too many to mention. But duty dictates that this expense should come directly from the treasury as a priority; most appropriately, it should come from the masses of the *dhimma*, the protected non-Muslims, since they do not make pilgrimage to the ancient House. It is stated in the *ḥadīth* sayings, "Regarding him who is able to make the pilgrimage but does not do so, let him die, if he wishes, a Jew or a Christian."

One of their poets said in praise of Quṣayy and his honour among his people.

> "Quṣayy was known, I swear it, as the 'gatherer'; through him God gathered together the tribes of Fihr.
>
> They filled the plain with glory and power and drove from us the satanic Banū Bakr."

Ibn Isḥāq related that when Quṣayy had finished his war, his brother Rizāḥ b. Rabīʿa left for his own country accompanied by his three paternal brothers, who were Ḥunn, Maḥmūd, and Julhuma by name. And Rizāḥ spoke the following verses in responding to Quṣayy:

> "When an envoy came from Quṣayy saying, 'Respond to your friend',
> We arose to him leading our fine horses, leaving aside the slow and overweight.
> We travelled with them by night till dawn, sheltering by day to survive.

They were speedy as sand-grouse to the water, as we answered Quṣayy's messenger.
We gathered men from al-Sirr[32] and the two Ashmadhs,[33] collecting tribesmen from each village.
What a band of horse that night, over a thousand, running free and fast,
When they passed by ʿAsjar and took the quick route from Mustanākh,
Skirting the edge of Wariqān and passing by al-ʿArj and a tribe encamped,
Overstepping the pasture, not tasting it, racing on, night-long, from Marr,
Keeping the colts near their dams to minimize their neighing.
When reaching Mecca, we destroyed the men tribe after tribe,
Switching them with our sword-blades, rendering them witless from all sides
Crushing them beneath our horses' hooves, as does the strong and mighty to the lowly.
We killed Khuzāʿa in their own home, and Bakr group by group.
We banished them from the Sovereign's land, so that they would never settle good land again,
We captured them in irons and quenched our vengeance thirst from all their tribes."

According to Ibn Isḥāq, when Rizāḥ returned home, God gave him increase. He also gave Hunn increase; they constitute the two tribes of ʿUdhra to this day.

Again according to Ibn Isḥāq, Quṣayy b. Kilāb said in that regard,

"I am the son of Banū Luʾayy, the defenders; my home is in Mecca, there was I raised,
And on to the plains, as Maʿad learned; with its lush pastures I was really content.
I would not have conquered it, had the sons of Qaydhar and al-Nābit not settled there.
Rizāḥ was my supporter and by him I came supreme; I fear no evil for as long as I shall live."

According to al-Umawī, citing al-Ashram from Abū ʿUbayda, from Muḥammad b. Ḥafṣ, Rizāḥ only arrived after Quṣayy had expelled Khuzāʿa. God knows best.

Section.

When Quṣayy grew old he entrusted all the prerogatives he had enjoyed – leadership of Quraysh and its honour of governing the provision of food and drink for the pilgrims, guardianship of the House, the issuance of banners, and the summoning of assemblies – to his son ʿAbd al-Dār, who was his oldest.

He only entrusted him with all these prerogatives because the rest of his brothers, ʿAbd Manāf, ʿAbd Shams, and ʿAbd had become noblemen during

32. A valley.

33. Two mountains between Medina and the town of Khaybar.

their father's rule and had attained great power and prestige. Thus Quṣayy wished for ʿAbd al-Dār to be equal to them in prestige and so gave him alone these powers. ʿAbd al-Dār's brothers did not dispute his action. But when they all had passed away their sons came into conflict about this and said, "Quṣayy only entrusted ʿAbd al-Dār with all that to equalize him with his brothers; we are entitled to what our fathers were due."

ʿAbd al-Dār's family replied, "This is a matter that Quṣayy decided in our favour, and we have the greater right."

And so a great dispute arose among them; and Quraysh split into two factions, one giving allegiance and alliance to the family of ʿAbd al-Dār, the other to the family of ʿAbd Manāf with whom they made a formal pact. Upon making the oath they placed their hands into a deep dish containing perfume. Then they went and wiped their hands on the corners of the *kaʿba*. This was thereafter known as the "Treaty of the Perfumed".

On the ʿAbd Manāf side there were the Quraysh tribes of Banū Asad b. ʿAbd al-ʿUzza b. Quṣayy, Banū Zuhra, Banū Taym, and Banū al-Ḥārith b. Fihr. On the side of ʿAbd al-Dār's descendants were Banū Makhzūm, Banū Sahm, Banū Jumaḥ, and Banū ʿAdī. The tribes of Banū ʿĀmir b. Luʾayy and Muḥārib b. Fihr remained separate from the rest, not allying with either side.

Ultimately they made peace, agreeing that the prerogatives of feeding and watering the pilgrims should be held by Banū ʿAbd Manāf, while those of guardianship of the *kaʿba*, issuance of banners, and calling of assemblies were to be held by Banū ʿAbd al-Dār. This arrangement became firm and permanent.

Al-Umawī related from al-Ashram, on the authority of Abū ʿUbayda that a number of the Khuzāʿa claim that after Quṣayy had married Ḥubbā daughter of Ḥulayl, he (Ḥulayl) found the guardianship of the *kaʿba* onerous and passed it on to his daughter Ḥubbā, appointing Abū Ghubshān Salīm b. ʿAmr b. Luʾayy b. Malkān b. Quṣayy b. Ḥāritha b. ʿAmr b. ʿĀmir as her trustee for it. Quṣayy purchased the guardianship of the *kaʿba* from him for a skin of wine and a young riding camel. And so there arose the saying, "A worse deal than that of Abū Ghubshān!" When Khuzāʿa saw this happen they attacked Quṣayy, who called for assistance from his brother; when he and his men arrived the issue was resolved as reported above. Ultimately Quṣayy passed on the prerogatives of protection and guardianship of the House, issuance of banners, calling of assemblies, and feeding and watering the pilgrims to his son ʿAbd al-Dār, as will be related in detail. The *ijāza*, giving permission to leave Muzdalifa, was established as a right of Banū ʿAdwān, the *nasīʾ*, the right of calendar intercalation, went to Fuqaym, while the Ṣūfa enjoyed that of *ijāza*, that is, of the *nafr*, the giving of the signal to leave Minā. All this information on the prerogatives of these people has been detailed above.

Ibn Isḥāq stated that Quṣayy had four sons and two daughters, the sons being ʿAbd Manāf, ʿAbd al-Dār, ʿAbd al-ʿUzzā, and ʿAbd, the daughters Takhmur and Barra. The mother of all these was Ḥubbā, daughter of Ḥulayl b. Ḥubshiyya b. Salūl b. Kaʿb b. ʿAmr, al-Khuzāʿī. It was from Ḥulayl that Quṣayy b. Kilāb took control over the Sacred House.

According to Ibn Hishām, ʿAbd Manāf b. Quṣayy had four sons, Hāshim, ʿAbd Shams, and al-Muṭṭalib, their mother being ʿĀtika daughter of Murra b. Hilāl. Another son of his was Nawfal b. ʿAbd Manāf, his mother being Wāqida, daughter of ʿAmr al-Māziniyya.

Ibn Hishām stated as well that ʿAbd Manāf also fathered Abū ʿAmr, Tumāḍir, Qulāba, Ḥayya, Rayṭa, Umm al-Akhtham, and Umm Sufyān.

Also according to Ibn Hishām, Hāshim b. ʿAbd Manāf had four (*sic*) sons and five daughters. The sons were named ʿAbd al-Muṭṭalib, Asad, and Abū Sayfī; the daughters were Naḍla, al-Shaffāʾ, Khālida, Ḍaʿīfa, Ruqayya, and Ḥayya. The mother of ʿAbd al-Muṭṭalib and Ruqayya was Salmā, daughter of ʿAmr b. Zayd b. Labīd b. Khidāsh b. ʿĀmir b. Ghanm b. ʿAdī b. al-Najjār from Medina. Ibn Hishām also gave the names of the mothers of the remaining children.

He stated that ʿAbd al-Muṭṭalib had ten sons and six daughters. The sons were al-ʿAbbās, Ḥamza, ʿAbd Allāh, Abū Ṭālib (whose name was ʿAbd Manāf and not ʿUmrān), al-Zubayr, al-Ḥārith, who was the first-born of his father who was therefore accorded his name, Jahl (whom some name as Ḥajl), who was nicknamed *al-Ghaydaq*, "the liberal", for his generosity, al-Muqawwim, Ḍirār, and Abū Lahab (whose name was ʿAbd al-ʿUzzā). His daughters' names were Ṣafiyya, Umm Ḥakīm al-Bayḍāʾ, ʿĀtika, Umayma, ʿArwā, and Barra. And Ibn Hishām also gave the names of their mothers. He stated that the mother of ʿAbd Allāh, Abū Ṭālib, al-Zubayr and all the girls except Ṣafiyya was Fāṭima, daughter of ʿAmr b. ʿĀʾidh b. ʿUmrān b. Makhzūm b. Yaqẓa b. Murra b. Kaʿb b. Luʾayy b. Ghālib b. Fihr b. Mālik b. al-Naḍr b. Kināna b. Khuzayma b. Mudrika b. Ilyās b. Muḍar b. Nizār b. Maʿad b. ʿAdnān.

He said further that ʿAbd Allāh fathered Muḥammad, the Messenger of God (ṢAAS), the lord of all Adam's children. His mother was Āmina daughter of Wahb b. ʿAbd Manāf b. Zuhra b. Kilāb b. Murra b. Kaʿb b. Luʾayy. He then gave mention of all her maternal forebears.

Ibn Hishām concluded that the Prophet (ṢAAS) was the most noble of Adam's children in worthiness and descent from both his father and his mother.

Previously recounted is the following statement of al-Awzāʿī on the authority of Shaddād Abū ʿAmmār from Wāthila b. al-Asqaʿ: "The Messenger of God (ṢAAS) said, 'God chose Kināna from Ishmael's progeny and Quraysh from Kināna, Hāshim from Quraysh, and myself from Hāshim.'" Muslim recounted this tradition.

There will follow hereafter an account of the noble birth of the Prophet (ṢAAS) and of the events and circumstances surrounding it. And in recounting his honoured ancestry there will be other useful information not here given, if God Almighty so wills it, and in Him is all trust and reliance.

An Account of a variety of events that occurred in the jāhiliyya.

It has already been recounted how Jurhum assumed control over the House from Banū Ismāʿīl out of envy for them because they were the children of their daughters. And similarly how it was that Khuzāʿa fell upon Jurhum and took over the House from them, and how ultimately its guardianship fell to Quṣayy and his sons, continuing in their hands until God sent his Messenger (ṢAAS) and how those prerogatives became established as they were.

Section: Information about a group of men famous in the jāhiliyya.

An Account of Khālid b. Sinān the ʿAbsite who lived in the inter-prophet period and who some allege was a prophet. But God knows best.

The *ḥāfiẓ* Abū al-Qāsim al-Ṭabarānī stated that Aḥmad b. Zuhayr al-Tasaturrī related, quoting Yaḥyā b. al-Muʿallā b. Manṣūr al-Rāzī, quoting Muḥammad b. al-Ṣalt, quoting Qays b. al-Rabīʿ, from Sālim al-Afṭas, from Saʿīd b. Jubayr, and from Ibn ʿAbbās as follows, "The daughter of Khālid b. Sinān came to the Prophet (ṢAAS) and he smoothed out his robe for her (to sit on), saying, 'Here's the daughter of a prophet whose people squandered him.'"

The *ḥāfiẓ* Abū Bakr al-Bazzār reported it from Yaḥyā b. al-Muʿalī b. Manṣūr, from Muḥammad b. al-Ṣalt, from Qays, from Sālim, from Saʿīd, from Ibn ʿAbbās, as follows, "Someone made reference to Khālid b. Sinān in the presence of the Messenger of God (ṢAAS) who commented, 'That was a prophet whose people squandered him.'"

Al-Bazzār then said, "And we have no direct reference of this *ḥadīth* to the Prophet other than in this form. Qays b. al-Rabīʿ was highly respected, though he was not regarded as having been a good memorizer. He had a son who would add extraneous material into the traditions he related. But God knows best." Al-Bazzār stated, "This *ḥadīth* was also related by al-Thawrī from Sālim al-Afṭas, transmitted forward indirectly from Saʿīd b. Jubayr."

The *ḥafiẓ* Abū Yaʿlā al-Mawṣilī stated that al-Muʿallā b. Mahdī al-Mawṣilī related to him, as did Abū ʿAwāna, from Abū Yūnis, from ʿAkrama and down to Ibn ʿAbbās, that a man from ʿAbs called Khālid b. Sinān said to his people, "I shall put out from you the fire of al-Ḥarratayn!" But one of his people responded, "O Khālid, you have only ever told us the truth; what have you to do with the fire of al-Ḥarratayn you claim you will extinguish?"

So Khālid went forth accompanied by some of his people, including ʿUmāra b. Ziyād, until they reached where the fire emerged from a fissure in the mountain. Khālid then drew a line at which he made them sit, saying, "If I am delayed, do not call for me by my name." As the fire spurted out, it looked like sorrel-red horses following one another. Khālid approached it and began beating it with his stick saying, "Badā, badā, badā kullu hudā; the son of the goatherdswoman claimed I won't come out from it bearing my clothes in my hand." Then he went inside the fissure with the fire. When he had been gone a long time, ʿUmāra b. Ziyād said to Khālid's people, "By God, if he were alive he would have come out to you by now!" Some said, "Call out to him by name."

The account continued, indicating that others replied, "He forbade us to call him by his name." But some did so and he emerged carrying his head, complaining, "Didn't I forbid you to call me by name? By God, you've killed me, so bury me! And if some donkeys pass, one of which is bobtailed, then exhume me and you'll find me alive."

They did bury him and some donkeys did pass by, one of them being bobtailed. So some wanted to exhume him as he had told them to do but ʿUmāra argued, "No don't exhume him. By God, Muḍar won't go around saying that we dig up our dead!" Khālid had also told them, "In my wife's possession there are two tablets into which you must look if you should have difficulties; if you do so you will find a response to your questions. But do not let a menstruating woman touch them." They therefore went to his wife and asked her about these tablets and she brought them out. However, she was in menstruation, and so whatever knowledge was in them had gone.

Abū Yūnus stated that Sammāk b. Ḥarb responded that the Prophet (ṢAAS) was asked about Khālid and he replied, "That was a prophet whose people squandered him."

Abū Yūnus also reported that Sammāk b. Ḥarb said that the son of Khālid b. Sinān came to the Prophet (ṢAAS) who told him, "Welcome to my brother's son!" This comment is traced back to Ibn ʿAbbās who makes no reference to his being a prophet. The accounts that do so cannot use this comment as a proof that he was a prophet. What is most probable is that he was a pious man with certain qualities and gifts. This is because if he had indeed lived in the inter-prophet period, it was firmly established as incontrovertible in the *ṣaḥīḥ* collection of al-Bukhārī that the Messenger of God (ṢAAS) stated, "The closest of men to Jesus son of Mary is myself, for there came no prophet between him and me." And if Khālid had lived earlier, he could not have been a prophet, because God Almighty stated, "that you may warn a people to whom no warner had come before you" (*sūrat al-Sajda*, XXXII, v.3).

A number of scholars have stated that God Almighty sent no prophet to the Arabs after Ishmael except Muḥammad (ṢAAS), the Seal of the Prophets mentioned by Abraham, God's true follower, who built the venerated *kaʿba* which God made the direction of prayer as a law for all the earth's people; and the other prophets announced to their peoples his coming, right on up to the last of them to do so, namely Jesus son of Mary, upon whom be peace.

And in this same way may be refuted the reports of al-Suhaylī and others concerning the dispatch to the Arabs of another prophet named Shuʿayb b. Dhī Muhdhim b. Shuʿayb b. Ṣafwān, lord of Madyan. Also the story that Ḥanẓala b. Ṣafwān was sent to the Arabs and that since both he and Shuʿayb had been disowned, God imposed Bukhtunaṣṣar (Nebuchadnezzar) over the Arabs who suffered from him killing and captivity similar to those endured by the Israelites; all this occurred in the time of Maʿad b. ʿAdnān.

What is evident is that these people were all good men advocating righteousness. But God knows best. We have previously given mention of ʿAmr b. Luḥayy b. Qamʿa b. Khindif in the account of Khuzāʿa following Jurhum.

An Account of Ḥātim al-Ṭā'ī, a good and generous man of the jāhiliyya *period.*

He was Ḥātim b. ʿAbd Allāh b. Saʿd b. al-Ḥashraj b. Imru' al-Qays b. ʿAdī b. Aḥzam b. Abū Aḥzam, the name of the last being Harūma b. Rabīʿa b. Jarwal b. Thaʿl b. ʿAmr b. al-Ghawth b. Ṭayyi' Abū Saffāna al-Ṭā'ī. Ḥātim was the father of ʿAdī b. Ḥātim *al-ṣaḥābī*, "the Companion of the Prophet". He was a generous man much praised in the *jāhiliyya* period, as was his son after the coming of Islam.

Ḥātim was a man of such distinction and generosity that many extraordinary events and strange accounts are associated with him. However, by these deeds he did not seek the grace of God or the hereafter but was motivated by desire for fame and recognition.

The *ḥāfiẓ* Abū Bakr al-Bazzār stated in his compilation of traditions that Muḥammad b. Muʿammar related to him, as did ʿUbayd b. Wāqid the Qaysite, as did Abū Naṣr who was al-Nājī, from ʿ Abd Allāh b. Dinār, from Ibn ʿUmar that Ḥātim was referred to in the presence of the Prophet (ṢAAS) and he commented, "That man wanted something, and he attained it."

This is a curious tradition. Al-Dārquṭnī said that ʿUbayd b. Wāqid was unique in transmitting it, on the authority of Abū Naṣr al-Nājī, whose name is said to have been Ḥammād.

According to Ibn ʿAsākir, Abū Aḥmad al-Ḥākim made a distinction between Abū Naṣr al-Nājī and Abū Naṣr Ḥammād and that he was not named "al-Nājī". Yet several accounts related by the *ḥāfiẓ* Ibn ʿAsākir refer to an "Abū Naṣr Shayba al-Nājī". But God knows best.

Imām Aḥmad (b. Ḥanbal) stated that Yazīd b. Ismāʿīl related to him, as did Sufyān, from Sammāk b. Ḥarb, from Marī b. Qaṭarī, from ʿAdī b. Ḥātim who stated that he said to the Messenger of God (ṢAAS); "My father was very generous to his kinsfolk and very active on their behalf; does he get something for that, some reward?" He responded, "Your father had sought something, and he attained it."

This tradition was similarly reported by Abū Yaʿlā, from al-Qawārīrī, from Ghandar, from Shuʿba, from Sammāk, in the form: "He responded, 'Your father had wanted something, and he got it.'" By this he meant reputation. Abū al-Qāsim al-Baghawī related it thus, from ʿAlī b. al-Jaʿd from Shuʿba.

In the *ṣaḥīḥ* tradition compendium it has been established that the three kinds of people by whom the fires of hell are fed include the man who spends his money (on others) so that he will be considered generous. His pay-off is in having that said of him on earth. So, too, is it with the scholar and the warrior. And in another tradition in the *ṣaḥīḥ* it tells how people asked the Messenger of God (ṢAAS) about ʿAbd Allāh b. Judʿān b. ʿAmr b. Kaʿb b. Saʿd b. Taym b. Murra, saying, "He was hospitable, freed slaves, and gave to charity; did that benefit him?" He responded, "But he never once said, 'O God, forgive me my sins on Judgement Day.'" This man was also one of those who were famous for their generosity, who gave food in years of famine and times of destitution.

The *ḥāfiẓ* Abū Bakr al-Bayhaqī stated that he was informed by the *ḥāfiẓ* Abū ʿAbd Allāh, Abū Bakr Muḥammad b. ʿAbd Allāh b. Yūsuf al-ʿUmānī, that Abū Saʿīd ʿUbayd b. Kathīr b. ʿAbd al-Wāḥid al-Kūfī related to him, as did Ḍirār b. Ṣurd, and ʿĀṣim b. Ḥamīd, from Abū Ḥamza al-Thamālī, from ʿAbd al-Raḥmān b. Jandab, from Kumayl b. Ziyād al-Nakhʿī who said that ʿAlī b. Abū Ṭālib exclaimed, "Glory be to God! How many a man acts pious for gain! How strange is someone who is approached by his Muslim brother in need yet does not see his way to doing good. For even if he did not hope for reward or fear punishment he ought to make haste in acting with nobility for it is such deeds that lead to success."

A man thereupon arose to ask him, "O Commander of the Believers, I pledge you my father and my mother, did you hear that from the Messenger of God (ṢAAS)?" ʿAli replied, "Yes. And I've a tale even better than that. When Ṭāʾī's women were brought in as captives, one of them was red-haired, cherry-lipped, smooth-skinned, slender-necked, fine-nosed, with a straight figure, raised head, full ankles, plump legs, rounded thighs, slim waist, slender sides and well-shaped body. I was much struck by her when I saw her and said I would request the Messenger of God (ṢAAS) to award her to me in my portion of the booty. But when she spoke I forgot her beauty for the eloquence I heard. She said, 'O Muḥammad, will you not release me and spare me the malicious gloating of the Arab tribes, for I am the daughter of the leader of my people. My father was guardian of our sacred objects, he relieved the distressed, fed the hungry, clothed the naked, gave generous hospitality, provided the best of food, spread peace abroad and never refused the request of the needy. I am the daughter of Ḥātim al-Ṭāʾī.'

"The Prophet (ṢAAS) replied, 'O girl, all that truly describes the believers. Had your father been a believer, we would certainly have been merciful to him. Release her, for her father was a man who loved to perform good deeds, and God Almighty loves good deeds.'

"At that Abū Burda b. Niyār arose and said, 'O Messenger of God, does God really love good deeds?'

"The Messenger of God (ṢAAS) replied, 'By him in whose hand is my soul, no one will enter heaven except by good deeds.'"

Abū Bakr b. Abū al-Dunyā stated that ʿUmar b. Bakr related to him, from Abū ʿAbd al-Raḥmān al-Ṭāʾī (his name being al-Qāsim b. ʿAdī) from ʿUthmān; from ʿArakī b. Ḥulays al-Ṭāʾī, from his father, from his grandfather (who was the brother of ʿAdī b. Ḥātim from his mother's side), that someone said to al-Nawār, wife of Ḥātim, "Tell us about Ḥātim."

She replied, "Everything about him was wonderful. Once we were afflicted with a year of utter desolation when the earth quaked, the skies filled with dust and wet nurses were too drained to suckle their children. The camels had become completely emaciated, their bones showing through, and not producing a drop of milk. And our money was all dried up.

"One interminable, cold night, with the small children writhing from hunger (their names were ʿAbd Allāh and ʿAdī and Saffāna), he said, 'By God, we don't have anything to pacify them with.' So he arose to one of the boys and lifted him up, while I went over to the girl to pacify her. And, by God, they only quietened down after a good part of the night had elapsed. After that we went to the other boy and rocked him until he became quiet, or almost so.

"Then we spread out a frayed Syrian rug we had and laid out the children on it, with me and him sleeping in the one room with the children in between us. Then he approached me, soothing me so I would sleep. I knew what he wanted, so I pretended to sleep. He asked, 'How are you? Have you fallen asleep?' I said nothing and he commented, 'I see that she has fallen asleep, but I'm not sleepy.'

"When the night became pitch black, the stars having almost disappeared and there was neither sound nor movement astir, the side of our tent was lifted. He called out, 'Who is there?' The person went away. At daybreak, or thereabouts, he again said, 'Who is there?' and a woman replied, 'It is your neighbour so-and-so, Abū ʿAdī; I have no one to turn to but you. I'm coming to you from my children who are moaning like wolves from their hunger. 'Bring them to me quickly,' he told her."

Al-Nawār went on, "I jumped up and exclaimed, 'What are you doing? Lie down! Your children are writhing from hunger and you've no means to soothe them, so what can you do for her and her children?' He responded, 'Be silent; by God, I will satisfy you, if God wills it.'"

She went on, "So in she came, carrying two children and with four others walking at her side, as though she were an ostrich surrounded by her chicks. Then he went over to his horse, thrust his spear in its upper chest and struck his flint and lit a fire. Next he brought a long knife and skinned the horse after which he handed the knife to the woman saying, 'After you.' Then he said, 'Now send your children.' And she did so. Then he said (to al-Nawār) 'You, evil woman, would you eat something before a poor man's children!'

"He then went all round to each one of them until they had all got up and approached the horse. Then he wrapped himself up in his cloak and stretched out to one side watching us. And, by God, he did not taste one bite himself, even though he was the most of all in need. And by next morning there was nothing of the horse left but bones and hooves!"

Al-Dārquṭnī stated that *Qāḍī* (judge) Abū ʿAbd Allāh al-Muḥāmilī related to him, as did ʿAbd Allāh b. Abū Saʿd, as did ʿUthaym b. Thawāba b. Ḥātim al-Ṭāʾī from his father, from his grandfather, that Ḥātim's wife said to Ḥātim, "O Abū Saffāna, I desire that you and I eat alone together, with no one else there." So he gave her instructions, and she moved her tent a *parasang*, a couple of miles, away from the rest. He ordered food and it was prepared, and the tent curtains were let down for him and for her. When the food was cooked, he took off his head-covering, then spoke these verses,

> "Do not you cook my pot with your curtains hiding it; for me, then, what you cook is forbidden.
>
> But at that hill light the fire with heavy wood if you do light it, not with quick kindling wood."

The narrator continued, "Then he drew aside the curtains, brought out the food and invited in the people. He and they then ate. She told him, 'You haven't fulfilled what you said.' And he responded, 'I couldn't bring myself to do it. My spirit was too noble to bring blame on me for this, when before I have always been generous.' He then spoke the following:

> 'I oppose the miser's spirit till I overcome it and leave alone that of the generous man, not battling it.
>
> My neighbour woman has no complaint of me except that I do not visit her when her husband is away.

My goodness shall attain her, and her husband will return to her, while her veils have not fallen short for her.'"

Ḥātim's verse includes the following:

"If I spent the night drinking and drinking in order to get drunk, may I never quench my thirst!
If I spent the night deceiving my neighbour to cheat with his wife, hiding by the dark, may I never be unseen!
Would I disgrace my neighbour woman and betray my neighbour?
By God, that I'll never do so long as I live."

And also:

"It never harmed my neighbour next to whom I live that his door had no curtain;
I look down when my neighbour's wife appears, until the women's quarters hide her again."

He also recited:

"It's not of my nature to curse a cousin or to reject someone's request,
And many an envious word I've heard for no wrongdoing on my part and said, 'Let it pass and spare me.'
They blamed it on my account but it never blemished me; my forehead never sweated for it.
The two-faced finds me free but does not imitate me when he leaves.
I overcome his evil and turn from him, preserving my repute and my faith."

And also he composed:

"Ask, O Umm Mālik, the wretched and cold if, when he comes to me between my fire and larder,
I smile on him. He is the first person served; on him I lavish charity, denying him not."

He also said:

"If you give your stomach its request, and your sexual desire too, they'll both together reach the utmost blame."

The judge Abū al-Faraj al-Muʿāfā b. Zakariyyāʾ al-Jarīrī said that al-Ḥusayn b. al-Qāsim al-Kawkabī related to him, as did Abū al-ʿAbbās al-Mubarrid that al-Thawrī told him, from Abū ʿUbayda, that when the following verses of al-Mutalammis reached Ḥātim al-Ṭāʾī,

"One of little wealth you can repair and he survive, but not the man of much corruption.
And preserving wealth is better than exhausting it and wandering abroad without provisions",

he said, "What's wrong with him, may God cut his tongue! Is he advising people to be miserly? Should he not have said,

> 'Generosity will not exhaust one's wealth before its going, nor stinginess increase the miser's wealth.
> So don't seek wealth through living miserly; for every day there's a blessing that comes anew.
> Do you not see that wealth comes and goes, and that He who gives to you is not far away.'"

The judge Abū al-Faraj commented, "He (Ḥātim) spoke well with those words, 'He who gives to you is not far away,' and if he had been a Muslim, good would have been hoped for him in the hereafter. For God stated in the Qur'ān, "Ask of God from His bounty" (*sūrat al-Nisā'*, IV, v.32) and also, "If my servants ask you about me (then say) that I am nigh and that I answer the call of those who pray to me" (*sūrat al-Baqara*, II, v.186).

And from al-Waḍḍāh b. Maʿbad al-Ṭā'ī comes the account that Ḥātim al-Ṭā'ī presented himself at the court of al-Nuʿmān b. al-Mundhir, who received and honoured him. Then upon his departure he gave him two camels loaded with gold and silver, as well as valued produce of his land. So off went Ḥātim, to be met by bedouins of the Ṭayyi' tribe as he approached home. They addressed him thus, "O Ḥātim, you've just come from the king, whereas we have come from our people in poverty!" Ḥātim responded, "Come and take what I have, and distribute it amongst you." They rushed forward to do so, taking and distributing the gifts of al-Nuʿmān. Then his maidservant, Ṭarīfa, came out to Ḥātim and said, "Both be pious and keep some for yourself; these people won't leave you a dinar or a dirham, a sheep or a camel." Ḥātim responded by speaking the verses,

> "Ṭarīfa said: 'You keep us no dirhams, though we are neither wasteful nor over-burdened with them.'
> If what we have is used up, then God will provide for us from someone else and it is not we who will provide for ourselves.
> No sooner does the dirham get acquainted with our rags than it passes on over and leaves again.
> If our dirhams were once to assemble together, they'd compete with one another for ways to give charity."

Abū Bakr b. ʿAyyāsh said that Ḥātim was once asked whether any other Arab was more generous than he and he replied, "All the Arabs are more generous than me!" Ḥātim then went on to relate that once he overnighted with a young Arab, an orphan, who had 100 sheep. So he slaughtered for him one ewe and when he brought it in and offered him its brain, Ḥātim commented, "What delicious brain!" Thereupon the young Arab kept on bringing him more and more of it until he told him he had had enough. Next morning Ḥātim found out that the young Arab had killed all 100 of the sheep and had nothing at all left for himself! Ḥātim was asked what he did then, and he replied, "However could I thank him enough if I were to do all in the world for him? But in any case, I did give him 100 of my very best camels."

Muḥammad b. Jaʿfar al-Kharāʾiṭī stated in his book *Makārim al-Akhlāq* (*Acts of Nobility of Character*), that al-ʿAbbās b. al-Faḍl al-Rabʿī related to him, as did Isḥāq b. Ibrāhīm, as did Ḥammād al-Rāwiyya and some elderly men of Ṭayyiʾ, that it is said that ʿAnṭara, daughter of ʿAfīf b. ʿAmr b. Imruʾ al-Qays, the mother of Ḥātim al-Ṭāʾī, could never hold on to anything due to her munificent generosity. Her brothers would restrain her but she ignored them. Since she was a woman of wealth they ultimately imprisoned her inside a house for a year, even feeding her there to make her change her behaviour. After a year they released her, believing she had reformed, and paid her over a portion of her money and told her to enjoy it. But a woman from Hawāzin who used to visit her came and asked her for money and she responded, "Take this money, for, by God, I've so suffered hunger myself, I'll spare no effort not to deny anyone who asks of me." Then she spoke the following verses,

"By my life, I have been so bitten before by hunger, that I'll spare no efforts never to deny the hungry,
So say now to this man blaming me, 'Spare me, and if you don't then chew on your own fingers!'
What can you tell your sister except your blame or the reproach of those who are misers.
What you witness today is only my nature, and how, O brother, should I abandon my nature?"

Al-Haytham b. ʿAdī stated, on the authority of Malḥān b. ʿArakī b. ʿAdī b. Ḥātim, on the authority of his father and his grandfather that he witnessed Ḥātim's excessive generosity and that Ḥātim had said to him, "Now, son, I pride myself on three qualities – I've never exposed a woman neighbour to suspicion, never given my trust and not fulfilled it, and no one has ever come to harm from me."

Abū Bakr al-Kharāʾiṭī said, "ʿAlī b. Ḥarb related to us, quoting ʿAbd al-Raḥmān b. Yaḥyā al-ʿAdawī, quoting Hishām b. Muḥammad b. al-Sāʾib al-Kalbī, on the authority of Abū Miskīn (otherwise known as Jaʿfar b. al-Muḥarrir b. al-Walīd) from al-Muḥarrir Mawlā Abū Hurayra, as follows: 'A party of men from the ʿAbd al-Qays tribe passed the grave of Ḥātim al-Ṭāʾī and came near by. One of them, Abū al-Khaybarī by name, went over and began running his foot over his grave, saying, "O Abū Jaʿd[34] give us hospitality!" One of his companions exclaimed, "What are you doing, talking to a decomposed corpse!" After darkness had fallen they went to sleep, but the man who had addressed Ḥātim awoke in a fright and began shouting, "Everyone, look to your mounts; Ḥātim came to me while I slept and spoke verses I've memorized that went:

34. Nickname of Ḥātim al-Ṭāʾī.

'O Abū al-Khaybarī, you're a man who brings disgrace and dishonour to the tribe.
You brought your companions to seek hospitality at a grave whose corpse had perished.
Do you wish to blame me when you stay here, while around you is the Ṭāyyīʾ tribe and their generosity?
We're ones to satisfy our guests, and delay the milking of their camels when they come to us.' " '[35]

"He (Abū Hurayra) went on: 'And then, to their surprise, the camel of the man who had spoken to the grave began hobbling on three legs. So they killed it and cooked and ate it, saying: "By God, Ḥātim hosted us both alive and dead!"

" 'Next morning they mounted their friend behind another rider and set off and were surprised to see a man waving to them as he approached on a camel, leading another behind him. "Which of you is Abū al-Khaybarī?" he asked. Abū al-Khaybarī identified himself and the man explained, "Ḥātim came to me in my sleep and told me he had hosted your companions with your camel, and so he asked me to bring you this mount. Take it!" And he gave it to him.' "

An Account of some matters relating to ʿAbd Allāh b. Judʿān.

His genealogy was ʿAbd Allāh, son of Judʿān, son of ʿAmr, son of Kaʿb, son of Saʿd, son of Taym, son of Murrah, lord of the Banū Taym. He was the nephew of the father of Abū Bakr *al-Ṣiddīq*, "the trusting", God bless him.

He was a noble knight during the era before Islam, one of those who gave generously to the needy.

At first he was poor and deprived, mean and sinful, so that his people, tribe, kinsfolk, and family all hated him, even his father too.

One day he went off into the outskirts of Mecca, aimless and miserable, and noticed a fissure in a mountain. He thought there might be something there that would harm him, so he approached it, so that he might die and so be relieved from his sufferings.

When he drew near it, he saw a serpent coming out towards him, darting at him. He tried to avoid it, jumping away, but it was no use. But when it was upon him, he saw it to be of gold, its eyes of sapphire. So he destroyed it, picked it up, and went into the cave. To his amazement, there he found the graves of some of the kings of Jurhum, including that of al-Ḥārith b. Muḍāḍ, who had long ago disappeared without trace. On their heads he found plaques of gold giving the dates of their death and the periods of their reigns. All about them were large quantities of jewels, pearls, gold, and silver. Of these he took what he wanted and left, after having marked the entry to the cave. When he reached his people

35. So that the guests can keep the milk of their camels for themselves.

he made gifts to them so that they loved him and then he became their leader. He would feed the people and when he ran out of valuables he would go off to the cave, get more and return. Of those who reported this were ῾Abd al-Mālik b. Hishām in his book *al-Tījān* (*The Crowns*), and Aḥmad b. ῾Ammār in the work entitled *Rayy al-῾Āṭish wa Uns al-Wāḥish* (*Quenching the Thirsty and Comforting the Lonely*). He had a watering trough from which mounted riders would feed; the trough was so large that a boy fell in and drowned.

Ibn Qutayba and others reported that the Messenger of God (ṢAAS) said, "I used to shelter in the shade of ῾Abd Allāh b. Jud῾ān's watering trough during the sweltering heat of midday."

In a *ḥadīth* relating to the death of Abū Jahl, the Messenger of God (ṢAAS) said to his Companions, "Look for him among the dead; you will recognize him by a scar on his knee. I was competing with him among the crowd at a feast given by Ibn Jud῾ān. I knocked him over and he fell against his knee which broke, the damage still being visible there on it." And they did find him just so.

People report that he used to feed people with dates and barley and with milk to drink until he heard the verses of Umayya b. Abū al-Ṣalt:

> "I've seen doers and their deeds, and found their noblest to be Banū al-Dayyān.
> Wheat mixed with honey is their food, not what Banū Jud῾ān entertain us with."

So Ibn Jud῾ān sent off 2,000 camels to Syria, and they returned bearing wheat, honey and butter. Then he had a man call out each night from the *ka῾ba* roof, "You're all to come to Ibn Jud῾ān's trough." Whereupon Umayya spoke the following:

> "He has one energetic fellow summoning (people) in Mecca, while another calls out from above its *ka῾ba*
> To come to large wooden platters filled with ears of wheat mixed with honey."

Yet despite all this, it is established in the *ṣaḥīḥ* tradition collection of Muslim (b. al-Hadjdjāj) that ῾Ā᾽isha said: "O Messenger of God, Ibn Jud῾ān used to donate food to eat and was hospitable to guests; will that benefit him on Judgement Day?" He replied, "No; he never once said: 'O my Lord, forgive me my sins on Judgement Day.'"

An Account of Imru᾽ al-Qays b. Ḥujr al-Kindī, author of one of the mu῾allaqāt *odes.*

His ode is the most magnificent and best known of them all, and it begins:

> "Halt here, both of you, and let us lament memory of a loved one and a dwelling . . ."

Al-Imām Aḥmad stated that Hushaym related to him, as did Abū al-Jahm al-Wāsiṭī, from al-Zuhrī, from Abū Salama, from Abū Hurayra, that the Messenger of God (ṢAAS) said: "Imruʾ al-Qays will be the company commander of the poets on their way to hell-fire!"

A large number of transmitters related this tradition from Hushaym, including Bishr b. al-Ḥakam, al-Ḥasan b. ʿArafa, ʿAbd Allāh b. Hārūn, the Commander of the faithful al-Maʾmūn, brother of al-Amīn, and Yaḥyā b. Maʿīn. Ibn ʿAdī considered the transmission chain to be through ʿAbd al-Razzāq from al-Zuhrī, but this would then be discontinuous and bad from another direction, through Abū Hurayra; and it would not be a reliable tradition except from the first chain of transmission.

The *ḥāfiz* Ibn ʿAsākir gave the genealogy of Imruʾ al-Qays as having been the son of Ḥujr, son of al-Ḥārith, son of ʿAmr, son of Ḥujr, the *ākil al-mirār*,[36] son of ʿAmr, son of Muʿāwiya, son of al-Ḥārith, son of Yaʿrub, son of Thawr, son of Murtaʿ, son of Muʿāwiya b. Kinda. He was also known as Abū Yazīd, Abū Wahb, and Abū al-Ḥārith al-Kindī. He lived in the regions of Damascus and mentioned a number of these in his poetry, as for example in the lines:

> "Halt here, both of you, and let us lament memory of a loved one and a dwelling at the winding ridges between al-Dakhūl and Ḥawmal,
>
> Tūḍiḥ and al-Miqrāt; its traces have not been erased by the interweaving winds from south and north."

These are well-known places in Ḥūrān.[37]

He then related, on a chain of authorities through Hishām b. Muḥammad b. al-Sāʾib al-Kalbī that Farwa b. Saʿīd b. ʿAfīf b. Maʿdī Karib related to him, from his father, from his grandfather, that while he and others were with the Messenger of God (ṢAAS) along came a delegation from Yemen. They said, "O Messenger of God, God gave us life by two verses from the poetry of Imruʾ al-Qays." He replied, "How so?" They explained, "We were making our way to visit you but lost our way *en route*, spending three days unable to get water. So we split up at the base of an acacia and a mimosa so that we each could die in the shade of a tree. When we were at our last gasp, there was a man speeding on his camel. When one of our men saw him, he spoke the following verses, the rider hearing them:

> 'And when she (the wild ass) says that the water was her desire but that the white of her veins was bloody[38]
>
> She made for the well at Ḍārij, its green slime shading it, overflowing.'[39]

36. One who ate the bitter desert plant *Centaurea calcitrapa*.

37. Ḥūrān is a plateau south of Damascus in Syria.

38. He implies that though the animal was thirsty, it was afraid that hunters might shoot it and that its veins would bleed.

39. Ḍārij was near where the ʿAbd tribe dwelt. The verse suggests that the animal headed for that well to be able to hide from hunters in the thick underbush.

"So the rider asked, 'Whose verses are those?' He saw our state of exhaustion. We answered, 'Imru᾽ al-Qays b. Ḥujr.' Then he said, 'By God, he did not lie; this is Ḍārij, where you are now.' So we looked, and there was the water about 50 arm's-lengths away. We slowly made our way to it on our mounts and found it just as Imru᾽ al-Qays had said, with 'green-slime shading it'.

"Then the Messenger of God (ṢAAS) commented, 'That's a man who is remembered on earth but forgotten in the next world, honoured in the former but ignored in the latter. In his hands he will carry the banner of the poets, leading them to hell-fire.'"

Al-Kalbī reported that Imru᾽ al-Qays advanced with his banners flying intending to battle Banū Asad after they had killed his father and passed by Tabāla. There was the shrine of Dhū al-Khalaṣa, an idol at which the Arabs would seek divine support. Imru᾽ al-Qays asked for prophecy and the arrow for negation came out. This then happened a second and a third time. At that he broke the arrows and struck them against the face of Dhū al-Khalaṣa, exclaiming: "You'd bite your father's penis! If your father were the man murdered, you'd not impede me!" He then launched a raid against Banū Asad and engaged them in swift battle.

And al-Kalbī commented that (from then on) until the arrival of Islam, support from Dhū al-Khalaṣa was not sought.

Some say that Imru᾽ al-Qays gave praise to the Byzantine emperor and asked his support and assistance in certain wars but did not receive encouragement from him. Consequently Imru᾽ al-Qays spoke verses against him, and it is said that the emperor gave him poison to drink and so killed him. Death came to him when he was beside the grave of a woman on a mountain called ῾Asīb and it was there he wrote the verses:

> "Oh neighbour, the shrine is near and I rest where a mountain cleft is established.
> Oh neighbour, we are strangers here and all strangers are of a common kin."

They say that the seven *mu῾allaqāt*, the select, displayed odes, were hung up on the *ka῾ba*. That was because when one of the Arabs composed an ode he would exhibit it to Quraysh. If they approved of it they would hang it on the *ka῾ba* in recognition of its worth. It is from this practice that the seven odes were gathered. The first of these, as previously noted, was by Imru᾽ al-Qays b. Ḥujr the Kindite, as previously mentioned. It begins:

> "Halt here, both of you, and let us lament memory of a loved one and a dwelling at the winding ridges between al-Dakhūl and Ḥawmal."

The second ode was by al-Nābigha al-Dhubyānī, whose given name was Ziyād b. Mu῾āwiya . He is also said to have been Ziyād b. ῾Amr b. Mu῾āwiya, who was the son of Ḍabbāb b. Jābir b. Yarbū῾ b. Ghayẓ b. Murra b.῾Awf b. Sa῾d

b. Dhubyān b. Baghīḍ. His ode begins:

> "Oh abode of Mayya at al-ʿAlyāʾ, the mountain top; your people have gone for so long and earlier generations dwelt there."

The third ode was by Zuhayr b. Abū Sulmā, also named Rabīʿa b. Riyāḥ al-Muzanī. It begins:

> "Are there still some voiceless remnants of Umm ʿAwfa's dwelling at the plain of al-Darrāj and al-Mutathallam?"

The fourth was composed by Ṭarafa b. al-ʿAbd b. Sufyān b. Saʿd b. Mālik b. Ḍubayʿa b. Qays b. Thaʿlaba, the son of ʿUkāba b. Ṣaʿb b.ʿAlī b. Bakr b. Wāʾil. It opens:

> "On the rocky ground of Thahmad, there are traces still of Khawla, visible like the shadow of an old tattoo on the back of a hand."

The fifth ode was by ʿAntara b. Shaddād b. Muʿāwiya b. Qurād b. Makhzum b. Rabīʿa b. Mālik b. Ghālib, the son of Quṭayʿa, the son of ʿAbs the ʿAbsite. It begins:

> "Have the poets left anything unsaid, or have you recognized the abode after using imagination?"

The sixth was by ʿAlqama b.ʿAbda b. al-Nuʿmān b. Qays, a member of Banū Tamīm. It opens:

> "Though your heart is burdened with care, there is joy in beautiful women; soon after youth comes time for greyness."

The seventh ode – and there are some who do not affirm it to have been one of the *muʿallaqāt*, as, for example al-Asmaʿī and others – is by Labīd, the son of Rabīʿa b. Mālik b. Jaʿfar b. Kilāb b. Rabīʿa b. ʿĀmir b. Ṣaʿṣaʿa b. Muʿāwiya b. Bakr b. Hawāzin b. Manṣūr b. ʿIkrima b. Khaṣafa b. Qays b.ʿAylān b. Muḍar. It begins:

> "The place where she dwelt at Minā; its water-troughs and its mountains have been deserted."

As for the ode of unknown authorship, according to Abū ʿUbayda, al-Asmaʿī, al-Mubarrid and others, it reads:

> "Is there any reply for one who asks at the ruins; or has it ever been accustomed to speak?"

It is a lengthy poem and has many fine lines.

SOME INFORMATION ABOUT UMAYYA B. ABŪ AL-ṢALT AL-THAQAFĪ; HE WAS A PRE-ISLAMIC POET WHO LIVED ON TO THE TIME OF ISLAM.

The *ḥāfiẓ* Ibn ʿAsākir said that his name was Umayya b. Abū al-Ṣalt, ʿAbd Allāh b. Abū Rabīʿa b. ʿAwf, the son of ʿUqda b. ʿIzza b. ʿAwf b. Thaqīf b. Munabbih b. Bakr b. Hawāzin, known as Abū ʿUthmān and some say Abū al-Ḥakam al-Thaqafī.

He was a pre-Islamic poet who went to Damascus before Islam. It is said that he was a righteous man and initially a man of the faith, but he turned away from it, and that God was referring to him in the words: "Tell them of him to whom we brought our signs, but he passed them by; so Satan followed him, and he went astray" (*sūrat al-Aʿrāf*, VII, v.175).

Al-Zubayr b. Bakkār said that Ruqayya daughter of ʿAbd Shams b. ʿAbd Manāf gave birth to Umayya the poet, the son of Abū al-Ṣalt, whose name was Rabīʿa b. Wahb b. ʿIlāj b. Abū Salama b. Thaqīf.

Others said that his father was a famous poet of Ṭāʾif, and that Umayya was their best poet.

ʿAbd al-Razzāq said that al-Thawrī stated that Ḥabīb b. Abū Thābit reported to him that ʿAbd Allāh b. ʿAmr said that by God's words: "Tell them of him to whom we brought our signs but he passed them by; so Satan followed him and he went astray", Umayya b. Abū al-Ṣalt was implied.

And thus did Abū Bakr b. Mardawayh, from Abū Bakr al-Shāfiʿī, from Muʿādh b. al-Muthannā, from Musaddad, from Abū ʿAwāna, from ʿAbd al-Mālik b.ʿUmayr, from Nāfiʿ b. ʿĀṣim b. Masʿūd. He said that he was in a circle in which was ʿAbd Allāh b. ʿAmr. One person there quoted the verse in the Qurʾān chapter *al-Aʿrāf*: "Tell them of him to whom we brought our signs but he passed them by." So he asked, "Do you know who he is?" Someone said: "Ṣayfī b. al-Rāhib." Someone else said, "No, he is Balʿam, an Israelite." "Incorrect," he replied. Someone asked, "Who, then?" "Umayya b. Abū al-Ṣalt," he answered.

Abū Ṣāliḥ and al-Kalbī said the same, and Qatāda reported it from several others.

Al-Ṭabrānī said that ʿAlī b.ʿAbd al-ʿAzīz related to him, quoting ʿAbd Allāh b. Shabīb al-Rabʿī, quoting Muḥammad b. Maslama b. Hishām al-Makhzūmī, quoting Ismāʿīl, the son of al-Ṭurayḥ b. Ismāʿīl al-Thaqafī, that his father told him on the authority of his father, from Marwān b. al-Ḥakam, from Muʿāwiya b. Abū Sufyān from his father, saying: "I and Umayya b. Abū al-Ṣalt went on business to Syria and whenever we stopped anywhere for the night Umayya would take out a sacred book he had and would read it to us. This went on until we stopped at a Christian village. So its people came to him, honoured him and gave him presents, and he went off with them to their houses.

"Late in the morning he came back, threw off his two garments and took out two black ones he had and dressed in them. He then asked me: 'Abū Sufyān, do you have access to any Christian scholar well versed in the Bible you could ask a question?' I replied, 'I've no interest in that; if such a person were to tell me something I wanted, I'd not trust him. And if he told me something I disliked, I'd certainly be very angry with him.'"

He went on, "So he went away and a Christian sheikh disputed with him. Then Umayya came in to me and said: 'What prevents you from going to this sheikh?' I replied that I was not of his religion, but Umayya responded, 'So what? You'd hear and see wonderful things from him.' Then he said: 'You're of Thaqīf, aren't you?' 'No,' I replied, 'but I am of Quraysh.' 'Well,' he asked, 'so what prevents you from going to the sheikh? He likes you, I swear it, and he'd counsel you.'

"Umayya then left and remained with them till he returned to us later that night; he undressed and lay down on his bed. But I swear he was restless!

"Next morning he was sad and depressed, his 'evening drink dropping on his morning draught' (as the saying goes) not speaking to us, nor we to him. Eventually he said, 'Won't you ride?' I responded: 'You want to leave then?' He replied, 'Yes.'

"So we rode away and travelled for two nights. Then on the third night he said: 'Wouldn't you like to talk, Abū Sufyān?' I replied, 'There's something you want to tell? I swear, I never saw anything like the way you came back from your friend.'

"'Well that's something you've nothing to do with; but it's to do with something that scared me about my *munqalab* (hereafter).'

"'Do you have a *munqalab* then?' I asked.

"'Yes, by God,' he replied, 'I'm to die then be brought back to life.'

"'Want to take my wager?' I asked.

"'What about?'

"'That you'll not be brought back nor be called to account.'

"He laughed, then said, 'Oh but yes, by God, Abū Sufyān; we certainly will be brought back, and then called to account so that one group can enter heaven and another hell-fire.'

"'And which group are you in according to what your friend told you?'

"'He has no knowledge of that, either in my case or his own.'

"We journeyed on for two more nights, with him wondering at me and me laughing at him, until we reached the Damascus valley. There we sold our goods, remaining there two months.

"Then we again journeyed on until we reached a Christian village, where we made a stop. When they saw him they came to him, gave him gifts and he went with them to their houses. He came back in the afternoon, put on his two garments and went to them. He returned later that night, threw off his clothes and fell on his bed. But I swear he did not sleep a wink.

"Next morning he was sad and depressed, not talking to us nor we to him. Then he said, 'Wouldn't you like to move on?'

"'Why yes,' I responded. So we travelled on several nights, with him still depressed. Eventually he spoke, asking, 'Abū Sufyān, would you like to travel on in advance of our companions?'

"'Would you like that?' I responded.

"'Yes,' he replied.

"So off we went and travelled one hour's distance ahead of our companions. Then he said: 'Let's go to a rock.'

"'What do you want,' I asked him and he replied, 'Tell me about ʿUtba b. Rabīʿa; does he avoid doing wrong or evil?'

"'Certainly, by God.'

"'Is he held in esteem by high and low, a central figure in the tribe?'

"'Yes.'

"'Do you know any man of Quraysh more noble than him?'

"'No, by God, I know of no one.'

"'Is he financially needy?' he asked.

"'On the contrary, he's a man of great wealth.'

"'How old is he?'

"'He's over a hundred,' I replied.

"'So nobility, age, and wealth have brought him contempt.'

"'Why should all that bring him contempt? No, by God, they benefit him.'

"'Just so; would you like to rest here?' he then asked.

"'I would,' I replied.

"So we rested till our fatigue passed. Then we travelled on till we alighted at the next rest station where we stayed. When it was night he spoke to me: 'Abū Sufyān.'

"'What do you want?' I asked.

"'Would you like to proceed as yesterday?'

"'Would you?' I asked.

"'Yes,' he replied.

"So on we went on two long-necked camels until we were ahead. He said: 'Let's go to a rock and talk again about ʿUtba b. Rabīʿa.'

"'Let's talk of him again,' I replied.

"'Does he avoid wrongdoing and evil and do good and order good be done?' he asked.

"'Yes, by God, all that he does.'

"'Is he wealthy?'

"'Yes, he's wealthy.'

"'Do you know of any man of Quraysh more central than him?'

"'No, no one.'

"'How old is he?' he asked.

"'He is over a hundred.'

"'So his age, nobility, and wealth have brought him contempt?'

"'Certainly not, by God; if you have something to say, then do so.'

"'No,' he replied, 'Just remember what I said, whatever results from it.'

"Then he went on: 'What so affected me was going to that scholar and asking him some things and then saying to him, "Tell me about the prophet who is expected."

"'He replied that he was an Arab; I responded that I knew that, and asked him from what group of Arabs.

"'He said: "He is from the people of a house to which the Arabs make pilgrimage."

"'I said, "We have a house to which the Arabs make pilgrimage."

"'He replied: "He is one of your brothers from Quraysh."

"'This had an impact on me, by God, like nothing ever had before, and the success of this world and the next left my grasp. I had wanted to be him. I asked him then:

"'"If so it will be, describe him to me."

"'"He is a man young when he entered old age; he started out avoiding wrongdoing and evil, doing good and ordering it. He is poor, respected by high and low and has a central position in the tribe. Most of his army are of angels."

"'"What is the sign of that?" I asked and he replied:

"'"After the death of Jesus son of Mary, peace be upon him, Syria suffered 80 earthquakes, each causing a disaster. One overall quake is left which will bring several disasters."'"

Abū Sufyān went on: "I responded: 'But, by God, that's silly; if God sent a messenger he would only take him away in age and honour.'

"Umayya spoke up, 'But by him whose name you invoked, that's how it is, Abū Sufyān. He is reiterating that the Christian's statement is true. Shall we rest here?'

"'Yes, I'd like that,' I responded."

He went on: "So there we stayed until our fatigue left us and we travelled on till we were a two-stage or two-nights' distance from Mecca. Then a rider caught us up from behind; we questioned him and he said: 'After you left, the people of Syria suffered an earthquake that devastated them and caused them heavy losses.'"

Abū Sufyān went on: "Then Umayya approached me and asked: 'So what do you think about what the Christian said, Abū Sufyān?'

"I replied: 'By God, it's my considered view that what your friend told you was right.'"

Abū Sufyān continued: "So we arrived at Mecca where I settled my current affairs, then left for Yemen on business, staying there five months before returning to Mecca.

"While there at my house people come to greet me and ask me about their goods. Eventually Muḥammad b. ʿAbd Allāh came to me; Hind was there with me playing with her children. He greeted me, welcomed me back and asked me about my journey and accommodations, but he did not enquire about his goods. Then he rose. I commented to Hind, 'By God, that surprises me! Every one of Quraysh who had goods with me asked me about them, but this man did not ask about his.'

"Hind asked: 'Don't you know what's going on with him?'

"Apprehensive, I asked her what, and she replied: 'He claims to be a messenger from God.'

"She dumbfounded me. I recalled what the Christian had said, and I shivered. Hind asked me what was the matter and I came to myself and said: 'This is crazy! He is too smart to say that.'

"'On the contrary,' she explained, 'he really is saying that and promulgating that. He also has followers in his religion.'

"'This is crazy,' I repeated."

Abū Sufyān continued: "I then went outside and while performing a ritual circumambulation of the *kaʿba* I met up with him. I said to him: 'Your goods totalled up to so-and-so and there were profits. Send someone to receive them; I won't be taking out the cut I charge my own people.'

"But he refused that, saying: 'Then I won't accept them.' I went on: 'Then send someone to take them and I will subtract the cut I get from my people.' So he did send for his goods and received them, while I had from him what I would take from others."

Abū Sufyān went on: "Soon thereafter I left for Yemen. Then I went to Ṭāʾif, where I stayed with Umayya b. Abū al-Ṣalt. He said he wanted to ask me something, and I enquired what. He said: 'Do you remember what the Christian said?'

"I replied: 'I do remember and it has come about.'

"'Who is he then?' he asked.

"'He is Muḥammad b.ʿAbd Allāh,' I replied.

"'The son of ʿAbd al-Muṭṭalib?'

"'Yes, the son of ʿAbd al-Muṭṭalib.' Then I related to him what Hind had said.

"'Well, God alone knows!' he exclaimed, and began sweating profusely.

"Then he said: 'By God, Abū Sufyān, perhaps it is him! The description certainly fits him. And if he has appeared while I'm alive, I'll seek from God success from him in absolution.'

"I then went off to Yemen and soon heard there of his appearance as a prophet. So I went forth until I reached Umayya b. Abū al-Ṣalt in al-Ṭā'if and asked: 'Oh Abū ʿUthmān, you must have heard about about what's going on with the man.'

"'It has come to pass, by my life.'

"'So how do you stand with him, Abū ʿUthmān?'

"He replied, 'I wasn't one to believe in any prophet coming from any tribe other than Thaqīf.'"

Abū Sufyān continued: "I went on again to Mecca which didn't take long since it was not far, and I found that his companions were being beaten and reviled.

"So I began asking myself: 'Where are his hosts of angels?' And I was assailed by the jealousies that enter people."

This (previous) anecdote was also reported by the *ḥāfiẓ* al-Bayhaqī in the book *al-Dalā'il* (*The Signs*) from a *ḥadīth* via Ismāʿīl b. Ṭurayḥ. But the sequence given by al-Ṭabrānī we have quoted is fuller and lengthier. But God knows best.

Al-Ṭabrānī stated that Bakr b. Aḥmad b. Nufayl related to him, quoting ʿAbd Allāh b. Shabīb, quoting Yaʿqūb b. Muḥammad al-Zuhrī, quoting Mujāshiʿ b. ʿAmr al-Asadī, quoting Layth b. Saʿd, from Abū al-Aswad Muḥammad b. ʿAbd al-Raḥmān from ʿUrwa b. al-Zubayr, from Muʿāwiya b. Abū Sufyān, from Abū Sufyān b. Ḥarb, who said that: "Umayya b. Abū al-Ṣalt had been (with me) at Ghāzza or Īliyā' and while we were returning home Umayya asked me: 'Abū Sufyān, would you like to go on in advance of our companions so that we can talk?'

"'Yes,' I agreed.

"So we did."

"Then he asked: 'What about ʿUtba b. Rabīʿa?'

"'Honoured by high and low.'

"'And does he avoid sin and evil deeds?'

"'Yes.'

"'Is he aged and of noble birth?'

"'Both aged and of noble birth.'

"'Nobility and age have brought him contempt!'

"'You lie; his increase in age brought him only increase in honour.'

"'Abū Sufyān, that's a word I've never heard anyone say to me since I reached awareness; don't rush to judgement before I tell you.'

"'Well then do so,' I responded.

"'In my books I would find reference to a prophet who would be sent from this area of ours and I thought – indeed I had no doubt – that I would be him. But when I enquired of scholars, he was to be of Banū ʿAbd Manāf. So I looked into Banū ʿAbd Manāf and the only person I found worthy of such a mission was ʿUtba b. Rabīʿa. And when you told me of his age, I knew that it was not him, since he had passed the age of 40 and had not received revelation.'"

Abū Sufyān went on: "So destiny struck its blow and revelation came to the Messenger of God (ṢAAS). And I left in a party of Quraysh on a business trip to Yemen, so I passed by Umayya and commented mockingly: 'Well Umayya, the prophet you were describing has emerged.'

"'Indeed he is true, you should follow him,' he replied.

"'But what prevents you from following him?' I enquired.

"'Nothing but the embarrassment before the women of Thaqīf. I have been telling them that I was him, then they would see me a follower of a young man of Banū ʿAbd Manāf!'

"Then Umayya continued: 'It's to me as though, Abū Sufyān, you've defied him then have been bound fast like a billy goat and taken to him for whatever judgement he might want.'"

ʿAbd al-Razzāq said that Maʿmar related to him, from al-Kalbī, as follows: "Umayya was once lying down with two of his daughters present when one of them got scared and screamed to him. 'What's wrong?' he asked her. She replied: 'I saw two eagles rip off the roof of the house. Then one of them swooped down on you and split open your belly while the other perched on top of the house. The latter asked: "Is he aware?" "Yes," was the response. "Is he pure?" the eagle asked again. "No," came the answer.'

"He then said: 'This was good expected of your father; but he did it not.'"

This was also told from another source in another way. Isḥāq b. Bishr said, from Muḥammad b. Isḥāq, from al-Zuhrī, from Saʿīd b. al-Musayyib and ʿUthmān b. ʿAbd al-Raḥmān, from al-Zuhrī, from Saʿīd b. al-Musayyib that al-Fāriʿa, sister of Umayya b. Abū al-Ṣalt, went to see the Messenger of God (ṢAAS) after the conquest of Mecca. She was a person of reason, intellect, and beauty, and the Messenger of God (ṢAAS) was much impressed by her. One day he asked her: "Fāriʿa, do you know any of your brother's poetry?" "Yes indeed; and even more remarkable than that is what I've seen."

She went on: "My brother was on a journey and after he left he appeared to me, and came and lay on my bed while I was stripping hair off a piece of hide I held. Suddenly two white birds – or what seemed like two white birds – appeared. One alighted at the high window while the other came in and descended on to him. The latter then made a split between his chest and his pubic region, put its hand inside him, drew forth his heart, placed it on its palm then sniffed it. The other bird then asked: 'Is he aware?' 'Yes, he's aware,' the second replied. 'Is he pure?' it asked again. 'He declined,' answered the second. Then it replaced his heart where it belonged and the wound was healed in the twinkling of an eye. Then the two birds were both gone.

"When I had seen that I went over to him and stirred him, saying: 'Do you feel anything?' He answered, 'No, except for some weakness in my body.'

"I had been alarmed at what I had seen and he asked, 'Why do I see you upset?'

"So I told him what had happened, and he responded: 'Goodness was wanted of me but was averted from me.' He then spoke the verses:

'My cares' distresses flowed on, blinding my eyes, my tears preceding,
From the certainty that had come to me, and I had been brought no disavowal conveyed by anyone who spoke (to me),
Will I be one of those blazed by fire surrounding them like a tent (by its smoke and flames)
Or will I dwell in the paradise promised the guiltless, its cushions piled high?
The two positions are not equal there, nor are actions equal in kind,
They are two groups, one who enter paradise, its gardens enfolding them,
And another group sent to hell, its installations paining them;
These hearts were long accustomed, whenever tending to good, to have barriers set up against them,
And these were diverted to misfortune away from the pursuit of paradise by a world which God will erase.
A slave who called for his soul and censured it, knowing that God, the acutely aware, is clearly watching,
What gives the spirit a desire for life? Even though it lives a while, death overtakes it.
One fleeing his fate will one day soon unexpectedly agree to it,
If you don't die exultant you will die decrepit; death has a cup and man must taste it.' "

She went on: "Then he continued on his journey, but only a little thereafter he was borne along in his bier. When news of it came to me I went to him and found him laid out in his burial winding-sheet. When I drew near him he emitted a deep sigh and stared; he looked up to the ceiling and raised his voice, saying:

"'*Labbaykumā*! *Labbaykumā*! At your service, at your service both of you; here I am before you both, not with money to ransom me nor with a clan to protect me.'

"He then lost consciousness, having emitted a deep sigh. So I said, 'The man has expired!'

"But he stared up to the ceiling and raised his voice, saying: 'At your service, at your service both; here am I before you both. Not innocent to seek forgiveness, nor with kinsfolk to achieve victory.'

"Then he lost consciousness, but suddenly emitted a deep sigh, stared up to the ceiling and said: 'At your service, at your service both, here am I before you both, blessed by good fortune but destroyed by wrongdoing.'

"Then he lost consciousness, but suddenly emitted a deep sigh and said, 'At your service, at your service you both, here I am before you both.

"'If, O Lord, you forgive, forgive *en masse*; what slave of yours has no pain.'

"Then he lost consciousness but soon emitted a deep sigh, and said: 'Each life, though it may last very long, is moving on but once till when it ceases.

"'Would that I were, before what appeared to me, shepherding goats in the mountain heights.'"

She went on: "And then he died. The Messenger of God (ṢAAS) told me: 'O Fāriʿa, your brother is like him to whom God brought his signs but he passed them by . . .' (to the end of the verse)" (*sūrat al-Aʿrāf*, VII, v.175).

Al-Khaṭābī spoke of the strangeness of this *ḥadīth*.

The *ḥāfiẓ* Ibn ʿAsākir related of al-Zuhrī that he said, "Umayya b. Abū al Ṣalt spoke the verse:

> 'Is there not a messenger to us from us who can inform us what is the distance of our ultimate goal from the beginning of our course.'"

Al-Zuhrī went on: "Then Umayya b. Abū al-Ṣalt left for Bahrain and the Messenger of God (ṢAAS) claimed prophecy. Umayya resided eight years in Bahrain then went to Ṭāʾif, where he asked people, 'What is Muḥammad son of ʿAbd Allāh saying?'

"They replied: 'He claims that he is a prophet; he is the one you were wishing for.'"

He continued: "So Umayya left for Mecca where he met him and asked: 'O son of ʿAbd al-Muṭṭalib, what is this you are saying?' He replied: 'I say that I am the Messenger of God, and that there is no God but Him.' Umayya said, 'I would like to speak with you; give me an appointment tomorrow.' 'Certainly, you have an appointment tomorrow,' came the reply. Umayya then asked: 'Would you like me to come alone or with a group of my friends?' 'Whichever you prefer,' responded the Messenger of God (ṢAAS). 'Then I will come with a group, and so you too come with a group,' concluded Umayya.

"So early morning Umayya appeared with a group from Quraysh while the Messenger of God (ṢAAS) came with a number of his Companions. They all sat down in the shade of the *kaʿba*. Umayya began by making an address, then spoke some rhyming prose, and recited some poetry. When he had finished the poetry, he said: 'Answer me then, son of ʿAbd al-Muṭṭalib.' At that the Messenger of God (ṢAAS) spoke the words, 'In the name of God the beneficent, the merciful, Yā Sīn. By the Qurʾān full of wisdom.' (*sūrat Yā Sīn*, XXXVI, v.1–2). When he had finished the chapter, Umayya arose suddenly and walked off, dragging his feet. The Quraysh men followed him, asking, 'Well, what do you have to say, Umayya?' 'I bear witness', replied Umayya, 'that he is right.' 'Will you follow him?' they asked. 'Until I look into his case,' he replied."

He continued: "Umayya went off to Syria and the Messenger of God (ṢAAS) left for Medina. Then, following the deaths of the people at the battle of Badr, Umayya returned from Syria and stayed at Badr. He travelled on to see the Messenger of God (ṢAAS). Someone asked Umayya: 'O Abū al-Ṣalt, what do you want?' 'I want Muḥammad,' he replied. 'What will you do?' he was asked. He replied, 'I believe in him and I will throw him the keys of this affair.' Someone asked him: 'Do you know who is in the burial pit?' 'No,' he answered. He was told: 'In it are ʿUtba b. Rabīʿa and Shayba b. Rabīʿa, your maternal uncle's sons, along with his mother Rabīʿa, daughter of ʿAbd Shams.'"

He went on: "So Umayya mutilated the ears of his riding camel and cut off its tail,[40] then stood over the pit and spoke the verses:

> 'What is in Badr – Mt. ʿAqanqal but chiefs and noble lords ...'
>
> (up to the end of the ode, which we will give in full in relating the history of the battle of Badr, if God wills it.)

"He then returned to Mecca and Ṭāʾif and left Islam."

The source then related the story of the two birds and that of his death as we have given. At his death he spoke the verses:

> "Each life, though it may last very long, is moving on but once till when it ceases.
>
> Would that I were before what appeared to me, shepherding goats in the mountain heights,
>
> So keep death before your vision and beware the destruction of fate, for fate has its evil demons
>
> Their claws attaining lions, wild bulls, and the young child with red eyes[41] at a lighthouse,
>
> And the mountain vultures, the fleeing gazelles, and the young ostrich, mixed in flock, thin."

He means in these verses that wild animals in the deserts do not escape death, nor do vultures living on mountain tops; death does not leave alone the young for their youth, nor the old for their age. Al-Khaṭābī and others have spoken of the rarity of these accounts.

Al-Suhaylī mentioned in his book *al-Taʿrīf wa al-Iʿlām* (*Identifying and Informing*) that Umayya b. Abū al-Ṣalt was the first who said, "bismika Allahumma", i.e. "in your name, O God". And concerning that he told a strange tale, as follows. He says that they were among a group of Quraysh who went away on a journey. They included Ḥarb b. Umayya, the father of Abū Sufyān. On their way they came across a snake and killed it. But that evening a spirit woman came to them and berated them for killing that snake. With her she had a

40. Presumably actions denoting his mourning for his relatives.
41. Presumably from weeping.

staff which she struck on the ground so hard that it completely stampeded their camels and they scattered in all directions. So off they went and chased them till they had them back. When they were all gathered, she again appeared, struck her staff on the ground and stampeded the camels. So off they went to search for them but having failed they asked Umayya, "By God, do you have any way out of our problem?" He replied, "No, by God, but I'll look into it." So they travelled on into that region hoping to find someone whom they could ask for some solution to their trouble. Eventually they saw a light ahead in the distance. When they arrived there they found an old man lighting a fire at the door of his tent. But he was in fact an evil spirit who was extremely tiny and ugly. They greeted him and he asked them what they wanted. (When they told him) he said: "When she comes to you, say: 'In your name, O God' and she will flee." So when the travellers had assembled their camels and she came for the third or fourth time, Umayya looked her in the face and said: "In your name, O God." She promptly fled in disarray. But the evil spirits attacked Ḥarb b. Umayya and killed him with that snake. His companions buried him there far from home or friend. On that subject the spirits spoke the verse:

> "The grave of Ḥarb is in a wasteland and there is no grave near that of Ḥarb."

Some people say that Umayya sometimes understood the languages of the animals. When passing some bird in his travel he would tell his companions, "This one says so-and-so." But they would say they did not know whether he spoke the truth. But once they passed by a flock of sheep from which an ewe and her kid had been separated. She turned to it and bleated, as though urging it to hurry. Umayya asked his companions whether they knew what it said and they replied that they did not. He explained: "She's saying, 'Let's hurry along so the wolf won't come and eat you up like one did your brother last year.'" The group moved quickly on and asked the shepherd whether a wolf had eaten a sheep in that area the previous year. He replied in the affirmative! One day, moreover, Umayya passed by a mule carrying a woman and raising its head to her and grumbling. Umayya said: "The mule is telling the woman that there's a needle in the saddle which she mounted on him." So they took the woman off, untied the saddle, and discovered there was a needle as he had said.

Ibn al-Sikkīt recounted that Umayya b. Abū al-Ṣalt was drinking when a crow cawed. Umayya said, "May you have dust twice in your mouth!" His companions asked Umayya what it was saying and he replied that it had said: "You'll drink that cup in your hand then die." At that point the crow cawed again and Umayya reported: "It says: 'The proof is that I'm going to fly down to this garbage pile, eat some and a bone is going to stick in my throat so I will die.'" At that the crow swooped down to the garbage pile, ate something, a bone lodged in its throat and it died!

Umayya said, "Well, he spoke the truth in this about himself but I'm going to see whether he was right about me or not." He then drank that cup in his hand, keeled over, and died!

The following anecdote is established in the *ṣaḥīḥ* collection in a *ḥadīth* of Ibn Mahdī from al-Thawrī from ʿAbd al-Mālik b. ʿUmayr, from Abū Salama, from Abū Hurayra who said that the Messenger of God (ṢAAS) said: "The truest word spoken by a poet is the verse of Labīd:[42]

'Is not all vain except God.'

"And Umayya b. Abū al-Ṣalt almost became a Muslim."

The Imām Aḥmad stated that Rawḥ related to him, quoting Zakariyāʾ b. Isḥāq, from Ibrāhīm b. Maysara, that he heard ʿAmr b. al-Sharīd say that al-Sharīd stated, "I was riding on the same camel as the Messenger of God (ṢAAS) when he asked me, 'Do you know any of the verses of Umayya b. Abū al-Ṣalt?' 'Why yes,' I replied. 'So recite them,' he asked. I then did recite a line and he went on asking for more, with me reciting till I had spoken a hundred lines for him. At that point the Prophet (ṢAAS) remained silent as did I."

This anecdote is similarly told by Muslim from a *ḥadīth* of Sufyān b. ʿUyayna from Abū Tamīm b. Maysara. In another line we have it from ʿAmr b. al-Sharīd from his father al-Sharīd b. Suwayd al-Thaqafī from the Prophet (ṢAAS). In some accounts the Messenger of God's words were, "If he had almost become a Muslim."

Yaḥyā b. Muḥammad b. Saʿīd stated that Ibrāhīm b. Saʿīd al-Jawharī related to him, quoting Abū Usāma, quoting Ḥātim b. Abū Ṣufra, from Simāk b. Ḥarb, from ʿAmr b. Nāfiʿ, from al-Sharīd al-Hamdānī (whose uncles were of Thaqīf) that he said, "We went off with the Messenger of God (ṢAAS) on the 'farewell pilgrimage'. While I was walking along one day I sensed the tread of a camel behind me and it was the Messenger of God (ṢAAS). He said: 'Al-Sharīd?' I replied, 'Yes.' Then he asked, 'Can't I give you a ride?' 'Why certainly,' I accepted. I was not tired but wanted the *baraka*, the blessing, of riding with the Messenger of God (ṢAAS). So he made his camel kneel and carried me, asking: 'Do you know any verses of Umayya b. Abū al-Ṣalt?' I replied in the affirmative and he asked me to recite them, which I did. 'I think he spoke a hundred verses,' he commented. Then he added, 'God has knowledge about Umayya b. Abū al-Ṣalt.'"

Ibn Saʿīd then stated, "This is a strange *ḥadīth*; and in what is related is that the Messenger of God (ṢAAS) said of Umayya: 'His poetry believed but his heart disbelieved.' God alone knows."

Imām Aḥmad stated: "ʿAbd Allāh b. Muḥammad – who was Abū Bakr b. Abū Shayba – related to us, quoting ʿAbda b. Sulaymān, from Muḥammad b. Isḥāq,

42. A poet mentioned earlier as one of the authors of the famous *muʿallaqāt* odes.

from Yaʿqūb b. ʿUtba, from ʿIkrima, from Ibn ʿAbbās, that the Messenger of God (ṢAAS) declared Umayya to be truthful in a piece of his poetry which says:

> 'As a man with a bull beneath his right foot, and an eagle for the other, and a lion in waiting;
> And the sun appears at the end of each night, its colour red in the morning and turning rosy;
> It is reluctant to arise for us, in its gentleness, unless tortured or else flogged.'"

The Messenger of God (ṢAAS) said (of this verse): "He spoke the truth."

In an account of Abū Bakr al-Hudhalī, from ʿIkrima, from Ibn ʿAbbās, he (the Prophet) said, "The sun never rises until it is urged up by 70,000 angels saying: 'Come on up! Come on up!' And it replies: 'I will not rise above any people who worship me to the exclusion of God.' When just about to rise a devil comes to the sun intending to divert it, but it rises between the devil's horns and burns him. And when the sun gathers itself for its setting it directs itself to God, the Almighty and Glorious. So a devil comes to it wishing to divert it from its obeisance but it sets between his horns and burns him."

Ibn ʿAsākir gives this anecdote at greater length.

In his poem on the throne-bearers, Umayya recited:

> "And there's many a bearer of one of the supports of his throne, who, were it not for the God of creation, would be fatigued and slow-moving,
> Standing on their feet, weary beneath it, their jugular veins trembling from the severity of their fear."

These verses were transmitted by Ibn ʿAsākir.

It is reported from al-Aṣmaʿī that he would recite the following verses of Umayya:

> "Glorify God, for He is worthy of glory; our Lord in heaven has been mighty.
> There in his great edifice that existed prior to man, above the heavens, where he laid down his throne.
> Longer it is than sight can see, before it you see *al-malāʾik* (the angels) bow down."

According to al-Aṣmaʿī, the word *al-malāʾik* (in the last line quoted), is the plural of *malak*, angel, while the word *al-ṣūr* (translated as "those bowing down") is the plural of *aṣwar*, meaning "bending the neck". These are they who bear the throne.

The following verses praising ʿAbd Allāh b. Judʿān of Taym are also from the poetry of Umayya b. Abū al-Ṣalt:

> "Should I make mention of my need or is your sensitivity enough for me; your nature is goodness
> And your knowledge of rights; you are of lofty status; refinement, high esteem, and majesty are yours.

You are a generous man whose fine character no morning or evening time can change.
You compete with the wind by your nobility and generosity when cold winter nights prevent the dog from staying outside (the tent).[43]
Your land is one of all nobility built by Banū Taym, and you are its sky.
Any man who one day praises you has in offering praise in itself reward enough."

Umayya offered him other verses of praise in his poetry.

This man ʿAbd Allāh b. Judʿān was a much praised, very noble, and famous man. He had a platter from which a rider could eat while on his mount, since it was so large and piled with food. He would fill it with the finest wheat mixed with butter and honey. He used to pay to free slaves and help the unfortunate. ʿAʾisha asked the Prophet (ṢAAS) whether all that would ultimately benefit him. But he replied: "He never once said the words: 'O Lord, forgive me my sins on Judgement Day!'"

Other fine lines of his poetry include:

"They do not plough the earth with wooden branches, when requests are made of them, as if seeking an excuse.[44]
Rather, when asked they uncover their faces and you see them cheerful with the finest of colouring.
And if the needy stay amidst their dwelling, they make him again a master of neighing horses and slaves,
And whatever dangerous enterprise to which you invite them, they block out the sun's rays with their knights."

This ends the biographical notice relating to Umayya b. Abū al-Ṣalt.

BAḤĪRĀ THE MONK.

It was he who perceived prophethood in the Messenger of God (ṢAAS) when he was with his uncle Abū Ṭālib and went to Syria in a company of merchants of Mecca. He was at that time 12 years of age. (Baḥīrā) saw a cloud shading him apart from the rest, so he made food for them and invited them to be his guests, as we will relate in the biography.

Al-Tirmidhī related an account which we discussed in detail therein. The *ḥāfiẓ* Ibn ʿAsākir recounted various testimonies and evidences relating to the biography of Baḥīrā, but did not recount what al-Tirmidhī told; and that is strange.

Ibn ʿAsākir reported that Baḥīrā lived in a village called al-Kafr situated some six miles from Baṣra. That is the place known as "Baḥīrā's monastery". And it is

43. Barking dogs and fires lit outside the tent in the desert were signals for passers-by that a tribe was encamped, and that guests were welcome to stop and rest, and enjoy hospitality there.

44. That is, by pretending to be too busy.

also said that he lived in a village called Manfaʿa in the plain of Balqāʾ, beyond Zayrā. But God knows best.

An Account of Quss b. Sāʿida al-Iyādī.

The *ḥāfiẓ* Abū Bakr Muḥammad b. Jaʿfar b. Sahl al-Kharāʾiṭī said in his book *Hawātif al-Jān* (*The Calls of the Spirits*) that Dāwūd al-Qanṭarī related to him, quoting ʿAbd Allāh b. Ṣāliḥ and Abū ʿAbd Allāh al-Mashriqī, from Abū al-Ḥārith al-Warrāq, from Thawr b. Yazīd, from Mūriq al-ʿIjlī, from ʿUbāda b. al-Ṣāmit that the latter said that when the delegation from the tribe of Iyād came to the Prophet (ṢAAS) he asked: "O members of the Iyād delegation, what happened to Quss b. Sāʿida al-Iyādī?" They replied, "He died, O Messenger of God." He commented, "Well, I once witnessed him at the ʿUkāẓ festival mounted on a red camel speaking words of strange and wonderful eloquence that I find I don't recall." A bedouin from the far back of the group came up to him and said: "I remember it, O Messenger of God," and the Prophet (ṢAAS) was pleased at this. "Yes", the man went on, "he was at the ʿUkāẓ festival on a red camel and saying, 'O people gather around, for all those who have passed away are gone. And things to come will come. Gloomy nights. Castle-filled skies. Seas that rage. Splendorous stars. Towering mountains. Flowing streams. In the heavens there is notice; on earth there is warning. How is it I see people pass away and do not return? Were they content to stay and did so? Or were they left and fell asleep? Quss swears by an oath beyond reproach, that God has a religion more pleasing than the one you follow.' Then he recited as follows:

> 'In those who first passed away in ages gone there are signs for us,
> Since I saw ways leading to death which had no beginnings,
> And I saw my people passing towards them, young and old alike,
> Not anyone who has passed on will come to you, nor will any of those who stay remain behind;
> I have become sure that I will inevitably pass on to where the people have gone.'"

This chain of authorities as given is strange. Al-Ṭabarānī related it from another line, stating in his book *al-Muʿjam al-Kabīr* (*The Great Encyclopedia*) that Muḥammad b. al-Sarrī b. Mahrān b. al-Nāqid al-Baghdādī related to him, quoting Muḥammad b. Ḥassān al-Sahmī, quoting Muḥammad b. al-Ḥajjāj, from Mujālid, from al-Shaʿbī, from Ibn ʿAbbās, that he said: "The delegation from ʿAbd al-Qays came to see the Prophet (ṢAAS) and he asked them, 'Which of you knows al-Quss b. Sāʿida al-Iyādī?' They replied, 'We all knew him, O Messenger of God.' 'Well, what's he done?' he asked. 'He died,' they told him. He went on: 'I'll never forget him at the ʿUkāẓ festival in the sacred month. He was on a red camel addressing the people in the words, "O people, gather, listen and take note. Those who live die. Those who die pass away. And what is to come will come. In heaven there is notice and on earth there is warning. A resting-place is put down and a roof is raised up. Stars move to and fro and seas do not empty. And Quss swore a true oath that if there be contentment in the matter, then discontent will follow! God has a religion more beloved by Him than that in which you engage. How is it I see people pass away and do not return? Were they content to stay and did so? Or were they left and fell asleep?" Then the Messenger of God (ṢAAS) asked, 'Can anyone among you recite his poetry?' One of them responded:

'In those who first passed away in ages gone there are signs for us.
Since I never saw ways leading to death which had no beginnings,
And I saw my people moving towards them, young and old alike,
The past will never return for me, nor will any of those who stay remain behind.
I have become sure I will inevitably pass on to where the people have gone.'"

The *ḥāfiẓ* al-Bayhaqī thus transmitted it in his book, *Dalāʾil al-Nubuwwa* (*Signs of the Prophethood*) in a line from Muḥammad b. Ḥasan al-Sahmī. And thus did we relate it in the fragment collected by al-Ustādh Abū Muḥammad ʿAbd Allāh b. Jaʿfar b. Darstawayh relating to Quss. He stated: "ʿAbd al-Karīm b. al-Haytham, the man from Dayr ʿĀqūl, related it to us from Saʿīd b. Shabīb, from Muḥammad b. al-Ḥajjāj Abū Ibrāhīm al-Wāsiṭī, a resident of Baghdad, known as *ṣāḥib al-harīsa* ('master of the beef and bulgar dish'). And he was called a liar by Yaḥyā b. Maʿīn and Abū Ḥātim al-Rāzī and al-Dārquṭnī. Also, more than one, including Ibn ʿAdī, accused him of fabricating the *ḥadīth*."

Al-Bazzār and Abū Nuʿaym related it from the account of this Muḥammad b. al-Ḥajjāj. And Ibn Darstawayh and Abū Nuʿaym recounted it by way of al-Kalbī, from Abū Ṣāliḥ, from Ibn ʿAbbās. And this chain is preferable to that preceding it. In this account it is Abū Bakr who tells the story in its entirety, both its poetry and prose, before the Messenger of God (ṢAAS).

And the *ḥāfiẓ* Abū Nuʿaym related it from a *ḥadīth* of Aḥmad b. Mūsā b. Isḥāq al-Khatmī. ʿAlī b. al-Ḥusayn b. Muḥammad al-Makhzūmī related to us, quoting Abū Ḥātim al-Sijistānī, quoting Wahb b. Jarīr, from Muḥammad b. Isḥāq, from al-Zuhrī, from Saʿīd b. al-Musayyab from Ibn ʿAbbās as follows: "A delegation from Bakr b. Wāʾil came to the Messenger of God (ṢAAS) and he asked them, 'What did your ally do whose name was Quss b. Sāʿida al-Iyādī?'" Then he recounted the anecdote at length.

Sheikh Aḥmad b. Abū Ṭālib al-Ḥajjār, the authority on lines of transmission and travel, recounted to us, on the basis of *ijāza*[45] if not *samāʿa*[46] that Jaʿfar b. ʿAlī al-Hamdānī told him the following tradition by *ijāza*, quoting the *ḥāfiẓ* Abū

45. Having heard it from a secondary source.
46. Having heard it himself from a named authority.

Ṭāhir Aḥmad b. Muḥammad b. Aḥmad b. Ibrāhīm al-Salafī, who told this account as having himself heard it directly. He stated that he read it from his Sheikh, the *ḥāfiẓ* Abū ʿAbd Allāh al-Dhahabī. Also Abū ʿAlī al-Ḥasan b. ʿAlī b. Abū Bakr al-Khallāl recounted it as one the latter had himself heard directly. He also said that he heard it directly from Jaʿfar b. ʿAlī, and also directly from al-Salafī. Also, Abū ʿAbd Allāh Muḥammad b. Aḥmad b. Ibrāhīm al-Rāzī informed us, quoting Abū al-Faḍl Muḥammad b. Aḥmad b. ʿĪsā al-Saʿdī, quoting Abū al-Qāsim ʿUbayd Allāh b. Aḥmad b. ʿAlī al-Muqrī', and it was also related to him by Abū Muḥammad ʿAbd Allāh b. Jaʿfar b. Darstawayh, the grammarian, by Ismāʿīl b. Ibrāhīm b. Aḥmad al-Saʿdī, the *qāḍī,* judge, of Fāris (Persia) by Abū Dāwūd Sulaymān b. Sayf b. Yaḥyā b. Dirham al-Ṭā'ī who was a man from Ḥarrān, by Abū ʿAmr Saʿīd b. Yarbuʿ, from Muḥammad b. Isḥāq. Abū Tālib was also told by some of our scholars on the authority of al-Ḥasan b. Abū al-Ḥasan al-Baṣrī, that the last mentioned said: "Al-Jārūd b. al-Muʿallā b. Ḥanash b. Muʿallā al-ʿAbdī was a Christian of great learning in the interpretation and analysis of the holy texts, an expert on the history and sayings of the Persians, well versed in philosophy and medicine, a man of evident good manners and culture, fine in appearance and of great wealth. He went to see the Prophet (ṢAAS) as a member of a delegation of men of sound judgement, maturity, eloquence, and scholarship from the tribe of ʿAbd Qays. When he approached the Prophet (ṢAAS) he stood before him, gestured towards him and spoke the verses:

'O Prophet of the right guidance, men have come to you through deserts and mirages,
Crossing down the flat open lands towards you, not counting fatigue for you as fatigue at all.
All the short-legged beasts greatly urged along in speed by our young she-camels,
The fine horses racing over the land, bolting with their mailclad warriors like stars, glinting,
Seeking to avert the suffering of an awful day, one of terror, pain, and great distress,
A day when all mankind will be brought together, a day separating out all who strayed in disobedience,
Moving towards a light from God, a proof, a favour and a grace to be attained,
God distinguished you with all good, O son of Āmina, through her; when (for others) good only comes and goes.
So, give your blessings in abundance, O proof of God, unlike the blessings of a false (prophet).'

"When he finished, the Prophet (ṢAAS) invited him to sit down close to himself and said, 'O Jārūd, both you and your people are late in coming.'

"Al-Jārūd responded, 'By my father and my mother, anyone late coming to you is indeed unfortunate, that being the greatest of faults, the worst of sins. But

I'm not one of those who saw you or heard of you, aggressed against you, and followed someone other than you. I now follow a religion of which you have knowledge. But I have come to you and here I am, abandoning it for your religion. Will that not have faults, sins, and misdeeds forgiven and please the Lord?'

"The Messenger of God (ṢAAS) replied, 'I will guarantee you that! So sincerely express your belief in the unity (i.e. monotheism) and give up the religion of Christianity.'

"Al-Jārūd replied: 'By my father and my mother, extend your hand, for I bear witness that there is no God but God alone and that He has no associate; and I testify that you are Muḥammad, His slave and His Messenger.'

"And so he accepted Islam, as did some of his people.

"And the Prophet (ṢAAS) was pleased at their accepting Islam and treated them with such honour and generosity as to make them very happy and delighted.

"Then the Messenger of God went over to them and asked, 'Does any one of you know Quss b. Sāʿida al-Iyādī?'

"Al-Jārūd replied: 'By my father and mother, we all know him. And I am one who knows a lot about him. Quss, O Messenger of God, was a fine Arab knight. He lived 600 years, of which he spent five lifetimes living in the wastelands and deserts, crying out the glory of God like Jesus did. He settled nowhere, had no home to shelter him and no neighbour to appreciate him. He dressed in hair-cloth and outdid the fasting ascetics. He never tired of his monastic ways, on his journeys living off ostrich eggs and befriending lions, enjoying the darkness, observing and considering, thinking and experiencing.

"'He therefore became one whose wisdom was legion, awe-inspiring things being discovered through him, and he attained the leadership of the disciples of Christ in reputation.

"'He was the first Arab to acknowledge God and to accept His unity. He devoted himself firmly to God, becoming fully convinced of life after death and of judgement. He warned of the evil of refusal and enjoined action before it was too late. He reminded of death and spoke of his acceptance of fate without either anger or pleasure. He visited graves and preached of resurrection day. He spoke verses in elegy. He gave thought to the fates and informed about the heavens and about nature. He talked of the stars and discussed the water. He described the seas and informed of ancient relics. He orated while riding and exhorted with perseverance. He admonished against grief and against an excess of anger. He wrote many sermons and made mention of all things terrible. He spoke compellingly in his orations, gave explanation in his writings, expressed fear of time, cautioned against weakness, exalted God's power, avoided any blasphemy, expressed yearning for the pure faith, and called for immersion in religious life and thought.

"'He is the person who said on the day of the *ʿUkāẓ* festival:

"East and west, orphans and groups, peace and war, dry and moist, brackish water or sweet, suns and moons, winds and rains, nights and days, females and males, lands and seas, seeds and plants, fathers and mothers, united and scattered, signs followed by signs, light and dark, abundance and nothingness, a Lord and idols, mankind has gone astray, the raising of a child, the burial of a dead one, the cultivation of a harvest, rich and poor, benefactor and evil-doer, woe to the indolent, let the worker improve his labour, and let the hopeful lose his hope. Nay; on the contrary He is one God, neither given birth nor a father. He both repeats and does for the first time. He makes to die and brings to life. He created male and female, Lord of the first life and of the after life.

"Moreover, O tribe of Iyād, where now are Thamūd and ʿĀd? Where are the fathers and their forefathers? Where now are those (who were) ill and those who visited them? To each is his appointed time. Quss swears by the Lord of mankind, and the one who flattens the smooth ground, you will be gathered individually, on assembly day, when horns will be blown and drums be beaten, when the earth will shine, and the preacher exhort and the despairing withdraw and the observer gazes out; woe to him who turns away from the truth most evident, and the shining light, and the great Judgement Day, on the day of separating, and the scales of justice, when He who decrees decides, and the apostle gives testimony, and the allies are far off, and the faults are apparent, and so one group goes to paradise, and one group to hell-fire."

"'It is he who spoke the verses:

"The heart passionately recalled and reflected: nights within which there are days.
And bucketsful pouring from storm clouds that burst forth with water, there being fire in their insides,
Their light blinded the eye and violent thunder was cast in east and west;
There are lofty castles possessed of wealth while others are empty and uninhabited.
There are unshakable mountains towering, and seas whose waters abound,
There are stars which flash in the dark of night which we see every day are revolved,
And then there is a sun urged on by moon of night, each pursuing the other and in motion.
There are the young, the hoary, and the old, all of them one day to meet above.
And there is plenty beyond the surmise of those whose mind is not perplexed.
All these I mentioned are signs of God for the souls of good guidance and wisdom."'"

Al-Ḥasan went on: "And the Messenger of God (ṢAAS) said: 'Whatever else I may forget, I will never forget him (Quss) at the ʿUkāẓ festival, standing up on a red camel and addressing the people: 'Gather around and listen, and having heard, be aware, benefit! And speak, and if you speak, tell the truth! He who lives dies, he who dies is gone, and all that is coming will come, rain and plants, the living and the dead, dark nights and skies with zodiac signs, and stars that shine, and seas that rage, and light and shade, and nights and days, and innocence and sins. There is knowledge in the heavens and lessons on earth such as to amaze even the perspicacious. There is a ground laid out, a roof raised up, stars that set, seas that do not empty, destinies drawing near, a treacherous fate, as sharp as a surgeon's knife and as accurate as a precise scale. Quss swears an oath, neither insincere nor sinning thereby, that if there be any pleasure in this mattter, then there will surely be discontent.' Then he said, 'O people, God has a religion which is more pleasing to him than this religion of yours you engage in. And this is its time, its epoch.' Then he said, 'How is it I see people go but not return? Were they content to stay and did so? Or were they left and fell asleep?'

"The Messenger of God (ṢAAS) then turned to some of his Companions and said, 'Which one of you can recite his verses to us?' Abū Bakr, the truthful, replied, 'By my father and my mother, I witnessed him on that day when he spoke the verses:

> "In those who went first in ages past are clear proofs for us.
> Since I saw ways leading to death which had no beginnings.
> And I saw my people moving towards them, young and old alike.
> The past will never come back to me, nor will any of those who stay remain behind;
> I have become sure that I will inevitably pass on to where the people have gone."'

"Then a tall, broad-shouldered, venerable old sheikh of ʿAbd Qays approached the Messenger of God (ṢAAS) and said, 'By my father and my mother, I saw something remarkable from Quss.'

"The Messenger of God (ṢAAS) asked, 'What was it you saw, O brother from ʿAbd Qays?'

"He explained: 'In my youth some camels I owned wandered off, so I hurried and followed their trail into rocky desert land where there were thorny twigs, wastelands of dead tree roots and palm trunks, waterlily ponds, and ostrich tracks and nests. While I passed along the trails in these high and low wastes, I came to a hilly area whose upper slopes were thick with thorn trees, their branches hanging low, their first fruits like seeds of pepper and heads of chamomile. Suddenly there was a bubbling spring, a green meadow, and a lofty tree. And there too was Quss b. Sāʿida at the base of that tree, standing with a stick in his hand. I approached him and said, "Good morning to you!" "Good morning to you likewise" he replied. There were many lions going down to drink at the water-hole. Whenever one tried to drink from the hole before another he would strike it with his stick and say: "Be patient! Wait till the one before you drinks!" I was absolutely amazed at that. He looked across at me and said, "Don't be afraid." Then I saw two graves with a mosque between them. I asked him, "What are these graves?" He replied, "They're the graves of two brothers who used to pray to God, Almighty and Glorious is He, at this spot. I remain here between their two graves, praying to God until I join them." I asked him, "But wouldn't it be better for you to join your people and enjoy their well-being and explain to them what it is they do that is evil?"

"''May your death make your mother grieve! Don't you know how Ishmael's sons abandoned the faith of their father and followed rival gods and venerated idols?"

"'Then he approached the graves and spoke the following verses:

> "O my two friends, arise; long have you lain. I urge you not to prolong your slumber;
> I see sleep between your skin and your bones, as though he who gives a drug to drink has given it to you.
> Is it from your long sleep that you do not respond to him who calls you, as though he who gives a drug to drink has given it to you?
> Do you not know that I am in Najrān alone, with no friend there but for you two?
> Living at your graves, not leaving night after night until your response is heard.
> I weep for you throughout my life, and what had the heartbroken gained that we wept for you both?
> If a soul were to be a ransom for the soul of another, I would strive to have my soul become ransom for you both
> As if death were the closest goal for my soul when death had come to you in your two graves."''"

Al-Ḥasan went on: "So the Messenger of God (ṢAAS) then said, 'God have mercy on Quss! He will be resurrected as a whole nation by himself on Judgement Day.'"

This tradition is very strange in this regard; and it is *mursal.*[47] However, al-Ḥasan did hear it from al-Jārūd. God knows best!

Al-Bayhaqī related it, quoting the *ḥāfiẓ* Abū al-Qāsim Ibn 'Asākir, from another route, from a *ḥadīth* of Muḥammad b. 'Īsā b. Muḥammad b. Sa'īd al-Qurashī al-Akhbārī, as follows: "My father related to us, quoting 'Alī b. Sulaymān b. 'Alī, from 'Alī b. 'Abd Allāh, from 'Abd Allāh b. 'Abbās, may God be pleased with them both, as follows: 'Al-Jārūd b. 'Abd Allāh came forward and recalled almost the same anecdote, at length, with much additional prose and poetry. In that account there is the story of the man whose camels went astray and he went to find them. The man recited, "So I stayed the night in a valley where I was scared for my life, having only my sword to rely on, watching the stars, peering into the blackness, until the night had gone its term and morning was almost breathing; I then heard someone speak aloud the verses:

> 'O you lying down in the pitch black of night, God has sent a prophet in the sacred sanctuary,

47. That is, its authority chain extends back to a successor rather than a Companion of the Prophet.

From Hāshim, a people of trust and honour, illuminating all most gloomy, dark and impenetrable.'"

"'The man continued, "I turned but saw no one and heard nothing else. So I then spoke the following:

'O you who speaks in darkest night, welcome indeed to you, a phantom who visited us!

Explain, may God give you guidance, in tone of words, what it is you urge that can be gained?'

"'"I then heard a clearing of the throat and a voice saying, 'The light has appeared; and falsehood has been defeated. For God has sent Muḥammad with righteousness, the master of the red mount, and the crown and the helmet, he of the shining visage, and the full eyebrows, and the eyes of marked contrast between the white of the cornea and the black of the iris, the man responsible for the words of the "shahāda", or testimony of the faith: "*lā ilāha illā Allāh*","there is no God but God". That person is Muḥammad, the one sent to the black and the white, to the people of the village and the people of the deserts.'" Then he recited the words:

"Praise be to God who did not create nature in vain;
He did not once leave us forsaken after Jesus, nor was He uncaring.
He sent among us Aḥmad, the best Prophet ever dispatched.
May God bless him whenever parties of men hurried (to seek audience with) him."'"

The same source attributes the following verses to Quss b. Sāʿida:

"O announcer of death and of the grave, in the tomb there are men in rags which are remnants of their clothing.

Leave them, for one day they will be called; and they, if they do waken from their sleep, will stay awake.

Until they revert to some state other than theirs, to a new creation similar to what they were before.

Some will be naked, some in their clothes, some of which will be new, some quickly frayed and tattered."

Also, al-Bayhaqī related it from Abū Muḥammad b. ʿAbd Allāh b. Yūsuf b. Aḥmad al-Asbahānī who said that Abū Bakr Aḥmad b. Saʿīd b. Fardakh al-Akhmīmī of Mecca related it to him, quoting al-Qāsim b. ʿAbd Allāh b. Mahdī, quoting Abū ʿAbd Allāh Saʿīd b. ʿAbd al-Raḥmān al-Makhzūmī, quoting Sufyān b. ʿUyayna, from Abū Ḥamza al-Thamālī, from Saʿīd b. Jubayr, from Ibn ʿAbbās. The latter related the anecdote and the recitation and said that they found at his head a sheet on which were the verses:

"O announcer of death and of the dead, in the tomb there are men in rags which are remnants of their clothing,

> Leave then, for one day they will be called, just as those who have fainted away at thunder will be aroused from their sleep.
>
> Some will be naked and others will be dead in their clothes, some of which are bluish and shabby."

So the Messenger of God (ṢAAS) said, "By Him who sent me with the truth, Quss did believe in Judgement Day!"

The origins of this tradition are well known; these other lines of transmission despite their weakness, are helpful in affirming the origin of the anecdote.

Abū Muḥammad b. Darstawayh commented upon the strangeness of what occured in this *ḥadīth*; most of it is obvious, if God Almighty wishes it so. We have drawn attention in our marginal commentary to what is extremely strange about it.

Al-Bayhaqī said that Abū Sa'd Sa'īd b. Muḥammad b. Aḥmad al-Shu'aythī informed him that Abū 'Amr b. Abū Ṭāhir al-Muḥammadabādhī related to him verbally that Abū Lubāba Muḥammad b. al-Mahdī al-Abyurdī related to him, quoting his father, quoting Sa'īd b. Hubayra, quoting al-Mu'tamir b. Sulaymān from his father, all from Anas b. Mālik, who said: "A delegation from Iyād went to the Prophet (ṢAAS) and he asked: 'What did Quss b. Sā'ida do?' They replied: 'He died.' He commented, 'Well, I heard some words from him I no longer recall.' Some of those present told him they remembered them, so he asked them to tell them. One of them responded, 'He stood up at the 'Ukāẓ festival and said, "O people, listen, hear, and take note. All those who live die. And all those who die pass away. And all that is to come will come. Dark nights. Skies with zodiac signs. Stars that shine. Seas that rage. Mountains tower above. Rivers flow. In heaven there is notice and on earth there is warning. I see people die and not return. Were they content to stay and did so? Or were they left and fell asleep? Quss swears an oath by God, not sinning thereby, that God has a religion which is more pleasing to Him than that you engage in." Then he recited the verses:

> "In those who went first in ages past are clear proofs for us.
> Since I saw ways leading to death for people which had no beginnings,
> And I saw my people moving towards them, young and old alike.
> I have become sure that I will inevitably pass on to where the people have gone."'"

Al-Bayhaqī then traces it back by other routes that we have referred to heretofore. After all of this, he then stated: "That *ḥadīth* was narrated from al-Kalbī from Abū Ṣāliḥ, from Ibn 'Abbās, with additions and deletions. It is also related via another way and with an incomplete line of transmission from al-Ḥasan al-Baṣrī. It is also related in abbreviated form in a *ḥadīth* from Sa'd b. Abū Waqqāṣ and Abū Hurayra." And I comment: also from 'Ubāda b. al-Ṣāmit, as given above, and 'Abd Allāh b. Mas'ūd, as related by Abū Nu'aym in his book *al-Dalā'il* (*The Signs*), from ʿAbd Allāh b. Muḥammad b. ʿUthmān al-Wāsiṭī, from Abū al-Walīd Ṭarīf, son of ʿUbayd Allāh the *mawlā* (freedman) of Abū Ṭālib of al-Mawṣil from Yaḥyā b. ʿAbd al-Ḥamīd al-Ḥammānī, from Abū Muʿāwiya, from al-Aʿmash, from Abū al-Ḍuḥā, from Masrūq, from Ibn Masʿūd, and he related it. And Abū Nuʿaym also related the *ḥadīth* of the aforementioned ʿUbāda and Saʿd b. Abū Waqqāṣ.

Then al-Bayhaqī stated, "And since the *ḥadīth* is related from other routes, even if some of them are weak, it shows that it did have an origin. But God knows best."

An Account of Zayd b. ʿAmr b. Nufayl, God be pleased with him.

He was Zayd b.ʿAmr b. Nufayl b.ʿAbd al-ʿUzzā b. Riyāḥ b. ʿAbd Allāh b. Qurẓ b. Razāḥ b. ʿAdī b. Kaʿb b. Luʾayy al-Qurashī al-ʿAdawī.

Al-Khaṭṭāb, father of ʿUmar b. al-Khaṭṭāb, was both his uncle and brother from his mother. That was because ʿAmr b. Nufayl had had a child by his father's wife after his father. She had had his brother al-Khaṭṭāb by Nufayl. Al-Zubayr b. Bakkār and Muḥammad b. Isḥāq told us of this.

Zayd b. ʿAmr gave up the worship of idols and abandoned their religion; he would only eat what had been slaughtered in the name of God alone.

Yūnus b. Bukayr stated on the authority of Muḥammad b. Isḥāq as follows: "Hishām b. ʿUrwa related to me, from his father, that Asmāʾ, daughter of Abū Bakr, said: 'I saw Zayd b. ʿAmr b. Nufayl leaning his back against the *kaʿba* saying, "O tribe of Quraysh, by Him in whose hand is Zayd's soul, not one of you apart from myself follows the religion of Abraham." Moreover, he would say, "O God, if only I knew the way most favoured by you, I would worship you by it, but I do not know." Also he would bow in prayer while on his mount.'"

Abū Usāma too related this, from Hishām, and added, "He would pray towards the *kaʿba* and say, 'My God is the God of Abraham, and my religion is that of Abraham.' He would give life back to girls about to be killed at birth, telling a man wishing to kill his daughter, 'Don't kill her. Give her to me to look after. When she grows up, you can take her back or if you wish give her up.'"

Al-Nasāʾī derived this account through Abū Usāma; and al-Bukhārī commented upon it saying, "And al-Layth said: 'Hishām b. ʿUrwa wrote to me about it from his father.'"

Yūnus b. Bukayr stated on the authority of Muḥammad b. Isḥāq, as follows, "There was a group of Quraysh who consisted of Zayd b. ʿAmr b. Nufayl, Waraqa b. Nawfal b. Asad b. ʿAbd al-ʿUzzā, ʿUthmān b. al-Ḥuwayrith b. Asad b. ʿAbd al-ʿUzzā, and ʿAbd Allāh b. Jaḥsh b. Riʾāb b. Yaʿmur b. Ṣabra b. Murra b. Kabīr b. Ghunm b. Dūdān b. Asad b. Khuzayma, whose mother was Umayya daughter of ʿAbd al-Muṭṭalib and whose sister was Zaynab, daughter of Jaḥsh whom the Prophet (ṢAAS) married after his *mawlā*, his freedman, Zayd b. Ḥāritha, as we will relate hereafter. These men were present among Quraysh when they were before an idol of theirs to which they would make sacrifice at one of their feast days. As they all gathered, this group of men met apart and agreed that they would make a secret pact of friendship with one another. One of them said, 'By God, you know that your people are doing nothing; they have strayed from the religion of Abraham and gone against it. Why worship some idol incapable of doing harm or good? Seek out for yourselves!'

"So they left, seeking and searching throughout the land to find the *ḥanifiyya*, the religion of Abraham.

"As for Waraqa b. Nawfal, he became a Christian and became learned in Christianity, seeking out its scriptures from its adherents until he acquired a great knowledge from those who follow the Bible.

"None of this group was a man more honourable in deed nor more dedicated than Zayd b.ʿAmr b. Nufayl. He gave up the idols and abandoned all the religions, of the Jews, the Christians, and all the sects except the *ḥanifiyya*, the religion of Abraham. He spoke of the unity of God alone and cast aside the gods beneath Him. He ate none of the meat his people slaughtered, and warned them of the judgement they would suffer from the practices they followed."

He went on: "Al-Khaṭṭāb so persecuted him that eventually Zayd left him by going to the heights of Mecca. So al-Khaṭṭāb assigned a group of young Quraysh thugs to watch him and told them not to let him enter Mecca. He never did so except without their knowledge, and when they found out they harmed him and evicted him violently, hating that he should spoil their religion for them or get others to join him in his own practice."

Mūsā b. ʿUqba stated that he heard someone he trusted give a report about Zayd b. ʿAmr b. Nufayl to the effect that he would criticize Quraysh for the slaughter of their beasts, saying, "Sheep were created by God and He brings down from the skies the water that makes vegetation grow for them from the earth, so why do you slaughter them in the name of gods other than God, denying all that and venerating them?"

Yūnus said, on the authority of Ibn Isḥāq: "Zayd b.ʿAmr b. Nufayl had determined to leave Mecca and travel across the land seeking the *ḥanafiyya*, the religion of Abraham. His wife Ṣafiyya, daughter of al-Ḥadramī, whenever she saw him preparing to make the departure he wished, would warn al-Khaṭṭāb b. Nufayl.

"Zayd did leave for Syria, enquiring and seeking the religion of Abraham among the people of the first holy book. They say he went on doing this until he covered al-Mawṣil and all Mesopotamia, finally reaching Syria and travelling throughout it. Eventually he came upon a monk in a church in the region of al-Balqāʾ who had, as they claim, much learning in Christianity. Zayd asked him about the *ḥanifiyya*, the religion of Abraham, and the monk replied, 'You are asking about a religion you'll not find anyone today to instruct you in. Those who had knowledge and familiarity with it have faded away and gone. But the emergence of a prophet draws near, his time having come.' Now Zayd had examined Judaism and Christianity, but had not been content with anything in them, and so he left quickly for Mecca after what the monk had told him. But when he was in Lakhm territory he was attacked and killed. Waraqa spoke the following verses eulogizing him:

> 'You followed the proper course and did right, O son of ʿAmr; and indeed you have avoided the ovens of hell,
> By your worshipping a Lord unlike any other and by your abandoning the idols of tyrants as they are,
> Man may indeed be reached by God's mercy, even though he be seventy valleys beneath the earth.' "

Muḥammad b. ʿUthmān b. Abū Shayba said, "Aḥmad b. Ṭāriq al-Wābishī related to us, quoting ʿAmr b. ʿAṭiyya, from his father, from Ibn ʿUmar, from Zayd b. ʿAmr b. Nufayl, that the latter worshipped God before the coming of Islam. He once came to a Jew and told him he wanted him to induct him into his religion. The Jew replied, 'I will not accept you in my religion until you experience your share of God's anger.' Zayd replied, 'It is from the anger of God that I am fleeing.'

"Zayd went on further till he came to a Christian, telling him he would like to engage with him in his religion. The Christian replied, 'I'll not accept you in my religion until you experience your share of false guidance.' Zayd replied, 'It is from false guidance that I flee.' The Christian then told him: 'I will show you the way to a religion in which, if you follow it, you will be rightly guided.' 'What religion is that?' asked Zayd. 'The religion of Abraham,' he replied. So Zayd said, 'O God, I swear to you that I will follow the religion of Abraham; in it I shall live and die.'

"When Zayd's story was referred to the Prophet (ṢAAS) he stated, 'He will be as a nation all by himself on Judgement Day.'"

Mūsā b. ʿUqba, on the authority of Sālim from Ibn ʿUmar, related approximately the same.

Muḥammad b. Saʿd stated: "ʿAlī b. Muḥammad b. ʿAbd Allāh b. Sayf al-Qurashī related to us, from Ismāʿīl, from Mujālid from al-Shaʿbī, from ʿAbd al-Raḥmān b. Zayd b. al-Khaṭṭāb as follows: 'Zayd b. ʿAmr b. Nufayl said, "I examined Judaism and Christianity and disliked them both. I travelled in Syria and the neighbouring lands and eventually came to a monk in a cell. I told him of my alienation from my own people and of my dislike for the worship of idols,

Judaism, and Christianity. He told me, 'I see you desire the religion of Abraham, O brother from the people of Mecca. You are searching for a religion that today no one adheres to, the religion of your father Abraham. He was a *ḥanīf*, neither a Jew nor a Christian. He prayed and prostrated himself in the direction of that house which is in your land. So you must go to your own country. God will send from your people in your land one who will bring the religion of Abraham, the *ḥanifiyya*; he is the most noble of creation in God's sight.'" ? "

Yūnus stated that Ibn Isḥāq said, "A member of the family of Zayd b.ʿAmr b. Nufayl related to me the following, 'Zayd used to say when he entered the *kaʿba*, "Here I am before you, really and truly, in worship, verity and submission. I turn in submission quoting Abraham, facing the *kaʿba*." He would stand as he would say, "O my God, I am submissive to you, fearful, and humble. Whatever painful task you impose, I will perform it. It is faith I desire, not vanity. He who journeys in the heat is not as one who naps in the afternoon."'"

Abū Dāwūd al-Ṭayālisī stated, "Al-Masʿūdī related to us, from Nufayl b. Hishām b. Saʿīd b. Zayd b. ʿAmr b. Nufayl al-ʿAdawī, on the authority of his father, from his grandfather, that Zayd b. ʿAmr and Waraqa b. Nawfal went off seeking religion and finally met a monk at al-Mawṣil. The monk asked Zayd, 'Where have you travelled from, O camel master?' 'From Abraham's building,' he replied. 'What are you seeking?' then asked the monk. 'I am seeking the religion,' replied Zayd. The monk responded, 'Go back; it is soon to appear in your land.'

"Zayd went on: 'Now Waraqa did adopt Christianity; but in my case, although I intended to become Christian he (the monk) would not accept me.' So Zayd returned home and spoke the words: 'Here I am before You, in truth, in worship and in submission. It is faith I desire, not vanity. Is he who journeys in the heat as one who naps in the afternoon? I believe in what Abraham believed in.' He also said, 'O my God, I am submissive to You, fearful, and humble. Whatever painful task You impose, I will perform it.' Then he would bow down and prostrate himself in prayer."

The account continues, "His son, by whom I mean Saʿīd b. Zayd, one of the *ʿashra*,[48] the ten, God bless him, said, 'O Messenger of God, my father was as you have seen and heard; seek forgiveness for him.' He replied, 'Yes; he will be raised up on Judgement Day as a nation, by himself.'"

It continues: "And Zayd b. ʿAmr b. Zayd came to the Messenger of God when the latter was in the company of Zayd b. Ḥāritha; the two men were eating from a dining-table set out for them. They invited Zayd b. ʿAmr to eat with them, but he replied, 'I am not one who eats what has been slaughtered on sacrificial stones.'"

48. *Al-ʿashra al-mubashshara* (the promised ten) denotes ten persons variously reported in non-canonical traditions as having been assured places in paradise. They include: Abū Bakr, ʿUmar, ʿUthmān, ʿAlī, Talḥa, Zubayr, ʿAbd al-Raḥmān b. ʿAwf, Saʿd b. Abī Waqqāṣ, and Sāʿid b. Zayd, along with the Prophet (ṢAAS).

Muḥammad b. Saʿd stated, "Muḥammad b. ʿAmr related to us, Abū Bakr b. Abū Sabra related to me, from Mūsā b. Maysara, from Ibn Abū Mulayka, from Ḥajar b. Abū Ihāb, as follows, 'I saw Zayd b.ʿAmr while I was at the idol named Bawāna, just after he had returned from Syria. He was observing the sun; when it set he approached the *kaʿba* and performed the prayer of two prostrations. Then he said, "This is the *qibla*, the prayer site, to which Abraham and Ishmael directed themselves. I do not worship a stone, nor pray to it, nor eat what was sarificed to it, nor will I seek the judgement of divining arrows. Yet I will pray towards this house till I die."

"'He would also perform the pilgrimage and station himself on Mt. ʿArafāt. He would also make the prayer call saying, "*Labbayk*! At Your service; there is no partner to You, nor any peer." Then he would leave ʿArafāt, walking and praying, saying, "*Labbayk*! At Your service, in worship and submission."'"

Al-Wāqidi stated, "ʿAlī b. ʿĪsā al-Ḥakamī related to me, from his father, from ʿĀmir b. Rabīʿa as follows, 'I heard Zayd b. ʿAmr b. Nufayl say, "I await the coming of a prophet from the progeny of Ishmael, then from the tribe of ʿAbd al Muṭṭalib. I do not see myself living to his time. But I have faith in him, assert his truthfulness, and testify that he is a prophet. If you live on a long time and see him, then tell him of my greetings to him. I will inform you of his qualities so that he will not be unknown to you." I replied, "Do so then."

" 'He continued, "He will be a man neither tall nor short with neither much nor little hair. Redness is never absent from his eye. He bears the mark of prophethood between his shoulders. His name is to be Aḥmad and this country will be the place of his birth and his mission. Then his people will expel him from it and will disapprove of his message until he will emigrate to Yathrib; and so his authority will appear. Take care that you are not deceived about him, for I have travelled all over seeking the religion of Abraham. And those of the Jews, Christians, and Magians to whom I made enquiry answered, 'That religion is behind you.' And they would describe him as I have described him to you and say, 'There is no prophet but him.'"'

"ʿĀmir b. Rabīʿa stated, 'And when I became a Muslim I informed the Messenger of God (ṢAAS) of the words of Zayd b.ʿAmr and did pass on his greetings to him. He returned such greeting to him and prayed for mercy for him, saying, 'I have seen him in paradise in long, flowing robes.'"

Al-Bukhārī stated in his *ṣaḥīḥ* collection in his account on Zayd b. ʿAmr b. Nufayl that Muḥammad b. Abū Bakr related to him that Fuḍayl b. Sulaymān related to us, quoting Mūsā b. ʿUqba, that Sālim related, from ʿAbd Allāh b. ʿUmar, that the Prophet (ṢAAS) met Zayd b.ʿAmr b. Nufayl in the lowlands of Baldaḥ, before revelation descended upon the Prophet. A meal was set out for the Prophet (ṢAAS) but he, Zayd, refused to eat of it. Then Zayd said, "I'm not going to eat from what you slaughter on your sacrificial stones; and I will only eat what has had the name of God spoken over it." Zayd b. ʿAmr would criticize Quraysh for the animal sacrifices they made, saying, "Sheep are created by God; He sends rain down from the skies and makes things grow for them from the earth. But then you slaughter them in the name of gods other than Him, denying all of that and venerating them!"

Mūsā b. ʿUqba said that Sālim b. ʿAbd Allāh related to him (indicating that he would not acknowledge what he related except that he spoke of it on the authority of Ibn ʿUmar) that Zayd b.ʿAmr b. Nufayl left for Syria enquiring after the religion he would follow and met a learned Jew whom he asked about his religion. Zayd said, "I'm inclined towards adopting your religion, so tell me of it." The man replied, "You will not be in our religion until you receive your share of God's anger." Zayd replied, "But it's only God's anger from which I flee; I bear none of God's anger, nor could I. Can you then direct me to something else?" He replied, "I don't know of anything – except for you to be a *ḥanīf*." "What", asked Zayd, "is a *ḥanīf*?" "The religion of Abraham, peace be upon him; he was neither a Jew nor a Christian and worshipped none but God."

So Zayd left and met a Christian scholar to whom he spoke as before. But the Christian replied, "You will not be of our religion until you take your share of the curses of God." Zayd replied, "But it's only from the curses of God that I flee. I do not at all ever bear the curses of God or His anger, nor could I. So would you direct me to something else?" "I don't know of anything, except for you to be a *ḥanīf*," the Christian answered. "What is a *ḥanīf*?" Zayd asked. "It is the religion of Abraham," the Christian answered; "he was neither a Jew nor a Christian and worshipped none but God."

Having considered their statement about Abraham, Zayd went outside and when he was in open country, he raised his hands and said, "O God, I testify that I follow the religion of Abraham."

Al-Bukhārī went on: "And al-Layth said, 'Hishām b. ʿUrwa wrote to me, on the authority of his father, and that of Asmāʾ daughter of Abū Bakr, may God be pleased with them both; he quotes her as having said, "I saw Zayd b. ʿAmr b. Nufayl standing leaning his back against the *kaʿba*, saying, 'O tribe of Quraysh, by God, none of you is in Abraham's religion except me.' And he used to give life back to a girl about to be killed at birth, saying to the man who wished to kill his daughter, 'Don't kill her; I will take care of providing for her.' Then he would take her away, and when she grew up he would tell her father, 'If you like, I'll either return her to you or provide for her.'"'" This brings to an end al-Bukhārī's account of Zayd.

This last anecdote was corroborated by the *ḥāfiẓ* Ibn ʿAsākir in a line of authority from Abū Bakr b. Abū Dāwūd from ʿĪsā b. Ḥammād, from al-Layth, from Hishām, from his father back to Asmaʾ, and his account is similar.

ʿAbd al-Raḥmān b. Abū al-Zinād said that on a line of authority from Hishām b. ʿUrwa, from his father, Asmāʾ said: "I heard Zayd b. ʿAmr b. Nufayl say, as he was resting his back against the *kaʿba*: 'O tribe of Quraysh, beware of adultery; it bequeaths poverty.'"

Here in his account Ibn ʿAsākir gave several very strange anecdotes, some of which are extremely implausible. Then he related from a variety of lines back to the Messenger of God (ṢAAS) as having said: "He will be raised up on Judgement Day as a nation all by himself." These accounts include the one by Muḥammad b. ʿUthmān b. Abū Shayba in which he indicated that Yūsuf b. Yaʿqūb al-Ṣaffār and Yaḥyā b. Saʿīd al-Umawī related to him, from Mujālid, from al-Shaʿbi, from Jābir, that the Messenger of God (ṢAAS) was asked about Zayd b. ʿAmr b. Nufayl having approached the *qibla* before the coming of Islam and saying, "My God is the God of Abraham, and my religion that of Abraham" and then making the prayer prostrations. The Messenger of God (ṢAAS) said, "That man will be gathered (on Judgement Day) as a nation all by himself between me and Jesus son of Mary." The chain of authorities for this is very good.

Al-Wāqidī stated that Mūsā b. Shayba related to him, from Khārija b. ʿAbd Allāh b. Kaʿb. b. Mālik, who said, "I heard Saʿīd b. al-Musayyab make reference to Zayd b.ʿAmr b. Nufayl with the words, 'He died while Quraysh were building the *kaʿba*, five years before the divine inspiration descended upon the Messenger of God (ṢAAS). And death came to him while he spoke the words, "I follow the religion of Abraham."' His son Saʿīd b. Zayd became a Muslim and a follower of the Messenger of God (ṢAAS). Once ʿUmar b. al-Khaṭṭāb and Saʿīd b. Zayd approached the Messenger of God (ṢAAS) and asked him about Zayd b.ʿAmr b. Nufayl and he responded, 'May God give him forgiveness and grant him mercy. He died following the religion of Abraham.' And after that day Muslims never failed to pray for forgivenesss and mercy for him whenever they mentioned his name. And then Saʿīd b. al-Musayyab himself spoke the words, 'May God grant him mercy and forgiveness.'"

Muḥammad b. Saʿd quoted al-Wāqidī as having said, "Zakariyyāʾ b. Yaḥyā al-Saʿdī related to me that he heard his father say, 'Zayd b.ʿAmr b. Nufayl died in Mecca and he was buried at the foot of Mt. Ḥirāʾ.'"

We, however, stated previously that he died in the land of al-Balqāʾ in Syria, when he was attacked by some men of the tribe of Lakhm who killed him at a place called Mayfaʿa. But God knows best.

Al-Bāghandī said, giving a line of authorities through Abū Saʿīd al-Ashajj, Abū Muʿāwiya, Hishām and his father, that ʿĀʾisha said, "The Messenger of God (ṢAAS) stated, 'I entered paradise and saw that Zayd b. ʿAmr b. Nufayl had two fine, lofty trees.'"

Among the verses of Zayd b. ʿAmr b. Nufayl, God have mercy on him, are the lines:

"To God I give my praise and homage, expressing a lasting joy that time will not fade.
To the Sovereign Lord all high, above whom there is none, a God to whom no other Lord can draw close."

It is also said that these lines are of Umayya b. Abū al-Ṣalt. But God knows best.

Among his verses affirming the oneness of God are the lines related by Muḥammad b. Isḥāq and al-Zubayr b. Bakkār, among others:

"I turn my face in submission to Him to whom the earth bearing heavy rocks submits;
He laid it down and when it settled He made it firm and level, then raised up the mountains above it.
I turn my face in submission to Him to whom the clouds bearing sweet cool water submit,
When they are drawn along to a place, they obey, and pour water down copiously upon it.
I turn my face in submission to Him to whom the wind, changing direction hither and yon, submits."

Muḥammad b. Isḥāq said, "I heard from Hishām b.ʿUrwa that, according to his father, Zayd b.ʿAmr spoke the verses:

"Is it one Lord or one thousand I'm to worship according to your calculations?
I have abandoned al-Lāt and al-ʿUzzā together; thus do all those who are firm and determined.
It is not al-ʿUzzā I worship, nor her daughters, nor do I visit the two idols of the ʿAmr tribe.
Nor do I worship Ghanm, though he was our Lord when I had little wisdom.
I was perplexed – and at night many things are strange that a sensible man understands well by day –
That God erased many men who lived in wickedness,
Yet gave long life to others through the faith of a people so that from them a young child could multiply,
And though a man may falter, one day he may be cured, as a green tree branch will leaf again,
But I worship the All-merciful, my lord, that the compassionate Lord may forgive my sins.
So preserve your fear of God your Lord; while you preserve it you will not be lost.
You will see that the abode of the innocent is paradise, and that there is a burning hell-fire for disbelievers,
Shame while alive and when they die they will suffer terrible torture."

This is the complete text of this poem as given by Muḥammad b. Isḥāq. Abū al-Qāsim al-Baghawī related it from Musʿab b. ʿAbd Allāh, from al-Ḍaḥḥāk b. ʿUthmān, from ʿAbd al-Raḥmān b. Abū al-Zinād.

Hishām b. ʿUrwa stated, from his father, that Asmāʾ, daughter of Abū Bakr, said, "Zayd b. ʿAmr b. Nufayl spoke the following verses:

> 'I have abandoned all spirits and demons; thus do all those who are firm and determined;
> It is not al-ʿUzzā I worship, nor her daughters, nor do I revere the two idols of the Ṭasam tribe.
> Nor do I worship Ghanm, though he was our lord when I had little wisdom,
> Is it one lord or a thousand I'm to worship according to your calculations?
> Do you not know that God erased many men who lived in wickedness,
> And gave long life to others through the faith of a people so that from them a young boy could grow up.
> And though a man may falter, one day he may be cured, as a green tree branch will leaf again.'"

Waraqa b. Nawfal spoke the following poetry:

> "You followed the proper course and did right, O son of ʿAmr, but indeed you have avoided the hot ovens of hell,
> For your worship of a Lord unlike any other and for your abandoning as they are the spirits of the mountains,
> I say that when I descend into some eerie place: have pity, do not let enemies appear before me.
> Have pity! For you are the hope of the spirits; and you are my God, our Lord, and my hope.
> Let the mercy of his Lord attain a man, even if he be seventy valleys down beneath the earth.
> I worship a Lord who responds, and I will not be seen worshipping someone who does not ever hear anyone calling.
> I say as I pray in every church: 'Blessed be You; I have indeed prayed much in Your name.'"

It has been stated earlier that Zayd b. ʿAmr b. Nufayl left for Syria along with Waraqa b. Nawfal, ʿUthmān b. al-Ḥuwayrith, and ʿUbayd Allāh b. Jaḥsh. All became Christians except Zayd, who adopted no religion but remained in his natural state of the worship of God alone and without partner, following as best he could the religion of Abraham, as we have mentioned.

As for Waraqa b. Nawfal, his story will be told in discussion of the beginnings of the divine mission.

As for ʿUthmān b. al-Ḥuwayrith, he remained in Syria until he died there while with Caesar. His story is very strange and was related by al-Umawī. In brief it is as follows. When he approached Caesar and complained to him of the treatment he had received from his own people, Caesar wrote for him to Ibn Jafna, the king of the Arabs of Syria, to the effect that he should provide an army to go with him to make war against Quraysh. He did decide to do so, but the bedouins wrote to him advising him against that action because of what they saw to be the greatness of Mecca, and also how God had treated the army that had come with the elephants. So Ibn Jafna invested him with a tunic dyed with poison and he was killed by it. Zayd b. ʿAmr b. Nufayl eulogized him in poetry recorded by al-Umawī which we have left out for brevity's sake.

His death occurred some three years before the mission of Islam. But God, All-glorious and Almighty is He, knows best.

An Account of some of the events that occurred in the time of the fatra,[49] *including the building of the* kaʿba.

It has been said that it was Adam who first built it. Such a statement comes down in a *ḥadīth* that is *marfūʿ*[50] and came on the authority of ʿAbd Allāh b. ʿAmr ; Ibn Lahīʿa is one of its chain of authorities and he is an authority considered *ḍaʿif*, weak.

The most credible of statements is that Abraham, *al-Khalīl*, "the true friend", peace be upon him, was the first who built it, as reported above. Simāk b. Ḥarb so related, from Khālid b. ʿArʿara back to ʿAlī b. Abū Ṭālib who said, "Then it collapsed, was rebuilt by *al-ʿamāliqa*, 'the giants', fell down and was built again by Jurhum; thereafter it collapsed and was rebuilt by Quraysh."

Here I will recount its being built by Quraysh; this occurred some five, or as some say fifteen, years before the coming of Islam. Al-Zuhrī stated, "The Messenger of God (ṢAAS) had by then attained puberty." Material related to all that will come in its proper place, if God wills it, and in Him there is trust.

An Account of Kaʿb b. Luʾayy.

Abū Nuʿaym related in a line from Muḥammad b. al-Haṣan b. Zabala, from Muḥammad b. Ṭalḥa al-Taymī, from Muḥammad b. Ibrāhīm b. al-Ḥārith back to Abū Salama who said, "Kaʿb b. Luʾayy would gather his people on Friday, a day Quraysh used to name *al-ʿarūba*, and he would address them as follows: 'And moreover you must listen, learn, understand, and know. Tranquil night, sunlit day; the earth is flat, the skies erected, the mountains bulwarks, the stars markers. The first are as the last, the female and the male, the couple, and whatever excites, all heads for decay. So respect your ties of relationship and preserve your kinship,

49. *Al-fatra* is a word given in Arabic to mean the period or the interval between two prophets. Here it refers to the interval between the life of Jesus and that of Muḥammad.

50. A tradition related by a Companion of the Prophet and reporting the latter's words or actions.

and make your wealth multiply. For did you ever see return someone who expired, or a dead person revived? The (eternal) abode is before you and thought is not what you express. Embellish and venerate your sanctuary and preserve it well; for to it glorious tidings will come. And from it will emerge a noble prophet.'

"Then he would say,

> 'Daytime and night, every day has a happening; the same to us whether by day time or night.
>
> They both bring events when they arrive and their coverings over us bring many blessings.
>
> The Prophet Muḥammad will come unexpectedly, and bring such news; believable indeed is their bearer.'

"Then he would say, 'By God, were I but part of them, by hearing and sight, by hand and foot, I would vigorously rise up like a camel, and charge into it like a stallion.'

"Then he would say, 'Would that I could witness the impact of his mission, when the tribe seeks the truth without vigour.'"

Between the death of Kaʿb b. Luʾayy and the mission of the Messenger of God (ṢAAS) there was a period of 560 years.

An Account of the re-digging of the well zamzam *by ʿAbd al-Muṭṭalib b. Hāshim, its whereabouts having been lost from the period when Jurhum filled and levelled it, up to his own time.*

Muḥammad b. Isḥāq stated, "ʿAbd al-Muṭṭalib was sleeping in the sacred enclosure when he received a vision ordering him to dig up *zamzam.*

"ʿAbd al-Muṭṭalib was the first to begin digging it, according to what was related to me by Yazīd b. Abū Ḥabīb al-Miṣrī from Marthad b. ʿAbd Allāh al-Yazanī, from ʿAbd Allāh b. Dhurayr al-Ghāfiqī, namely, that the last mentioned heard ʿAlī b. Abū Ṭālib, God be pleased with him, telling how ʿAbd al-Muṭṭalib had been ordered to dig *zamzam.* ʿAlī reported ʿAbd al-Muṭṭalib as saying: 'I was sleeping in the sanctuary when a vision came to me and said, "Dig *ṭība*!" "But what's *ṭība*?" I asked. But it vanished.

"'Next day when I again went to my bed and slept, he came again and said, "Dig *barra*!" "But what's *barra*?" I asked. But it vanished.

"'Next day when I again went to my bed and slept, he came again and said, "Dig *al-maḍnūna*!" "But what's *al-maḍnūna*?" I asked. But it vanished.

"'Next day when I again went to my bed and slept, he came again and said, "Dig *zamzam*!" "But what's *zamzam*?" I asked. "It will never fail or dry up; it will water the grand pilgrim. It lies between the dung and the blood, near the nest of the crow with the white leg and the ants' nest."'

"The matter having been clarified and he having been directed to its location, and knowing that he had been spoken to in truth, he took up his pick-axe next day and went off in the company of his son al-Ḥārith b. ʿAbd al-Muṭṭalib, his only son at that time. So he dug down for it and when the coping stone appeared to ʿAbd al-Muṭṭalib he let out a cry of praise for God. Quraysh therefore knew that he had achieved his purpose so they came and told him, 'O ʿAbd al-Muṭṭalib, that is the well of our father Ishmael; we have a right to it, so make us partners in it with yourself.' 'I will do no such thing; I was specifically assigned to this without you; I was given it from among you all,' he replied. They asked again, 'Treat us fairly; we'll not leave you alone till we share with you in it.' ʿAbd al-Muṭṭalib replied, 'Then appoint someone of your choice for me to ask to adjudicate the matter with you.' 'The woman diviner of the Banū Saʿd b. Hudhaym,' they suggested. ʿAbd al-Muṭṭalib agreed; the woman lived in the uplands of Syria.

"So ʿAbd al-Muṭṭalib mounted up with a company of men of the Banū Ummaya, along with members of each tribe of Quraysh and they all left. The earth at that time was waterless and having travelled some distance ʿAbd al-Muṭṭalib and his friends had used up their water. They were so thirsty that they became convinced they were doomed. They therefore asked the other party for water, but they refused, saying, 'We're in a waterless desert and we fear for ourselves a similar plight that afflicts you.' ʿAbd al-Muṭṭalib then said, 'I think each man should dig a grave for himself with the strength he has remaining, so that when anyone dies his friends can put him in the hole and cover him up, and so on till there is only one man left. Better the loss (without burial) of one than that of a whole company.' 'What you instruct is good,' they agreed.

"So each man dug himself a hole, and they sat down to await death from thirst. But then ʿAbd al-Muṭṭalib told his companions, 'By God, our casting ourselves down by our own hands like this for death without searching the land and exerting ourselves is truly weakness; God may well provide us water somewhere in this land. Mount up!' So they did so. But when ʿAbd al-Muṭṭalib urged his mount up, a spring of sweet water burst up from beneath its hoof! ʿAbd al-Muṭṭalib made exclamations of God's greatness, as did his companions; he and they dismounted, drank, and filled their water flasks. Then ʿAbd al-Muṭṭalib called the Quraysh tribesmen who had been watching all this, saying, 'Come on over to the spring. God has given us water.' So they came and drank, all filling their flasks. They then said, 'Judgement has been made, by God, in your favour against us! We won't ever dispute with you over *zamzam*. He who gave you this water in this desert is also He who gave you *zamzam*. So return to your drawing of water, it being your right.'

"So he and they all went back without consulting the diviner. And Quraysh gave ʿAbd al-Muṭṭalib free access to *zamzam*."

Ibn Isḥāq stated, "And that is the account I heard on the authority of ʿAlī b. Abū Ṭālib concerning *zamzam*."

He also said, "I heard someone relate a tradition that ʿAbd al-Muṭṭalib was told, when ordered to dig *zamzam*:

'Then pray for abundant water without impurities to quench God's pilgrims at all the sacred sites.

'There's nothing to fear so long as it provides.'

"Having been told so, ʿAbd al-Muṭṭalib went to Quraysh and said to them, 'You should know that I have been ordered to dig *zamzam*.' They asked, 'And was it explained to you where it lies?' When he responded in the negative, they told him, 'Then go back to your bed where you had your vision. For if it in truth came from God, it will be made clear to you, whereas if it came from Satan, it will not reappear to you.' ʿAbd al-Muṭṭalib did return and slept and did receive a visitation, being told: 'Dig *zamzam*. You will not regret if you do dig it. It is an inheritance from your most mighty Father. It will never fail or dry up. It will water the grand pilgrim. Like fleeing ostriches, it will never be divided. A truth-sayer vows it to a benefactor. It will be an inheritance and a secure contract. It is not as some things you might have known. And it lies between the dung and the blood.'"

Ibn Isḥāq went on, "It is claimed that when this was said to ʿAbd al-Muṭṭalib, he asked, 'Then where is it?' He was then told that it was near the ants' nest where the crow would peck the next day. But God knows whether that was so.

"Next day ʿAbd al-Muṭṭalib went with his son al-Ḥārith, his only son at that time (al-Umawī added: 'along with his servant Aṣram') and found the ants' nest and the crow pecking near by, between the two idols Isāf and Nāʾila, at which Quraysh would make sacrifice. So he brought his pick-axe to dig where he had been told. But Quraysh stood in his way saying, 'By God, we'll not allow you to dig down between our two idols to which we make sacrifice.' ʿAbd al-Muṭṭalib addressed his son al-Ḥārith, 'Protect me so I can dig, for by God I shall carry on and do what I was ordered.' When Quraysh realized that he would not back down, they made way for him to dig and left him alone. He had not been digging for long before the coping stone appeared and he acclaimed the greatness of God, knowing that truth had been spoken to him. Persisting in the digging, he found there two golden gazelles that Jurhum had buried, along with some white metal swords and some breast-plates.

"Quraysh then addressed him, 'O ʿAbd al-Muṭṭalib, we have a right to share in this.' 'No,' he replied, 'but let us decide what is equitable between us. Let us use divinatory arrows over it.' 'What shall we do then?' they asked. He replied, 'I will make two arrows for the *kaʿba*, two for myself, and two for you. Whoever has his arrows come out for something, that he shall have. Whoever has his arrows left behind gets nothing.' They agreed that this was fair. So he made two yellow arrows for the *kaʿba*, two black ones for himself, and two white ones for them. Then he gave the arrows to the diviner at the site of the idol Hubal, who was to cast them. And Hubal was the largest of their idols; that was why Abū Sufyān said at the battle of Uḥud, 'Arise, O Hubal!', referring to that idol. So ʿAbd al-Muṭṭalib said a prayer to God."

Yūnus b. Bukayr recounted, from Muḥammad b. Isḥāq, that ʿAbd al-Muṭṭalib began saying:

> "O God, You are the much-praised King; my Lord; You are the one who initiates and repeats,
> The one who is firmly holding the rocky mountain; from You comes all that is new or that is old.
> If You wish, You give inspiration as You want, to find the place of the ornaments and the steel.
> So make clear today what You wish; I have made a vow to Him who decides
> Give it, O my Lord, to me, and I'll not go back."

"The diviner cast the arrows and the two yellow ones went towards the gazelles, giving them to the *kaʿba*, the two black ones came out for the swords and armour, making them for ʿAbd al-Muṭṭalib, but the two arrows for Quraysh remained behind. So ʿAbd al-Muṭṭalib hammered down the two swords into a door for the *kaʿba* into which he incorporated the two golden gazelles. This was, so they say, the first decoration of gold the *kaʿba* had."

Thereafter ʿAbd al-Muṭṭalib took charge of providing water from *zamzam* to the pilgrims. And Ibn Isḥāq and others relate that Mecca had many wells in it prior to the appearance of *zamzam* at the time of ʿAbd al-Muṭṭalib. Ibn Isḥāq, moreover, enumerated and named them, and told their whereabouts in and around Mecca as well as those who dug them. His account of this concludes, "*Zamzam* overshadowed all the other wells, their customers preferring to go to it, because of its proximity to the holy mosque, the superiority of its water over the rest, and its having been the well of Ishmael, son of Abraham. The ʿAbd Manāf tribe expressed because of it a superiority over all Quraysh as well as all the other Arabs."

It is established in the *ṣaḥiḥ* collection of Muslim in the material relating to the adoption of Islam by Abū Dharr, that the Messenger of God (ṢAAS) said the following about *zamzam*: "It is the taste supreme. It is the cure of disease."

The Imām Aḥmad (Ibn Hanbal) said, "ʿAbd Allāh b. al-Walīd related to us, on the authority of ʿAbd Allāh b. al-Muʿmil, from Abū al-Zubayr, from Jābir b. ʿAbd Allāh, that the Messenger of God (ṢAAS) said, 'The water of *zamzam* is for what is drunk from it.'"

Ibn Māja related this also, from a *ḥadīth* of ʿAbd Allāh b. al-Muʾmil. They spoke it and gave its wording as: "The water of *zamzam* is for what is drunk to it." Suwayd b. Saʿīd related it from ʿAbd Allāh b. al-Mubārak, from ʿAbd al-Raḥmān b. Abū al-Mawālī, from Muḥammad b. al-Munkadir, from Jābir, from the Prophet (ṢAAS) who said, "The water of *zamzam* is for what is drunk to it." However, Suwayd b. Saʿīd is a weak link. The tradition as preserved from Ibn al-Mubārak from ʿAbd Allāh b. al-Muʾmil is as given above. Al-Ḥākim related it from Ibn ʿAbbās in the form "The water of *zamzam* is for what is drunk to it." And this is questionable. But God knows best.

Similarly, Ibn Māja and al-Ḥākim relate that Ibn ʿAbbās said to a man, "When you drink from *zamzam* face the *kaʿba* and repeat the name of God. Then breathe deeply three times and drink from it until you are full. When finished, give praise to God. For the Messenger of God (ṢAAS) said, 'The evidence of the differences between us and the hypocrites is that they do not drink to the fill from the water of *zamzam*.'"

And it is related from ʿAbd al-Muṭṭalib that he said, "O God, I do not allow a person to wash with it; it is for people to drink *ḥillun*, 'freely available', *wa*, 'and', *ballun*, 'allowed'."[51]

Some learned scholars report this from al-ʿAbbās b. ʿAbd al-Muṭṭalib but in fact it came from ʿAbd al-Muṭṭalib himself, for it was he who restored *zamzam* as stated above. But God knows best.

Al-Umawī wrote in his *Maghāzī* work as follows: "Abū ʿUbayd related to us, Yaḥyā b. Saʿīd informed us, from ʿAbd al-Raḥmān b. Ḥarmala, that the last mentioned said that he heard Saʿīd b. al-Musayyab relate that ʿAbd al-Muṭṭalib b. Hāshim remarked when he dug *zamzam*, 'I do not allow a person to wash with it; it is freely available and allowed for a person to drink it.' To that purpose he had two basins for it, one for drinking, the other for the prayer ablution. At that point he said, 'I do not allow a person to wash with it, deeming it inappropriate for the mosque to be washed in.'"

According to Abū ʿUbayd, al-Asmaʿī stated that his saying *wa ballun* is an *itbāʿ*,[52] "corroboration of the preceding word", *ḥillun*. But Abū ʿUbayd objected that an *itbāʿ* cannot occur with the *waw* of conjunction (*wa* meaning "and") but it is used because, as Muʿtamir b. Sulaymān had indicated, *ballun* in the language of Ḥimyar means *mubāḥ*, i.e. "allowed".

Abū ʿUbayd then said, "Abū Bakr b. ʿAyyāsh related to us, from ʿĀsim b. Abū al-Nujūd, that he heard Zirr (say) that he heard al-ʿAbbās state, 'I do not allow a person to wash in it.'" And ʿAbd al-Raḥmān b. Mahdī related to us, as did

51. Discussion of these words *hillun wa ballun* follows in the text. Also, another meaning of the word *ballun* is "for wetting".

52. In Arabic grammar *itbāʿ* is intensification by repetition of a word with its initial consonant changed.

Sufyān, from ʿAbd al-Raḥmān b. ʿAlqama, that the last mentioned heard Ibn ʿAbbās say the same."

And this tradition relating back to both of them is true; it has them so saying in their own era with the purpose of informing and establishing what ʿAbd al-Muṭṭalib had specified when he dug it; thus it does not contradict the preceding account. But God knows best.

The rights to providing water for the pilgrims remained with ʿAbd al-Muṭṭalib as long as he lived, thereafter passing to his son Abū Ṭālib for a period. Then it so happened that he became impoverished for a while and went into debt to his brother al-ʿAbbās for 10,000 from one year to the next. Abū Ṭālib spent the money on matters relating to watering the pilgrims, and when the next year arrived he had nothing left. So he asked his brother for a loan of 14,000 to the following year, at which time, he promised, he would repay the total debt. But al-ʿAbbās agreed only on condition that if Abū Ṭālib did not repay it, control of the well would transfer to himself. To this Abū Ṭālib agreed.

When the next year arrived Abū Ṭālib had nothing to give to al-ʿAbbās and so he relinquished control of the well to him. Thereafter it went to ʿAbd Allāh, al-ʿAbbās' son, then to ʿAlī b. ʿAbd Allāh b. ʿAbbās, to Dāwūd b. ʿAlī, to Sulaymān b. ʿAlī and to ʿĪsā b. ʿAlī. Then al-Manṣūr took it over and entrusted its control to his *mawlā*, his freed slave, Abū Ruzayn. Al-Umawī gave this account.

An Account of ʿAbd al-Muṭṭalib's vow to sacrifice one of his sons.

Ibn Isḥāq stated, "It is claimed that when ʿAbd al-Muṭṭalib received such opposition from Quraysh over the digging of *zamzam*, he vowed that if ten sons were born to him who grew up and protected him, he would sacrifice one of them for God at the *kaʿba*.

"Eventually he had ten sons grown up whom he knew would give him protection. Their names were al-Ḥārith, al-Zubayr, Ḥajl, Ḍirār, al-Muqawwim, Abū Lahab, al-ʿAbbās, Ḥamza, Abū Ṭālib, and ʿAbd Allāh. He assembled them and told them of his vow and asked them to honour his pledge to God, Almighty and All-glorious is He. They obeyed, and asked him what he wanted them to do. He asked each of them to take an arrow, write his name on it and return to him.

"They did so and he went with them inside the *kaʿba* to the site of their god Hubal where there was the well in which offerings to the *kaʿba* would be placed. There, near Hubal, were seven arrows which they would use for divining a judgement over some matter of consequence, a question of blood-money, kinship, or the like. They would come to Hubal to seek a resolution, accepting whatever they were ordered to do or to refrain from."

The outcome was that when ʿAbd al-Muṭṭalib came to seek judgement with the arrows from Hubal, the one with the name of his son ʿAbd Allāh came forth. He was his youngest boy and the one he loved most, but ʿAbd al-Muṭṭalib took his son ʿAbd Allāh by the hand, drew out his knife, and went up to Isāf and Nāʾila[53] to sacrifice him. At this Quraysh left their meeting-places and asked him what he intended to do. When he replied that he was going to sacrifice ʿAbd Allāh, they, along with ʿAbd Allāh's brothers, said, "By God, do not sacrifice him without seeking forgiveness for him; if you do this men will keep bringing their sons to sacrifice and how could that go on?"

Yūnus b. Bukayr related from Ibn Isḥāq that al-ʿAbbās was the one who drew ʿAbd Allāh out from beneath his father's foot when he had placed it on him to sacrifice him. And it is said that he scarred his face so badly that it remained visible there till he died.

Thereafter Quraysh advised that ʿAbd al-Muṭṭalib should go to the Hijāz where there was a woman diviner who had an attendant spirit, and that he should consult her. "That", they said, "is the best you can do. If she then orders you to sacrifice him, do so; but if she tells you to do something that provides you a way out, then accept it."

So they left for Medina, where they found that the diviner whose name was Sajāḥ, as Yunus b. Bukayr reported from Ibn Isḥāq, was at Khaybar. They rode off again and went to her and sought her advice, ʿAbd al-Muṭṭalib telling her of the whole problem regarding him and his son. She told them: "Leave me today, until my attendant spirit comes and I can ask him."

They left her and ʿAbd al-Muṭṭalib prayed to God. Next day they went back to her and she informed them that she had had a message. "How much is the blood-money you prescribe?" she asked. "Ten camels," they told her, that being then the case. "Then go back to your land and present your man as an offering and do the same with ten camels. Then cast arrows to decide between him and them. If the divining arrow points to him then add to the number of camels until your god is satisfied; if it points to the camels, then sacrifice them in his place. That way you will please your god and save your man."

So they went back to Mecca and, when they had agreed to do as she had said, ʿAbd al-Muṭṭalib said prayers to God. Then they offered up ʿAbd Allāh and the ten camels as sacrifice and cast the arrow. It came out against ʿAbd Allāh so they added ten more camels and tried once more. Again it came out against him and they added ten more, then kept on doing so until the camels reached one hundred in number. When they next cast the arrow it came out for the camels. At that point the men of Quraysh told ʿAbd al-Muṭṭalib, who was standing near Hubal praying to God, "It's all over! Your God is pleased, O ʿAbd al-Muṭṭalib." It is

53. Two idols referred to earlier.

claimed that he then replied, "No, not until I cast the arrows three times." So they did cast three times, the arrow always indicating the camels, which were slaughtered and left there for anyone to take without hindrance. And Ibn Hishām reported "And it is said, for any wild beast to take as well."

It is otherwise related that when the number of camels reached 100 the arrow was still against ʿAbd Allāh, so they added another 100, making 200, and the same thing happened. Likewise it did with 300. It was then that the arrow came out against the camels, whereupon ʿAbd al Muṭṭalib slaughtered them. But the first account is the true one. Though God knows best.

Ibn Jarīr related, from Yūnus b. ʿAbd al-Aʿlā, from Ibn Wahb, from Yūnus b. Yazīd, from al-Zuhrī from Qabīṣa b. Dhuʾayb that Ibn ʿAbbās was asked for advice by a woman who had vowed to sacrifice her son at the *kaʿba*. He told her to sacrifice 100 camels instead and related to her the above account about ʿAbd al-Muṭṭalib. She then asked ʿAbd Allāh b. ʿUmar but he gave her no legal decision, simply refraining from doing so. The problem then reached Marwān b. al-Ḥakam, who was the governor of Medina. He said, "Neither of them gave a correct decision." He then ordered the woman to perform whatever acts of charity she could, forbidding her from sacrificing her son and not ordering her to slaughter any camels. And the people accepted Marwān's judgement in the matter. But God knows best.

An Account of ʿAbd al-Muṭṭalib's marriage of his son ʿAbd Allāh to Āmina bint Wahb al-Zuhriyya.

Ibn Isḥāq stated: "ʿAbd al-Muṭṭalib then left, holding his son ʿAbd Allāh by the hand. They passed, it is claimed, a woman of Banū Asad b. ʿAbd al-ʿUzzā b. Quṣayy who was named Umm Qattāl; she was the sister of Waraqa b. Nawfal b. Asad b. ʿAbd al-ʿUzzā b. Quṣayy and had been there at the *kaʿba* . She stared into the face of ʿAbd Allāh and asked him where he was going. 'With my father,' he replied. 'If you will have me now,' she said, 'you can have the like number of camels that were sacrificed for you!' 'But I am with my father, and I may not oppose him or leave him,' he answered."

ʿAbd al-Muṭṭalib took him further on till they reached Wahb b. ʿAbd Manāf b. Zuhra b. Kilāb b. Murra b. Kaʿb b. Luʾayy b. Ghālib b. Fihr who was at that time leader of Banū Zuhra in both age and honour. He agreed to marry to ʿAbd Allāh his daughter Āmina, who was then the woman most highly regarded among his people.

It is claimed that ʿAbd Allāh consummated the marriage then and there, and that she conceived the Messenger of God (ṢAAS). Afterwards he left her and passed again by the woman who had made a proposition to him. He asked her,

"How come you're not making me the offer today you did yesterday?" She replied, "The light you bore yesterday has left you, and I need you no more." She had heard from her brother Waraqa b. Nawfal who had become a Christian and studied the Scriptures, that there was to be a prophet come to that nation, and she wanted him to be born to her. So God made him of the finest and most noble lineage, as the Almighty put it, in the Qur'ān, "And God knows best where to place His prophethood" (*sūrat al-Anʿam*, VI, v.124). We will relate the birth itself in detail.

And among the verses spoken by Umm Qattāl expressing her disappointment at her failure to get what she had wanted are the following lines related by al-Bayhaqī from Yūnus b. Bukayr from Muḥammad b. Isḥāq, God be pleased with him:

"And so on to Banū Zuhra, where they were, and to Āmina who bore a boy
She sees *al-Mahdī*, the right-guided, when he mounted her, and a light that had preceded him ahead . . ."

and so on to the lines:

"All creation, all mankind, were hoping for him to lead the people as an Imām, rightly guided.
God shaped him from a light, making it pure, its glow taking the gloom from us.
That is the work of your lord who singled him out, whether he would move ahead one day or stay
He guides the people of Mecca after faithlessness, enjoining thereafter the fast."

Abū Bakr Muḥammad b. Sahl al-Kharā'iṭī said that ʿAlī b. Ḥarb related to him, as did Muḥammad b. ʿUmāra al-Qurashī, as did Muslim b. Khālid al-Zanjī, as did Ibn Jurayj from ʿAṭā' b. Abū Ribāḥ, from Ibn ʿAbbās that the latter said, "When ʿAbd al-Muṭṭalib went off with his son ʿAbd Allāh to arrange his marriage, he passed by a woman diviner of the Tibāla people who had adopted the Jewish faith and read the Scriptures, her name being Fāṭima daughter of Murr al-Khathʿamiyya. She saw the light of prophethood on ʿAbd Allāh's face and said, 'Young man, would you like to have me now and let me give you 100 camels?' ʿAbd Allāh replied with the verse,

'I'd rather die than do the forbidden, and staying here is not allowed, I clearly see.
So how could we do what you desire?'"

Then ʿAbd Allāh passed on with his father who married him to Amīna daughter of Wahb b. ʿAbd Manāf b. Zuhra; and he stayed three nights with her. Then he had an urge to accept the woman's offer so he went to her. "Well, what did you do after (seeing) me?" she asked. And he told her. She then said: "By God, I'm not a woman of doubtful morals; but I did see a light in your face, and I wanted it to be in me. But God refused to put it anywhere other than He wished." Then Fāṭima spoke the following verses:

"I saw a sign shine forth, glistening like raindrops in dark storm clouds,
Which appeared to me as a light illuminating all around it, as the full moon shines forth.
And I hoped to attain it, a source of pride I could capture, but not everyone who strikes his flint lights fire,
For God is what a Zuhriyya woman took, though your two garments are what she seized; but she did not know that."

She also spoke the verses:

"O Banū Hāshim, it came off from your brother to Umayna (Āmina) as they were passionately consummating their marriage,
As the lamp when it dies down leaves behind its wicks, stained with oil,
Not all the wealth a man holds is achieved by resoluteness, nor is what escapes him always from lassitude.
So be moderate in pursuing what you want; good luck and misfortune contending together should suffice you,
Suffice you either a hand tight closed or a hand laid open, fingers stretched.
When Umayna (Āmina) got from him what she had, she received from him an honour, never to come again."

And Imām Abū Nuʿaym, the *ḥāfiẓ*, in his book *Dalāʾil al-Nubuwwa* (*Signs of the Prophethood*), related on a chain from Yaʿqūb b. Muḥammad al-Zuhrī, from ʿAbd al-ʿAzīz b. ʿUmrān, from ʿAbd Allāh b. Jaʿfar, from Ibn ʿAwn, from al-Miswar b. Makhrama, from Ibn ʿAbbās as follows: "ʿAbd al-Muṭṭalib went to Yemen on a winter's journey and stayed with a Jewish high priest. ʿAbd al-Muṭṭalib said, 'And one of the monks – by that he meant a scholar of the Scriptures – said to me, "O ʿAbd al-Muṭṭalib, would you allow me to look at a certain part of you?" "Yes, if it be nothing shameful," I replied. Then the man opened up one of my nostrils and looked inside it, and did the same with the other one, saying, "I swear that in one of your hands you will have power and in the other prophethood. But we find that to be in the Banū Zuhra, so how can that be?" I replied that I did not know. The man then asked, "Do you have a *shāʿa*?" I asked him what he meant by this word *shāʿa* and he replied, a wife. I replied that I did not at that time and he said, "Well, when you go back marry someone from them (i.e. Banū Zuhra)."'

"So when ʿAbd al-Muṭṭalib did return home he married Hāla, daughter of Wahb b. ʿAbd Manāf b. Zuhra, and she gave birth to Ḥamza and Ṣafiyya. Then ʿAbd Allāh son of ʿAbd al-Muṭṭalib married Āmina daughter of Wahb and she gave birth to the Messenger of God (ṢAAS).

"When ʿAbd Allāh married Amīna, the men of Quraysh commented, 'He won out', i.e. ʿAbd Allāh beat out or defeated his father ʿAbd al-Muṭṭalib."

THE BOOK OF THE LIFE OF THE MESSENGER OF GOD (ṢAAS).

An Account of his life story, his battles and raids, the delegations to him, and his natural qualities, his virtues, and the features distinguishing him.

CHAPTER: AN ACCOUNT OF HIS NOBLE ANCESTRY AND THE EXCELLENCE OF HIS HIGH LINEAGE.

God Almighty's words were: "God knows best where to place His prophethood" (*sūrat al-Anʿām*, VI, v.124).

When Heraclius, the Roman emperor, asked Abū Sufyān questions relating to the qualities of the Prophet (ṢAAS), he wanted to know how good his lineage was in his people. Abū Sufyān replied, "He does indeed have good lineage in us." Heraclius commented, "Thus are the messengers given their missions within the ancestry of their own people." He meant from among peoples with the highest reputation and the most numerous tribal connections. May God's blessing be upon them all.

He was the best of Adam's sons, their pride on earth and the hereafter. He was known as the father of al-Qāsim and of Ibrāhīm, as Muḥammad, as Aḥmad, as *al-Māḥī*, "the Abolisher", the one by whom disbelief was abolished, as *al-ʿĀqib*, "the Ultimate" after whom no prophet would follow, as *al-Ḥāshir*, "the Gatherer", i.e. he at whose feet the people would gather, as *al-Muqaffī*, "the Tracker", as *nabī al-Raḥma*, "the Prophet of Mercy", as *nabī al-Tawba*, "the Prophet of Repentance", as *nabī al-Malḥama*, "the Prophet of the Fierce Battle", as *khātim al-nabīyyīn*, "the Seal of the Prophets", as *al-fātiḥ*, "the Conqueror", as *Ṭāhā*, as *Yāsīn*, and as *ʿAbd Allāh*, "God's Servant".

According to al-Bayhaqī some authorities added more names to these. He said, "In the Qurʾān, God named him *rasūl*, 'messenger', *nabī*, 'prophet', *ummī*, 'unlettered', *shāhid*, 'witness-giver', *mubashshir*, 'bringer of good tidings', *nadhīr*, 'admonisher', *dāʿī ilā Allāh bi idhnihi*, 'he who calls to God with His permission', *sirāj munīr*, 'illuminating lamp', *raʾūf raḥīm*, 'kind and compassionate', and *mudhakkir*, 'reminder'. And God made him mercy, a blessing, and a guide."

We will give the accounts relating to the names attributed to him (ṢAAS) in a chapter we will include after the completion of the biography. For on this subject many traditions have come down, responsibility for gathering them having been assumed by two of the great *ḥuffāẓ* Abū Bakr al-Bayhaqī and Abū al-Qāsim b. ʿAsākir. Some people have written works specifically on these names, some going so far as to gather as many as 1,000. But the great legal scholar Abū Bakr b. al-ʿArabī al-Mālikī, who interpreted the words of al-Tirmidhī in his book *ʿĀriḍat al-Aḥwadhī* (*The Expert's Clear Review*), gives 64 such names. But God knows best.

He was the son of ʿAbd Allāh who was in turn the youngest son of his father ʿAbd al-Muṭṭalib; ʿAbd Allāh was the man who lay down to be sacrificed but was ransomed by 100 camels, as previously explained.

Al-Zuhrī said, "And ʿAbd Allāh was the most handsome man in Quraysh. He was brother to al-Ḥārith, al-Zubayr, Ḥamza, Ḍarār, Abū Ṭālib, whose own given name was ʿAbd Manāf, Abū Lahab, whose given name was ʿAbd al-ʿUzzā, al-Muqawwim, whose given name was ʿAbd al-Kaʿba, though some say these were two men, Ḥajl, whose given name was al-Mughīra, al-Ghaydāq, a man of great generosity whose given name was Nawfal, though some say that was Ḥajl. These, then, were the paternal uncles of the Prophet (ṢAAS).

"His aunts numbered six; they were Arwā, Barra, Umayma, Ṣafiyya, ʿĀtika, and Umm Hakīm, she being al-Bayḍā', 'the white woman'. We will talk of all of these later, if God wills it.

"All of these were children of ʿAbd al-Muṭṭalib, whose own name was Shayba, 'grey', so known because of his grey hair; alternatively his name Shayba, meant 'the one praised for his generosity'. However, he was known as ʿAbd al-Muṭṭalib because when his father Hāshim had passed through Medina on a trading mission to Syria, he had stayed at the house of ʿAmr b. Zayd b. Labīd b. Ḥarām b. Khidāsh b. Khindaf b. ʿAdī b. al-Najjār al-Khazrajī al-Najjārī who was the leader of his tribe. Hāshim was much taken with ʿAmr's daughter Salmā and asked her father to engage her in marriage. He did so but on condition that she should remain there with him. Some say that the condition was that she should only give birth there with him in Medina. When Hāshim returned from Syria he consummated marriage with her and took her with him to Mecca. When he next went away on business she was pregnant and he took her with him, leaving her in Medina. Hāshim then went off to Syria but died at Ghazza . When Salmā gave birth to her child she named him Shayba. He remained there with his maternal uncles of the Banū ʿAdī b. al-Najjār for seven years.

"Then his uncle al-Muṭṭalib b. ʿAbd Manāf came and secretly took him away from his mother and returned with him to Mecca. When people there saw them both on his mount they asked him who the boy was and he replied, 'My *ʿAbd*, my servant!' Then they all came up and welcomed the boy, addressing him consequently as ʿAbd al-Muṭṭalib, i.e. al-Muṭṭalib's servant, and the name stuck to him.

"He rose to a great position of leadership among Quraysh, becoming their most honoured chief. They united behind him and in him rested the rights of *al-saqāya* and *al-rifāda*,[54] as had been the case with al-Muṭṭalib. It was al-Muṭṭalib who dug out the well *zamzam*, which had been covered up since the Jurhum era. He was the first to decorate the *kaʿba* with gold, overlaying its doors with those two golden gazelles he found in *zamzam* along with the two white-metal swords."

According to Ibn Hishām, ʿAbd al-Muṭṭalib was brother to Asad, Naḍla, Abū Ṣayfī, Ḥayya, Khālida, Ruqayya, al-Shaffāʾ and Daʿīfa. All these were children of Hāshim. His real name was ʿAmr, but he was called Hāshim, i.e. "the crusher", because he would crush bread with meat and broth for his people during years of famine, as Maṭrūd b. Kaʿb al-Khuzāʿī said in his ode; the poem is alternatively attributed to al-Zabaʿrā Wālid ʿAbd Allāh. The verses are:

> "ʿAmr is he who crushed the bread and meat for his people, the people of Mecca suffering drought and hunger.
>
> He received charge of both expeditions, the winter caravan and that of the summers."

This related to his having been the first to institute the two expeditions, of winter and of summer; he was the oldest of his father's children. Ibn Jarīr related that he was the twin brother of ʿAbd Shams, and that Hāshim came forth with his leg attached to his twin brother's head, which was only separated after blood had flowed between them. People said that that signified wars between their progeny; and so there occurred the confrontation between Banū al-ʿAbbās and Banū Umayya b. ʿAbd Shams in the year 133 AH.

Their third brother, al-Muṭṭalib, was his father's youngest boy; their mother was ʿĀtika, daughter of Murra, son of Hilāl.

The fourth of the siblings was Nawfal, born to another mother named Wāqida daughter of ʿAmr of the tribe of Māzin. These brothers ruled their people after their father; they were known as *al-mujīrūn*, "the protectors". That is because they negotiated safe conduct for their people of Quraysh with the kings of the neighbouring lands so that they could enter them for trading. Hāshim won safe passage from the rulers of Syria, Byzantium, and Ghassān; ʿAbd Shams won the same from the Great Negus, the emperor of Abyssinia; Nawfal gained it for them from the Chosroes, while al-Muṭṭalib received it from the kings of Ḥimyar.

It was of them that a poet composed the lines,

> "O you, man, changing your luggage, have you not dismounted at the family of ʿAbd Manāf?"

54. The provision of water and food to the pilgrims.

Hāshim enjoyed the rights of feeding and watering the pilgrims following his father, and it is to him as well as to his brother al-Muṭṭalib, that his kinsfolk claimed relationship. The two men were as one during both the pre- and post-Islamic periods, never differing. They (and their progeny) all together constituted one multi-sided tribe. But the progeny of their brothers ʿAbd Shams and Nawfal separated out. That is why Abū Ṭālib stated in his ode:

> "God requited us Abd Shams and Nawfal as a punishment for evil, immediate, not delayed."

No family from one father is known who were so far removed from one another in their deaths as they were. Hāshim died in Ghazza in Syria, ʿAbd Shams died in Mecca, Nawfal in Salmān in Iraq, while al-Muṭṭalib, known as "the moon" for his fine looks, died in Radman on the way to Yemen. These, then are the four famous brothers, Hāshim, ʿAbd Shams, Nawfal, and al-Muṭṭalib.

They did have a fifth brother who was not famous. He was known as Abū ʿAmr, his own name being ʿAbd, from the name ʿAbd Quṣayy. People called him ʿAbd b. Quṣayy; he died childless. This is what al-Zubayr b. Bakkār and others said. They also had six sisters whose names were Tamāḍur, Ḥayya, Rīṭa, Qilāba, Umm al-Akhtham, and Umm Sufyān.

All these, then, were children of ʿAbd Manāf. Manāf was the name of an idol, and the original name of ʿAbd Manāf was "al-Mughīra". He took the leadership during his father's time, and his nobility was unexcelled. He was the brother of ʿAbd al-Dār who was his father's eldest son. To him he delegated various appointments, as told above. There were also ʿAbd al-ʿUzzā, ʿAbd, Barra, and Takhmur, the mother of them all being Ḥubbā, daughter of Ḥulayl b. Ḥubshiyya b. Salūl b. Kaʿb b. ʿAmr the Khuzāʿī. Her father was the last of the kings of Khuzāʿa who were the guardians of the *kaʿba*. All were descendants of Quṣayy, whose given name was Zayd. He was known as Quṣayy because his mother had married Rabīʿa b. Ḥarām b. ʿUdhra after his father; Rabīʿa travelled with her to his own land while her son was still young, and Quṣayy was so named because of this, i.e. "little stranger". He later, when fully grown, returned to Mecca and united Quraysh into one, having gathered them together from all parts of the land. He removed Khuzāʿa's power from the House (the *kaʿba*) and expelled them from Mecca, thus restoring what was right. He became absolute ruler over Quraysh and controlled the feeding and watering of the pilgrims, systems he established, along with the *sadāna*, *the ḥijāba*, and *al-liwā*.[55] And his house was where public meetings were held, all of which is explained above. It is due to this that a poet spoke the line:

55. These offices referred, respectively, to the keeper of the *kaʿba*, the chamberlain, and the hoisting of the banner.

"Quṣayy, by my life, was known as a 'gatherer together'; through him God gathered up all the tribes of Fihr."

He was the brother of Zuhra, both being sons of Kilāb, who was the brother of Taym and of Yaqẓa Abū Makhzūm. All three were sons of Murra, who was the brother of ʿAdī and Huṣayṣ.

All of these were progeny of Kaʿb. It was he who used to address his people each Friday and announce to them the glad tidings of the coming of the Messenger of God (ṢAAS), reciting poetry to that effect as we have given above. Kaʿb was brother to ʿĀmir, Sāma, Khuzayma, Saʿd, al-Ḥārith, and ʿAwf, the seven being sons of Luʾayy, brother of Taym al-Adram. These latter two were sons of Ghālib, brother of al-Ḥārith and Muḥārib. These three were sons of Fihr who was the brother of al-Ḥārith, both of them being sons of Mālik. He was the brother of al-Ṣalt and Yakhlud, who were sons of al-Naḍr who was given due credit for bringing Quraysh together into the right way, as we have shown heretofore. He was the brother of Mālik, Malkān, ʿAbd Manāt, and others. All these were born to Kināna, brother of Asad, Asada, and al-Hawn, sons of Khuzayma who was brother to Hudhayl. These two were sons of Mudrika, whose name was ʿAmr who was brother to Ṭābikha whose name was ʿĀmir, and to Qamaʿa. These three were sons of Ilyās; his brother was ʿAylān who fathered all of Qays. These two were sons of Muḍar, brother of Rabīʿa. These two men were known as *al-Sarīḥān*, the candid ones, of the line of Ishmael; they had brothers named Anmār and Iyād who went to Yemen. These four were sons of Nizār, brother of Quḍāʿa, according, that is, to a group of those who consider Quḍāʿa to have been Ḥijāzī and ʿAdnānī in line, as we have explained above. These last two, Nizār and Quḍāʿa, were sons of Maʿad b. ʿAdnān.

This genealogy, described as above, is without dispute among scholars. All the tribes of the Arabs of Ḥijāz combine in this line of descent. That is why Ibn ʿAbbās and others comment on the Qurʾanic verse, "Say, I shall not ask of you all any other reward than that of love for those related" (*sūrat al-Shūrā*, XLII, v.23) by implying that there was not a single subtribe of Quraysh devoid of linear connection with the Messenger of God (ṢAAS).

Ibn ʿAbbās, God be pleased with him, was correct and conservative in saying as he did. Namely, that all the ʿAdnān Arab tribes relate to him through their fathers' lines and many through their mothers' lines as well, as Muḥammad b. Isḥāq and others showed through their tracing of all his mothers and of those of the rest back through their maternal lines at great length.

Ibn Isḥāq, God have mercy on him, and the *ḥāfiẓ* Ibn ʿAsākir recorded all this.

In our comments above on the biography of ʿAdnān we gave details of his descent and matters relating thereto. He was very definitely of Ishmael's line, though there is some variance in the number of generations between them, as is shown in accounts we explained above. But God knows best.

We also reported the rest of the genealogy back from ʿAdnān to Adam, along with the ode of Abū al-ʿAbbās al-Nāshiʾ incorporating that material. All this was in the material relating to the Arabs of Hijāz, our thanks be to God.

The Imām Abū Jaʿfar b. Jarīr, God have mercy on him, gave a very useful, succinct, and accurate account of that in the opening part of his history.

We have one *ḥadīth* relating to his descent from ʿAdnān actually spoken when he was on the *minbar*, the pulpit, but God knows how authentic it is. The *ḥāfiẓ* Abū Bakr al-Bayhaqī said that Abū al-Ḥasan ʿAlī b. Aḥmad b. ʿUmar b. Ḥafṣ, the reciter in Baghdad, informed him that Abū ʿĪsā Bakkār b. Aḥmad b. Bakkār related to him, as did Abū Jaʿfar Aḥmad b. Mūsā b. Saʿd in a transcription dated 296, quoting Abū Jaʿfar Muḥammad b. Abān al-Qalānisī, quoting Abū Muḥammad ʿAbd Allāh b. Muḥammad b. Rabīʿa al-Qaddāmī, quoting Mālik b. Anas, from al-Zuhrī, from Anas, and from Abū Bakr b. ʿAbd al-Raḥmān b. al-Ḥārith b. Hishām as follows: "It reached the Prophet (ṢAAS) that some men of Kinda were claiming relationship to him, so he stated, 'Al-ʿAbbās and Abū Sufyān b. Ḥarb would say that only to make us look bad; we will never deny our forefathers. We are Banū al-Naḍr b. Kināna.'"

The account states that the Prophet gave an address as follows: "I am Muḥammad son of ʿAbd ʿAllāh b. ʿAbd al-Muṭṭalib b. Hāshim b. ʿAbd Manāf b. Quṣayy b. Kilāb b. Murra b. Kaʿb b. Luʾayy b. Ghālib b. Fihr b. Mālik b. al-Naḍr b. Kināna b. Khuzayma b. Mudrika b. Ilyās b. Muḍar b. Nizār. And whenever people divided off into two groups God placed me in the better. I was born from my two parents and was tainted by none of the debauchery of the era before Islam. I was the product of true marriage, not fornication, right down from Adam to my father and my mother. I am the best of you in spirit and the best of you in parentage."

This tradition is a very strange one from Mālik. Al-Qaddāmī alone transmits it, and he is a weak authority. Nevertheless we will give several testimonies in support of it from other sources.

Regarding his having said, as above, "I was the product of true marriage, not fornication", ʿAbd al-Razzāq stated that Ibn ʿUyayna informed him, from Jaʿfar b. Muḥammad, that his father Abū Jaʿfar al-Bāqir making reference to the Qurʾanic verse, "A messenger has come to you from yourselves" (*sūrat al-Tawba*, IX, v.128) said that, "He was not tainted at all by his birth during the *jāhiliyya*, the pre-Islamic era"; and the Messenger of God (ṢAAS) said, "I was the product of true marriage, not fornication." This tradition is very incomplete in its transmission.

The same was related by al-Bayhaqī from al-Ḥākim, from al-Aṣamm, from Muḥammad b. Isḥāq al-Ṣanʿānī, from Yaḥyā b. Abū Bukayr, from ʿAbd al-Ghaffār b. al-Qāsim, from Jaʿfar b. Muḥammad, from his father, that the Messenger of God (ṢAAS) said, "God produced me from a true marriage, not from fornication."

Ibn ʿAdī related it with a complete transmission chain as follows, "Aḥmad b. Ḥafṣ related to us, as did Muḥammad b. Abū ʿAmr al-ʿAdanī al-Makkī, as did Muḥammad b. Jaʿfar b. Muḥammad b. ʿAlī b. al-Ḥusayn, saying, 'My father testified to me, on the authority of his father and his grandfather, as having heard from ʿAlī b. Abū Ṭālib that the Prophet (ṢAAS) said, "I was the product of true marriage, not fornication, from Adam right on up to when my father and mother had me. And I was not at all tainted by the fornication of the *jāhiliyya*."'"

This is a strange tradition from this line of transmission and can scarcely be credited.

Hushaym said, "Al-Madīnī related to me, from Abū al-Ḥuwayrith, from Ibn ʿAbbās, that the Messenger of God (ṢAAS) said, 'Nothing of the fornication of the *jāhiliyya* was born in me; I was born from nothing but a true marriage, just like the true marriage of Islam.'"

This too is strange. The *ḥāfiẓ* Ibn ʿAsākir passed it on, then substantiated it by a tradition of Abū Hurayra, and there is weakness in its transmission from him. But God knows best.

Muḥammad b. Saʿd said, "Muḥammad b. ʿUmar informed us, quoting Muḥammad b. ʿAbd Allāh b. Muslim, from his uncle al-Zuhrī, from ʿUrwa, from ʿĀʾisha who said that the Messenger of God (ṢAAS) said, 'I was born from a true marriage, not fornication.'"

Moreover Ibn ʿAsākir passed down from a tradition of Abū ʿĀṣim, from Shabīb, from ʿIkrima, from Ibn ʿAbbās who with reference to the Qurʾanic verse "your ever-changing presence among those who prostrate in prayer" (*sūrat al-Shuʿarāʾ*, XXVI, v.219) quoted the Prophet as saying, "from prophet to prophet until I was brought forth as a prophet." He related this on the authority of ʿAṭāʾ.

Muḥammad b. Saʿd said, "Hishām b. Muḥammad al-Kalbī informed us, from his father who said, 'I wrote out some 500 maternal ancestors for the Prophet (ṢAAS) and found fornication in not one of them, nor anything relating to (the evil ways) of the *jāhiliyya*.'"

It is established in the *ṣaḥīḥ* collection of al-Bukhārī from a *ḥadīth* of ʿAmr b. Abū ʿAmr from Saʿīd al-Maqbirī, from Abū Hurayra who said, "The Messenger of God (ṢAAS) stated, 'I was sent on through the best of generations of humankind, age after age, until I received my mission in the century in which I lived.'"

In the *ṣaḥīḥ* of Muslim, from a tradition of al-Awzāʿī from Shaddād Abū ʿAmmār, from Wāthila b. al-Asqaʿ, comes the statement of the Messenger of God (ṢAAS): "God chose Ishmael from the children of Abraham, Banū Kināna from the tribe of Ishmael, Quraysh from the tribe of Kināna, Banū Hāshim from Quraysh, and myself from Banū Hāshim."

The Imām Aḥmad (Ibn Hanbal) stated that Abū Nuʿaym related to him, from Sufyān, from Yazīd b. Abū Ziyād, from ʿAbd Allāh b. al-Ḥārith b. Nawfal, from al-Muṭṭalib b. Abū Wadāʿa, who said that Al-ʿAbbās stated, "Certain things the people were saying reached the Prophet (ṢAAS) so he mounted the pulpit and asked, 'Who am I?' They replied, 'You are the Messenger of God.' He replied, 'I am Muḥammad b. ʿAbd Allāh b. ʿAbd al-Muṭṭalib; God devised creation and made me part of his best creatures. He made them all into two groups, placing me in the better of them. He created the tribes and placed me in the best one, subdivided them into *buyūt* (clans) and placed me in the best one. And so I am the best of you both in clan and in spirit.'" May God's grace and blessings be upon him always and forever till Judgement Day!

Yaʿqūb b. Sufyān said that ʿUbayd Allāh b. Mūsā related to him, from Ismāʿīl b. Abū Khālid, from Yazīd b. Abū Ziyād, from ʿAbd Allāh b. al-Ḥārith b. Nawfal, from al-ʿAbbās b. ʿAbd al-Muṭṭalib, who said, "I once said, 'O Messenger of God, when Quraysh meet one another they do so joyfully, but when they meet us it is as if we don't know them.' The Messenger of God (ṢAAS) became extremely angry when he heard that and said, 'By Him in whose hand is the soul of Muḥammad, faith will never enter the heart of any man until he loves you all for the sake of God and his Messenger.'

"I commented, 'O Messenger of God, Quraysh sat recalling their lines of genealogy and you they compared to a date palm in a hole in the ground.'

"The Messenger of God (ṢAAS) responded, 'On the day when God created man he placed me among the best of them. Then when He divided them into tribes He placed me in the best one. And when He made the *buyūt*, clans, he placed me in the best one. And so I am the best of them in spirit and the best in clan.'"

Abū Bakr b. Abū Shayba related it from Ibn Fuḍayl from Yazīd b. Abū Ziyād, from ʿAbd Allāh b. al-Ḥārith, from Rabīʿa b. al-Ḥārith who said, "(The comment) reached the Prophet (ṢAAS) and he responded to it as above." But he (i.e. Rabīʿa b. al-Ḥārith) made no mention of al-ʿAbbās.

Yaʿqūb b. Sufyān said that Yaḥyā b. ʿAbd al-Ḥamīd related to him, as did Qays b. ʿAbd Allāh, from al-Aʿmash, from ʿAlīla b. Rubʿī from Ibn ʿAbbās, who said: "The Messenger of God (ṢAAS) stated, 'God divided creation into two parts and placed me in the better of them. This relates to His words (in the Qurʾān) "and those of the right" and "those of the left". And I am of those of the right, indeed the best one of them. God then split these two parts into thirds placing me in the best third. This relates to His words "those of *al-maymana*" (the right wing) and to "*al-sābiqūn, al-sābiqūn*" (those in the forefront). I am one of those in the forefront; indeed I am the best of them.

"'Then He made those thirds into tribes and placed me in the best of them. That relates to His words, "We made you into peoples and tribes so that you would know one another; the most noble of you in God's sight are the most pious. God is indeed knowing, informed" (*sūrat al-Ḥujurāt*, XLIX, v.13). And I am the most pious of Adam's sons and the most noble of them with God. Without boast.

"'God then made the tribes into *buyūt*, clans, and placed me in the best of them. This relates to God's words. "God wants only to remove from you what is unclear, O people of the house, purifying you thoroughly" (*sūrat al-Aḥzāb*, XXXIII, v.33). And I and the people of my house are purified of sin.'"

This *ḥadīth* is somewhat strange and objectionable.

Al-Ḥākim and al-Bayhaqī related from a *ḥadīth* from Muḥammad b. Dhakwān, the uncle of the son of Ḥamād b. Zayd, from ʿAmr b. Dīnār, from Ibn ʿUmar who said, "We were sitting in the courtyard of the Prophet (ṢAAS) when a woman passed by. Someone said, 'That's the daughter of the Messenger of God (ṢAAS)!' Abū Sufyān then commented, 'Muḥammad's presence in Banū Hāshim is like a sweet basil plant amidst rotten garbage!' The woman hurried off and informed the Prophet (ṢAAS).

"Soon the Messenger of God (ṢAAS) arrived, his face showing his anger. He said, 'What's the meaning of certain statements reaching me about people? God created all seven heavens and chose the highest for whomsoever of his creatures he wished to dwell there. Then he created all living things and chose from them mankind. From mankind he chose the Arabs and from them Muḍar. From Muḍar he chose Quraysh and from them the Banū Hāshim. From Banū Hāshim he chose me. I am the choicest of the chosen; so whoever loves the Arabs, it is through loving me that he loves them. Whoever hates the Arabs, it is through hating me that he hates them.'"

This too is a strange *ḥadīth*.

It is established in the *ṣaḥiḥ* collection of al-Bukhārī that the Messenger of God (ṢAAS) said, "I am (to be) lord of Adam's sons on Judgement Day, without boasting."

Al-Ḥākim and al-Bayhaqī recounted from a *ḥadīth* of Mūsā b. ʿUbayda that ʿAmr b. ʿAbd Allāh b. Nawfal related to him from al-Zuhrī, from Abū ʿUsāma or Abū Salama, from ʿĀʾisha, God bless her, who said that the Messenger of God (ṢAAS) stated, "Gabriel said to me, 'I searched the earth from east to west but found no man superior to Muḥammad; and I searched the earth from east to west but found no tribe superior to the Banū Hāshim.'"

The *ḥāfiẓ* al-Bayhaqī said, "These traditions, even though the transmitters of some are unreliable, do substantiate one another. And the message of all does relate back to the *ḥadīth* of Wāthila b. al-Asqaʿ. But God knows best."

On this subject Abū Ṭālib spoke the following verses in praise of the Prophet (ṢAAS):

"Were Quraysh to gather one day to boast, ʿAbd Manāf would be their heart and core,
And if the chiefs of ʿAbd Manāf were assessed, their most noble and ancient of line would be from Hāshim,
Were they to boast one day, then Muḥammad would be the one chosen from their inmost, and their pride.
Quraysh, all and sundry of them, plotted against us, but they did not succeed and were confounded;
Since ancient days we reject injustice and if others turned away in contempt we set them straight.
Each day we protect their sanctuary from evil, repelling from their refuges all seeking them;
By us the dried-out branches are revived, their roots becoming moist and growing under our protection."

Abū al-Sakn Zakariyyāʾ b. Yaḥyā al-Ṭāʾī said in the famous anecdote ascribed to him: "ʿUmar b. Abū Zuḥr b. Ḥaṣīn said, on the authority of his grandfather Ḥamīd b. Munhib, that his grandfather Khuraym b. Aws stated, 'I went away to join the Messenger of God (ṢAAS) and came to him at his camp at Tabūk. I had become a Muslim. I heard al-ʿAbbās b. ʿAbd al-Muṭṭalib say, "Oh Messenger of God, I would like to speak verses in your praise." The Messenger of God (ṢAAS) replied, "Speak on and may God not block your tongue." So he recited,

"Before this you were pleasantly in the shade (of paradise) in a place where leaves clustered above.
Then you came down to this land; no human you, no embryo, no clot.
A droplet, rather, riding (Noah's) vessel, the deep having bridled an eagle and his family.
Being carried from loins to womb, one world passing, another surface appearing,
Until your supreme house encompassed Khindaf[56] so lofty (in honour), beneath her all other beings.
When you were born the earth glowed, the horizon shining with your light.
So we are in that illumination and that light, making our way upon the paths of righteousness."'"

This poem has been ascribed to Ḥassān b. Thābit.

The *ḥāfiẓ* Abū al-Qāsim b. ʿAsākir recounted in a line of transmission from Abū al-Ḥasan b. Abū Ḥadīd as follows that Muḥammad b. Abū Naṣr informed him, ʿAbd al-Salām b. Muḥammad b. Aḥmad al-Qurashī told him, Abū Ḥaṣīn Muḥammad b. Ismāʿīl b. Muḥammad al-Tamīmī related to him, as did Muḥammad b. ʿAbd Allāh al-Zāhid al-Khurāsānī, as did Isḥāq b. Ibrāhīm b. Sinān, as did Sallām b. Sulayman Abū al-ʿAbbās al-Makfūf al-Madāʾinī, as did

56. Khindaf was the wife of Ilyās, mother of Mudrika, referred to earlier in the lineage from which the Prophet descended.

Warqāʾ b. ʿUmar, from Ibn Abū Nājīḥ from ʿAṭāʾ and Mujāhid from Ibn ʿAbbās who said, "I posed the following question to the Messenger of God (ṢAAS), 'Where were you, may my parents be your ransom, when Adam was still in paradise?' He replied, smiling so broadly all his teeth could be seen, 'I was in his loins. Then the vessel carried me into the loins of my father Noah, who cast me out into the loins of my father Abraham. My parents never once engaged in fornication. God went on transporting me from respectable loins to chaste wombs, pure and unsullied, and whenever a line split I was always in the better half. God has covenanted prophethood in me and made Islam my pact. He made mention of me in the Torah and in the Bible. All the prophets made clear my qualities; the earth brightens with my light and the dark clouds with my face. He taught me His Book and gave me honour in His heaven. He cut off for me one of His own names; the enthroned One is Maḥmūd, while I am Muḥammad and Aḥmad. He promised me that He would reward me with a garden and with *al-kawthar*, the river of paradise, that He would make me the first intercessor and the first for whom there was intercession. He drew me forth, moreover, out of the best marriage for my people, and they are those who give much praise, enjoin good deeds and prohibit sin.'"

Ibn ʿAbbās stated, "Ḥassān b. Thābit spoke the following verses about the Prophet (ṢAAS):

> 'Before this you were pleasantly in the shade, and in a place where the leaves are plaited together,
> Then you dwelt in this land; no human you, no embryo, no clot,
> Purified, riding the vessel, the deep flood having bridled an eagle and his family,
> You were carried from loin to womb; whenever one surface passed, another appeared.'

"So the Prophet (ṢAAS) said, 'May God have mercy on Ḥassān!' And ʿAlī b. Abū Ṭālib commented, 'Ḥassān deserves paradise, by the Lord of the *kaʿba*!'"

The *ḥāfiẓ* Ibn ʿAsākir then stated: "This tradition is very strange!"

And I say, it is highly objectionable. And it is well established that these verses are by al-ʿAbbās, God be pleased with him. They were, moreover, passed on from a tradition of Abū al-Sakn Zakariyyāʾ b. Yaḥyā al-Ṭāʾī, as above.

I also comment that some claim that the verses are of al-ʿAbbās b. Mardās al-Salamī. But God knows best.

An observation: The *qāḍī* ʿIyād stated in his book *al-Shifāʾ* (*Healing*): "Regarding the name 'Aḥmad' mentioned in the (holy) Books and of whom the prophets gave glad tidings, God in His wisdom prevented anyone to be named by it before Him, so that no confusion or doubt should descend on those weak of heart."

Similarly with "Muḥammad" as well; none of the Arabs or any other people was named by it until shortly before his birth word was spread that a prophet would be sent whose name would be "Muḥammad". And so a small Arab group did give their sons that name hoping that one of them would be he. But God knows best where to place His message.

These were "Muḥammad" b. Uḥayḥa b. al-Julāḥ al-Awsī, "Muḥammad" b. Maslama al-Anṣārī, "Muḥammad" b. Barrāʾ al-Bakrī, "Muḥammad" b. Sufyān b. Mujāshiʿ, "Muḥammad" b. Ḥumrān al-Juʿfī, and "Muḥammad" b. Khūzaʿī al-Sulmī; no seventh person was so named.

It is said that the first person named "Muḥammad" was Muḥammad b. Sufyān b. Mujāshiʿ; in Yemen they say, however, that it was "Muḥammad" b. al-Yaḥmud of Azd.

Moreover, God protected those so named from claiming the prophethood or others from claiming it for them. Not one of them showed any manifestation that would cause anyone to suspect of such, until the two signs were realized in him (ṢAAS) "signs that could not be denied", that being His expression.

CHAPTER ON THE BIRTH OF THE MESSENGER OF GOD (ṢAAS).

He was born on a Monday. This is from what is related by Muslim in his *ṣaḥīḥ* collection, from a *ḥadīth* told by Ghaylān b. Jarīr from ʿAbd Allāh b. Maʿbad al-Zimmānī, from Abū Qatāda to the effect that a bedouin said, "O Messenger of God, what do you say about fasting on Mondays?" He replied, "That is the day I was born, and the day I was first sent revelation."

The Imām Aḥmad said, "Mūsā b. Dāwūd related to us, as did Ibn Lahīʿa, from Khālid b. Abū ʿUmrān, from Ḥanash al-Sanʿānī, from Ibn ʿAbbās who said, 'The Messenger of God (ṢAAS) was born on a Monday. He received the prophethood on a Monday, left Mecca for Medina as an emigrant on a Monday, arrived at Medina on a Monday, died on a Monday, and raised up the stone on a Monday.'"

Only Aḥmad gives the tradition thus, but ʿAmr b. Bukayr related it from Ibn Lahīʿa with an addition of the words, "The Qurʾanic *sūrat al-Māʾida* (Ch. V) was revealed on a Monday, with the words, "This day have I completed for you your religion" (V, v.3).

Some others relate it thus from Mūsā b. Dāwūd with a further addition, "The battle of Badr was on a Monday." Yazīd b. Ḥabīb was one of those who stated this. But it is highly objectionable.

According to Ibn ʿAsākir what is generally accepted is that the battle of Badr and the revelation of "This day have I completed for you your religion" both occurred on a Friday. And Ibn ʿAsākir spoke the truth.

ʿAbd Allāh b. ʿAmr recounted, from Kurayb, from Ibn ʿAbbās who said, "The Messenger of God (ṢAAS) was born and died on a Monday."

Similar reports from different lines of transmission also have Ibn ʿAbbās saying that he was born on a Monday.

This, then, is a matter without dispute, namely that he was born on a Monday. Unlikely, indeed in error, is the view of those who say he was born on Friday, the 17th day, the month of Rabīʿ al-Awwal. This idea was transmitted by the *ḥāfiẓ* Ibn Diḥya from what he had read in the book: *Iʿlām al-Ruwāt bi Aʿlām al-Hudā* (*Informing the Narrators of the Signs of Righteousness*) written by certain Shiʿites. But then Ibn Diḥya proceeded to denigrate this account; and it is appropriate to criticize it since it contradicts authenticated tradition.

Most people believe that the birth occurred in the month of Rabīʿ al-Awwal, and, it is said, on the second day thereof. Ibn ʿAbd al-Barr stated this in his exhaustive study and al-Wāqidī related it from Abū Maʿshar Nujayḥ b. ʿAbd al-Raḥmān al-Madanī.

Some say that it occurred on the 8th of the month. Al-Ḥumaydī related it so from Ibn Ḥazm. Mālik, ʿUqayl, and Yūnis Ibn Yazīd, and others related this from al-Zuhrī, from Muḥammad b. Jubayr b. Muṭʿim.

Ibn ʿAbd al-Barr recounted that the historians had verified this, and the great *ḥāfiẓ* Muḥammad b. Mūsā al-Khawārizmī so determined it. The *ḥāfiẓ* Abū al-Khaṭṭāb b. Diḥya considered it likely in his book: *al-Tanwīr fī Mawlid al-Bashīr al-Nadhīr* (*Enlightenment on the Birth of the Warner and the Bearer of Glad Tidings*).

And it is said, in an account transmitted by Ibn Diḥya in his book, that it occurred on the 10th of the month; Ibn ʿAsākir related this from Abū Jaʿfar al-Bāqir as did Mujālid from al-Shaʿbī, as above.

The birth is also said to have come on the 12th of the month. Ibn Isḥāq states this. Ibn Abū Shayba relates this too in his compilation, on the authority of ʿAffān, from Saʿīd b. Mīnāʾ, from Jābir and from Ibn ʿAbbās, the latter two having stated, "The Messenger of God (ṢAAS) was born in the 'year of the elephant', on Monday the 12th of Rabīʿ al-Awwal. On that same day he received his mission, was carried up to heaven, emigrated from Mecca, and died. And this is what is widely known to most people; but God knows best."

He is also said to have been born on the 17th, as Ibn Diḥya reported from some of the Shīʿa. But also on the 8th, Ibn Diḥya so stating from the writing of the *wazīr*, the government minister, Abū Rāfiʿ, son of the *ḥāfiẓ* Abū Muḥammad b. Ḥazm, from his father. What is correct about the account of Ibn Ḥazm, the first, that it occurred on the 8th, is as al-Ḥumaydī recounted from him; this is best established.

There is a second account, namely that he was born in Ramaḍān. Ibn ʿAbd al-Barr transmitted this from al-Zubayr b. Bakkār. This is a very strange statement. Its basis is the fact that he doubtless received revelation in Ramaḍān, at the beginning of the 40th year of his life. And so his birth should be in Ramaḍān. However, this is debatable. But God knows best.

Khaytham b. Sulaymān, the *ḥāfiẓ*, related from Khalaf b. Muḥammad Kirdaws al-Wāsiṭī, from al-Muʿallā b. ʿAbd al-Raḥmān, from ʿAbd al-Ḥamīd b. Jaʿfar, from al-Zuhrī, from ʿUbayd Allāh b. ʿAbd Allāh, from Ibn ʿAbbās who said, "The Messenger of God (ṢAAS) was born on a Monday in *Rabīʿ al-Awwal* and revelation of his prophethood came down to him on Monday, the first of *Rabīʿ al-Awwal*; also the Qurʾān chapter *al-Baqara* (*The Cow*; II) was revealed on a Monday in Rabīʿ al-Awwal."

This is very strange. It is Ibn ʿAsākir who related it.

Al-Zubayr b. Bakkār stated, "His mother became pregnant with him during *ayyām al-tashrīq*, the celebratory feast days,[57] in the vale of Abū Ṭālib, near *al-jumrat al-wusṭā*, the central stoning pile at Minā. He was born in Mecca in the house known as that of Muḥammad b. Yūsuf, brother of al-Ḥajjāj b. Yūsuf, on the 12th of Ramaḍān."

The *ḥāfiẓ* Ibn ʿAsākir recounted this from a line through Muḥammad b. ʿUthmān b. ʿUqba b. Makram, from al-Musayyab b. Sharīk, from Shuʿayb b. Shuʿayb, from his father, from his grandfather, who said, "The Messenger of God (ṢAAS) was conceived on the day of *ʿĀshūrāʾ*, the 9th or 10th day of Muḥarram, and he was born on Monday, the 12th of Ramaḍān in the 23rd year after the attack on Mecca by the troops with elephants."

Other sources relate that al-Khayzurān, the mother of Hārūn al-Rashīd, when she performed the pilgrimage, ordered the conversion of this house into a mosque. It is known by her name to this day.

Al-Suhaylī gave the date of his birth as the 20th of Nisān, April. This was the most appropriate time and season; and that was in the year 882 of the era of Alexander, according to those who use astronomical almanacs.

And they claim that the ascendant was at twenty degrees from Capricorn, and that Jupiter and Saturn were joined together at a position within three degrees of Scorpio, a position in the middle of the heavens. This was in correspondence with the stages of Aries. The birth occurred as the moon first arose at the beginning of the night. Ibn Diḥya transmitted all this; but God knows best.

According to Ibn Isḥāq, his birth occurred in the year of the elephant.

And this is what is well known to the people at large. Ibrāhīm b. al-Mundhir al-Ḥizāmī said, "And this is something about which our scholars have no doubt, the fact that he was born in the year of the elephant; and that he received his mission as a prophet at the beginning of the 40th year after the attack with elephants."

57. The term was applied to the three days following the Day of Immolation during the Ḥajj festival.

Al-Bayhaqī related this as well from a tradition of Abū Isḥāq al-Sabīʿī, from Saʿīd b. Jubayr from Ibn Abbās who said, "The Messenger of God (ṢAAS) was born in the year of the elephant attack."

Muḥammad b. Isḥāq stated, "Al-Muṭṭalib b. ʿAbd Allāh b. Qays b. Makhrama related, from his father, from his grandfather Qays b. Makhrama, who said, 'The Messenger of God (ṢAAS) and I were born in the year of the elephant attack; our births were contemporaneous.'"

ʿUthmān, may God be pleased with him, asked Qubāth b. Ashyam, brother of Banū Yaʿmur b. Layth, "Were you the greater[58] (in age) or was the Messenger of God (ṢAAS)?" He replied, "The Messenger of God (ṢAAS) was 'greater' than me, but I was earlier in birth. I saw the elephants' droppings when still green and changing (in colour)." Al-Tirmidhī related this, as did al-Ḥākim from a *ḥadīth* of Muḥammad b. Isḥāq.

Ibn Isḥāq stated: "The Messenger of God (ṢAAS) was 20 in the year of *ʿukāẓ*."

He also said, "*Al-fijār*[59] took place 20 years after the elephant attack. The building of the *kaʿba* was done 15 years after *al-fijār*, and the divine mission came about 5 years after its building."

Muḥammad b. Jubayr b. Muṭʿim stated, "Ukāẓ occurred 15 years after the 'elephant' battle, the building of the *kaʿba* 10 years thereafter, and the mission 15 years after that."

The *ḥāfiẓ* al-Bayhaqī related from a tradition of ʿAbd al-ʿAzīz b. Abū Thābit al-Madinī as follows: "Al-Zubayr b. Mūsā related to us on the authority of Abū al-Ḥuwayrith, saying, 'I heard ʿAbd al-Mālik b. Marwān say to Qubāth b. Ashyam al-Kinānī al-Laythī, "O Qubāth, which of you, you or the Messenger of God (ṢAAS) was *akbar*?" He replied, "The Messenger of God (ṢAAS) was *akbar* (i.e. greater) than me, but I was *asann*, older. The Messenger of God (ṢAAS) was born during the year of the elephant attack, but I was aware enough to recall my mother standing with me upon the elephant's dung while it was still changing (in colour). And the Messenger of God (ṢAAS) became a Prophet at the beginning of 40 years thereafter."'"

Yaʿqūb b. Sufyān said, "Yaḥyā b. ʿAbd Allāh b. Bukayr related to us, Nuʿaym, meaning Ibn Maysara, related to us, from certain others, from Suwayd b. Ghafla, that the last-mentioned stated, 'I am contemporary in birth with the Messenger of God (ṢAAS); I was born in the year of the elephant attack.'"

Al-Bayhaqī stated, "It is related from Suwayd b. Ghafla that he said, 'I am younger than the Messenger of God (ṢAAS) by two years.'"

58. The word *akbar* is used which may mean "older" or "greater"; hence the exchanges in the accounts that follow.

59. Battles at ʿUkāẓ between Arab tribes during months when warfare was proscribed.

Ya'qūb said: "And Ibrāhīm b. al-Mundhir related to us, as did 'Abd al-'Azīz b. Abū Thābit, (and) 'Abd Allāh b. 'Uthmān b. Abū Sulaymān al-Nawfalī related to me, from his father, from Muḥammad b. Jubayr b. Muṭ'im, saying, 'The Messenger of God (ṢAAS) was born in the year of the elephant attack, and the Ukāẓ incident occurred 15 years later. The *ka'ba* was built early in the 25th year after the elephant attack, and the Messenger of God (ṢAAS) became a Prophet at the beginning of the 40th year after that attack.'"

The outcome is that the Messenger of God (ṢAAS) was, according to majority opinion, born in the year of the elephant attack. Some say the birth occurred one month after that event, others say 40 days, yet others 50 days, which is the most favoured date.

And according to Abū Ja'far al-Baqīr, the arrival of the elephants was half-way through the month of al-Muḥarram, while the birth of the Messenger of God (ṢAAS) occurred 55 days thereafter.

But others say that, on the contrary, the elephant attack occurred ten years before the birth of the Messenger of God (ṢAAS). Ibn Abzā stated this.

The attack is also said to have occurred 23 years before his birth; this is what Shu'ayb b. Shu'ayb related from his father from his grandfather, as stated above. Alternatively, the birth is said to have come 30 years after the attack; Mūsā b. 'Uqba stated this, from al-Zuhrī, God be pleased with him. And Mūsā b. 'Uqba himself, God be pleased with him also, chose this date.

Abū Zakariyyā' al-'Ijlānī stated that the birth came 40 years after the attack; Ibn 'Asākir recounted this, something very strange.

Even stranger is the statement of Khalīfa b. Khayyāṭ who said, "Shu'ayb b. Ḥibbān related to me, from 'Abd al-Wāḥid son of Abū 'Amr, from al-Kalbī, from Abū Ṣāliḥ, from Ibn 'Abbās as follows: 'The Messenger of God (ṢAAS) was born 15 years before the elephant attack.'" This statement is unique, objectionable, and considered weak as well.

Khalīfa b. Khayyāṭ stated, "The consensus is that he was born, peace be upon him, in the year of the elephants' attack."

A DESCRIPTION OF HIS NOBLE BIRTH (ṢAAS).

It has been told above how 'Abd al-Muṭṭalib sacrificed the 100 camels, God having saved him from fulfilment of his vow to sacrifice his son 'Abd Allāh. This was in accord with what He had decreed of old, that the *nabī al-ummī*, the unlettered Prophet (ṢAAS) the "seal of the prophets", and the lord of all the progeny of Adam would appear. Thereafter, as explained, He arranged the marriage of 'Abd Allāh to the most noble of the women of Quraysh, Āmina, daughter of Wahb b. 'Abd Manāf b. Zuhra al-Zuhriyya. And when the groom took her as his wife and consummated the marriage, she became pregnant with the Messenger of God (ṢAAS).

Umm Qattāl, Raqīqa, daughter of Nawfal, sister of Waraqa b. Nawfal, saw the sign of light appear between ʿAbd Allāh's eyes before he united with Āmina. She wished for it to be transmitted to herself, because of all the tidings she had heard from her brother foretelling the coming of Muḥammad (ṢAAS) and that his time was near; she therefore offered herself to ʿAbd Allāh. Some authorities add "To have him marry her". That does seem most likely. But God knows best. But ʿAbd Allāh resisted her and when that dazzling light had gone to Āmina after he consummated marriage with her, it seems that he regretted not having accepted what Umm Qattāl had offered. And so he approached her to have her repeat her offer. But she now said she had no need of him and was sad at what she had missed. She therefore recited on that subject the fine and eloquent poetry we quoted above. The chaste abstinence of ʿAbd Allāh was not to his own credit but to that of the Messenger of God (ṢAAS); it reflected the words of God Almighty, "God knows best wherein to place His mission" (*sūrat al-Anʿam*, VI, v.124).

The tradition, from a good transmission line, has already been given that the Prophet (ṢAAS) stated, "I was born of marriage, not fornication."

What is intended here is (to say) that after his mother had conceived him his father died and he remained a foetus in his mother's womb, as it is generally understood.

Muḥammad b. Saʿd stated that Muḥammad b. ʿUmar, he being al-Wāqidī, related to him, as did Mūsā b. ʿUbayda al-Yazīdī, as did Saʿīd b. Abū Zayd, from Ayyūb b. ʿAbd al-Rahmān b. Abū Ṣaʿṣaʿa, as follows: "ʿAbd Allāh b. ʿAbd al-Muṭṭalib went off to Ghazza in a Quraysh trading caravan. When they finished their business they left there and passed through Medina. By then ʿAbd Allāh was sick and he asked that he be left there in the company of Banū ʿAdī b. al-Najjār to whom he was related.

"He stayed there with them sick for one month while his friends continued back to Mecca. There ʿAbd al-Muṭṭalib asked them about his son ʿAbd Allāh and they told him of how he was sick and they had left him with his relatives of Banū ʿAdī b. al-Najjār. ʿAbd al-Muṭṭalib sent to him his oldest son al-Ḥārith, but the latter found that ʿAbd Allāh had died and been buried in the house of al-Nābigha. And so al-Ḥārith returned to his father and told him this.

ʿAbd al-Muṭṭalib and his brothers and sisters all grieved terribly at his loss.

The Messenger of God (ṢAAS) was at that time still a foetus; Abd Allāh, son of ʿAbd al-Muṭṭalib, was 25 when he died."

Al-Wāqidī asserted, "This is the most firmly based of the accounts of the death of ʿAbd Allāh and of his age that we have."

Al-Wāqidī also said, "Maʿmar related to me from al-Zuhrī that ʿAbd al-Muṭṭalib sent ʿAbd Allāh to Medina to purchase dates for them but he died."

Muḥammad b. Saʿd said, "Hishām b. Muḥammad b. al-Sāʾib al-Kalbī told us from his father as well as from ʿAwāna b. al-Ḥakam that they had both said that ʿAbd Allāh b. ʿAbd al-Muṭṭalib died after the Messenger of God (ṢAAS) had reached 28 months; and it is also said he was 7 months old."

Muḥammad b. Saʿd stated, "The first account is better established, namely that when he died the Messenger of God (ṢAAS) was still a foetus."

Al-Zubayr b. Bakkār said, "Muḥammad b. Ḥasan related to me, from ʿAbd al-Salām, from Ibn Kharbudh, as follows, ʿAbd Allāh died in Medina when the Messenger of God (ṢAAS) was 2 months old. His mother died when he was 4 years of age, and his grandfather when he was 8. And so he was entrusted to his uncle, Abū Ṭālib."

What al-Wāqidī considered more probable and the *ḥāfiẓ* Muḥammad b. Saʿd wrote, was that when his father died the Messenger of God (ṢAAS) was still a foetus in his mother's womb.

And this is the epitome and highest rank of being an orphan.

In the *ḥadīth* literature occur the words, "and the visions of my mother who saw, as she bore me, a light came forth from her that lit up the castles of Syria."

Muḥammad b. Isḥāq stated that Āmina, daughter of Wahb and mother of the Messenger of God (ṢAAS), used to say that when she became pregnant with the Messenger of God (ṢAAS), a voice told her: "You are pregnant with the lord of this nation; when he drops to the ground (in birth) say the words, 'I invoke for him the protection of the One God, from the evil of all who envy, from everyone committed to his oath and every prowling slave; may a champion protect me, for he is with the All-praised and All-glorious One, until I see him come into view.

"'And the proof of that is a light accompanying him that will fill the castles of Buṣrā in Syria. And at his birth, then call him Muḥammad, for in the Torah his name is "Aḥmad" and the hosts of earth and heaven give him *ḥamd*, praise. In the Gospels his name is "Aḥmad", the hosts of heaven and earth giving him *ḥamd*, praise. And his name in the Qurʾān is "Muḥammad", "the praised one."'"

But these traditions require that she had a vision when she became pregnant with him, that a light was emanating from her by which the castles of Syria were illuminated. And then, when she gave birth to him, she actually saw by her eyes a realization of that, just as she had seen beforehand, as told here. But God knows best.

Muḥammad b. Saʿd stated that Muḥammad b. ʿUmar, he being al-Wāqidī, informed him that Muḥammad b. ʿAbd Allāh b. Muslim related to him, from al-Zuhrī, what follows. Al-Wāqidī also stated that Mūsā b. ʿAbda related to him the following, from his brother and Muḥammad b. Kaʿb al-Quraẓī; as did ʿAbd Allāh b. Jaʿfar al-Zuhrī, from his aunt Umm Bakr, daughter of al-Miswar, from her father; as did ʿAbd al-Raḥmān b. Ibrāhīm al-Mazanī and Ziyād b. Ḥashraj, from Abū Wajza; as did Maʿmar from Abū Nujayḥ, from Mujāhid; as did Ṭalha b. ʿAmr from ʿAṭāʾ from Ibn ʿAbbās. The accounts of some of these correlate with those of others. These accounts state that Āmina daughter of Wahb said, "I became pregnant with him (meaning the Messenger of God (ṢAAS)) and he caused me no difficulties up to when I gave birth to him. When he was separated from me a light emerged along with him that lit all between east and west. Then he dropped to the ground, resting upon his hands, and took up a handful of earth which he gripped tight, raising his head towards heaven."

Some sources word this tradition, "he dropped down resting upon his knees and there emerged with him a light by which were illuminated the castles and market-places of Syria, even so that the necks of the camels at Buṣrā could be seen, while he raised his head towards heaven."

The *ḥāfiẓ* Abū Bakr al-Bayhaqī said that Muḥammad b. ʿAbd Allāh, the *ḥāfiẓ*, informed him, quoting Muḥammad b. Ismāʿīl, quoting Muḥammad b. Isḥāq, and Yūnus b. Mubashshir b. al-Ḥasan, quoting Yaʿqūb b. Muḥammad al-Zuhrī, quoting ʿAbd al-ʿAzīz b. ʿImrān, quoting ʿAbd Allāh b. ʿUthmān b. Abū Sulaymān b. Jubayr b. Muṭʿim, from his father, from Ibn Abū Suwayd al-Thaqafī, from ʿUthmān b. Abū al-ʿĀṣ as follows: "My mother told me that she witnessed the giving of the birth by Āmina daughter of Wahb to the Messenger of God (ṢAAS) the night the birth occurred." She said, "All I could see in the house was light. As I looked I saw the stars coming so close that I said that they were going to fall on me!"

The *qāḍī* (judge) ʿIyād recounted, from al-Shaffāʾ, mother of ʿAbd al-Raḥmān b. ʿAwf, that she was his midwife and that she said that when he dropped into her hands and first made a sound, she heard a voice say, "May God have mercy on you!" And (she said) that a light shone from him by which the castles of Byzantium could be seen.

Muḥammad b. Isḥāq said that when she gave birth to him she sent her slave girl to ʿAbd al-Muṭṭalib, his father having died while she was pregnant (it is also said that ʿAbd Allāh died when the Prophet (ṢAAS) was 28 months old, and God knows best which account is true) to say to him, "A boy has been born to you, so look to him."

When ʿAbd al-Muṭṭalib came to her she related to him what she had seen when she bore him, what she had been told about him, and what she had been ordered to name him.

So ʿAbd al-Muṭṭalib took him in to Hubal; inside the *kaʿba*, and stood and prayed, thanking God the Almighty and Glorious, and speaking the verses,

"Praise be to God who gave me this fine, wonderful boy,
Who already in the cradle leads all boys; I entrust his safety to the pillared House (*kaʿba*),

Until he becomes the epitome of young men, until I see him fully grown.
I seek his protection from all who hate, and from the envious and the unstable,
From those with ambition but eyeless, until I see him highly eloquent;
You are he who was named in the Qurʾān, in books whose meanings are well established,
(Your name being) ʿAḥmad, written upon the tongue."

Al-Bayhaqī stated, "Abū ʿAbd Allāh the *ḥāfiẓ* informed us, quoting Abū Bakr Muḥammad b. Aḥmad b. Ḥātim al-Darābardī, of Merv, Abū ʿAbd Allāh al-Būshanjī related to us, quoting Abū Ayyūb Sulaymān b. Salama al-Khabāʾirī, quoting Yūnus b. ʿAṭāʾ b. ʿUthmān b. Rabīʿa b. Ziyād b. al-Ḥārith al-Ṣaddāʿī, of Egypt, quoting al-Ḥakam b. Abān, from ʿIkrima, from Ibn ʿAbbās, from his father al-ʿAbbās b. ʿAbd al-Muṭṭalib, God bless him, as follows. "The Messenger of God (ṢAAS) was born circumcised and with his umbilical cord severed. His grandfather ʿAbd al-Muṭṭalib was amazed at this and found favour in him, saying, 'This son of mine is sure to be important.' And so he was."

There is dispute over the veracity of this.

The *ḥāfiẓ* Ibn ʿAsākir told it, from an account of Sufyān b. Muḥammad al-Maṣṣīṣī, from Hushaym, from Yūnus b. ʿUbayd, from al-Ḥasan, from Anas, as follows: The Messenger of God (ṢAAS) said, "One way God honoured me was in my being born already circumcised, so that no one saw my private parts."

He (Ibn ʿAsākir) then related it on a line of transmission from al-Ḥasan b. ʿArafa, on the authority of Hushaym.

He thereafter related it from Muḥammad b. Muḥammad b. Sulaymān, he being al-Bāghandī, who said that ʿAbd al-Raḥmān b. Ayyūb al-Ḥimṣī related to him, quoting Mūsā b. Abū Mūsā al-Maqdisī, that Khālid b. Salama related to him, from Nāfiʿ, from Ibn ʿUmar, that the latter said, "The Messenger of God (ṢAAS) was born circumcised and with his umbilical cord detached."

Abū Nuʿaym stated that Abū Aḥmad Muḥammad b. Aḥmad al-Ghitrīfī related to him, quoting al-Ḥusayn b. Aḥmad b. ʿAbd Allāh al-Mālikī, quoting Sulaymān b. Salama al-Khabāʾirī, quoting Yūnus b. ʿAṭāʾ, quoting al-Ḥakam b. Abān, quoting ʿIkrima, from Ibn ʿAbbās, from his father al-ʿAbbās, as follows, "The Messenger of God (ṢAAS) was born circumcised and with his umbilical cord detached. This amazed his grandfather ʿAbd al-Muṭṭalib and he found favour in him, saying, 'This son of mine is sure to be important.' And so he was."

Some authorities claim authenticity for this tradition for the lines of transmission it has; some even claim for it the status of *mutawātir*.[60] However, this is debatable.

60. The term connotes a tradition related by consecutive testimonies and therefore one of evident authenticity.

The word *makhtūn* given in these traditions means "having the foreskin cut off"; the word *masrūr* means "having had the umbilical cord from his mother severed".

The *ḥāfiẓ* Ibn ʿAsākir related from ʿAbd al-Raḥmān b. ʿUyayna al-Baṣrī as follows, "ʿAlī b. Muḥammad al-Madāʾinī al-Salmī related to us, quoting Salama b. Muḥārib b. Muslim b. Ziyād, from his father, from Abū Bakra, that Gabriel circumcised the Prophet (ṢAAS) when he cleansed his heart."

This is extremely strange.

It is also said that it was his grandfather ʿAbd al-Muṭṭalib who circumcised him and held a celebration for him to which he gathered all Quraysh. But God knows best.

Al-Bayhaqī said that Abū ʿAbd Allāh the *ḥāfiẓ* informed us, quoting Muḥammad b. Kāmil al-Qāḍī – verbally – that Muḥammad b. Ismāʿīl – meaning al-Salmī – related to him that Abū Ṣāliḥ ʿAbd Allāh b. Ṣāliḥ related to him that Muʿāwiya b. Ṣāliḥ told him, from Abū al-Ḥakam al-Tanūkhī as follows: "When a child was born to Quraysh they would entrust it to some Quraysh women till next morning. They would place an upside-down pottery vessel over it. When the Messenger of God (ṢAAS) was born, ʿAbd al-Muṭṭalib entrusted him to the women and they did put over him an upside-down pottery vessel. When they came to him next morning they discovered that the vessel had split into two pieces and fallen away from him. They found him there with his eyes wide open gazing up to heaven! When ʿAbd al-Muṭṭalib arrived they told him, 'We never saw a newborn child like him! We discovered that the vessel had split in two away from him and found him open-eyed and gazing up to heaven!' He commented, 'Take care of him; I hope he will be of importance, or that he will achieve good.'"

On the seventh day he made sacrifice for him and invited Quraysh to see him. When they had feasted, they asked, "O ʿAbd al-Muṭṭalib, what have you thought of naming this son of yours you have honoured?" "I have named him Muḥammad," he replied. "Why", they asked, "have you preferred him not to have one of the names of his kinsfolk?" "Because I wanted God to praise him in heaven and His creatures to praise him on earth," he replied.

Language scholars say, "All that invites the qualities of good is named 'Muḥammad'." As the poet said,

> To you, blameless as you are, I have urged on my mount, to him who is the glorious and noble master, the one 'Muḥammad'" (i.e. "the laudable one").

Some scholars say that God, the Almighty and Glorious, encouraged them to name him Muḥammad for the praiseworthy qualities he possessed; so that word and deed be joined and that the name and the one named be appropriately congruent in form and concept. As his uncle Abū Ṭālib composed – and the verse is also attributed to Ḥassān –

> "God took a part of His own name for him, to honour him; for He of the throne is named 'Maḥmūd' (i.e. he to whom praise is due) while he is 'Muḥammad'."

We will report the various names and qualities by which he (ṢAAS) is known, these being his evident qualities and pure virtues, the evidences of his prophethood, and the attributes of his status. All these we will give at the end of the biography, if God wills it so.

The *ḥāfiẓ* Abū Bakr al-Bayhaqī said that Abū ʿAbd Allāh the *ḥāfiẓ* informed him that Abū al-ʿAbbās Muḥammad b. Yaʿqūb related to him, quoting Aḥmad b. Shaybān al-Ramalī, quoting Aḥmad b. Ibrāhīm al-Ḥubalī, quoting al-Haytham b. Jamīl, quoting Zuhayr, from Muḥārib b. Dithār, from ʿAmr b. Yathribī, from al-ʿAbbās b. ʿAbd al-Muṭṭalib, as follows: "I said: 'O Messenger of God, it was a sign of your prophethood that encouraged me to join your religion. I saw you in the cradle whispering to the moon and gesturing to it with your finger. And it would move in the direction you indicated.' He replied, 'I would talk to it and it to me and it would distract me from crying. And I would hear its palpitations when it would prostrate beneath God's throne.'"

He (Abū Bakr al-Bayhaqī) then said, "He (Aḥmad b. Ibrāhīm Ḥubalī) transmitted only this one tradition, and he is not known."

Section: On the signs that occurred on the night of the birth of the Prophet (ṢAAS).

In the section on *Hawātif al-Jān* (*The Cries of the Spirits*), we told of the downcast faces of many of the idols and how they fell from their places on that night, and of what the Negus, the king of Abyssinia, saw. Similarly we have reported the appearance of the light that came with him that even lit up the castles of Syria when he was born, and how he dropped into a kneeling position and raised his head to heaven. We told also how the vessel split asunder from above his honoured face, what was seen by the light in the house where he was born and how the stars came down close to them, and other such events.

Al-Suhaylī related from the Qurʾān commentary of Baqī b. Makhlid, the *ḥāfiẓ*, that Satan let out four cries. One came when he was cursed (by God); another when he was sent down from heaven; a third when the Messenger of God (ṢAAS) was born; and the fourth when *sūrat al-Fātiḥa*, the opening verse of the Qurʾān, came down.

Muḥammad b. Isḥāq said that Hishām b.ʿUrwa would tell traditions on the authority of his father, that came from ʿĀʾisha, who once said, "There was a Jew who resided in Mecca and did business there. On the night when the Messenger of God (ṢAAS) was born, the man addressed a gathering of Quraysh with the words, 'O Quraysh, did a birth occur among you this night?' They replied that they did not know. He then exclaimed, 'Well, God is very great; if that should have missed you, then no matter. Do look, and remember what I am telling you. This night a prophet has been born to this last nation; between his shoulders there is a mark consisting of successive lines of hair looking like a horse's mane. He will not suckle for two nights and this is because a spirit will have put his finger into his mouth and prevented him from suckling.'

"The gathering broke up at this with all amazed at what he had told them. When they returned to their homes each one told his family. And they responded, 'By God, a child was born to ʿAbd Allāh, son of ʿAbd al-Muṭṭalib, a boy they named "Muḥammad".' The people then gathered and asked one another, 'Did you hear what the Jew said, and have you heard of the birth of the boy?' They then hurried off to the Jew and told him the news. He asked them to go with him, so that he could see the boy. They left together and took him in to Amīna, saying, 'Bring out your son for us.' She did so and they uncovered his back. There they saw the mark and the Jew fell down in a faint. When he came to, they asked him what was the matter with him. He replied, 'By God, prophecy has left Israel's tribe; are you glad with it, O Quraysh? He will so empower you that news of it will spread from east and west!'"

Muḥammad b. Isḥāq said that Ṣāliḥ b. Ibrāhīm b. ʿAbd al-Raḥmān b. ʿAwf related to him, from Yaḥyā b. ʿAbd Allāh b. ʿAbd al-Raḥmān b. Saʿd b. Zurāra, as follows, "Certain trustworthy men of my tribe told me that Ḥassān b. Thābit once said, 'I was a mature lad of seven or eight, capable of understanding all I saw and heard, when one morning a Jew in Yathrib began shouting for the attention of his people. When they gathered about him – I heard all that myself – they asked him what the matter was. He replied, "The star has risen beneath which 'Aḥmad' will be born this night."'"

The *ḥāfiẓ* Abū Nuʿaym related in the book, *Dalāʾil al-Nubuwwa* (*Signs of the Prophethood*), from a tradition of Abū Bakr b. ʿAbd Allāh al-ʿĀmirī, from Sulaymān b. Suḥaym and Dhurayḥ b. ʿAbd al-Raḥmān, both of their accounts coming from ʿAbd al-Raḥmān b. Abū Saʿīd, from his father, who said that he heard Abū Mālik b. Sinān say: "I came one day to talk with Banū ʿAbd al-Ashhal, with whom we then had a truce, and heard the Jew Yūshuʿ say, 'The time approaches for the coming of a prophet named Aḥmad who will arise from the sanctuary.' Khalīfa b. Thaʿlaba al-Ashhalī asked him, sarcastically, 'How might you describe him?' He responded, 'A man neither short nor tall, with fine, light eyes; he wears a full cloak and rides a donkey, carries his sword over his shoulder and to this land will he migrate.'"

Abū Mālik went on, "When I returned to my own people and expressed at that time my surprise at what Yūshuʿ had been saying, I heard one of our own men comment, 'So is it Yūshuʿ who alone says that? All the Jews of Yathrib are saying the same!'"

Abū Mālik continued, "I thereafter left and visited the Banū Qurayẓa whom I found in assembly discussing the Prophet (ṢAAS). Al-Zubayr b. Bāṭā said, 'The red star has risen and it only ever rises on the departure or emergence of a prophet. And the only one left is Aḥmad; this will be the place to which he will migrate.' And Abū Saʿīd said, 'When the Prophet (ṢAAS) eventually arrived my father told him this story, and the Messenger of God (ṢAAS) commented, "If al-Zubayr had adopted Islam, then his fellow Jewish leaders would also have done so; but they all followed him."'"

Abū Nuʿaym said that ʿUmar b. Muḥammad related to him, quoting Ibrāhīm b. al-Sindī, quoting al-Naḍr b. Salama, quoting Ismāʿīl b. Qays b. Sulaymān b. Zayd b. Thābit, from Ibrāhīm b. Yaḥyā b. Thābit, who said that he heard Zayd b. Thābit say, "The Jewish rabbis of the Banū Qurayẓa and al-Naḍīr would discuss the description of the Prophet (ṢAAS), and when the red star arose, they said that it was for a prophet after whom there would be no other, that his name was Aḥmad and that he would migrate to Yathrib. But when the Messenger of God (ṢAAS) ultimately arrived in the town they denied him, expressing their envy and disbelief."

This story is also given by the *ḥāfiẓ* Abū Nuʿaym in his book from other lines of transmission, and may God be praised.

Abū Nuʿaym and Muḥammad b. Hibān said that Abū Bakr b. Abū ʿĀṣim related to them, quoting Wahb b. Baqiyya, quoting Khālid, from Muḥammad b. ʿAmr, from Abū Salama and Yaḥyā b. ʿAbd al-Raḥmān b. Ḥāṭib, from Usāma b. Zayd who said that Zayd b. ʿAmr b. Nufayl stated, "A priest of Syria once told me, 'A prophet has come in your land. While he was arriving, his star arose. So go home, believe in him and follow him!'"

An Account of the shaking of the palace, and of the falling of the balconies, the extinguishing of the fires, the visions of the Magian supreme priest, and other such signs.

The *ḥāfiẓ* Abū Bakr Muḥammad b. Jaʿfar b. Sahl al-Kharāʾiṭī stated in the book, *Hawātif al-Jān* (*The Cries of the Spirits*), that ʿAlī b. Ḥarb related to him, quoting Abū Ayyūb Yaʿlā b. ʿImrān, from the family of Jarīr b. ʿAbd Allāh al-Bajalī quoting Makhzūm b. Hāniʾ al-Makhzūmī, from his father who reached the age of 150 years, as follows, "When it was the night in which the Messenger of God (ṢAAS) was born Chosroe's domed palace shook and 14 balconies upon it fell down. Also the 'fire of Persia' went out, having not done so for a thousand years before, and Lake Sāwa emptied. A Magian priest saw (in a dream) wild camels leading pure-bred horses that had crossed the Tigris river and spread into their land. This greatly alarmed Chosroe when he told him of it next morning; he put on a brave front and pretended lack of concern but then decided not to conceal it from his governors. He therefore summoned them, put on his crown, and sat upon his throne. Then he had them brought in and when they gathered around him he said, 'Do you know why I have summoned you?' They replied that all they knew was that their king wanted to tell them something. At that point a message came telling of the extinguishing of the fire, news that further upset the king. He then told them what he (the priest) had seen and what had alarmed him.

"The supreme priest explained, 'Last night I saw, may God save the realm, a vision.' He then recounted his vision of the camels and the king asked him how he interpreted it. He replied that it concerned some event occurring over in the territory of the Arabs who would understand it better than they themselves.

"Thereupon the king wrote a message, saying, 'From Chosroe, king of kings, to al-Nuʿmān b. al-Mundhir: Greetings. Send me some man learned in what I wish to question him about.' Al-Nuʿmān then dispatched to him ʿAbd al-Masīḥ b. ʿAmr b. Ḥayyān b. Buqayla al-Ghassānī. When he arrived Chosroe asked him, 'Do you have knowledge of what I wish to question you about?' ʿAbd al-Masīḥ replied, 'Let the king inform or question me as however he wishes; if I have knowledge of it (then good), otherwise I will inform him of someone who does know.'

"So Chosroe told him what he had been informed and ʿAbd al-Masīḥ replied, 'An uncle of mine named Saṭīḥ who lives in the uplands of Syria will have knowledge of that.' Chosroe then told him to go to this man to ask him what he wanted to know and then to return with the explanation.

"ʿAbd al-Masīḥ left but Saṭīḥ, by the time he reached him, was on his death-bed. ʿAbd al-Masīḥ greeted him and talked to him, but Saṭīḥ made no reply. So ʿAbd al-Masīḥ then spoke the following verses:

> 'Has the noble lord of Yemen gone deaf or does he hear; or has he died, the ultimate reins (death) having him in tow.
>
> O he who determines the course, one that would exhaust anyone, your visitor is the local sheikh of the Sunan family.
>
> His mother is of the family of Dhiʾb ('wolf') b. Ḥajan (crooked of staff, evil-eyed) vicious of fang, raucous to the ear.
>
> White, full of cloak and body, a messenger from the king of the Persians, travelling by night till deep slumber.
>
> Carried over the earth by a strong, large she-camel, tireless, unawed by thunder or vicissitudes of time.
>
> Lifting me with a bump and dropping me with a crash, bare of breast and lower back,
>
> Enveloped by a gale of manure dust, as though blasting from the two sides of a mountain.'

"When Saṭīḥ heard those verses he raised his head and said, 'Why, it's ʿAbd al-Masīḥ, ridden here on a tireless mount, who's come to Saṭīḥ, looking down at my death-bed; you've been sent by the king of the Sassanians, because of the shaking of his palace, the extinguishing of the fires, and the visions of the priest who saw wild camels leading pure-bred horses that had crossed the Tigris and spread into their lands.

"'O ʿAbd al-Masīḥ, when many recitations have been made and the sceptre-bearer has appeared, the Samāwa valley flooded, Lake Sāwa dried up, and the fires of Persia gone out, then Syria is Syria no more for Saṭīḥ. Of them there shall reign kings and queens to the number of their balconies; all that will be, will be.'

"At that Saṭīḥ died, right then and there. So ʿAbd al-Masīḥ mounted his camel, saying the following verses:

> 'Get going, for you are decisive and expeditious; separation and change do not alarm you.
> If the rule of the Sassanians is ending (so be it), for man is all stages and periods of time,
> They may have achieved a status whose power mighty lions dread,
> Of whom was Bahrām of the Tower and his brothers, the al-Hurmuzān, and Sābūr and Sābūr.[61]
> People are indeed changeable; knowing that one of them has become destitute he is then despised and abandoned,
> And many are the people who are (erroneously) influenced by what they hear, as if distracted by playing flutes.
> However, should they see someone with riches and prosperity, then they are to him closely associated. This has been the secret of life, well preserved and repeatedly validated (they say), that's the province and concern of the unknown,
> And good and evil stick always as a pair; for good is pursued relentlessly, evil avoided.'

"When ʿAbd al-Masīḥ came in to Chosroe and told him what Saṭīḥ had said, Chosroe replied, 'So, until 14 of us have ruled, many things can happen!'

"Ten of their kings did rule in a period of four years and the remainder ruled on until the caliphate of ʿUthmān, God be pleased with him."

Al-Bayhaqī related this from an account of ʿAbd al-Raḥmān b. Muḥammad b. Idrīs, from ʿAlī b. Ḥarb al-Mūṣilī in similar form.

The last of their kings, the one from whom rule was wrested, was Yazdajard b. Shahriyār b. Abrawīz b. Hurmuz b. Anūshirwān; it was the last mentioned in whose era the domed palace shook. His forebears had ruled for 3,164 years. The first of their kings was Juyūmart b. Umaym b. Lāwadh b. Sām b. Noah. Mention of the lives of Shiqq and Saṭīḥ have been given above.

61. Bahrām, Sābūr, and Sābūr were Sassanian kings. Al-Hurmuzān was a famous Persian military leader.

Regarding this man Saṭīḥ, the *ḥāfiẓ* Ibn ʿAsākir stated in his history: "His name was al-Rabīʿ b. Rabīʿa b. Masʿūd b. Māzin b. Dhiʾb b. ʿAdī b. Māzin b. al-Azd. He was known as al-Rabīʿ b. Masʿūd; his mother was Radʿa daughter of Saʿd b. al-Ḥārith al-Ḥajūrī."

Other accounts of his ancestry also exist. He lived at al-Jābiyya.[62]

Moreover, he (Ibn ʿAsākir) related from Abū Ḥātim al-Sijistānī that the latter heard some sheikhs, among whom were Abu ʿUbayda and others say, "He (Saṭīḥ) came after Luqmān b. ʿĀd. He was born at the time of the torrent of al-ʿArim and he lived on to the era of King Dhū Nuwās, a period of some 30 generations. He dwelt in al-Baḥrain. The tribe of ʿAbd Qays claimed him as theirs, as also did Azd. Most authorities claim him to have been of Azd; we do not know from whom he was descended. His descendants, however, say he was from Azd."

It is related of Ibn ʿAbbās that he said, "No one in all mankind was like Saṭīḥ; he was like flesh on a butcher's block, devoid of bones or sinew except for his head, his eyes, and his hands. He folded up from feet to neck like a garment. And the only part of him that moved was his tongue."

Others say that when he became angry he would puff up and sit.

Ibn ʿAbbās recounted that when Saṭīḥ went to Mecca he was met by a group of their leaders among whom were ʿAbd Shams and ʿAbd Manāf, sons of Quṣayy. They questioned him on a variety of matters and he responded to them frankly. They asked him how it would be at the end of time and he replied, "Take this from me and as God's inspiration to me, you are now, Arabs, in an age of decrepitude in terms of both your vision and that of foreigners. You have neither knowledge nor understanding. After you there will arise those with understanding. They will seek after all ranges of knowledge and they will destroy the idols, pursue the worthless, fight the non-Arabs, and go in search of the spoils of war. What will happen ultimately and for ever, will be that a right-guided prophet will surely draw you forth from this land and lead you to the truth. He will refute Yagūth and the lies, be innocent of worship of the devil, and pray to one Lord alone. Then God will take him unto Himself, giving him praise and the best abode, one lost to the world but seen there in heaven. Then *al-Ṣiddīq* ('the trusting', i.e. the first Caliph Abū Bakr) will follow him; when he gives judgement he will speak aright, and there will be no rush nor rupture in restoring rights. He will be followed by *al-Ḥanīf* ('The Sincere', i.e. the second Caliph, ʿUmar), the noble and demanding lord. He will be the 'host supreme' and best arbiter of the faith." He then made mention of (the third Caliph) ʿUthmān and his murder, and of the rule thereafter of the Umayyads and the ʿAbbāsids and all the disturbances and wars that followed. Ibn ʿAsākir traces his line of transmission back to Ibn ʿAbbās, in all its length.

62. Said to have been a man-made ditch filled with drinking-water for the camels.

We stated previously his comment to Rabīʿa b. Naṣr, king of Yemen, and how Saṭīḥ described the vision he had had before he was himself told of it. And then we related how he predicted the disturbances and the changes of government that would occur in Yemen before reaching Sayf b. Dhū Yazan. Rabīʿa b. Naṣr then asked whether that rule would hold or be broken and Saṭīḥ replied it would end. The king asked who would end it, and Saṭīḥ responded, "A pure prophet to whom inspiration comes from the Almighty." When asked from which tribe the prophet would come, he replied, "From the progeny of Ghālib b. Fihr b. Mālik b. al-Naḍr; and the rule shall be in his people till the end of time." "And shall there be an end to time?" the king asked. "Yes, indeed," was the reply, "on that day the first and the last shall be gathered and the good rejoice while the evil suffer." "Is what you are telling me really true?" the king asked. "Yes", Saṭīḥ replied, "by the dawn and the dusk and by the moon when it becomes full, what I have told you is indeed true." And Shiqq was in complete agreement with all this, using different phraseology, as we have shown above.

Among the verses of Saṭīḥ are the lines,

> "Act in God's piety in secret and in public, and never deceitfully pretend good faith.
> And always be a protector and shield for those neighbouring you when fate's misfortunes befall them."

That poetry was transmitted by the *ḥāfiẓ* Abū ʿAsākir. Al-Muʿāfā b. Zakariyyāʾ al-Jarīrī, moreover, cited that and stated, "Stories relating to Saṭīḥ are many, and several scholars have collected them. What is well known is that he was a soothsayer and gave information about the Prophet (ṢAAS) and described both his qualities and his mission. And it is related to us through a chain of authorities God alone can judge, that the Prophet (ṢAAS) was asked about Saṭīḥ and responded, "He was a prophet, squandered by his own people."

Regarding this tradition, my own comment is that it is without foundation in any of the established works of Islam. I do not consider its authority chain to be well founded; one similar to it is given relative to Khālid b. Sinān al-ʿAbsī and it too lacks veracity.

What is evident in these expressions points to Saṭīḥ having had excellent knowledge, and they do evince believability. But he did not survive on after the coming of Islam, as al-Jarīrī maintained. In this regard, he tells us that Saṭīḥ told his nephew, "O ʿAbd al-Masīḥ (if) when many recitations have been made, and the sceptre-bearer has appeared, the Samāwa valley has flooded, Lake Sāwa dried up, and the fires of Persia gone out, then Syria is Syria no more for Saṭīḥ; then kings and queens will reign to the number of their balconies; and all that will be, will be." At that Saṭīḥ died then and there. This was after the birth of the Messenger of God (ṢAAS) by a month or, a *shayʿa*, a portion thereof, that is, less than that.

His death occurred in a part of Syria contiguous to the land of Iraq; and God alone knows the truth about Saṭīḥ and what became of him.

Ibn Ṭarār al-Jarīrī relates that he lived 700 years. Others say he lived 500; yet others 300. But God knows best.

Ibn ʿAsākir related that a king once asked Saṭīḥ about the family origin of a young man about whom there was some disagreement. He therefore informed him of the facts at length and with wit and eloquence. The king then asked Saṭīḥ to tell him about how he knew all that. Saṭīḥ replied, "This knowledge of mine does not come from me, not by guesswork or by thought; I took it from a brother of mine who heard inspiration on Mt. Sinai." The king then asked, "Have you seen your brother, this genie; is he with you and won't he depart from you?" Saṭīḥ replied, "He will cease to exist when I do. I only ever pronounce what he says."

As stated previously, he and Shiqq b. Muṣʿab b. Yashkur b. Rahm b. Basr b. ʿUqba, the other diviner, were both born on the same day. They were carried to the fortune-teller, Ṭarīfa, daughter of al-Ḥusayn al-Ḥamīdiyya, and she spat into their mouths. And so they inherited divination from her. She died that very same day. Saṭīḥ was half-human. It is said that Khālid b. ʿAbd Allāh al-Qusrī was of his progeny. Shiqq died a very long time before Saṭīḥ.

Regarding ʿAbd al-Masīḥ b. ʿAmr b. Qays b. Ḥayyān b. Buqayla al-Ghassānī, the Christian, he was very long-lived.

The *ḥāfiẓ* Ibn ʿAsākir gave his life story in his history, saying therein that it was he who made the peace treaty for al-Ḥīra with Khālid b. al-Walīd; he gave at length the story of their contact. Also he reported that ʿAbd al-Masīḥ once ate by his own hand some rapid-acting poison, but that no harm came to him. This was because as he took it he spoke the words, "In the name of God; and by God, Lord of the earth and the heaven, who (ensures that) no harm will come when His name is invoked." He then ate it, swooned, and beat his hands on his chest. He poured with sweat and then, God bless him, recovered. Verses other than those previously quoted are also attributed to ʿAbd al-Masīḥ.

Abū Nuʿaym said that Muḥammad b. Aḥmad b. al-Ḥasan related to us, quoting Muḥammad b. ʿUthmān b. Abū Shayba, quoting ʿUqba b. Makram, quoting al-Musayyab b. Sharīk, quoting Muḥammad b. Sharīk, all on the authority of Shuʿayb b. Shuʿayb, from his father and from his grandfather, as follows, "At Marr al-Dhahrān there was a certain monk from Syria named ʿAyṣā. He was under the protection of al-ʿĀṣ b. Wāʾil. God had given him great knowledge and placed in him many qualities for the people of Mecca, qualities of goodness, kindness, and learning.

"He kept to a cell he had and came down to Mecca every year to meet the people and to say to them, 'O people of Mecca, soon there will be born among you a child to whom the Arabs will look for guidance and who will hold sway over the foreigners. This is his time. Whoever has contact with him and follows him will achieve success, while those in contact with him who oppose him will experience failure. By God, I did not leave the land of fine wine, leavened bread, and security and come to live in the land of hunger, poverty, and fear for any reason other than to seek him.'

"No birth in Mecca ever occurred without his asking about it, but he would always say, 'He's not come yet.' When people would ask for a description of him, he would decline. He would hide that information because of what he knew the future leader would experience from his tribe, fearing for himself that it might some day result in harm, however slight, to him.

"When the morning arrived of the day when the birth of the Messenger of God (ṢAAS) occurred, ʿAbd Allāh son of ʿAbd al-Muṭṭalib went out to see ʿAyṣā. He stood at the foot of the monk's cell and called out, 'Hallo there, ʿAyṣā.' The response came, 'Who is there?' 'I am ʿAbd Allāh,' he replied. Then ʿAyṣā looked down at him and said, 'Be his father! The child I used to tell you of has been born, and on a Monday. He shall also receive God's mission on a Monday, and he will die on a Monday.'

"Abd Allāh replied, 'Well, this morning a boy was born to me.' 'And what have you named him?' the monk asked. 'Muḥammad.' 'By God,' exclaimed ʿAyṣā, 'I wanted the child to be born among you, the people of the House (the *kaʿba*), because of three factors of which we know. Those were that his star arose yesterday, that he was born today, and that his name is Muḥammad. Go to him, for he whom I used to foretell is your son.' ʿAbd Allāh asked, 'How do you know he is my son? Perhaps some other child will be born today.' 'Your son,' the monk replied, 'has got the right name. And God has never been one to confuse scholars; it is a proof. And a (further) sign of that is the fact that he is currently in pain. He will suffer for three days. Then for three days he will show hunger and after that be cured. So you hold your tongue; for no one ever before has been the object of the envy (there will be) for him, no one has been the object of such hatred as he will have. If you live until his mission appears and he announces himself, then you will experience from your people what you will only endure by patience and in humility. So hold your tongue and protect him.' ʿAbd Allāh then asked, 'What will his life-span be?' 'Whether his life be long or short, he will not attain seventy. He will die a short span before that, in his sixties, at age 61 or 63, at an age average for his people.'"

The account goes on, "The Messenger of God (ṢAAS) was conceived on the 10th of *muḥarram* and born on Monday, the 12th of Ramaḍān, 23 years after the attack of those with elephants."

Thus did Abū Nuʿaym relate it; and there is some strangeness in the account.

An Account of the rearing and suckling of the Prophet (ṢAAS).

Umm Ayman, whose given name was Baraka, reared him. The Prophet (ṢAAS) had inherited her from his father. When he grew up he emancipated her and married her to his *mawlā*, his freed-slave, Zayd b. Ḥāritha. She gave birth to Usāma b. Zayd, God be pleased with them all.

The Prophet (ṢAAS) was suckled, as well as by his mother, by the freed-slave of his uncle Abū Lahab who was named Thuwayba, and later by Ḥalīma al-Saʿdiyya.

Al-Bukhārī and Muslim extracted in their two *ṣaḥīḥ* tradition collections from a *ḥadīth* of al-Zuhrī, from ʿUrwa b. al-Zubayr, from Zaynab daughter of Umm Salama, from Umm Ḥabība daughter of Abū Sufyān, as follows. She said, "O Messenger of God, marry my sister, Abu Sufyān's daughter." According to Muslim's account the words used were, "my sister ʿAzza, Abū Sufyān's daughter."

The Messenger of God (ṢAAS) replied, "Would you like that then?" She replied, "Yes; I'm not unmarried (and available) for you. And the person who shares best with me in goodness is my sister."

The Prophet (ṢAAS) responded, "But that would not be permissible for me."

She commented, "We are discussing your marrying Abū Salama's daughter." Also in an account the words, "Durra, Abū Salama's daughter," are given.

"You mean Umm Salama's daughter?"

"Yes," I replied.

"But", he explained, "even if she were not under my care in my household, she would not be permitted for me. She is my niece by suckling. Her father Abū Salama and I were both suckled by Thuwayba. So don't propose your daughters or your sisters for me."

Al-Bukhārī's account adds, "ʿUrwa said, 'And Thuwayba was a *mawlat*, a freed-slave woman of Abū Lahab whom he had emancipated. So she suckled the Messenger of God (ṢAAS).'"

And when Abū Lahab was dead, one of his family, greatly disappointed, was shown him. The man asked him, "What happened to you?" Abū Lahab replied, "I experienced nothing good after (leaving) you, except for being given to drink from this for my having emancipated Thuwayba." And he pointed to the hollow between his thumb and adjoining fingers.

Al-Suhaylī and others report that the one who saw him was his brother al-ʿAbbās. And this occurred a year after the death of Abū Lahab, after the battle of Badr. Their account relates that Abū Lahab said to al-ʿAbbās, "It (i.e. the punishment of hell) is alleviated for me on Mondays."

This is explained as being because when Thuwayba told him the news of the birth of his nephew Muḥammad, son of ʿAbd Allāh, he emancipated her at once. And he was rewarded thus for that.

An Account of the suckling of the Prophet (ṢAAS) by Ḥalīma, daughter of Abū Dhu'ayb of the Sa'd tribe, and of the signs of the prophethood and of blessedness apparent on him.

Muḥammad b. Isḥāq said, "Ḥalīma daughter of Abū Dhū'ayb was asked to suckle him. Abū Dhu'ayb's given name was 'Abd Allāh b. al-Ḥārith b. Shijna b. Jābir b. Rizām b. Nāṣira b. Fuṣayya b. Naṣr, b. Sa'd b. Bakr b. Hawāzin b. Manṣūr b. 'Ikrima b. Khaṣafa b. Qays 'Aylān b. Muḍar.

"And the name of the foster father of the Messenger of God (ṢAAS), that is Ḥalīma's husband, was al-Ḥārith b. 'Abd al-'Uzzā b. Rifā'a b. Mallān b. Nāṣira b. Sa'd b. Bakr b. Hawāzin.

"His foster-brother was 'Abd Allāh b. al-Ḥārith; and Unaysa and Khidāma daughters of al-Ḥārith were his foster-sisters. The last named was known as 'al-Shaymā'; and it is said that she would cradle the Messenger of God (ṢAAS) along with her mother while he was with them."

Ibn Isḥāq went on to report that Jahm b. Abū Jahm (the *mawlā*, the freed-slave, of a woman of the Banū Tamīm who lived with al-Ḥārith b. Ḥāṭib, who was known as "the *mawlā* of al-Ḥārith b. Ḥāṭib"), told him that someone related to him from someone who heard 'Abd Allāh b. Ja'far b. Abū Ṭālib say that it was related to him that Ḥalīma, daughter of al-Ḥārith, had said, "I arrived at Mecca along with other women (al-Wāqidī told, with a chain of authorities, that they were ten in number from Banū Sa'd b. Bakr who acted as foster-mothers along with her) from Banū Sa'd looking for babies to suckle; it was a year of famine. I arrived on a dark grey she-ass worn out from riding. With us I had a boy of our own, and an old milch camel which, I swear, wasn't giving a drop of milk. That whole night, along with that boy of ours, we did not sleep at all. There was nothing in my breast of use to him and nothing in our milch camel to feed him. We did, however, have hopes of rain and relief. So on I went on that old ass of mine, which lagged behind the other riders because of its weakness and its thirst, much to their annoyance.

"So we arrived in Mecca and, I swear, I don't know of one woman of ours who was not offered the Messenger of God (ṢAAS); but all refused him when it was said that he was an orphan. We refused him saying, 'What good could his mother do for us? What we want is some help from the boy's father; what could his mother do for us?' I swear, every single one of my women companions, all except me, did take a baby to suckle.

"Having found no one except him and being assembled to leave, I said to my husband, al-Ḥārith b. 'Abd al-'Uzzā, 'By God, I hate to go back amongst my companions without having a baby to suckle. I'll go off to that orphan and take him.' He replied, 'It's not your duty to do so; and so perhaps God will bring us some blessings through him.' And so I went off and got him; and the fact is, by God, I only took him because I couldn't find anyone else.

"No sooner had I taken him and brought him back to my baggage than my breasts welcomed him, giving him all the milk he wanted. He drank till he was satisfied and his foster-brother drank his fill too. My husband then went over to that old milch camel of ours and, to his surprise, she was full. He milked her and we both drank till we were satisfied. We then spent a fine night together.

"Next morning my husband said, 'Ḥalīma, by God I really think you've taken a person who is blessed! You see what a fine, happy night we passed when we took him? May God Almighty go on bringing us more benefit yet!'

"We then left to return to our own land. And, I swear, my she-ass went off ahead of all the other riders, with not a single donkey able to catch up with her. Eventually my women companions said, 'Hey there, O daughter of Abū Dhu'ayb! Is that the she ass you were riding when you left with us?' I replied, 'Yes indeed, it's her.' They commented, 'Well, by God, something's really happened to her!'

"Eventually we were back in Banū Sa'd territory, and I knew no other part of God's earth more barren than it is. But my goats would graze free, then leave the grazing, satisfied and full of milk and we would milk them as ever we wished. And this while no one around us, near or far, had their ewes give so much as a drop of milk, their ewes always going hungry. Finally the others said to their shepherds: 'Woe on you! Just watch where the flock of Abū Du'ayb's daughter grazes. You graze along with them.' And this they would do, theirs grazing where mine went, but their flocks remained hungry, not giving a drop of milk, while mine were satisfied and full so we could milk them as much as we wanted.

"And God went on blessing us this way, and we recognized it. Then he reached two years of age. He was already growing up a very fine boy, not like the other children. I swear that by age two he was a sturdy boy, so we took him to his mother; we were very covetous of him because of having seen the blessings he had brought. When his mother saw him I told her, 'Let us bring back this son of ours some other year. We are concerned he might catch a disease from Mecca.' We kept on at her until she agreed and sent him off with us and we stayed with him for two or three months more.

"Then one time he was out behind our dwellings with one of his foster-brothers with our animals. Suddenly that foster-brother came in greatly agitated and said, 'That Quraysh brother of mine! Two men dressed in white came to him, laid him down, and split open his abdomen!'

"At this his father and I rushed outside towards him. We found him standing there, his colour pale. His foster-father hugged him and asked, 'What's wrong, son?' He replied, 'Two men dressed in white came to me. They laid me down and opened my abdomen. Then they drew something from inside it and threw it away . After that they put my abdomen back as before.' So we took the boy back with us and his foster father said, 'Ḥalīma, I'm afraid my foster son has become afflicted; let's hurry and give him back to his family before what we fear does develop.' So we did take him back. His mother was very surprised to see him and when we gave him over to her she said, 'So why did you bring him back, nurse? You both wanted to have him so much.' 'No, it's nothing,' we replied, 'it's just that God has relieved us of our task. We did our duty. We're afraid some harm or accident may befall him, so we are returning him to his own people.' His mother insisted, 'What's going on with you both! Tell me truthfully what's worrying you!' She would not leave us alone till we told her what had happened. She asked, 'Are you afraid for him from Satan? Absolutely not; Satan won't get to him. By God, this son of mine has a great future before him. Should I tell you what happened with him?' 'Please do,' we asked. 'Well,' she explained, 'when I was pregnant with him, he was the lightest child I ever bore. And when carrying him I saw in my sleep a light emanating so bright it lit up the castles of Syria! And then, when he was born, he came out in a manner that babies never do, drew himself up on his arms and lifted his head up to heaven. So leave him, and don't worry.'"

This account has been related through various other lines as well, and it is one of the best known, and most frequently told by the biographers and early historians.

Al-Wāqidī said that Ma'ādh b. Muḥammad related to him, from 'Aṭā' b. Abū Rabbāḥ, from Ibn 'Abbās, as follows, "Ḥalīma once went out to seek the Prophet (ṢAAS) and she found their animals to be sleeping in the sun. Him she found with his sister. She asked, 'Why outside in this heat?' His sister replied, 'My brother doesn't get hot; I saw a cloud shading him that stopped when he did and moved when he did, till he came to this spot.'"

Ibn Isḥāq said that Thawr b. Yazīd related to him, from Khālid b. Ma'dān, from the Companions of the Messenger of God (ṢAAS) that the Companions once asked him to tell them about himself. He responded, "I am the one called for by my father Abraham, the glad tidings foreseen by Jesus, peace be upon them both. When she bore me my mother saw that a light came from inside her that illuminated the castles of Syria. I was suckled by the tribe of Sa'd b. Bakr and while I was among some of our animals two men dressed in white came, carrying a golden basin filled with ice. They laid me down, cut open my abdomen and took out my heart. This they split and extracted from it a black clot that they threw away. They then washed my heart and insides with that ice until clean. Having put it back as before, one of them said to his companion, 'Weigh him against ten of his nation.' He did so, but I outweighed them. He then said, 'Weigh him against a hundred of his nation.' This he did but I outweighed them. He said, 'Weigh him against a thousand.' The other man did, but

I outweighed them too. The first man then said, 'Leave him now, for even if you weighed him against his entire nation, he would outweigh them!'"

This has a fine, strong chain of authorities.

Ibn Isḥāq also narrated that Abū Nuʿaym, the *ḥāfiẓ*, related this story in his work *al-Dalāʾil* (*The Signs*) by way of ʿUmar b. al-Ṣubḥ, known as Abū Nuʿaym, from Thawr b. Yazīd, from Makḥūl, from Shaddād b. Aws, in a much lengthened version. But this ʿUmar b. Ṣubḥ should be ignored, for he was a liar who was accused of invention. For this reason we will not mention the text of the tradition, for it gives no pleasure.

Ibn Isḥāq then said that Abū ʿAmr b. Ḥamdān related to him, quoting al-Ḥasan b. Nafīr, quoting ʿAmr b. ʿUthmān, quoting Baqiyya b. al-Walīd, from Buḥayr b. Saʿīd, from Khālid b. Maʿdān, from ʿAbd al-Raḥmān b. ʿAmr al-Salamī, from ʿUtba b. ʿAbd Allāh, as follows. A man asked the Prophet (ṢAAS), "What was it happened to you first, O Messenger of God?" He replied, "My wet-nurse was from the Banū Saʿd b. Bakr. One time a son of hers and I went off with our flock without taking any food with us. So I said, 'Hey brother, go back and get us some food from our mother's home.' So my brother hurried away while I stayed with the animals. Then two white birds like eagles came along and one said to the other, 'Is that he?' 'Yes,' the other replied. Then they both swooped down, took hold of me and laid me out on my back. They then split my abdomen, extracted my heart, cut it open, and took out from it two black clots. One bird said to his companion, 'Bring me some ice water.' And with it they cleaned my insides. The first bird then said, 'Now get some cold water.' With that they washed my heart. Then the bird said, 'Bring me *al-sakīna* (quietude).' This they sprinkled into my heart. The one said to the other, 'Sew it up.' So he did that and then placed on my heart the seal of prophethood. After that one bird said to the other, 'Place him in one balance scale and a thousand of his people in the other.' And when I looked up, there were the thousand above me, and I was concerned that some of them might tumble down on to me. Then the bird said, 'If his whole nation were balanced against him, he would still outweigh them.' Then both birds went away, leaving me there. I was tremendously afraid and raced off to my foster-mother and told her what had happened. She was afraid I'd lost my mind and exclaimed, 'God protect you!' Then she got an ass of hers ready for travel and put me on it. She rode behind me and we travelled till we reached my mother. She then said, 'Well, I've fulfilled my pact and agreement.' She then told my mother what had happened, but it didn't shock her. She said, 'What I saw was that a light came from inside me that lit up the castles of Syria.'"

Aḥmad related it from a tradition told by Baqiyya b. al-Walīd. ʿAbd Allāh b. al-Mubārak and others similarly told this from Baqiyya b. al-Walīd.

Ibn ʿAsākir related it through Abū Dāwūd al-Ṭayālisī. Jaʿfar b. ʿAbd Allāh b. ʿUthmān al-Qurashī related to him that ʿUmayr b. ʿUmar b. ʿUrwa b. al-Zubayr informed him as follows, "I heard ʿUrwa b. al-Zubayr relate from Abū Dharr al-Ghifārī who said that he asked, 'O Messenger of God, how were you informed that you were a prophet and when did you become convinced that you were one?' He replied, 'O Abū Dharr, two angels came to me when I was in one of the valleys of Mecca. One of them dropped down to the ground, while the other remained suspended between heaven and earth. One said to the other, "Is that he?" "Yes, it's he." The one said, "Weigh him against another man." He did so, and I outweighed him.'"

He then told it till the end, recounting how his chest was opened and sewn up and the seal was placed between his shoulders. He then said, "Then finally they turned away from me, as if their work was fully done."

Moreover Ibn ʿAsākir gave it from Ubayy b. Kaʿb in similar words, and from Shaddād b. Aws in a more simple form than that.

And it is established in the *ṣaḥīḥ* collection of Muslim through Ḥammād b. Salama, from Thābit, from Anas b. Mālik that the Messenger of God (ṢAAS) was visited by Gabriel, on whom be peace, while he was playing with the other boys. Gabriel took him, laid him down, split his heart open, took it out and withdrew a black clot from inside it, saying, "That's the devil's lot!" Then he washed it in a golden basin with water from (the well called) *zamzam*. He then mended it and put it back in its place. The other boys raced off to his mother – meaning his nurse – and told her, "Muḥammad has been killed!" When they met him he was very pale. Anas stated, "And I used to see the mark of the sewing on his chest."

Ibn ʿAsākir related this through Ibn Wahb, from ʿAmr b. al-Ḥārith, from ʿAbd Rabbihī Ibn Saʿīd, from Thābit al-Banānī, from Anas, to the effect that prayer was prescribed in Medina and that two angels came to the Messenger of God (ṢAAS), took him to *zamzam*, split open his abdomen, took out his insides and put them in a basin of gold, washed them in *zamzam* water then filled his insides with wisdom and knowledge.

And the tradition also comes through Ibn Wahb, from Yaʿqūb b. ʿAbd al-Raḥmān al-Zuhrī, from his father, from ʿAbd al-Raḥmān b.ʿĀmir b. ʿUtba b. Abū Waqqās, from Anas, who said, "The Messenger of God (ṢAAS) was visited three nights. (A voice) said: 'Take him who is the best of them and their leader.' So they took the Messenger of God (ṢAAS), conducted him to *zamzam*, opened his abdomen, brought a gold bowl, washed out his insides then filled them with wisdom and faith."

This is substantiated by the account of Sulaymān b. al-Muqhīra, from Thābit, from Anas.

In the two *ṣaḥīḥ* collections it is given through Sharīk b. Abū Nimr, from Anas, and also from al-Zuhrī from Anas, from Abū Dharr and Qatāda from Anas, and from Mālik b. Ṣaʿṣaʿa from the Prophet (ṢAAS) in the recounting of *al-Isrāʾ* (the ascension to heaven), as the story of the laying open of his chest (as occurring) on that night, and its being washed with *zamzam* water.

There is no denying the probability of that occurring twice, once when he was young and once on the night of the ascension in preparation for his going to join the heavenly assemblage of angels, and of conferring with and appearing before the Lord, the Almighty, Glorious, Blessed, and Exalted one.

Ibn Isḥāq stated, "The Messenger of God (ṢAAS) used to tell his Companions, 'I am the most Arab of you all; I am of Quraysh and was suckled by Banū Saʿd b. Bakr.'"

Ibn Isḥāq reported, "When Ḥalīma was returning him to his mother after he had been weaned, she passed with him by a caravan of Christians. They came up to him, turned him around in their hands and said, 'We must take this boy to our king; he is a person of great importance.' And Ḥalīma managed to evade them only after great effort."

He reported also that when Ḥalīma was returning him fearing some harm had come to him, as she approached Mecca she lost him and could not find him. So she went to his grandfather ʿAbd al-Muṭṭalib, and he and a group of men went off to search for him. It was Waraqa b. Nawfal and another man of Quraysh who found him and brought him to his grandfather. He put him on his shoulders and circumambulated (the *kaʿba*), praying to God for the boy's protection, and then returned him to his mother Amīna.

Al-Umawī related through ʿUthmān b. ʿAbd al-Raḥmān al-Waqqāsī, a weak authority, from al-Zuhrī, from Saʿīd b. al-Musayyab, the story of the birth of the Prophet (ṢAAS), and of his being suckled by Ḥalīma with a course different from that of Muḥammad b. Isḥāq. He stated that ʿAbd al-Muṭṭalib ordered his son ʿAbd Allāh to take the baby and go around the quarters of the bedouin to find a foster-mother for him. He did so and eventually hired Ḥalīma to suckle him. He recounted that the boy stayed with her for six years, being brought each year to visit his grandfather. When the opening of his chest occurred while he was with them, she took him back and he lived with his mother until he was eight, when she died. Thereupon his grandfather ʿAbd al-Muṭṭalib took charge of him, but he too died when the Prophet (ṢAAS) was ten. Then his two uncles, his father's two brothers al-Zubayr and Abū Ṭālib, took responsibility for him. In his early teens his uncle al-Zubayr took him to Yemen. His account states that on that journey they saw signs (of his prophethood). One of these was that a stallion camel had made its way some distance along a valley through which the party was passing. When the stallion saw the Messenger of God (ṢAAS), it knelt down and rubbed its chest on the ground and so he mounted it. Another sign was that they came to a stream in violent flood but God Almighty dried it up so that they could cross it. Thereafter his uncle al-Zubayr died; at that time he was fourteen and Abū Ṭālib alone took charge of him.

What is implied here is that the blessedness of the Prophet (ṢAAS) came down upon Ḥalīma al-Saʿdiyya and her family, when he was young and then his virtues reverted to the people of Hawāzin when he took them prisoners after their battle; that occurred a month following the capture of Mecca. They were related to him because of his being suckled among them. He therefore released them, taking pity on them, and treating them with kindness, as will be related in full in its proper place, if God wills it.

Concerning the battle with Hawāzin, Muḥammad b. Isḥāq related from ʿAmr b. Shuʿayb, from his father, from his grandfather, who said, "We were with the Messenger of God (ṢAAS) at the battle of Hunayn and when he seized their properties and took them prisoners, a delegation from Hawāzin who had accepted Islam came to him at al-Jiʿrāna[63]. They said, 'O Messenger of God, we are one family and tribe. You know well what misfortune has befallen us. Have mercy on us, and may God have mercy on you.' Their spokesman Zuhayr b. Ṣurad then arose and said, 'O Messenger of God, those prisoners you have in the stockades are your aunts and your nurses who looked after you. If we had suckled Ibn Abū Shamar or al-Nuʿmān b. al-Mundhir and then we were to suffer from them what we have from you, we would have hoped for their help and kindness. And yet you are the most honourable of men.' He then recited the verses:

'Have pity on us, O Messenger of God, in kindness; for you are the man we plead with and implore.
Have pity on a tribe ruined by fate, their whole divided, their fortune adversely changed,
Which has left us to cry out in sorrow; a people in whose hearts there is gloom and tragedy,
Unless you ward it off with kindnesses you spread forth, O most superior of men in wisdom when it is tested.
Have pity on women you once sucked, your mouth filled with their pure milk,
Have pity on women you once sucked, for then whatever happens will sustain your reputation.
Do not make us as those who scattered and died; spare us, for we are a tribe of fame.
We give thanks for kindnesses even if not redeemed, and after this day we will have a store (of good will).'"

This story is also related through ʿUbayd Allāh b. Rumāḥis al-Kalbī al-Ramlī from Ziyād b. Ṭāriq al-Jashamī, from Abū Ṣarad Zuhayr b. Jarwal, who was the leader of his people. The last-mentioned stated, "When the Messenger of God (ṢAAS) took us prisoners at the battle of Ḥunayn he was separating the men from the women. So I jumped up, stood before him and spoke some verses to him, reminding him of the time when he was a boy and grew up among Hawāzin who suckled him:

63. A place between Mecca and al-Ṭāʾif.

'Have mercy on us, Messenger of God, in gentleness, for you are the man we hope for and await.

Have mercy on a people ruined by fate, their whole divided, their fortune adversely changed,

The fighting left us a war-cry only of sadness; a people in whose hearts there is gloom and tragedy.

Unless you ward it off with kindness you spread forth, O most superior of men in wisdom when he is tested

Have pity on women you used to suck, your mouth filled with their pure milk;

When you were a small child you used to suck them and then whatever happens will sustain your reputation.

Do not make us as those who scattered and died; spare us for we are a tribe of fame.

We give thanks for kindness, even if disavowed, for after this day we will have store (of goodwill);

Dress in forgiveness those you used to suck, your mothers; for acts of forgiveness become widely known.

We hope for forgiveness from you; dress these people in it, if forgive you will, and then be triumphant.

So forgive and may God forgive you from whatever you fear on Judgement Day when victory shall be given you.'

"The Messenger of God (ṢAAS) then said, 'Whatever prizes were due myself or the family of ʿAbd al-Muṭṭalib, that goes to God and to you all.' *Al-anṣār*[64] then said, 'And what was to be for us we give to God and to his Messenger (ṢAAS).'"

It will be later told how he set them free; they were 6,000, men and women combined. He gave them many camels and people. So that Abū al-Ḥusayn b. Fāris said, "The value of what he gave them that day totalled 500,000 dirhams."

All this then came from his early blessings on earth: what blessings, then, will he bestow on those who follow him in the next world!

Division

After recounting the return of the Prophet (ṢAAS) to his mother Amīna following his suckling by Ḥalīma, Ibn Isḥāq told how the Messenger of God (ṢAAS) stayed with his mother Āmina, daughter of Wahb, and his grandfather ʿAbd al-Muṭṭalib in the care and trust of God. And God nurtured him like a fine plant for the honour He intended for him. When he reached the age of six his mother Āmina daughter of Wahb died.

Ibn Isḥāq stated, "ʿAbd Allāh b. Abū Bakr b. Muḥammad b. ʿAmr b. Ḥazam related to me that Amīna, the mother of the Messenger of God (ṢAAS), died

64. *Al-anṣār* is a term denoting the Muslims of Medina who granted the Prophet refuge following his migration from Mecca.

when he was six at al-Abwāʾ, a place between Mecca and Medina. She had taken him to visit his uncles of the tribe of ʿAdī b. al-Najjār and died when she was returning with him to Mecca."

Al-Wāqidī related, with chains of authorities, that the Prophet (ṢAAS) was taken by his mother to Medina, in the company of Umm Ayman, when he was six years old and that she visited his uncles.

Umm Ayman said, "One day two Jews of Medina came to me and said, 'Bring out Aḥmad for us to see.' They then looked at him and turned him around in their hands. Then one of them said to the other, 'This is the Prophet of this nation. And this shall be the abode of his refuge, where very many will be taken prisoner and many will be killed.'

"When his mother heard this she was afraid and left. And it was at al-Abwāʾ that she died, on her way home."

The Imām Aḥmad said that Ḥusayn b. Muḥammad related to us, quoting Ayyūb b. Jābir, from Simāk, from al-Qāsim b. ʿAbd al-Raḥmān, from Ibn Burayda, from his father (Burayda) who said, "We left along with the Messenger of God (ṢAAS) and travelled until we reached Waddān. Then he told us to wait there until he returned. He went off and later returned looking grave. Then he said, 'I went to the grave of Muḥammad's mother and asked my Lord for intercession for her. But He would not allow me that. I had forbidden you from visiting graves; do visit them. Similarly I had forbidden you from eating the flesh of sacrificed animals after three days had passed; do eat and take what you want. I had forbidden you from drinking from these vessels; do drink as you will.'"

Al-Bayhaqī related this tradition through Sufyān al-Thawrī, from ʿAlqama b. Yazīd, from Sulaymān b. Burayda from his father as follows: "The Prophet (ṢAAS) went over to the site of a grave and the other men sat down around him. He began to move his head as though addressing someone, and then he wept. ʿUmar went over to him and asked, 'What is making you weep, O Messenger of God?' He replied, 'This is the grave of Āmina daughter of Wahb. I asked my Lord for permission to visit her grave and he gave permission. I also asked for forgiveness for her, but this He refused me. Sympathy for her overwhelmed me and so I wept.' And I never saw an occasion of greater weeping than that."

He was corroborated by Muḥārib b. Dithār, from (Ibn) Burayda, from his father.

Moreover al-Bayhaqī related from al-Ḥākim, from al-Aṣamm, from Baḥr b. Naṣr, from ʿAbd Allāh b. Wahb that Ibn Jurayj related to us, from Ayyūb b. Hāniʾ, from Masrūq b. al-Ajdaʿ, from ʿAbd Allāh b. Masʿūd as follows, "The Messenger of God (ṢAAS) went off to look at graves and we went with him. He told us to sit down and we did. Then he walked on till he stopped at one grave. He spoke to it at length and then there arose a lamentation and weeping from the Messenger of God (ṢAAS). And we all wept at his crying so.

"Then the Messenger of God (ṢAAS) came over to us and was met by ʿUmar b. al-Khaṭṭāb who said, 'O Messenger of God, what made you weep? It made us weep and scared us.'

"Then he came and sat down with us and asked, 'My weeping scared you, did it?' 'Indeed yes,' we replied. He explained, 'The grave you saw me addressing was that of Āmina, daughter of Wahb. I asked my Lord's permission to visit it and he allowed me. Then I asked His permission to seek forgiveness for her, but this He did not permit me. Then there were revealed to me the verses:

> "It is not for the Prophet and for those who believe to ask forgiveness for idolaters, even if related to them, once it has become clear to them that those are going to hell. Abraham's seeking pardon for his father resulted only from a promise he had made him; and when it became clear to Abraham that he (his father) was an enemy of God, he (Abraham) disowned him. Abraham was certainly soft of heart, long-suffering" (*sūrat al-Tawba*, IX, v.113, 114). And I was affected by the emotion a son feels for his mother; that it was made me weep.'"

A unique tradition, one they (the major scholars of the traditions) did not propagate.

Muslim related from Abū Bakr b. Abū Shayba, from Muḥammad b. ʿUbayd, from Yazīd b. Kaysān, from Abū Ḥāzim, from Abū Hurayra as follows: "The Prophet (ṢAAS) visited his mother's grave; he wept and this made those with him weep too. Then he said, 'I asked my Lord's permission to visit my mother's grave and He allowed me. I also asked his permission to seek forgiveness for her, but he did not permit me. So do visit graves; they will remind you of death.'"

Muslim related, from Abū Bakr b. Abū Shayba, from ʿAffān, from Ḥammād b. Salama, from Thābit, from Anas, that a man asked, "O Messenger of God, where is my father?" He replied, "In hell-fire." Then when the man turned away, he called out to him: "My father and yours are both in hell."

Al-Bayhaqī related from a tradition of Abū Nuʿaym al-Faḍl b. Dukayn, from Ibrāhīm b. Saʿd, from al-Zuhrī, from ʿĀmir b. Saʿd, from his father as follows, "A bedouin came to the Prophet (ṢAAS) and said, 'My father used to give to charity, and so on and so forth. So where is he now?' He replied, 'In hell-fire.'

"The bedouin appeared angered at that and asked, 'Well, Messenger of God, and where's your father?' He replied, 'Whenever you pass by the grave of an unbeliever, warn him of hell-fire.'

"Thereafter the bedouin accepted Islam and said, 'The Messenger of God (ṢAAS) put a heavy burden on me; when I pass the grave of an unbeliever, I never fail to warn him of hell-fire!'"

A unique tradition, and one they (the major scholars of the traditions) did not propagate.

The Imām Aḥmad said, "Abū ʿAbd al-Raḥmān related to us, as did Saʿīd – he being Ibn Abū Ayyūb – as did Rabīʿa b. Sayf al-Maʿāfirī, from Abū ʿAbd al-Raḥmān al-Ḥublī, from ʿAbd Allāh b. ʿAmr as follows, "While we were walking with the Messenger of God (ṢAAS) he noticed a woman he did not think he recognized. When half-way across the street he stopped until she reached him. Surprisingly, it was Fāṭima, the daughter of the Messenger of God (ṢAAS). He said, 'Fāṭima what brings you out of your house?' She replied, 'I came to visit the family in this house, expressing my condolences to them for their dead.' He commented, 'Perhaps you went as far as *al-kudā* (the grave) with them.' She replied, 'God forbid that I would have gone to that with them, having heard what you have said about that.' He went on, 'Well, if you had gone that far with them you would not see paradise until your father's grandfather sees paradise!'"

Aḥmad also related this, as did Abū Dāwūd, al-Nasāʾī, and al-Bayhaqī from a *ḥadīth* of Rabīʿa b. Sayf b. Māniʿ al-Maʿāfirī al-Ṣanamī al-Iskandarī. Al-Bukhārī said the tradition has faults. Al-Nasāʾī said there was nothing wrong with it. Once he said "It is trustworthy." But in another account that it was "weak". Ibn Ḥabbān made mention of it in *al-Thiqāt* and said, "He made a lot of errors." Al-Dārquṭnī stated that it was "sound". Ibn Yūnus stated in the *Tārīkh Miṣr* (*History of Egypt*) that "there are faults in his narration." He died in approximately 120 AH.

And what is meant by *al-kudā* is the "grave". And it is also said to mean "lamentation".

What the tradition means is that ʿAbd al-Muṭṭalib died while still being a member of pre-Islamic society; this contrasts with the views of some of the Shīʿa about him and Abū Ṭālib. This will be dealt with in the material on the death of Abū Ṭālib.

Al-Bayhaqī stated, after relating these traditions in his work *Dalāʾil al-Nubūwwa* (*Signs of the Prophethood*), "And how would the father and grandfather of the Prophet (ṢAAS) not be in such circumstances regarding the hereafter when they used to worship idols until they died, and they did not follow the religion of Jesus son of Mary upon whom be peace? Yet their having been unbelievers did not impair the lineage of the Prophet (ṢAAS), because marriages between unbelievers were valid. Did not many men adopt Islam, along with their wives, but not have either to renew their marriage contracts or to separate from their wives, since these would similarly be allowed under Islam? And to God goes all success." Thus ended his comments.

My own comment is, that the relating by the Prophet (ṢAAS) that his own parents and his grandfather ʿAbd al-Muṭṭalib were in hell does not contradict the tradition related from him via various authorities that those who lived during the interregnum between the emergence of two prophets, children, the insane, and the deaf would all be put to the test in the assemblies on Judgement Day. This we laid out with chapter and verse in our Qurʾān exegesis dealing with the Almighty's words: "and We have never punished before sending a prophet" (*sūrat al-Isrāʾ*, XVII, v.15). There will be some among these groups who will respond and others who will not. Those people, then, will be among those who will not respond; there is no inconsistency here, grace and praise be to God.

As for the tradition related by al-Suhaylī about which it was mentioned that there are persons in its lineage who are unknown, traced back to the son of Abū al-Zinād, from ʿUrwa from ʿĀʾisha, God bless her, that the Messenger of God (ṢAAS) asked his Lord to bring his parents back to life and that God did so and that they expressed faith in him; this is a highly unreliable tradition. Even though all this would be possible in terms of the power of God Almighty. However, what is well established in the *ṣaḥīḥ* collections does contradict this tradition. And God knows best.

Division

Ibn Isḥāq stated, "When the Messenger of God (ṢAAS) lived with his grandfather ʿAbd al-Muṭṭalib b. Hāshim – that is, after the death of his mother Āmina daughter of Wahb – a spread would be set out for ʿAbd al-Muṭṭalib in the shade of the *kaʿba*. His sons would seat themselves around his spread until he would come to it. But none of his sons would actually sit upon it, out of respect for him. The Messenger of God (ṢAAS), when a young boy, would come along and sit down on it. Then his uncles would take him to remove him from it, but ʿAbd al-Muṭṭalib would say, if he saw them doing that, 'Leave my son (*sic*) alone; he has great things ahead of him.' Then he would sit down with him on his spread, rub his back, and it would please him to watch what he would do."

Al-Wāqidī said that Muḥammad b. ʿAbd Allāh related to him, from al-Zuhrī, as did ʿAbd Allāh b. Jaʿfar from ʿAbd al-Wāḥid b. Ḥamza b. ʿAbd Allāh, and Hāshim b. ʿĀṣim al-Aslamī from al-Mundhir b. Jahm, and Maʿmar from Ibn Abū Najiḥ from Mujāhid and ʿAbd al-Raḥmān b. ʿAbd al-ʿAzīz from Abū al-Ḥuwayrith, and Ibn Abū Sabra from Sulaymān b. Saḥīm, from Nāfiʿ, from Ibn Jubayr, the narration of some interfering with that of others, as follows: "The Messenger of God (ṢAAS) used to live with his mother Amīna daughter of Wahb and when she died his grandfather ʿAbd al-Muṭṭalib took him to himself, treating him with a closeness and kindness he had not shown to his own son. He would allow and encourage him to come close to him, and the boy would go in to him when he was alone or asleep. He would sit down on his spread, and ʿAbd al-Muṭṭalib would say when he saw him do this, "Leave my son alone; he will establish a kingdom.'"

A group of men from Banū Mudlij said to ʿAbd al-Muṭṭalib, "Take good care of him; for we have never seen anyone with so noble a lineage as his." So ʿAbd al-Muṭṭalib said to Abū Ṭālib: "Listen to what these men are saying." And Abū Ṭālib did take care of him.

ʿAbd al-Muṭṭalib said to Umm Ayman – who had suckled him – "O Baraka, do not neglect my son. I found him with some boys close to the lote-tree; and the People of the Book (i.e. Christians and Jews) claim that my boy will be the Prophet of this nation."

ʿAbd al-Muṭṭalib used never to eat without saying, "Bring my son." And he would be brought to him.

And when death approached ʿAbd al-Muṭṭalib he charged Abū Ṭālib with the care and safe-keeping of the Messenger of God (ṢAAS).

Then ʿAbd al-Muṭṭalib died and was buried at al-Ḥajūn.

Ibn Isḥāq stated, "And when the Messenger of God (ṢAAS) was eight, his grandfather ʿAbd al-Muṭṭalib died." He also stated that ʿAbd al-Muṭṭalib had summoned his daughters and told them that they should compose elegies for him; these daughters were called Arwā, Umayma, Barra, Ṣafiyya, ʿĀtika, and Umm Ḥakīm al-Bayḍā'.

Ibn Isḥāq mentioned their poems and what they said in mourning their father, all while he listened, before he in fact died. Their words of mourning were extremely eloquent. He described that in great detail.

Ibn Hishām said, "I never met any scholar of poetry who knew these verses."

Ibn Isḥāq stated, "And when ʿAbd al-Muṭṭalib b. Hāshim died, control over providing water for the pilgrims and over *zamzam* went after him to al-ʿAbbās who was the youngest of his brothers.

This control remained his until the coming of Islam, after which the Messenger of God (ṢAAS) confirmed it for al-ʿAbbas.

The Messenger of God (ṢAAS) was with his uncle Abū Ṭālib after having been with his grandfather ʿAbd al-Muṭṭalib. This was because the latter had placed him in trust of his uncle and because Abū Ṭālib was the full brother of his father ʿAbd Allāh, the mother of both having been Fāṭima daughter of ʿAmr b. ʿĀ'idh b. ʿImrān b. Makhzūm."

Ibn Isḥāq went on: "Abū Ṭālib was the one who took charge of the Messenger of God (ṢAAS); he cared for him completely."

Al-Wāqidī stated that Maʿmar told him, from Ibn Najīh, from Mujāhid; and that Maʿādh b. Muḥammad al-Ansārī related to him from ʿAṭā', from Ibn ʿAbbās, as did Muḥammad b. Ṣāliḥ and ʿAbd Allāh b. Jaʿfar, as did Ibrāhīm b. Ismāʿīl b. Abū Ḥabība, the account of each of these corresponding with one another, as follows: "When ʿAbd al-Muṭṭalib died Abū Ṭālib took the Messenger of God (ṢAAS) to live with him.

"Abū Ṭālib was not wealthy; he loved the boy very much, more so than his children. The boy slept always by his side and went wherever he did.

"Abū Ṭālib had very great and unusual depth of affection for him. He would give the boy's food special attention. And if his own children ever ate, alone or as a group, without the boy's presence, they would remain unsatisfied, whereas when the Prophet would eat with them they would be well satisfied. When serving his family a daytime meal he would tell them to wait till the boy's arrival. When the Messenger of God would arrive and eat with them, they would get satisfied, and part of the food would remain uneaten. But if he did not eat with them they would remain unsatisfied. Abū Ṭālib would say, 'You are clearly blessed.'

"In the morning the other boys would arise bleary-eyed and dishevelled while the Messenger of God (ṢAAS) would get up bright-eyed and with his hair in place."

Al-Ḥasan b. ʿArafa stated that ʿAlī b. Thābit related to him from Ṭalḥa b. ʿAmr that the latter heard ʿAṭāʾ b. Abū Rabbāḥ report having heard Ibn ʿAbbās say, "Abū Ṭālib's family would get up in the morning with bleary, dirty eyes, while the Messenger of God (ṢAAS) would get up bright-eyed and with his hair neatly groomed."

Early each morning Abū Ṭālib would bring to the boys their food platter and they would all sit down and snatch at it. The Messenger of God (ṢAAS), however, would keep his hand away and not grab at the food along with them. When his uncle saw this he set food aside for him alone.

Ibn Isḥāq said, "Yaḥʿyā b. ʿAbd Allāh b. al-Zubayr related to me that his father told him that there was a certain man of Lihb who could predict the future. Whenever he came to Mecca the men of Quraysh would take their boys to him to see and predict their futures."

He went on, "So Abū Ṭālib brought the Messenger of God (ṢAAS) to him when he was still a boy, along with some others. The fortune-teller looked at the Messenger of God, but then something engaged his attention. When finished with that, he said, 'Bring that boy over to me!' When Abū Ṭālib saw how interested the man was in him, he took him away. Then the man exclaimed, 'Woe on you! Bring back to me that boy I saw earlier; by God, he has a big future ahead of him!'

"But Abū Ṭālib hurried away with him."

Section: The journey of the Prophet (ṢAAS) with his uncle Abū Ṭālib away to Syria and on what transpired with the monk Baḥīrā.

Ibn Isḥāq stated that thereafter Abū Ṭālib left with a trading caravan for Syria. As he was preparing to depart and assembling the goods, the Messenger of God (ṢAAS) began to miss him badly, or so they claim.

So Abū Ṭālib took pity on him and said words to the effect that, "By God, I'll take him away with me and never be parted from him, just as he will not be parted from me!"

He did leave with him. Eventually the caravan made a halt at Buṣrā in Syria, where there was a monk named Baḥīrā living in a cell. He was very learned in Christianity; the cell he lived in had always been occupied by some monk who would acquire their Christian learning from a book, as they claim, which they had passed down in inheritance from one elder to the next.

They stopped that year near Baḥīrā, as they had often done previously without his paying them attention. When they halted, then, near his cell, this time he made a lot of food for them. This, they claim, was because of a vision he had seen while he was in his cell; he had seen the Messenger of God (ṢAAS) approaching in the caravan, with a cloud casting its shade only on him. When they had arrived they had dismounted in the shade of a tree near the monk. When he looked up at the cloud he saw it was shading the tree, the branches of which were extending out over the Messenger of God (ṢAAS) so that he was shaded beneath them.

When Baḥīrā saw this he came down from his cell and, having ordered food which was then prepared, he sent word over to the travellers saying, "O Quraysh, I have prepared food for you and would like you all to come over, great and small, and freemen or slaves."

One Quraysh man commented to him, "By God, Baḥīrā, you've put yourself to much trouble today! You've never done this for us, even though we've passed by you here often before. Why today?"

Baḥīrā replied, "You are right; before it was as you say. But you are my guests, and I wanted to honour you and so have prepared you some food. I want all of you to eat of it."

So they gathered around him. But the Messenger of God (ṢAAS), because of his youth, was left behind with the baggage, beneath the tree.

When Baḥīrā saw them he did not see the quality he had seen and known to be the boy's. So he said, "O Quraysh let not any one of you be left out of my feast."

They replied, "O Baḥīrā, the only one left out who ought to have come to you is a boy; he is the youngest of our party and he remained behind with the baggage." Baḥīrā insisted. "Do not do this; call him over and let him attend this feast along with you."

One of the Quraysh party exclaimed, "By al-Lāt and al-'Uzzā it really is a shame on us that Muḥammad son of 'Abd Allāh son of 'Abd al-Muṭṭalib be kept back from eating the food among us."

Then he went over to the boy, brought him back, and sat him down among the rest.

When Baḥīrā saw him he began to scrutinize him very intently, looking at various parts of his body and finding certain qualities in him. Finally, when all had finished dining and had dispersed, Baḥīrā went up to the boy and said,

"Boy, by al-Lāt and al-ʿUzzā I charge you to answer what I will ask you." Baḥīrā only used these words because he had heard the boy's people swearing by these two gods.

They claim that the Messenger of God (ṢAAS) told him: "Don't ask me anything by al-Lāt and al-ʿUzzā; for, by God, I hate nothing more than them." So Baḥīrā said, "By God, would you tell me about what I ask you?" So the boy told him to ask whatever he liked.

The monk then asked him various questions about his sleep, habits, circumstances, and so on; and the Messenger of God (ṢAAS) responded. And what Baḥīrā heard matched the description he expected.

Then he looked at the boy's back and saw the seal of prophethood between his shoulders, in the very place according to the description he had.

Having concluded this, he went over to the boy's uncle Abū Ṭālib and asked, "What relation is he to you?" "He is my son," he replied.

Baḥīrā objected, "He's not your son. This boy can't have a living father."

"Well," Abū Ṭālib replied, "he's actually my nephew."

"And what happened to his father?" the monk asked.

"He died while the boy's mother was still pregnant with him."

"Now you're telling the truth," the monk went on. "Take your brother's son back to his own country and guard him from the Jews. For, by God, if they see him and know what I know, they will do him evil. This nephew of yours has a great future before him; take him back soon to his own country."

So his uncle Abū Ṭālib left with him for Mecca quickly, as soon as he had finished his business in Syria.

Ibn Isḥāq stated, "They claim, according to what people said, that Zurayr, Tammām, and Darīs – all believers in the Scriptures – had also seen what Baḥīrā noticed in the Messenger of God (ṢAAS) on that trip with his uncle Abū Ṭālib. They tried to get him, but Baḥīrā kept them away from him, making reference to God and to the description of him and mention of him they would find in the Holy Scripture, as well as the statement that they would not succeed in getting him. They recognized the reference he was making to them, and since they believed what he said they let the boy alone and went away."

Yūnus b. Bukayr recalled, on the authority of Ibn Isḥāq, that Abū Ṭālib spoke three odes on this subject.

This is how Ibn Isḥāq related this sequence of events, but he gave no chain of authorities for it. A similar account also came down by way of a *musnad marfūʿ*.[65]

The *ḥāfiẓ* Abū Bakr al-Kharāʾiṭī stated that ʿAbbās b. Muḥammad al-Dūrī related to him, as did Qarād Abū Nūḥ, as did Yūnus, from Ibn Isḥāq, from Abū

65. The term denotes a tradition attributed to the Prophet that has a complete line of transmission.

Bakr b. Abū Mūsā, from his father, as follows: "Abū Ṭālib went off to Syria along with the Messenger of God (ṢAAS) and a number of Quraysh elders. When they reached a point overlooking the monk – meaning Baḥīrā – they went down and untied their baggage. The monk then came out to them, whereas previously when they had passed by he had not come out or even turned towards them."

He went on, "He came down, then, as they were untying their baggage, and walked among them until he came and took the Prophet (ṢAAS) by the hand and said, 'This is the Lord of all mankind!'"

In the account of al-Bayhaqī the phrase he used was longer, saying also, "This is the Messenger of the Lord of the worlds; God sent him as a mercy to all mankind."

Some of the Quraysh elders then asked him, "What is it you know?" He replied, "When you looked down from the mountain road every single tree and every rock bent down in worship. And they would only prostrate themselves before a prophet. And I know him by the mark of prophethood below the cartilage of his shoulder blades."

He then went back and prepared food for them. When he brought it, the boy was tending to the camels. The monk told them to send for him. As he approached a cloud was shading him, and as the boy came near the others the monk exclaimed, "See; there is a cloud above him!" When the boy arrived he found that the others had preceded him to the shade of the tree, but when he sat down the shade moved out over him. The monk commented, "Just look how the tree's shade moved over him!"

While Baḥīrā was standing there urging them not to take him into Byzantine territory, saying that when they saw him the Romans would recognize him by his description and would kill him, he turned around and, to his surprise, saw seven Romans who had arrived. He greeted them and asked why they had come. They replied, "We have information that there's this prophet who will come forth this month and so we have been sending men along each route; news we had of him brought us along this route of yours." "Do you", Baḥīrā asked, "have anyone superior to you coming along behind you?" They replied, "No; it's just the information we had about him brought us along this road of yours." Baḥīrā then asked them, "Have you ever known any matter God wished to bring about that anyone was able to reverse?" They said they had not, and then they pledged him allegiance and stayed with him there at Baḥīrā's place.

The account goes on, reporting that the monk then asked, "I abjure you by God to tell me, which of you is his guardian?" "Abū Ṭālib," they replied.

Baḥīrā kept on admonishing him (Abū Ṭālib) until he took the boy back (to Mecca); Abū Bakr sent Bilāl along with him and the monk provisioned him with cake and oil.

Thus al-Tirmidhī told it, from Abū al-ʿAbbās al-Faḍl b. Sahl al-Aʿraj, from Qarād Abū Nūḥ. Al-Ḥākim, al-Bayhaqī, and Ibn ʿAsākir derive it through Abū al-ʿAbbās Muḥammad b. Yaʿqūb al-Aṣamm from ʿAbbās b. Muḥammad al-Dūrī.

And thus too did more than one *ḥāfiẓ* relate it from an account of Abū Nūḥ ʿAbd al-Raḥmān b. Ghazwān al-Khuzāʿī, their *mawlā*, their freed slave. He was known as al-Ḍabbī, and also as Qarād; he lived in Baghdad and was one of those "trustworthy sources" vouched for by al-Bukhārī. A number of legal scholars and *ḥufāẓ* declare him trustworthy, and I never knew anyone who impugned him. Nevertheless, there are unique aspects to this account of his.

Al-Tirmidhī stated: "The tradition is good, though unusual. We know of it only from this account."

ʿAbbās al-Dūrī said, "There is no one in the world who relates it apart from Qarād Abū Nūḥ; Aḥmad b. Ḥanbal, God have mercy on him, heard this from him, and Yaḥyā b. Muʿīn similarly for its unique and unusual quality." Al-Bayhaqī and Ibn ʿAsākir related it.

My comment is that one strange aspect to the tradition is its being attributed back to the Companions, whereas Abū Mūsā al-ʿAshʿarī only came forward (into Islam) in the year of the battle of Khaybar, in the seventh year of the *hijra*. This view does not reflect Ibn Isḥāq's statement that includes him amongst those who emigrated to Abyssinia from Mecca.

By all estimations the story was attributed (back to the Prophet); the incident occurred, as some sources maintain, when the Messenger of God (ṢAAS) was 12 years old. Perhaps Abū Mūsā received it from the Prophet (ṢAAS), in which case it would be very accurate. Or he could have received it from some of the major Companions, God be pleased with them. Alternatively the incident might have been well known and often mentioned and the narrator took it from knowledge widely current.

The second strange aspect is that the cloud was not referred to in any account more reliable than this one. The third problem relates to the words: "Abū Bakr sent Bilāl along with him." If the age of the Prophet (ṢAAS) at that time was twelve, then Abū Bakr would have been nine or ten. Bilāl's age would have been less than that. And where was Abū Bakr at that time? And where was Bilāl? Both (being there) would be strange, certainly, unless it be said that this occurred when the Messenger of God (ṢAAS) was full grown. This would mean that the trip took place later than it is supposed, or that the statement that he was twelve at the time is inaccurate; al-Wāqidī related the incident contingent upon that. Yet al-Suhaylī stated on the authority of certain sources, that the age of the prophet (ṢAAS) at the time was nine. So God knows best.

Al-Wāqidī stated that Muḥammad b. Ṣāliḥ related to him, as did ʿAbd Allāh b. Jaʿfar and Ibrāhīm b. Ismāʿīl b. Abū Ḥabība, from Dāwūd b. al-Ḥusayn, as follows: "When the Messenger of God (ṢAAS) reached the age of twelve, his uncle Abū Ṭālib took him along to Syria in the caravan he was accompanying to engage in business there. They made a halt with the monk Baḥīrā, who made some statements in confidence to Abū Ṭālib. Baḥīrā told him to look after the boy and Abū Ṭālib sent him back to Mecca. The Messenger of God lived as a youth with Abū Ṭālib, while God protected him and preserved him from the evils of the *jāhiliyya* period for the honour He wished for him."

When he grew up he was consequently the most honourable man of his people, the best in character, the most noble in his relationships, the best neighbour, the most prudent, trustworthy and truthful, and the man most removed from immorality or harmfulness. He was never seen to do anyone harm or to quarrel with anyone, so that his people named him *al-Amīn*, "the trustworthy one" because of all the fine qualities God had joined together in him.

Abū Ṭālib protected and cared for him, aided and assisted him until his death.

Muḥammad b. Saʿd stated, "Khālid b. Maʿdān told us, Muʿtamir b. Sulaymān related to us, that he heard his father relate from Abū Mijliz that ʿAbd al-Muṭṭalib or Abū Ṭālib – Khālid was unsure which one – said, that when ʿAbd Allāh died he was sorry for Muḥammad and never went away on any trip without taking him with him. And when he was on the way to Syria and stopped to set up camp, a monk came to him there and said, 'You have a man of goodness among you.' Then he said, 'Where is the father of this boy?' The reply was given, 'I am his guardian' (or it was said, 'he is his guardian'). The monk commented: 'Take care of this boy; do not take him to Syria. The Jews are jealous, and I fear for him from them.' He was told, 'It is not you who are saying that but God himself.' So he did take him back, and said, 'O God, I place Muḥammad in your care!' Then he died."

The Story of Baḥīrā.

Al-Suhaylī related, quoting the biographical writings of al-Zuhrī, that Baḥīrā was a Jewish high priest.

My comment is, that it appears from the course of the story that he was a Christian monk. But God knows best.

From al-Masʿūdī comes the information that he was a man of the ʿAbd al-Qays tribe, and that his name was Jirjis.

In the work *al-Maʿārif* (*Knowledge*) of Ibn Qutayba it states, "A voice was heard in the *jāhiliyya* period, shortly before Islam, calling out the words, 'O yea, the finest of men on earth are three: Baḥīrā, Riʾāb b. al-Barrāʾ al-Shannī, and the third is still awaited." The third and one awaited was the Messenger of God (ṢAAS).

Ibn Qutayba stated, "*Al-ṭish* is always seen at the graves of Riʿāb al-Shannī and of his son who came after him." This word, *al-ṭish*, means light rain.

Section: On the early upbringing and raising of the Messenger of God (ṢAAS) and how God cared for him and protected him; how he had been an orphan and God gave him a home and destitute and God enriched him.

Muḥammad b. Isḥāq stated, "And so the Messenger of God (ṢAAS) became a youth under the care and protection of God who saved him from the evils of the *jāhiliyya* because of the honour and mission He wished for him. When he grew up he was the finest man among his people, the best of them in character and repute, the best of neighbours, the most prudent, the most honest in speech and most trustworthy, and the one most removed from immorality and those characteristics that corrupt men, which he avoided because of his nobility."

Consequently the name by which he was known among Quraysh was none other than *al-Amīn*, "the trustworthy", because of the fine qualities God had joined in him.

The Messenger of God (ṢAAS), as I was told, used to relate about those (pre-Islamic) practices, matters from which God had protected him in his youth and time of ignorance. He said, "Once I happened to be amongst some Quraysh boys carrying some stones for those games boys play. Each of us was exposed, having taken up his shirt and fastened it around his neck to carry stones in. I was running along with them in this way and having fallen behind I suddenly received a very painful slap from someone who spoke the words, 'Put your shirt on properly!' So I took it and put it back on properly and began carrying the stones around my neck with my shirt on, alone among my friends."

This anecdote is similar to the one in the *ṣaḥīḥ* collection relating to the building of the *kaʿba*, when he and his uncle al-ʿAbbās were hauling (stones). If not the same, it certainly precedes that and is seemingly preparing for it. But God knows best.

ʿAbd al-Razzāq said that Ibn Jurayj informed him, quoting ʿAmr b. Dīnār, that he heard Jābir b. ʿAbd Allāh say, "When the *kaʿba* was being built, the Messenger of God (ṢAAS) went off to transport stones. Al-ʿAbbās said to the Messenger of God (ṢAAS), 'Put your shirt over your shoulder for the stones.' He did so, but fell to the ground and his eyes were drawn up to heaven. Then he got up and said, 'It was my shirt.' So it was put back on him properly."

The two traditionalists brought this *ḥadīth* out in the two *ṣaḥīḥ* collections, from an account of ʿAbd al-Razzāq. They also extrapolated it from an account of Rawḥ b. ʿUbāda from Zakariyyāʾ b. Abū Isḥāq, from ʿAmr b. Dīnār from Jābir to the same effect.

Al-Bayhaqī said that the *ḥāfiẓ* Abū ʿAbd Allāh and Abū Saʿīd b. Abū ʿAmr informed him that Abū al-ʿAbbās Muḥammad b. Yaʿqūb told them that Muḥammad b. Isḥāq al-Ṣāghānī related to him, quoting Muḥammad b. Bukayr al-Ḥaḍramī, quoting ʿAbd al-Raḥmān b. ʿAbd Allāh al-Dashtakī, quoting ʿAmr b. Abū Qays, from Simāk, from ʿIkrima, who said that Ibn ʿAbbās related to him from his father that he would carry stones to the *kaʿba* when Quraysh was building it. Quraysh divided up into two groups, with the men transporting the stones and the women the mortar mix.

He went on: "I was with my nephew, carrying the rocks, wearing our shirts around our necks; when we came up to other people we covered up. While I was walking along with Muḥammad in front of me, he fell down and stretched out flat on his face. I hurried along, threw down my rocks; meanwhile he was looking up to heaven. 'What's wrong?' I asked. He got up and took his shirt, saying, 'I was forbidden from walking uncovered.'" Ibn ʿAbbās went on, "I hid this from the others for fear they would say (he) was mad."

Al-Bayhaqī related from a tradition of Yūnus b. Bukayr, from Muḥammad b. Isḥāq, that Muḥammad b. ʿAbd Allāh b. Qays b. Makhrama related to him, from al-Ḥasan b. Muḥammad b. ʿAlī b. Abū Ṭālib, from his father and from his grandfather, ʿAlī b. Abū Ṭālib, who said that he heard the Messenger of God (ṢAAS) say, "I wasn't interested in performing those things with women that people during the *jāhiliyya* used to do; except, that is, on two nights on which God, Almighty and Glorious is He, restrained me.

"One evening I and a young man of Mecca were watching some sheep belonging to some people there. I said to him, 'Would you keep an eye on my sheep so I can go into Mecca and spend an evening there like other lads?' 'Sure,' he replied. So I went into town and stopped at the first house where I heard the music of tambourines and flutes. I asked what was going on and was told that a man and woman had married. So I sat down to watch. But God struck my ears and, I swear, next thing I knew I was being awakened by the sun's touch. I went back to my friend, who asked what I had done. I replied, 'I didn't do a thing.' Then I told him what I had seen.

"Then one other night I asked him to watch my sheep so I could go to a party. He agreed, so I went off to Mecca and heard the same as I had the previous occasion. Again I was told that there was a marriage and so sat down to watch. But God again struck my ears and, I swear, I was later awakened by the sun's touch.

"When I returned to my friend he asked what I had done. 'Not a thing,' I replied, and then I told him what had happened. And, by God, I never tried or returned to anything like that thereafter right up to when Almighty and Glorious God honoured me with His prophethood."

This is a very strange tradition. It could be about ʿAlī himself, with the final words "up to when Almighty and Glorious God honoured me with his prophethood" having been added. But God knows best.

This scholar Ibn Isḥāq is mentioned by Ibn Ḥibbān as being a very reliable source. Some authorities claim him to be an author of a *ṣaḥīḥ* collection of traditions. In his supplementary notes, this sheikh of ours commented on this, "I don't fully stand behind this." But God knows best.

The *ḥāfiẓ* al-Bayhaqī said that the *ḥāfiẓ* ʿAbd Allāh related to him, quoting Abū al-ʿAbbās Muḥammad b. Yaʿqūb, quoting al-Ḥasan b. ʿAlī b. ʿAffān al-ʿĀmirī, quoting Abū Usāma, quoting Muḥammad b. ʿAmr, from Abū Salama and Yaḥyā b. ʿAbd Raḥmān b. Ḥāṭib, from Usāma b. Zayd, from Zayd b. Ḥāritha, who said, "There was a brass idol called ʿIsāf and Nāʾila which the polytheists would touch as they performed their circumambulation. The Messenger of God (ṢAAS) said 'Don't touch it.'"

Zayd continued, "Well, as we went round (again) I told myself I would touch it to see what would happen. When I did so, the Messenger of God (ṢAAS) asked me, 'Were you not forbidden to do that?'"

Al-Bayhaqī said that others added, from Muḥammad b. ʿAmr, giving a chain of authorities, that Zayd said, "By Him who honoured him and revealed to him the Holy Book, he (the Prophet) never saluted an idol right up to when God Almighty honoured him as He did and gave revelation to him."

We earlier made reference to the comment of the Messenger of God (ṢAAS) when Baḥīrā put a question to him invoking al-Lāt and al-ʿUzzā: "By God, do not question me by invoking them! I hate nothing so much as them!"

As for the tradition given by the *ḥāfiẓ* Abū Bakr al-Bayhaqī, Abū Saʿd al-Mālīnī informed us, Abū Aḥmad b. ʿAdī, the *ḥāfiẓ* told us, Ibrāhīm b. Asbāṭ related to us, as did ʿUthmān b. Abū Shayba, as did Jarīr, from Sufyān al-Thawrī, from Muḥammad b. ʿAbd Allāh b. Muḥammad b. ʿUqayl, from Jābir b. ʿAbd Allāh, God bless him, as follows: "The Prophet (ṢAAS) used to attend the ceremonies of the polytheists along with them. But once he heard two angels behind him, one saying to the other, 'Let's move up and stand right behind the Messenger of God (ṢAAS).' But the other objected, 'How can we stand right behind him when he is in the habit of saluting idols?'"

He went on, "And thereafter he never again attended such ceremonies with the polytheists."

This is a tradition several authorities deny being attributed to ʿUthmān b. Abū Shayba. Regarding it Imām Aḥmad commented: "His brother would never speak any such words."

Al-Bayhaqī related from various sources that his meaning was that he witnessed those who saluted idols, and that that was before God made revelation to him. But God knows best.

We previously reported a tradition from Zayd b. Ḥāritha to the effect that he abstained from witnessing the ceremonies of the polytheists until God honoured him with His mission.

It is established in the tradition that he did not participate in the assembly at al-Muzdalifa during the night on Mt. ʿArafāt. Indeed he did not assemble with the people at ʿArafāt.

Similarly Yūnus b. Bukayr said, from Muḥammad b. Isḥāq, that ʿAbd Allāh b. Abū Bakr related to him, from ʿUthmān b. Abū Sulaymān, from Nāfiʿ b. Jubayr b. Muṭʿim, from his father Jubayr who said, "I saw the Messenger of God (ṢAAS) while he was a member of his people's religion. He would station himself there on a camel of his at ʿArafāt, among his people until he raced away with them, God the Almighty and Glorious giving him blessing thereby."

Al-Bayhaqī stated, "The meaning of the words 'a member of his people's religion' refers to the remnants of the heritage of Abraham and Ishmael, on both of whom be peace. The Prophet (ṢAAS) never at any time associated with Allāh any other god."

I also comment, that from these words of (al-Bayhaqī) it is to be understood that he did attend the assembly at ʿArafāt before he received revelation. And it was this that was a "blessing" to him from God the Almighty and Glorious.

The Imām Aḥmad related this tradition from Yaʿqūb, from Muḥammad b. Isḥāq. The words he used were: "I saw the Messenger of God (ṢAAS) before he received revelation while he was positioned on a camel of his with his people on ʿArafāt so that he would move forward with them, this being a blessing from God."

The Imām Aḥmad said that Sufyān related to him, from ʿAmr, from Muḥammad b. Jubayr b. Muṭʿim, from his father, saying, "I lost track of a camel of mine in the ʿUrana valley (close to ʿArafāt) and went off to look for it. I found the Prophet (ṢAAS) in the assembly there. I said, 'He's one of the *ḥums* (a word used for Quraysh). What's he doing here?'"

They both derived this from a tradition of Sufyān b. ʿUyayna to that effect.

An Account of how the Prophet (ṢAAS) witnessed the war known as al-fijār, *the sacrilegious war.*

Ibn Isḥāq said, "The 'sacrilegious' war raged at a time when the Messenger of God (ṢAAS) was 20. It was named the *fijār* (sacrilegious) war because the two tribes Kināna and Qays ʿAylān acted as though the sacred month (when warfare was disallowed) was open for them to fighting. The leader of Quraysh and of Kināna was Ḥarb b. Umayya b. ʿAbd Shams. Early in the day of the battle, Qays were defeating Kināna, but by midday the victory had gone to Kināna over Qays."

Ibn Hishām stated, "When the Messenger of God reached 14 – or 15 – as Abū ʿUbayda the grammarian related to me, from Abū ʿAmr b. al-ʿAlā', the 'sacrilegious' war broke out between Quraysh and its Kināna supporters and Qays ʿAylān.

"What started it was that ʿUrwa al-Raḥḥāl b. ʿUtba b. Jaʿfar b. Kilāb b. Rabīʿa b. ʿAmr b. Ṣaʿṣaʿa b. Muʿāwiya b. Bakr b. Hawāzin had given a passing permission to a trading caravan of musk which belonged to al-Nuʿmān b. al-Mundhir. And so al-Barrāḍ b. Qays, one of the tribe of Ḍumra b. Bakr b. ʿAbd Manāt b. Kināna asked, 'Are you going to apply the same against Kināna's will?' 'Yes,' was the reply, 'and against everyone.'

"So ʿUrwa al-Raḥḥāl set out with the trading party and al-Barrād left too, seeking to catch him unawares. When the party reached the high ground of Tayman Dhū Ṭilāl, ʿUrwa became careless and al-Barrāḍ fell upon him and killed him; this was during the sacred month. Consequently the warfare became known as 'sacrilegious'." Al-Barrāḍ spoke the following verses about all this:

> "There's many a tragedy that distressed people before me that I, O Banū Bakr, stood firm against.
> Thereby I destroyed the houses of Banū Kilāb and humbled the freed slaves to submission.
> I raised my fist against him at Dhū Ṭilāl and he dropped like a felled tree."

Labīd b. Rabīʿa b. Mālik b. Jaʿfar b. Kilāb also composed the lines:

> "Tell Banū Kilāb, if you chance on them, and ʿĀmir, that there are some who can master disasters,
> Tell Banū Numayr, if you chance on them, and the dead man's uncles of Banū Hilāl,
> That the expected al-Raḥḥāl now rests at Tayman Dhū Ṭilāl."

Ibn Hishām continued, "A man arrived and told Quraysh of it, saying, 'Al-Barrād has killed ʿUrwa, and during the sacred month, at ʿUkāẓ.' They then rode off, unbeknown to Hawāzin. When Hawāzin learned of this they pursued them and caught up with them before they reached the sacred territory. They engaged in battle till nightfall but then they went inside the sacred territory and Hawāzin gave up on them.

"They met for several days after that battle, with the people going forth under various banners with a leader from each of the tribes of Quraysh and Kināna, and a leader from each of the tribes of Qays.

"The Messenger of God (ṢAAS) was present at some of these battles, his uncles having taken him with themselves. The Messenger of God (ṢAAS) said, 'I was giving arrows to my uncles.' That is, he would gather for them the arrows their enemy had shot at them."

Ibn Hishām said, "The account of the 'sacrilegious' war is very long, longer than I have recounted. But I have been deterred from recounting it because it would have interrupted the telling of the biography of the Messenger of God (ṢAAS)."

Al-Suhaylī said that *al-fijār* is spelt with an "i" after the "f", in the like form to *qitāl*, fighting. The *fijār* wars among the Arabs totalled four, and al-Mas‘ūdī gave reference to all of them.

He went on, "The last of them was this one involving al-Barrāḍ. The fighting in it consisted of four battles: the battle of Shamṭa, and the battle of al-‘Ablā᾽, both near ‘Ukāẓ, and the battle of al-Sharb, which was the major battle. It was this one that the Messenger of God (ṢAAS) attended. For this battle the chieftains of Quraysh and Banū Kināna, respectively Ḥarb b. Umayya and his brother Sufyān, made a pact not to take to flight. On that occasion Qays were defeated, except for Banū Naḍr who held out. The fourth battle was at al-Ḥarīra, near Nakhla. Then they made an agreement to meet the following year at ‘Ukāẓ. When they assembled to fulfil this appointment ‘Utba b. Rabī‘a rode out on his camel and called out: 'O tribe of Muḍar, what is it you are fighting for?' Hawāzin replied, 'What are you suggesting?' 'Peace,' he replied. 'How,' they asked. He said, 'We pay you blood-money for your dead, and will leave people hostage with you to guarantee payment; and we will forgo our blood-money you owe.' 'Who will guarantee us that?' 'I will,' he replied. 'And who are you?' they demanded. 'I am ‘Utba b. Rabī‘a,' he told them.

"On that basis peace was made, and they sent out to them 40 men, including Hākim b. Ḥizān. And when Banū ‘Amr b. Ṣa‘ṣa‘a saw the guarantee hostages in their hands they gave up their claims and the 'sacrilegious' war was at an end."

Al-Umawī gave an account of the "sacrilegious" wars and the battles that occurred, detailing them at length, his information deriving from al-Athram, who was al-Mughīra b. ‘Alī, from Abū ‘Ubayda Ma‘mar b. al-Muthannā.

CHAPTER: HOW THE MESSENGER OF GOD (ṢAAS) WITNESSED THE PACT OF *AL-FUḌŪL*.

The *ḥāfiẓ* al-Bayhaqī said that Abū Sa‘d al-Mālīnī told him, Abū Aḥmad b. ‘Adī, the *ḥāfiẓ*, related to him, quoting Yaḥyā b. ‘Alī b. Hāshim al-Khaffāf, quoting Ismā‘īl b. ‘Aliyya, from ‘Abd al-Raḥmān b. Isḥāq, from al-Zuhrī, from Muḥammad b. Jubayr b. Muṭ‘im from his father, that the Messenger of God (ṢAAS) said, "I was a witness, with my uncles, to the pact of *al-muṭayyabīn* and I would not have wanted to renege – or some such word – for the very choicest herd."

He (al-Bayhaqī) said that this tradition was related in these words also by Bishr b. al-Mufaḍḍal, from ‘Abd al-Raḥmān.

He also said that Abū Naṣr b. Qatāda related to him, quoting Abū ‘Amr b. Maṭar, quoting Abū Bakr b. Aḥmad b. Dāwūd al-Samnānī, quoting Mu‘allā b. Mahdī, quoting Abū ‘Awāna, all from ‘Umar b. Abū Salama, from his father, from Abū Hurayra, that the Messenger of God (ṢAAS) said. "The only pact I witnessed Quraysh make was that of *al-muṭayyabīn*. And I'd not have abrogated it in return for the choicest herd."

He said that *al-muṭayyabīn* referred to Hāshim, Umayya, Zahra, and Makhzūm.

Al-Bayhaqī said, "This explanation is also interpolated within the tradition, but I do not know who it was who said it."

Some biographers maintain that he was referring to the *fuḍūl* pact; for the Prophet (ṢAAS) was not yet born at the time of the *muṭayyabīn* pact.

In my view, there is no disputing that. The fact is that Quraysh did conclude a treaty following the death of Quṣayy. They disputed the fact of Quṣayy having left to his son ʿAbd al-Dār the right to control provision of food and drink to the pilgrims, raising the banner at the *kaʿba*, its guardianship, and the convening of the assembly. The tribe of ʿAbd Manāf disputed them these prerogatives and various of the Quraysh tribes gave alliance and help for victory to one or other side.

So the partisans of Abd Manāf brought a bowl filled with *al-ṭīb*, nutmeg powder, into which they placed their hands and swore allegiance to one another. When they had done so, they wiped their hands over the corners of the house (the *kaʿba*). They were therefore named the *muṭayyabīna*, as mentioned above; this took place long ago.

But what is meant by this alliance, is the treaty of *al-fuḍūl*, a word meaning "the excess" or "remnants". This was sworn in the home of ʿAbd Allāh b. Judʿān, as al-Ḥumaydī related it, from Sufyān son of ʿUyayna, from ʿAbd Allāh, from Muḥammad and ʿAbd al-Raḥmān, two sons of Abū Bakr. They stated that the Messenger of God (ṢAAS) said, "I witnessed in the house of ʿAbd Allāh b. Judʿān a treaty to which I would have responded positively if, during Islam, I had been invited to participate in it. They made an agreement to return any excess to those who had owned it, and that no one should take unfair advantage over anyone."

The authorities stated that the *fuḍūl* pact was concluded 20 years before the prophethood, in the eleventh month, Dhū al-Qaʿda, that date being some four months after the *al-fijār* war. That was because the *al-fijār* occurred in Shaʿbān, the eighth month of the same year.

The *al-fuḍūl* treaty was reputed the most fair and honourable pact reached among the Arabs. The first man who suggested and advocated it was al-Zubayr, son of ʿAbd al-Muṭṭalib. The cause for it was that a man from Zabīd brought some goods to Mecca and these were brought from him by al-ʿĀṣ son of Wāʾil who held back some of what was due to him. So the man from Zabīd complained about him to his allies who were the tribes of ʿAbd al-Dār, Makhzūm, Jumaḥ, Sahm, and ʿAdī b. Kaʿb, but they declined to help him against al-ʿĀṣ son of Wāʾil and instead they roughed him up and drove him away. Having experienced such ill-treatment, the man from Zabīd approached Abū Qubays at daybreak, while Quraysh were in their assemblies around the *kaʿba*, and called out at the top of his voice:

> "O heirs of Fihr, there's a man being wronged of his goods, right here in the middle of Mecca, far from his own home and people.
> "A man dishevelled and deprived, who has not completed his pilgrimage; fellow men, I'm right here at the very heart of the *ḥijr*.[66]
> "The sacrosanct is for those whose nobility is complete; there is nothing sacrosanct for the robe of the immoral and treacherous."

At this arose al-Zubayr b. ʿAbd al-Muṭṭalib and said, "This matter can't be ignored."

So the men of Hāshim, Zuhra, and Taym b. Murra assembled in the home of ʿAbd Allāh b. Judʿān who prepared food for them. They established their pact in Dhū al-Qaʿda, a sacrosanct month, agreeing and swearing by God that they would act in unison with any wronged person against the wrongdoer until his rights were fulfilled, for so long as the sea makes wool wet and the mountains Thabīr and Ḥirāʾ remain firmly set in their place and that they would comfort (people) as long as they are alive.

Quraysh named that pact *al-fuḍūl*, saying, "Those men went into that matter *fī faḍl*, i.e. 'to excess'. Afterwards they walked over to al-ʿĀṣ b. Wāʾil and took away from him the goods of the man from Zabīd and returned them to him."

Al-Zubayr b. ʿAbd al-Muṭṭalib spoke the following verses about this pact:

> "I swore, Let's make a pact against them, though we're all members of one tribe.
> We'll call it *al-fuḍūl*; if we make a pact by it the stranger could overcome those under local protection,
> And those who go around the *kaʿba* will know that we reject injustice and will prevent all things shameful."

Al-Zubayr also spoke the following:

> "*Al-fuḍūl* made a pact and alliance that no evildoer shall dwell in Mecca's heart.
> This was a matter they firmly agreed and so the protected neighbour and the unprotected stranger are safe among them."

Qāsim b. Thābit related, in a curious *ḥadīth* that, "A man of Khathʿam came to Mecca either as a pilgrim or to perform the *ʿumra* (the 'minor pilgrimage'), and brought with him a daughter of his named al-Qatūl, an exceedingly modest girl. But Nabīh b. al-Ḥajjāj seized her and took her away from him. So the man of Khathʿam said, 'Who will help me against this man?' He was advised to invoke the pact of *al-fuḍūl*.

66. The space on the north-west side of the *kaʿba* enclosed by the curved wall, the *ḥāṭim*.

"So he stood at the *kaʿba* and called out, 'O you who made the pact of *al-fuḍūl*!' Men flocked to him from all sides, their swords unsheathed and shouting, 'Help is here; what's the matter?' He told them how Nabīh had wronged him by taking his daughter from him by force.

"The men went with him to Nabīh's house and he came out to them. They told him, 'Bring the girl out! You know who we are and the pact on which we've agreed!' 'I'll do it,' he replied, 'But let me enjoy her tonight!' 'Certainly not, by God,' they insisted, 'and there will be no intercourse!' So he brought her out to them speaking the verses:

> "My friends are gone, and I have not greeted al-Qatūl; I did not say to them a pleasant farewell,
>
> For the *al-fuḍūl* reiterated that they protect her; yet I still see myself not fearing the *al-fuḍūl*.
>
> Don't think, girl, that I, that evening the riders left, did not feel disregarded by their going."

And lines other than these were also given.

It has been said that this was known as the "pact of *al-fuḍūl*" merely because it was like an agreement reached by the Jurhum tribe that similarly favoured victims over oppressors. There were those of their leaders who advocated this, each one of whom bore the name "Faḍl". They were al-Faḍl b. Faḍala, al-Faḍl b. Wadāʿa, and al-Faḍl b. al-Ḥārith. This is what Ibn Qutayba stated. Others give the names as al-Faḍl b. Sharāʿa, al-Faḍl b. Bidāʿa and al-Faḍl b. Qudāʿa. It was al-Suhaylī, God be pleased with him, who reported this.

Muḥammad b. Isḥāq b. Yasār said, "Tribes of Quraysh suggested making a pact and assembled for that purpose in the house of ʿAbd Allāh b. Judʿān because of his high reputation and age.

"The pact made there at his house was between Banū Hāshim, Banū ʿAbd al-Muṭṭalib, Banū Asad b. ʿAbd al-ʿUzzā, Zuhra b. Kilāb, and Taym b. Murra. They made a pact and agreement that they would support any man in Mecca who was wronged, whether from their own people or someone who had merely come there, against whoever had wronged him, and that they would ensure that his rights be upheld.

"Quraysh named that agreement the 'pact of *al-fuḍūl*'."

Muḥammad b. Isḥāq said that Muḥammad b. Zayd b. al-Muhājir b. Qunfudh of Taym related to him that he heard Ṭalḥa b. ʿAbd Allāh b. ʿAwf al-Zuhrī say that the Messenger of God (ṢAAS) stated, "I witnessed in the house of ʿAbd Allāh b. Judʿān a pact made that I wouldn't have exchanged for the choicest herd; and if it had been suggested after Islam, I would have responded positively to it."

Ibn Isḥāq said that Yazīd b. ʿAbd Allāh b. Usāma b. al-Hādī al-Laythī related to him that Muḥammad b. Ibrāhīm b. al-Ḥārith of Taym told him that there was between al-Ḥusayn b. ʿAlī b. Abū Ṭālib and al-Walīd b. ʿUtba b. Abū Sufyān – al-Walīd being at that time governor of al-Medina, having been appointed over it by his uncle Muʿāwiya b. Abū Sufyān – a dispute over some property they owned at (the village of) Dhū al-Marwa. It seems that al-Walīd was using his power to take advantage of al-Ḥusayn. So al-Ḥusayn told him, "I swear by God that you will either justly recognize my rights or I will draw my sword and stand up in the mosque of the Messenger of God (ṢAAS) and invoke the pact of *al-fuḍūl*."

Ibn Isḥāq continued, "So ʿAbd Allāh b. al-Zubayr, who was with al-Walīd when al-Ḥusayn made this statement, said, 'And I too swear by God that if he does invoke it, I'll draw my sword and stand there with him until he gets his justice or we'll all die together.'"

Ibn Isḥāq stated that when al-Miswar b. Makhrama b. Nawfal al-Zuhrī and ʿAbd al-Raḥmān b. ʿUthmān b. ʿUbayd Allāh of Taym heard of the incident, they gave similar responses.

And when al-Walīd b. ʿUtba heard what had been said, he treated al-Ḥusayn justly and made him content.

Section: On the marriage of the Prophet (ṢAAS) to Khadīja, daughter of Khuwaylid b. Asad b. ʿAbd al-ʿUzzā b. Quṣayy.

Ibn Isḥāq stated, "Khadīja daughter of Khuwaylid was a merchant woman of stature and wealth. She would employ men to trade her goods on a profit-sharing basis.

"When she heard of the truthfulness, trustworthy nature and fine character of the Messenger of God (ṢAAS), she sent for him and proposed that he should take some of her goods on a trading venture to Syria; she offered him better terms than she did other merchants and suggested he be accompanied by a youth in her employment whose name was Maysara.

"The Messenger of God (ṢAAS) accepted this offer and set off with her goods, in the company of Maysara. When they reached Syria, the Messenger of God (ṢAAS) made a halt beneath the shade of a tree near the cell of a certain monk. This monk looked out at Maysara and said, 'Who is that man resting beneath the tree?' Maysara responded, 'He is of Quraysh, those who guard the sanctuary.' The monk responded, 'No one but a prophet has ever stopped beneath that tree.'

"The Messenger of God (ṢAAS) then sold his wares, the goods that he had brought, and bought those things he wanted. Thereafter he set off in a caravan for Mecca, Maysara accompanying him.

"At midday when it was fiercely hot, Maysara would see, so they say, two angels shading him from the sun as he travelled forward on his camel.

"When he reached Mecca and brought the goods back to Khadīja, she sold them for twice their cost or thereabouts. Maysara related to her what the monk had said, and how he had seen the angels giving him shade.

"Now Khadīja was a decisive, noble, and intelligent lady, as well as possessed of all the other fine qualities God had endowed her with. When Maysara told her all this she sent for the Messenger of God (ṢAAS) and said to him, so they say, 'Cousin, I am interested in you because of your being related to me, because of your high reputation among your people, and because of your trustworthiness, fine character and truthfulness.' She then offered herself to him in marriage.

"Khadīja was the highest-born, most respected and wealthiest woman in Quraysh. All her people were covetous of all that and would have attained it if they could.

"When she said this to the Messenger of God (ṢAAS), he reported it to his uncles. One of these, Ḥamza, went off with him to visit Khuwaylid b. Asad and made an engagement between them. Thereafter the Prophet (ṢAAS) did marry her."

Ibn Hishām stated, "He gave her 20 young female camels as a dowry. She was the first woman he married. And he married no other woman until she died."

Ibn Isḥāq said, "It was she who bore all the children of the Messenger of God (ṢAAS) except for Ibrāhīm. His sons from her were al-Qāsim, by whose name he was known, as 'Abū al-Qāsim', 'father of Qāsim' that is. Al-Ṭayyib and al-Ṭāhir were his other sons. His daughters were named Zaynab, Ruqayya, Umm Kulthūm, and Fāṭima."

Ibn Hishām stated, "The first-born of the boys was al-Qāsim, then came al-Ṭayyib, followed by al-Ṭāhir. The first-born girl was Ruqayya, followed by Zaynab, Umm Kulthūm, and Fāṭima, in that order."

Al-Bayhaqī stated, from al-Ḥākim that he read, by the hand of Abū Bakr b. Abū Khaythama, that Musʿab b. ʿAbd Allāh al-Zubayrī related to him, saying, "The eldest of his sons was al-Qāsim. Then came Zaynab, followed by ʿAbd Allāh, Umm Kulthūm, Fāṭima, and Ruqayya. The first of his children to die was al-Qāsim, followed by ʿAbd Allāh. Khadīja is said to have died at age 65 or at age 50, the latter being more likely."

Others say that al-Qāsim attained an age when he could ride, even on light, swift camels but then he died, after the call to prophethood.

Others say he died while still unweaned. The Messenger of God (ṢAAS) said, "In heaven there is a place for him where he can complete his suckling."

However, it is well known that this statement applied to (his son) Ibrāhīm.

Yūnus b. Bukayr stated that Ibrāhīm b. ʿUthmān related to him from al-Qāsim from Ibn ʿAbbās, who said, "Khadīja gave birth from the Messenger of God

(ṢAAS) to two boys and four girls. These were al-Qāsim, ʿAbd Allāh, Fāṭima, Umm Kulthūm, Zaynab, and Ruqayya."

Al-Zubayr b. Bakkār said, "It was ʿAbd Allāh who was known as 'al-Ṭayyib' (the good) and 'al-Ṭāhir' (the pure). He was given these appellations because he was born after the call to prophethood. His other sons died before his mission. All his daughters were born prior to the call to the prophethood, and emigrated with him (ṢAAS)."

Ibn Hishām stated, "Ibrāhīm was born to Maria the Copt who was presented to the Prophet (ṢAAS) by al-Muqawqis, governor of Alexandria; she was from (the Upper Egypt town of) Kūrat Anḍāʾ."

We will discuss the wives and children of the Messenger of God (ṢAAS) in a separate section at the end of this biography, if God Almighty wills it; and in Him we trust.

Ibn Hishām said, "The Messenger of God (ṢAAS) was 25 years of age when he married Khadīja, according to the account of several scholars, including Abū ʿAmr al-Madanī."

Yaʿqūb b. Sufyān stated, "I wrote down, from Ibrāhīm b. al-Mundhir, the following: ʿUmar b. Abū Bakr al-Muʿammilī related to me that more than one authority related to him that ʿAmr b. Asad married Khadīja to the Messenger of God (ṢAAS) when he was 25 years of age and Quraysh were building the *kaʿba*."

Similarly, al-Bayhaqī transmitted from al-Ḥākim that the age of the Messenger of God (ṢAAS) when he married Khadīja was 25 and that she was then 35. It is also said that she was 25.

Al-Bayhaqī stated, in a chapter entitled: "The employment the Messenger of God had before he married Khadīja" as follows:

"Abū ʿAbd Allāh the *ḥāfiẓ* narrated to us, quoting Abū Bakr b. ʿAbd Allāh, quoting al-Ḥasan b. Sufyān; and Suwayd b. Saʿīd related to us, quoting ʿAmr b. Abū Yaḥyā b. Saʿīd al-Qurashī, from his grandfather Saʿīd, from Abū Hurayra who said that the Messenger of God (ṢAAS) stated, 'God never sent anyone to be a prophet without his having been a shepherd for sheep.' His Companions asked him, 'And you too, O Messenger of God?' He replied, 'I shepherded them for Meccans at al-Qarārīṭ.'"

Al-Bukhārī related it from Aḥmad b. Muḥammad the Meccan, from ʿAmr b. Yaḥyā.

Thereafter al-Bayhaqī related the same tradition by way of al-Rabīʿ b. Badr, a weak link, from Abū al-Zubayr, from Jābir who said that the Messenger of God (ṢAAS) said, "My wage from Khadīja for two expeditions was a young she-camel."

Al-Bayhaqī related, through Ḥammād b. Salama, from ʿAlī b. Zayd, from ʿAmmār b. Abū ʿAmmār, from Ibn ʿAbbās who said, "Khadīja's father married the Messenger of God (ṢAAS) to her at a time when he (her father) was – and I think this is what he said – drunk!"

Then al-Bayhaqī stated that Abū al-Ḥusayn b. al-Faḍl al-Qaṭṭān related to him, as did ʿAbd Allāh b. Jaʿfar, as did Yaʿqūb b. Sufyān, who said that he was told by Ibrāhīm b. al-Mundhir, and by ʿUmar b. Abū Bakr al-Muʿammilī and by ʿAbd Allāh b. Abū ʿUbayd b. Muḥammad b. ʿAmmār b. Yāsir, from his father from Muqsim b. Abū al-Qāsim, the *mawlā* of ʿAbd Allāh b. al-Ḥārith b. Nawfal, that ʿAbd Allāh b. al-Ḥārith related to him that ʿAmmār b. Yāsir, whenever he heard people discussing the marriage of the Messenger of God (ṢAAS) to Khadīja and embellishing it as they did, would tell them, "I know better than anyone else about his marriage to her. I was his companion and his close friend. One day I was out with the Messenger of God (ṢAAS) and when we came to al-Ḥazura we passed by Khadīja's sister who was seated on a fine-coloured camel she had for sale. She called to me and I went over to her, while the Messenger of God (ṢAAS) stood there waiting for me. She said, 'Would that friend of yours like to marry Khadīja?'

"So I went back to him and told him and he responded, 'Indeed I certainly would!'

"I then reported to her what the Messenger of God (ṢAAS) had said and she suggested, 'Come and visit us tomorrow.' When we did so next day we found that they had slaughtered a cow and dressed Khadīja's father in ceremonial clothes; and his beard had been dyed yellow. I spoke with her brother and he with his father, who had been drinking wine. The brother told him of the Messenger of God (ṢAAS) and of his reputation and asked him if he would conduct his marriage. And so he did marry him to Khadīja. They cooked the cow and we ate from it, after which her father went to sleep. When he woke up he was sober and he said, 'What's this I'm wearing, what's this yellow and why this food?' His daughter who had spoken to ʿAmmār replied, 'It was your son-in-law Muḥammad son of ʿAbd Allāh who gave you the ceremonial outfit and he who presented the cow to you, and we slaughtered it when you married him to Khadīja.'

"He denied having concluded this marriage with him and stormed off, shouting, to al-Ḥijr. Banū Hāshim brought out the Messenger of God (ṢAAS) and they all went off to talk to him. Khadīja's father demanded, 'Where's this man of yours you claim I married to Khadīja?' The Messenger of God (ṢAAS) made his presence known to him. Having looked at him, her father then said, 'If I already performed his marriage, then so be it. If I didn't before, I do so now!'"

Al-Zuhrī stated in his works of biography that her father married her to him when he was drunk. His account is similar to the foregoing. Al-Suhaylī (similarly) related it.

Al-Mu῾ammilī stated, "What is generally agreed upon is that it was her uncle, ῾Amr b. Asad, who married her to him."

This is what al-Suhaylī preferred. He related so on the authority of Ibn ῾Abbās and ῾Ā᾽isha. The latter said, "Khuwaylid had died before *al-fijār*, the 'sacrilegious' war. It was he who had fought against Tubba῾ when he wanted to remove the 'black stone' to Yemen. Khuwaylid and a group from Quraysh had prevented him from doing so. Then Tubba῾ had a nightmare about it, changed his mind, and left the 'black stone' where it was."

Ibn Isḥāq related at the end of his biography that Khadīja's brother, ῾Amr b. Khuwaylid, was the one who married her to the Messenger of God (ṢAAS), but God knows best.

Division

Ibn Isḥāq stated that Khadīja, daughter of Khuwaylid, had informed Waraqa b. Nawfal b. Asad b. ῾Abd al-῾Uzzā b. Quṣayy, who was her cousin and a Christian who had studied the Scriptures and human knowledge, of what her young employee (Maysara) had told her of what the monk had said, and how he had seen the two angels shading him. Waraqa had then told her, "If this is true, Khadīja, then Muḥammad is the Prophet of this nation. I learned that a prophet was expected for this nation, and this is his time." These were approximately the words he used.

Thereafter Waraqa had impatiently awaited his coming, asking how long it would be. He spoke the following verses on the subject:

> "I persisted, being persistent in recalling both a worry that often inspired my tears,
> And a description from Khadīja, following (another) description; my waiting has been long, O Khadīja,
> In the heart of Mecca, with my hoping because of your words that I would see some solution.
> From what you related as the words of a priest who was a monk whom I would hate to be wrong,
> That Muḥammad will one day prevail and defeat whomever opposes him,
> Making a light appear in the land by which he will bring change to all creation.
> Those who oppose him will meet defeat, while those who aid him will achieve success.
> Would that I be there to witness, for I'll be the first of them in participating.
> Participating in that which Quraysh will hate, however much they bluster in their Mecca.
> I aspire, through him whom they all hate, to reach the Enthroned One, even if they descend, aside.
> Is it not folly to disbelieve in Him who chooses, He who raised the stars?
> If they and I survive, things will happen at which the disbelievers will be sorely discomfited.

Even if I perish, so does every man meet from the fates with destruction and death."

Waraqa also spoke the following lines, according to the account given of him by Yūnus b. Bukayr from Ibn Isḥāq:

"Will you leave early in the morning, or late tonight, or in the evening, there being a fire alight in your heart from your concealing your sadness?

At parting from a people whom I do not like to leave, as if after two days' journey away they seem very far removed.

And at true information related about Muḥammad, told about him when he was elsewhere by an honest man.

The man came back to you, O best of free women, whom you had sent to the Ghawr lowland and to the plateaux of the Najd ranges.

To the markets of Buṣrā with the mounts that left early, bent over with their loads, slow-moving.

He tells us of things good, through his knowledge; and truth has doors for which keys exist.

That ʿAbd Allāh's son, Aḥmad, is being sent to all people everywhere.

My belief is that he will be sent to tell the truth, just as God's two servants Hūd and Sāliḥ were sent

And Moses, and Abraham, until his glory shall be witnessed and widely spread abroad by report, very clear;

And there shall follow him the tribes of Luʾayy and Ghālib, their young and their grey leaders alike.

If I survive till his era reaches the people, then I will give glad tidings of love.

If not, O Khadīja, then you should know that I shall be travelling the wide earth, far from your land."

Al-Umawī added the lines:

"Following the religion of Him who established all things, He who had virtue far greater than all men.

And erected a secure building in Mecca, whose lamplight glitters in the dark,

A meeting place for all the various tribes, a place to which the tired, fine mounts hurry,

Standing tall like arrows of fine wood, the sinews winding around them suspended above their pastern-joints."

Other verses of this, as given by Abū al-Qāsim al-Suhaylī in his work *al-Rawḍ* (*The Gardens*) are the following:

"I gave advice to the tribes, telling them 'I came to warn, so let no one deceive you.'

Do not worship any God other than your creator, and if others call you, then say, 'We are in conflict with you.'

Glory everlasting be to Him of the throne; both the waters and the dry land glorified Him before us.

All things beneath the sky are subjugated before Him; no one should oppose His dominion.
Nothing that you see has its splendour last, but God remains, though wealth and progeny perish.
With his treasures, one day Hurmuz did not prevail, and the tribe of ʿĀd sought eternity, but they did not last.
Nor Solomon either, for the winds blew him away, and all spirits and men too, a waste land between them.
Where are those kings whose glory was such that delegations would come to them from all parts?
A great basin is up there where, without falsehood, all must gather one day, just as they did."

He then said, "Abū al-Faraj similarly attributed these to Waraqa." He also commented that some of these verses are also considered to have been by Umayya b. Abū al-Salṭ.

I would also add that we have been told that ʿUmar b. al-Khaṭṭāb, God bless him, used sometimes to quote some of these verses. But God knows best.

Section: On Quraysh having rebuilt the kaʿba *five years before the coming of the prophethood.*

Al-Bayhaqī recounts the building of the *kaʿba* to have been before the marriage of the Prophet (ṢAAS), to Khadīja.

However, it is widely known that the building by Quraysh of the *kaʿba* took place some ten years following their marriage, as we have stated.

Al-Bayhaqī begins by relating the *kaʿba*'s construction as having occurred in the time of Abraham, as we have stated in our earlier account of him. He gives the *ḥadīth* of Ibn ʿAbbās recorded in the *ṣaḥīḥ* collection of al-Bukhārī and also makes reference to some of the accounts attributed to Israeli legends regarding the construction of the *kaʿba* in Adam's lifetime.

But that is not correct, for the plain statement in the Qurʾān establishes that Abraham was the first person to begin building it, the first to establish it. Moreover its site was revered before that, honoured, and cared for throughout time. God Almighty stated,

"The first 'house' established for mankind was the one in Bekka (Mecca), blessed and a guidance for the worlds. In it there are clear signs. (There is) the stone on which Abraham stood. Whoever enters it shall be safe. Men owe it to God to make pilgrimage to the House, (all) those who can afford to do so" (*sūrat Āl-ʿImrān*, III, v.96, 97).

In the two *ṣaḥīḥs* it is said of Abū Dharr that he stated, "I asked, 'O Messenger of God, which mosque was established first?' He replied, 'The *al-Ḥaram* mosque (the 'Holy Mosque' in Mecca) 'Which one next?' I enquired. 'The *al-Aqṣā* mosque' (the 'further mosque', in Jerusalem). 'How many years intervened?', I asked. 'Forty years', he replied."

We have earlier addressed this issue and the fact that the *al-Aqṣā* mosque was established by (the tribe of) Israel, by Jacob, peace be upon him.

In both *ṣaḥīḥ* collections it is stated: "This land was made sacred by God when he created the heavens and the earth. It is made sacred by the sanctity of God until Judgement Day."

Al-Bayhaqī stated that Abū ʿAbd Allāh, the *ḥāfiẓ*, informed him, as did Abū ʿAbd Allāh al-Ṣaffār, Aḥmad b. Mahrān, ʿUbayd Allāh, and Isrāʾīl, from Abū Yaḥyā, from Mujāhid, from ʿAbd Allāh b. ʿAmr as follows, "The house (of worship) existed 2,000 years before the earth: 'And lo! the earth was laid out' (*sūrat al-Inshiqāq*, LXXXIV, v.3). "It was," he said, "laid out beneath it."

He said, "And Manṣūr traced this account back to Mujāhid."

I consider this very strange. It is as though it comes from the two baggage camels seized by ʿAbd Allāh b. ʿAmr at the battle of Yarmuk which were transporting Israeli legends, from which he used to relate; they told of strange and objectionable things.

Then al-Bayhaqī stated that Abū ʿAbd Allāh, the *ḥāfiẓ*, informed him, quoting Abū Jaʿfar Muḥammad b. Muḥammad b. Muḥammad b. ʿAbd Allāh al-Baghdādī, quoting Yaḥyā b. ʿUthmān b. Ṣāliḥ, as did Abū Ṣāliḥ al-Juhanī, quoting Ibn Lahīʿa, from Yazīd b. Abū al-Khayr, from ʿAbd Allāh b. ʿAmr b. al-ʿĀṣ that the Messenger of God (ṢAAS) said, "God sent down Gabriel to Adam and Eve, and told them: 'Build a house of worship for me.' Gabriel drew it out for them and Adam began digging while Eve transported until the water spoke to him, calling out from beneath him, 'That's enough, Adam!' When they had finished building, God revealed to him that he should circumambulate it. He was told, 'You are the first man, and this is the first house.' Thereafter the centuries succeeded one another until Noah made pilgrimage there. Further centuries went by until Abraham constructed its foundations."

Al-Bayhaqī stated, "Ibn Lahīʿa is the only one transmitting this tradition in this way."

I consider him to be a weak source. If its transmission had stopped directly with ʿAbd Allāh b. ʿAmr it would have been a stronger and more authentic tradition. But God knows best.

Al-Rabīʿ stated that al-Shāfiʿī informed him, as did Sufyān, from Ibn Abū Labīd, from Muḥammad b. Kaʿb al-Quraẓī – or someone else – that he (the Prophet, ṢAAS) said, "Adam performed the pilgrimage and the angels met him and told him, 'Your sacrifice made has been successful. We made pilgrimage 2,000 years before you!'"

Yūnus b. Bukayr stated that Ibn Isḥāq said, "Buqayya – or, he said, someone trustworthy of Medina – related to me, from ʿUrwa b. al-Zubayr that he (the Prophet) said, 'There has never been a prophet who has not made pilgrimage to the *kaʿba* – except, that is, for Hūd and Ṣāliḥ.'"

But I have elsewhere reported their pilgrimage to it; by which I meant their having made pilgrimage to its site, even though it was not yet built. But God knows best.

After this al-Bayhaqī reported the *ḥadīth* from Ibn ʿAbbās giving in full the story of Abraham, upon whom be peace; it is included in the *ṣaḥīḥ* collection of al-Bukhārī.

Al-Bayhaqī then related from the *ḥadīth* of Simāk b. Ḥarb, on the authority of Khālid b. ʿArʿara, as follows: "A man asked ʿAlī about God's statement (in the Qur'ān): 'The first house (of worship) established for mankind was the one in Bekka (Mecca), blessed and a guidance for the world' and asked whether it really was the first house built on earth.

"He replied, 'No, but it was the first one in which blessings and guidance for all mankind were in place, along with the stone on which Abraham stood; and whoever enters it is safe. And if you like, we can tell you how it was constructed.

"'Almighty God sent a revelation to Abraham, saying, "Build for me a house on earth!" This command disturbed him greatly. So God sent down *al-sakīna*, which is a strong wind with a head to it. Head and wind pursued one another until finally stopping. Thereupon the gale whirled around itself at a certain spot, like the coils of a snake. So Abraham built (there) until he reached the position for the stone. He then said to his son: "Help me by finding a stone." He searched for one and brought it, but found that the 'black stone' had already been set in place. He asked his father, "Where did you get that?" "Someone came who wouldn't rely on your building. Gabriel brought it from heaven." So he finished it.

"'Time passed and it fell down. So the *ʿamāliqa* (the giants) rebuilt it and when it next collapsed it was Jurhum who reconstructed it.

"'Again it collapsed and Quraysh rebuilt it, the Messenger of God (ṢAAS) being a young man at that time. When they wanted to lift into place the 'black stone' they fell into a dispute who should do so. They agreed they would let the first person to come along that street decide. It was the Messenger of God (ṢAAS) who came by first, so he decided for them to place it in a piece of cloth, so that all the tribes would lift it to its place.'"

Abū Dāwūd al-Ṭayālisī said that Ḥammād b. Salama and Qays and Sallām related to him, all on the authority of Simāk b. Ḥarb, from Khālid b. ʿArʿara, from ʿAlī b. Abū Ṭālib who said, "When the *kaʿba* fell down after Jurhum, Quraysh rebuilt it. And when they wanted to position the stone they fell into a dispute with one another. So they agreed that the first person to come in the door should do it.

"The Messenger of God (ṢAAS) came in through the Banū Shayba door. He told them to bring a robe in the centre of which he placed the stone. Then he ordered each subtribe to take hold of an edge of the cloth. They then lifted it up and the Messenger of God (ṢAAS) took the stone and positioned it."

Yaʿqūb b. Sufyān said that Aṣbugh b. Faraj related to him, as did Ibn Wahb, from Yūnus from Ibn Shihāb as follows: "When the Messenger of God (ṢAAS) reached puberty a woman set alight to the *kaʿba*. A spark from her fire lit some of the cloth covering of the *kaʿba* and it burned. So they tore it down and rebuilt it up to that point in the corner where a dispute arose among Quraysh as to which of the tribes should be entrusted with raising it.

"They agreed to appoint as arbitrator the first person who came up to them. It was the Messenger of God (ṢAAS) who did so, he being a youth, and he was wearing a leopardskin sash. They asked him to decide the issue and he told them to get the corner piece, which was placed in a cloth. Then he asked the leader of each tribe to come forward and gave each one a side of the cloth while he climbed up. They lifted it up and he put the corner piece in position.

"As he increased in age he became only more pleasing, and so they gave him the sobriquet *al-Amīn*, 'the trustworthy', even before revelation came down to him. They adopted the practice of never slaughtering a camel for sacrifice without seeking him, and he would say a prayer over it for them."

The context of this tradition is good, it being from the biographies written by al-Zuhrī.

One strange element in it is the wording "when he reached puberty". For it is well known that this occurred when the Messenger of God (ṢAAS) was 35. This is established by Muḥammad Ibn Isḥāq b. Yasār, God bless him.

Mūsā b. ʿUqba stated that the building of the *kaʿba* occurred 15 years prior to the prophethood. Similarly, Mujāhid agreed, as did ʿUrwa, Muḥammad b. Jubayr b. Muṭʿim and others. But God knows best.

Mūsā b. ʿUqba said, "There was a period of 15 years between the 'sacrilegious' war *al-fijār* and the building of the *kaʿba*."

I observe that *al-fijār* and the pact of *al-fuḍūl* came in one year, when the Messenger of God (ṢAAS) was 20. This fact substantiates what Muḥammad b. Isḥāq said. But God knows best.

Mūsā b. ʿUqba said: "Quraysh were motivated towards rebuilding the *kaʿba* because water would flood in from its top, from above the earth roof with which it was covered and which was in disrepair. Consequently they were concerned that water might leak inside.

"Also, a man named Mulayḥ had stolen the *kaʿba*'s incense and they wanted to rebuild it taller and raise its door so that only those they wished could enter it.

"They therefore established a fund for the costs and hired workers and then went there one morning to tear it down, despite their concern and apprehension that God might prevent them from doing what they wanted.

"The first man to start and to take down a piece of it was al-Walīd b. al-Mughīra. When they saw what al-Walīd had done the others followed by doing the same; they levelled it and were pleased to have done so.

"When they wanted to begin rebuilding it, they brought the workmen, but not one of them would set foot anywhere before it.

"They claimed that they saw a snake encircling the building completely, its head reaching back to its tail. They were terrified of it and afraid that what they were doing would destroy them.

The *kaʿba* had been their haven and safe refuge from others as well as a source of their pride. Because of their confusion and worry at what had happened to them, al-Mughīra b. ʿAbd Allāh b. ʿAmr b. Makhzūm stood up and reminded them of the advice and orders he had given them, namely that they should not dispute or envy one another in rebuilding it, but should divide it into quarters and use no ill-gotten money in its construction.

"When they had decided to proceed, the snake disappeared up into the sky, and they could see that this was the work of God, Almighty and All-powerful is He."

His account also states that some people maintain that a bird picked it up and tossed it away towards Ajyad.[67]

Muḥammad b. Isḥāq b. Yasār said, 'When the Messenger of God (ṢAAS) reached 35 Quraysh reached an agreement to rebuild the *kaʿba*. They did so because they were concerned about reroofing it, being afraid its roof would collapse since it was made only of stones set above its frame. They also wanted to make it taller as well as reroof it.

"That was because some men had stolen the *kaʿba*'s treasure which had been kept in a well in its middle. The man who was found in possession of the treasure was Duwayk, a freed-man of Banū Mulayḥ b. ʿAmr b. Khuzāʿa. Consequently Quraysh cut off his hand.

"Quraysh claims that those who stole it planted it with Duwayk.

"The sea had cast ashore at Jidda a ship belonging to a Byzantine trader. The ship had broken up, so they took its wood to use for the *kaʿba*'s roof."

Al-Umawī said, "This ship belonged to the emperor of Byzantium and was carrying building materials, marble, wood, and metal. The emperor had sent this off with Baqum the Byzantine for the church the Persians had burned belonging to the Abyssinians. When it had reached its anchorage at Jidda God had sent a gale which destroyed it."

67. Ajyad is a mountain at Mecca.

Ibn Isḥāq said, "In Mecca there was a Copt who was a carpenter and so they had available to them some of what was needed to repair it.

"There was a serpent that would emerge from the *kaʿba*'s well into which they would drop every day the sacrificial offerings. It would emerge and sun itself on the *kaʿba*'s wall. They were all afraid of it, because whenever anyone approached it, it would raise its head, move its coils audibly and open its mouth. One day as it lay on the *kaʿba*'s wall as was its habit, God sent down a bird which snatched it up and flew away with it.

"At this Quraysh said, 'Now we can hope that God is pleased at our plan. We have a local carpenter, and wood, and God has taken care of the serpent.'"

Al-Suhaylī recounted, on the authority of Razīn, that a thief had entered the *kaʿba* during the Jurhum era to steal its treasure but that the well had caved in on him. Some men had come and lifted him out and retrieved what he had taken. After that, a serpent resided in the well, its head as big as that of a young goat, its belly white and its back black. It had lived there for 500 years. This was the serpent mentioned by Muḥammad b. Isḥāq.

Muḥammad b. Isḥāq stated, "When they had agreed on demolishing and rebuilding it, Abū Wahb b. ʿAmr b. ʿĀʾidh b. ʿAbd b. ʿImrān b. Makhzūm (whose name according to Ibn Hishām was ʿĀʾidh b. ʿImrān b. Makhzūm) went and removed a stone from the *kaʿba* but it flew straight out of his hand back to its position. So he said, 'O Quraysh, in rebuilding it, use only money that you have fairly earned. Nothing gained from prostitution, usury, or injustice against any person must enter it.'"

(Some) people attribute this statement to al-Walīd b. al-Mughīra b. ʿAbd Allāh b. ʿUmar b. Makhzūm. Ibn Isḥāq, moreover, was inclined to believe that the man who said this was Abū Wahb b. ʿAmr. He said that he was the maternal uncle of the father of the Prophet (ṢAAS), and a very highly regarded and honourable man.

Ibn Isḥāq said, "Then Quraysh divided up the *kaʿba*. The side with the door was entrusted to the tribes of ʿAbd Manāf and Zuhra, that between the 'black stone' corner and the Yemeni corner went to the Banū Makhzūm, along with various other Quraysh tribes. The back of the *kaʿba* went to the tribes of Jumaḥ and Sahm; the *ḥijr* (shrine) side was entrusted to the tribes of ʿAbd al-Dār b. Quṣayy and Asad b. ʿAbd al-ʿUzzā, while the ʿAdī b. Kaʿb were assigned the *rahw al-ḥaṭīm*, the enclosed slope around the walls.

"But the people were apprehensive about demolishing it and were very scared of it. So al-Walīd b. al-Mughīra said, 'I shall begin demolishing it.' And he took up a pick-axe and set about it, saying, 'O God, it is not to be feared. O God, good is all we want.'

"He then demolished some of the side where two *rukn*, the sacred corners, are. That night everyone expected something bad would happen and said, 'Let's keep watch on him and if he comes to harm we'll not demolish any more of it and we'll repair it just as it was. But if nothing happens to him, then God will have been pleased by our action in destroying it.'

"Early next morning al-Walīd recommenced his work of demolition, and the others joined in with him. Eventually they had demolished it down to the foundations established by Abraham, peace be upon him. They uncovered some green rocks interlocking together like teeth."

In the *ṣaḥīḥ* of al-Bukhārī an account from Yazīd b. Rūmān gives the phrase "interlocking together like camels' humps". And al-Suhaylī said, "I consider the wording in the biography 'like teeth' to be imaginary." But God knows best.

Ibn Isḥāq stated, "A certain reciter of traditions related to me as follows, 'A man of Quraysh, who were demolishing the *kaʿba*, put his crowbar between two stones to remove one of them and when the stone moved all Mecca shook, so they stopped working on that foundation.'"

Mūsā b. ʿUqba stated, "ʿAbd Allāh b. ʿAbbās claimed that leaders of Quraysh related that when they had assembled to extract stones to set up the (stations of) Abraham and Ishmael, upon both of whom be peace, one of their tribesmen began removing one of the stones from the original foundation. When he lifted it up, not knowing that it was from the original foundation, the onlookers saw a light emitting from beneath it that almost dazzled the man's sight. Then the stone jumped out of his hand and dropped back into its place. The man and the other builders were terrified. But when the stone again hid from them what was beneath it they went back to their building, saying, 'Don't move that stone, or any of those next to it.'"

Ibn Isḥāq stated, "It was related to me that Quraysh found in the corner a document with Syriac writing on it and they did not know what it was until a Jew read it to them. It said, 'I am God, Lord of Bakka (Mecca). I created it the day I created the heavens and the earth and formed the sun and the moon. I have set seven trusty angels around it. It will not cease to exist until its *akhshabāhā* (a word Ibn Hishām interpreted to mean "its two mountains") disapppear, a blessing to its people in their water and their milk.'"

Ibn Isḥāq stated, "It was related to me that they found in the shrine a document stating, 'Mecca is God's holy House. Its sustenance shall come from three paths; let it not be first desecrated by its own people.'"

He also stated that Layth b. Abū Sulaym claimed that they had found a stone in the *kaʿba* 40 years before the coming of the mission of the Prophet (ṢAAS) – if what they said is true – on which was written, "He who plants good shall harvest joy; he who plants evil shall harvest regret. If you do evil things, shall you be rewarded with good things? Indeed so, just as grapes are harvested from thorns!"

Saᶜīd b. Yaḥyā al-Umawī stated that al-Muᶜtamir b. Sulaymān al-Raqqī related to him, from ᶜAbd Allāh b. Bishr al-Zuhrī, with a chain of authorities back to the prophet (ṢAAS), who said, "In the shrine three slates were found. On the first was written, 'It is I, God, Lord of Bakka; I made it when I made the sun and the moon and I have set seven trusty angels around it. And I have blessed its people in the meat and in the milk.'

"On the second it said, 'I am God, Lord of Bakka. I created *al-raḥim*, kinship, which I derived from my name, (*Raḥīm*, (meaning) merciful and compassionate). He who acts kindly to his kin, so will I treat; he who severs his ties of kinship, so will I treat.'

"On the third was written: 'I am God, Lord of Bakka. I created goodness and evil and I predetermine. Joy shall be for those who bring good, and woe upon those who bring evil!'"

Ibn Isḥāq continued, "Then the tribes of Quraysh gathered stones to rebuild it, each one collecting them separately.

"They built it up until it reached the place for the (black) stone but then fell into dispute about it. Each tribe wanted to raise it into its position, regardless of the rest. Eventually they broke up, established alliances, and readied to do battle. Banū ᶜAbd al-Dār brought a bowl full of blood and they and Banū ᶜAdī b. Kaᶜb b. Luʾayy made a pact to fight to the death, placing their hands into that bowl of blood. And so they were known as the 'blood-lickers'.

"Quraysh remained in this confrontation for four or five nights, then they met together in the mosque, debated one another but divided into equal sides.

"Some scholars of the traditions claim that Abū Umayya b. al-Mughīra b. ᶜAbd Allāh b. ᶜUmar b. Makhzūm, who was at that time the oldest man in all Quraysh, said, 'O Tribe of of Quraysh, resolve your dispute by agreeing that the first man who enters by the door of this mosque will decide the issue.' They agreed.

"The first man to enter was the Messenger of God (ṢAAS) and when they saw him they said, 'This is *al-Amīn*, "the trustworthy"; we are satisfied. This is Muḥammad.' When he reached them and they told him of the problem, the Messenger of God (ṢAAS) said: 'Bring me a robe.' One was brought to him and he took the cornerpiece (the 'black stone') and placed it on the robe. Then he said, 'Let each tribe grasp one side of the cloth. Then all raise it up.' This they did until it was at the right spot, whereupon the Messenger of God (ṢAAS) himself positioned it. Then they built above it."

Quraysh used to refer to the Messenger of God (ṢAAS) as "the trustworthy".

Imām Aḥmad stated that ᶜAbd al-Ṣamad related to him, quoting Thābit – meaning Abū Yazid – quoting Hilāl – meaning Ibn Ḥabbān – from Mujāhid from his *mawlā*, whose name was al-Sāʾib b. ʿAbd Allāh, that the last-mentioned related to him that he was one of those who built the *kaʿba* before the coming of Islam. He stated, "I had a stone I had sculpted that I worshipped besides God. I used to bring clotted milk unfit for myself and pour it over it. Then a dog would lick it off, raise its hind leg and urinate on it. We continued building until we reached the position for the (black) stone, but no one knew where it was. But then it was seen among our rocks looking like a man's head with a face almost distinguishable. A leader of Quraysh said, 'We'll position it.' But others said they too would do it. People suggested an arbitrator be appointed and they agreed that he should be the first man to appear from the mountain road. And it was the Messenger of God (ṢAAS) who arrived, and those there commented, 'Well, it's the "trustworthy" who's come.' They talked to him and he placed it on a cloak. He then summoned their head men and they lifted it up while he, (ṢAAS) placed it in its position."

Ibn Isḥāq stated, "At the time of the Prophet (ṢAAS), the *kaʿba* measured 18 cubits and was covered by Egyptian-woven Qabāṭī cloth. Later it was covered by *al-burūd*[68] cloths. The first to clothe it with the *dibāj* silk brocade was al-Ḥajjāj b. Yūsuf."

My comment is that they left out of it the *ḥijr* area that was six or seven cubits long in the direction of Syria. They had insufficient funds for that; that is, they were not able to rebuild it on Abraham's foundations. They constructed one door for the *kaʿba* on the east side, placing it high up so that not everyone could get inside. This allowed them to permit inside only those they wished.

It has been established in both *ṣaḥīḥ* collections, on the authority of ʿĀʾisha, God be pleased with her, that the Messenger of God (ṢAAS) told her: "Don't you know that your people had insufficient funds for the expenses? If it were not for the fact that your people were only recently unbelievers, I would have torn down the *kaʿba* and made for it one door on the east and another on the west. And I would have included the *ḥijr* area within it."

This was how Ibn Zubayr rebuilt it, just as the Messenger of God (ṢAAS) had indicated. It was done in the utmost splendour and beauty, one complete whole on the foundations of al-Khalīl (Abraham). It had two doors at ground level, on the east and west sides, and people would enter through one and exit through the other.

When he had executed Ibn al-Zubayr, al-Ḥajjāj wrote to the Caliph of the time, ʿAbd al-Mālik b. Marwān, concerning what Ibn Zubayr had done; and they believed that he had made the changes on his own authority.

And so it was ordered that it be restored to its original state. They set to work on the "Syrian" wall, tearing it down and removing the (black) stone, laying out

68. *Al-burūd* is the name given to striped-cloth sheets.

its stones on the *kaʿba* floor. Then its door was raised and the western door was blocked off; the eastern one was left as it was. When it was the time of al-Mahdī – or his son al-Mansūr – he (the ruler) sought advice from Mālik on rebuilding it as it had been remodelled by Ibn al-Zubayr. But Mālik, God be pleased with him, said, "I hate for the rulers to treat it like a plaything."

And so he left it as it was; it remains the same to this day.

As for the *masjid al-ḥarām*, the sacred mosque at Mecca, the first man to remove the buildings around the *kaʿba* was ʿUmar b. al-Khaṭṭāb, God be pleased with him. He purchased them from their owners and demolished them. When ʿUthmān ruled he bought other houses which he added to it. When Ibn al-Zubayr succeeded, he reinforced it, improved its walls, and increased the number of its doors. But he was not able to make any additions to increase its size.

When ʿAbd al-Mālik b. Marwān seized power he made the walls of the sacred mosque taller and ordered that the *kaʿba* be covered by the *dibāj*. The one who carried out this order was al-Ḥajjāj b. Yūsuf.

We have elsewhere related the history of the building of the House and the traditions that came down about that in our exegesis of the *sūrat al-Baqara* (Qurʾān, II) in reference to the verse: "When we ordered Abraham to raise the foundations of the house along with Ishmael" (verse 127). Our explanation of this is lengthy and exhaustive and whoever wishes could write it down here. And all praise and power be to God.

Ibn Isḥāq stated, "When they had finished the construction, having built it as they wished, al-Zubayr b. ʿAbd al-Muṭṭalib spoke the following verses about the serpent that caused Quraysh to be afraid of rebuilding the *kaʿba*:

> "I was amazed at the eagle aiming straight for the serpent when it was in an excited state.
> It used to make a rustling sound, and sometimes it would dash out;
> When we began the building it increased our awe of the structure and we were scared.
> When we were too afraid to drive it away an eagle came, swooping straight down at it.
> It grasped it tight, then left the building to us; there being nothing else in its way.
> Together we assembled to begin the building, for which we already had the foundations and the soil;
> Next morning its foundations were raised, our men wearing no clothes.
> The Lord ennobled Banū Luʾayy through it and there's no denying their founding it.
> Banū ʿAdī had also assembled there, and Murra who were preceded by Kilāb.
> The Lord thereby established us in glory, and it is from God that reward is requested.'"

We earlier treated in a separate passage how God protected the Messenger of God (ṢAAS) from the bad practices of the pre-Islamic era. He and his uncle al-ʿAbbās used to transport stones and when he (ṢAAS) positioned his loincloth over his shoulder beneath the stones, he was forbidden from doing so and therefore reverted to his former practice.

Division

Ibn Isḥāq related how Quraysh began the practice of calling themselves *al-Ḥums*, a word implying intensity in religion, and intolerance.

This is because they gave extreme veneration to the holy places, to the extent that they required people not to leave there on the night of the procession to ʿArafāt. They would say, "We are men of the holy places, the *ḥaram*, and the *Quṭṭān*, those who dwell at God's house."

They would not make the halt on Mt. ʿArafāt, though they knew that was the wish of Abraham, peace be upon him, in order not to abandon the corrupt innovative practices they themselves established. They would not put away for storage sour cheese made from milk or butter, or clarify fat while they were in a state of ritual uncleanliness. While in this state, they would not enter any tent made of hair, and would seek shelter from the sun only under tents made of leather. Similarly they prevented those making the greater or smaller pilgrimage from eating any but Quraysh food while in that state, and these people could only circumambulate wearing Quraysh clothes. If one of these pilgrims could not find a gown from one of the *Ḥums*, who were Quraysh either by birth or by having joined Quraysh from Kināna and Khuzāʿa, they would have to circumambulate naked, even if they were women. A woman who happened to go round in this manner would place her hand over her vagina and recite:

> "Today all or part may appear, but visible though it may be, I do not make it available!"

If anyone who had access to the garment of a *Ḥums* person were too proud to use it, then he could go round in his own clothes, but when he had finished he had to throw them aside; thereafter, they could not be used again, either by them or by anyone else, nor ever touched. The Arabs used to call such clothes *al-luqā*, "cast-offs". A certain poet spoke the lines:

> "How sad it is, my returning to it, it being like a proscribed thing cast off before the pilgrims."

Ibn Isḥāq stated, "They continued in these practices until God sent Muḥammad (ṢAAS) and revealed the Qur'ān to him, as a retort to them and their innovations. God said, 'Hasten forth from the place where people hasten from' (*sūrat al-Baqara*, II, v.199). By this is meant the masses of the Arabs from ʿArafāt. And also that same verse reads, 'and ask the forgiveness of God; surely God is forgiving, merciful.'"

As we have previously shown, the Messenger of God (ṢAAS) would make the halt at ʿArafāt before he received his prophethood, this being an award granted by God to him.

God also revealed to him a response to their practice of forbidding people certain actions and foods in the words, "O mankind, attend to your dress at every prayer meeting and eat and drink, but do not be extreme. God does not love extremists. Say, 'Who made forbidden clothing (from) God that He brought forth for His worshippers, along with all good provisions?'" (*sūrat al-Aʿrāf*, VII, v.31–2).

Ziyād al-Bakkāʾī stated from Ibn Isḥāq, "But I don't know whether their making these innovations preceded or followed the battle of the elephant."

THE BOOK OF THE APOSTLESHIP OF THE MESSENGER OF GOD (ṢAAS) AND AN ACCOUNT OF SOME OF THE PREDICTIVE SIGNS THEREOF.

Muḥammad b. Isḥāq, God bless him, stated: "Jewish Rabbis, Christian priests and Arab soothsayers all spoke of the Messenger of God (ṢAAS) before his mission as the time for it approached.

"The rabbis and the priests found in their books descriptions of him and of his time along with inferences relating to him from their prophets."

God Almighty said, "Those who follow the Messenger, the prophet, the *ummī*, "the unlettered", to whom they will find written reference in the Torah and the Bible requiring them to do good and warning them of evil, allowing them the good things and forbidding them the bad, removing the burden and chains formerly upon them; so those who believe in him, honour him and aid him and follow the light that was sent down with him, those will be successful" (*sūrat al-Aʿrāf*, VII, v.157).

God Almighty stated, "And when Jesus son of Mary said, 'O children of Israel, I am God's messenger to you, bringing affirmation of the Torah before me and giving tidings of a prophet who will come after me whose name will be Aḥmad'" (*sūrat al-Ṣaff*, LXI, v.6). And God Almighty said, "Muḥammad is the Messenger of God. And those with him are those who are very severe against the unbelievers, compassionate with one another. You shall see them bowing down, prostrating themselves, seeking grace from God, and approval. They have marks on their faces from their prostrations. That is their likeness in the Torah and in the Bible. (They are) like plants. (God) brings forth their sprouts and then strengthens them and thickens them so they stand straight on their stalks. He pleases the planters to discomfort through them the unbelievers. God gave promise of forgiveness and great reward to those who believe in him and perform righteous deeds" (*sūrat al-Fatḥ*, XLVIII, v.29).

And God Almighty said, "When God made the covenant with the Prophets, saying, 'I gave you the Scripture and wisdom, then there will come unto you a messenger confirming what you possess; you shall believe in him and render him help.' He said, 'Do you agree and accept my covenant as binding to you?' They replied, 'We affirm.' He said, 'So bear witness and I along with you am a witness'" (*sūrat Āl-ʿImrān*, III, v.81).

In the *ṣaḥīḥ* of al-Bukhārī there is a *ḥadīth* from Ibn ʿAbbās that states, "God never sent down a prophet without entering into a covenant upon him (to the effect that) if Muḥammad were sent down his mission when he was (already) living, then he (that prophet) would believe in him and aid him. God ordered him to take a covenant to his people that if Muḥammad were given his mission during their lifetime, then they should believe in him, aid him, and follow him."

This confirms that all prophets had talked about him and were commanded to follow him.

Abraham, upon whom be peace, stated in the prayer he made about the people of Mecca, "O our Lord! Send among them as a messenger one of their own people, who will recite to them Your signs and teach them the scriptures and wisdom and purify them. You are the mighty one, the wise" (*sūrat al-Baqara*, II, v.129).

Imām Aḥmad said that Abū al-Naḍr related to him, quoting al-Faraj b. Faḍāla, quoting Luqmān b. ʿĀmir, who said that he heard Abū Umāma say, "I asked the Prophet, 'O Messenger of God, what was the beginning of your mission?'

"He replied, 'The prayer of my father Abraham, the glad tidings from Jesus, and my mother's seeing a light emitting from her that illuminated the castles of Syria.'"

Muḥammad b. Isḥāq said that just such a statement was related to him from Thawr b. Yazīd, from Khālid b. Maʿdān, from the Companions of the Prophet (ṢAAS).

By this is meant his wanting to refer to the beginning of his mission among his people and the spreading and expanding of his fame. And so he made mention of the prayer of Abraham, to whom the Arabs trace their descent. Then the prediction of Jesus, the 'Seal' of the prophets of the tribe of Israel, as mentioned before. This shows that there were other prophets between these two who also gave tidings of his coming.

Regarding (the assembly of) the archangels, their cognizance of him was widespread and well known before the creation of Adam, upon whom be prayers and peace. Imām Aḥmad stated that ʿAbd al-Raḥmān b. Mahdī related to him, quoting Muʿāwiyya' b. Ṣāliḥ, from Saʿīd b. Suwayd al-Kalbī, from ʿAbd al-Aʿlā b. Hilāl al-Salamī, from al-ʿIrbāḍ b. Sāriyya who stated, "The Messenger of God (ṢAAS) said, 'For God I am the Seal of the prophets; Adam was well made in His likeness. And I shall tell you of the first of it: my father Abraham's prayer, the prediction of Jesus about my coming, and the visions seen by my mother, as well as by the mothers of the believers.'"

Al-Layth related this from Muʿāwiyya' b. Ṣāliḥ who said, "When she delivered him, his mother saw a light from him that illuminated the castles of Syria."

Imām Aḥmad also said, "ʿAbd al-Raḥmān related to us, as did Manṣūr b. Saʿd, from Badīl b. Maysara, from ʿAbd Allāh b. Shaqīq, from Maysara al-Fajr, who stated, 'I asked, O Messenger of God, when did you become a prophet?' He replied, 'When Adam was between the spirit and the body.'"

Aḥmad is the sole source of these.

ʿUmar b. Aḥmad b. Shāhīn related this in the work entitled *Dalāʾil al-Nubuwwa* (*Signs of the Prophethood*) from a *ḥadīth* of Abū Hurayra who stated, "ʿAbd Allāh b. Muḥammad b. ʿAbd al-ʿAzīz – meaning Abū al-Qāsim al-Baghawī – related to us, as did Abū Hammām al-Walīd b. Muslim, from al-Awzāʿī, and I was told by Yaḥyā from Abū Salama, from Abū Hurayra, who said that the Messenger of God (ṢAAS) was asked, 'When was it made your duty to become a prophet?' He replied, 'Between the making of Adam and the breathing of the spirit into him.'"

It was related on another line of authorities from al-Awzāʿī who used the words "and Adam was formed in his likeness".

It was also related from al-Baghawī, from Aḥmad b. al-Miqdām, from Baqiyya b. Saʿīd b. Bashīr, from Qatāda, from Abū Hurayra, relating to the words of Almighty God, "And when we made a covenant with the prophets, and with you, and with Noah" (*sūrat al-Aḥzāb*, XXXIII, v.7) that the Messenger of God (ṢAAS) stated, "I was the first of the prophets to be created and the last of them to be sent."

And from a *ḥadīth* of Abū Muzāḥim, on the authority of Qays b. al-Rabīʿ, from Jābir, from al-Shaʿbī, from Ibn ʿAbbās, that someone asked, "O Messenger of God, when were you a prophet?" He replied, "While Adam was between spirit and body."

The Arab soothsayers had been told by the devils from the *jinn* things overheard by them while they were still not prevented from so doing by having stars cast at them. Soothsayers, male and female, continued mentioning such matters, without the Arabs giving any credence to them, until God Almighty sent him, and there occurred those things they had talked of and so recognized.

When the time of the Messenger of God and his prophethood approached, the devils were screened from overhearing and they were prevented from occupying those seats from which they used to overhear. Stars were hurled at them, and the devils knew that that was because of an order coming from God, the Almighty and Glorious.

On this subject God sent down to his messenger (ṢAAS) the words, "Say: it has been revealed to me that a group of *jinn* listened and then said, 'We heard a wonderful Qurʾān which guides towards the right, and we believed in it. And we will never associate any other god with our Lord'" (*sūrat al-Jinn*; LXXII, v.1–2).

We have given prior explanation to all that in our *Tafsīr*, exegesis of the

Qurʾān, as well as to God's words, "And when we directed (mention) towards you (of) a group of *jinn* who listened to the Qurʾān. And when they came to it, they said, 'Listen silently!' And when it was over they turned back to their people warning them, and saying: 'O people ours, we have heard a book sent down after Moses verifying what came before it, guiding towards the truth, and to the straight path'" (*sūrat al-Aḥqāf*, XLVI, v.29, 30). All this too we elucidated there.

Muḥammad b. Isḥāq stated that Yaʿqūb b. ʿUtba b. al-Mughīra b. al-Akhnas related to him that he was told that the first Arabs to be afraid at (seeing) the stars being thrown was the tribe of Thaqīf. They consulted one of their men on the subject, whose name was ʿAmr b. Umayya, one of Banū ʿIlāj, he being the most shrewd and astute of all Arabs. They asked him, "O ʿAmr, don't you see what's going on in the heavens, all those stars being thrown about?"

He replied, "I certainly do. Keep watch and if the ones being cast are most prominent stars, the ones by which men are guided on land and sea, and by the rising and setting of which the seasons of summer and winter are marked, for the good of men in their lives, then, by God, it means the end of the world, and the destruction of all creation. If it is other stars, while the prominent stars remain firm in their place, then it is occurring for some purpose God intends for mankind. So what could that be?"

Ibn Isḥāq said, "A certain scholar related to me that a woman of Banū Sahm known as al-Ghayṭala who had been a soothsayer before the coming of Islam was visited one night by her other world contact who swooped down beneath her, then said, 'I know what I know; a day of slaying and slaughtering.' When she told Quraysh of this they asked, 'What does he mean?'

"When he came to her on another night, swooping down beneath her, he said, 'Ravines! What ravines? In them, down their sides, Kaʿb will fall.' When this reached Quraysh they said, 'What does this mean? This is something that will happen; look to see what it will be.'

"But they could not interpret it until the battles of Badr and Uḥud took place in 'ravines'; then they knew what it was the spirit had told her."

Ibn Isḥāq stated, "ʿAlī b. Nāfiʿ al-Jurashī related to me that Janb, a tribe from Yemen, had a soothsayer before Islam came. And when news of the Messenger of God (ṢAAS) spread among the Arabs, Janb asked their soothsayer, 'Find out about this man for us' and they assembled (to hear him) at the foot of his mountain.

"When the sun rose he came down to them and stood leaning on a bow he had. Then, having gazed up for a long time into the sky, he began to leap about. Then he spoke: 'O people, God has honoured Muḥammad by choosing him. He has purified his heart and his insides. But, O people, his stay among you will be short.' He then hurried back up his mountain, returning whence he had come."

Thereafter Ibn Isḥāq mentions the story of Siwād b. Qārib. We have postponed giving it until the section on The Cries of the Spirits.

Division

Ibn Isḥāq stated that ʿĀṣim b. ʿAmr b. Qatāda related to him, from some of his tribe, as follows: "One of the things that brought us into Islam – along with the mercy of God Almighty and His guidance – was what we heard from a Jew. We were at that time polytheists and worshipped idols, while they, the Jews, were people with Scriptures who had knowledge we did not. There was always enmity between us and them and if ever we bested them in some way they disliked they would tell us, 'The time is near for a prophet; he will now be sent, and with him we will kill you just as Ād and Iram were killed.'

"We heard that from them often.

"So when God sent His messenger (ṢAAS) we responded positively when he invited us to God, and became aware of what their threats to us meant. We therefore hastened to him before them and believed in him, while they disbelieved in him.

"Concerning us and them this verse was sent down: 'And when there came to them a book from God verifying what they had, though they formerly prayed for victory against those who disbelieved; and when there came to them that which they knew, they disbelieved in it. And so may God's curse be upon the disbelievers'" (*sūrat al-Baqara*, II, v.89).

Warqāʾ stated, from Ibn Abū Najīh from ʿAlī al-Azdī that the Jews used to say: "O God send us this prophet who will judge between us and the people who seek victory by him." It was al-Bayhaqī who related this.

Thereafter it was related through ʿAbd al-Mālik b. Hārūn b. ʿAnbara, from his father, from his grandfather, from Saʿīd b. Jubayr, from Ibn ʿAbbās, who said, "The Jews were at Khaybar battling Ghaṭafān, but whenever battle was joined the Jews of Khaybar were defeated. So the Jews resorted to this prayer, saying, 'O God, we will ask you by Muḥammad's rightness, the Prophet, the *ummī*, "the unlettered", whom you promised us you would send at the end of time, if you will give us victory over them.'"

The report went on to say that when they met in battle and they spoke this prayer they defeated Ghaṭafān.

Yet when the Prophet (ṢAAS) was sent, they disbelieved in him. And so God, Almighty and Glorious is He, revealed the words, "they formerly prayed for victory against those who disbelieved."

ʿAṭiyya related approximately the same from Ibn ʿAbbās, and also said that ʿIkrima used similar words.

Ibn Isḥāq stated that Ṣāliḥ b. Ibrāhīm b. ʿAbd al-Raḥmān b. ʿAwf related to him, from Maḥmūd b. Labīd, from Salama b. Salām b. Waqsh, who was at the battle of Badr, who said, "We had a Jewish neighbour from Banū ʿAbd al-Ashhal and he came out of his house one day to us. At that time, I was the youngest of my household; I was wearing a fur gown I had and was lying in it in the courtyard of my family's house.

"The Jew talked of the resurrection, the Day of Judgement, the reckoning, the scales, paradise, and hell-fire.

"This he told to polytheists, idolaters who did not believe in any life after death.

"They replied, 'Come on, now! You really think people can be sent, after their death, to some place where there is a paradise, and a fire where they will be punished for their deeds?'

"'Yes indeed,' he replied, 'and by Him by whom oaths are sworn, anyone going into that fire would prefer being placed in the hottest oven in the house, and having it covered over him, and he being let out of it only next day.'

"'Good gracious! But what proof is there?' they asked.

"'A prophet is being sent from hereabouts in these lands,' he replied, and gestured over towards Mecca and Yemen.

"'When will we see him?' they enquired.

"He looked over at me, I being the youngest one there, and said, 'If this lad lives a normal lifespan, he'll live to his time.'"

Salama said, "And a day and a night had scarcely passed thereafter until God sent the Messenger of God (ṢAAS) who lived among us. And so we believed in him. But he (the Jew) disbelieved in him out of evil and envy.

"So we asked him, 'What now then; aren't you the one who told us certain things about him?'

"'Yes,' he replied, 'but he's not the one.'"

This anecdote was also related by Aḥmad, from Yaʿqūb from his father, from Ibn ʿAbbās. And al-Bayhaqī told it from al-Ḥākim with a chain of authorities through Yūnus b. Bukayr.

Abū Nuʿaym related in *al-Dalāʾil* (*The Signs*), from ʿĀṣim b. Umar b. Qatāda, from Maḥmūd b. Labīd, from Muḥammad b. Salama, saying, "In the tribe of ʿAbd al-Ashhal there was only one Jew, whose name was Yūshaʿ. When I was still a boy, wearing a waist-wrapper, I heard him say, 'The time is near for a prophet to be sent to you from somewhere over near this building.' And he pointed over at God's temple, saying, 'And whoever lives till then, let him believe in him.'

"And the Messenger of God (ṢAAS) was sent and we accepted Islam, while he, living there among us, did not, out of envy and evil."

We have already given the account of Abū Saʿīd, from his father, about this Yūshaʿ's having told of the coming of the Messenger of God (ṢAAS) and of having given his description. Also we told of al-Zubayr b. Bāṭā's account of the appearance of a star at the birth of the Messenger of God (ṢAAS).

Al-Ḥākim related this anecdote from al-Bayhaqī with a chain of authorities through Yūnus b. Bukayr.

Ibn Isḥāq said that ʿĀṣim b. ʿUmar b. Qatāda related to him about a sheikh of Banū Qurayẓa who asked him, "Do you know how it came about that Islam was accepted by Thaʿlaba b. Saʿya and Usayd b. Saʿya along with Asad b. ʿUbayd, all of Banū Hudal, brothers of Banū Qurayẓa, with whom they had lived in the days before Islam but who then became their masters after Islam?"

ʿĀṣim said, "I do not." Whereupon the sheikh told him, "A Jew from Syria called Ibn al-Hayyibān came to us some years before the arrival of Islam and lived among us. And by God, I never knew a non-Muslim (one who does not perform the five daily prayers) better than him. Well, he was living there with us at a time of drought, so we asked him, 'Please, Ibn al-Hayyibān, pray for rain for us!' But he replied, 'No, by God, I'll not do that until you pay me.' 'How much?' we asked. 'A *ṣāʿa* weight of dates or two *mudd* weights of barley.' 'We'll pay it,' we agreed.

"He then went out with us to the top of our parched land and prayed for rain for us. And by God, he no sooner got up but clouds came and it rained! Yet others had done that once, twice, and thrice!

"Later his death came while he lived with us. When he knew he was dying, he said, 'O Jews, what do you think it was that brought me from a land of wine and bread to one of poverty and hunger?' 'You know that best,' we replied. He then said, 'I only came to this country because I expected the arrival of a prophet whose time is near. This land is where he will take refuge. And I had hoped that he would be sent so that I could follow him. His time is near for you. But don't hasten to him, O Jews, for he is sent to shed the blood and capture the women and children of those who oppose him. And that (hurrying to him) will not prevent him treating you thus.'

"And when the Messenger of God (ṢAAS) was sent, he besieged Banū Qurayẓa. Those grown men who had been young boys at the earlier occasion addressed their people, saying, 'O Banū Qurayẓa, he is, by God, the prophet foretold to you by Ibn al-Hayyibān.' They replied, 'He is not.' The men insisted, saying, 'Yes he is. He has just his description.' So they went down and accepted Islam, and by doing so saved their blood, their property, and their people."

Ibn Isḥāq commented, "This account reached us from Jewish rabbis."

Earlier we gave an account of the arrival at Medina of the Tubbaʿ of Yemen, Abū Karib Tubbān Asʿad, and of his siege of it; and how those two rabbis came out to him and told him, "You shall have no path to it. It will be the place of refuge for a prophet at the end of time", and how that made him turn away from the town.

Abū Nuʿaym told in his work, *al-Dalāʾil* (*The Signs*), on a line of authorities through al-Walīd b. Muslim, that Muḥammad b. Ḥamza b. Yūsuf b. ʿAbd Allāh b. Sallām related to him, from his father and grandfather, the following, "ʿAbd Allāh b. Sallām stated that God having wished good guidance for Zayd b. Saʿya, Zayd said, 'All marks of the prophethood were there as expected for me to recognize on the face of Muḥammad (ṢAAS) when I looked at him, except that there were two I had not explored in him: that his patient wisdom preceded his ignorance, and that the more ignorance was directed at him, the more his patient wisdom increased.'

"He stated further, 'I used to be nice to him so that I could mix with him and get to know his wisdom and his foolishness.'

"He then told a story of his having made an advance payment to the Prophet (ṢAAS) for profit. He went on, 'And when the time for the loan was due, I went to him and grabbed him by the closure of his cloak and gown, he being then at a funeral with some of his Companions. I also glared at him in an ugly fashion and said, "O Muḥammad, aren't you going to pay me my due? By God, I never knew you of the tribe of ʿAbd al-Muṭṭalib to be late payers!"

"'ʿUmar stared over at me, his eyes rolled like revolving celestial bodies. Then he said, "You enemy of God! Do you dare say to the Messenger of God (ṢAAS) what I am hearing and do what I am seeing? By Him who sent him with the truth, if I were not wary of his blaming me, I would cut off your head with my sword!"

"'Meanwhile, the Messenger of God (ṢAAS) was looking at ʿUmar, smiling quietly with gentleness. Then he said, "ʿUmar, both he and I were in need of something other than that from you; you should have told me to pay up properly, and him to behave better. Take him away, ʿUmar, and pay him his due. And give him 20 *ṣāʿ*'s weight of dates as a bonus!"'

"And so Zayd b. Saʿya, may God be pleased with him, became a Muslim. He was present with the Messenger of God at all the battles, and he died in the year of Tabūk, God bless him."

Then Ibn Isḥāq, God be pleased with him, recounted how Salmān al-Fārisī, "the Persian", God bless him, became a Muslim. He stated that ʿĀṣim b. ʿUmar b. Qatāda the *anṣārī*, the "helper", related to him, from Maḥmūd b. Labīd, from ʿAbd Allāh b. ʿAbbās, who said that Salmān al-Fārisī told him as follows, "I was a Persian from Isfahan and dwelt in a village called Jayy. My father was the headman of the village and I was the one he most loved of all creatures; his affection for me was so strong that he kept me closeted in his house like a slave-girl.

"I took pains to be a good Magian, and became the keeper of the fire, the one who lights it and never for a moment lets it go out.

"My father owned a large farm and one day, when he was busy constructing a building, he said to me, 'Son, I'm too busy to leave here today for the farm, so you go and look to it.' And he told me certain things he wanted. Then he told me, 'Don't be away from me too long. If you are I'll be more concerned about you than about my farm or work, and you'll keep me from everything else.'

"So I left for the farm as he had told me and on my way I passed by a church for Christians and heard their voices as they prayed there. I didn't know anything about other people, because my father had kept me shut up at home. So when I heard their voices I went in to them to find out what they were doing. When I saw them I was much impressed with their prayers and wanted to join them. I said to myself, 'This, by God, is better than the religion we have.'

"So I didn't leave them until sunset and neglected to go to my father's farm.

"I asked them, 'Where is the origin of this religion?' 'In Syria,' they replied.

"I then went back to my father who had sent people to look for me and had been distracted from all his work. When I arrived he asked, 'Well, son, where were you? Didn't I ask you to do something?' 'O Father,' I replied, 'I went by some people praying in a church of theirs and I was much impressed by what I saw of their religion. So I stayed with them till sunset.'

"'Son, there's no good in that religion. Your religion and that of your forefathers is better than it.'

"'But no,' I replied, 'I swear by God theirs is better than ours.'

"My father was afraid for me and set chains on my legs and imprisoned me in his house. So I sent a message to the Christians saying, 'If a caravan comes to you from Syria send word to me about them.'

"A caravan did arrive from Syria and the Christians came and told me about them. I said to them, 'When they finish their business and are about to return home, then tell me.'

"When they were ready to go home they let me know and I threw the shackles off my legs and left with them. When we arrived in Syria, I asked, 'Who is the most learned man in this religion?' 'The bishop in the church,' they replied.

"So I went to him and said, 'I really like this religion, and I want to join you and to serve you in your church, to learn from you and to pray with you.'

"'Come on in,' he invited me.

"So I joined him. But he was an evil man, demanding alms from his people and whatever they collected he would store away for himself and not give to the poor. Eventually he had gathered seven jars of gold and silver.

"I hated him mightily for what I saw him doing.

"Then he died, and the Christians assembled to bury him. I told them, 'This was an evil man. He demanded alms from you but when you brought it to him he stored it away for himself and gave none of it to the poor.'

"They asked me, 'How do you know that?' and I replied that I could take them to his treasure. 'Do so!' they told me, so I showed them where it was and they brought out seven jars filled with gold and silver. When they saw it they said, 'We'll never give him burial!' And so they crucified and stoned him.

"Then they brought another man to take his place. And," said Salmān, "I never saw a man who did not attend the five prayers who was better than he, nor more ascetic, nor more enthusiastic about the afterlife, nor more devoted both day and night. I loved him as I had never loved before.

"So I stayed with him for a time and then his death approached. I asked him, 'Since I've been with you I've loved you as never before. But now what you know to be God's decree is approaching, so to whom do you entrust me? And what are your orders to me?'

"'My son,' he replied, 'I don't know anyone who has done as I have. People have either died or changed or abandoned most of their prior practices, except for one man in Mawṣil; he practises as I did. Join him.'

"So when he died and was buried, I joined the leader of al-Mawṣil. I told him, 'So-and-so enjoined me at his death to come to you; he told me you are as he was.' 'Stay with me,' I was invited.

"I did so and found him the best of men, like his friend. But soon he was to die. And when death was near for him, I told him, 'So-and-so entrusted me to you and told me to join you. Now God's decree, as you know, is near for you, so whom do you recommend to me, and what are your orders to me?' 'My son,' he replied, 'I don't know anyone else who is as we were, except one man at Naṣībīn, so join him.'

"When he did die and was buried, I joined the bishop at Naṣībīn and told him my story and what my two masters had ordered me. 'Stay with me,' he said. And so I did so, finding him extremely good, as his two colleagues had been. But, I swear by God, death soon approached him too, so I asked him, 'So-and-so recommended one man to me, who recommended me to another, who recommended me to you. Whom do you recommend for me, and what are your orders?'

"'My son,' he said, 'I don't know anyone who is still as we were whom I can recommend, except for one man at ʿAmūriyya in Byzantium. He is as we were. If you wish, go to him.'

"When he died and was buried, I joined the bishop of ʿAmūriyya, and related to him my story. He said, 'Stay with me.' So I did stay there, and he was the best of men, as well-directed and fine in his behaviour as his predecessors had been.

"I worked hard and earned well and eventually I had some cows and a small goat. But then God's decree came for him too and I told him, 'So-and-so recommended someone to me, who recommended me to another, he to another, then he to another and so on until you were recommended me. To whom do you recommend me and what are your orders?'

"'My son,' he replied, 'I don't know anyone who is as we were to whom to send you. But the time is near for a prophet being sent with Abraham's religion who will come forth in the land of the Arabs. He will move to refuge to somewhere with date-palms growing between two scorched, rocky plains. He has signs that are unmistakable. He eats things given to him as gifts but not alms. And between his shoulders there is the seal of prophethood. If you can go there, do so.'

"Then he died and was buried, and I stayed in ʿAmūriyya for the length of time God wished.

"Eventually a group of merchants of the Kalb tribe passed by and I asked them to take me to the land of the Arabs and offered them my cows and goat. They agreed, so I gave them to them and they took me with them as far as Wādī al-Qurā. There they did me evil by selling me as a slave to a Jew. There with him I saw palm trees and hoped that might be the land my master had described.

"While I was there with him he received a visit from a cousin of his of Banū Qurayẓa from Medina. He sold me to him, who bore me off to Medina. And I swear by God, as soon as I saw it I recognized it as my friend had described it to me. And there it was I stayed.

"Then the mission came to the Messenger of God (ṢAAS), who remained in Mecca without me hearing any report of him, busy as I was in the toil of slavery. But then he took refuge in Medina.

"One day I was doing some work for my master at the top of a palm tree, with him sitting there underneath, when a cousin of his came and stopped there. 'Hey there, so-and-so,' the cousin said, 'God damn those *anṣār* of Banū Qayla! They are assembled at Qibāʾ in support of a man come from Mecca whom they claim to be a prophet.'"

Salmān continued, "When I heard this I began to tremble, so much I thought I would fall down on top of my master! So I climbed down the tree and began questioning his cousin.

"This angered my master and he slapped me hard. Then he asked, 'What's this to do with you? Get back to your work!'

"'It's nothing,' I replied, 'I just wanted to clarify what he said.'"

Salmān went on: "I had put aside some food, so that evening I took it to the Messenger of God (ṢAAS) he being at Qibāʾ, and went in to see him, saying, 'I heard you were a good man and that you have with you some companions who are strangers and needy. This is some food I have to give as alms, and I consider you have more right to it than anyone else.'

"I then handed it to him and the Messenger of God (ṢAAS) said to his companions, 'Eat it then.' He himself took none.

"This is one test passed," I told myself.

"Then I left him and saved up some more, while the Messenger of God (ṢAAS) was moving on towards Medina. I then went to him again and said, 'I noticed you didn't eat from the food I gave as alms. This is a present I wish to honour you with.'

"The Messenger of God (ṢAAS) did eat from this and told his companions to do the same, which they did.

"And again I said to myself: 'That makes it two!'

"I then went to the Messenger of God (ṢAAS) when he was at Baqīʿ al-Gharqad, the cemetery, where he had followed the funeral procession of one of his companions. He was wearing two cloaks, sitting there among his companions. I greeted him, then came round behind him to look at his back to find out if I could see the mark my former master had described to me. When the Messenger of God (ṢAAS) saw me go behind him he knew I was trying to establish something of what had been described to me. So he threw off his cloak from his back and I looked at the sign and recognized it. I then prostrated myself before him, kissing him and weeping. The Messenger of God (ṢAAS) then told me, 'Turn around!' So I stood up in front of him and told him my story as I have to you, O Ibn ʿAbbās.

"The Messenger of God (ṢAAS) then wanted his companions to hear my story."

Thereafter Salmān was so engaged at his work as a slave that he missed participation with the Messenger of God (ṢAAS) at the battles of Badr and Uḥud.

Salmān continued, "Eventually the Messenger of God (ṢAAS) said to me, 'Salmān, write!' So I wrote out for my master an agreement that I would plant 300 palm trees watered by a well and pay 40 ounces (of gold). The Messenger of God (ṢAAS) then said to his companions, 'Help your brother.' So they helped me, one man with 30 seedlings, another with 20, another with 15, and another with 10, each one participating as he could, until I had all the 300 together. Then the Messenger of God (ṢAAS) told me, 'Now Salmān, go and dig the holes for them. When you have finished come to me so that I can plant them with my own hands.'

"So I dug and my companions helped me and when we had finished I went and told him. He then went out with me to them and we began handing him the seedlings which the Messenger of God (ṢAAS) himself planted. When we had finished, and this I swear by Him in whose hands Salmān is, not one of those plants died.

"I had now settled up for the palm trees but was still in debt for the money. Now the Messenger of God (ṢAAS) was given a quantity of gold the size of a chicken's egg from a mine. He said, 'Hasn't the Persian done accounts?' I then said a prayer for him. Next, he said, 'Take this and pay off what you owe, Salmān.'

"I asked him, 'Where will this stand relative to what I owe, O Messenger of God?' He said, 'Take it, for God will pay your debt with it.' So I took it and weighed it for them and, I swear by Him in whose hand Salmān is, it was 40 ounces! So I gave my debt in full.'

"And Salmān was set free."

"And", concluded Salmān, "I was present with the Messenger of God (ṢAAS) at the battle of *al-khandaq* ('the trench') as a free man, and never missed another battle where he participated."

Ibn Isḥāq continued, "Yazīd b. Abū Ḥabīb related to me, from a man from the ʿAbd al-Qays tribe, from Salmān, who said, 'When I asked, "Where will this stand relative to what I owe, O Messenger of God?" he took it (the gold nugget), turned it over on his tongue and then said, "Take it; pay them in full with this." And so I did and with it paid off the 40 ounces.'"

Muḥammad b. Isḥāq stated that ʿĀṣim b. ʿUmar b. Qatāda related to me that a reliable authority told him from ʿUmar b. ʿAbd al-ʿAzīz b. Marwān who said that it was related to him about Salmān that when he, Salmān, was telling his story to the Messenger of God (ṢAAS), he said that the bishop of ʿAmūriyya told him, "Go this way and that in Syria, and there you will find a man who dwells between two thickets. Every year he emerges from one of these and then is accosted by people who are sick. Every one of these for whom he says a prayer is cured. So ask him about this religion you're seeking. And he will tell you about it."

Salmān said, "So I left and travelled to the place he had described and I found people gathered there with their sick waiting until the night the man would move out from one of the thickets towards the other. (When he came out) the people there overwhelmed him and every sick person for whom he prayed was cured. They beat me to him and I couldn't get near him till he entered the thicket he was heading for, when I touched his shoulder. 'Who is that?' he asked and turned towards me. I replied, 'God have mercy on you! Do tell me about the *ḥanifiyya*, Abraham's religion!'

"'You're asking me about something people don't enquire about nowadays. The time is near for the coming of a prophet who will be sent down with that religion; he will be one of the people of the sanctuary. Go to him and he will take you to it.' He then went into the thicket.

"At this the Messenger of God (ṢAAS) commented: 'If you have told me the truth, O Salmān, you have met Jesus son of Mary!'"

That, then, is how this anecdote is worded. There is (in its chain of authorities) one man of questionable reliability, he being Sheikh ʿĀṣim b. ʿUmar b.

Qatāda. That link is also said to have been al-Ḥasan b. ʿUmāra. The tradition is also missing a link, indeed untraceable, between ʿUmar b. ʿAbd al-ʿAzīz and Salmān, may God be pleased with him.

As for his words, "If you have told me the truth, O Salmān, you have met Jesus son of Mary," these are very strange, if not unacceptable. For the period involved must, by all accounts, be one of 400 years, perhaps even 600 years by the solar calendar. The longest anyone suggests that Salmān lived is some 350 years. Al-ʿAbbās b. Yazīd al-Baḥrānī related that the consensus of his elders was that he lived for 250 years; they differed as to whether it could have been as much as 350 years. But God knows best. And it seems that he was saying, "You met a (good) follower of Jesus, son of Mary." And that could well be true.

Al-Suhaylī stated, "The man of questionable reliability (in the above chain of authorities) is al-Ḥasan b. ʿUmāra, a weak authority. But if he was correct, then there is nothing unacceptable about it. Because Ibn Jarīr related that Jesus came down again to earth after he had been resurrected and that he found his mother and another woman weeping at the cross of the crucified man. Jesus told them that he had not been killed, and after that he sent his disciples."

He went on: "And if it is possible that he came down once, then it is possible he did so many times. Moreover there is his evident return when he broke the cross and killed the pig and thereafter married a woman of Banū Jidhām and finally was buried in a chamber of the grave (usually referred to as the garden) of the Messenger of God (ṢAAS)."

Al-Bayhaqī related in his book *Dalāʾil al-Nubuwwa* (*Signs of the Prophethood*) this story of Salmān by way of Yūnus b. Bukayr, from Muḥammad b. Isḥāq as previously given. And he also related it from al-Ḥākim, from al-Aṣamm b. Yaḥyā b. Abū Ṭālib.

ʿAlī b. ʿĀṣim related to us, as did Ḥātim b. Abū Ṣufra, from Simāk b. Ḥarb, from Yazīd b. Ṣūḥān, that he heard Salmān relating how his accepting Islam first occurred. Salmān made a lengthy account of how he had originated in Rāmhurmuz and that he had a wealthy brother who was older than himself. He himself was poor and under his brother's care, and the son of the headman of Rāmhurmuz was his friend, with whom he would visit a teacher. And his friend also used to call upon some Christian worshippers who lived in a cave. Salmān asked his friend to take him to visit them, but the reply was, "You're just a young man, and I'm afraid that you will betray them and that my father will kill them." And so he made him promise that he would not do anything his friend would not like.

So he accompanied his friend and they (the Christians) were six or seven in number. And they looked as if, from all their praying, their souls had left them; they fasted by day and stayed up (praying) at night, and ate trees or whatever they found.

He related of them that they believed in all the previous messengers from God and that Jesus was a worshipper of God, His messenger, and the son of His slave-girl and that God aided him with miracles.

They told him, "Boy, you have a Lord; and will have an afterlife. Awaiting you there is to be a heaven and a hell. And those people who worship fires are unbelievers and in error. God is not pleased with what they do, and they are not in his religion."

Thereafter Salmān went to them often with his friend and eventually joined them totally. But then the ruler of that land expelled them, and he was the father of the young man who had visited them with Salmān. The ruler imprisoned his son at home. Salmān presented their religion to his older brother but the latter said, "I'm personally just busy with making my living."

So Salmān went away with them, and they entered the church at al-Mawṣil, whose people made them welcome. "Then", continued Salmān, "they wanted to leave me there with those people, but I refused to do anything but accompany them. So then they went further until they came to a mountain valley, and the monks of that region hurried down to greet them and to be with them. The monks asked them how it had been away, and also enquired about me, and they praised me highly."

Then there arrived a man much respected among them who addressed them and gave all due praise to God. He made mention of the messengers and what assistance they were given. He also talked of Jesus son of Mary and how he was the slave of God and His Messenger. He enjoined them to be good and forbade them evil. Then when his former companions wished to go further on, Salmān kept with this man and followed him. He would fast by day and stay up at night (praying) from one Sunday to the next. He would go out before them and give them sermons, enjoining good and forbidding evil. This went on for a long period and then he wished to visit Jerusalem, and Salmān accompanied him there.

Salmān went on, "As he walked he would turn towards me, draw near, preach to me, and tell me that I had a Lord, that there were heaven, hell, and an accounting before me, reminding me of approximately what he would preach to the congregation on Sundays. One time he told me, 'O Salmān, God will send a messenger whose name is Aḥmad. He will come up out of Tihāma; he will eat a gift, but not alms. And between his shoulders there will be a seal of prophethood. This is the time now approaching when he will appear. I am an old man, and I don't think I will live until his coming. But if you do, then believe in him and follow him.' 'But what', I asked, 'if he tells me to abandon your faith and practices?' He replied, 'No matter what he orders you, he brings the truth with him, and the wish of the Most Merciful One is in what he says.'"

Salmān then related their arrival in Jerusalem and that his companion worshipped at various places there. Before he went to sleep, the priest told him to wake him up when the shadow arrived at a certain place. But Salmān let him rest a little longer than he had requested and when he awoke he first praised God then reproached Salmān for not having done as he requested. They then left Jerusalem and (Salmān's account continues), "A cripple begged, 'O worshipper of God, I asked of you when you arrived, but you gave me nothing. I am now asking you again.' The priest looked but found no one else. So he took him by the hand and said, 'Stand up, in the name of God.' The man did so, and there was nothing wrong with him, no diseases at all; he was moving as if with the slightest limp. The priest then told me, 'O, worshipper of God, load up my baggage for me so I can go off to my own people and tell them the good tidings.' I got busy doing this, but when I wanted to go over to him, I could not find him. I did not know where he had gone. And whenever I asked anyone about him, they told me, 'He's out ahead of you.'

"Eventually I was met by a caravan of Arabs of Banū Kalb and I made enquiry of them. When they heard my accent one man made his camel kneel and mounted me up behind him, and they brought me to their land.

"There they sold me, and a Christian woman bought me and put me to work in a garden she had.

"Then the Messenger of God (ṢAAS) arrived."

Salmān related after this how he went to see him (the Prophet) and gave him alms, then a gift to test what his companion had told him, and asked to see the seal. When he did see it he believed at once and informed the Messenger of God (ṢAAS) what he had been told.

The account then tells of the Messenger of God (ṢAAS), having summoned Abū Bakr, "the trusting", who bought Salmān from the woman and then set him free.

Salmān went on: "Later I asked the Messenger of God one day about the Christians' religion. He replied, 'There's no good in them.' I remembered all those I had accompanied and in particular that good man who had been in Jerusalem with me, and so his words had great impact on me. Then God sent down to the Messenger of God (ṢAAS) the statement: 'Certainly you will find that the people the most violent in their enmity to those who believe are the Jews along with polytheists. And you will find that the closest of people in friendship to those who believe are those who say, "We are Christians." That is because there are priests and monks among them and because they do not behave with conceit' (*sūrat al-Mā'ida*, V, v.82).

"The Messenger of God (ṢAAS) summoned me, and I was afraid when I came. When I sat before him he recited, 'In the name of God the most compassionate, the most merciful. "That is because there are priests and monks among them, and because they do not behave with conceit." Then he said, 'O Salmān, those whom you accompanied, and your friend as well, were not Christians; they were Muslims.' I replied, 'By Him who sent you with the truth, he certainly did order me to follow you.' And when I said, 'But what if he tells me to leave your religion and your practices?' he did say, 'Yes; do leave that, for the truth, and what pleases God is whatever he orders you.'"

In this passage there are many strange elements and some differences with the text cited by Muḥammad Ibn Isḥāq. Ibn Isḥāq's is stronger in its chains of authorities, better in its narrative, and closer to that related by al-Bukhārī in his *ṣaḥīḥ* collection. The latter relies on the *ḥadīth* of Mu῾tamar b. Sulaymān b. Tarkhān al-Taymī, from his father, from Abū ῾Uthmān al-Nahdī, from Salmān al-Fārisī. That account relates dozens of interactions, from master to master, that is, from teacher to teacher, and from guide to guide. But God knows best.

Al-Suhaylī said, "There were 30 changes in all, from one master to the next." But God knows best.

Similarly the *ḥāfiz* Abū Nu῾aym abbreviated the account of Salmān's conversion in his work *al-Dalā᾽il* (*The Signs*). In it he gave many different chains of authorities, and many different phrases. In some of these the name of the woman who made the contract about him was named Ḥalbasa. But God knows best.

An Account of certain strange events relating thereto.

Abū Nu῾aym stated in *al-Dalā᾽il* that Sulaymān b. Aḥmad related to him, quoting Muḥammad b. Zakariyyā᾽ al-Ghalābī, quoting al-῾Alā᾽ b. al-Faḍl b. ῾Abd al-Mālik b. Abū al-Sawiyya al-Minqarī, as did ῾Abbād b. Kassīb, from his father, from Abū ῾Atwāra al-Khuzā῾ī, from Sa῾īr b. Sawāda al-῾Āmirī, who said, "I was in love with one of the finest ladies of the tribe. For her I rode every kind of mount, difficult and submissive alike, leaving no place untried in my hopes of business and profit. I left Syria with goods and produce I wanted to sell to the crowds of pilgrims and Arabs and so entered Mecca one very dark night. I stayed until night was over and when I lifted my head I could see a pavilion over against the top of the mountain quilted out of heavy cloth from al-Ṭā᾽if. Animals were being slaughtered and others brought. People were eating and others encouraging the cooks to hurry up. There, too, was a man calling loudly from a hilltop, saying, 'O pilgrims, come on over and eat lunch!' There was also a little man over on a path calling out, 'O pilgrims, if you have eaten, pass on till supper.' I was amazed by what I saw and went over there seeking the group's leader. One man saw what I wanted and told me, 'Straight ahead!'

"Then I saw an old man whose cheeks were very red and who seemed to have a star shining forth from his forehead. He had twisted around his head a black turban from beneath the folds of which his head-parting appeared, sesame seed in colour." (Some accounts give the wording as "sitting on a chair of black *samāsim* wood with a saddle cushion beneath it.") "In his hand he lightly held a rod. All around him sheikhs were sitting, their heads held down, and not one of them was saying a word. Information had reached me in Syria that this was the time for the arrival of the *ummī* (unlettered) Prophet, so when I saw this man I thought it was he. So I said to him, 'Peace be upon you, O Messenger of God!' He replied in anger, 'Stop that! No! I wish I were he.' I asked, 'Who is that sheikh?' 'That's Abū Naḍla, Hāshim b. ʿAbd Manāf.' So I turned away, saying, 'Now that is glory! Not like that of the house of Jafna!'"

By this he meant the Arab kings of Syria of the Ghassān tribe, who were known as the Āl (family of) Jafna. The office he was describing relative to Hāshim was that of the *rifāda*, namely the feeding of the pilgrims.

Abū Nuʿaym said that ʿAbd Allāh b. Muḥammad b. Jaʿfar related to him, quoting Muḥammad b. Aḥmad b. Abū Yaḥyā, quoting Saʿīd b. ʿUthmān, quoting ʿAlī b. Qutayba al-Khurāsānī, quoting Khālid b. Ilyās, from Abū Bakr b. ʿAbd Allāh b. Abū al-Jahm, from his father from his grandfather, who said that he heard Abū Ṭālib relate the following about ʿAbd al-Muṭṭalib. He said, "While I was sleeping in the *ḥijr* enclosure, I had visions that scared me really badly. I went to a Quraysh soothsayer and I was wearing a silk shawl and my long hair was brushing my shoulders. When she looked at me, she knew from my face that something was changed; at that time I was the leader of my tribe. She said, 'What is wrong with our master that he has come to us, his face so changed? Is he afraid of some fateful happening?' 'Indeed I am,' I replied.

"Now she never first addressed anyone before they kissed her right hand. She would then place that hand on top of her head and the person would tell her what he wanted. I did not do that because I was the chief of my tribe.

"So I then sat down and said, 'As I lay sleeping last night in the *ḥijr* I had a vision of a tree having grown up, its head touching the sky and its boughs touching both the east and the west. And I never saw any light shine more brightly, 70 times brighter than the sun's light. I saw the Arabs and the non-Arabs alike prostrate before it, while it grew broader, taller, and more dazzling all the time, sometimes dimming but then gleaming again. I saw a group of men of Quraysh who had grasped its branches, while another group of them wanted to cut it down. When they came near it they were fended away by a young man more good and handsome than I had ever seen before. And he was breaking their backs and gouging their eyes. I raised my hand to have my share of the tree but the young man stopped me. 'But who is to have it, then?' I asked. He replied, 'It is for those who climbed it, and they were there before you.' At that I woke up in a fright.

"I saw that the expression on the face of the soothsayer had now altered. She said, 'If your vision was true, then a man will emerge from your offspring who will rule both east and west, a man whom all will follow.'"

After that he – ʿAbd al-Muṭṭalib, that is – said to Abū Ṭālib: "Maybe you are to be that person."

Abū Ṭālib used to tell this anecdote after the birth of the Messenger of God, following his receiving his mission. Then he said, "As God knows best, the tree was Abū al-Qāsim, the Trustworthy." Someone asked Abū Ṭālib, "So don't you believe?" He replied, "Shame and disgrace!"

Abū Nuʿaym stated that Sulaymān b. Aḥmad related to him, quoting Muḥammad b. Zakariyyā' al-Ghalābī, quoting al-ʿAbbās b. Bakkār al-Ḍabbī, quoting Abū Bakr al-Hudhalī, from ʿIkrima, from Ibn ʿAbbās that al-ʿAbbās said, "I went off in a caravan to Yemen to trade. In that party was Abū Sufyān b. Ḥarb. When we were in Yemen I used to prepare the food one day and then go off with Abū Sufyān and others. Then next day Abū Sufyān would prepare the food and do the same as I had. One day when I was to prepare it, he asked, 'Abū al-Faḍl, how would you like to go to my house and send your food to me?' I agreed.

"So I went with the group to his place and I sent off for the food. When everyone had finished eating, they left but he kept me there. He asked, 'Abū al-Faḍl, are you aware that your brother's son claims to be the Messenger of God?' I replied, 'Which one of my brother's sons?' Abū Sufyān said, 'Would you evade me? Which of your brother's sons would it have to be saying that except one?' 'Nevertheless, which one?' I asked. 'He is Muḥammad b. ʿAbd Allāh,' he replied. 'He's done that?' I enquired. 'He certainly has,' he insisted.

"He then took out a letter to him from his son Ḥanẓala b. Abū Sufyān which said, 'This is to tell you that Muḥammad stood up in the open space and said, 'I am the Messenger of God; I summon you to God, Almighty and Glorious is He!' Al-ʿAbbās replied, 'O Abū Ḥanẓala, I think he's telling the truth!'

"'Easy does it, O Abū al-Faḍl! By God, I don't like him saying that. (Yet) I don't fear any harm for us from his saying that, O son of ʿAbd al-Muṭṭalib. By God, Quraysh is always saying something or other is yours, and there's purpose behind each of them! Have you heard of that, Abū al-Faḍl?' 'Yes, I have,' I replied. So he said, 'You're cursed with this, by God!' 'Maybe we're blessed with it,' I responded."

Al-ʿAbbās went on: "It was only a few days thereafter that ʿAbd Allāh b. Ḥudhāfa brought that information, he being a believer. That news spread in all the assemblies of Yemen. Abū Sufyān used to attend one assembly in Yemen where a rabbi would talk. And the Jew said to him, 'What's this news? I've heard that you have among you the uncle of the man who has been saying these things.'

"Abū Sufyān replied, 'Yes, that's true. I am his uncle.' The Jew asked, 'His father's brother?' 'Yes,' Abū Sufyān told him. 'Well tell me about him,' he said.

"'Don't ask me,' he responded. 'I am not at all pleased at him making that claim, and I don't want to find fault with him, though there are others better than him.'"

"The Jew noticed that Abū Sufyān did not want to diminish his support nor to criticize him.

"'He has no ill will towards the Jews, or the Torah,' the Jew commented."

Al-ʿAbbās stated: "Having been invited by the rabbi, I went and sat in at one of their meetings the next day. Abū Sufyān b. Ḥarb was there along with the rabbi. I said to the rabbi, 'I've been told that you asked my cousin about one of our men who claims to be the Messenger of God (ṢAAS) and that he told you he was his uncle. But he is not his uncle but his cousin. I'm his uncle, his father's brother.'

"'You're his father's brother?' he asked and I stated I was.

"He then approached Abū Sufyān and asked, 'Did he tell the truth?' 'Yes, he did,' he replied.

"Then I said, 'Ask me some questions, and if I lie, he can refute me.'

"He came over to me and said, 'I ask you now, has your brother's son sexual desires or immoral behaviour?'

"'Certainly not, by the God of ʿAbd al-Muṭṭalib,' I replied, 'and he has never lied or cheated. Among Quraysh he is known as "the Trustworthy".'

"'Does he write by his own hand?' he asked."

Al-ʿAbbās thought it would be better for him if he did write by his own hand, and he wanted to say he did. But then he remembered Abū Sufyān's being there and how he would call him a liar and refute him. So al-ʿAbbās replied, "No, he doesn't write."

He continued, "The rabbi jumped up, and his loose robe fell down as he exclaimed, 'Jews will be slaughtered, Jews killed!'"

Al-ʿAbbās went on, "And when we returned home, Abū Sufyān said, 'O Abū al-Faḍl, the Jews are terrified of your nephew.' I asked him, 'Well, having seen what you have, do you believe in him? If it's true, you could be there early; but if it's not, you'd only be among others like you.'

"He replied: 'I'll not believe in him till I see horses high up on Mt. Kadāʾ.'"

"'What do you mean?' I asked. 'Just a phrase that came to mind,' he replied. 'Except that I know that God won't allow horsemen to climb up on Kadāʾ.'"

Al-ʿAbbās said, "But when the Messenger of God (ṢAAS) conquered Mecca and we looked up at the horsemen high on Kadāʾ, I said, 'Well Abū Sufyān, remember what you said?'

"'Yes,' he replied, 'I certainly do. And thanks be to God for guiding me to Islam.'"

This account is excellent, fully illuminated by the light of truth, even though some people cast doubts on some who reported it. But God knows best.

We have previously given the story of Abū Sufyān's contact with Umayya b. Abū al-Ṣalt and it is similar to that given here. It is one of the strangest and best authenticated of stories, and one that is clear.

Also there will come the story of Abū Sufyān with Heraclius, the King of Byzantium, when the former was asked to describe the Messenger of God (ṢAAS) and how he then thus gave proof of his truthfulness, prophethood, and mission. The King replied, "I knew he was coming, but did not realize he was one of you. If I had known I would survive to his time, I would have striven to meet him. If I had been with him, I would have washed his feet. And if what you say is true, he will govern wherever these two feet of mine are placed." So did it happen, all power and praise be to God.

The *ḥāfiẓ* Abū Nu'aym gave more instances with lengthy and better reports relating to monks, rabbis, and Arabs; may God have mercy on him and bless him.

The Story of 'Amr b. Murra al-Juhanī.

Al-Ṭabarānī stated that 'Alī b. Ibrāhīm al-Khuzā'ī al-Ahwāzī related to him, quoting 'Abd Allāh b. Dāwūd b. Dalhāth b. Ismā'īl b. 'Abd Allāh b. Sharīḥ b. Yāsir b. Suwayd, the Companion of the Messenger of God (ṢAAS), quoting his father, from his father Dalhāth, from his father Ismā'īl, that his father 'Abd Allāh related to him from his father, that his father Yāsir b. Suwayd related to him from 'Amr b. Murra al-Juhanī, who said, "I went on a pilgrimage before the coming of Islam. In my dream, when I was in Mecca, I saw a shining light emerging from the *ka'ba*, and going as far as the mountains of Yathrib and the fertile slopes of Yanbu'. I heard a voice coming from amidst the light saying, 'The shadows are dispersed, the light shines bright, and the Seal of the Prophets has been sent.'

"Then another light shone, so that I could see to the castles of al-Ḥīra and to *Abyaḍ al-Madā'in*, Chosroe's palace. I heard a voice from that light calling, 'Islam has appeared! The idols are destroyed! And all is made whole!'

"I awoke with a start and called out to my people, 'By God, something is certainly going to happen in this tribe of Quraysh!' And I told them what I had seen.

"When we reached home, the news came that a man called Aḥmad had received a mission. So I went to him and told him what I had seen. He then said to me, 'O 'Amr b. Murra, I am the Prophet sent to all mankind; I summon them to Islam, order them to shed blood and to bring reconciliation, to pray to God and reject idols, to make the pilgrimage to the *kaʿba*, to fast the month of Ramaḍān, one month out of twelve. For those who respond, there is paradise; for those who rebel, the fire. So have faith, O ʿAmr, and God will protect you from the terror of hell!'

"I said, 'I give testimony that there is no God but God, and that you are the Messenger of God. I have faith in your message as to what is permitted and prohibited, even though that offends many peoples.' I then recited to him verses that I had spoken when I heard of him. We had an idol whom my father worshipped, and I went and destroyed it. Then I joined the Prophet (ṢAAS), speaking the verses,

> 'I gave witness that God is truth, and that I am the first to abandon stone worship.
> I busied myself taking flight to you, crossing wild deserts and sand wastes
> To accompany the best of men in spirit and line, the messenger of mankind's Lord above the stars.'

"The Prophet (ṢAAS) said, 'Welcome to you indeed, O ʿAmr b. Murra.' And I replied, 'O Messenger of God, send me to my people so that God may favour them through me as He did me through you.'

"So he sent me to them, saying, 'Behave with kindness and speak the truth. Be you not churlish, nor arrogant, nor envious.'"

He told how he came to his people, and summoned them to the teachings of the Messenger of God (ṢAAS) and they all accepted Islam, except for one of their men. ʿAmr then went with them to the Messenger of God (ṢAAS) who greeted and welcomed them. He wrote for them a document as follows:

"In the name of God the Most Merciful and Beneficent. This document is a safe-passage from God through the words of the Messenger of God (ṢAAS) through a truth-telling document and a veracious spokesman, sent with ʿAmr b. Murra al-Juhanī to Juhayna b. Zayd. For you there shall be the lowlands and the slopes, the depths and the sides of the valleys. You shall cultivate their produce and drink their pure water, provided that you affirm that you shall forsake one-fifth (of the harvest) and keep praying the five prayers. (Your rich shall pay the alms to the poor): one ewe for each forty sheep and one ewe for each five camels, or two ewes for any combination thereof. The rich shall not be eligible to receive charity. And God will bear witness that we so agreed, and the Muslims attending will bear witness. (This document is) handwritten by Qays b. Shammās."

He then gave some verses spoken by ʿAmr b. Murra on that subject, as is depicted in the great *musnad ḥadīth* collection. In God we trust, and upon Him we rely.

And God Almighty said, "And when we made a covenant with the prophets and with you and with Noah and Abraham and Moses and Jesus son of Mary, and we made a firm covenant with them" (*sūrat al-Aḥzāb*, XXXIII, v.7).

Many of our early ancestors said, "When God made his covenant with mankind the day he said, 'Am I not your Lord?', he made a special agreement with the prophets. And He affirmed that that group (consisted) of five great law-giving prophets, the first of whom was Noah and the last Muḥammad (ṢAAS)."

The *ḥāfiẓ* Abū Nuʿaym informed us in his book the *Dalāʾil al-Nubuwwa* (*Signs of the Prophethood*) through various routes from al-Walīd b. Muslim, that al-Awzāʿī related to him, as did Yaḥyā b. Abū Kathīr, from Abū Salama, from Abū Hurayra, who said that the Prophet (ṢAAS) was asked, "When was the prophethood required of you?" He replied, "Between the creation of Adam and the blowing of the spirit into him."

Al-Tirmidhī related it similarly through al-Walīd b. Muslim. He defined it as "good, but unique as a *ḥadīth* from Abū Hurayra; we know of it only from that line".

Abū Nuʿaym stated that Sulaymān b. Aḥmad related to him, quoting Yaʿqūb b. Isḥāq b. al-Zubayr al-Ḥalabī, quoting Abū Jaʿfar al-Nufaylī, quoting ʿAmr b. Wāqid, from ʿUrwa b. Ruwaym, from al-Ṣunabiḥī, saying that ʿUmar said, "O Messenger of God, when were you made a prophet?" He replied, "While Adam was being formed in the clay."

He then related it from a *ḥadīth* of Naṣr b. Muzāḥim from Qays b. Rabīʿ, from Jābir al-Juʿfī, from al-Shaʿbī, from Ibn ʿAbbās, who said that someone asked, "O Messenger of God, when were you (made) a prophet?" He replied, "While Adam was between soul and body."

In the tradition we gave in the story of Adam when God extracted from his loins his progeny, He singled out the prophets by a light between their eyes. It is apparent – but God knows best – that it (i.e. the light) was commensurate with their levels and ranks in God's view. If that be the case, then the light of Muḥammad (ṢAAS) was greater, stronger, and more evident than that of all the rest.

And this is a great and obvious distinction and indication of his nobility and high worth.

And to that effect there is the *ḥadīth* spoken by Imām Aḥmad who said that ʿAbd al-Raḥmān b. Mahdī related to him, as did Muʿāwiya b. Ṣāliḥ from Saʿīd b. Suwayd al-Kalbī, from ʿAbd al-Aʿlā b. Hilāl al-Salamī from al-ʿIrbad b. Sāriyya, who said that the Messenger of God (ṢAAS) stated, "In God's view I was the Seal of the Prophets while Adam was still within his clay. And I shall tell you of the first of it – the prayer of my father Abraham, the glad tidings of Jesus regarding me, the visions my mother saw, and similarly those that the mothers of the believers see."

Al-Layth and Ibn Wahb related this from ʿAbd al-Raḥmān b. Mahdī, and ʿAbd Allāh b. Ṣāliḥ from Muʿāwiya b. Ṣāliḥ, who added, "his mother saw, when she delivered him, a light from him that illuminated the castles of Syria."

Imām Aḥmad stated that ʿAbd al-Raḥmān related to him, as did Manṣūr b. Saʿīd, from Badīl, from ʿAbd Allāh b. Shaqīq, from Maysara al-Fajr, who stated that he said, "O Messenger of God, when were you a prophet?" And he replied, "While Adam was between spirit and body."

The line of transmission of this tradition is also excellent.

Ibrāhīm b. Tahmān related it similarly, along with Ḥammād b. Zayd and Khālid al-Hadhdhāʾ from Badīl b. Maysara.

Abū Nuʿaym related it from Muḥammad b. ʿUmar b. Aslam, from Muḥammad b. Bakr b. ʿAmr al-Bāhilī, from Shaybān, from al-Ḥasan b. Dīnār, from ʿAbd Allāh b. Sufyān, from Maysara al-Fajr, who said that he asked, "O Messenger of God, when were you a prophet?" He replied, "While Adam was between spirit and body."

The *ḥāfiẓ* Abū Nuʿaym stated in his book *Dalāʾil al-Nubuwwa* (*Signs of the Prophethood*) that Abū ʿAmr b. Ḥamdān related to him, quoting al-Ḥasan b. Sufyān, quoting Hishām b. ʿAmmār, quoting al-Walīd b. Muslim, from Khulayd b. Daʿlaj, and Saʿīd, from Qatāda, from al-Ḥasan, from Abū Hurayra, from the Prophet (ṢAAS), about Almighty God's words, "And when we made a covenant with the Prophets." He said, "I was the first of the Prophets in creation, and the last of them to be sent."

He then related it from Hishām b. ʿAmmār from Baqiyya, from Saʿīd b. Nusayr, from Qatāda, from al-Ḥasan, from Abū Hurayra, traced back similarly.

He also related it through Saʿīd b. Abū ʿArūba and Shaybān, from Qatāda who said, "It was related to us that the Messenger of God (ṢAAS) said the like." And this account is very firm and reliable. But God knows best.

This acknowledges the extremely high regard in which he is held among the heavenly host of angels, that he is recognized among them for having been the Seal of the Prophets even before the soul was blown into Adam. This is because God's knowledge of that was prior, most assuredly before the creation of the earth and heaven. And so all that remained necessary was to make reference to the recognition there was among the heavenly hosts. But God knows best.

Abū Nuʿaym reported from a *ḥadīth* of ʿAbd al-Rāziq from Maʿmar, from Ḥammām, from Abū Hurayra, the *ḥadīth* being agreed upon as stating, "We are those who will have precedence at Judgement Day and who will be judged before the other creatures, even though they were brought the Scriptures before we were, we receiving them after them."

Abū Nuʿaym added at the end, "And he (ṢAAS) was the last of them to receive a mission, and through him the prophethood ended. He will take precedence on Judgement Day, because he was the first covenanted for prophethood."

He then said, "That *ḥadīth* depicts the high honour of the Messenger of God (ṢAAS) regarding God's appointing him to the prophethood before the completion of the creation of Adam. It is likely that it is this affirmation that

God conveyed to His angels, of what there was previously in His knowledge, and His judgement of sending a mission to him till the end of time."

This comment is in agreement with what we previously stated. And so all praise be to God.

In his interpretation of the *ḥadīth* of ʿAbd al-Raḥmān b. Zayd b. Aslam – about which there is some controversy – al-Ḥākim related from his father, from his grandfather, from ʿUmar b. al-Khaṭṭāb, God be pleased with him, that the Messenger of God (ṢAAS) said, "When Adam committed sin, he said, 'O God, I ask you for Muḥammad's sake, won't you forgive me?' God replied, 'O Adam, how did you know Muḥammad when I haven't created him yet?' Adam replied, 'O Lord, because when you created me with your own hand and blew life into me from your spirit, I raised my head and saw on the foundations beneath the throne the writing, "There is no God but God. Muḥammad is the Messenger of God." I knew that you would never have added to your own name anyone but the most precious to you of your creation.' God replied, 'You have spoken the truth, O Adam; he is to me the most precious of my creation. And since you asked in his name, you have my forgiveness. Were it not for Muḥammad, I would not have created you.'"

Al-Bayhaqī said, "ʿAbd al-Raḥmān b. Zayd b. Aslam alone gave this tradition, and it is weak. But God knows best.

God Almighty said, "And when God made a covenant with the prophets, saying, 'I brought you the Scripture and wisdom, then a Messenger will come unto you verifying what you have. Let you believe in him well, and aid him!' He said, 'Have you agreed, and accepted my covenant in that?' They replied, 'We have agreed.' He said, 'Then bear witness and I too along with you will bear witness. Whoever revokes this hereafter, those are sinners!'" (*sūrat Āl-ʿImrān*, III, v.81–2).

ʿAlī b. Abū Ṭālib and ʿAbd Allāh b. ʿAbbās, God bless them, said, "God never sent any prophet without first making a covenant with him (to the effect that) if Muḥammad (ṢAAS) was sent when that prophet was alive, then he would believe in him and aid him. And He ordered him to convey the covenant to his people, that if Muḥammad was sent while they were living, they really would believe in him and aid him to make him victorious."

This is a recognition and an affirmation of his honour and high stature among all the religions and upon the tongues of all the prophets. It is an announcement to them and from them of his being a Messenger to the end of time and of his being the most noble of the messengers and the Seal of the Prophets.

And God has made plain all the facts about him, all information, all secrets pertaining to him. He made his splendour very clear, as well as facts of his birth and homeland through the words of Abraham the "true friend", peace be upon him, when he finished building the *kaʿba*: "O our Lord, send among them a Messenger from among themselves who will recite to them your signs and teach them the Scripture and wisdom, and purify them. You are the Mighty and the Wise" (*sūrat al-Baqara*, II, v.129).

The first clear and evident sign of his status among the people of the earth came, then, on the tongue of Abraham, the "true friend", the prophet, the next most honoured by God after Muḥammad (ṢAAS).

This why Imām Aḥmad said that Abū al-Naḍr related to him, quoting al-Faraj, meaning Ibn Faḍāla, as did Luqmān b. ʿĀmir, who said that he heard Abū Amāma say that he once asked, "O Messenger of God, what was the beginning of your mission?" He replied, "It was the prayer of my father Abraham, the glad tidings of Jesus, and my mother's seeing a light emitting from her that illuminated the castles of Syria."

Imām Aḥmad alone gave this tradition, and none of the authors of the six (canonical) books (of traditions) included it.

The *ḥāfiẓ* Abū Bakr b. Abū ʿĀṣim related in his book *al-Mawlid* (*The Birth*) through Baqiyya, from Ṣafwān b. ʿAmr, from Ḥajar b. Ḥajar, from Abū Marīq, that a bedouin asked, "O Messenger of God, what event was it that began your prophethood?" He replied, "God took from me the covenant, as he took covenants from the other prophets." And the mother of the Messenger of God (ṢAAS) saw in her sleep that a light was emitting from between her feet that lit up the castles of Syria.

Imām Muḥammad b. Isḥāq b. Yasār stated that Thawr b. Yazīd related to him from Khālid b. Maʿdān, from the Companions of the Messenger of God (ṢAAS) that they, the Companions, asked, "O Messenger of God, tell us about yourself." He replied, "The prayer of my father Abraham, the glad tidings of Jesus, and (the fact that) my mother saw, when she was pregnant, that a light came from inside her that illuminated Buṣrā in Syria."

The chain of authorities of this tradition is also excellent.

It contains good news for the people of our community in the lands of Buṣrā. It is the first place in Syria to receive the light of the prophethood; and to God all praise and favour are due. That is why it was the first city of Syria to be conquered. It was taken peacefully during the caliphate of Abū Bakr, God be pleased with him. The Messenger of God (ṢAAS) travelled there twice in the company of his uncle Abū Ṭālib when he was a boy of 12. It was there the story of Baḥīrā the monk was set, as we have related above. The second time he was with Maysara, the freed man of Khadīja, while on a trading expedition on her behalf. Also, it has the spot where the camel known as the camel of the Messenger of God (ṢAAS) had knelt. Its remains are still there, so they say. Eventually its remains were gathered, and a mosque, famous to this day, was built over it. That is the town where the necks of the camels lit up from the light of the fire that came from Ḥijāz in the year 654, according to the statement made by the Messenger of God (ṢAAS), who said, "A fire leaves Ḥijāz that illuminates the necks of the camels at Buṣrā."

And God Almighty stated, "Those who follow the Prophet, the *ummī* (unlettered), whom they find written down with them in the Torah and the Gospel, who orders people to be good and forbids them evil, and who makes lawful for them good things and makes unlawful foul things, who removes from them their burden and the chains that were upon them. And so those who believe in him and honour him and help him and who follow the light that came down with him, those shall be successful" (*sūrat al-Aʿrāf*, VII, v.157).

Imām Aḥmad stated that Ismāʿīl related to him, from al-Jurayrī, from Abū Ṣakhr al-ʿUqaylī, who said that a bedouin told him that he had brought in some merchandise to Medina while the Messenger of God (ṢAAS) was still alive. And when he had finished selling it, he told himself that he should meet that man and listen to him.

The bedouin said, "He met me when he was walking between Abū Bakr and ʿUmar. I followed them until they came to a Jew holding and reading the Torah, and consoling himself with it at the death of a son of his, the best and most handsome of boys. The Messenger of God (ṢAAS) asked him, 'I beg of you, by Him who sent down the Torah, do you see in your Scripture any description of me and my place of origin?' The man made a gesture with his head, meaning, 'no'. But his (dead) son spoke, saying, 'But yes, by Him who sent down the Torah, we do find in our Scriptures a description of you and of your place of origin! I bear witness that there is no God but God, and that you are the Messenger of God.' And so he said, 'Keep away the Jew from your brother.' Then he (the Prophet) took care of winding the dead boy in his shroud and performed the prayers for the dead over him."

This chain of authorities is excellent, and there are testimonies to its veracity in the *ṣaḥīḥ* from Anas b. Mālik.

Abū al-Qāsim al-Baghawī stated that ʿAbd al-Wāḥid b. Ghiyāth, Abū Baḥr that is, related to him, quoting ʿAbd al-ʿAzīz b. Muslim, quoting ʿĀṣim b. Kulayb, from his father, from al-Ṣallatān b. ʿĀṣim, who related that his uncle said that he was seated with the Prophet (ṢAAS) when he gazed over at a certain man, a Jew wearing a shirt, trousers, and sandals. The Prophet (ṢAAS) began talking to him. The man asked, "O Messenger of God . . ." The Messenger of God (ṢAAS) responded, "Are you witnessing that I am the Messenger of God?" "No," the man said. The Messenger of God (ṢAAS) then asked him, "Do you read the Torah?" "Yes," the man replied. He asked, "Do you read the Gospel?" "Yes, the man replied. "And the Qurʾān?" "No," the Jew replied. "But if you want, I will." The Prophet (ṢAAS) then asked, "In what you read of the Torah and the Gospel, do you find me to be a prophet?" The man answered, "We do find a description of you and of your place of origin. When you came, we hoped you would be one of us. But when we saw you we knew that you were not he." The Messenger of God (ṢAAS) then asked, "Why is that, O Jew?" He replied, "We find it to be written down that, 'There will enter paradise from his nation 70,000'. But with you we see only a few men."

The Messenger of God (ṢAAS) then responded, "My nation is far greater in number than 70,000, and 70,000 more again."

This is a unique *ḥadīth* from such a source, and they (the scholars) have not promulgated it.

Muḥammad b. Isḥāq stated, from Sālim, the freed-man of ʿAbd Allāh b. Muṭīʿ, from Abū Hurayra who said that some Jews came to the Messenger of God (ṢAAS) who said, "Bring out your most knowledgeable man." They replied, "He is ʿAbd Allāh b. Ṣūriyā." The Messenger of God (ṢAAS) sat with him alone and adjured him by his religion and by God's blessings to them, by God who had fed them with manna and quails and shaded them with clouds. "Do you know me as the Messenger of God?" the Prophet (ṢAAS) asked. "Yes indeed, by God," the Jew responded. "And my people know what I know. You are fully apparent in the Torah. But they are envious."

"So what prevents you (from believing)?" he asked.

"I just hate to disagree with my people," the Jew replied. "Maybe they will follow you and accept Islam, then I will."

Salama b. al-Faḍl stated, from Muḥammad b. Isḥāq, from Muḥammad b. Abū Muḥammad, from ʿIkrima, from Ibn ʿAbbās, to the effect that he used to say that the Messenger of God (ṢAAS) wrote to the Jews of Khaybar as follows, "In the name of God the most merciful and beneficent, from Muḥammad, the Messenger of God, the companion and brother of Moses and the corroborator of the message Moses brought. God stated to you, 'O Jews, people of the Torah, you will find in your book the fact that Muḥammad is the Messenger of God; and those who are with him are violent against unbelievers, compassionate among themselves. You see them bowing down and prostrating themselves, desiring grace and approval from God. They have marks on their faces from the effects of prostration. That is how they are compared in the Torah and in the Gospel. (They are) like a plant that emits its shoot, then strengthens it so that it thickens and stands straight on its stem. He (God) gives the sowers delight so that He may enrage through them the unbelievers. God has promised forgiveness and great reward to those of them who believe and do good' (*sūrat al-Fatḥ*, XLVII, v.29). I adjure you by God by that which has come down to you, and by Him who fed manna and quails to your forebears and tribes, who dried up the sea for your forefathers to save you from Pharaoh and his deeds, can you not tell us whether you find in God's revelations to you (the fact) that you should believe in Muḥammad? And if you do not discover that in your Scriptures, then there is no hatred for you. (But now) what is right has become clear from what is error. And I call you to God and to his Prophet (ṢAAS)."

Muḥammad b. Isḥāq b. Yasār related in his book *al-Mubtada'* (*The Beginning*) from Sa'īd b. Bashīr, from Qatāda, from Ka'b al-Aḥbār, and others related from Wahb b. Munabbih, that Bukhtunaṣṣar (Nebuchadnezzar), after he had destroyed Jerusalem and kept the Jews in subjugation for seven years, saw strange visions in a dream that terrified him. And so he assembled his soothsayers and wise men and questioned them about those visions of his. They suggested, "If the King first tells us of them, then we can interpret them." But he replied, "I've forgotten them. And if you don't tell me in three days about them, I'll kill the lot of you!"

Off they went very fearful of his threat. Daniel, in gaol at the time, heard of this and told the gaoler, "Go and tell the King, 'We have a man who has knowledge of your visions and can interpret them.'"

So he went to tell the King who summoned Daniel. When he entered, Daniel did not bow down to him, so the King demanded, "What prevents you from prostrating before me?" Daniel replied, "God brought me knowledge, and ordered me not to bow to anyone but Him." Bukhtunaṣṣar then said, "I like those who fulfil their duty to their masters. Tell me about my vision."

Daniel said to him, "You saw a huge idol, its feet on the ground and its head in the sky. Its upper part was of gold, its middle of silver, its lower part of brass, its legs of iron and its feet of clay. While you were looking at it, delighted by its beauty and the intricacy of its workmanship, God cast down a stone from heaven which hit the top of its head and crushed it completely. Its gold, silver, brass, iron, and clay became mixed together so that it seemed to you that even if all men and all the spirits were to try to differentiate its components they would fail. When you looked at the stone that had been thrown, you saw it get bigger and bigger until it filled all the earth so that all you could see was it and the sky."

Bukhtunaṣṣar said, "You are right. That is the vision I saw. What does it mean?"

"Well", replied Daniel, "the idol represents various nations, early, intermediate, and late in time. The stone by which the idol was struck is a religion God will send and reveal to these nations at time's end. And God will send a prophet, an *ummī*, from the Arabs who will conquer with it all the nations and all the religions, as you saw the stone destroy the various components of the idol. It will overcome all the nations and religions, just as you saw the stone overwhelm the entire earth. God will purify the truth and annihilate falsehood through it. Through it He will guide those in error. He will teach the illiterate, strengthen the weak, uplift the humble, and give victory to the disadvantaged."

The account ends the story by Bukhtunaṣṣar releasing the Israelites through Daniel, peace be upon him.

Al-Wāqidī related, with a chain of authorities from al-Mughīra b. Shuʿba, the story of the latter's going to al-Muqawkis, King of Alexandria, and of being questioned by him about the qualities of the Messenger of God (ṢAAS) similarly to how Heraclius asked Abū Sufyān Ṣakhr b. Ḥarb. He related how he questioned the Christian bishops in the churches for a description of the Messenger of God (ṢAAS) and how they did so. It is a long story that is related by the *ḥāfiẓ* Abū Nuʿaym in *Dalāʾil al-Nubuwwa* (*Signs of the Prophethood*).

It is established in the *ṣaḥīḥ* that the Messenger of God (ṢAAS) went past some Jewish schools and asked them, "O Jews, accept Islam. For, by Him in whose hand is my soul, you will certainly find description of me in your scriptures."

Imām Aḥmad stated that Mūsā b. Dāwūd related to him, quoting Fulayḥ b. Sulaymān, from Hilāl b. ʿAlī, from ʿAṭāʾ b. Yasār who said that he met ʿAbd Allāh b. ʿAmr b. al-ʿĀṣ and asked him, "Describe to me the qualities of the Messenger of God (ṢAAS) that are in the Torah." He replied, "Certainly. He is, by God, referred to in the Torah as he is in the Qurʾān. 'O Prophet, we have sent you to give witness, to bring good tidings, and to warn, and to protect the illiterate. You are my slave and my messenger. I have named you *al-Mutawakkil*, "the manager", a man not rough or uncouth nor one who shouts loudly in the markets. A man who does not pay back evil with evil, but one who forgives and pardons. God will not take him until they set the deviant community aright by them saying, "There is no God but God." By him He will open blind eyes, deaf ears, and closed hearts.'"

Al-Bukhārī related this from Muḥammad b. Sinān from Fulayḥ. He also related it from ʿAbd Allāh (who was the son of Rajāʾ, or as others say the son of Ṣāliḥ) from ʿAbd al-Azīz b. Abū Salama, from Hilāl b. ʿAllūya, and his text is similar to this, with additions.

Ibn Jarīr related it from a *ḥadīth* of Fulayḥ, from Hilāl, from ʿAṭāʾ. His account adds the words, "And ʿAṭāʾ said, 'I met Kaʿb and asked him about that, and he did not disagree by so much as a letter; though he said, "among the merchants". And he gave the line of authorities as Saʿīd, from Hilāl, from ʿAṭāʾ from ʿAbd Allāh b. Salām.'"

The *ḥāfiẓ* Abū Bakr al-Bayhaqī stated that Abū al-Ḥusayn b. al-Mufaḍḍal al-Qaṭṭān related to him, quoting ʿAbd Allāh b. Jaʿfar, quoting Yaʿqūb b. Sufyān, quoting Abū Ṣāliḥ, quoting al-Layth, quoting Khālid b. Yazīd, from Saʿīd b. Abū Hilāl b. Usāma, from ʿAṭāʾ b. Yasār, from Ibn Sallām, who used to say, "We do find a description of the Messenger of God (ṢAAS) in the wording, 'We have sent you as a man to witness and to bring tidings, to warn and to protect the illiterate. You are My slave and My messenger. I have named him *al-Mutawwakil*, "the manager"; he will be neither rough nor uncouth nor one who shouts loudly in the markets. He will not requite evil with the same but will pardon and make allowance. And He will not take him until he sets the deviant community aright by having them bear witness that there is no God but God. By him He will open blind eyes, deaf ears, and closed hearts.'"

ʿAṭāʾ b. Yasār stated, "Al-Laythī informed me that he heard Kaʿb al-Aḥbār say the same as Ibn Sallām."

My comment is, that this tradition from ʿAbd Allāh b. Sallām is similar, though the account from ʿAbd Allāh b. ʿAmr is lengthier. However, he found at the battle of Yarmuk two bags full of the books of the people of the Scriptures, and he used to talk about them a great deal.

And it should be recognized that many of our forebears used to apply the word "Torah" to the books of the peoples of the scriptures. These are in their view more comprehensive than those God revealed to Moses. This fact is attested from the *ḥadīth*.

Yūnus stated from Muḥammad b. Isḥāq that Muḥammad b. Thābit b. Shuraḥbīl related to him, from Ibn Abū Awfā, from Umm al-Dardāʾ who said that she asked Kaʿb al-Aḥbar: "How do you find the description of the Messenger of God (ṢAAS) in the Torah?"

"We find him as Muḥammad the Messenger of God; his name is *al-Mutawwakil*. He is not rough nor uncouth nor one who shouts loudly in the markets. He has been given the keys. Through him, God will give sight to eyes that are damaged, and hearing to ears that are dulled. He will set right twisted tongues, through him, until they give witness that there is no God but God, one and without partner. And through him He will aid and protect the ill-treated."

And this is also related from Kaʿb from a different chain of authorities.

Al-Bayhaqī related, from al-Ḥākim, from Abū al-Walīd al-Faqīh, from al-Ḥasan b. Sufyān who indicated that ʿUtba b. Mukrim related to him, quoting Abū Qaṭan ʿAmr b. al-Haytham, quoting Ḥamza b. al-Zayyāt, from Sulaymān al-Aʿmash, from ʿAlī b. Mudrik from Abū Zurʿa, from Abū Hurayra, that regarding the wording, "And you were not besides Mt. Ṭūr when we called" the tradition gives, "it was called out to them, 'O nation of Muḥammad, I have responded to you before you called to me, and have given to you before you asked me.'"

Wahb b. Munabbih mentioned that God revealed to Dāwūd (David) in the Book of Psalms, "O Dāwūd, there will come after you a prophet named Aḥmad and Muḥammad, a truthful man, a lord; I will never be angry with him, and he will never make me angry with him. I have forgiven him before he disobeyed me, both his previous and his later sins. His nation is forgiven. I have made gifts to them similar to those I gave to the prophets, and imposed duties upon them that I imposed upon the prophets and the messengers, so that they will come to me on Judgement Day with their light like that of the prophets."

The text continues until the words, "O Dāwūd, I have given preference to Muḥammad and to his nation above all the nations."

Knowledge of the existence of reference to him in the books of the peoples of the Scriptures, a fact known to the religion, is essential. And many verses of the holy Qurʾān give proof of that and we have, praise be to God, made reference to those in the proper places.

One such verse is, "(As for) those to whom we gave the Scripture before it, they believe in it. And when it is recited to them, they say, 'We believe in it. It is the truth from our Lord. We were already submitting Muslims before it'" (*sūrat al-Qaṣaṣ*, XXVII, v.52–3).

And Almighty God said, "Those to whom we have brought the book know him as they know their sons. (Yet) a group of them certainly conceal the truth, though they know it" (*sūrat al-Baqara*, II, v.146).

Almighty God also said, "Those who were given the knowledge of it prostrate themselves on their faces when it is recited to them and they say, 'Glory be to our Lord; the promise of our Lord is fulfilled'" (*sūrat al-Isrāʾ*, XVII, v.107–8). This means that if it were the promise of our Lord that Muḥammad (ṢAAS) exists and be sent, then that is an indisputable fact. And all praise to Him capable of whatever he wishes; there is nothing he is incapable of doing.

And the Almighty said, making reference to the priests and monks, "And when they hear what was revealed to the Messenger, you see their eyes overflow with tears for the truth they recognize. They say, 'O God, we believe, so write us down among those bearing witness' (*sūrat al-Māʾida*, V, v.83).

In the story of the Negus, Salmān, ʿAbd Allāh b. Salām and others, as will come hereafter, there are many testimonials to this effect. And all praise and power are to God.

In the explanatory notes relating to the lives of the prophets (in the text *al-Bidāya wa al-Nihāya*: *The Beginning and the End*) we referred to their descriptions of the mission of the Messenger of God (ṢAAS), of his towns of birth and of refuge, and of his nation. These occur in the accounts of Moses, Isaiah, Jeremiah, Daniel, and others.

Almighty God has related of the last of the prophets of the Israelites, Jesus, son of Mary, that he stood up among his people and addressed them as follows, "I am the Messenger of God to you, verifying what is in the Torah that came before me and announcing the coming of a messenger who will come to you after me and whose name is Aḥmad" (*sūrat al-Ṣaff*, LXI, v.6).

And in the Gospel there are the tidings of *al-Fārqalīt*, "the Paraclete",[69] by whom Muḥammad (ṢAAS) is meant.

Al-Bayhaqī related from al-Ḥākim, from al-Aṣamm, from Aḥmad b. ʿAbd al-Jabbār, from Yūnus b. Bukayr, from Yūnus b. ʿAmr, from al-ʿĪzār b. Ḥarb, from ʿĀʾisha, God be pleased with her, that the Messenger of God (ṢAAS) said, "It is written in the Gospel (that he will be) not rough, nor uncouth, not one who shouts loudly in the markets, and does not repay evil with the like, but rather who pardons and forgives."

Yaʿqūb b. Sufyān stated that Fayḍ al-Bajalī related to him, quoting Salām b. Miskīn, from Muqātil b. Ḥayyān who said that the Almighty and Glorious God revealed to Jesus, son of Mary, as follows: "Serve me well and listen and obey, O Son of the pure, chaste, virgin. We have created you without a physical father and have made you a sign for the worlds, so worship me. And explain to the people of Surān, in Syraic, and tell those around you that I am the existent truth that will not pass away. Believe in the Arab *ummī* (unlettered) Prophet; he who has the camel, and wears a *midraʿa* (outer garment), and a turban that is his crown, and sandals, and has a cane that is his staff. His hair is curly, his brow is broad, his eyebrows are joined, his eyes are large, his lashes are fine, his eyes are black, his nose is curved, his cheeks are distinct, and his beard is full. The sweat of his face is like pearls; from him the scent of musk emanates. His neck is like a silver vessel, and along his collarbone gold seems to flow. He has hairs that grow long and soft from his throat down to his navel, his stomach bearing no other hair. He is broad of fingers and toes. He overshadows all when he is with others. When he walks he seems to emerge from the rock and flow from a stream. He has few progeny, as if he wanted males as his offspring."

This is also how al-Bayhaqī related this account, through Yaʿqūb b. Sufyān.

Al-Bayhaqī related that ʿUthmān b. al-Ḥakam b. Rāfiʿ b. Sinān said, "Some of my older male relatives told me that they had in their possession a document they had inherited before Islam and still had when God brought Islam. When the Messenger of God (ṢAAS) came to Medina they told him of it and brought it to him. In it was written, 'In the name of God, His words are truth while those of evil-doers shall perish. This statement is for a nation that will come at the end of time who will wash their extremities and wear a loincloth around their waists. They will plunge into the seas after their enemies. They will perform prayers that would have saved Noah's people from the flood if spoken then, and ʿĀd's people would not have been destroyed by the wind, and Thamūd's would not have been destroyed by the shouting. In the name of God, His words are truth,

69. For the interpretation of the Comforter or "Paraclete" (The Gospel according to John, 15.23 ff) as referring to the Prophet (ṢAAS), see Ibn Isḥāq, *Sīrat Rasūl Allāh*, Vol. I (Turāth al-Islam series), ed. M. al-Saqqā et al., p. 233. A Guillaume's trans., *The Life of Muhammad* (Oxford University Press, 1955), p. 104, may also be consulted.

while those of evil-doers shall perish.' The document then recounted another story. The Messenger of God (ṢAAS) was astonished at what was read to him from it."

We recounted, regarding the verse in *sūrat al-Aʿrāf*, "whom they find written down along with them in the Torah and the Gospel" (VII, v.157) the story of Hishām b. al-ʿĀṣ al-Umawī when (Abū Bakr) al-Ṣiddīq sent him with a group of men to Heraclius, calling upon him to worship God, Almighty and Glorious is He. He related how Heraclius brought out for them pictures of the prophets in a piece of cloth, from Adam to Muḥammad (ṢAAS). It showed how they had all looked. Then he related how, when he brought out the picture of Muḥammad (ṢAAS) Heraclius stood up to show his respect for him. He then sat down again and gazed at it, contemplating it closely. The group then asked him where he had obtained the picture and he responded, "Adam asked his Lord to show him all the prophets he had produced. And God did reveal their pictures to him. They were kept in the treasury of Adam, peace be upon him, where the sun sets. And *Dhū al-Qarnayn* (Alexander) took them out and gave them to Daniel."

The account continues, "Heraclius then stated, 'O how I wish I could leave my kingdom and were a slave to the worst of your kings till I die.' He then dismissed us, giving us generous gifts, and we left."

When the group returned to Abū Bakr and related to him what they had seen, how he had rewarded them, and what he had said, he wept and said, "Poor man! If God had wished good for him, He would have done so." Then he said, "The Messenger of God (ṢAAS) related to us that they and the Jews would find among them the description of Muḥammad (ṢAAS)."

Al-Ḥākim related this tradition in full. It is written down here from the exegesis. Al-Bayhaqī related it in *Dalāʾil al-Nubuwwa* (*Signs of the Prophethood*).

Al-Umawī stated that ʿAbd Allāh b. Ziyād related to him from Ibn Isḥāq who said that Yaʿqūb b. ʿAbd Allāh b. Jaʿfar b. ʿAmr b. Umayya related to him, from his father, from his grandfather ʿAmr b. Umayya, who said, "I brought in some slaves from the Negus who had given them to me. They said, 'O ʿAmr, if we saw the Messenger of God, we would recognize him without you telling us.' Abū Bakr passed by, so I asked them, 'Is that he?' 'No,' they replied. ʿUmar went by and I asked, 'Is that he?' 'No,' they responded.

"We went inside the house and the Messenger of God (ṢAAS) went by and then they called out to me, 'O ʿAmr that is the Messenger of God (ṢAAS).' When I looked I saw it was he, yet no one had told them so. They recognized him from the writings they had."

We previously recounted the warning made by Sabaʾ to his people, and how he had announced to them the coming of the Messenger of God (ṢAAS) in poetry we gave earlier in his biography. So there is no need to repeat it. Also we earlier recounted the words of the two rabbis to Tubba‘, the Yemeni, when he besieged the people of Medina, telling him that it was to be the place of refuge for a prophet at the end of time. And so he retired from the city and composed verses that include his salutations to the Prophet (ṢAAS).

The Story of Sayf b. Dhū Yazan the Ḥimyarite and his foretelling the coming of the *ummī* Prophet.

The *ḥāfiẓ* Abū Bakr Muḥammad b. Ja‘far b. Sahl al-Kharā᾽iṭī stated in his book *Hawātif al-Jānn* (*Calls of the Jinn*) that ‘Alī b. Ḥarb related to him, quoting Aḥmad b. ‘Uthmān b. Hakīm, quoting ‘Amr b. Bakr – who was the son of Bakkār al-Qa‘nabī – from Aḥmad b. al-Qāsim, from Muḥammad b. al-Sā᾽ib al-Kalbī, from Abū Ṣāliḥ, from ‘Abd Allāh b. ‘Abbās who said that when when Sayf b. Dhū Yazan came to power over Abyssinia (Ibn al-Mundhir said that his name was al-Nu‘mān b. Qays), that being two years after the birth of the Messenger of God (ṢAAS), a delegation of Arabs, including poets, went to congratulate and praise him and to recognize his achievements.

Among those who went to him was one delegation from Quraysh that included ‘Abd al-Muṭṭalib b. Hāshim, Umayya b. ‘Abd Shams, ‘Abd Allāh b. Jud‘ān, and Khuwaylid b. Asad, along with other Quraysh leaders. They went to Ṣan‘ā᾽ to see him, but he was in Ra᾽s Ghumdān to which Umayya b. Abū al-Ṣalt made reference in the line of poetry:

> "Drink up, may you enjoy it, with your crown raised upon your head at Ra᾽s Ghumdān, a home for you to stay in."

The chamberlain went in to him and told the King where they were and he gave them permission to attend him. When ‘Abd al-Muṭṭalib arrived he asked to speak with the King, who replied, "If you are a man who speaks before kings, then I give you permission to do so now." ‘Abd al-Muṭṭalib responded, "God has placed you, O King, in a high, impregnable, lofty, and splendid position, having given you growth in a spot where your roots have developed strong and well, firmly established, and eminently branched, in the most noble of lands, the best of origins. You are, may you be immune to curses, the King of the Arabs, their springtime that their land brings to growth, the head of the Arabs to which you give leadership, their pier upon which they depend, their refuge to which people have recourse. Your forebears were the best ever, and from them you came to us as the best successor. None with such forebears could fail, none perish with you as their successor. O King, we are the people of God's sanctuary, the custodians of His house. He who delighted you by removing the cares that oppressed us has brought us up to you, and so we are a delegation of congratulation, not of complaint."

The King asked, "And who are you who speak?"

He replied, "I am ʿAbd al-Muṭṭalib b. Hāshim." "Our sister's son?" "Yes." "Approach then." When he had done so the King addressed him and the delegation, saying, "Welcome indeed to you; may you enjoy your stay and find us generous hosts. The King has heard your speeches and of your kinship and accepted your petition. You are welcome at all times. You will be honoured as long as you stay, and awarded gifts when you leave."

The Arab delegation then went off to the guest quarters where they stayed a month having no access to the King but not being given permission to leave. He then again turned his attention fully to them and sent for ʿAbd al-Muṭṭalib with whom he sat alone, close by himself. He then said, "O ʿAbd al-Muṭṭalib, I am going to reveal to you a secret I know that I would not reveal to anyone else. But I believe you worthy of it and will tell you of it. Let you keep it to yourself until God makes His purpose known. For God will achieve His goal.

"I have found in the hidden book and the treasured knowledge we preserve and protect for ourselves alone certain information of vital and critical importance that affects the honour and virtue of mankind in general, your community in particular, and you in person."

ʿAbd al-Muṭṭalib asked, "O King, the like of you brings joy and good! What is it, O he for whom company after company of bedouins would sacrifice themselves?"

He replied, "When a youth is born in Tihāma who has a sign upon him, a birthmark between his shoulders, he shall have leadership and through him you shall have primacy till Judgement Day."

ʿAbd al-Muṭṭalib exclaimed, "May you be immune to curses, I have been better rewarded than any visitor before! And were it not for the great dignity, honour and glory of the King, I would ask him whose coming it is he is announcing such as to bring such joy to me."

Ibn Dhū Yazan responded, "This is the time for his birth, or he may have already been born. His name is to be Muḥammad. His father and his mother will die and his grandfather and his uncle will care for him, and hold him always dear. God will send him plainly and He will make us his helpers, through whom God will give power to His allies, humble His enemies, strike people down everywhere, render permissible the most precious of things on earth, destroy the idols, extinguish the fires, worship the All-Merciful, rout out the devil, his word being final, his rule being justice, demanding goodness and acting it, averting from evil and abolishing it."

ʿAbd al-Muṭṭalib responded, "O King, may your power increase, your glory rise, your kingdom last, and your life be long, such is my origin. And so if power is coming to me plainly, then it has all become somewhat clear to me."

Ibn Dhū Yazan responded, "By the House that has a screen and the marks on the idols, you O ʿAbd al-Muṭṭalib are, without doubt, his grandfather."

ʿAbd al-Muṭṭalib fell down prostrate in worship. The King then said, "Lift your head, calm yourself, and be content. Did you have any prior sense of what I told you?"

"O King," he replied, "I had one son in whom I delighted and whose fond companion I was. I married him to a noble lady of his tribe, Āmina b. Wahb, and she had a son I named Muḥammad. But his father died, then his mother, and I and his uncle brought him up."

Ibn Dhū Yazan then said, "What I told you is as you told me. Take care of your boy and protect him from the Jews; for they are his enemies. God will give them no path to him. Keep what I have told you from the group with you, for I am concerned that they or their children may feel some rivalry at your having the leadership and so scheme and plot his destruction. If I were not aware that I will die before his mission, I would take my men and cavalry and go to Yathrib, the seat of his reign. For I find in previous knowledge and the Scriptures that it will be in Yathrib that he will establish his power, there that he will find those to aid him, and there that his grave will be. If I were not concerned with protecting him from curses and from bodily harm, I would make public all about him despite his youth and would have crushed the Arabs' nobles and leaders under his foot. But I am charging you with that since I do not find inadequate those who are with you."

He then ordered that each one of them be presented with ten male and ten female slaves, one hundred camels, two sets of fine, striped clothing, five rotls of gold, ten rotls of silver, and a receptacle filled with ambergris.

For ʿAbd al-Muṭṭalib he ordered ten times that amount. He told him to come back to him after one year, but Ibn Dhū Yazan died before the year had passed.

ʿAbd al-Muṭṭalib used often to say, "O Tribe of Quraysh, let not any one of you envy me the generosity of the king's gift, large though it was, for it will not last forever. But do envy me the repute, honour and pride there will be for me and for my ancestors to come."

He would be asked, "When will that be?" And he would then reply, "It will one day be known, though after some period."

On this subject Umayya b. ʿAbd Shams spoke the verses,

> "We brought away good counsel, carrying it in bags on our mounts and on the saddle bags of camels, male and female;
>
> Their grazing grounds stripped bare, rising high up to Ṣanʿāʾ from a deep ravine,
>
> Leading us to Ibn Dhū Yazan, their appetite carrying them across the scant fodder of the road,
>
> Feeding in their imagination on the lightning flashing constantly.
>
> When they reached Ṣanʿāʾ they stayed in the home of the king and of ancient dignity."

The *ḥāfiẓ* Abū Nuʿaym related it thus in *al-Dalāʾil* (*The Signs*) through ʿAmr b. Bakīr b. Bakkār al-Qaʿnabī. Then Abū Nuʿaym said, "I was told on the authority of Abū al-Ḥasan ʿAlī b. Ibrāhīm b. ʿAbd Rabbihi b. Muḥammad b. ʿAbd al-ʿAzīz b. ʿAfīr b. ʿAbd al-ʿAzīz b. al-Ṣafar b. ʿAfīr b. Zurʿa b. Sayf b. Dhū Yazan who said it was related to him by his father Abū Yazan Ibrāhīm, and by his uncle Aḥmad b. Muḥammad Abū Rajāʾ, and his uncle Muḥammad b. ʿAbd al-ʿAzīz and by ʿAbd al-Azīz b. ʿAfīr, from his father, from Zurʿa b. Sayf b. Dhū Yazan the Ḥimyarite who said, 'When my grandfather Sayf b. Dhū Yazan gained control over Abyssinia . . .'," and he related it in full.

Abū Bakr al-Kharāʾiṭī stated that Abū Yūsuf Yaʿqūb b. Isḥāq al-Qalūsī related to him, quoting al-ʿAlāʾ b. al-Faḍl b. Abū Sawiyya that he was informed by his father from his father ʿAbd al-Mālik b. Abū Sawiyya, from his grandfather Abū Sawiyya, from his father Khalīfa, who said that he asked Muḥammad b. ʿUthmān b. Rabīʿa b. Sawāʾa b. Khathʿam b. Saʿd, how was it his father named him Muḥammad. He replied that he asked his father the same question, and he replied, "Four men from Banū Tamīm, including myself, went on a trip. The group consisted of myself, Sufyān b. Mujāshiʿ b. Dārim, Usāma b. Mālik b. Jundab b. al-ʿAqīd and Yazīd b. Rabīʿa b. Kināna b. Ḥurbūṣ b. Māzin. We travelled to see Ibn Jafna, the King of Ghassān. When we were overlooking Syria we alighted at a stream where there were some small trees and we talked together. A monk overheard our conversation and, as he looked down on us, he said, 'That language (of yours) is not the speech of this country.' We replied, 'No, we're from a tribe of Muḍar.' 'From which subtribe?' he asked. 'From Khindif,' we told him. 'Very soon will be the mission of a prophet who will be the very last one of all prophets. Hurry to him and take your chances with him and you'll be wise.' We asked him, 'What is his name?' 'His name is Muḥammad,' he replied.

He went on, "When we came back from the land of Ibn Jafna each one of us had a son and each one named his Muḥammad."

This means that each of them wanted his own son to be this Prophet whose coming had been foreseen.

The *ḥāfiẓ* Abū Bakr al-Kharāʾiṭī stated that ʿAbd Allāh b. Abū Saʿd related to him, quoting Ḥāzim b. ʿAqqāl b. al-Zahr b. Ḥabīb b. al-Mundhir b. Abū al-Ḥuṣayn b. al-Samawʾal b. ʿĀdiyā, quoting Jābir b. Jaddān b. Jamīʿ b. ʿUthmān b. Sammāk b. al-Ḥuṣayn b. al-Samawʾal b. ʿĀdiyā that when death was close to al-Aws b. Ḥāritha b. Thaʿlaba b. ʿAmr b. ʿĀmir, his people of Ghassān gathered around him and said, "You know that God's decree for you is near. We used to tell you in your youth to get married, but you refused. This brother of yours, al-Khazraj, has five sons, but you have none other than Mālik." He replied, "No one shall perish who has left behind the like of Mālik. He who is capable of drawing fire out of stone is capable of giving progeny to Mālik, and fine heroic progeny too. Everyone, in any case, is headed for death."

He then went to Mālik and said, "O son, (if it is a matter of choice, then choose) death over infamy, punishment over blame, stoicism over rage. The grave is better than poverty. And those few in number are those humiliated. Those who can attack are those who can escape. And defending women is part of being honourable. Time is of two days – one for you and one against. If it's going for you, don't overdo it, if against you don't give up. Either state will exhaust itself. Neither crowned kingship nor despised ridicule are permanent. Greet your day well, and God will bless you." He then spoke the following verses:

"I witnessed the taking of prisoners at the battle of Al-Muḥarriq, and I lived (to see) God's punishment for the sin (of Thamūd) at al-Ḥijr

I never saw any man, king or pauper, who was not on his way to the grave.

All glory be to Him who destroyed Thamūd and Jurhum; He will leave for me my progeny till time's end,

So that they will delight the kin of ʿAmr b. ʿĀmir (and protect them) against those who seek revenge.

And even if time had not worn me out and turned my head grey – for greyness comes with age –

We do have a Lord sitting high upon his throne who knows what good and evil there will be.

Has it not come to my people that God has a message by which good and happy people can succeed

When the Messenger was sent out from Ghālib's tribe at Mecca, between Mecca and al-Ḥijr?

There; so seek his victory for your country, O tribe of ʿĀmir, for happiness is in victory."

Thereupon, so the account states, he died.

CHAPTER ON THE CRIES OF THE SPIRITS, CONSISTING OF WHAT WORDS OF INSPIRATION THE SPIRITS GAVE TO THE TONGUES OF SOOTHSAYERS, AND WHICH WERE TO BE HEARD BY THE IDOLS.

We previously reported the words of Shiqq and Saṭīḥ to Rabīʿa b. Naṣr, King of Yemen, announcing the coming of the Messenger of God (ṢAAS) of his being,

"A chaste messenger to whom revelation comes from the All-High."

Regarding his birth, there would come the words of Saṭīḥ to ʿAbd al-Masīḥ, "when many recitations have been made, Lake Sāwa dried up, and the sceptre-bearer has appeared", by which he was referring to the Messenger of God (ṢAAS), as we will explain in detail.

Al-Bukhārī stated that Yaḥyā b. Sulaymān al-Juʿfī related to him, quoting Ibn Wahb, quoting ʿAmr – he being Muḥammad b. Zayd – that Sālim told him from

ʿAbd Allāh b. ʿUmar who said, "I never heard ʿUmar ever say of anything, 'I think it so' without it being as he thought it would."

"While ʿUmar b. al-Khaṭṭāb was seated one day, a handsome man passed by. ʿUmar said, 'Either I'm mistaken or that man has not adopted Islam, or maybe he was a soothsayer. Bring him to me.'

"So he was summoned and told the same. He commented, 'I never thought I would meet a Muslim man in the manner I did today!'

"'I invite you to tell me about yourself.'

"'I was a soothsayer in the old days before Islam,' he told him.

"'And what was the strangest thing your female *jinni* friend, your channel, brought you?'

"'Once, in the market, she came to me and I recognized that she was in a state of panic. She said, "Do you not see the spirits and their despondency, their despair after their decadence, and their clinging to their fast mounts and to the cloth under their saddles?"

"ʿUmar said, 'He spoke true. While I was asleep near their gods a man came with a calf that he sacrificed. And I then heard a voice cry out louder than any I had ever heard before. It said, "O Jalīḥ, a success! An eloquent man! He says, 'There is no God but God!'" Everyone jumped up, and I said, "I'll not leave till I know what's behind this!" Then (the voice) called out, "O Jalīḥ, a success, an eloquent man! He says 'There is no God but God!'" So I arose, and soon thereafter it was said, 'This was a prophet.'"

Al-Bukhārī alone gave this tradition.

The man speaking here was Sawwād b. Qārib al-Azdī, called al-Sadūsī, of the people of al-Sarāt of the Balqāʿ mountains. He had the honour of being a Companion and envoy of the Prophet (ṢAAS). Abū Ḥātim and Ibn Mandah stated that Saʿīd b. Jubayr and Abū Jaʿfar Muḥammad b. ʿAlī quoted him. Al-Bukhārī said, "He had the honour of being a Companion." Similarly Aḥmad b. Rūḥ al-Bardhaʿī, the *ḥāfiẓ*, included his name among the Companions, quoting al-Dārquṭnī and others besides these two. The *ḥāfiẓ* ʿAbd al-Ghanī b. Saʿīd al-Miṣrī said that his name was spelled, "Sawād", not "Sawwād" b. Qārib. ʿUthmān al-Waqqāṣī related from Muḥammad b. Kaʿb al-Quraẓī that he was a Yemeni noble man.

Abū Nuʿaym mentioned him in *al-Dalāʾil* (*The Signs*). The account relating to him was also told by others at greater length but based upon al-Bukhārī's account.

Muḥammad b. Isḥāq stated that a reliable source related to him, from ʿAbd Allāh b. Kaʿb, the freed-man of ʿUthmān b. ʿAffān, that it was told to him that ʿUmar b. al-Khaṭṭāb, God be pleased with him, was one day sitting in the mosque of the Messenger of God (ṢAAS) when an Arab came in looking for him. When ʿUmar looked at him he commented, "That man is still a polytheist, still an unbeliever, or maybe he was a soothsayer before Islam."

The man greeted him, then sat down. ʿUmar addressed him, "Have you become a Muslim?" "Oh yes, O Commander of the Faithful," the man replied. "Were you a soothsayer before Islam?" ʿUmar asked.

The man replied, "Glory be to God, O Commander of the Faithful, you're casting suspicion on me; and you are receiving me with words I never heard you use to any other of your subjects since you came to power."

"O God, forgive me," exclaimed ʿUmar. "Before Islam we were involved in things far worse than that. We worshipped idols and adopted images until God favoured us with His Messenger and with Islam."

"Yes, by God, O Commander of the Faithful. I was a soothsayer before Islam."

"Then tell me what your channel had informed you."

"It came to me one month or so before Islam and said, 'Do you not see the spirits and their despondency, their despair for their religion, and their clinging to their fast mounts and to the cloth under their saddles?'"

Ibn Isḥāq commented that the preceding quotation was rhymed prose and not poetry.

"At that, ʿUmar said, addressing the people around him, 'I swear, I was once near an idol, before Islam, along with a group of Quraysh. An Arab had sacrificed a calf and we were waiting for him to divide it up so we would have our share. Then I heard a voice louder than I had ever heard before coming out from the calf's belly. This was a month or so before Islam. The voice said, 'O Dharīḥ, success is won! A man is crying out and saying, "There is no God but God."'"

Ibn Hishām commented, "Another version has the words as, 'A man is crying out, his language eloquent, and saying, "There is no God but God."'"

He went on, "A scholar learned in poetry recited to me the lines,

> 'I was surprised at the spirits and their grief and their gripping their cloth-blankets on their mounts
> Heading for Mecca, seeking guidance, for the believing spirits are not like the impure ones.'"

The *ḥāfiẓ* Abū Yaʿlā al-Mawṣilī stated that it was related to him by Yaḥyā b. Ḥijr b. al-Nuʿmān the Syrian, and also by ʿAlī b. Manṣūr al-Anbārī, from Muḥammad b. ʿAbd al-Raḥmān al-Waqqāṣī, from Muḥammad b. Kaʿb al-Quraẓī, who said that while ʿUmar b. al-Khaṭṭāb, God bless him, was one day seated, a man passed him by and someone asked, "O Commander of the Faithful, do you know this passer-by?" "Who is he?", he asked. They replied, "That is Sawwād b. Qārib whose channel came to him and told him about the rising of the Messenger of God (ṢAAS)."

ʿUmar sent for him and asked him whether he was Sawwād b. Qārib, and the man replied that he was.

"Are you still a soothsayer, as you were?" asked ʿUmar.

The man became angry and replied, "No one greeted me that way since I became a Muslim, O Commander of the Faithful."

"O glory be to God!" exclaimed ʿUmar, "the polytheism we used to follow was far worse than the soothsaying you were involved in! But tell me what it was your channel told you of the coming of the Messenger of God (ṢAAS)."

"Certainly, O Commander of the Faithful. One night I was between sleep and wakefulness when my channel came to me, kicked me and said, 'Up you get, O Sawwād b. Qārib, listen to what I have to say and comprehend, if you can. A messenger has been sent from the tribe of Luʾayy b. Ghālib calling people to God and to His worship.' He then recited these verses,

> 'I was surprised at the spirits and their intentions and their gripping their saddle-bags on their mounts
> Heading for Mecca, seeking guidance, for the honest spirits are not like the lying ones.
> So head to the finest men of Hāshim, their best men are not like their hindmost.'

"I told it, 'Let me sleep. I'm very sleepy now.'

"The next night back he came and kicked me, saying, 'Up you get, O Sawwād b. Qārib, and listen to what I am saying. And comprehend, if you can. A messenger has been sent from the tribe of Luʾayy b. Ghālib, calling men to God and to His worship.' He then recited these verses,

> 'I was surprised at the spirits and their knowledge, and their gripping their baggage on their mounts
> Heading for Mecca, seeking guidance, for believing spirits are not like those that disbelieve.
> So head for the finest men of Hāshim, amidst their hills and rocks.'

"'Leave me alone to sleep,' I pleaded, 'I'm very sleepy.'

"The third night, again it came and kicked me, saying, 'Up you get, O Sawwād b. Qārib, and listen to what I am saying. And comprehend, if you can. A messenger has been sent from the tribe of Luʾayy b. Ghālib, calling men to God and to His worship.' He then recited the verses,

> 'I was surprised at the spirits and their perceptions, and their gripping their cloth blankets on their mounts
> Heading for Mecca, seeking guidance, for the gracious of the spirits are not like the foul ones.
> So head for the finest men of Hāshim, and raise your eyes to their head.'

"So I got up, saying, 'God has put my heart to the test.' I readied my camel for travel and went off to the city – by which he meant Mecca – and there I saw the Messenger of God (ṢAAS) amidst his Companions. I approached him and said, 'Listen to what I have to say, O Messenger of God.' 'Let's hear it,' he replied. So I recited to him the following verses.

'My channel came to me after rest and sleep, and I never experienced him to be untruthful.
Three nights and each time he would say, "A messenger has come out to you of (the tribe of) Lu᾿ayy b. Ghālib".
So I tucked up my waist-wrapper, for travel, and my strong and swift she-camel carried me across the deserts
And I bear witness that there is nothing besides God, and that you are safe from any conqueror
And that you are the messenger with closest access of all to God, O you born of the finest and best of men.
So order us to do whatever you are told, O best man ever to walk, even if what comes is such as to make the hair grey;
Intercede for me when intercession time comes, for none but you can help Sawwād b. Qārib.'

"The Messenger of God (ṢAAS) and his Companions were most pleased at what I had said, their pleasure being evident in their faces.

"῾Umar b. al-Khaṭṭāb jumped from his place and came close to him and said, 'I wanted to hear that from you. Can your channel come to you today?'

"But after I had read the Qur᾿ān, then never again; God's book does away with any need for spirits.

"῾Umar then said, 'Once we were in a quarter of Quraysh known by their name of the Dharīḥ family. They had sacrificed a calf and the butcher was cutting it up when we heard a voice emitting from its stomach. We could not see anything (there), however. It said, 'O family of Dharīḥ, success is won. A voice is crying out, its tongue eloquent, giving witness that there is no God but God.'"

This account is abbreviated, as that of al-Bukhārī shows. They do substantiate that the one hearing the voice from the calf was ῾Umar b. al-Khaṭṭāb. But God knows best.

The *ḥāfiẓ* Abū Bakr Muḥammad b. Ja῾far b. Sahl al-Kharā᾿iṭī stated, in his work that he compiled on the cries of the spirits, that Abū Mūsā ῾Imrān b. Mūsā al-Mu᾿addib related to him, quoting Muḥammad b. ῾Imrān b. Muḥammad b. ῾Abd al-Raḥmān b. Abū Laylā, quoting Sa῾īd b. ῾Ubayd Allāh al-Waṣṣābī, from his father, from Abū Ja῾far Muḥammad b. ῾Alī, who said that Sawwād b. Qārib al-Sadūsī came in to ῾Umar b. al-Khaṭṭāb, God be pleased with him, and the latter said to him, "By God, O Sawwād b. Qārib, I adjure you to say whether nowadays your soothsaying benefits you." He replied, "Glory be to God, O Commander of the Faithful, you've never greeted anyone else the way you have me!" "Glory be to God indeed, O Sawwād," he replied, "our polytheistic practices were worse than your soothsaying. By God, O Sawwād, I've heard a most strange account relating to you." "Yes indeed, O Commander of the Faithful, strange it certainly was." "Tell me about it," asked ʿUmar.

"Well, I was a soothsayer before Islam. One night when I was asleep, my channel came to me, kicked me and said, 'O Sawwād, listen to what I will tell you.' 'Go on,' I said. It then recited,

> 'I was surprised at the spirits and their concern, and how they gripped their blankets on their mounts
> Heading for Mecca seeking guidance, for those of them that believe are not like those that are evil.
> So travel to the best of Hāshim and raise your eyes to their head.'

"But I went to sleep, not caring at all what he had said. Then he came back the second night, kicked me and said, 'Up you get, Sawwād b. Qārib and listen to what I say.' 'Well let's hear it,' I said. He then recited,

> 'I was surprised at the spirits and their intentions and their gripping their saddlebags on their mounts
> Heading for Mecca, seeking guidance, for the honest spirits are not like the lying ones.
> So head for the finest man of Hāshim, for their foremost men are not like their hindmost.'

"His words did intrigue me, somewhat, but I went to sleep. The third night he came again, kicked me and said, 'O Sawwād b. Qārib, are you going to comprehend or not?"

"'How?' I asked. He explained, 'A prophet has come forth in Mecca calling for worship of his Lord. Go and join him. Listen to what I tell you.' 'Let's hear it,' I said. Then he recited,

> 'I was surprised at the spirits and their fright, and how they gripped their cloth blankets to their mounts
> Heading for Mecca, seeking guidance, for the spirits who believe are unlike those who disbelieve.
> So travel to the best of Hāshim, between their hills and rocks.'

"So I realized that God wished me well. I went and got a striped garment I had, unsewed it, put it on and placed my feet in the saddle stirrups of my camel and rode off till I reached the Prophet (ṢAAS). He then suggested to me that I become a Muslim, and I did so. I told him what had happened, and he said, 'When the Muslims are all gathered, tell them this.' So when all were assembled, I got up and recited the following verses,

> 'My channel came to me after rest and sleep, and I never knew him to be untruthful;
> Three nights, and each time he would say, "A messenger has come to you out of Luʾayy b. Ghālib."

So I tucked up my waist-wrapper for travel, and my strong and swift she-camel carried me across the deserts,
And I know that there is nothing besides God, and that you are safe from any conqueror
And that you are the Messenger with closest access of all to God, O you born of the finest and best of men.
So order us to do whatever you are told, O best messenger, even if what comes is such as to make the hair grey.'

"The Muslims," he concluded, "were delighted with this."

"Well," asked ʿUmar, "do you have any sense of that now?" "Since God has taught me the Qurʾān now, then no."

Muḥammad b. al-Sāʾib al-Kalbī related this anecdote from his father, from ʿUmar b. Ḥafṣ. He said that when Sawwād b. Qārib came to ʿUmar, the latter asked, "O Sawwād b. Qārib, what remains from your being a soothsayer?"

He got angry and retorted, "O Commander of the Faithful. I don't think you greeted any Arab like that before."

When ʿUmar saw the anger in his face, he said, "Look Sawwād, the polytheism we were previously involved in was worse." Then he went on, "Tell me, Sawwād, that story I've so wanted to hear from you."

"Certainly. Once I was tending some camels of mine at al-Sarāt. One night when I was asleep a channel I had came to me, kicked me and said, 'Up you get, Sawwād b. Qārib! A prophet has appeared in Tihāma who calls people to the truth and to the straight path.'" He then related the story as given above, adding one last line to the poetry. It read:

"And intercede for me on a day when no relative than you will be of any use for Sawwād b. Qārib."

The Messenger of God (ṢAAS) told him: "Go to your people and speak these verses to them."

The *ḥāfiẓ* Ibn ʿAsākir related this story through Sulaymān b. ʿAbd al-Raḥmān, from al-Ḥakam b. Yaʿlā b. ʿAṭāʾ al-Muḥāribī, from ʿAbbād b. ʿAbd al-Ṣamad, from Saʿīd b. Jubayr who said that Sawwād b. Qārib al-Azdī recounted to him, "I was sleeping up on a mountain of al-Sarāt when someone came and kicked me . . ." And he went on to tell the story too.

It was also related through Muḥammad b. al-Barrāʾ, from Abū Bakr b. ʿAyyāsh, from Abū Isḥāq from al-Barrāʾ, who said that Sawwād b. Qārib stated, "I was living in India when one night my channel came to me . . ." and he told the whole story. Then, after reciting the final piece of poetry, he said, "And the Messenger of God (ṢAAS) laughed so loud his back teeth were visible, and he commented, 'You did well, Sawwād!'"

Abū Nuʿaym stated in his book *Dalāʾil al-Nabuwwa* (*Signs of the Prophethood*) that ʿAbd Allāh b. Muḥammad b. Jaʿfar related to him, quoting

ʿAbd al-Raḥmān b. al-Ḥasan, quoting ʿAlī b. Ḥarb, quoting Abū al-Mundhir Hishām b. Muḥammad b. al-Sāʾib, from his father, from ʿAbd Allāh al-ʿUmānī, who said that they had a man called Māzin b. al-ʿAḍūb who was custodian of an idol at a village called Samāyā, in ʿUmān. Banū al-Ṣāmit revered this idol, along with Banū Ḥuṭāma and Muhra, who were related to Māzin through his uncles on his mother's side, her name being Zaynab d. ʿAbd Allāh b. Rabīʿa b. Khuwayṣ, of Banū Namrān.

Māzin said, "One day we brought a ewe to the idol for slaughter, it being our sacrifice, and I heard a voice emanating from the idol saying, 'O Māzin, hear and rejoice. Goodness has emerged and evil been submerged. A prophet has been sent from Muḍar with God's greatest religion. Abandon something carved from stone and you will be saved from scorching fire.'

"I was extremely scared to hear this.

"Then, a few days later, we sacrificed another ewe, and heard a voice from the idol say, 'Come to me, come close and hear what you cannot ignore. This is a prophet who has been sent; he has brought truth revealed. Believe in him so that you will avoid the heat of a fire that will flame, a fire set alight by the stone.'"

Māzin continued, "This is amazing, I thought. And this is good intended for me. Then a man from Ḥijāz arrived, and I asked him what news there was back home. He replied, 'A man called Aḥmad has emerged who tells everyone who comes to him to respond to God's Messenger.'"

"This news relates to what I heard, I thought. So I rushed to the idol and broke it into small pieces. I then mounted up and rode off to the Messenger of God (ṢAAS). God then opened my heart to Islam, which I accepted. I spoke the verses,

> 'I broke Yājur into pieces, there now being a Lord through whom we would see false guidance and delusion,
>
> Through the Hāshimite, who led us out of our error, his religion having been unknown to me.
>
> O rider, tell ʿAmr and its brothers that I detest those who said, "My Lord is Yājir."'"

By ʿAmr here he means al-Ṣāmit, the silent one. By "brothers" he means Ḥuṭāma.

"I said, 'O Messenger of God, I'm a man who is crazy for pleasure, for women and wine. But now the years are pressing hard, the money is gone, the concubines have thinned out, and I have no son. Please pray to God to alleviate my suffering, to make us modest, and to grant me a son.'

"The Prophet (ṢAAS) then spoke a prayer: 'O God, exchange his pleasure-seeking with Qurʾān readings, his immorality with morality, his sin and corruption with chastity, make him modest, and grant him a son.'"

Māzin went on: "And so God alleviated my suffering and ʿUmān became fertile. I married four noble women, learned by heart a portion of the Qurʾān, and God granted me my son Ḥayyān." He then recited the verses:

> "My mount galloped towards you, O Messenger of God, traversing the deserts from ʿUmān to al-ʿArj,
> So that you would intercede for me, O you who are the best of those who walked on earth; and God would forgive me, and I return victorious.
> To people whose religion I contradict; their beliefs and likes are different from mine.
> I was a man crazy over wine and women all my youth, until my boyhood almost wore out;
> He substituted fear and anxiety for the wine, and gave me chastity for immortality, and reinforced my virtue.
> So my interest and intent turned to the holy fight, and to God I direct my fasting, to God my pilgrimage."

He went on, "So when I came back to my people, they censured me and cursed me, and set one of their poets to attack me. And I realized that if I responded in like kind, I would only harm myself.

"So I moved away from them. Then a great delegation of them came to me; I had been formerly in charge of their affairs. They told me, 'O Cousin, we hate what has happened. If you can put it all aside, then return and be in charge of our affairs. And we'll not bother you or whatever is in your religion.'

"So I did return with them and spoke the lines,

> 'Your hatred for us is bitter in taste, whereas our dislike for you, O my people, tasted like buttermilk;
> Time (fate) would not notice if your faults were laid out, but all of you when our faults are extolled are keenly aware;
> Our poet does not answer you back, while your poet is eloquent and flamboyant in cursing us.
> Towards you, you should know, there is in (our) hearts only irritation, while in yours there is hatred and loathing.'"

Māzin ended: "Then God led them all to Islam."

The *ḥāfiẓ* Abū Nuʿaym related from a *ḥadīth* of ʿAbd Allāh b. Muḥammad b. ʿUqayl, from Jābir b. ʿAbd Allāh, who said, "The first news of the mission of the Messenger of God (ṢAAS) in Medina was as follows. A certain woman of Medina had a channel who would come to her in the form of a white bird. It alighted on a wall they had and she asked it, 'Why don't you come on down so that we can talk together and exchange news?' It replied, 'A Prophet has been sent in Mecca who has prohibited fornication. And so our pleasure is prevented.'"

Al-Wāqidī stated that ʿAbd al-Raḥmān b. ʿAbd al-ʿAzīz related to him, from al-Zuhrī, from ʿAlī b. al-Ḥusayn, as follows, "The first news that arrived in Medina about the Messenger of God (ṢAAS) was that a woman called Fāṭima had a channel (a male *jinn*) that came to her one day but stood on a wall. She asked it, 'Aren't you coming down?' 'No, a Messenger has been sent who has prohibited fornication,' he replied.

"One of the early Muslims related the same account also. He mentioned that the woman's channel was called Ibn Lūdhān, and stated that he had been absent from her a long time, and then when he did come she reproached him and he replied, 'I went to the Messenger and heard him forbidding fornication; so good-bye to you!'"

Al-Wāqidī stated that Muḥammad b. Ṣāliḥ related to him, from ʿĀṣim b. ʿUmar b. Qatāda who said that ʿUthmān b. ʿAffān stated, "We left in a camel caravan for Syria, before the Messenger of God (ṢAAS) received his mission. When we were on the outskirts of Syria where a female soothsayer lived, she stood in our way and said that her channel came to her and stopped at her door. So she asked him to come in, but he replied, 'There's no way for that; Aḥmad has come forth and an unendurable situation has arisen.'"

ʿUthmān continued, "Then I left and, upon returning to Mecca discovered that the Messenger of God (ṢAAS) had announced his mission in Mecca and was calling people to God the Almighty and Glorious."

Al-Wāqidī stated that Muḥammad b. ʿAbd Allāh al-Zuhrī related to him, saying, "It used to be that inspired voices were heard; but when Islam came these were banned."

There was a woman of Banū Asad named Saʿīra who had a spirit companion. When it learned that inspired voices were not being allowed, he came to her and entered her chest where he made such an uproar that she lost her mind. From inside her chest he began shouting, "Embracing has been banned. Companionship has been abolished! And an unendurable situation has arisen! Aḥmad has forbidden fornication."

The *ḥāfiẓ* Abū Bakr al-Kharāʾiṭī stated that Abd Allāh b. Muḥammad al-Balawī – in Egypt – related to him, quoting ʿUmāra b. Zayd, quoting ʿĪsā b. Yazīd, from Ṣāliḥ b. Kīsān, from someone who told it to him, from Mirdās b. Qays al-Sadūsī, who said, "I was present with the Prophet (ṢAAS) when the subject of soothsaying came up and the changes that had occurred in it as a result of his coming forth. I said to him, 'O Messenger of God, some of that used to go on among us. I can tell you about a slave-girl we had called al-Khulaṣa about whom nothing but good was known until she came to us and said, "O tribe of Daws something very strange has happened to me; did you ever know anything except good (about me)?" We asked, "What's wrong?" She replied, "I was out with my sheep when a cloud overshadowed me, and I had some strange experience, some sense of a man with a woman. I was afraid I might be pregnant." Eventually came the time for her to give birth, and she did produce a boy who had lop-ears like those of a dog. He remained with us till the age when he would play with other boys. Then one day he jumped into the air, threw off his waist wrapper and began screaming out at the top of his voice, saying, 'Yā wayla, yā wayla, yā ʿawla yā ʿawla, woe on the sheep, woe on Fahm who is the fire brand, there are horsemen, by God, behind the mountain path, and among them are youths who are handsome, noble."'

"So we mounted up, our weapons ready, and asked, 'O you, woe to you, what do you see?' He asked, 'Is there some menstruating girl among you?' 'Who can find one for us?' we asked. An old sheikh of ours said, 'Yes, I have a daughter of a chaste mother.' We told him to bring her at once. So the sheikh brought the girl and (he) went up the mountain, telling her: 'Throw off your clothes and go out in front of them.' He then told our men, 'Follow on after her.' Then he said to one of our men called Aḥmad b. Ḥābis, 'O Aḥmad b. Ḥābis you get the first rider!' So Aḥmad charged and struck the first rider, felling him. And they were defeated and we plundered them. Then we built a house over them which we named 'Dhū al-Khulaṣa'. And this boy never told us anything that did not come out as he said.

"Until your mission, that is, O Messenger of God. One day he told us, 'O tribe of Daws, Banū al-Ḥārith b. Kaʿb has encamped.' So we rode off, with him telling us, 'Urge your horses on at speed, and stuff the enemy into their graves! Sweep them away in the morning and drink wine in the evening!'

"We met them in battle, but they utterly defeated us. So when we returned to him we demanded, 'What's wrong with you? What have you done to us?' When we looked at him we saw his eyes all red and his ears standing straight up. He was absolutely furious, almost exploding with anger. Then he left.

"We rode away and eventually forgave him, and nothing happened for a while. Then he summoned us and said, 'How would you like to go on a raid that will give you glory, and provide you fine booty so that you'll have a real treasure?' 'We need that more than anyone,' we replied. So he said, 'Then mount up.' We did so and asked, 'What next?' He replied: 'Attack Banū al-Ḥārith b. Maslama!' Then he said, 'Stop.' So we did, and he said, 'Attack Fahm!' Then he went on, 'But you've no bad blood with them; attack Muḍar; they have horses and cattle.' Then he said, 'No; attack Durayd b. al-Ṣimma. They're few in number and under protection.' Then he said, 'No; instead go after (the tribe of) Kaʿb b. Rabīʿa. first, lodge them at the estate of ʿĀmir b. Saʿṣaʿa, then do battle with them!'

"So we engaged them in battle but they defeated us, indeed humiliated us. So when we returned we asked him, 'Woe on you! What are you doing to us?' He replied, 'I just don't know; he who was telling me the truth is now lying to me. Imprison me in my house for three days, then come back.'

"We did that. Then, after three days, we returned to him and let him out. And to our surprise he was like a stone of fire! He said, 'O Daws, heaven is protected! And the best of prophets has come forth!' 'Where?' we asked. 'In Mecca; and I am dying, so bury me on a mountain top, for I shall burst into flames. If you leave me (unburied) I will be a source of your shame. When you see me catch fire and flame, then throw three stones at me and with each one say, "In your name, O God." Then I will die down and go out.'

"And he did die and burst into flame! We did what he had told us, throwing three stones and saying after each one 'O God, in your name!' And he did die down and go out.

"Things went on as before until the pilgrims came and told us of your mission, O Messenger of God."

Very strange!

Al-Wāqidī related to us, from his father, from the son of Abū Dhi'b, from Muslim b. Jandab, from al-Naḍr b. Sufyān al-Hudhalī, from his father, who said, "We left for Syria on a camel caravan and when we were between al-Zarqā' and Muʿān, having stopped there to rest for the night, along came a horseman, seemingly somehow between earth and sky, who called out, 'Get up, all you who sleep! This is no time to rest! Aḥmad has come forth and put all the spirits to flight!'

"We were terrified, though brave men we were, all having heard this.

"So we travelled back to our people and when we arrived we found them discussing a conflict in Mecca among Quraysh about a Prophet who had come forth from among them, from the ʿAbd al-Muṭṭalib family, whose name was Aḥmad."

Abū Nuʿaym related this.

Al-Kharā'iṭī stated that ʿAbd Allāh b. Muḥammad al-Balawī – in Egypt – related to him, quoting ʿUmāra b. Zayd, ʿAbd Allāh b. al-ʿAlā', quoting Yaḥyā b. ʿUrwa, from his father, who said that a group from Quraysh, including Waraqa b. Nawfal b. Asad b. ʿAbd al-ʿUzzā b. Quṣayy, Zayd b. ʿAmr b. Nufayl, ʿAbd Allāh b. Jaḥsh b. Ri'āb and ʿUthmān b. al-Ḥuwayrith, were once at a place where they had an idol around which they would assemble. That particular day they had set aside as a holiday each year. They would worship it and make sacrifice of camels to it and then feast, drink wine, and say prayers to it. When they went into it that night, they saw it to be overturned onto its face. They disliked that, so they took it and set it back up as before. Soon, however, it tumbled over violently, but they set it back straight as before. Again, for a third time, it fell over.

Seeing this they were both amazed and very worried. ʿUthmān b. al-Ḥuwayrith said, "Why is it turning upside down so much? This must be because something has happened." This was occurring during the night when the Messenger of God (ṢAAS) was born.

ʿUthmān then spoke the following verses,

> "O festival idol, around whom assemble the chiefs of delegations come from far and near,
> You turn upside down if defeated; tell us why. Is this unimportant, or do you turn in anger?
> If this is for some sin we have committed, we will acknowledge it and give up this sin,
> But if you have been defeated and turned over in abasement, then among idols you are no Lord, no master."

They then set the idol back in its position. When they did so, a great voice rang out from inside the idol, saying,

> "It fell over because of a newly born, light from whom illuminated all the mountain sides of all the earth, in east and west,
> To which all the idols, without exception, fell down and at which the hearts of all the kings of the earth, without exception, trembled in fear.
> And the fires of all the Persians died down and went out, the king of the Persians himself spending a night of great anxiety.
> The soothsayers of the unknown having been abandoned by their spirits, from them no information coming, true or false.
> O Quṣayy, come back from your error, come over to Islam and to the wide-open house."

When they heard this they conferred together in private and some of them said, "Let us be truthful to one another and keep our secret among one another."

All of them said, "Yes indeed!"

Waraqa b. Nawfal told them, "By God, you all know that your people have no religion. They have made an enormous mistake and abandoned Abraham's religion. What purpose is there in a stone you circumambulate that does not hear, nor see, nor can do any good or harm? O my people, adopt a religion!"

The account proceeds, "And so thereupon they left, travelling all over asking about the *ḥanifiyya*, the religion of Abraham, God bless him."

As for Waraqa b. Nawfal, he became a Christian, studied the Scriptures and so became very learned.

ʿUthmān b. al-Ḥuwayrith travelled to the emperor, became a Christian and lived there in high estate with him.

Zayd b. ʿAmr b. Nufayl tried to leave but was gaoled. Eventually, however, he did leave, travelling far and wide till he reached al-Raqqa, in the Arabian peninsula. There he met a learned monk whom he told what he wanted to know. Then the monk said, "You are seeking a religion to which you won't find anyone to lead you. But the time is near for a prophet who will come forth from your land and who will be sent with the *ḥanifiyya* religion."

When he was told this Zayd headed back for Mecca but the Lakhmites attacked and killed him.

As for ʿAbd Allāh b. Jaḥsh, he stayed in Mecca until the Prophet (ṢAAS) was sent. He left thereafter with the others who went to Abyssinia. Once there, he became a Christian and abandoned Islam. He remained there till he died, still a Christian.

There is testimony for this in the earlier account given of the life of Zayd b. ʿAmr b. Nufayl.

Al-Kharāʾiṭī stated that Aḥmad b. Isḥāq b. Ṣāliḥ Abū Bakr al-Warrāq related to him, quoting ʿAmr b. ʿUthmān, quoting his father, quoting ʿAbd Allāh b. ʿAbd al-ʿAzīz, quoting Muḥammad b. ʿAbd al-ʿAzīz, from al-Zuhrī, from ʿAbd al-Raḥmān b. Anas al-Sulamī, from al-ʿAbbās b. Mirdās who said he was one day busy impregnating a milch-camel at midday when a white dove appeared before him with a rider on its back all dressed in clothing as white as milk. The rider said to him, "O ʿAbbās b. Mirdās, don't you see that the heavens have assembled their guards, that war has choked on its own breath, that the mounts have their riding blankets saddled, and that there (has come) he who brought piety and devotion on Monday, the night of the third day, the master of the furthest-riding camel?"

Al-ʿAbbās then said, "So I returned in a fright, very scared by what I had seen and heard. Then I went to an idol we had called al-Ḍimār that we used to worship; it would address us from inside its belly. I swept up all around it, anointed it and kissed it, and then a voice sounded from inside it saying,

> 'Tell all the tribes of Sulaym that al-Ḍimār is gone, and that the people of the mosque have triumphed.
> Al-Ḍimār is dead, though once he was worshipped, before prayer with the Prophet Muḥammad.
> He who inherited the prophethood and the right path following the son of Mary is from Quraysh, rightly guided.'"

He continued, "So off I went until I reached my people and told them what had happened. Then I left, along with 300 of my men of Banū Ḥāritha, to join the Messenger of God (ṢAAS), who was at Medina. We entered the mosque and when the Messenger of God (ṢAAS) saw me he said, 'O ʿAbbās, how did your acceptance of Islam come about?' I then told him the story. He was delighted, and thereupon I and my men all adopted Islam."

The *ḥāfiẓ* Abū Nuʿaym related this in the *al-Dalāʾil* (*The Signs*) from an account of Abū Bakr b. Abū ʿĀṣim, from ʿAmr b. ʿUthmān.

He then recounted it again through al-Aṣmaʿī, who said, that al-Waṣṣāfī related to him, from Manṣūr b. al-Muʿtamir, from Qabīṣa b. ʿAmr b. Isḥāq al-Khuzāʿī, from al-ʿAbbās b. Mirdās al-Sulamī, who said, "My adoption of

Islam first came about this way. My father Mirdās, when near death, recommended to me an idol named Ḍimār he had. So I placed it in a building and established a visitation time, once each day. Now when the Prophet (ṢAAS) came forth, I heard a voice calling out through the night that scared me. So I hurried to Ḍimār seeking its help and heard a voice coming from its belly that said,

'Tell to the tribe of all Sulaym that *al-Anīs* (the close friend)[70] is gone and that the people of the mosque live on.

"'Ḍimār has perished, and he was once worshipped, before the Scripture (was sent) to the Prophet Muḥammad.

"'He who has inherited the prophethood and the right path, after the son of Mary, is from Quraysh, rightly guided.'"

He went on, "I kept this from my people. After they had returned from the battle (of the siege of Medina) I was out with my herd on the side of the ravine at Dhāt ʿIrq, asleep, when I heard a voice. Then I saw a man riding on a dove's wing and saying, 'The light appeared on the night before Tuesday along with (the birth of) the master of the she-camel named *al-ʿAdbāʾ*,[71] at the house of Banū al ʿAnqāʾ.' And another voice, from the left, replied, 'Tell the disheartened spirits that the mount has put on its saddle blankets, that heaven has been protected by its guards.'

"I jumped up in fright at this and knew that Muḥammad was a messenger. So I rode my mare as fast as I could till I reached him and pledged him my allegiance. Then I went off, burned Ḍimār in fire, returned again to the Messenger of God (ṢAAS) and recited to him the following verses:

> 'By your life, by my making Ḍimār as partner with the Lord of the worlds
>
> And by my leaving the Messenger of God with the Aws tribe around him, those being his helpers;
>
> I am like someone who left the easy ground and sought out the difficult one, to find his path into the most difficult of matters,
>
> So I believed in God, whose servant I am, and opposed those who have begun seeking destruction.
>
> And I turned my face towards Mecca, seeking to declare allegiance to the blessed Prophet of the most noble men,
>
> A Prophet who came to us after Jesus, with a message of truth in which there is the conclusive word.
>
> Entrusted with the Qurʾān, the first Intercessor and the first Messenger to respond to the angels,
>
> He restored the bonds of Islam after they had been broken, making them firm and establishing the rituals.

70. He is referring to the idol Ḍimār.
71. The camel of the Prophet (ṢAAS) was so named.

I meant you, O best man of all the world; you have been situated at the top of all heights and possessed all eminence and honour.

You are the purified one of Quraysh; when they fade away you will remain blessed for the ages.

When the two tribes Kaʿb and Mālik trace their lineage we find you of pure descent, and your fertile women too.'"

Al-Kharāʾiṭī stated that ʿAbd Allāh b. Muḥammad al-Balawī, in Egypt, related to him, quoting ʿUmāra b. Zayd, quoting Isḥāq b. Bishr and Salama b. al-Faḍl, from Muḥammad b. Isḥāq who said that it was related to him by a sheikh from among the Companions whose name was ʿAbd Allāh b. Maḥmūd, from the family of Muḥammad b. Maslama, that he said that he was informed that men of Khathʿam used to say, "This is what drew us to Islam. We used to be a people who worshipped idols. One day we were at an idol of ours when a group came to seek the idol's advice in settling a dispute among them. Suddenly a voice called out to them:

'O people possessed of bodies, old men and young alike, what are you with your perplexed minds to rely on idols for judgements?

Are all of you in confusion, sleeping, or do you not see what I see: a shining light, clearing up the darkness, has emerged to view from Tihām?

That is a prophet, Lord of mankind, who has brought Islam after disbelief.

The All-Merciful has honoured him by making him a leader, and a messenger whose words are truthful.

The most just of all judges, he commands prayer and fasting

And piety and reconciliation and drives people away from evil.

And from immorality, idol worship, and sin; he is from Hāshim among the elite of leaders

Announcing (his mission) in the sacred land.'

"And when we heard this, we broke away from the idol, came to the Prophet (ṢAAS) and accepted Islam."

Al-Kharāʾiṭī stated that ʿAbd Allāh al-Balawī related to him, quoting ʿUmāra, quoting ʿUbayd Allāh b. al-ʿAlāʾ, quoting Muḥammad b. Akbar, from Saʿīd b. Jubayr, that there was a man from the Banū Tamīm called Rāfiʿ b. ʿUmayr, a highly skilled tracker, the best of all men in travelling at night, and the most intrepid in danger. The Arabs therefore used to call him "Duʿmūṣ of the Arabs", a name implying his skill in following a trail and his bravery. He recounted how he first adopted Islam, as follows, "One night I was travelling over deep sand when I felt very sleepy. So I dismounted, tied my camel down, rested my head on its leg and went to sleep. Before falling asleep I said a prayer: 'I seek protection from the master (spirit) of this valley against being harmed or disturbed by evil spirits.' In my sleep I saw a young man creeping up on my camel, a spearhead in his hand with which he was going to stab her in the throat. At that I awoke in alarm and, though I looked in all directions, I could see nothing. I told myself it was just a dream. So I went back into a light sleep and saw the same as I had before. Again I awoke, walked all around my camel but saw nothing. Once more I slept, saw the same and awoke to find my camel trembling. Again I slept, saw the vision once more and awoke to find my camel in a disturbed state. I turned around and there was a young man just like I had seen in my dream, carrying a spearhead in his hand which was being restrained by an old man who was reciting:

> 'O Mālik b. Muhalhil b. Dithār, easy does it, my mantle and waist-wrapper be your ransom,
> Leave the human's camel alone, don't harm it and choose instead whatever of my bulls you want.
> You're showing me a side of yourself I never knew, not to honour my relationship to you and my honour.
> Going up to him with a poisoned spearhead! Woe to you for doing so, O Abū al-Ghaffār.
> If it were not for shame and your family being neighbours, I'd tell you things of me I've not disclosed.'

"After he had spoken thus, the young man responded:

> 'Did you want to raise and drop our reputation for no contemptible action, O Abū al-'Izār?
> They never in the past had a lord among them; it is Banū al-Akhyār who are best.
> So go your way, O Mu'akbar; however, the protector was Muhalhil b. Dithār.'

"While they were thus disputing three bulls emerged from the wilderness and the old man said to the young one, 'Go on now, nephew, just take any one of these you want in compensation for the camel of my human friend here.' So the young man did take one bull and left with it. Then the old man turned to me and said, 'When you go down into some valley or other and are afraid, then say, "I take refuge in God, the Lord of Muḥammad, from the terror of this valley." Don't seek the protection of any spirit because they're all finished.' I asked him, 'Who is this Muhammad?' He replied, 'He is an Arab prophet, neither of the east nor of the west, who was sent down on a Monday.' 'Where does he live?' I asked. 'Yathrib, where there are palm trees', he replied. So I rode off on my mount as soon as dawn broke and rode on and on till I entered Medina (i.e. Yathrib). The Messenger of God (ṢAAS) saw me and he told me my story before I told him anything about it! He invited me into Islam, and I did accept Islam."

Sa'īd b. Jubayr commented, "We used to think that it was about him that God revealed the words, 'There were human men who used to seek protection from spirit men, and so made them more malicious'" (*sūrat al-Jinn*, LXXII, v.6).

Al-Kharāʾiṭī related, through Ibrāhīm b. Ismāʿīl b. Ḥammād b. Abū Ḥanīfa, from Dāwūd b. al-Ḥusayn, from ʿIkrima, from Ibn ʿAbbās, from ʿAlī, who said, "If you should be in a valley where you fear lions, then say 'I seek protection from Daniel and the well against the evil of the lion.'"

Al-Balawī recounted, from ʿUmāra b. Zayd, from Ibrāhīm b. Saʿd, from Muḥammad b. Isḥāq who said that Yaḥyā b. ʿAbd Allāh b. al-Ḥārith related to him, from his father, from Ibn ʿAbbās, the story of ʿAlī's killing the *jinn* in the well which had a flag that was at al-Juḥfa. This happened when the Messenger of God (ṢAAS) sent him to get water; they (the *jinn*) wanted to prevent him and so they cut up the bucket. He then went down to them; this is a long and very objectionable story. But God knows best.

Al-Kharāʾiṭī stated that it was related to him by Abū al-Ḥārith Muḥammad b. Muṣʿab the Damascene and others, and also by Sulaymān, son of the daughter of Sharaḥbīl the Damascene, and by ʿAbd al-Quddūs b. al-Ḥajjāj, as by Khālid b. Saʿīd, from al-Shaʿbī, from a man who said that he was once attending an assembly with ʿUmar b. al-Khaṭṭāb. There also present were a group of the Companions of the Prophet (ṢAAS), who were discussing the virtues of the Qurʾān. One of them referred to the final verses of *sūrat al-Nahl* (XVI). Another suggested *sūrat Yā Sīn* (XXXVI). ʿAlī said, "How about the *Āyat al-Kursī*? ('The Throne Verse', *sūrat al-Baqara*, II, v.255). It has 70 words, each one of which has a blessing."

One of those present was ʿAmr b. Maʿdī Karib who was never lost for a comment. He asked, "Where do you stand regarding the invocation, 'In the name of God, the most Merciful, the most Beneficent'?" ʿUmar said, "Tell us an anecdote, O Abū Thawr?" (addressing ʿAmr).

He responded, "One time, before Islam, I felt terribly hungry, so I urged on my horse into the wilderness, but all I found were some ostrich eggs. As I went further I came across a bedouin sheikh in a tent with a girl beside him who was as beautiful as the rising sun. He also had some young goats. I addressed him, saying, 'Surrender, may your mother be bereft of you!' He raised his head to me and replied, 'Now lad, if you need hospitality, then dismount. If you want help, I'll help you.' But I replied, 'Surrender!' He then recited the following verses,

> 'We offered you hospitality out of kindness on our part, but you were not converted, in ignorance, acting as the unlucky do.
>
> You came and insulted us and were rude. And your throat would be slashed before you get what you hoped to get from my daughter.'"

He went on: "And then all of a sudden he leapt at me, saying, 'In the name of God, the Most Merciful, the Most Beneficent.' Suddenly I felt as if I were beneath him in submission. He then asked, 'Well, shall I kill you or let you go?' 'Let me go,' I said. Then he stood back from me. But at that point my spirit persuaded me to try again, so I said, 'Surrender! May your mother be bereft of you!' He responded with the verses:

> 'In the name of God and the All-Merciful, we were victorious there, and by the Most Beneficent it was we conquered.
>
> But the determination of a haughty man will do no good when once we go forth to battle.'

"He then leapt at me, while I was there under him in submission. 'Well,' he said, 'should I kill you or let you go?' 'Let me go,' I replied. He stood back from me and I hurried some small distance away. But then I said to myself, 'O ʿAmr, can this old sheikh really defeat you? By God, better you be dead than alive.' So I went back to him and said again, 'Surrender! May your mother be bereft of you!' Again he leapt at me, saying, 'In the name of God, the most Merciful and Beneficent,' and again I suddenly found myself there in submission beneath him. Again he asked, 'Should I kill you or let you go?' Again I replied, 'Let me go.' 'Impossible! Now girl, bring me the sharp dagger.' She brought it to him and he lopped off my forelock! When the Arabs defeated a man and lopped off his forelock they would be placing him into servitude. So I stayed with him for a time as his servant. He then said to me, 'O ʿAmr, I want you to ride out into the desert with me. I have fear of you yet am fully confident in the words, "In the name of God, the most Merciful, the most Beneficent."'

"So off we went till we came to a valley that was overgrown, awesome and spirit-ridden. He cried out at the top of his voice, 'In the name of God, the most Merciful and Beneficent!' Immediately every bird there left its cover and flew off. He repeated the same cry and every single lion there fled its den. Again he made the cry and all of a sudden there before us was an Abyssinian who had come out at us from the valley, standing there like a tall palm tree. The sheikh said to me, 'O ʿAmr, when you see us both go off alone together, then say, "May my master overcome him through the words 'In the name of God, the most Merciful, the most Beneficent.'"' But when I saw them alone together I said, 'May my master overcome him through al-Lāt and al-ʿUzzā.' So the sheikh did nothing. He then came back to me and said, 'You realize you disobeyed me?' 'Yes,' I replied, 'but I won't do it again.' He then said, 'When you see us alone together, then say, "May my master overcome him through the words 'In the name of God, the most Merciful, the most Beneficent.'"' 'All right,' I agreed. So when I saw them go off alone together I did say, 'May my master overcome him through (the words) "In the name of God, the most Merciful, the most Beneficent."' The sheikh then threw himself upon the Abyssinian, sliced at him with his sword, slit his stomach open and drew out from his insides something in the form of a black candle. He then said, 'O ʿAmr, this is his deceit and his rancour.' He then asked me, 'Do you know who this girl is?' 'No,' I answered.

'This', he replied, 'is al-Fāriʿa, daughter of al-Salīl al-Jurhumī, a leader of the demon spirits. Those are all her people, her relatives. Every year one man of them makes an attack on me, but God helps me defeat him through the words, 'In the name of God, the most Merciful, the most Beneficent."' He then said, 'You saw how I treated that Abyssinian. Now I'm really hungry, so get me something to eat.' I rode my mount off into the desert but only found some ostrich eggs. These I brought back for him but found him asleep. Beneath his head there was something that looked like a piece of wood. When I drew it out it was a sword, its size being one hand-span by seven. I struck his legs off with one blow which severed them along with his feet. He sat up on his haunches and cried out, 'May God destroy you! How treacherous you are, traitor!'"

ʿUmar then asked, "What did you do then?"

"Well," ʿAmr replied, "I just kept hitting him till I had chopped him up into little bits." He remained silent in sorrow a while, then went on, reciting the verses:

"Through deceit and from close by you took Islam's brother; I never heard the like in Arabs of former times.

(Even) the non-Arabs would be shamed in their honour to do as you did; may you perish for what you did to this able Lord.

Yet I am amazed that you were able to murder him; and that you did not care how (well) he treated you when you sinned.

He was a chief who had forgiven you often and whose hands clung to you at his place of death.

Yet if I had been acting during Islam as they have done to polytheists and those of the cross,

Then you would have attained by my justice a terrible fate such as to make its sufferer call out in grief and woe."

"And what happened to the slave girl?" he asked. ʿAmr replied, "I then went to her. When she saw me, she said, 'What happened to the sheikh?' 'The Abyssinian killed him,' I replied. 'You lie!' she cried. 'You killed him, by betraying him!' Then she recited the verses:

'O eyes, weep well for the brave warrior, then weep copious droplets more;

Do not tire of weeping, for fate has deceived you (in taking) a trustworthy man who had truth and was patient.

A man who was pious, stately and wise, a man worthy of glory on Judgement Day.

How sad I am that you let ʿAmr live, for time has given you up to your fate.

By my life, if you had not sought him out in betrayal, you would have faced a lion as sharp as a sword.'

"What she said greatly angered me so I drew my sword and entered the tent to kill her. But in the tent I found no one. So I herded up the cattle and came home."

This is a curious anecdote.

It is obvious that the sheikh was a demon spirit, one of those that adopted Islam and learned the Qurʾān, one thing he used being the invocation "In the name of God the most Merciful, the most Beneficent." He would seek protection by speaking it.

Al-Kharāʾiṭī stated that ʿAbd Allāh b. Muḥammad al-Balawī related to him, quoting ʿUmāra b. Zayd, saying that ʿAbd Allāh b. al-ʿAlāʾ related to him, from Hishām b. ʿUrwa, from his father, from his grandmother Asmāʾ, daughter of Abū Bakr, who said, "Zayd b. ʿAmr b. Nufayl and Waraqa b. Nawfal used to tell how they went to the Negus after the retreat of Abraha from Mecca. They would say, 'When we went in to him, he told us, "O you two men of Quraysh, tell me truthfully. Was there born among you a boy whose father wanted to sacrifice him and who had divining arrows cast about him, but who was saved and had many camels sacrificed for him?"

"'Yes,' we replied. 'Do you have knowledge of him then, and of what became of him?' We replied, 'He married a woman named Āmina, daughter of Wahb; he left her pregnant then went away.' 'Do you know if a child was born or not?'

"Waraqa b. Nawfal replied, 'I will tell you, O King. I had spent a night at an idol of ours around which we used to circumambulate and worship. Suddenly I heard a voice emanating from its belly that said, "The Prophet is born and so the kings are abased, falsehood is averted and polytheism is dead."

"'The idol therupon tipped over on to its face.'

"Zayd b. ʿAmr b. Nufayl then spoke, 'I had a similar experience, O King.' 'Let's hear it,' he was told. He related as follows, 'On just such a night as he told of, I left my people, who were talking about Amīna's being pregnant, and went to Mt. Abū Qubays, wanting to be alone there because of something that was bothering me. Suddenly I saw a man descend from the skies who had two green wings. He stood atop Mt. Abū Qubays, then looked down over Mecca and said, 'Satan is humiliated and the idols are cast down. The 'Trustworthy One' is born.' He then spread out a cloth he had with him and floated away on it to the east and west. I saw that he had lit up all beneath the sky and a light was shining so brightly that it almost blinded me. I was awed by what I had seen. The man who had called out flapped his wings and flew down to the *kaʿba*, a light shining from him that illuminated all Tihāma. He then spoke, "The earth is aflame and has reached its springtime." He then gestured towards the idols that were in the *kaʿba* and they all fell down.'

"The Negus said, 'Let me tell you now what happened to me. I was asleep that same night you mentioned, alone in a pavilion, when out from the ground came a neck and a head which said, "Woe has befallen the warriors with elephants! flocks of birds cast clay stones at them. The criminal aggressor al-Ashram has perished! And the *ummī* prophet has been born, he from Mecca, from the sacred quarter. Whoever responds to him will be glad; whoever scorns him will be sad." He then entered the earth and was gone. I tried to scream, but couldn't say a word. I then tried to get up, but could not do so. I struck the pavilion with my hand and my family heard this and came to me. I told them, "Keep the Abyssinians away from me." They did so. And then I regained use of my tongue and feet.'"

If God Almighty wills it, I will now give accounts, in the stories relating to the birth, concerning the visions of Chosroe of the collapse of 14 balconies of his palace, of the extinguishing of his fires, of the visions of his soothsayer, and Saṭīḥ's interpretation of these through the help of ʿAbd al-Masīḥ.

The *ḥāfiẓ* Abū al-Qāsim b. ʿAsākir related in his history work dealing with the life of al-Ḥārith b. Hāniʾ b. al-Mudlij b. Ibn al-Miqdād b. Zamal b. ʿAmr al-ʿUdhrī, from his father, from his grandfather, from his father, from Zamal b. ʿAmr al-ʿUdhrī, who said, "The Banū ʿUdhra had an idol called Ṣamām whom they venerated. And it was kept with Banū Hind b. Ḥirām b. Ḍabba b. ʿAbd b. Kabīr b. ʿUdhra, its guardian being a man called Ṭāriq. People used to make sacrifice near it. When the Messenger of God (ṢAAS) came forth we heard a voice that said, 'O Banū Hind b. Ḥirām, the truth has come forth and Ṣamām has gone; Islam has done away with idol worship.' We were very alarmed and awed by this. Nothing more happened for several days, but then we heard a voice saying, 'O Ṭāriq; the truth-telling Prophet has been sent with spoken inspiration. A man has emerged in the land of Tihāma announcing the truth; those who support him will live secure, while those who desert him will regret it. This now is my farewell until Judgement Day.'

"'At that', Zamal said, 'the idol fell forward on its face. So I bought a riding camel and rode off to the Messenger of God (ṢAAS) along with a group of my tribesmen. I recited to him the following verses:

> 'To you, O Messenger of God, I directed (my mount), driving it hard over high rough ground and sandy lowlands
> To give strong help to the best of men, to tie a rope of yours to my own,
> And I testify that there is nothing besides God, and that I will worship Him so long as my shoes weigh down my feet.'

"'So I accepted Islam and pledged my allegiance to him. We told him what we had heard, and he responded, "That was demon-spirit talk."'

"He then said, 'O you Arabs, I am the Messenger of God to you and to all mankind. I call upon you to worship God alone. I tell you I am his Messenger and his servant and that you must make pilgrimage to the *kaʿba*, fast for one month out of twelve, that being Ramaḍān. Those of you who respond to me shall have paradise as your abode. Whoever opposes me will have hell-fire as his final destiny.'

"He went on, 'So we accepted Islam and he made a pact with us. He wrote a document for us as follows: "In the name of God, the most Merciful and most Beneficent; this is from Muḥammad, the Messenger of God, to Zamal b. ʿAmr and to those in particular who accepted Islam with him. I am sending him to his people intentionally. Whoever accepts Islam is on the side of God and his Messenger. Whoever refuses can have a truce for two months. Witnessed by ʿAlī b. Abū Ṭālib and Muḥammad b. Maslama al-Anṣārī."'"

Ibn ʿAsākir at this point made the comment, "Very strange!"

Saʿīd b. Yaḥyā b. Saʿīd al-Umawī stated in his history of the Prophet's wars that Muḥammad b. Saʿīd – meaning his uncle – told him that Muḥammad b. al-Munkadir said that he was told that Ibn ʿAbbās said that a demon-spirit called out to Abū Qubays, saying,

> "O people of Fihr! May God find your views repugnant; how petty minds and intelligence are
> When they disregard those slandering the religion of their fathers, those noble guardians!
> He has allied with the spirits, the spirits of Buṣrā against you, along with the men of the palm trees and the forest
> You are about to see the horsemen running (right and left) swiftly killing people in sheepskin garments.
> Is there any noble man among you, who has the spirit of a free man, a man of illustrious parents and relatives,
> A man to strike a blow that will be a warning and a rupture from anxiety and worry?"

Ibn ʿAbbās stated, "This poetry became a refrain for the people of Mecca, and they would recite it to one another. The Messenger of God (ṢAAS) said, 'This is a devil who speaks to people through the idols; his name is Misʿar; and God will confound him.' Nothing else happened for three days and then a voice cried out on the mountain:

> 'We killed Misʿar in three days when he disgraced the spirits and advocated evil.
> I slashed at his head with a sharp sword drawn because he reviled our Prophet made pure.'

"The Messenger of God (ṢAAS) then said, 'This is a genie whose name is Samij; when he believed in me, I renamed him ʿAbd Allāh; he told me he spent three days searching for him (Misʿar).' ʿAlī said, 'May God reward him well, O Messenger of God.'"

The *ḥāfiẓ* Abū Nuʿaym stated in the *al-Dalāʾil* (*The Signs*) that ʿAbd Allāh b. Muḥammad b. Jaʿfar related to him, quoting Abū al-Faḍl Muḥammad b. ʿAbd al-Raḥmān b. Mūsā b. Abū Ḥarb al-Ṣaffār, quoting ʿAbbās b. al-Faraj al-Riyāshī, quoting Sulaymān b. ʿAbd al-ʿAzīz b. Abū Thābit, from his father, from ʿAbd al-Ḥamīd b. Bahrām, from Shahr b. Ḥawshab, from Ibn ʿAbbās, from Saʿd b. ʿUbāda, who said, "The Messenger of God (ṢAAS) sent me on a mission to Haḍramawt[72] before his migration. On the way, during the night, I heard a voice cry out,

> 'O Abū ʿAmr, insomnia afflicted me, sleep fled and slumber was impossible
> At thought of a group of men who came before and now are gone; and all mankind have their palaces disappear.
> They passed away, moving to their deaths, destined (to their graves) not to a watering place.
> They left, while I remained behind, alone, with no one to assist me,
> Futile, unable to even deal with an issue that a child could handle (with ease).
> After all, I am not remaining with a people whose tombs are like those of Thamūd
> And ʿĀd and the centuries are all equal to death, all being mere stalks after harvest.'

"Another voice then called out, 'O Kharʿab, "soft twig", has wonder taken your senses? Wonderful, wonderful things are happening between Zahra and Yathrib.'

"'What's happened there, O Shāḥib?' He replied, 'The Prophet of peace has been sent with the best of words to all of humanity. And he has left the holy places for the date palms and forts.'

"He asked, 'What's it all about, this Prophet with a mission, the Revealed Scripture and this "chosen" *ummī*?' He replied, 'He is a descendant of Luʾayy b. Ghālib, son of Fihr b. Mālik b. al-Naḍr b. Kināna.' The second voice replied, 'O what a pity! I'm too old for this, my time is all gone. Al-Naḍr b. Kināna and I used to aim at the same target, drink cold milk together. Early one cold morning I accompanied him out from Dawḥa; he arose with the sun and set with it too, with him telling what he heard and verifying what he saw. If this man is of his descent then the sword is sheathed, fear has gone, sexual immorality is over, and usury is no more.'

"'Then tell me what will be?' He replied, 'Distress, misery, and hunger are over. Strength and bravery are over, except for what is to remain in the tribe of Khuzāʿa. Oppression, sufferings, along with high character are gone, except for what is to remain in the tribes of Khazraj and Aws. Conceit and arrogance are gone too, along with calumny and perfidy, except for what is to remain in Banū Bakr, meaning Ibn Hawāzin. Regrettable and sinful deeds are over, except for what is to remain in Khathʿam.'

"'Tell me what else will be?' He replied, 'If goodness is defeated and the free woman suppressed, then leave the land of migration. If the peace is disrupted and family ties are broken, then leave the holy land.' 'Tell me what will be?' He replied, 'Were it not for ears that hear, eyes that shine, I would tell you what

72. Part of south-western Arabia, on the Arabian Sea.

would fill you with dread.' Then he went on, 'Nowhere have I slept in peace, O Ibn Ghawt, without a morning arriving for us.'

"He went on: 'And then he screamed like a woman in labour. Dawn then broke and I went to look. And what I saw was a small iguana and a snake, both dead.

"It was only through this incident that I learned that the Messenger of God (ṢAAS) had migrated to Medina."

Abū Nu'aym then related this story from Muḥammad b. Ja'far, from Ibrāhīm b. 'Alī, from al-Naḍr b. Salama, from Ḥassān b. 'Ubāda b. Mūsā, from 'Abd al-Ḥamīd b. Bahrām, from Shahr, from Ibn 'Abbās, from Sa'd b. 'Ubāda, as follows, "After we pledged our allegiance to the Messenger of God (ṢAAS) on *'Aqaba* night, I left for Ḥadramawt on business. That having been concluded, I started back. Some distance along the way I fell asleep and awoke in a fright to hear a voice shouting, 'O Abū 'Amr, insomnia has afflicted me, sleep has fled and my slumber is interrupted.'" And he recounted the whole incident as given above.

Abū Nu'aym stated that Muḥammad b. Ja'far related to him, quoting Ibrāhīm b. 'Alī, quoting al-Naḍr b. Salama, quoting Abū Ghazīyya Muḥammad b. Mūsā, from al-'Aṭṭāf b. Khālid al-Waṣṣābī, from Khālid b. Sa'īd, from his father, who said that he heard Tamīm al-Dārī say, "I was in Syria when the Messenger of God (ṢAAS) received his mission. I left on some business and on the way night fell. I said, 'I claim to be under the protection of the chief spirit of this valley for this night.' When I went to bed, I heard someone I could not see calling out, 'Seek God's protection. For no spirit can give anyone protection from God.' 'By God,' I exclaimed, 'what are you saying?' The voice replied, 'The Messenger of the *ummīs*, the Messenger of God, has come forth. We prayed behind him at al-Ḥajūn. We accepted Islam and became his followers. The tricks of the demon-spirits are over, and they have been pelted with shooting stars. Hurry to Muḥammad, the Messenger of the Lord of the worlds, and accept Islam.'"

Tamīm went on, "When morning came I went on to Ayyūb's monastery, where I asked to see a monk and told him what had happened. He said, 'They spoke the truth to you. He is leaving the holy place, and the place where he is migrating is holy. He is the best of prophets. Do not let anyone beat you to him.'"

Tamīm continued, "I took the trouble to travel hurriedly until I reached the Messenger of God (ṢAAS) and then accepted Islam."

Ḥātim b. Ismā'īl stated, from 'Abd Allāh b. Yazīd al-Hudhalī, from 'Abd Allāh b. Sā'ida al-Hudhalī, from his father, who said, "We were at our idol named Suwā', having brought some sheep of ours to him. They consisted of 200 ewes that were afflicted with mange. We brought them close to him seeking his blessing. Then I heard a voice calling out from the belly of the idol, 'The tricks of the demon-spirits are no more; we have been pelted with shooting stars – all for a Prophet whose name is Aḥmad!'

"'You have misled us, by God!' I exclaimed. I turned the face of my sheep away, urging them towards my people, and I then saw a man who told me of the appearance of the Prophet (ṢAAS)."

Abū Nuʿaym mentioned this account as such, without elaboration. He then stated that ʿUmar b. Muḥammad b. Jaʿfar related to him, quoting Ibrāhīm b. al-Sindī, quoting al-Naḍr b. Salama, quoting Muḥammad b. Maslama al-Makhzūmī, quoting Yaḥyā b. Sulaymān, from Ḥakīm b. ʿAṭāʾ al-Ẓafarī, who is of Banū Sulaym, descended from Rāshid b. ʿAbd Rabbihī, from his father, from his grandfather, from Rāshid b. ʿAbd Rabbihī, who said, "The idol known as Suwāʿ was at al-Miʿlāt, one of a group worshipped by the tribes of Hudhayl and Banū Ẓafar b. Sulaym." Banū Ẓafar dispatched Rāshid b. ʿAbd Rabbihī with a gift for Suwāʿ from Sulaym.

Rāshid went on, "At dawn I attended an idol before the idol Suwāʿ. As I did so, all of a sudden a voice rang out from its belly, 'How strange! How very strange that a prophet should come forth from the family of ʿAbd al-Muṭṭalib who would ban fornication, usury and sacrificing to idols! And the skies are being guarded and we are being pelted by shooting stars! How strange! How very strange!' Then another idol screamed out from deep within itself, 'Al-Ḍimār has been abandoned, and he used to be worshipped! The Prophet Aḥmad has come forth. He says the prayers, orders the payment of alms, fasting, piety, and kindness to relatives.' Then another voice shouted from the belly of another idol:

> 'He who has inherited the prophethood and the true religion after Mary's son is of Quraysh, rightly guided
>
> A prophet come to inform of what is past, and what is today the truth, or tomorrow.'"

Rāshid went on: "Next dawn I attended Suwāʿ and there were two jackals licking all around it and eating what had been sacrificed to it. And they were directing their urine on to it."

At this Rāshid b. ʿAbd Rabbihī spoke the verse:

> "Is this a lord upon whose head two jackals urinate? Whoever has jackals urinate upon him is disgraced!"

"This occurred at the time of the emergence of the Prophet (ṢAAS), his migration to Medina and his acceptance by the people. And so Rāshid left and made his way to the Prophet (ṢAAS) in Medina, taking along a dog he had with him. Now at that time Rāshid's name was *Ẓālim*, tyrant, evil-doer, and that of his dog *Rāshid*, rightly guided. The Prophet (ṢAAS) asked him what his name was. He replied 'Ẓālim'. 'And what is your dog's name?' 'Rāshid,' he replied.

'Well,' said the Prophet (ṢAAS), 'Now your name is Rāshid and your dog's Ẓālim!' And the Prophet (ṢAAS) laughed.

"And so Rāshid pledged his allegiance to him and remained in Mecca with him. He then made a request to the Messenger of God (ṢAAS) to receive the land fees for Wahāṭ, and he described it to him. The Messenger of God (ṢAAS) gave him the land fees right for the heights above Wahāṭ, along with control over *shaʿwa al-faras*, the 'horse bridle', monument and over the rituals there of throwing stones at it three times. He presented him with a waterskin filled with water and spat in it. He told him, 'Empty it out at the top of the tract, and don't deny people access to its overflow.' And so he did. He therefore channelled the water into an open ditch which still flows to this day. Around it he planted palm trees. It is said that all Wahāṭ uses it for their water supply and that the people there call it 'the water of the Messenger of God (ṢAAS).' The people of Wahāṭ also wash in it. Rāshid's stone-casting site was attended by many travelling parties, called the 'caravans of the stone'. One morning Rāshid went to Suwāʿ and demolished it."

Abū Nuʿaym stated that Sulaymān b. Aḥmad related to him, quoting ʿAlī b. Ibrāhīm al-Khuzāʿī al-Ahwāzī, quoting Abū Muḥammad ʿAbd Allāh b. Dāwūd b. Dalhāth b. Ismāʿīl b. Musriʿ b. Yāsir b. Suwayd, the Companion of the Messenger of God (ṢAAS), from his father, from his father Dalhāth from his father Ismāʿīl, that the father of the last-mentioned, ʿAbd Allāh, related to him from his father Musriʿ b. Yāsir that his father Yāsir related to him, from ʿAmr b. Murra al-Juhannī who used to tell the following, "Once, before Islam, I went on pilgrimage with a party from my tribe. At Mecca, during my sleep, I saw a blinding light emitting from the *kaʿba*, so strong that it lit up Mt. Yathrib and the mountains overlooking the town. I heard a voice in the light that said, 'The shadows have been dispelled, the light now shines bright, and the last of the prophets has been sent.'

"Then another light shone forth by which I could see the castles of al-Ḥīra and Chosroe's palace. I also heard a voice in the light that called out, 'Islam has appeared, the idols have been demolished and reconciliation has come.'

"I awoke with a start and said to my people, 'By God, in this Quraysh quarter something tremendous is going to happen!' And I told them what I had seen. When we got back home a man arrived who told us that someone named Aḥmad had received a mission. I went to that man, and told him what I had seen. He told me, 'O ʿAmr b. Murra, I have been dispatched to all mankind to invite them into Islam, to command them not to shed blood, to bring about reconciliation, to worship God, to reject the idols, to make pilgrimage to the *kaʿba*, and to fast one month in twelve, Ramaḍān that is. For those who respond there will be paradise. Whoever disobeys will go to the fire. So you, ʿAmr b. Murra, you believe and God will spare you from the fires of hell.'

"I therefore said, 'I bear witness that there is no God but God and that you are the Messenger of God. I believe in all you have brought us regarding what is lawful and what is disallowed, even though that will give offence to many people.' I then recited to him some verses I had composed when I had heard of him. We used to have an idol, and my father was its guardian. I went to it and demolished it and then joined up with the Prophet (ṢAAS). I recited,

'I bore witness that God is truth and that I will be the first to abandon the stone idols;
I then hurried to depart to you, travelling over ravines and flat lands towards you.
To attend the very best of men in spirit and in ancestry, the messenger of man's sovereign above the stars.'

"The Prophet (ṢAAS) responded, 'Welcome indeed, O ʿAmr b. Murra.' I replied, 'O Messenger, may my father and mother be sacrifice for you! Send me back to my own people, so that God may give me to benefit them as he has given you to me.'

"So he did send me to them, saying, 'Speak only what is right; do not be harsh, nor arrogant, nor envious.'

"When I went to my people, I told them, 'O you, Banū Rifāʿa, and you too, Banū Juhayna, I am a messenger to you from the Messenger of God. I invite you to paradise and warn you of the fire. I command you not to shed blood, to enourage reconciliation, to worship God, to reject the idols, to make pilgrimage to the *kaʿba*, to fast during Ramaḍān, one month in twelve. Those who respond will go to paradise. Those who disobey will go to the fires. O people of Juhayna, God, all praise be to Him, has made you better than your forebears. He made you hate, in your state of ignorance, the obscene practices which others have found acceptable. They used to unite two sisters, men would marry their fathers' wives, and they would allow warfare during the sacred month. So respond to this Prophet (ṢAAS) sent to you from Banū Luʾayy b. Ghālib, and you will attain respect on earth and honour in the hereafter. Hurry! Hurry to do this, so that you will find favour with God.'

"They did all respond, except for one man. He arose and said, 'O ʿAmr b. Murra, may God embitter your life for you! Do you order us to reject our gods and break apart our community by abandoning the religion of our forefathers in favour of what this Qurayshite from Tihāma advocates? No; and you are neither welcome nor honoured here!' He then spoke the verses,

'Ibn Murra has come here and made a speech, but it's not a speech of someone wanting goodness.
I consider his words and deeds will be one day, however long the wait, mere winds.
Are we to deprecate our elders now gone? Whoever seeks for that will never achieve success.'

"To that ‘Amr b. Murra responded, 'Whoever is the liar, may God embitter his life, silence his tongue, and blind his sight!'

"'Amr b. Murra went on: 'And by God, by the time he died his mouth had dropped, he had lost all taste for food, and he was blind and dumb.'

"'Amr b. Murra and those others of his people who had accepted Islam then went to the Prophet (ṢAAS). He welcomed and honoured them and wrote for them a document, the text of which was as follows, 'In the name of God, the most Merciful, the most Beneficent, this document is from God through the tongue of the Messenger of God and is a trustworthy document, a spoken truth, (sent) with ‘Amr b. Murra al-Juhanī to Juhayna b. Zayd: "You shall have the low-lying flat and fertile lands and the sides and backs of the valleys, and all their vegetation and their pure water to drink. Provided that you forsake one fifth (of the harvest), and perform the five daily prayers. Your rich shall pay alms (to the poor): one ewe for each forty sheep, and one ewe for each five camels, or two ewes for any combination thereof. The rich shall not be eligible to receive charity. The Muslims present here witness this document (written by) Qays b. Shammās, may God bless them all."'"

That was when ‘Amr b. Murra spoke the following verses,

"Did you not see that God has made his religion apparent and made plain the proof of the Qur᾽ān to ‘Āmir,

A document from the Merciful one, a light for our community and our descendants in desert and town alike.

To the best of all walking on the earth, its very best when troubles loom thick.

We obeyed the Messenger of God when the enemy tribes were torn apart by sharp swords and valiant knights.

We are a tribe walled about by our glory, when during warfare the heads of great men are brought in.

We are the warriors, entertain the battle with strong arms and shining swords in the hands of our valiant raiders;

Around him you see the *anṣār*, his followers, protecting their prince with their spearpoints and the flats of their swords;

When warfare goes on at every great event, grinding with its mill the strongest of lions,

His complexion remains serene, his face gleaming like the light of the full moon amidst the stars."

Abū ‘Uthmān Sa‘īd b. Yaḥyā al-Umawī stated in his *Maghāzī* collection that ‘Abd Allāh related to him, quoting Abū ‘Abd Allāh, quoting al-Mujālid b. Sa‘īd, and al-Ajlaḥ, from al-Shi‘bī, quoting a sheikh of Juhayna, who said, "One of our men became extremely sick, so ill that we dug his grave and prepared to bury him. He passed out, then opened his eyes and came to again and asked, 'Have you dug my grave?' 'Yes,' we told him. He then asked, 'What did al-Fuṣal do?'

making reference to a cousin of his. We replied, 'Ṣāliḥ passed by a while ago and asked after you.' 'He's soon going to be put in my grave; a spirit came to me after I became unconscious and said, "Weep to Hubal; don't you see your grave is being made ready and that your mother is almost bereft of you? What do you think? Supposing we were to reverse it away from you and then filled the grave with stones and threw in it al-Fuṣal who passed by and said he would take your place, thinking he would not do so. Will you thank your Lord and pray and abandon the religion of those who worship idols and who go astray?" "Yes," I replied. The voice said, "Get up; you are made healthy."'"

He went on, "So the man was cured and al-Fuṣal died and was put in his grave."

Al-Juhaynī stated, "And I saw that man of the Juhayna tribe after that; he was praying, cursing the idols and striking them."

Al-Umawī said that ʿAbd Allāh related to him, saying that once, when ʿUmar b. al-Khaṭṭāb, God be pleased with him, was in a gathering where they were discussing the spirits Khuraym b. Fātik al-Asadī said, "Should I tell you how I came to adopt Islam?" "Yes, do," he said.

"I was once searching for a young she-camel of mine, following a trail of hers that went up and down till finally I was at Abraq al-ʿAzzāf. There I tied my camel-mount down and spoke the words, 'I claim protection from the chief spirit of this place; I claim protection from the leader of this valley.' When I had done so, a voice called out the following verses,

> 'Woe to you! Seek protection with the Lord of majesty, glory, exaltation, and precedence
> And then recite verses from (*sūrat*) *al-Anfāl*, saying that God is One, and do not worry.'

"I was dumbfounded, but once regaining my wits, I said,

'O voice what is it you say? Is it truth you have, or falsehood? Make plain, may God guide you, what is the way?'

"It spoke again:

> 'This is the Messenger of God, he who does good deeds, at Yathrib, who calls to salvation,
> Who commands piety, prayer and restrains people from sins.'

"I said, 'I'll not rest till I come to him, and believe in him.' I then set my foot in the stirrup of my mount and spoke the verses,

> 'Guide me, guide me on the right course, may you never hunger or lack shelter so long as you live.
> May you never cease being a lord of strength; don't keep the good you were granted from all the spirits as long as you live.'

"He replied,

> 'May God accompany you and lead your mount; may He enhance your wage and protect your soul;
> Believe in Him, may my Lord grant you success, and give him a great victory as he will you.'

"'Who are you; may God forgive you. Tell me so I can inform him when I come to him.' He replied, 'I am Mālik b. Mālik and am his chief over the spirits of Naṣībīn. Your camel is being protected until I reunite it with your people, if God wills it.'"

The narrator went on, "So I travelled on till I reached Medina; it was a Friday and people were on their way to the mosque. There the Prophet (ṢAAS) was upon the *minbar*, the pulpit, looking wonderful as he addressed the congregation. I told myself I would make my camel kneel at the door of the mosque until he prayed. Then I would go in to him, accept Islam and tell him of it. When I had set my camel down, out to me came Abū Dhar who said, 'Welcome, indeed welcome! We heard of your having become a Muslim, so come on in and pray.'

"I did so, and later went to the Messenger of God (ṢAAS) and he told me of my accepting Islam. I commented, 'Praise be to God!' He said, 'By the way, your friend did keep faith with you, that being his nature. He did lead your camel back to your people.'"

Al-Ṭabarānī related this anecdote in his discussion of the life of Khuraym b. Fātik in his encyclopedia. There he stated that al-Ḥusayn b. Isḥāq al-Yasīrī related to him, quoting Muḥammad b. Ibrāhīm al-Shāmī, quoting ʿAbd Allāh b. Mūsā al-Iskandarī, quoting Muḥammad b. Isḥāq, from Saʿīd b. Abū Saʿīd al-Maqburī, from Abū Hurayra, who said that Khuraym b. Fātik said to ʿUmar b. al-Khaṭṭāb, "O Commander of the Faithful, may I tell you how I came to accept Islam?" "Certainly," he replied.

He then recounted it as above except for saying, "Then Abū Bakr al-Ṣiddīq, 'the trusting', came out and said, 'Come inside. We have heard about your accepting Islam.' I replied, 'But I don't know how to cleanse myself properly.' So he taught me how and afterwards I went in to the mosque where I saw the Messenger of God (ṢAAS) looking really happy and saying, 'There is no single Muslim who has performed the ablutions, and done so properly, who then has prayed, learned it by heart and understood it, who will not enter paradise.'

"ʿUmar then told me, 'Bring us some proof of this (your conversion) or I will punish you severely.' So a sheikh of Quraysh, ʿUthmān b. ʿAffān, testified on my behalf and his testimony was accepted."

The same source then related this anecdote from Muḥammad b. ʿUthmān b. Abū Shayba, from Muḥammad b. Taym, from Muḥammad b. Khalīfa, from Muḥammad b. al-Ḥasan, from his father, who said, "ʿUmar b. al-Khaṭṭāb said to Khuraym b. Fātik, 'Tell me some *ḥadīth* I will enjoy.'" He then related the story exactly as in the first version.

Abū Nuʿaym stated that Sulaymān b. Aḥmad related to him, quoting Abū ʿAbd al-Mālik Aḥmad b. Ibrāhīm al-Qurashī al-Dimashqī, quoting Sulaymān b. ʿAbd al-Raḥmān, the son of Shuraḥbīl's daughter, quoting Ismāʿīl b. Ayyāsh, from Yaḥyā b. Abū ʿAmr al-Shaybānī, from ʿAbd Allāh b. al-Daylamī, who said that a man came to Ibn ʿAbbās and said, "We have heard that you, in reference to Saṭīḥ, maintain that God created him. But why would He have created of mankind anyone like him?" He replied, "Yes, God did create Saṭīḥ al-Ghassānī out of flesh over strips of palm bark. He had no bones or sinews except for his skull and his two hands. He was folded over from his feet to his collarbone as a robe is folded; the only part of him that moved was his tongue. When he wanted to travel to Mecca, he was carried on a board and brought there. Four men of Quraysh went out to greet him, they being ʿAbd Shams and Hāshim, the sons of ʿAbd Manāf b. Quṣayy, al-Aḥwaṣ b. Fihr, and ʿUqayl b. Abū Waqqāṣ. They pretended different identities and told him, 'We are men of Jumaḥ who have come to you. We heard of your arrival so thought we would come to you; our doing so is a right of yours and a duty of ours.' ʿUqayl presented him with an Indian platter and a straight Rudaynī lance which were placed by the door of the holy *kaʿba* to determine whether or not Saṭīḥ would see them.

"Saṭīḥ spoke: 'O ʿUqayl, give me your hand.' ʿUqayl did so and Saṭīḥ continued, 'O ʿUqayl, by the hidden world, by Him who forgives sins, by the pact that is fulfilled and by the *kaʿba* that is built, you have presented me with a gift, the Indian platter and the straight Rudaynī spear.' They replied, 'You are right, O Saṭīḥ!' He then said, 'By Him who brings joy, by the rainbow, by all other joys, by the orphan lying prostrate, by the palm trees, the fresh plants, and by the dates, the crow as it passed by presented itself and made known that your group is not of Jumaḥ, and that their ancestry is of great Quraysh.' They replied, 'You are right, O Saṭīḥ! We are of those who guard the holy *kaʿba*; we have come to visit you because of what we have learned of your knowledge. So tell us what will happen in this time of ours and what will come hereafter; perhaps you do have knowledge of that.'"

He replied, "Now you are telling the truth! Take the following from me and from what God has inspired me with. You, O Arabs, are in the age of senility; your mental perception is the same as that of the non-Arabs. You have neither knowledge nor understanding. But from your descendants there will come people of understanding who will seek out all kinds of knowledge. They will destroy the idols, reach the dam, kill foreigners, and seek after booty."

They then asked, "But who will those men be, Saṭīḥ?" He replied, "By the pillared house, by security, and by tranquillity, after you there will be your descendants; it is they who will destroy the idols, forbid the worship of Satan, worship the All-Merciful alone, spread the best of all religions, honour the building (the *ka‘ba*), and ask judgements of the young heroes."

"Whose progeny will they be?" they asked.

"By the most noble of all, by Him who communicates with the nobles, by Him who moves the winding dunes, by Him who multiplies by doubling, thousands will arise from the line of ‘Abd Shams and ‘Abd Manāf, and there will be disputation over this."

"O Saṭīḥ," they commented, "what misery there will be for them, from what you tell us you know. From what land will those men come?"

He replied, "By Him who will remain everlasting, by Him who will reach eternity, there will come forth from this land a young man who will guide to what is right, who will reject the idol Yaghūth and illusion, who will be innocent of worshipping what is repugnant; he will worship one Lord alone. And then God will cause him to die, with all praise. From the earth he will be missed; in heaven he will be witnessed. After him *al-ṣiddīq* ("the trusting", i.e. Abū Bakr) will come to rule; when he judges he speaks the truth and in restoring right he is neither foolish nor intemperate. Then he will be followed to power by *al-ḥanīf*, ("the true believer", i.e. the Caliph ‘Umar), he who puts to the test and is lordly, a man who disavows violent language, who gives hospitality to guests, and who is wise and prudent in his judgements. Then there will follow him a man who will be demanding and invite others to the cause, and various groups and factions will assemble about him. Then they will kill him out of envy and rage; the old man will be seized and hacked to pieces and men will speak orations over him.[73] Then will follow *al-nāṣir*, "the protector", a man who will confuse right opinion with that of the unfriendly ones. Soldiers will rule over the earth. Then after him his son will reign, and take what he gathers yet gain little praise. He will consume his wealth and eat alone. Those after him of his progeny will expand that wealth. Following him will rule a number of kings; doubtless there will be much blood spilled over them. After them will come the beggars, who will soon be folded up like cloth. Then will come a strong and ruthless man, who destroys justice, subjugates Egypt and conquers the earth with brutality. Then will come a man short of stature, who will have a mark on his back, die violently and so good-bye! Then for a while a young man will rule who will leave the kingdom ruined. His brother will succeed him and continue the same way, concerning himself with wealth-gathering and speech-making. After him a fool will rule, a worldly, comfort-loving and spoiled man. His intimates and family will advise him, then rise up against him, depose him from rule and kill him. Then after him will rule *al-sābi‘*, "the seventh", who will leave the kingdom a wasteland. His sons in his rule will be like those who are deformed, all of them. After that,

73. The assassinated Caliph ‘Uthmān is clearly implied.

every destitute fellow will hunger for rule. He will be followed by the greedy one. A group of Qaḥṭān will favour Nizār when they meet at Damascus, in two groups between Bunyān and Lubnān. Yemen at that time will consist of two parties, those engaging in consultation, and those holding back. Nothing will be seen except failure and disintegration, prisoners in chains surrounded by swords and horses. Thereafter dwellings will be demolished, widows will be plundered, pregnant women will miscarry, and earthquakes will occur. Wā'il will seek the Caliphate and Nizār will be furious. Slaves and evil men will be favoured, while the best of men will be in disfavour. Prices will rise, in the month of Ṣafar, and people will kill each other. Then they will move into trenches which will have hair-cloth and trees to block the rivers, and he will defeat them early in the day. The best will appear, but neither sleep nor decision will avail them. (This will continue) until he enters one of the chief cities, where death and fate will overcome him. The archers will come and assemble on foot, to kill the mail-clad warriors and to capture the defenders. The evil-doers will perish; there he will be seized, at the headwaters. Then religion will die out, all things fall into disarray, the Scriptures are disbelieved, the bridges are demolished, and the only ones who escape are those on islands in the seas. Then the seeds will go bad, the bedouin will appear, there not being among them anyone to warn them against what is immoral and sinful, at a time of great difficulty, if people had decency, but alas! Wishful thinking will do no good."

They asked, "What then, Saṭīḥ?" He replied, "Then there will appear a man from the people of Yemen, a man like a strong, thick rope, and through him God will abolish dissension."

The above material is a strange relic. We have recorded it here for its peculiarity, and for the references to the dissensions and battles it includes.

The story of Shiqq and Saṭīḥ with Rabīʿa b. Naṣr, king of Yemen, and how he announced the coming of the Messenger of God (ṢAAS) has been given above. Similarly we already recounted the story of Saṭīḥ with his nephew ʿAbd al-Masīḥ, when the king of the Banū Sāsān sent him when the palace was shaken, the fires were extinguished, and the high priest had his visions. All that occurred on the night of the birth of him who, by his *sharīʿa*, superseded all other religions.

CHAPTER ON THE MANNER OF THE BEGINNING OF THE REVELATION TO THE MESSENGER OF GOD (ṢAAS) AND AN ACCOUNT OF THE FIRST REVELATION TO HIM FROM THE GLORIOUS QUR'ĀN.

This occurred when he was 40 years of age.

Ibn Jarīr recounted, from Ibn ʿAbbās and Saʿīd b. al-Musayyib, that his age at the time was 43.

Al-Bukhārī stated that Yaḥyā b. Bukayr related to him, quoting al-Layth, from ʿUqayl, from Ibn Shihāb, from ʿUrwa b. al-Zubayr, from ʿĀʾisha, God be pleased with her, who said, "The first indication of revelation to the Messenger of God (ṢAAS) came in the form of true visions in his sleep. Every vision he had came like the breaking of dawn.

"He then developed a liking for solitude. He would spend time alone in the cave Ḥirāʾ, where he would seek religious purification through devotions. He would stay there many nights and then return to his family for more provisions to continue doing so; then he would come down to Khadīja and repeat the same.

"Eventually the truth came to him while he was there in that cave Ḥirāʾ.

"The angel came and told him, 'Read!' He replied, 'I don't read.' He then said, 'The angel then overpowered me and choked me until I could bear it no more, and then he released me. Again he said, 'Read!' Again I replied, 'I don't read.' Once more he overpowered me and choked me till I could bear it no more, then he released me and said, 'Read!' I replied, 'I don't read.' Again he overpowered me and choked me a third time until I could bear it no more. Then he released me and said, 'Read in the name of your Lord who created; He created man from a clot. Read! Your Lord is the most noble, He who taught by the pen. He taught man what he did not know' (*sūrat al-ʿAlaq*, XCVI, v.1–5).

"The Messenger of God (ṢAAS) returned home with this, his heart palpitating. He went in to Khadīja, daughter of Khuwaylid, and said, 'Wrap me up! Wrap me up!' They did so until the terror left him.

"He then spoke to Khadīja, telling her what had happened, saying, 'I was afraid for myself.'

"Khadīja replied, 'Oh no! I swear by God He would never abuse you. You maintain family ties, you are hospitable to guests, you support the weak, provide for the poor and help out when tragedy strikes.'

"Khadīja then hurried off with him to Waraqa b. Nawfal b. Asad b. ʿAbd al-ʿUzzā, who was her cousin. He had earlier become a Christian, and used to write the Hebrew script, copying out from the Bible in Hebrew whatever God inspired him to write. He was an old man by then, and he was blind.

"Khadīja told him, 'O cousin! Listen to your nephew!' Waraqa then addressed him, 'O nephew, what did you see?' The Messenger of God (ṢAAS) then told him what he had seen. Waraqa commented, 'This was the angel Gabriel who used to come down to Moses. How I wish I were a young man again! I hope I am still alive when your people exile you!' The Messenger of God (ṢAAS) exclaimed, 'Are they to exile me?' 'Yes,' he replied, 'no one has ever received what you have without being treated as an enemy. If I am alive when your time comes, I will give you every help.'

"Not long thereafter Waraqa died, and the revelation waned for a period, so that the Messenger of God (ṢAAS) was so depressed – as we have been told –

that he would frequently feel like throwing himself down from the summits of high mountains. Whenever he reached the top of a mountain, to throw himself down, Gabriel would appear and say, 'O Muḥammad, you are in truth the Messenger of God!' This would relieve his distress and he would return down. And if the inspiration was again long in coming, he would feel and do the same."

Another account gives the same wording, except that it substitutes the word "when" for the word "whenever" above.

The account is given in full in this way in the *Bāb al-Taʿbīr* (*The Chapter on Expression*) in al-Bukhārī's work.

Ibn Shihāb stated that Abū Salama b. ʿAbd al-Raḥmān informed him that Jābir b. ʿAbd Allāh al-Anṣārī said, in relating matters concerning the revelation period, that the Prophet (ṢAAS) said, "While I was walking, I heard a voice from the sky. I raised my sight and there was the angel who had come to me at Ḥirāʾ seated on a throne between the sky and the earth. I was terrified and returned home, saying, 'Wrap me up! Wrap me up!' And so God revealed the verse, 'O you who are all wrapped up! Arise and give warning! And glorify your Lord! Purify your garments! And shun idolatry!' (*sūrat al-Muddaththir*, LXXIV, v.1–5). And the revelation became stronger and continued uninterrupted."

Al-Bukhārī added that ʿAbd Allāh b. Yūsuf and Abū Ṣāliḥ gave this tradition a further link, from al-Layth. And Hilāl b. Raddād added a link, from al-Zuhrī. Yūnus and Maʿmar, moreover, gave in the prior text the word *bawādir*, "emotions", in place of the word *fuʾād*, "heart".

This tradition was related by Imām al-Bukhārī, God be pleased with him, in various parts of his work. We have discussed it at length in our first commentary on al-Bukhārī, in the book on *The Beginnings of the Revelation*, in terms of both its chain of authorities and its text. And to God is all praise and grace.

In his *ṣaḥīḥ* collection, Muslim derives this tradition from an account of al-Layth, and through Yūnus and Maʿmar from al-Zuhrī, just as al-Bukhārī attributes it to their authority. In our own commentaries we referred to the additions made by Muslim and to his accounts of it. And to God be praise. Muslim's account of the above goes as far as the above words of Waraqa, "I will give you every help."

The statement, given above, of ʿĀʾisha, mother of the believers, that, "the first indication of revelation to the Messenger of God (ṢAAS) came in the form of true visions. Every vision he had came like the breaking of dawn" corroborates what Muḥammad b. Isḥāq b. Yasār related from ʿUbayd b. ʿUmayr al-Laythī, to the effect that the Prophet (ṢAAS) said, "And Gabriel brought me while I was asleep a piece of silk brocade cloth with writing on it. He told me, 'Read!' I replied, 'What should I read?' Thereupon he choked me till I thought it meant death. But then he released me." He related the rest of ʿĀʾisha's statement in the same words.

This came as a prelude to the awakening that followed. The Prophet (ṢAAS) is reported to have expressly stated this in the book on the *maghāzī*, the military campaigns, by Mūsā b. ʿUqba, from al-Zuhrī; therein it states that he saw all that in a dream, and that the angel appeared to him thereafter when he was awake.

The *ḥāfiẓ* Abū Nuʿaym al-Aṣbahānī stated in his work *Dalāʾil al-Nubuwwa* (*Signs of the Prophethood*) as follows, "Muḥammad b. Aḥmad b. al-Ḥasan related to us, quoting Muḥammad b. ʿUthmān b. Abū Shayba, quoting Janāb b. al-Ḥārith, quoting ʿAbd Allāh b. al-Ajlaḥ, from Ibrāhīm, from ʿAlqama b. Qays, who said, 'The first visitation to prophets is during their sleep, so that they will remain calm; revelation comes thereafter.' This comment comes directly from ʿAlqama b. Qays himself. It is an appropriate one that is substantiated by both what preceded and what followed it."

A DISCUSSION OF THE AGE OF THE PROPHET (ṢAAS) AT THE TIME OF HIS RECEIVING THE MISSION AND THE DATE THEREOF.

Imām Aḥmad stated that Muḥammad b. Abū ʿAdī related to him, from Dāwūd b. Abū Hind, from ʿĀmir al-Shaʿbī, that the Messenger of God (ṢAAS) received his mission when he was 40 years old. The angel Isrāfīl was entrusted with his prophethood for three years, during which he would teach him words and facts; the Qurʾān was not revealed then. After those three years Gabriel was entrusted with his prophethood and the Qurʾān was revealed through his voice over a 20-year period, 10 in Mecca and 10 in Medina. The Prophet (ṢAAS) died when he was 63 years old.

This chain of authorities back to al-Shaʿbī is a correct one. It establishes that Isrāfīl was entrusted with him for a 3-year period after his age of 40, and that Gabriel came thereafter.

Sheikh Shihāb al-Dīn Abū Shāma, however, has stated, "ʿĀʾisha's account does not refute this. It is possible that first of all he did receive visions, and that Isrāfīl was put in charge of him during the period he spent alone in Ḥirāʾ, casting words at him at speed and not actually staying with him, and teaching him gradually. This was so until Gabriel came to him and taught him, after having throttled him three times. And so ʿĀʾisha related what had happened to him with Gabriel and did not tell what had occurred with Isrāfīl in order to shorten the account. Or she did not know about the story of Isrāfīl."

Imām Aḥmad stated that Yaḥyā b. Hishām recounted to him, from ʿIkrima, from Ibn ʿAbbās who said, "The Qurʾān was revealed to the Prophet (ṢAAS) when he was 43 years of age. He stayed in Mecca for 10 years and lived in Medina for 10. He died at the age of 63."

Yaḥyā b. Saʿīd and Saʿīd b. al-Musayyib related the same. Then both Aḥmad b. Ghundar and Yazīd b. Hārūn related from Hishām, from ʿIkrima, from Ibn

ʿAbbās, that he said, "The Messenger of God (ṢAAS) received his mission and the Qurʾān was revealed to him when he was 40 years old. He stayed in Mecca for 13 years, and in Medina for 10. He died at the age of 63."

Imām Aḥmad stated that ʿAffān related to him, quoting Ḥammād b. Salama, quoting ʿAmmār b. Abū ʿAmmār, from Ibn ʿAbbās who said, "The Prophet (ṢAAS) lived in Mecca for 15 years, for 7 of which he was seeing the light and hearing the voice, and then for 8 years while he was receiving revelation. He lived in Medina for 10 years."

Abū Shāma stated, "The Messenger of God used to see strange visions before his mission."

On this same subject there is the material in the *ṣaḥīḥ* collection of Muslim, on the authority of Jābir b. Samura, who said that the Messenger of God (ṢAAS) stated, "I know a rock in Mecca that would greet me before I received my mission. I still know it now." The statement ended thus.

The Messenger of God (ṢAAS) only preferred the seclusion and being alone from his people because of the clear error in which he saw them engaged. This was in their worshipping and prostrating before idols. His liking for being alone increased as God's revelation to him came closer (ṢAAS).

Muḥammad b. Isḥāq recounted, from ʿAbd al-Mālik b. ʿAbd Allāh b. Abū Sufyān b. al-ʿAlāʾ b. Ḥāritha – who was, he said a very attentive listener – from a certain scholar who said, "The Messenger of God (ṢAAS) used to go out to Ḥirāʾ for one month every year and pray alone, he being one of those Quraysh men who would, in the *jāhiliyya*, practise this prayer in seclusion. He would feed the poor who would come to him. Having left there he would not re-enter his own home without first circumambulating the *kaʿba*."

This was related similarly from Wahb b. Kaysān, to the effect that he heard ʿUbayd b. ʿUmayr telling ʿAbd Allāh b. al-Zubayr a similar account.

This shows that it was a custom for religious-minded men of Quraysh to go and stay on Ḥirāʾ for prayer. This is why Abū Ṭālib spoke the following line in his famous ode:

> "By Thawr and by Him who established Thabīr in its place, and by those who ascend to Ḥirāʾ, and then descend."

This is the correct form for the recitation of this verse, as mentioned by al-Suhaylī, Abū Shāma and our Sheikh, the *ḥāfiẓ* Abū al-Ḥajjāj al-Mizzī, God be pleased with them all. Some reciters made a mistake in this verse, making it read, "and by those who go up to ascend in *ḥar*, 'heat', and descend." This version is weak and incorrect. Though God alone knows best.

The word Ḥirāʾ is sometimes treated as contracted or lengthened, declined or indeclinable. It is a mountain in the heights over Mecca, three miles distant from it, to the left side of the path to Minā. It has a summit that overlooks the *kaʿba* to one side, and the cave is on that side. How splendid is the verse of Ruʾba b. al-ʿAjjāj:

> "But no, by the Lord of the secure (pigeons) dwelling (at the *kaʿba*), and by the Lord of a corner Ḥirāʾ, sloping downwards . . ."

The explanation (by al-Bukhārī) that *al-Taḥannuth* means devotion, is one interpreted from the context. Otherwise, the truth of *al-Taḥannuth*, as interpreted from its form, lies in what al-Suhaylī suggested, namely, "entering into *al-ḥinth*", i.e. sin or perjury. However, a few words in the language were heard to mean "the departure from" rather than "entering into". These words have a form like the verb *taḥannatha*, i.e. "he left the state of *ḥinth*". Examples would be *taḥawwaba*, i.e. "he abstained from crime", and *taḥarraja*, i.e. "he kept away from sin", and *taʾaththama*, i.e. "he abstained from iniquity". Similarly there is *tahajjada*, a word meaning to give up *al-hujūd*, sleep to attend prayer. Also there are *tanajjasa*, "he left an impure state", i.e. he cleaned himself, and *taqadhdhara*, "he avoided foul actions". Abū Shāma cited this example.

Ibn al-Aʿrābī was asked about his interpreting *yataḥannathu* as meaning "he performs his devotions", and he replied, "Well, I don't actually know that, but there is the example of *yataḥannafu*, derived from the word *al-ḥanifiyya*, signifying the religion of Abraham, peace be upon him."

Ibn Hishām stated, "The Arabs say *al-taḥannuth* and *al-taḥannuf* (as having the same meaning), where the letter *f* has replaced the letter *th*. This is similar to the change from *jaddafa* to *jadhdhafa*, both meaning "he rowed a boat". As Ruʾba's verse goes,

> ". . . if my stones were with *al-ajdhāf* . . .", by which he means *al-ajdāth* (the graves).

Abū ʿUbayda related to me that the bedouin say *fumma* for *thumma*, meaning "then".

I would add that some commentators say *wa fūmuhā* when they mean *wa thūmuhā*, when referring to *thūm*, i.e. "garlic".

The scholars differ over the devotion to prayer of the prophet (ṢAAS) before his mission, whether he was following some religion, and what that was.

Some say that it was the religion of Noah.

Others suggest that of Abraham, it being the most similar as well as the most powerful.

Others say that of Moses, yet others that of Jesus.

Others say that all that is established is that he did have a religion, and that he followed and observed it.

For the interpretation of these statements and the circumstances in which they were made, one should look elsewhere in works on the origins of Islamic jurisprudence. But God knows best.

The words "eventually the truth came suddenly to him while he was in the cave Ḥirāʾ" mean that it came to him abruptly and unexpectedly. As God stated, "And you had no hope that the Book would be delivered to you, but it is a mercy from your Lord" (*sūrat al-Qaṣaṣ*, XXVIII, v.86).

The first portion of this holy chapter, namely "Read in the name of your Lord who created; He created man from a clot. Read! Your Lord is the most noble, He who taught by the pen. He taught man what he did not know" (*sūrat al-ʿAlaq*, XCVI, v.1–5) was the first part of the Qurʾān revealed, as we established in the commentary and in what will follow; it came on a Monday.

It has been similarly affirmed in the *ṣaḥīḥ* collection of Muslim, on the authority of Abū Qatāda, that the Messenger of God (ṢAAS) was asked about fasting on Mondays. He replied, "That is a day on which I was born, and a day on which I received revelation."

Ibn ʿAbbās stated, "Your prophet Muḥammad (ṢAAS) was born on a Monday, and he was made a prophet on a Monday."

ʿUbayd b. ʿUmayr, Abū Jaʿfar al-Baqīr, and several other scholars similarly stated that he received revelation on a Monday; this is a matter undisputed among them.

It is said, moreover, that that occurred during the month of Rabīʿ al-Awwal; it has also been previously stated from Ibn ʿAbbās and Jābir that he was born on the 12th of Rabīʿ al-Awwal, received his mission on the same date, and also on that day he was raised to heaven.

It is also widely believed that he received his mission in Ramaḍān, as has been stated by ʿUbayd b. ʿUmayr, Muḥammad b. Isḥāq and others.

Ibn Isḥāq stated this, using as evidence God's statement "the month of Ramaḍān, during which the Qurʾān was revealed as a guidance to mankind" (*sūrat al-Baqara*, II, v.185). And it is said that this was on the 10th.

Al-Wāqidī attributed to Jaʿfar al-Bāqir, to whom his chain of authorities extended, the words, "The beginning of the revelation to the Messenger of God (ṢAAS) occurred on Monday, the 17th of Ramaḍān; others, however, say it was the 24th."

Imām Aḥmad stated that Abū Saʿīd, a freed-man of the Banū Hāshim, related to him, quoting ʿUmrān Abū al-ʿAwwām, from Qatāda, from Abū al-Malīḥ, from Wāthila b. al-Asqaʿ, that the Messenger of God (ṢAAS) said, "The tablets of Abraham were revealed on the first night of Ramaḍān, the Torah on the 6th of Ramaḍān, and the Bible on the 13th of Ramaḍān, while the Qurʾān was revealed on the 14th of Ramaḍān."

Ibn Mardawayh related much the same in a tradition back to the Prophet

(ṢAAS) that is based on the authority of Jābir b. ᶜAbd Allāh.

Therefore, a majority of the Companions and followers of the Prophet (ṢAAS) have concluded that the *laylat al-qadar*, the "night of destiny", was the 24th.

Regarding Gabriel's order "Read!", the reply was, "I don't read." The truth is that this statement, "I don't read", is a negation, that is, it implies, "I am not a man who knows how to read well." Among those who prefer this interpretation are al-Nawawī and, before him, Sheikh Abū Shāma.

Those who interpret this as interrogatory are incorrect, because the prefixed *bā᾽*, as in *mā anā biqārī*, i.e. "I don't read", is not added if the intent is to affirm.

The first interpretation is substantiated by what Abū Nuᶜaym related from a *ḥadīth* that comes down through al-Muᶜtamir b. Sulaymān from his father who said that the Messenger of God (ṢAAS) said, fearful and shaking, "I have never read a document; I don't do that well. I neither read nor write." And so Gabriel seized him and choked him violently. He then released him and told him, "Read!" Muḥammad (ṢAAS) then replied, "I don't see anything to read; and I don't read, or write."

It is also read in the form *fa ghaṭṭanī* or *wa ghaṭṭanī* in the two *ṣaḥīḥ* collections, or *qad ghaṭṭanī*. These all mean "he choked me". The phrase *ḥattā balagha minnī al-juhd*, "till I could bear it no more", is read either with a *ḍamma* or with a *fatḥa* on the *j* (i.e. *al-juhd* or *al-jahd*); also with a *fatḥa* or a *ḍamma* on the third letter, *d*, for either the nominative or the accusative case (i.e. *al-juhdu* or *al-juhda*). He, Gabriel, did this to him three times.

Abū Sulaymān al-Khaṭṭābī stated, "Gabriel only did that to test his patience and to discipline him so that he would be agreeable to bear the burdens of prophethood placed upon him. Because of these burdens he would be gripped by a feverish condition and have a high temperature, that is, he would breathe hard and sweat profusely."

Others say that Gabriel acted in this way for various reasons. He wanted to awaken him to the gravity of what was being placed upon him by treating him in such a distressing fashion. As God Almighty stated, "We are indeed placing upon you a heavy message" (*sūrat al-Muzzammil*, LXXIII, v.5). This is why, when revelation came to him, his face would turn red and he would breathe heavily and fast, like a young camel, while his forehead would stream with perspiration on an extremely cold day.

Regarding the statement quoted above, "The Messenger (ṢAAS) returned home to Khadīja with this, his heart palpitating", there is a variant reading of *bawādir* for the word *fu᾽ād*, "heart", that is. Abū ᶜUbayda explains this word as referring to the flesh between the shoulder and the neck. Others interpret the word as referring to veins that tremble because of fear.

Some readings substitute the word *baādiluhu*, singular *bādila* or *bādil*, for that which palpitates. This would refer to the area between the neck and the collarbone. Others interpret it as the base of the breast, or as the flesh of the breast. There are also other interpretations of the word.

Regarding the phrase, "Wrap me up! Wrap me up!", when his terror had calmed he asked Khadīja, "What is wrong with me? What was it appeared to me?" and then related what had happened. He then said, "I was afraid for myself." This was because he had witnessed something he had never experienced or imagined before.

That was why Khadīja said to him, "Be of good cheer! Oh no! I swear by God, He would never abuse you." The word for "abuse" here is from *al-khizy* (disgrace); others say the word is from *al-ḥuzn*, meaning sadness, that is, "He would never sadden you."

This statement relates to her knowledge of the fine behaviour characteristics God had instilled in him, and that those endowed with the qualities of goodness would not be abused in this world or the hereafter.

She then made reference to those exemplary traits that made his fine character. She said, "You maintain family ties, you are truthful." The Prophet (ṢAAS) was famous for that among those both who agreed and disagreed with him.

The words *wa taḥmilu al-kalla*, i.e, "you carry the burden", that is, you do so for others imply "you provide for those in need what will alleviate their burden of supporting their family".

The phrase *wa taksibu al-maʿdūma*, translated here as "you provide for the poor", means that you hurry to do good by giving to the poor before others do so. The poor are called by the term *al-maʿdūm* because they are lacking in their lives, their existence or "non-existence" (a meaning also of this word) being the same. As a certain poet said,

> "He who is relieved by death did not die; there are those who are dead though they are still living."

Abū al-Ḥasan al-Tihāmī said, as was reported from him by *al-qāḍī*, the judge, ʿIyāḍ, in the exegesis of Muslim,

"The poor can be considered dead, their clothing a threadbare winding-sheet, their shelter the grave."

Al-Khaṭṭābī stated, "The correct text is *tuksib al-muʿdim*, meaning 'you give generously to them' or that you provide earnings for the poor by giving them money by which they can live."

Our teacher, the *ḥāfiẓ* Abū al-Ḥajjāj al-Mizzī, preferred to interpret "al-maʿdūm" here as referring to the money being given, that is he gave money to those without it.

Some interpret this phrase to mean, "you earn by doing business with goods that are *maʿdūm*", meaning unavailable, or valuable and scarce. But this is far-fetched and contentious and contrived without basis. Such interpretations are rarely found laudable and ʿIyāḍ and al-Nawawī and others find these interpretations weak. But God knows best!

The words *wa taqrī al-ḍayf* translated above as "you are hospitable to guests", mean that you honour them by offering them food and good accommodation.

The phrase *tuʿīnu ʿalā nawāʾib al-ḥaqq* (the final word here being also given as *al-khayr*) translated above as "and help them out when tragedy strikes", means that if someone is struck by misfortune, you assist them; that is, you stand by them till they find some means of livelihood.

Regarding the words, "Khadīja then hurried off with him to Waraqa b. Nawfal . . . he was an old man by then, and blind."

We gave some information concerning Waraqa in material above relating to Zayd b. ʿAmr b. Nufayl, God have mercy on him. We told how he had become a Christian before the coming of Islam and how he had left and travelled to Syria accompanied by Zayd b. ʿAmr, ʿUthmān b. al-Ḥuwayrith and ʿUbayd Allāh b. Jaḥsh. All of these became Christians because they found Christianity to be at that time the religion closest to the truth.

Zayd b. ʿAmr b. Nufayl, however, considered that there were certain innovations, changes, corruptions and interpretations that had occurred in it that prevented him from embracing it. The rabbis and monks told him, moreover, about a prophet whose time was near.

He therefore returned seeking information about this, while continuing to believe in one God, as he had before. But death cut him down before the mission of Muḥammad (ṢAAS).

Waraqa b. Nufayl did adopt Christianity, and used to try to prognosticate it in the Messenger of God (ṢAAS) as we have said above, from the way in which Khadīja would describe and characterize him. She told Waraqa of the fine, pure qualities he had, and of the signs and indications there were upon him.

Therefore when there occurred as above, she took the hand of the Messenger of God (ṢAAS) and said, "O Cousin, listen to what happened to your nephew." And when the Messenger of God (ṢAAS) related to him what he had seen, Waraqa replied, "By the All-Glorious God, this was the angel Gabriel who came down to Moses!"

He did not mention Jesus, though he came later, after Moses, because the system of religion of Muḥammad (ṢAAS) was to be a completion and fulfilment of that sent to Moses, upon both of whom be peace. The valid opinion of the scholars, in what they say on this point, is that the *sharīʿa* complemented, and also abrogated, certain things in the system of Moses. As God said, "And so that I may make permissible to you some of what was forbidden to you" (*sūrat Āl-ʿImrān*, III, v.49).

This comment made by Waraqa is similar to that made by the spirits, namely, "O our people, we have heard a book revealed after Moses verifying what was before it, guiding to the truth and to the straight path" (*sūrat al-Aḥqāf*, XLVI, v.30).

Waraqa then commented, "How I wish I were a young man again!" This implies, "How I wish I were a lad endowed with faith, useful knowledge, and good work to do."

The phrase: "I hope I am still alive when your people exile you", implies "so that I can leave with you and help you".

To this the Prophet (ṢAAS) responded, "Are they to exile me?" According to al-Suhaylī he said this because to be parted from one's homeland is very painful. To this Waraqa replied, "Yes, no one has ever received what you have received without being treated as an enemy. If I am alive when your time comes, I will give you every help." That is, "I will strive hard to help you always."

The words, "Not long thereafter Waraqa died" mean that his death came shortly after this event; may God have mercy on him and bless him. For what is told of him here constitutes credence in what had occurred, faith in the revelation that had come, and good intent for the future.

The Imām Aḥmad stated that Ḥasan related to him, from Ibn Lahīʿa, quoting Abū al-Aswad, from ʿUrwa, from ʿĀʾisha, that Khadīja asked the Messenger of God (ṢAAS) about Waraqa b. Nawfal. He replied, "I saw him; and on him I saw white clothing. And if he were among those of hell, he would not have on white clothing."

This chain of authorities is good, but al-Zuhrī and Hishām related it from ʿUrwa in an incomplete line. So God alone knows best.

The *ḥāfiẓ* Abū Yaʿlā recounted, from Shurayḥ b. Yūnus, from Ismāʿīl, from Mujāhid, from al-Shaʿbī, from Jābir b. ʿAbd Allāh, that the Messenger of God (ṢAAS) was asked about Waraqa b. Nawfal and he replied, "I saw him; and I saw on him white clothing. I observed him in the heart of paradise and he was wearing a silken robe."

He was asked about Zayd b. ʿAmr b. Nufayl, and he replied, "He will be resurrected on Judgement Day as one nation by himself." He was asked about Abū Ṭālib and he replied, "I drew him forth from a deep pool in hell to a shallow shore of it."

He was asked about Khadīja because she died before the rules and ordinances prescribed in the Qurʾān. He said, "I saw her beside a river in paradise in a house made of reeds where there was no noise or hardship."

The chain of authorities for this is good, and there are testimonies corroborating some of it in the *ṣaḥīḥ* collections. But God knows best.

The *ḥāfiẓ* Abū Bakr al-Bazzār stated that ʿUbayd b. Ismāʿīl related to him, quoting Abū Usāma, from Ḥishām b. ʿUrwa, from his father, from ʿĀʾisha, who said that the Messenger of God (ṢAAS) said, "Do not revile Waraqa; I have seen a garden or two for him."

Ibn ῾Asākir related this similarly from a *ḥadīth* of Abū Sa῾īd al-Ashajjī, from Abū Mu῾āwiyyā᾿, from Hishām, from his father, from ῾Ā᾿isha, and this chain of authorities is excellent. And it is also told in a similar way through a chain that is incomplete.

The two *ḥufāz* al-Bayhaqī and Abū Nu῾aym related in both their works entitled *Dalā᾿il al-Nubuwwa* (*Signs of the Prophethood*) from a *ḥadīth* of Yūnus b. Bukayr, from Yūnus b. ῾Amr, from his father, from ῾Amr b. Sharaḥbīl, that the Messenger of God (ṢAAS) said to Khadīja, "When I was left to myself, I heard a cry and, by God, I feared that something terrible was going to happen."

She replied, "God forbid! He would never do anything to you! By God, you behave with loyalty, you maintain the ties of kinship, and speak truthfully."

And when Abū Bakr came in, the Messenger of God (ṢAAS) was no longer there so she recounted it all to him, saying, "Good old friend, go with Muḥammad to Waraqa."

When the Messenger of God came in, Abū Bakr took his hand and said, "Let's go at once to Waraqa." He asked, "Who told you?" "Khadīja." And so they went at once to Waraqa and related it to him. The Messenger of God (ṢAAS) told him, "When I am all alone I hear a voice behind me saying, 'Muḥammad! O Muḥammad!' So I rush off outside." Waraqa told him, "Don't do that. When it comes, stay right there to hear what it says to you. Then come and tell me." And when he was alone, the voice did call out again, saying, "Muḥammad! O Muḥammad! Say, 'In the name of God the most Merciful, the most Beneficent; praise be to God, Lord of the worlds . . ." And it continued right on (to the end of the *sūrat al-Fātiḥa*; I) to the words, *wa lā al-ḍālīna*, 'nor those who go astray'. It then said, "Say: 'There is no God but God!'"

So he went to Waraqa and told him that. Waraqa replied, "Rejoice, then rejoice again! I bear witness that you are he of whom the son of Mary spoke. What you have is like what came to the angel Gabriel for Moses. You are a Prophet from God. You will be ordered into the struggle some time hereafter. And if I live that long, I will fight along with you!"

When he died the Messenger of God (ṢAAS) said, "I saw the priest in heaven wearing silken garments, because he believed in me and believed what I said." He was referring to Waraqa.

This text is from al-Bayhaqī, and its chain of authorities is not fully complete. It is also strange that according to this account it was the *surat al-Fātiḥa* (Qur᾿ān, I) that was revealed first.

We have given above some of the poetry of Waraqa that shows his concealed faith in him, his confidence in it and his dedication to it. This was when Khadīja told him what had happened when the Messenger of God (ṢAAS) had been with the youth Maysara, and how the cloud had been sheltering him in the extreme heat. Waraqa spoke some verses on that occasion, as we have already given above. These were:

"I persisted, being determined to recall both a matter that often inspired my tears
And a description from Khadīja, following (another) account; my waiting has been long, O Khadīja.
In the heart of Mecca, with my hoping because of your words, that I would see some solution.
From what you related as the words of a priest who was a monk, words I would hate to be wrong,
That Muḥammad will one day prevail and defeat whomever opposes him
Making a light appear in the land by which he will bring change to all creation.
Those who oppose him will meet defeat, while those who aid him will achieve success.
Would that I be there to witness, for I'll be the first of them in participating.
Sharing in that which Quraysh will hate, however much they bluster in their Mecca.
I aspire, through him whom they all hate, to reach the Enthroned One, even if they descend, aside.
Is it folly to not disbelieve in Him who chooses, He who raised the stars?
If they and I survive, things will happen at which the disbelievers will be sorely discomfited."

He also spoke the following verses in another ode:

"By news of veracity you foretold of Muḥammad, telling them about him, an adviser being absent,
Informing that the son of ʿAbd Allāh, Aḥmad, is sent to all men on earth.
My thought of him is that he will be sent to speak the truth, just as the two slaves Hūd and Ṣāliḥ were sent
And Moses and Abraham, so that a brightness will be seen and a clear emanation of the truth.
And there will follow him the two tribes of Luʾayy b. Ghālib, both the young men and the lordly greybeards.
And if I survive until his age arrives for man, then I will greet him in joy and love.
If not, then I will certainly, O Khadīja please know this, be travelling somewhere above the broad earth."

Yūnus b. Bukayr stated, on the authority of Ibn Isḥāq, that Waraqa also spoke the following:

"If it be true, O Khadīja, then know that your account to us means that Aḥmad is sent.
And Gabriel will bring to him, Michael being with them both, from God a revelation that relieves the heart sent down.
Through him there will succeed those who have success through repentance, and through him will suffer those in distress, those deceived and led astray.

Two groups of them there will be: one will go to God's gardens, and the other will be kept in pain within the enclosures of hell.

If they call out in woe therein, iron staffs will be inserted in their heads in succession, and be put in flames.

And so, glory be to Him at whose order the winds blow, and Who in all time does as He wishes,

He whose throne is above all the heavens, and He whose decrees made for those He has created may not be changed."

And Waraqa also said,

"O for men and the changes of time and fate, though in whatever God decrees there is no change

Until Khadīja calls me to tell her of a matter I see will come to people unawares.

She told me of something of which I had in the past, long, long ago already heard,

That Aḥmad would be visited by Gabriel and told, "You are sent forth to humankind."

And I replied,

"Perhaps what you wish for, God will fulfil for you; so hope for good and be patient!

Send him to us that we may question him about what it is he sees asleep, and when awake."

So when he came to us, he gave a wondrous speech, so as to make the skin creep, and the hair stand tall.

(He said) "I saw God's trusted servant facing me, in a figure made complete from the most magnificent of forms.

Then he continued on, while fear made me panic for what would save me from the anguish I was in."

I said, "I think, and I don't know if what I think will come true, that he will be sent forth to recite chapters to be revealed,

"And it will pain you if you call openly to them to engage in the struggle with neither inducement nor threat."

In his *al-Dalāʾil* (*The Signs*) the *ḥāfiẓ* al-Bayhaqī gave the text of these verses thus: I have doubts over whether they truly stem from Waraqa. But God knows best.

Ibn Isḥāq stated that ʿAbd al-Mālik b. ʿAbd Allāh b. Abū Sufyān b. al-ʿAlāʾ b. Jāriyya al-Thaqafī related to him – and he had a fine ear and memory – on the authority of a scholar, that the Messenger of God (ṢAAS), after God wished to honour him by the beginning of the prophethood, would walk far off to do his business, out of sight of dwellings. As he went off into the pathways of Mecca and deep into its valleys, every rock and tree he passed would greet him, saying, "Peace be upon you, O Messenger of God!" Hearing this, he would turn all around yet see nothing but the trees and rocks. This situation prevailed, with him seeing and hearing as long as God wished, until ultimately Gabriel brought God's honour upon him during Ramaḍān in Ḥirā'.

Ibn Isḥāq stated that Wahb b. Kaysān, the freed-man of the Zubayr tribe, related to him, that he heard ʿAbd Allāh b. al-Zubayr say to ʿUbayd b. ʿUmayr b. Qatāda al-Laythī, "Tell me, ʿUbayd, how was the beginning of the mission of the Messenger of God (ṢAAS) when Gabriel first came to him?" ʿUbayd replied, in my presence, talking to ʿAbd Allāh b. al-Zubayr and the others there with him, "The Messenger of God (ṢAAS) used to take up residence in Ḥirā' in seclusion for one month each year. This practice, known as *al-taḥannuth*, i.e. 'pious devotion', was one performed by Quraysh before the coming of Islam.

"While the Messenger of God (ṢAAS) was dwelling there for that month of each year, he would feed all the poor who came to him. When the period of that month of devotion was concluded, the first thing he would do was go to the *kaʿba*, circumambulating around it seven times or so before proceeding to his own home.

"This was so until that month came of the year when God honoured him with his mission. That month, it being Ramaḍān, he went off as usual for his devotions at Ḥirā', his family accompanying him. Then came the night when God did honour him with his mission, thereby having mercy on all men. Gabriel came to him then with the command of God Almighty.

"The Messenger of God (ṢAAS) said, 'He came to me while I was asleep, carrying a brocade cloth with writing upon it. He told me, "Read!" "Read what?" I asked. He then choked me so hard I thought I would die, but he released me and said, "Read!" "Read what?" I asked, so he choked me so hard I thought I would die. He then released me and said, "Read!" I asked, "What should I read?" I only said this to spare myself his doing the same to me again.

"'Then he said, "Read; in the name of your Lord who created. He created man from a clot. Read! Your Lord is the most noble, He who taught by the pen. He taught man what he did not know."

"'So I recited this, and then he had finished with me and left me. I awoke from my sleep, and it was as though a document had been inscribed into my heart.'

"He went on: 'I then went off into the mountains where I heard a voice from the sky saying, "O Muḥammad, you are the Messenger of God, and I am Gabriel!"

"'I raised my head up to the sky to look, and there was Gabriel in the image of a man, with his feet placed evenly across the horizons of the sky. He was saying, "O Muḥammad, you are the Messenger of God, and I am Gabriel."

"'I stood there looking up at him, neither advancing nor retreating, and began turning my head in all directions, but wherever I looked I still saw him.

"'I remained standing there thus, neither advancing nor retreating, until Khadīja sent her messengers to look for me. And they went all the way to Mecca and returned again to her while I still stood there where I was. Then he (Gabriel) left me.

"'I now returned to my family and sat down close beside Khadīja. She asked me, "Where were you, O father of al-Qāsim? I swear, I sent my messengers all the way to Mecca and back looking for you."

"'I then told her what I had seen, and she said, "Rejoice and be brave; by Him in whose hands Khadīja is, I hope you will be the prophet of this nation."'

"She then arose, dressed, and went off to Waraqa b. Nawfal to tell him what the Messenger of God (ṢAAS) had reported to her. Waraqa exclaimed, 'Holy of Holies! By Him in whose hands Waraqa is, if you have told me the truth, Khadīja, the Archangel Gabriel has come to him just as he did to Moses. He is to be the prophet of this nation! Tell him to be brave!'

"Khadīja returned to the Messenger of God (ṢAAS) and told him what Waraqa had said.

"When the Messenger of God (ṢAAS) had completed his period of secluded devotion, he did as always, going first to the *kaʿba* and circumambulating it. There he met Waraqa b. Nawfal who was also performing the circumambulation, and Waraqa asked him, 'O nephew, tell me what you saw and heard.'

"He did tell him, and Waraqa commented, 'By Him who bears my soul in His hand, you certainly will be the Prophet of this nation. You have been visited by the Archangel who came to Moses. You will certainly be called a liar, reviled, sent into exile and fought. If I live till that time, I will give God my help, and He will know it.' Waraqa then brought his head down over him, and kissed him on the top of his head. The Messenger of God (ṢAAS) thereupon went off home."

This is the account given by ʿUbayd b. ʿUmayr, just as we have told it. It serves as a prelude to the awakening that followed it, and introduces the statement of Khadīja, God bless her, who said, "Whenever he saw visions they came to him as the breaking of dawn."

It is probable that this dream came after what he had seen while awake on the morning following that same night. It is also possible it came some time after that. God knows best.

Mūsā b. ʿUqba stated, from al-Zuhrī, from Saʿīd b. al-Musayyab, as follows, "From what we have been told, the first thing he saw – meaning the Messenger of God (ṢAAS) – were visions God revealed to him while he was asleep. These greatly disturbed him and he told his wife Khadīja of them. God protected her from scepticism about them, opening her heart to belief. And so she said, 'Rejoice! For God has never done anything but good.'

"Thereafter he went off, but returned later to tell her how he had seen his stomach split open, and it had been washed and cleaned and all restored as before. To this she said, 'By God, I swear that this is good; so rejoice!'

"Then Gabriel appeared before him while he was on the heights above Mecca, sitting him down on a wonderful seat of honour. The Prophet (ṢAAS) used to say, 'He sat me down on a rug of *durnūk*, velvet, that was decorated with pearls and precious stones.' Gabriel then announced to him the mission from God the Almighty and Glorious, and put the Messenger of God (ṢAAS) at ease. Gabriel then said to him, 'Read!' He replied, 'How shall I read?' Gabriel answered, 'Read: in the name of your Lord who created. He created man from a clot. Read! your Lord is the most noble, He who taught by the pen. He taught man what he did not know.'"

He went on, "And people claim that 'O you who are all wrapped up!' is the first *sūrat* revealed to him. But God knows best."

He went on, "And the Messenger of God (ṢAAS) accepted the mission from his Lord, and obeyed the commandment Gabriel had brought him from God.

"And when he was returning back home, every tree and rock he passed greeted him. And so he went back to his family in good spirits, convinced that he had seen something stupendous. When he went in to see Khadīja, he said, 'You remember what I told you I saw in a vision? Well, Gabriel has now appeared plainly before me. My Lord, Almighty and Glorious is He, sent him to me.' He then told her what Gabriel had told him to do and what he had heard him say. She responded, 'Rejoice! For God will never bring you anything but good. And so accept the order that has come to you from God, for it is the truth. And rejoice, for you are in truth the Messenger of God.'

"She then left her home and set off to visit a youth who belonged to ʿUtba b. Rabīʿa b. ʿAbd Shams, a Christian originally from Nineveh, who was called ʿAddās. She said to him, 'I adjure you by God to tell me, do you have any knowledge about Gabriel?' He replied, 'Holy! Holy! How is it that mention is made of Gabriel in this land, all of whose people are idol worshippers?' She replied, 'Tell me what you know of him!' 'Gabriel', he replied, 'is God's trusty servant, God's intercessor between Himself and the prophets. He it was who accompanied Moses and Jesus, upon both of whom be peace.'

"Khadīja then came back from visiting him and went to see Waraqa b. Nawfal. She told him of what had happened to the Prophet (ṢAAS) and what Gabriel had commanded to him. Waraqa said to her, 'O fond daughter of my brother, I just don't know. Perhaps your companion is the prophet who is awaited by the People of the Book (i.e. Scriptures), about whom they find it written in their Torah and Bible. But I swear by God, that if this is he and he openly proclaims his mission while I am still live, I will express my dedication to

God by obedience to His Messenger and by giving him every assistance in maintaining fortitude and in achieving victory.'

"Thereafter Waraqa, God have mercy on him, died."

Al-Zuhrī stated, "Khadīja was the first person to believe in God and to give credence to His Messenger (ṢAAS)."

The *ḥāfiẓ* al-Bayhaqī stated, after having given the account we have reported above, "The reference here to his stomach being split open probably refers to his relating what was done to him when he was a boy, that is, its being opened while he was with Ḥalīma. It is also possible that it was split open a second time, and then again a third, when he was transported up to heaven. But God knows best."

The *ḥāfiẓ* Ibn ʿAsākir related in his biography of Waraqa, with a chain of authority back to Sulaymān b. Ṭarkhān al-Taymī, as follows, "We have heard that God Almighty sent Muḥammad as a Prophet at the start of the 50th year after the rebuilding of the *kaʿba*.

"The first aspect of God's making him a Prophet and honouring him, was a vision he saw. He related that to his wife Khadīja, daughter of Khuwaylid, and she told him, 'Rejoice! For, I swear by God, He will never do you anything but good.'

"One day when he was in the cave Ḥirāʾ, where he would seclude himself from his people, Gabriel came down to him. As he approached, the Messenger of God (ṢAAS) was mightily afraid, so Gabriel placed one hand on his chest and the other on his back between his shoulders and said, 'O God, unburden him, and give him relief! Cleanse his heart! O Muḥammad, rejoice! For you are the Prophet of this nation. Read!' The Prophet of God (ṢAAS) then replied, trembling with fear, 'I have never read any document; I don't read well. I neither write nor read.'

"At this Gabriel took hold of him and choked him hard, then released him and said, 'Read!' And the same happened as before. Then Gabriel seated him upon a soft rug of the *durnūk* type of such richness and splendour as to remind him of pearls and precious stones. Gabriel then told him, 'Read: in the name of your Lord who created . . .' and so on to the end of the verses. He then said to him, 'O Muḥammad, do not be afraid. You are the Messenger of God!'

"Then he left. The Messenger of God (ṢAAS) was overcome by anxiety and he asked himself, 'What am I to do? And what can I say to my people?'

"The Messenger of God (ṢAAS) then arose afraid, but Gabriel appeared before him in all his splendour. And so the Messenger of God (ṢAAS) saw a sight that filled him with wonder, and Gabriel told him, 'O Muḥammad, be you not afraid! Gabriel is God's messenger. Gabriel is God's messenger to His prophets and His messengers. Be secure in God's nobility. You are the Messenger of God.'

"As the Messenger of God (ṢAAS) went home every tree and rock bowed down before him, saying, 'Peace be upon you, O Messenger of God!' And so his soul was calmed, and he was sure of God's having honoured him. When he reached his wife Khadīja, she saw from his face that something had happened, and that scared her. She arose to him and, when close, began wiping his face and saying, 'You've probably been seeing and hearing things like those before today.'

"He replied, 'O Khadīja, you know what I've been seeing in my sleep and the voice I've been hearing while awake and that so disturbed me? It was Gabriel! He has appeared plainly before me, spoken to me and made me read some words that gave me fear. He then came back to me and told me that I am the prophet of this nation. So I came back home and on my way trees and rocks turned to me and said, "Peace be upon you, O Messenger of God!"'

"Khadīja said, 'Rejoice! For, by God, I well know that God will not do you anything but good. I bear witness that you are the prophet of this nation whom the Jews await. My servant Nāsiḥ and the monk Baḥīrā both told me this and advised me more than 20 years ago to marry you.' And she stayed with the Messenger of God (ṢAAS) until he had eaten, drunk, and laughed.

"She then went off to see the monk, who lived close by to Mecca. When she drew near and he recognized her, he said, 'What is wrong, O mistress of all the women of Quraysh?' She replied, 'I have come to you for you to tell me about Gabriel.'

"He replied, 'Glory be to God, our most holy Lord! How is it that Gabriel is mentioned here, in this land whose people worship idols? Gabriel is the trusted servant of God, and his envoy to His prophets and to His messengers. It is he who was the companion of Moses and Jesus.'

"And so she knew how much God was honouring Muḥammad.

"Then she went to a slave of ʿUtba b. Rabīʿa called ʿAddās, and questioned him. He told her the same as the monk had, and more besides. He said, 'Gabriel was with Moses when God drowned Pharaoh and his men. He was also there when God spoke to Moses on Mt. al-Ṭūr. And he it was who accompanied Jesus, son of Mary, and he through whom God aided Jesus.'

"She then left ʿAddās and went to Waraqa b. Nawfal whom she asked about Gabriel. He told her the same. He then asked her what was the matter, and she made him swear not to divulge what she would tell him. He so swore, and she told him, 'The son of ʿAbd Allāh related to me – and he is truthful and never, I swear it, either told a lie or was accused of lying – that Gabriel came down to him in Ḥirāʾ, told him he was the prophet of this nation, and made him recite some verses he had been sent with.'

"Waraqa was dumbfounded at this, and said, 'If Gabriel has actually placed his feet upon earth, he has done so for the best of people thereupon. And he never came down for anyone except a prophet. For he is the companion of all the prophets and messengers, the one whom God sends down to them. I believe what you tell me of him. Send for ʿAbd Allāh's son, so that I may question him, hear what he says and talk to him. I am afraid it may be someone other than Gabriel, for certain devils imitate him and by so doing can mislead and corrupt some men. This can result in a man becoming confused and even crazy whereas before he had been of sound mind.'

"Khadīja arose and left him, confident that God would never do anything but good to her husband. So she returned to the Messenger of God (ṢAAS) and told him what Waraqa had said. God Almighty then sent down the words: '*Nūn*. By the pen, and what they write! You are not, by grace of God, mad!' and so on to the end of these verses (*sūrat al-Qalam*, LXIII, v.1). He then told her, 'Absolutely not, by God! It was Gabriel!' She told him, 'I'd like you to go to him and inform him, so that God might give him guidance.'

"The Messenger of God (ṢAAS) did go to Waraqa who asked him, 'Did he who came to you appear in lightness or in the dark?' The Messenger of God (ṢAAS) described Gabriel to him and his majesty, and what he had revealed to him.

"Waraqa then said, 'I bear witness that that was Gabriel, and that these were words spoken by God. He has ordered you to convey certain things to your people. It is a matter of prophethood, and if I live on into your era, I will follow you.' He then said, 'Rejoice, O son of ʿAbd al-Muṭṭalib!'

The account went on, "And Waraqa's words became widely known, along with the fact that he had given credence to the Messenger of God. This fact distressed most of his people.

"And thereafter the revelation faltered. So people said, 'If he had come from God, he would have continued. But God is displeased with him.' And so God sent down the *sūras* of *al-Ḍuḥā* (XCIII) and *A Lam Nashrah* (*al-Inshirāḥ*, XCIV) in all their entirety."

Al Bayhaqī stated that the *ḥāfiẓ* Abū ʿAbd Allāh related to him, quoting Abū al-ʿAbbās, quoting Aḥmad b. ʿAbd al-Jabbār, quoting Yūnus, from Ibn Ishāq and Ismāʿīl b. Abū Ḥakīm, the freed-man of the Zubayr family, who related to him that Khadīja, daughter of Khuwaylid, said once to the Messenger of God (ṢAAS) regarding his explanation of how God honoured him with his prophethood, "O cousin, can you tell me about this companion who comes to you when he actually does come?" "Yes," he replied. "Then do tell me when he comes," she asked.

And while the Messenger of God (ṢAAS) was with her, he was visited by Gabriel. When the Messenger of God (ṢAAS) saw him, he said, "Khadīja, this is Gabriel." "Do you see him now?" she asked. "Yes, I do," he replied. "Now come over and sit by my right side." He changed his position and sat. She asked,

"Do you see him now?" "Yes," he replied. "Now change your position and sit in my lap." When he did this, she asked, "Well, do you see him now?" "Yes," he replied. She then exposed her head and removed her veil, while the Messenger of God (ṢAAS) still sat there in her lap. Then she asked, "Do you see him now?" "No," he answered. "This is no devil then, cousin; this is an angel! Take heart and rejoice!" She then believed in him and gave witness that it was the truth he brought.

Ibn Isḥāq stated, "I told ʿAbd Allāh b. Ḥasan this story and he commented, 'I heard my mother Fāṭima relate this account from Khadīja, except that I heard her say, 'She took the Messenger of God (ṢAAS) inside her shift, and it was then that Gabriel, upon whom be peace, went away.'"

Al-Bayhaqī stated, "This was something that Khadīja did to settle the matter, to preserve her faith and affirm her credence."

The Prophet (ṢAAS) was secure in what Gabriel had said to him, in the verses he had revealed to him which we have recounted several times, and in the fact of the trees and rocks having made salutation to him.

Muslim stated in his *ṣaḥīḥ* collection that Abū Bakr b. Abū Shayba related to him, quoting Yaḥyā b. Bukayr, quoting Ibrāhīm b. Ṭahmān, and Simāk b. Ḥarb, from Jābir b. Samura, God be pleased with him, that the Messenger of God (ṢAAS) said, "I know one rock in Mecca that used to greet me even before I received my mission; I still know it now."

Abū Dāwūd al-Ṭayālisī stated that Sulaymān b. Muʿādh related to him, from Simāk b. Ḥarb, from Jābir b. Samura, that the Messenger of God (ṢAAS) said, "There is in Mecca a rock that used to greet me on the nights when I was receiving my mission; I recognize it when I pass by it."

Al-Bayhaqī related, from a tradition of Ismāʿīl b. ʿAbd al-Raḥmān al-Suddī al-Kabīr, from ʿAbbād b. ʿAbd Allāh, from ʿAlī b. Abū Ṭālib, God be pleased with him, who said, "We were with the Messenger of God in Mecca, walking in various parts of the town, and no tree nor mountain received him without saying, 'Peace be upon you, O Messenger of God.'"

And in another account he said, "When I entered the valley in his company, he would not pass by a single rock or tree without its saying, 'Peace be upon you, O Messenger of God'; I heard this."

Division

Al-Bukhārī stated in his account given above, "then the revelation waned, so that the Messenger of God (ṢAAS) was so depressed, as we have been told, that he would often feel like throwing himself down from the summits of high mountains. Whenever he reached the top of a mountain to throw himself down, Gabriel would appear to him and say, 'O Muḥammad, you are in truth the Messenger of

God.' This would relieve his distress and he would return down. And if the revelation was again long in coming, he would feel and do the same. When he would reach the mountain summit, Gabriel would appear and speak to him as before."

In both the *ṣaḥīḥ* collections there is a tradition from ʿAbd al-Razzāq, from Maʿmar, from al-Zuhrī, who said that he heard Abū Salama ʿAbd al-Raḥmān relate from Jābir b. ʿAbd Allāh, who said that he heard the Messenger of God (ṢAAS) talking about the intermission in the revelation, say, "While I walked, I heard a voice from heaven. I raised my sight towards the sky and there I saw the angel who came to me in Ḥirāʾ, seated upon a throne amidst the sky. I knelt down before him in fear, right down to the ground, then went to my family and said, 'Wrap me up! Wrap me up!' And so God sent down, 'O you who are wrapped up! Arise and give warning! And glorify your Lord! Purify your garments! And shun idolatry!' (*sūrat al-Mudaththir*, LXXIV, v.1–5).

"He went on, 'And then the revelation became stronger and continued uninterrupted.'"

The above verse was the first of the Qurʾān sent down after the intermission in revelation, though not the very first of all, which was the verse, "Read: in the name of your Lord who created" (*sūrat al-ʿAlaq*, XCVI, v.1).

It is established on the authority of Jābir that the first verse to be revealed was, "O you who are wrapped up." It is perhaps appropriate to interpret his words as we have suggested, for in the sequence of what he states, there is evidence for the angel having come down earlier, as he recognized him from earlier. Moreover, in Jābir's words making reference to the "intermission in the revelation", there is a proof that revelation did precede this instance. But God knows best.

It is established in both the *ṣaḥīḥ* collections, from an account of ʿAlī b. al-Mubārak, as well as in the works of Muslim and al-Awzāʿī, both of whom also quote Yaḥyā b. Abū Kathīr as having said, "I asked Abū Salama b. ʿAbd al-Raḥmān, 'Which part of the Qurʾān was revealed before?' He replied, 'The verse, "O you who are wrapped up."'"

"I asked, 'And the verse, "Read in the name of your Lord who created?" He replied, 'I asked Jābir b. ʿAbd Allāh which verse of the Qurʾān came earliest, and he replied, "It was 'O you who are wrapped up.' So I asked him, 'What about "Read in the name of your Lord who created?"' and he answered, 'The Messenger of God (ṢAAS) said, "I spent a month in seclusion in Ḥirāʾ and when it was over I went down into the heart of the valley. I heard a voice calling out to me and I looked ahead, behind me and to left and right, but I saw nothing. Then I looked up at the sky and there he was, on a throne in the air. I was seized by a trembling" – or he used the word "anxiety" instead of the word "a trembling" – and went on to Khadīja. She ordered them and they wrapped me up. And then God revealed the verse, 'O you who are wrapped up . . .' and so on till the verse, 'and purify your garments.'"'"

According to a variant account he used the words, "And there was the angel who had come to me in Ḥirāʾ seated on a throne between the heavens and the earth, and I knelt down before him."

This is a plain reference to his prior coming to him and to his having made revelation from God to him, as we have stated. But God knows best.

There are some who claim that the first revelation that came after the intermission was the *sūrat* beginning, "By the morning hours and by the night when it darkens, your Lord has not forsaken you, nor is He displeased" (*sūrat al-Ḍuḥā*, XCIII, v.1–3) and so on to the end of the *sūrat*. This is what Muḥammad b. Isḥāq stated.

Some Qurʾān reciters state that this is why the Messenger of God (ṢAAS) said the words "*Allāhu Akbar*" ("God is most Great!") when he received the first part of it, out of joy.

This statement is suspect, since it is refuted by the previous account of the two authors of the *ṣaḥīḥ* collections, to the effect that the first to·be revealed of the Qurʾān after the intermission was, "O you who are wrapped up" but that the *sūrat* beginning "by the morning hours" came after another intermission of a few nights.

This is established in both *ṣaḥīḥ* collections and elsewhere, as well as from the account of al-Aswad b. Qays, from Jandab b. ʿAbd Allāh al-Bajalī, who said, "The Messenger of God (ṢAAS) was indisposed and did not get up for one, two or several nights. A woman commented, 'So your spirit soon abandoned you, then!' And so God revealed the verses, 'By the dawn and by the night when it darkens, your Lord has not forsaken you, nor is He displeased.'"

And it was thereby that the revelation transpired for mankind, whereas it was by the former circumstances that the prophethood came about.

Some authorities state that the intermission lasted for approximately two years, or two years and a half.

What is apparent – though God alone knows best – is that it was a period comparable to that related to Mikāʾīl; al-Shaʿbī and others made this observation.

This does not refute that Gabriel first brought him revelation, in the verses, "Read in the name of your Lord who created."

Thereafter Gabriel became associated with him, following the revelation of "O you who are wrapped up, arise and give warning! And glorify your Lord. Purify your garments! And shun idolatry!"

Thereafter the revelation intensified and continued; that is, it came uninterrupted, little by little.

At this time the Messenger of God (ṢAAS) began devoting himself totally to the mission, with energy and determination. He summoned all to God, both near and far, slaves and free men alike. And all of intelligence, excellence, and good favour believed in him, while all who were stubborn and intransigent continued to oppose and disobey him.

Abū Bakr al-Ṣiddīq, "the trusting", was the first free man to believe in him, while ʿAlī b. Abū Ṭālib was the first youth to do so.

The first woman to believe was Khadīja, daughter of Khuwaylid, his wife.

Of the freed men, the *mawālī*, his own *mawlā* Zayd b. Ḥāritha al-Kalbī was the first. May God be pleased with all the above.

We have previously written about the faith of Waraqa b. Nawfal, and how he reacted to the revelation and died during the intermission period. May God be pleased with him.

Section: On preventing the demons and evil spirits from eavesdropping when the Qurʾān was revealed, so that none of them would acquire any of it, even so much as a syllable, and deliver it through the speech of his human associates, which would have led to complications and a confusion of the truth.

It was God's mercy, grace and kindness to His creation that He excluded them from heaven. God Almighty spoke of them in His words, "and that we tried heaven, but found it filled with a strong guard and shooting stars. We used to sit in seats there to listen, but now any of us who eavesdrops finds a shooting star in wait. And we do not know whether harm is meant for those on earth, or whether their Lord intends guidance for them" (*sūrat al-Jinn*, LXXII, v.8–10).

The Almighty said, "And the devils have not brought it down. This would not be right for them; and they could not. They are kept away from hearing it" (*sūrat al-Shuʿarā*, XXVI, v.210–12).

The *ḥāfiẓ* Abū Nuʿaym stated that Sulaymān b. Aḥmad – he being al-Ṭabarānī – related to him, quoting ʿAbd Allāh b. Muḥammad b. Saʿīd b. Abū Maryam, quoting Muḥammad b. Yūsuf al-Firyābī, quoting Isrāʾīl, on the authority of Abū Isḥāq, from Saʿīd b. Jubayr, from Ibn ʿAbbās, who said, "The devils would ascend to heaven to listen to the revelation. Having memorized the statement, they would then make nine additions to it. The statement itself would be true, but their additions thereto would be false.

"When the Prophet (ṢAAS) was given his mission, their seats were denied them. They complained of this to Satan. And prior to that they did not have shooting stars fired at them. Satan told them, 'This is due to some event on earth.'

"He therefore sent his forces down and they found the Messenger of God (ṢAAS) standing between two mountains and praying. They went back to him (Satan) and told him. He then said, 'That is what has occurred on earth.'"

Abū ʿUwāna gave an account from Abū Bishr, from Saʿīd b. Jubayr, from Ibn

ʿAbbās, who said, "The Messenger of God (ṢAAS) left with others on a trip to the market of ʿUkāẓ. At this time the devils were being denied access to information from heaven and shooting stars had been sent against them. The devils had returned to their own people who asked them what was wrong. They replied, 'We've been denied access to information from heaven, and shooting stars have been fired at us.' Their people told them, 'This has to be because something has happened. So go and search the ends of the earth!'

"One group set off towards Tihāma and passed over a date plantation where he was, while on their way to ʿUkāẓ. He was with his Companions there performing the dawn prayer. When the devils overheard the Qurʾān, they listened to it and said, 'It is this that has denied us access to information from heaven.'

"So they returned home and told the rest: 'O our people, we have heard a wonderful Qurʾān that leads to right guidance; we believe in it, and will never associate another deity with our Lord' (*sūrat al-Jinn*, LXXII, v.1–2). And so God revealed to His Prophet (ṢAAS) the words: 'Say: "It was revealed to me that a group of *jinn* listened and said, 'We have heard a wonderful Qurʾān'"' (*sūrat al-Jinn*, LXXII, v.1)."

This account was included in both *ṣaḥīḥ* collections.

Abū Bakr b. Abū Shayba stated that Muḥammad b. Fuḍayl related to him, from ʿAṭāʾ b. al-Sāʾib, from Saʿīd b. Jubayr, from Ibn ʿAbbās, who said, "Every single tribe of *jinn* had places where they would sit and listen. When revelation began the angels would hear a sound like that of metal being cast against stone.

"When the angels heard this, they would fall down prostrate and not raise their heads until revelation had come. When it had, they would ask one another, 'What was it your Lord said?' And if it related to matters in heaven, they would say, 'He spoke the truth; and He is the All-High, the Almighty.' But if it related to matters on earth, dealing with the future, with death or other worldly affairs, they would talk about it and say, 'It would be so, and such.' The devils would listen to this and transmit it down to their human companions.

"Now when the Prophet Muḥammad (ṢAAS) received his mission, they were chased away with shooting stars. The first to learn of this were the tribe of Thaqīf. Those with livestock began making sacrifice. Those with sheep would slaughter one each day, those with camels would slaughter one similarly. They made haste to their flocks to do this. But some said, 'No, don't do this. If it is the stars people use to find their way, (then it is right to make sacrifice) but otherwise it is just happening because of some specific event.' When they looked, they found that nothing had happened to the stars used for navigation. And so they ceased making sacrifice.

"And God sent the *jinn* into motion, and they heard the Qurʾān. When they were there present, they said, 'Listen carefully!'

"The devils would go off to Iblīs (Satan) and inform him. He told them, 'This is some event that has occurred on earth. Therefore bring me some dust from every part of it.' And when they brought him some from Tihāma, he said, 'This is the site of the event.'"

Al-Bayhaqī related this tradition, quoting al-Ḥākim, through Ḥammād b. Salama, from ʿAṭāʾ b. al-Sāʾib.

Al-Wāqidī stated that Usāma b. Zayd b. Aslam related to him, from ʿUmar b. ʿAbdān al-ʿAbsī, from Kaʿb, who said, "No stars had been cast since the ascension of Jesus until the time when the Messenger of God (ṢAAS) became a prophet. Quraysh then saw sights they never before witnessed. And so they began releasing their flocks and freeing their slaves, thinking that it meant the end of the world. News of these actions of theirs reached the people of al-Ṭāʾif, and Thaqīf did the same (as Quraysh).

"What Thaqīf had done became known to the slave of Yālayl b. ʿAmr, and he asked them, 'Why have you done what I see?' They replied, 'There have been shooting stars, and we have seen them falling from the sky.' He observed, 'But it's hard to replace properties once they have gone; don't be in a hurry and observe. If they are stars that are recognized, then it does mean destruction for us. But if they are stars that were unknown stars, then it's all because of some event that has occurred.'

"So they made observations, found they were unknown stars and told him of this. He commented, 'Well, there's still some time left then. This is because of the appearance of a prophet.'

"Soon thereafter Abū Sufyān b. Ḥarb came for his animals and ʿAbd Yālayl went to him and told him about the stars. Abū Sufyān then commented, 'Muḥammad son of ʿAbd Allāh has come forth and made a claim that he is a prophet who has been sent.' ʿAbd Yālayl then said, 'Well, that's why there have been shooting stars.'"

Saʿīd b. Manṣūr stated, from Khālid b. Ḥusayn, from ʿĀmir al-Shaʿbī, who said, "The stars were not cast until the Messenger of God (ṢAAS) received his mission. People then released their flocks and set free their slaves. So ʿAbd Yālayl said, 'Observe; and if it is stars that are known, it means the end of mankind is near. But if they are not known, then it is happening because of some event that has occurred.' And so they did make observations and found them to be unknown. They therefore ceased what they had been doing and soon thereafter news came to them of the emergence of the Prophet (ṢAAS)."

Al-Bayhaqī and al-Ḥākim gave the wording of this account through al-ʿAwfī from Ibn ʿAbbās, he having said: "The world's heavens had not been guarded over throughout the period between Jesus and Muḥammad (ṢAAS)."

Perhaps what is meant by this negative statement is that the heavens had not been under strict guard. This must be held more likely, because of what is well established in a *ḥadīth* through ʿAbd al-Razzāq, from Maʿmar, from al-Zuhrī, from ʿAlī b. al-Ḥusayn, from Ibn ʿAbbās, God be pleased with him, who said, "On one occasion when the Messenger of God was sitting down, a shooting star occurred and it became light. He then asked, 'What was it you used to say when shooting stars were going on?' They replied, 'We would say: "A great man has died; a great man is born."' He commented, 'No, but . . .' He then made the statement we reported elsewhere (in part one of the work *al-Bidāya wa al-Nihāya* (*The Beginning and The End*), relating to the creation of the heavens and the stars therein at the first Creation. And all praise be to God.

Ibn Isḥāq related the story of the shooting stars in his biography of the Prophet (ṢAAS). Of the leader of Thaqīf, he said that he used the words, regarding observation of the stars, "(to see) whether they are the most prominent stars of the skies, or other ones". But Ibn Isḥāq named this man as ʿAmr b. Umayya. God knows best.

Al-Suddī stated, "The heavens were only guarded when there was a prophet on earth, or when a religion of God was appearing. The devils, prior to Muḥammad (ṢAAS), used to take seats in the skies above the world and overhear what was going on in heaven.

"When God sent Muḥammad (ṢAAS) as a prophet, one night they had stars shot at them. This terrified the people of al-Ṭāʾif, and they told one another that the people of heaven had been destroyed! This was because of the violence of the fires in the sky and the great variety of the shooting stars. So they began setting their slaves free and releasing their livestock. At this ʿAbd Yālayl b. ʿAmr b. ʿUmayr told them, 'Woe upon you, O people of Ṭāʾif! Secure your property and observe the most prominent stars. If you see them to be still set in their places, then the people of heaven are not destroyed, but it's all because of the son of Abū Kabsha.[74] But if you don't see them there, then the people of heaven have perished.'

"And when they looked, they did still see them and so they secured their property.

"That night the devils were terrified and went to Satan and he told them, 'Bring me a handful of earth from every place.' When they did so, he sniffed it and said, 'Your man is in Mecca.'

"He then dispatched seven of the spirits of Naṣībīn and they came to Mecca and found the Messenger of God (ṢAAS) in the Harām (Holy) Mosque reciting the Qurʾān. They approached him so eager to hear it that their bodies almost touched him. They then accepted Islam, and God sent down revelation to his Prophet (ṢAAS) about them."

74. The unbelievers of Mecca used to refer to the Prophet as "the son of Abū Kabsha".

Al-Wāqidī stated that Muḥammad b. Ṣāliḥ related to him, from the son of Abū Ḥakīm – by whom he meant Isḥāq – from ʿAṭāʾ b. Yasār, from Abū Hurayra, who said, "When the Messenger of God (ṢAAS) received his mission, all the idols were overturned. So the evil spirits went and told him (Satan), 'Every single idol on earth has been overturned.' He responded, 'This is due to a Prophet who has been given a mission. Look for him in villages in the countryside.' They did so, but reported to him that they could not find him. He then said, 'I'll do it.' And so he went off and looked for him. A voice called out to him, 'Go to *Janbat al-Bāb*' – the 'gate quarter' – meaning Mecca. He looked for him there and found him at *Qarn al-Thaʿālib*. Satan then went off to the devils and told them, 'I found him, and Gabriel was with him. What's your opinion?' They answered, 'We'll make earthly pleasures delightful in people's eyes and so make them covet them.' 'So no problem then,' he commented."

Al-Wāqidī stated that Ṭalḥa b. ʿAmr related to him, from Ibn Abū Mulayka, from ʿAbd Allāh b. ʿAmr, who said, "When the day came when the Messenger of God (ṢAAS) became a Prophet, the devils were denied access to heaven and shooting stars were fired at them. So they went to Satan and when they told him this he commented, 'Some event has occurred. This is a Prophet who has come forth to them in the Holy Land, the place where the tribe of Israel came from.'

"So the devils went off to Syria, then returned and told him, 'There's no one there.' Satan responded, 'I'll do it.'

"Then he went off to look for him in Mecca. And there was the Messenger of God in Ḥirāʾ, and Gabriel was there with him. Satan returned to his evil spirits and told them, 'Aḥmad has received his mission and Gabriel is with him. What is your opinion?' They replied, 'Earthly delights; we'll make them attractive to people.' He replied, 'That will do it.'"

Al-Wāqidī said that Ṭalḥa b. ʿAmr related to him, from ʿAṭāʾ, from Ibn ʿAbbās, who said, "The devils used to listen to the revelation. And when Muḥammad (ṢAAS) was assigned to his mission, they were prevented from doing so. They complained about this to Satan, and he responded, 'Some event has occurred.' He then went on up above Abū Qubays, the very first mountain placed on the face of the earth, and saw the Messenger of God (ṢAAS) at prayer behind the shrine. He told himself, 'I'll go on down and break his neck!' So he strutted off towards him. But Gabriel was there with him, and charged out at Satan sending him flying in all directions. So the devil took to his heels."

Both al-Wāqidī and Abū Aḥmad al-Zubayrī also related this, from Rabbāḥ b. Abū Maʿrūf, from Qays b. Saʿd, from Mujāhid. Their account was similar, with the variation, "Gabriel kicked the devil and threw him down to Aden."

Section: On the manner in which the revelation came to the Messenger of God (ṢAAS).

It has previously been related how Gabriel came to him on both the first and second occasions.

Mālik stated, from Hishām b. ʿUrwa, from his father, from ʿĀʾisha, God bless her, that al-Ḥārith b. Hishām asked the Messenger of God (ṢAAS) "O Messenger of God, how does revelation come to you?"

He replied, "Sometimes it comes like the ringing of a bell, it being then most painful. When it leaves me I remain conscious of what he spoke. Sometimes the angel appears before me as a man who addresses me, and I am fully aware of what he is saying."

ʿĀʾisha, God bless her, stated, "I saw him (ṢAAS) when revelation came to him on the extremely cold day. Then it left him, and his forehead was bathed in perspiration."

The authors of the two *ṣaḥīḥ* collections derived this *ḥadīth* from the account of Mālik.

Imām Aḥmad related it from ʿĀmir b. Ṣāliḥ, from Hishām b. ʿUrwa in a similar manner.

ʿAbda b. Sulaymān and Anas b. ʿIyyād related it similarly from Hishām b. ʿUrwa.

Ayyūb al-Sakhtiyānī related it from Hishām, from his father, from al-Ḥārith b. Hishām who said, "I asked the Messenger of God (ṢAAS), 'How does revelation come to you?'" He related the same *ḥadīth* as above, but made no reference to ʿĀʾisha.

In the *ḥadīth al-ʾifk*[75] she stated, "By God, the Messenger of God (ṢAAS) did not get up, nor did any member of the family leave, until revelation came down to him. He underwent the agony that used to seize him (on such occasions) with sweat emerging like pearls from him, even though it was a winter's day, because of the heavy burden of the revelation that came down upon him."

Imām Aḥmad stated that ʿAbd al-Razzāq related to him, quoting Yūnus b. Salīm, who said that Yūnus b. Yazīd dictated to him, from Ibn Shihāb, from ʿUrwa b. ʿAbd al-Raḥmān b. ʿAbd al-Qārī, who said, "I heard ʿUmar b. al-Khaṭṭāb say, 'When revelation came down to the Messenger of God (ṢAAS), it would be heard like the buzzing of a bee near his face.'"

The tradition in its entirety was recounted in the section[76] on the revelation of the Qurʾānic verse, "and the believers have succeeded" (*sūrat al-Muʾminūn*, XXIII, v.1).

75. ʿĀʾisha's account relating to certain slanderous charges made against her, see Volume III.

76. See Ibn Kathīr: *Tafsīr al-Qurʾān al-Karīm* (*The Exegesis of the Glorious Qurʾān*), Vol 3, p.237.

Al-Tirmidhī related this, quoting al-Nasāʾī from ʿAbd al-Razzāq.

After giving it, al-Nasāʾī commented, "It is objectionable; we know of only Yūnus b. Salīm as having related it, and him we do not recognize."

In the *ṣaḥīḥ* collection of Muslim and others, it is recounted by al-Ḥasan, from Ḥiṭṭān b. ʿAbd Allāh al-Raqāshī, from ʿUbāda b. al-Ṣāmit, who said, "The Messenger of God (ṢAAS) would become in pain when revelation came to him, and his face would look very serious." According to one account, this wording should be "and his eyes would close; we recognized that in him."

In both *ṣaḥīḥ* collections there is the account of Zayd b. Thābit that relates to the circumstance when the verse "Those of the believers who sit still are not on equality with . . ." (*sūrat al-Nisāʾ*, VI, v.95) was revealed; and when the son of Umm Maktūm complained of his disabilities, the next verse came down: "except for those with disabilities".

His account states, "The Messenger of God (ṢAAS) was seated with his thigh right next to mine while I was writing. When revelation came, his leg almost crushed mine."

In the *ṣaḥīḥ* collection of Muslim, there is an account by Ḥammām b. Yaḥyā, from ʿAṭāʾ, from Yaʿlā b. Umayya, who is quoted as saying, "Umar said to me, 'Would you like to look at the Messenger of God (ṢAAS) while revelation is coming to him?' He raised the edge of his robe from his face while he was receiving revelation at al-Jiʿrāna, and he was all flushed. And he would moan like a newborn calf."

It was established in the two *ṣaḥīḥ* collections from a *ḥadīth* of ʿĀʾisha relating to when revelation came concerning the *ḥijāb* (the wearing of the veil) that Sawda went out thereafter to the privies, by night. ʿUmar spoke to her, saying, "We can recognize you, O Sawda!" She then went back to the Messenger of God (ṢAAS) and questioned him, while he was sitting having supper and holding his milk (mug) in his hand. God then sent down revelation to him, while the milk was in his hand. He then raised his head and said, "You women have been given permission to go out and attend to your needs."

This shows that revelation did not fully absent his feelings from him. This is proven by his being seated; and the milk, moreover, did not drop from his hand (ṢAAS)!

Abū Dāwūd al-Ṭayālisī stated that ʿAbbād b. Manṣūr related to him, quoting ʿIkrima, from Ibn ʿAbbās, who said, "When revelation came down, the body and face of the Messenger of God would become pale; he would ignore those with him, and none of them would address him."

In the collection of traditions made by Aḥmad and others, there is an account of Ibn Lahīʿa in which he states, "Yazīd b. Abū Ḥabīb related to me, from ʿAmr b. al-Walīd, from ʿAbd Allāh b. ʿAmr, who said, 'I asked, "O Messenger of God, can you feel revelation coming?" He replied, "Yes; I hear ringing sounds. Then

I recover. And never once did I receive revelation without thinking that my soul was being seized by it."'"

Abū Yaʿlā al-Mawṣilī stated that Ibrāhīm b. al-Ḥajjāj related to him, quoting ʿAbd al-Wāḥid b. Ziyād, quoting ʿĀṣim b. Kulayb, quoting his father, from his uncle al-ʿIlyān b. ʿĀṣim, who said, "We were with the Messenger of God (ṢAAS) when revelation came to him. When this happened, he could still see and his eyes remained open, while his hearing and his heart were made empty for what would come to him from God, Almighty and Glorious is He."

Abū Nuʿaym related, from a tradition of Qutayba that ʿAlī b. Ghurāb related to him, from al-Aḥwaṣ b. Ḥakīm, from Abū ʿAwāna, from Saʿīd b. al-Musayyib, from Abū Hurayra, who said, "When revelation came down to the Messenger of God, he would get a headache and would cover his head with the henna plant."

This is a very strange *ḥadīth*.

Imām Aḥmad stated that Abū al-Naḍr related to him, quoting Abū Muʿāwiya Sinān, from Layth, from Shahr b. Ḥawshab, from Asmāʾ, daughter of Yazīd, who said: "I was holding the reins of al-ʿAḍbāʾ, the camel of the Messenger of God (ṢAAS), when the whole text of the *sūrat al-Māʾida* (Qurʾān, V) was revealed to him. The camel's back almost gave way beneath the weight of it."

Abū Nuʿaym related this from a *ḥadīth* of al-Thawrī, from Layth b. Abū Salīm.

Imām Aḥmad also stated that Ḥasan related to him, quoting Ibn Lahīʿa, quoting Jabr b. ʿAbd Allāh, from Abū ʿAbd al-Raḥmān al-Ḥubalī, from ʿAbd Allāh b. ʿAmr, who said, "The *sūrat al-Māʾida* was revealed to the Messenger of God (ṢAAS) while he was riding on his camel. It could not carry him, so he dismounted."

Ibn Mardawayh related, from a *ḥadīth* of Ṣabāḥ b. Sahl, from ʿĀṣim al-Aḥwal, who said, "Umm ʿAmr related to me, from her uncle, that he was on a journey with the Messenger of God (ṢAAS) when the *sūrat al-Māʾida* was revealed to him. The camel's neck was broken because of the weight of it."

The implications of this are strange.

It is established, moreover, in both *ṣaḥīḥ* collections that the *sūrat al-Fatḥ* (Qurʾān, XLVII) was revealed to the Messenger of God (ṢAAS) when he was returning from al-Ḥudaybiyya, riding on his camel. It came at various times, according to the circumstances. But God knows best.

We have earlier given an account of the kinds of revelation that came to him (ṢAAS) in the early part of our exegesis of al-Bukhārī's work, along with the comments of al-Ḥalīmī and other Imāms, God be pleased with them all.

Division

God Almighty stated, "Do not move your tongue with it, to speak it in haste. It is up to Us to put it together, and to recite it. So when We do recite it, follow its recitation. And then, it is up to Us to explain it" (*sūrat al-Qiyāma*, LXXV, v.16–19).

And the Almighty said, "And do not make haste with the recitation, before its revelation to you has been completed. And say, 'O God, increase me in knowledge!'" (*sūrat Ṭāhā*, XX, v.114).

This was in the beginning. Due to his eagerness to receive from the angel what God the Almighty and Glorious had revealed to him, he used to join him through recitation. God Almighty therefore ordered him to listen on until the revelation was completed. He assured him He would store it in his chest and enable him to recite and announce it. God also said He would clarify and explain it and enable him to understand it.

For this reason He stated, "And do not make haste with the recitation, before its revelation to you has been completed. And say, 'O God, increase me in knowledge!'"

And He said, "Do not move your tongue with it, to speak it in haste. It is up to Us to put it together" – in your chest, that is – "and to recite it." That is, and you shall recite it. "So when We do recite it" – that is, when the angel recites it to you – "follow its recitation." That is, listen to it and consider it. And then, "it is up to Us to explain it." This is equivalent to saying, "O God, increase me in knowledge!"

In both *ṣaḥīḥ* collections there is a tradition of Mūsā b. Abū ῾Ā᾿isha, from Sa῾īd b. Jubayr, from Ibn ῾Abbās, who said, "The Messenger of God would suffer great strain from revelation. He would move his lips and so God sent down to him, 'Do not move your tongue with it, to speak it in haste. It is up to Us to put it together, and to recite it.' He said 'to put it together' in your breast and then you will recite it. 'And so when We do recite it, follow its recitation.' And hear it, and listen to it. 'And then, it is up to Us to explain it.'"

He went on, "And when Gabriel came to him he would bow his head; and when he left he would recite it just as God the Almighty and Glorious had promised him."

Division

Ibn Isḥāq stated, "Thereafter revelation came frequently to the Messenger of God (ṢAAS) and he fully believed in what he was receiving from God. He accepted it willingly and because of it received both the approbation and blame of other men.

"Prophethood brings burdens and troubles that can only be borne by messengers who are strong and determined through the power and aid of God. Their burdens arise from the reactions of men to them that result from what it is that God the Almighty and Glorious has brought them.

"The Messenger of God did continue to fulfil God's orders despite the opposition and harm he met from his people."

Ibn Isḥāq went on, "And Khadīja, daughter of Khuwaylid, believed in him and God's messages to him, and helped him.

"She was the first person to believe in God and His Messenger, and to believe in God's message to him.

"In this God alleviated His Messenger's burdens; whenever he suffered some unpleasant reaction or painful rejection, God would comfort him through her. When he came back to her she would give him strength and alleviate his pain. She would express her belief in him and make light of the opposition to him; may God bless and comfort her!"

Ibn Isḥāq continued to say that Hishām b. ʿUrwa related to him, from his father, from ʿAbd Allāh b. Jaʿfar, who said that the Messenger of God (ṢAAS) stated, "I was commanded to tell Khadīja the glad tidings of a house made of *qaṣab*, one where there would be no rancour and no trouble."

In the two *ṣaḥīḥ* collections this *ḥadīth* is derived from an account of Hishām.

Ibn Hishām explained that the word *qaṣab* in this *ḥadīth* means hollowed-out pearls.

Ibn Isḥāq went on, "The Messenger of God (ṢAAS) began, in secret, to inform all of his people whom he could trust about all that prophethood with which God had honoured him and His servants."

Mūsā b. ʿUqba stated, from al-Zuhrī, "Khadīja was the first person to believe in God and in His Messenger; and this was even before prayer was made obligatory."

I make the comment that by this is meant the five daily prayers (that were enjoined) on the occasion of the *laylat al-isrāʾ*, the "night journey". As for the origin of prayer, it was (already) made necessary during the lifetime of Khadīja, God bless her, as we will explain.

Ibn Isḥāq stated, "Khadīja was the first person to believe in God, His Messenger, and the mission he brought.

"Gabriel came to the Messenger of God (ṢAAS) when prayer was made incumbent upon him; he made a mark with his heel on the side of the valley and a spring of water from *zamzam* gushed forth. Then Gabriel performed the ablution, along with Muḥammad, peace be upon them both. He then bowed in prayer twice and made four prostrations. Thereafter the Prophet (ṢAAS) went home, God having much comforted him and brought him what he wanted. He took Khadīja's hand and led her to the well and there performed the ablution as Gabriel had done. He then made two bows in prayer and four prostrations. Thereafter Khadīja and he would perform the prayer in secret."

I wish to comment that Gabriel's prayer on this occasion was different from the prayers he performed twice at the *kaʿba*. Then he explained the five times for prayer to him, from first to last. This came after they had been made obligatory following the *laylat al-isrāʾ*.

Explanation of this will come later, if God wills it, and in Him is all trust, all reliance.

Section: Concerning the first persons to accept Islam; also reference to those of the Companions and others who were early in becoming Muslims.

Ibn Isḥāq stated, "And then ʿAlī son of Abū Ṭālib, God be pleased with him, came the following day while they were both praying. ʿAlī asked, 'O Muḥammad, what are you doing?' He replied, 'It is God's religion that he has chosen for Himself and sent forth to His messengers. And so I summon you to God alone, He who has no partner, and to pray to Him, and to renounce al-Lāt and al-ʿUzzā.'

"ʿAlī replied, 'This is something I never heard before today. I'm not going to decide anything before I tell Abū Ṭālib about it.'

"The Messenger of God was reluctant to have him expose his secret before he himself made it public. So he told him, 'O Alī, even if you don't accept Islam, do keep the matter secret.' ʿAlī therefore did nothing that night. Then God placed Islam in the heart of ʿAlī, and he went next morning to the Messenger of God and asked him, 'What was it you proposed to me, O Muḥammad?' The Messenger of God (ṢAAS) then said, 'Bear witness that there is no God but God alone; He has no partner. And renounce al-Lāt and al-ʿUzzā, and disavow any peers.'

"ʿAlī did this and accepted Islam; but he was afraid of Abū Ṭālib's displeasure whenever he went to the Prophet (ṢAAS) and so he kept his acceptance of Islam a secret he did not divulge.

"Ibn Ḥāritha, Zayd that is, then became a Muslim and they went on thus (in secret) for approximately one month, during which ʿAlī frequently visited the Messenger of God (ṢAAS). A favour God had previously granted ʿAlī was his having been brought up in the care of the Messenger of God (ṢAAS) before the coming of Islam."

Ibn Isḥāq stated that Ibn Abū Nājīḥ related to him, from Mujāhid, who said, "One matter in which God favoured ʿAlī was that Quraysh had a period of great crisis. Abū Ṭālib had a large family and so the Messenger of God (ṢAAS) said to his uncle, al-ʿAbbās, a man who was among the wealthiest of the Banū Hāshim, 'O ʿAbbās, your brother Abū Ṭālib has a large family, and you know how this crisis has affected everyone. So let us go and relieve him of the burden of some of his family.' And so the Messenger of God (ṢAAS) took ʿAlī and added him to his own family. And he was still living with the Messenger of God (ṢAAS) when God sent him his prophethood. And so it was that ʿAlī followed him, and believed in him and his message."

Yūnus b. Bukayr related, from Muḥammad b. Isḥāq, who said that Yaḥyā b. Abū al-Ashʿath al-Kindī, a scholar from al-Kūfa, related to him, quoting Ismāʿīl

b. Abū Iyās b. ʿAfīf, from his father, from his grandfather ʿAfīf, this ʿAfīf being the brother of al-Ashʿath b. Qays on his mother's side, who said, "I was a businessman and went to Minā during the pilgrimage season. Al-ʿAbbās b. ʿAbd al-Muṭṭalib was also a merchant, and I went to him to buy and sell from him.

"While we were engaged in this, a man came out of a tent and began praying towards the *kaʿba*. And then a woman came out and also began to pray, then a boy emerged and prayed along with the man. I asked, 'O Ibn ʿAbbās, what is this religion? We don't know what religion this is.'

"He replied, 'This is Muḥammad, son of ʿAbd Allāh. He claims that God has sent him and that the treasures of Chosroe and Caesar will be opened up for him. That is his wife, Khadīja, daughter of Khuwaylid, and the boy is his nephew ʿAlī, son of Abū Ṭālib, and he believes in him.'

"ʿAfīf then commented, 'O how I wish I had then believed in him; I would then have been the second!'"

Ibrāhīm b. Saʿd gave a similar account, from Ibn Isḥāq, which gives the wording, "when a man came out of a tent near by. He looked up at the sky and when he saw the sun declining to set, he began to pray." He then recounted how Khadīja stood there behind him.

Ibn Jarīr stated that Muḥammad b. ʿUbayd al-Muḥāribī related to him, quoting Saʿīd b. Khuthaym, from Asad b. ʿAbda al-Bajalī, from Yaḥyā b. ʿAfīf, who said, "I went to Mecca before the coming of Islam and stayed with al-ʿAbbās b. ʿAbd al-Muṭṭalib. When the sun rose and hung high in the sky as I was overlooking the *kaʿba*, a young man approached. He looked up at the sky then went to the *kaʿba* and stood there facing it. A boy soon arrived and stood there to his right, and shortly thereafter a woman came and stood behind them. The man bowed down and so did the boy and the woman. Then the man stood up straight and so did the boy and the woman. Next the man made a prostration and they both did, along with him.

"I said, 'O ʿAbbās, this is a strange business!'

"'It is,' he agreed. 'Do you know who that is?' 'No,' I replied. 'That is Muḥammad, son of ʿAbd Allāh, grandson of ʿAbd al-Muṭṭalib, my brother's son. Do you know who the boy is?' 'No,' I answered. 'That is ʿAlī son of Abū Ṭālib, God be pleased with him. Do you know who the woman is standing behind them?' 'No,' I replied. 'That is Khadīja, daughter of Khuwaylid, my nephew's wife.'

"This man told me that your Lord, the Lord of the heavens and the earth, ordered him to do what you see them performing. By God, I know of no other on the face of the whole earth who engages in this religion except for these three!"

Ibn Jarīr stated that Ibn Ḥumayd related to him, quoting ʿĪsā b. Sawāda b. Abū al-Juʿd, quoting Muḥammad b. al-Munkadar and Rabīʿa b. Abū ʿAbd al-Raḥmān, and Abū Ḥāzim and al-Kalbī, all of whom said, "ʿAlī is the first man to accept Islam."

Al-Kalbī stated, "He accepted Islam at the age of nine."

Ibn Ḥumayd related to us, quoting Salama, from Ibn Isḥāq, who said, "The first male who believed in the Messenger of God (ṢAAS) and prayed with him was ʿAlī, son of Abū Ṭālib. At the time he was ten years of age and he had been under the care of the Messenger of God (ṢAAS) before the coming of Islam."

Al-Wāqidī stated that Ibrāhīm related to him, from Nāfiʿ, from Ibn Abū Nājīḥ, from Mujāhid, who said, "ʿAlī accepted Islam when he was ten."

Al-Wāqidī stated, "Our companions were in agreement that ʿAlī accepted Islam one year after the Messenger of God became a prophet."

Muḥammad b. Kaʿb stated, "The first of this nation to accept Islam was Khadīja. The first two men to do so were Abū Bakr and ʿAlī, ʿAlī having done so before Abū Bakr. ʿAlī hid his faith because of his fear of his father, until his father joined him and asked, 'Have you accepted Islam?' ʿAlī replied, 'Yes.' 'Then give your cousin all help and aid,' he told him."

Abū Bakr al-Ṣiddīq, "the trusting", was the first man to openly declare his acceptance of Islam.

Ibn Jarīr related in his work of history, from a *ḥadīth* of Shuʿba, from Abū Balj, from ʿAmr b. Maymūn, from Ibn ʿAbbās, who said, "The first person to pray was ʿAlī."

ʿAbd al-Ḥamīd b. Yaḥyā related to us, quoting Shurayk, from ʿAbd Allāh b. Muḥammad b. ʿUqayl, from Jābir, who said, "The Prophet (ṢAAS) received his mission on a Monday and ʿAlī prayed on Tuesday." And he related, from a *ḥadīth* of Shuʿba from ʿAmr b. Murra, from Abū Ḥamza – a supporter from Medina – who said he heard Zayd b. Arqam say, "The first man to accept Islam along with the Messenger of God (ṢAAS) was ʿAlī son of Abū Ṭālib."

He went on, "I mentioned this to al-Nakhʿī, but he refuted it and said, 'It was Abū Bakr who first accepted Islam.'"

He then said that ʿUbayd Allāh b. Mūsā related to him, quoting al-ʿAlāʾ, from al-Minhāl b. ʿAmr, from ʿAbbād b. ʿAbd Allāh, who said, "I heard ʿAlī say, 'I am the slave of God and the brother of His Messenger. And I am the grand *ṣiddīq*, "trusting one". No one can say this after me without being a liar and a fabricator. I prayed seven years before the people did.'"

Ibn Māja recounted this similarly, from Muḥammad b. Ismāʿīl al-Rāzī, from ʿUbayd Allāh b. Mūsā al-Fahmī – who was a *shīʿī* and a man accepted as a fully reliable source for traditions – from al-ʿAlāʾ b. Ṣāliḥ al-Azdī of Kūfa, a man also considered reliable. However, Abū Ḥātim said of him that he was from the old aristocracy of the *shīʿa*. And ʿAlī b. al-Madīnī stated, "al-ʿAlāʾ related objectionable accounts. Al-Minhāl b. ʿAmr is trustworthy, while his teacher, Sheikh ʿAbbād b. ʿAbd Allāh – of the Asad tribe and from Kufa – is weak." Moreover al-Bukhārī stated, "There is some question about him." Ibn Ḥabbān referred to him as trustworthy.

This tradition is objectionable in any case. ʿAlī, God be pleased with him, would not have said this. How could he have prayed seven years before the people? This is simply unimaginable. But God knows best.

Others said that the first man of this nation to accept Islam was Abū Bakr, "the trusting".

Combining these various accounts we see that Khadīja was the first woman to accept Islam, the leader of the pack, as it were, and also she preceded the men. Among slaves, the first to accept Islam was Zayd b. Ḥāritha. And the first boy to accept Islam was ʿAlī b. Abū Ṭālib; he was young then and had not reached puberty – as generally believed. These were then the family of the Prophet.

The first free man to accept Islam was Abū Bakr, "the trusting". His conversion was more beneficial than that of those mentioned before because he was a highly respected leader, an honoured chief of Quraysh and a man of wealth. He became a missionary for Islam and was very much liked and admired for spending money in the service of God and His Messenger. Details of this activity will follow.

Yūnus stated, from Ibn Isḥāq, "Then Abū Bakr met the Messenger of God (ṢAAS) and asked him, 'Is it true what Quraysh are saying, Muḥammad? About you abandoning our gods, ridiculing our intellects, and calling our ancestors pagans?'

"The Messenger of God (ṢAAS) responded, 'Yes indeed. I am the Messenger of God, and His Prophet. He sent me to deliver his message and to invite you to God by the truth. For, I swear, God is the truth. I call upon you, O Abū Bakr, to believe in God alone, in Him who has no associate. And I call upon you to worship none but Him, and to devote yourself to obeying Him.'

"He then recited the Qurʾān to him. And he neither confirmed nor refused.

"Then he did accept Islam, disavowed the idols, repudiated the other gods, and affirmed the truth of Islam. When Abū Bakr went home he was a believer, a man of the faith."

Ibn Isḥāq stated that Muḥammad b. ʿAbd al-Raḥmān b. ʿAbd Allāh b. al-Ḥusayn of Tamīm related to him that the Messenger of God (ṢAAS) said, "I never called upon any man to embrace Islam without him expressing reluctance, hesitation, and argument except Abū Bakr. He did not *ʿakam* ("hold back") from Islam when I told him of it, nor did he hesitate at all."

Here *ʿakam* means *talabbatha*, i.e. "he delayed".

That which Ibn Isḥāq stated, that "he neither confirmed nor refused", is objectionable. For Ibn Isḥāq and others have told how he (Abū Bakr) was the friend of the Messenger of God (ṢAAS) before his mission. He was known for his truthfulness, trustworthiness, fine disposition, and excellent qualities. These prevented him from lying to other mortals, so how could he ever have given the lie to God?

Therefore, from the mere fact of his telling him that God had sent him, Abū Bakr promptly believed him, not holding back or delaying at all.

We have recounted the manner of his becoming a Muslim in the book we devoted to his biography in which we emphasized his many qualities. That book we followed with another biography, of ʿUmar, the *fārūq* (i.e. he who differentiated truth from falsehood). In these works we recorded the various sayings of each of these men attributed to the Prophet (ṢAAS) along with legal decisions and pronouncements he made. These writings total three volumes; all praise and credit be to God for these.

In the *ṣaḥīḥ* collection of al-Bukhārī there is a *ḥadīth* from Abū al-Dardāʾ relating to the feud that existed between Abū Bakr and ʿUmar, may God be pleased with them both. In it he states that the Messenger of God (ṢAAS) said, "God sent me to you and you all said, 'You lie!' But Abū Bakr said, 'He spoke the truth.' And he dedicated himself and his fortune to me. Will you then leave this friend of mine to me?" He said this twice. And afterwards he was done no harm.

This is a direct text that he was the first to accept Islam. God be pleased with him!

Al-Tirmidhī and Ibn Ḥibbān recounted, from a *ḥadīth* of Shuʿba, from Saʿīd al-Jarīrī, from Abū Naḍra, from Abū Saʿīd, who said that Abū Bakr, "the trusting", may God be pleased with him, said, "Am I not the most worthy of people for it? Am I not the first person to accept Islam? Is that not my distinction?"

Ibn ʿAsākir recounted, through Bahlūl b. ʿUbayd, that Abū Isḥāq al-Sabīʿī related to him, from al-Ḥārith, who said that he heard ʿAlī say, "The first man to accept Islam was Abū Bakr, 'the trusting'. The first man to pray with the Prophet (ṢAAS) was ʿAlī b. Abū Ṭālib."

Shuʿba stated, from ʿAmr b. Murra, from Abū Ḥamza, from Zayd b. Arqam, who said, "The first man to pray with the Prophet (ṢAAS) was Abū Bakr, 'the trusting'."

Aḥmad related this, quoting al-Tirmidhī and al-Nasāʾī from a *ḥadīth* of Shuʿba. And al-Tirmidhī stated, "It is a good and reliable *ḥadīth*."

We previously gave Ibn Jarīr's quotation of this *ḥadīth* through Shuʿba, from ʿAmr b. Murra, from Abū Ḥamza, from Zayd b. Arqam, who said, "The first to accept Islam was ʿAlī b. Abū Ṭālib."

ʿAmr b. Murra stated, "I mentioned this to Ibrāhīm al-Nakhʿī, but he denied it. He said, 'The first to accept Islam was Abū Bakr.'"

Al-Wāqidī stated, giving chains of authority from Abū Arwā al-Dawsī and Abū Muslim b. ʿAbd al-Raḥmān, along with a group of authorities, to the effect that the first to accept Islam was Abū Bakr, "the trusting".

Yaʿqūb b. Sufyān stated that Abū Bakr al-Ḥumaydī related to us, quoting Sufyān b. ʿUyayna, from Mālik b. Mighwal, from a man who said, "Ibn ʿAbbās was asked, 'Who was it who first believed?' He replied, 'It was Abū Bakr, "the trusting". Have you not heard the lines of Ḥassān (b. Thābit):

> 'When talking of grief at loss of a man to be trusted, recall your brother Abū Bakr for what he did.
>
> He was the best of men, the most just and honourable after the Prophet, and the most worthy, for what he bore
>
> The one who came next, the second, praised was sight of him, he the first of the people to believe in the messengers.
>
> He lived fully praised, following God's will at the order of his friend who passed away, without deviation.'"

Abū Bakr b. Abū Shayba recounted this. One of our sheikhs related to us, from Mujālid, from ʿĀmir, who said, "I asked Ibn ʿAbbās – or Ibn ʿAbbās was asked – which one of the people was the first to accept Islam? He replied, 'Haven't you heard the verses of Ḥassān b. Thābit?' He then recited them."

Al-Haytham b. ʿAdī related this account similarly from Mujālid, from ʿĀmir al-Shaʿbī who said, "I asked Ibn ʿAbbās, and he referred to it."

Abū al-Qāsim al-Baghawī said that Surayj b. Yūnus related to him, quoting Yūsuf b. al-Mājishūn, who said, "Our sheikhs, including Muḥammad b. al-Munkadir, Rabīʿa b. Abū ʿAbd al-Raḥmān, Ṣāliḥ b. Kaysān and ʿUthmān b. Muḥammad, concluded without any doubt, that the first of our people to accept Islam was Abū Bakr, 'the trusting', God be pleased with him."

My own comment is, that this agreed with the views of Ibrāhīm al-Nakhʿī, Muḥammad b. Kaʿb, Muḥammad b. Sīrīn and Saʿd b. Ibrāhīm. That is what is generally accepted by the majority of scholars of orthodox religion.

Ibn ʿAsākir recounted of Saʿd b. Abū Waqqāṣ and Muḥammad b. al-Ḥanafiyya, that they both agreed that, "He was not the very first to accept Islam, but he was in fact the best of all in faith."

Saʿd said that five persons accepted Islam before he did.

It is established in the *ṣaḥīḥ* collection of al-Bukhārī, from a *ḥadīth* of Hamām b. al-Ḥārith, from ʿAmmār b. Yāsir, who said, "I saw the Messenger of God (ṢAAS) and with him there were only five slaves, two women and Abū Bakr."

The Imām Aḥmad and Ibn Māja recounted from a *ḥadīth* of ʿĀṣim b. Abū al-Nujūd, from Zirr, from Ibn Masʿūd, who said, "There were seven persons who were first to openly accept Islam. They were the Messenger of God (ṢAAS) Abū Bakr, ʿAmmār and his mother Sumayya, Ṣuhayb, Bilāl, and al-Miqdād.

"Now the Messenger of God (ṢAAS) was protected by God through his uncle, and Abū Bakr by God through his tribe. But the rest of them were taken away by the idol worshippers who mounted chains on them and roasted them in the sun. All except Bilāl gave way under this treatment; he, however, attached no importance to himself in suffering in God's cause. His people considered him valueless, so they handed him over to the children who began parading him through the streets of Mecca, while he shouted, 'One! One!'"

Al Thawrī recounted this as such from Manṣūr, from Mujāhid, with an incomplete line of transmission.

Ibn Jarīr related that he was informed by Ibn Ḥumayd that Kināna b. Jabala related to him, from Ibrāhīm b. Ṭahmān, from Ḥajjāj, from Qatāda, from Sālim b. Abū al-Jaʿd, from Muḥammad b. Saʿd b. Abū Waqqās, who said, "I asked my father, 'Was Abū Bakr the first one to accept Islam?' 'No,' he replied. 'More than 50 others accepted Islam before he did. But his Islam was the best of all.'"

This *ḥadīth* is objectionable in both its content and its chain of authorities.

Ibn Jarīr said that others stated that the first person to accept Islam was Zayd b. Ḥāritha. Then he related, moreover, through al-Wāqidī from Ibn Abū Dhiʾb, who asked al-Zuhrī, "Who was the first woman to accept Islam?" "Khadīja," he replied. "And the first man?" "Zayd b. Ḥāritha," was his answer.

ʿUrwa, Sulaymān b. Yasār and others said the same, that the first man to accept Islam was Zayd b. Ḥāritha.

Abū Ḥanīfa, God be pleased with him, responded by combining these statements and concluding that the first free man to accept Islam was Abū Bakr, that Khadīja was the first woman, Zayd b. Ḥāritha the first slave, and ʿAlī b. Abū Ṭālib the first boy. God be pleased with them all.

Muḥammad b. Isḥāq stated, "When Abū Bakr accepted Islam and announced this fact, he prayed to God the Almighty and Glorious. Abū Bakr was a man admired by his people, a well-liked and easy-going man. He knew more than anyone about the genealogy of Quraysh and of the good and bad in their history. He was a business man of fine character and charity.

"His people would come and consult with him on all kinds of matters because of his knowledge, his business experience and the pleasantness of his company.

"He soon began inviting those he trusted of his friends and associates to join him in accepting Islam.

"I have been told that those who accepted Islam through him were: al-Zubayr b. al-ʿAwwām, ʿUthmān b. ʿAffān, Ṭalḥa b. ʿUbayd Allāh, Saʿd b. Abū Waqqāṣ and ʿAbd al-Raḥmān b. ʿAwf, God be pleased with them.

"They all went, accompanied by Abū Bakr, to the Messenger of God (ṢAAS) who explained Islam and its correctness to them and recited to them from the Qurʾān; they then believed.

"These eight men were the earliest to accept Islam. They prayed and believed in the Messenger of God (ṢAAS) and in the mission he had received from God."

Muḥammad b. ʿUmar al-Wāqidī stated that Al-Ḍaḥḥāk b. ʿUthmān related to him, from Makrama b. Sulaymān al-Wālibī, from Ibrāhīm b. Muḥammad b. Abū Ṭalḥa, who said that Ṭalḥa b. ʿUbayd Allāh said, "I attended the trade fair at Buṣrā and there, in his cell, was a monk who called out, 'Ask the Meccans at the fair whether any man of them is from the holy quarter.'"

Ṭalḥa stated, "I replied, 'Yes; I am.' The monk then asked, 'Has Aḥmad come forth yet?' I asked, 'Who is Ahmad?' He responded, 'He is the son of ʿAbd Allāh b. ʿAbd al-Muṭṭalib; this is the month during which he will appear. He is the last of the prophets. He will come forth from the holy quarter and go into exile to a place of date-palms, stony tracts, and salty earth. Be sure not to let anyone precede you to him.'"

Ṭalḥa went on, "His words deeply impressed me. So I left quickly for Mecca. There I asked, 'Is there any news?' People replied, 'Yes indeed; Muḥammad son of ʿAbd Allāh, "the trustworthy", has declared himself a prophet. And he has Abū Bakr b. Abū Quḥāfa as a follower.'"

Ṭalḥa continued, "So I went off to Abū Bakr and asked him, 'Have you really become a follower of this man?' 'Yes,' he replied. 'And you should go off to him, see him and follow him. He is calling to the truth.'" Then Ṭalḥa told him what the monk had said.

Abū Bakr then took Ṭalḥa with him and they went in to see the Messenger of God (ṢAAS). Ṭalḥa then accepted Islam and told the Messenger of God (ṢAAS) what the monk had said; he was delighted to hear this.

When Abū Bakr and Ṭalḥa had accepted Islam they were seized by Nawfal b. Khuwaylid b. al-ʿAdawī, who was known as "the lion of Quraysh". He tied both men together with one rope; and Banū Taym did nothing to protect them. For this reason Abū Bakr and Ṭalḥa were known as "the bondsmen". And the Prophet (ṢAAS) spoke the words, "O God, save us from the evil of al-ʿAdawī's son." It was al-Bayhaqī who recounted this.

The *ḥāfiẓ* Abū al-Ḥasan Khaythama b. Sulaymān al-Aṭrabulsī stated that ʿUbayd Allāh b. Muḥammad b. ʿAbd al-ʿAzīz al-ʿUmarī, the *qāḍī*, judge, of al-Miṣṣīṣa, related to him, quoting Abū Bakr ʿAbd Allāh b. ʿUbayd Allāh b. Isḥāq b. Muḥammad b. ʿUmrān b. Mūsā b. Ṭalḥa b. ʿUbayd Allāh, quoting Abū ʿUbayd Allāh, quoting ʿAbd Allāh b. Muḥammad b. ʿUmrān b. Ibrāhīm b. Muḥammad b. Ṭalḥa, who said that his father Muḥammad b. ʿUmrān related to him, from al-Qāsim b. Muḥammad b. Abū Bakr, on the authority of ʿĀʾisha, God be pleased with her, who said, "Abū Bakr went to see the Messenger of God (ṢAAS); he had been his friend before the coming of Islam. On meeting him, Abū Bakr said, 'O Abū al-Qāsim, you have been missed from your tribe's councils; and people are charging you with disloyalty to your forebears.'

"The Messenger of God replied, 'I am the Messenger of God and I summon you to God!' When he had finished speaking Abū Bakr accepted Islam. The Messenger of God (ṢAAS) then left him, and there was no man between Mecca's two mountains happier than he was at Abū Bakr accepting Islam.

"Abū Bakr went thereafter to ʿUthmān b. ʿAffān, Ṭalḥa b. ʿUbayd Allāh, al-Zubayr b. al-ʿAwwām and Saʿd b. Abū Waqqāṣ, and they all accepted Islam.

"Next day he brought ʿUthmān b. Maẓʿūn, Abū ʿUbayda b. al-Jarrāḥ, ʿAbd al-Raḥmān b. ʿAwf, Abū Salama b. Abd al-Asad, and al-Arqam b. Abū al-Arqam, and they all accepted Islam. God be pleased with them!"

ʿAbd Allāh b. Muḥammad stated that his father Muḥammad b. ʿUmrān related to him, from al-Qāsim b. Muḥammad, from ʿĀʾisha, who said, "When the Companions of the Prophet (ṢAAS), 38 men in number, met, Abū Bakr urged the Messenger of God (ṢAAS) to proclaim Islam openly, but he replied, 'O Abū Bakr, we are only few in number.'

"However, Abū Bakr kept urging until the Messenger of God (ṢAAS) did appear openly (as a Muslim). Then the Muslims separated off into different areas of the mosque, each man in his own tribe, and Abū Bakr arose to address the assembly, while the Messenger of God (ṢAAS) remained seated. He was the first man to make a speech calling people to God and to His Messenger (ṢAAS). The polytheists were very angry at Abū Bakr and the Muslims and caused violent fights all over the mosque. Abū Bakr was trampled underfoot and severely beaten. The sinner ʿUtba b. Rabīʿa went over to him and began beating him with a pair of old sandals with which he cut up his face and then so trampled Abū Bakr's body that he was badly injured.

"After this Banū Taym arrived and engaged in the fight and the idolaters withdrew from Abū Bakr. Men of Banū Taym then carried Abū Bakr away in a cloth to his house, convinced that he was dying. After that they went back into the mosque and said, 'By God, if Abū Bakr dies we are going to kill ʿUtba b. Rabīʿa!'

"They then returned to Abū Bakr. Thereafter Abū Qaḥāfa, and the Taym tribesmen kept talking to Abū Bakr until, late in the day, he spoke back. He said, 'How is the Messenger of God (ṢAAS)?' But they upbraided and attacked him verbally and rose to leave, telling his mother Umm al-Khayr, 'Be sure to give him something to eat or drink.' When she was alone with him she fretted over him, but he began saying, 'How is the Messenger of God (ṢAAS)?' She replied, 'I swear, I don't know anything about your friend.' He asked, 'Please go to Umm Jamīl, al-Khaṭṭāb's daughter, and ask her about him.'

"She went out to visit Umm Jamīl and said to her, 'Abū Bakr asks you about Muḥammad b. ʿAbd Allāh.' She replied, 'I don't know Abū Bakr nor Muḥammad b. ʿAbd Allāh. But if you like I will go with you to your son.' She agreed and took her to where Abū Bakr lay stretched out near death. Umm Jamīl went over to him and let out a scream, shouting, 'By God, they've done this to you for the sake of a crowd of sinners and disbelievers! I just hope God takes vengeance for you on them!'

"He asked, 'How is the Messenger of God (ṢAAS)?' She replied, 'This is your mother, here listening.' He insisted, 'You need fear nothing from her.' She then said, 'He is safe and sound.' 'Where is he?' Abū Bakr asked. 'In the house of Ibn al-Arqam,' she told him.

"He commented, 'God has made it incumbent on me not to taste food or to drink until I go to the Messenger of God (ṢAAS).'

"They did nothing until things had quietened down and people were calm again. They then helped him outside, he leaning upon them, and took him in to see the Messenger of God (ṢAAS) who greeted him with embraces and kisses, as did the other Muslims. The Messenger of God (ṢAAS) was extremely moved by his state. Abū Bakr commented, 'I swear by my mother and father, O Messenger of God, I'm not in bad shape, except for what that sinner did to my face. But here is my mother, who is always so kind to her son. You are blessed by God; please invite her to come to God, and pray to Him for her, to save her, through yourself, from hell-fire.'

"And the Messenger of God (ṢAAS) prayed for her and invited her to God, and so she did accept Islam.

"They stayed with the Messenger of God (ṢAAS) there in that house for a month, all 39 men of them.

"Ḥamza b. ʿAbd al-Muṭṭalib had accepted Islam the day when Abū Bakr was beaten.

"The Messenger of God (ṢAAS) said a prayer for ʿUmar b. al-Khaṭṭāb – or for Abū Jahl b. Hishām. ʿUmar awoke next morning – the prayer having been made on Wednesday – and that day, Thursday, accepted Islam. The Messenger of God (ṢAAS) shouted out, along with all the household, the words *Allāhu Akbar*, 'God is most Great', so loudly at this that they could be heard in the very heights of Mecca.

"Abū al-Arqam, a man who was blind and a disbeliever, then came out saying, 'O God, forgive my young son ʿUbayd al-Arqam, for he has apostacized.'

"ʿUmar arose and asked, 'O Messenger of God, why do we conceal our faith though we follow the truth, while their religion is displayed openly even though they follow falsehood?' He replied, 'O ʿUmar, we are but few, and you saw what happened to us.' ʿUmar responded, 'By Him who sent you with the truth, I'll never attend a meeting with disbelievers without declaring my faith there.'

"He then left, and circumambulated the *kaʿba*, passing by some Quraysh men who were waiting for him. Abū Jahl b. Hishām asked, 'So-and-so claims you've turned heretic.' ʿUmar responded, 'I bear witness that there is no God but God alone, who has no associate, and that Muḥammad is His servant and His Messenger!'

"The polytheists charged at him and he attacked ‘Utba, getting him down and beating him. He poked his fingers into the eye of ‘Utba, who began to scream. The attackers withdrew at this and ‘Umar got up. Whenever anyone came near him he would grab some nearby old chief until the people gave up attacking him. He then attended those meetings he used to frequent, and there gave expression to his faith.

"Thereafter he went to the Prophet (ṢAAS), having vanquished them, and said, 'Do not worry, by my father and mother! By God, I swear I've been to every meeting I used to attend as a polytheist and at every one I've expressed my faith without fear or reservation!'

"So the Messenger of God (ṢAAS) went outside, ‘Umar leading the way, along with Ḥamza b. ‘Abd al-Muṭṭalib, and circumambulated the *ka‘ba* and performed the noon prayer as a believer. He then went back to the house of al-Arqam, ‘Umar accompanying him. After that ‘Umar went off alone and thereafter the Prophet (ṢAAS) left too."

But the truth is that ‘Umar only accepted Islam after those who migrated for Abyssinia had left, an event that occurred in the sixth year of the mission. Reference to this will be made in the proper place, if God wills it.

We have examined the manner in which Abū Bakr and ‘Umar accepted Islam, God be pleased with them both, in the volume devoted solely to their biography. There we dealt with the subject fully; all praise be to God.

It is established in the *ṣaḥīḥ* collection of Muslim, from a tradition of Abū Amāma, from ‘Amr b. ‘Abasa al-Sulāmī, God be pleased with him, who said, "I came to the Messenger of God (ṢAAS) at the beginning of his mission, while he was in Mecca; he was in hiding at the time. I asked him, 'What are you?' He replied, 'I am a prophet.' 'But what is a prophet?' I asked. 'God's Messenger,' he replied. I asked, 'Was it God who sent you?' 'Yes,' he answered. 'With what did he send you?' I then asked. He replied, 'With the command: Worship God alone; He has no associate. Destroy the idols. And make firm ties of kinship.' I commented, 'Well, that's fine what he sent you with. Who are your followers in this?' He replied, 'A free man and a slave.'"

By this he meant Abū Bakr and Bilāl. He went on, "‘Amr used to say, 'I thought myself one quarter of Islam.'

"And so I did accept Islam and said, 'Shall I follow you then, O Messenger of God?' He replied, 'No; join your own people. When you are informed I have gone public, then follow me.'"

It is said that the statement of the Prophet (ṢAAS), "a free man and a slave", has a generic meaning. To interpret it by reference to Abū Bakr and to Bilāl alone would be doubtful, for a group of men had accepted Islam before ‘Amr b. ‘Absa. And Zayd b. Ḥāritha had accepted Islam before Bilāl. Perhaps he referred to being "one fourth of Islam" by his own knowledge alone, because the believers were concealing their Islam at this time, few of their close relatives being aware of it, let alone strangers and bedouins from the desert. But God knows best.

In the *ṣaḥīḥ* collection of al-Bukhārī, through Abū Usāma, from Hāshim b. Hāshim, there is a *ḥadīth* from Saʿīd b. al-Musayyab, who said, "I heard Abū Isḥāq Saʿd b. Abū Waqqāṣ say, 'No one accepted Islam that same day I did. For seven days I remained one third of Islam.'"

His statement "no one accepted Islam the same day I did" presents only a simple issue. It was recounted by some to read: "except on the day I accepted Islam". This would be problematic, for it suggests that no one preceded him in accepting Islam. And it is well known that Abū Bakr, ʿAlī, Khadīja, and Zayd b. Ḥāritha accepted Islam before he did. Similarly, more than one authority, including Ibn al-Athīr, have reached a consensus that these people did precede in accepting Islam. Abū Ḥanīfa, God be pleased with him, gives textual evidence that each of these did accept Islam before those of his kind. But God knows best.

As for the above statement, "For seven days I remained one-third of Islam", this is problematic. I do not know how to explain it, except for his having made the statement based on his knowledge alone. But God knows best.

Abū Dāwūd al-Ṭayyālisī stated that Ḥammād b. Salama related to him, from ʿĀṣim, from Zarr, from ʿAbd Allāh, who is Ibn Masʿūd, who said, "When I was a youth I used to tend flocks for ʿUqba b. Abū Muʿīṭ in Mecca. The Messenger of God (ṢAAS) and Abū Bakr came out and joined me, having escaped from the polytheists. He said – or they both said – 'Do you have any milk you could give us to drink, lad?' I replied, 'But I'm entrusted with it; I can't give it to you to drink.' He then asked, 'Do you have a young ewe that hasn't yet been served by a ram?' 'Yes, I do', I replied.

"I brought the ewe over to them and Abū Bakr tethered it. Then the Messenger of God (ṢAAS) took hold of its udder and said a prayer. The udder filled and Abū Bakr brought a hollowed stone and the Prophet (ṢAAS) poured milk into it. He then drank, quoting Abū Bakr, and poured some for me too. He now spoke to the udder and told it to contract, which it did.

"Later I went to the Messenger of God (ṢAAS) and said, 'Teach me some of this good speech,' meaning the Qurʾān. He replied, 'Consider yourself a well-taught young man.' I then took from his mouth 70 *suras* regarding which no one can challenge me."

This is how Imām Aḥmad related this anecdote, from ʿAffān, from an account of it by Ḥammād b. Salama.

Al-Ḥasan b. ʿArafa also recounted it, from Abū Bakr b. ʿAyyāsh, from ʿĀṣim b. Abū al-Nujūd.

Al-Bayhaqī stated that Abū ʿAbd Allāh, the *ḥāfiẓ*, related to him, quoting Abū ʿAbd Allāh b. Baṭṭa al-Aṣbahānī, quoting al-Ḥasan b. al-Jahm, quoting al-Ḥusayn b. al-Faraj, quoting Muḥammad b. ʿUmar, quoting Jaʿfar b. Muḥammad b. Khālid b. al-Zubayr, from his father – or from Muḥammad b. ʿAbd Allāh b. ʿAmr b. ʿUthmān – who said, "The acceptance of Islam by Khālid b. Saʿīd b. al-ʿĀṣ was early; he was the first one of his brothers to accept Islam.

"The beginnings of his becoming Muslim was that he saw himself in a dream placed on the brink of a fire, the size of which was so great as only God could have known. In his sleep he had a vision as though someone were pushing him towards it. Then he saw the Messenger of God (ṢAAS) grip him by his waist-wrappers (so that) he would not fall. He awoke in a fright from his sleep and said, 'I swear by God that this was a vision of the truth.'

"When he met Abū Bakr b. Abū Qaḥāfa, he told him of this and Abū Bakr replied, 'This was indeed the Messenger of God (ṢAAS): follow him. You will follow him and enter into Islam with him. Islam will prevent you from falling into it (the fire) though your father will do so.'

"And so he joined the Messenger of God (ṢAAS) who was at Ajyad, and asked him, 'O Messenger of God, O Muḥammad, to what do you call (people)?' He answered, 'I invite you to come to God, the One, He who has no associate, and (to bear witness) that Muḥammad is His slave and His Messenger, and for you to abandon your practice of worshipping rocks that cannot hear, nor harm, nor see, nor benefit, nor know who it is who worship them and who do not.'

"Khālid said, 'I do bear witness that there is no God but God, and that you are the Messenger of God.' The Messenger of God (ṢAAS) was delighted at his accepting Islam.

"Khālid then went away and his father learned of his accepting Islam. So he sent after him and had him brought back. His father reprimanded him and beat him with a club he held in his hand so hard that he broke it upon his head. He swore, 'By God, I'll prevent you from getting food!' Khālid responded, 'If you do so, God will provide me what I shall live by.'

"He then went off to the Messenger of God (ṢAAS) whom he served and stayed with."

An Account of how Ḥamza, son of ʿAbd al-Muṭṭalib, God be pleased with him, the uncle of the Prophet (ṢAAS), accepted Islam.

Yūnus b. Bukayr quoted Muḥammad b. Isḥāq as saying that a man of the Aslam tribe – a man with a fine memory – related to him that Abū Jahl blocked the path of the Messenger of God (ṢAAS) at al-Ṣafā, and reviled and cursed him, inflicting insults on his religion. This was reported to Ḥamza b. ʿAbd al-Muṭṭalib, who then went up to Abū Jahl and, standing right there over him, gave him a terrible beating with his bow on the head that fractured his skull.

Quraysh men of Banū Makhzūm tribe approached Ḥamza to give Abū Jahl help against him. They said to Ḥamza, "So, we see you're turning heretic then!"

"And who's going to prevent me?" demanded Ḥamza, "when I now see clearly and can testify that he is the Messenger of God (ṢAAS) and that what he says is the truth. I'll not retract, so you just go on and stand in my way, if you're serious!"

Abū Jahl then spoke up, "Leave Abū ʿUmara alone; I swear, I really did badly insult his nephew."

When Ḥamza accepted Islam Quraysh knew that the Messenger of God (ṢAAS) had gained strength and was protected, and so they refrained from some of their previous treatment of him. Ḥamza spoke some verses on this subject.

Ibn Isḥāq stated, "Then Ḥamza went home where Satan came to him and said, 'You, a Quraysh chief, have followed this heretic and abandoned the religion of your forefathers! Death is best for you for what you've done!'

"Ḥamza then addressed his inner self, saying, 'O God, if what I've done was right, then make me believe it in my own heart! Or else find me some way out of my predicament!'

"He then spent a night worse than he ever had before due to the whisperings of the devil.

"Next morning he went to the Messenger of God (ṢAAS) and said to him, 'O nephew, I've fallen into a trap from which I don't know how to escape. I don't know whether continuing as I am is wiser for me, or whether it's a terrible mistake. Please talk to me. I really need you to talk to me, nephew.'

"And so the Messenger of God went over to him and talked and preached to him, telling him both what frightened and cheered him. God placed in his heart faith at what he was told by the Messenger of God (ṢAAS).

"Ḥamza therefore said, 'I do truly bear witness that you are telling the truth. Make your faith public, O nephew; for, by God, I would not like to own what is under the sky while keeping to my former religion.'"

So Ḥamza was one of those through whom God fortified the faith.

Al-Bayhaqī related it thus from al-Ḥākim, from al-Aṣamm, from Aḥmad b. ʿAbd al-Jabbār, from an account given by Yūnus b. Bukayr.

An Account of how Abū Dharr, God be pleased with him, came to accept Islam.

The *ḥāfiẓ* al-Bayhaqī stated that the *ḥāfiẓ* Abū ʿAbd Allāh related to him, quoting Abū ʿAbd Allāh Muḥammad b. Yaʿqūb, also a *ḥāfiẓ*, quoting al-Ḥusayn b. Muḥammad b. Ziyād, quoting ʿAbd Allāh b. al-Rūmī, quoting al-Naḍr b. Muḥammad, quoting ʿIkrima b. ʿAmmār, from Abū Zumayl Simāk b. al-Walīd, from Mālik b. Marthad, from his father, from Abū Dharr, who said, "I was a quarter of Islam. Three persons accepted Islam before myself, and I was the fourth. I went to the Messenger of God and said, 'Peace be upon you, O Messenger of God. I bear witness that there is no God but God, and that Muḥammad is the Messenger of God.' I then saw the face of the Messenger of God (ṢAAS) radiate with pleasure."

This is an abbreviated account.

Al-Bukhārī stated, regarding the acceptance of Islam by Abū Dharr, that ʿAmr b. ʿAbbās related to him, quoting ʿAbd al-Raḥmān b. Mahdī, from al-Muthannā, from Abū Jamra, from Ibn ʿAbbās, who said that when news of the mission of the Messenger of God (ṢAAS) reached Abū Dharr, he said to his brother, "Ride off into that valley and bring me information about this man who claims that he is a prophet to whom information comes from heaven. Listen to what he says, then come back to me."

The brother then left, came to the Prophet (ṢAAS), heard his words, then returned to Abū Dharr. He told him, "I saw him advocating ethical behaviour, and delivering speech that was not poetry."

Abū Dharr told him, "You've not solved my problem."

He then equipped himself for a journey, carrying a large, full waterskin, and left for Mecca. There he went to the mosque and looked for the Messenger of God (ṢAAS) but did not know how to recognize him and he was reluctant to ask after him. When night came and he lay down to rest, ʿAlī saw him and realized he was a stranger. Abū Dharr followed him without either man asking the other any questions. Next morning when he arose, Abū Dharr carried off his waterskin and provisions to the mosque, where he remained all day without the Prophet (ṢAAS) seeing him. When night came, he set out his bedding. ʿAlī passed by and exclaimed, "Isn't it high time the man knew his house!" He then helped him up and took him home, neither man asking the other any questions.

The third day the same thing happened and again ʿAlī accommodated him. But this time ʿAlī asked him, "Won't you tell me what brought you here?" Abū Dharr replied, "I will if you'll promise faithfully to guide me." ʿAlī agreed and so Abū Dharr explained. ʿAlī then told him, "He is truth; he is the Messenger of God (ṢAAS). Tomorrow morning follow me and if I see anything that makes me fearful for you, I will get up as if I need to urinate. If I leave, follow me and go where I do."

ʿAlī did this and Abū Dharr followed on behind him and accompanied him when he went in to the Prophet (ṢAAS). Abū Dharr heard him speak and he accepted Islam then and there.

The Prophet (ṢAAS) then told him, "Go back to your people and tell them; then wait till you hear from me."

But Abū Dharr replied, "No, by Him who sent you with the truth, I'll shout it out in full public!"

He then left and went to the mosque, where he shouted at the top of his voice, "I bear witness that there is no God but God, and that Muḥammad is the Messenger of God!" At that everyone there set about beating him till they laid him low.

Then al-ʿAbbās came and, bending over him, exclaimed, "Woe unto you! Don't you realize that he is from Ghifār, and that your trade route is to Syria?" He then rescued Abū Dharr from them. But the next day Abū Dharr did the same and was again attacked and then saved by al-ʿAbbās.

This is the story as told by al-Bukhārī.

Abū Dharr's acceptance of Islam is elaborated in the *ṣaḥīḥ* collections of Muslim and elsewhere.

Imām Aḥmad stated that Yazīd b. Hārūn related to him, quoting Sulaymān b. al-Mughīra, quoting Ḥumayd b. Hilāl, from ʿAbd Allāh b. al-Ṣāmit, who quoted Abū Dharr as saying, "We – that is I, my brother Anīs, and our mother – left our tribe of Ghifār because they used to disregard the restrictions of the holy month.

"We took up residence with an uncle of ours who was a man of wealth and status; he honoured us and treated us extremely well. But his family envied us and told him, 'If you were to go away from your people, Anīs would take your place over them.'

"Our uncle then came to us and reported what he had been told. I then said to him, 'You've cancelled out all your prior generosity to us. We'll have no communion with you henceforth.'

"So we assembled our herd of camels and set off with them, while our uncle covered himself up in his robe and began to weep.

"We rode on until we made camp on the outskirts of Mecca. My brother Anīs then made a wager, betting our flock of camels and an additional number equal to our herd. He (and his competitor) then went to a diviner who decided in favour of Anīs. Anīs returned to us with our herd and a like one."

Abū Dharr continued, "Now, my nephew, I had been praying for three years prior to meeting the Messenger of God (ṢAAS)." I asked, "To whom?" "To God." "In which direction?" "Wherever God directed me. And I would pray each evening till deep into the night, when I find myself under my blanket, until the sun would rise."

"Well any way," Anīs said, "I have business in Mecca; await me until I return." He left and was away for what seemed a long time, then he came back. I asked him, "What kept you?" He said, "I met a man who claimed that God had sent him with your religion." "And what do people say of him?" I asked. "They say that he is a poet and a soothsayer." Anīs was himself a poet.

He went on, "Anīs commented, 'I've heard soothsayers and he does not speak like them. And I've checked his utterances against the measures of poetry and, by God, it doesn't fit anyone's tongue as poetry. And, I swear, he is truthful, whereas the rest are liars.'

"I asked him, 'Could you stand in for me while I leave?' 'Yes,' he replied, 'but watch out for the Meccans. They have pilloried and berated him.'

"So I left and went to Mecca, where I asked a weak-looking man, 'Where is the one people refer to as the heretic?' But he pointed at me and the people of that valley pelted me with clods of earth and bones until I was injured with wounds and fainted. When I got up later, I was like a red pole. I made my way to *zamzam*, drank its water and washed the blood off myself. I then positioned myself between the *ka῾ba* and its hangings. And there I stayed, O nephew, for 30 days and nights without sustenance except for water from *zamzam*. But I gained weight and developed folds of fat on my belly, finding no evidence on my body of the emaciation of starvation.

"One night when the moon was very bright and the Meccans were fast asleep, there were only two women circumambulating the *ka῾ba*. As they came past me they were saying prayers to the gods Isāf and Nā᾽ila. I commented, 'Make one of them have intercourse with the other!' This did not deter them, so I then said, 'They're just like bits of wood, but I'd not lean on them!'

"At this they scurried away, wailing, 'If only one of our menfolk were here!'

"'The Messenger of God (ṢAAS) and Abū Bakr, on their way down from the mountain, met these women and asked them what was the matter. 'It's that heretic between the *ka῾ba* and its hangings.' They asked them what I had said, and the women replied, 'He said a real mouthful to us!'

"The Messenger of God (ṢAAS) and his Companion then came along, kissed the stone, circumambulated the *ka῾ba*, then prayed. I went over to him and was the first person to address him with the greeting of the community of Islam. He replied, 'Peace be upon you, and God's mercy. Who are you?' I told him I was from the Ghifār tribe. He brought his hand to his forehead in a gesture of surprise and I told myself, 'He dislikes my being from Ghifār!'

"I made as if to take him by the hand, but his Companion pushed me away, knowing him better then I did.

"The Prophet (ṢAAS) then asked, 'How long have you been here?' 'I've been here for 30 days and nights,' I answered.

"'And who has been feeding you?' he asked.

"'There's been nothing except *zamzam* water, but I've gained so much weight that I developed folds of fat on my belly. And I feel no emaciation from hunger.'

"The Messenger of God (ṢAAS) then said, 'It's blessed! Wonder food!'

"Abū Bakr then asked, 'Please, O Messenger of God, permit me to give him some food tonight.' And he agreed.

"The Prophet (ṢAAS) then left and I went with them. Abū Bakr opened a gate and began picking some grapes from Ṭā'if for us. And that was the first food I ate there. I stayed some time in Mecca.

"Then the Messenger of God (ṢAAS) told me, 'I have been directed to go to a land of palm trees, none other than Yathrib, I believe. Will you go and inform your people about me? Perhaps God will benefit them through you, and give you reward among them too.'

"So I left and rejoined my brother Anīs. He asked me, 'What did you do?' 'What I did was, I accepted Islam and believed.'

"He commented, 'I've nothing against your religion. I too accept Islam and believe.'

"We then went to our mother and she said, 'Well, I've nothing against your religion. I accept Islam and believe.' We then packed up and rejoined our tribe of Ghifār, and some of them accepted Islam before the Messenger of God migrated to Medina. Khufāf b. Aymā' b. Rakhṣa the Ghifārī led them as he was their chief at that time. The remainder of them said, 'If the Messenger of God (ṢAAS) comes, we will accept Islam.'

"And the Messenger of God (ṢAAS) did come and the remainder of them did accept Islam. Then the Aslam tribe arrived and said, 'O Messenger of God, we'll accept Islam just as our Ghifār brothers did.'

"The Messenger of God (ṢAAS) commented, 'God has *ghafara*, "forgiven", Ghafar, and God has *salama*, "made peace with", Aslam!'"

Muslim related this from Hudba b. Khālid from Sulaymān b. al-Mughīra in much the same words. The story of Abū Dharr's acceptance of Islam is also told in another way, along with strange additions. But God knows best.

The account of the acceptance of Islam by Salmān al-Fārisī has been given previously in the book recounting the miraculous signs of the mission of the Prophet (ṢAAS).

An Account of the acceptance of Islam by Ḍimād.

Muslim and al-Bayhaqī related a *ḥadīth* of Dāwūd b. Abū Hind, from ʿAmr b. Saʿīd, from Saʿīd b. Jubayr, from Ibn ʿAbbās, who said that Ḍimād came to Mecca, he being a man of the Azd tribe from Shanū'a. He used to say incantations to protect people from those winds. He overheard some Meccan fools saying, "Muḥammad is crazy." He asked them, "Where is this man? Perhaps God will cure him at my hands."

He recounted, "I met Muḥammad and said, 'I use incantations against these winds. And God cures at my hands whomever He wishes. Do come along.'

"Muḥammad (ṢAAS) replied, 'Praise be to God! We praise Him and seek His help. Whomever God leads aright, no one can lead astray. Whomever God leads astray, no one can lead aright. I bear testimony that there is no God but God alone who has no associates.' He repeated this three times."

Ḍimād said, "I swear, I have heard the speech of soothsayers, sorcerers, and poets, but I never heard the like of these words. Give me your hand and I'll pledge you my allegiance in Islam."

The Messenger of God accepted his pledge and asked him, "For your tribe too?" "Yes, for my tribe too," he agreed.

The Prophet (ṢAAS) dispatched an army that passed by the people of Ḍimād. The army commander asked his troops, "Have you seized anything from these people?" One of the men replied, "I did take one strong-backed camel from them." He ordered the man, "Give it back to them; they are from the tribe of Ḍimād."

In another account Ḍimād said to the Prophet (ṢAAS), "Repeat these words of yours to me; they are the epitome of oratory."

Abū Nuʿaym devoted a long chapter in his work *al-Dalāʾil* (*The Signs*) to accounts of the prominent men who accepted Islam. He gave it in fine detail, may God have mercy on him and reward him.

Ibn Isḥāq gave a list of the names of the Companions, God be pleased with them, who accepted Islam early on. He stated, "Then Abū ʿUbayda accepted Islam, as did Abū Salama, al-Arqam b. Abū al-Arqam, ʿUthmān b. Maẓʿūn, ʿUbayda b. al-Ḥārith and Saʿīd b. Zayd, along with his wife Fāṭima, daughter of al-Khaṭṭāb.

Also there were Asmāʾ, daughter of Abū Bakr, and ʿĀʾisha, also daughter of Abū Bakr, when she was young.

As well there were Qudāma b. Maẓʿūn, ʿAbd Allāh b. Maẓʿūn, Khabbāb b. al-Aratt, ʿUmayr b. Abū Waqqāṣ, ʿAbd Allāh b. Masʿūd, Masʿūd b. al-Qārī, Salīṭ b. ʿAmr, ʿAyyāsh b. Abū Rabīʿa, along with his wife Asmāʾ, daughter of Salama b. Mukharriba of the Taym tribe, and Khunays b. Hudhāqa, and ʿĀmir b. Rabīʿa.

Then there were ʿAbd Allāh b. Jaḥsh, Abū Aḥmad b. Jaḥsh, Jaʿfar b. Abū Ṭālib, along with his wife Asmāʾ daughter of ʿUmays.

Others included Ḥāṭib b. al-Ḥārith and his wife Fāṭima, daughter of al-Mujallil, and also Ḥaṭṭāb b. al-Ḥārith and his wife Fukayha, daughter of Yasār, Maʿmar b. al-Ḥārith b. Maʿmar al-Jumaḥī, and al-Sāʾib b. ʿUthmān b. Maẓʿūn, al-Muṭṭalib b. Azhar b. ʿAbd Manāf and his wife Ramla, daughter of Abū ʿAwf b. Ṣubayra b. Saʿīd b. Sahm, al-Naḥḥām, whose name was Nuʿaym b. ʿAbd Allāh b. Asīd, ʿĀmir b. Fuhayra, the freed-man of Abū Bakr, Khālid b. Saʿīd, Umayna, daughter of Khalaf b. Asʿad b. ʿĀmir b. Bayāḍa, of Khuzāʿa, and

Ḥāṭib b. ʿAmr b. ʿAbd Shams, Abū Ḥudhayfa b. ʿUtba b. Rabīʿa, Wāqid b. ʿAbd Allāh b. ʿArīn b. Thaʿlaba of Tamīm, allies to Banū ʿAdī.

Also there were Khālid b. al-Bukayr, ʿĀmir b. al-Bukayr, ʿĀqil b. al-Bukayr, Iyās b. al-Bukayr b. ʿAbd Yālayl b. Nāshib b. Ghīra, of the tribe of Saʿd b. Layth. The given name of ʿĀqil (a word meaning "wise") had originally been Ghāfil (a word meaning "heedless") and so the Messenger of God (ṢAAS) had renamed him ʿĀqil. These were all allied to the tribe of ʿAdī b. Kaʿb.

Also there were ʿAmmār b. Yāsir and Ṣuhayb b. Sinān.

Thereafter people began accepting Islam in large numbers, men and women both, so that it became a prominent subject of discussion in Mecca.

Ibn Isḥāq stated, "God then ordered his Messenger (ṢAAS), after three years of his mission, to announce it openly and to remain firm against the evil of the polytheists.

"The Companions of the Prophet (ṢAAS) would go off along mountain trails when they prayed, to hide this from their people.

"While Saʿd b. Abū Waqqāṣ was at prayer, along with a small group of others, on a mountain trail, some polytheists came at them. They upbraided them, reviled them for what they were doing, and attacked them.

"Saʿd struck one man with a camel's jawbone and cut him open; this was the first blood spilled in Islam."

Al-Umawī related this incident at length in his *maghāzī* study of the early campaigns, through al-Waqqāṣī, from al-Zuhrī, from ʿĀmir b. Saʿd, from his father. His account states that the man wounded was ʿAbd Allāh b. Khaṭal, God damn him.

CHAPTER: GOD'S COMMAND TO HIS MESSENGER (ṢAAS) TO ANNOUNCE HIS MISSION PUBLICLY.

This chapter deals with God's command to his Messenger (ṢAAS) to announce publicly his mission to high and low and how He told him to be patient and stoical, and to oppose those who remain stubborn, mendacious and ignorant even after the evidence had been brought against them and the Messenger had been sent to them. It also mentions the damages they had done to him and to his Companions, may God bless them all.

God Almighty stated, "And warn those of your people closest to you and bring down your wing to protect those believers who follow you. And if they disobey you, say, 'I am innocent of what you do'. Put your trust in the Almighty and All-Merciful, who sees you when you arise and when you turn about among those prostrating in prayer; He is the All-Hearing, the All-Knowing" (*sūrat al-Shuʿarāʾ*, XXVI, v.214–20).

And the Almighty stated, "It is surely a message to you and to your people, and you will all be questioned" (*sūrat al-Zukhruf*, XLIII, v.44).

Also He stated, "He who imposed the Qur'ān upon you will bring you back to an after life" (*sūrat al-Qaṣaṣ*, XXVIII, v.85). This means, He who has made a demand upon you and has required you to announce the Qur'ān will return you to the hereafter, which is the *ma'ād*, the afterlife, and He will question you about that. As the Almighty stated, "And, by your Lord, we will question them all for what they have done" (*sūrat al-Ḥijr*, XV, v.92–3).

The verses and statements concerning this are numerous, and we have given these in detail in our *Exegesis*. We addressed this issue at length in commenting on the verse, "And warn those of your people closest to you" in *sūrat al-Shu'arā'*, XXVI, v.214. There we gave many references to that.

On this subject, Imām Aḥmad stated that 'Abd Allāh b. Numayr related, from al-A'mash, from 'Amr b. Murra, from Sa'īd b. Jubayr, from Ibn 'Abbās, who said, "When God sent down, 'And warn those of your people closest to you', the Prophet (ṢAAS), went up on Mt. Ṣafā and called out, 'Ya Ṣabāḥā!'

"People gathered there around him; they consisted of men who had come to him themselves and others who had sent messengers.

"The Messenger of God (ṢAAS) addressed them, saying, 'O tribe of 'Abd al-Muṭṭalib, O tribe of Fihr, O tribe of Ka'b! If I were to tell you that there were horsemen on the heights of this mountain who planned to attack you, don't you think you would believe me?' 'Yes,' they replied. He then announced, 'Well, I am come to warn you of a terrible punishment.'

"Abū Lahab, God damn him! said, 'Damn you! May you perish all day long! You called us here for this?'

"And so God, the Almighty and Glorious, revealed 'Damn the hands of Abū Lahab! Damn him!'" (*sūrat al-Lahab*, CXI, v.1).

Both of the sources gave this *ḥadīth* from an account of al-A'mash in similar form.

Aḥmad stated that Mu'āwiya b. 'Amr related to him, quoting Zā'ida, quoting 'Abd al-Mālik b. 'Umayr, from Mūsā b. Ṭalḥa, from Abū Hurayra, who said that when this verse, "And warn those of your people closest to you" was revealed, the Messenger of God (ṢAAS) summoned the people of Quraysh, high and low alike, and told them, "O Quraysh, save yourselves from hell-fire! O tribe of Banū Kalb, save yourselves from hell-fire! O tribe of 'Abd al-Muṭṭalib, save yourselves from hell-fire! O Fāṭima, daughter of Muḥammad, save yourself from hell-fire! For I, I swear by God, have nothing to protect you from God, except the fact that you have kinship (to me) for which I shall care."

Muslim related this from a *ḥadīth* of 'Abd al-Mālik b. 'Umayr, and it was published in both *ṣaḥīḥ* collections from an account of al-Zuhrī, from Sa'īd b.

al-Musayyib and Abū Salama, from Abū Hurayra. The account has other provenances from Abū Hurayra in the *musnad* collection of Aḥmad and elsewhere.

Aḥmad also stated that Wakīʿ b. Hishām related to him, from his father, from ʿĀʾisha, God bless her, who said, "When there was revealed the verse, 'And warn those of your people closest to you' the Messenger of God (ṢAAS) arose and said, 'O Fāṭima, daughter of Muḥammad! O Ṣafiyya, daughter of ʿAbd al-Muṭṭalib! O family of ʿAbd al-Muṭṭalib! I have nothing to protect you from God; ask whatever you will from my wealth.'" Muslim also related this.

The *ḥāfiẓ* Abū Bakr al-Bayhaqī stated in his work *al-Dalāʾil* (*The Signs*) that Muḥammad b. ʿAbd *al-ḥāfiẓ* related to him, quoting Abū al-ʿAbbās Muḥammad b. Yaʿqūb, quoting Aḥmad b. ʿAbd al-Jabbār, quoting Yūnus b. Bukayr, from Muḥammad b. Isḥāq, who said that someone who concealed his name from him told him that he heard ʿAbd Allāh b. al-Ḥārith b. Nawfal relate from Ibn ʿAbbās, from ʿAlī b. Abū Ṭālib, who said, "When there was revealed to the Messenger of God (ṢAAS) the verses, 'And warn those of your people closest to you and bring down your wing to protect those believers who follow you', the Messenger of God (ṢAAS) said, 'I realized that if I announced it to my people I would see from them what I would hate, and so I kept silent. Then Gabriel, peace be upon him, came to me and said, 'O Muḥammad, if you do not act as your Lord has ordered you, He will punish you with hell-fire.'"

ʿAlī continued, "So he called for me and said, 'O ʿAlī, God has commanded me to warn my closest relatives. So prepare for us a sheep on a platter of food, along with a large pot of milk, then assemble Banū ʿAbd al-Muṭṭalib for me.'

"I did so and they assembled on that day. There were 40 men, more or less; among them there were his uncles Abū Ṭālib, Ḥamza, and al-ʿAbbās, along with Abū Lahab, the vile polytheist.

"I served the food platter to them and the Messenger of God (ṢAAS) took from it a piece of meat, split it with his teeth and tossed it in all directions, saying, 'Eat, in the name of God!' Everyone ate until satiated, nothing being seen left but the marks of their fingers. No one ate like that ever before! Then the Messenger of God (ṢAAS) said, 'Now give them to drink, ʿAlī!' So I brought the large pot of milk, and they drank it up till they were full. I swear, no one ever drank that way before!

"When the Messenger of God (ṢAAS) was on the point of addressing them, Abū Lahab, God damn him! forestalled him by saying, 'Well, what a feast your host served to you to eat!' At that they dispersed without the Messenger of God (ṢAAS) addressing them.

"Next day the Messenger of God (ṢAAS) said, 'Prepare for us the same food and drink as yesterday; that fellow forestalled me by saying what he did before I could address them.'

"I did so, then gathered them for him and the Messenger of God (ṢAAS) did as he had the previous day. They ate till they were full; I swear, none of them ate like that ever before! Then the Messenger of God (ṢAAS) said, 'Give them to drink, ῾Alī!' So I brought them the pot and they drank of it till they were satiated. I swear, none of them drank like that before!

"When the Messenger of God (ṢAAS) was about to address them, Abū Lahab, God damn him! forestalled him by saying, 'Well, what a feast your host served to you to eat!' So they dispersed without the Messenger of God (ṢAAS) addressing them.

"Next day the Messenger of God (ṢAAS) told me, '῾Alī, prepare food and drink for us as you did yesterday. This fellow forestalled me by saying what you heard before I could address the people.'

"I did so and assembled them again. The Messenger of God (ṢAAS) acted as he had the day before. They ate till they were satiated, and then I served them from the pot until they were full. I swear, I never saw people eat and drink like that!

"Then the Messenger of God (ṢAAS) spoke, 'O Family of ῾Abd al-Muṭṭalib, I know of no Arab man, by God, who brought his people anything better than I have brought you. I have brought you what deals with this world and the afterlife as well.'"

Al-Bayhaqī related this anecdote in this way through Yūnus b. Bukayr, from Ibn Isḥāq, from a sheikh of uncertain identity, from ῾Abd Allāh b. al-Ḥārith.

Abū Ja῾far b. Jarīr related it from Muḥammad b. Ḥumayd al-Rāzī, from Salama b. al-Faḍl al-Abrash, from Muḥammad b. Isḥāq, from ῾Abd al-Ghaffār Abū Miryam b. al-Qāsim, from al-Minhāl b. ῾Amr, from ῾Abd Allāh b. al-Ḥārith, from Ibn ῾Abbās, from ῾Alī. His account is similar but adds after the words, "I have brought forth for you the good of this world and the next", "And God has ordered me to call upon you to come to Him. And whoever of you will aid me in this matter I must consider my brother." And so on.

῾Alī continued, "But everyone drew back from that. Since I was the youngest, had the most bleary eyes, the largest stomach and the shortest legs, I called out, 'O Prophet of God, I will be your *wazīr* (i.e. your deputy) in this!'

"The Prophet (ṢAAS) took me by the neck and said, 'This is my brother' and so on and so forth, 'so listen to him and obey him!'

῾Alī went on, "Everyone began laughing and saying to Abū Ṭālib, 'He has ordered you to listen to your son and to obey him!'"

Abd al-Ghaffār b. al-Qāsim Abū Maryam is the sole authority for this account, and he was a liar and a *shī῾ī* whom ῾Alī b. al-Madīnī and others accused of inventing the *ḥadīth*; the other scholars consider him a weak source.

But Ibn Abū Ḥātim related, in his work of exegesis of the Qur᾽ān, from his father, from al-Ḥusayn b. ῾Īsā b. Maysara al-Ḥārithī, from ῾Abd Allāh b. ῾Abd al-Quddūs, from al-Aʿmash, from al-Munhāl b. ʿAmr, from ʿAbd Allāh b. al-Ḥārith, who said, "'ʿAlī stated, 'When the verse "And warn those of your people closest to you" was revealed, the Messenger of God (ṢAAS) said to me, "Make me a leg of lamb on a platter of food and a beaker of milk, and invite Banū Hāshim for me." I did invite them and on that occasion they were 40, give or take a man.'"

This account is much the same up to the words, "Then the Messenger of God (ṢAAS) forestalled them in speaking and asked, 'Which of you will settle my debt for me, and be my successor for my family?'"

ʿAlī went on. "They were all silent. Al-ʿAbbās kept quiet because he feared the issue might involve his money. And I kept quiet because of al-ʿAbbās's age.

"The Prophet (ṢAAS) repeated his question and al-ʿAbbās kept silent and, witnessing this, I said, 'I will, O Messenger of God!' 'You?' he replied.

ʿAlī explained, "At that time I was the most homely looking person there. I was bleary eyed, had a large stomach and short legs."

This wording of the anecdote substantiates the previous one, except that it does not have Ibn ʿAbbās as one of the chain of authorities. But God knows best.

Imām Aḥmad related in his *musnad* collection from a *ḥadīth* of ʿAbbād b. ʿAbd Allāh al-Asadī and Rabīʿa b. Nājīdh from ʿAlī an account approximating to the former, or giving testimony to it. But God knows best.

His statement in this *ḥadīth*, "Which of you will settle my debt for me, and be my successor for my family" carries the implication "if I should die". It seems that the Messenger of God (ṢAAS) feared that if he announced his mission to the Arab polytheists they might kill him. He therefore wanted to establish that whoever came in his place thereafter would be beneficial to his family and fulfil his obligations. But God removed his concern at that with His words, "O Messenger, announce what has been revealed to you from your Lord. If you do not, then you will not have fulfilled your mission. God will protect you from the people" (*sūrat al-Māʾida*, V, v.67).

The outcome was that the Messenger of God (ṢAAS) continued to call upon people to believe in God Almighty day and night, secretly and openly, without anyone being able to deter, dissuade, or prevent him. He followed people everywhere, into their celebrations, meetings and gatherings, to the fairs and to the pilgrimage stations. Everyone he met, free man or slave, weak or powerful, rich or poor he urged; as far as he was concerned all were equal and alike.

Violent and powerful Quraysh polytheists inflicted harm both verbal and physical upon the Messenger of God (ṢAAS) and upon those powerless individuals who followed him.

One of the most violent of those opposed to him was his uncle Abū Lahab; his full name was ʿAbd al-ʿUzzā b. ʿAbd al-Muṭṭalib. His wife, Umm Jamīl, was named Arwā, daughter of Ḥarb b. Umayya, the sister of Abū Sufyān.

Another uncle, Abū Ṭālib b. ʿAbd al-Muṭṭalib, was at variance with Abū Lahab, for he favoured the Messenger of God (ṢAAS) above all other men for his fine qualities. He treated him with the utmost compassion and kindness and gave him his support and protection. In doing this he was in opposition to his own people, even though he shared their religion and their friendship. God had, however, put his heart to the test by making him love the Prophet (ṢAAS) by natural disposition rather than for religious reasons.

His persisting in the religion of his people was, in fact, an expression of the wisdom of Almighty God and a factor in the protection He was affording to His Messenger. For if Abū Bakr had accepted Islam, he would have no longer held any weight or leadership among the Quraysh polytheists; they would have held no respect for or fear of him. They would have penalized him and done him verbal and actual harm. For your Lord determines and establishes whatever He wills! And He has divided up His creation into many different types and kinds.

Both these uncles, Abū Ṭālib and Abū Lahab, were infidels. But whereas the former will be at the very surface of the fire, the latter will be deep down in its lowest depths. About him God made revelation in one of the chapters of the Qurʾān to be recited from the pulpit and read in sermons and prayers. It contains information that he will roast in flaming hell-fire, along with his wife, that "firewood hawker".[77]

Imām Aḥmad stated that Ibrāhīm b. Abū al-ʿAbbās related to him, quoting ʿAbd al-Raḥmān b. Abū al-Zinād, from his father who said that a man named Rabīʿa b. ʿAbbād of Banū al-Dīl, who had been an idol-worshipper and had accepted Islam, recalled, "I saw the Messenger of God, before the coming of Islam, at the fair of Dhū al-Majāz, and he was saying, 'O you people, say, "There is no God but God", and you will prosper.' There were people gathered all around him, while behind him stood a mean-looking, squint-eyed man wearing two plaits who was saying, 'He's a lying Sabian!' This man followed him wherever he went. I asked who he was and was told it was his uncle, Abū Lahab."

Imām Aḥmad and al-Bayhaqī both also related this anecdote from a *ḥadīth* in similar form from ʿAbd al-Raḥmān b. Abū al-Zinād.

Al-Bayhaqī also stated that Abū Ṭāhir al-Faqīh related to us, quoting Abū Bakr Muḥammad b. al-Ḥasan al-Qaṭṭān, quoting Abū al-Azhar, quoting Muḥammad b. ʿAbd Allāh al-Anṣārī, quoting Muḥammad b. ʿUmar, from Muḥammad b. al-Munkadar, from Rabīʿa al-Dīlī, who said, "I saw the Messenger of God (ṢAAS) at Dhū al-Majāz following people into their dwellings urging them to believe in God, while behind him went a squint-eyed man with scarred cheeks who was saying, 'O people, let not this fellow entice you away from your religion, the religion of your forefathers!'

"I asked, 'Who is he?' And I was told, 'That's Abū Lahab.'"

77. A reference to the words of *sūrat Abū Lahab*, CXI, v.4.

He then related this anecdote through Shuʿba, from al-Ashʿath b. Salīm, from a man of Kināna, who said, "I saw the Messenger of God (ṢAAS) at the Dhū al-Majāz fair. He was saying, 'O people, say "There is no God but God" and you will prosper.' There was a man standing there behind him scattering dust on him. It was Abū Jahl, and what he was saying was, 'O people, let not this fellow entice you away from your religion. He just wants you to give up worship of al-Lāt and al-ʿUzzā.'"

This anecdote states it was Abū Jahal, but it is obvious that it was Abū Lahab. We will give details of his biography when we report his death, which occurred after the battle of Badr. If God Almighty wills it, so shall it be.

Abū Ṭālib, as will be apparent from both his actions and his qualities, was a man of great natural kindness and compassion. He showed this by his support for the Messenger of God (ṢAAS) and for his Companions, God bless them all.

Yūnus b. Bukayr stated that he was informed from Ṭalḥa b. Yaḥyā, from ʿAbd Allāh b. Mūsā b. Ṭalḥa, that ʿUqayl b. Abū Ṭālib related, "Quraysh came to Abū Ṭālib and said, 'This nephew of yours is disturbing our meetings and our mosque; keep him away from us!' He asked me, 'O ʿUqayl, go and bring me Muḥammad.' So I went off and brought him out from a *kanas*.' This word means a "tent"; or he might have used the word *khanas*, a "hide-out", or alternatively as some say, a "small house". He arrived back at midday in the full heat. When he came in, Abū Ṭālib told him, 'These relatives of yours charge that you are annoying them in their meetings and in their mosque. Stop annoying them!'

"At this the Messenger of God (ṢAAS) gazed upwards to the sky and asked, 'Do you see that sun?' 'Yes,' they replied. He then said, 'I'm no more capable of stopping that than you are of getting a flame from it.'

"Abū Ṭālib then said, 'By God, I swear that my nephew never lied. So go home!'"

Al-Bukhārī related this story in his history, from Muḥammad b. al-ʿAlāʾ, from Yūnus b. Bukayr. And al-Bayhaqī related it from al-Ḥākim, from al-Aṣamm, from Aḥmad b. ʿAbd al-Jabbār in the same words.

Moreover al-Bayhaqī related it through Yūnus, from Ibn Isḥāq, who stated, "Yaʿqūb b. ʿUtba b. al-Mughīra b. al-Akhnas related to me that he was told that when Quraysh made this complaint to Abū Ṭālib, he sent for the Messenger of God (ṢAAS) and told him, 'O nephew, your relatives have come to me and told me this and that. Do right by me and by yourself by not burdening me with what neither you nor I could bear. Stop telling your relatives what they dislike hearing!'

"The Messenger of God (ṢAAS) thought that Abū Ṭālib's attitude towards himself and his Muslims had changed and that his support for them had weakened. And so he addressed Abū Ṭālib as follows, 'O uncle, if the sun were placed in my right hand and the moon in my left, I would not give up this matter until either God gives me success in it, or I perish in its pursuit.' The Messenger of God (ṢAAS) then broke down into tears.

"When he turned to leave, Abū Ṭālib said, having seen how deeply the Messenger of God (ṢAAS) had been moved, said to him, 'O nephew!' When he turned to him, he said, 'Continue as before; do as you like. By God, I will never abandon you for any reason.'"

Ibn Isḥāq stated that Abū Ṭālib spoke the following verses on that subject:

> "By God, they'll never get their gang to you until I'm laid to rest, buried in the ground.
>
> Carry on with your work that is beyond reproach; rejoice, and may you be content in doing so.
>
> You invited me, and I knew you were advising well; you spoke the truth, and you were ever trustworthy.
>
> You offered a religion I knew to be the best religion of mankind.
>
> Were it not for people's blame and anger, you'd find me giving it my favour openly."

Al-Bayhaqī stated, "Ibn Isḥāq related various verses of Abū Ṭālib on that subject."

All this gives evidence that God Almighty gave the prophet (ṢAAS) His protection through his uncle, even though he differed in his religion. And God had protected him when his uncle was not there; God's will is final and unchallenged.

Yūnus b. Bukayr stated that Muḥammad b. Isḥāq related to him, quoting a man originally from Egypt some 40 years previously, from 'Ikrima, from Ibn 'Abbās, a long anecdote relating what transpired between the polytheists of Mecca and the Messenger of God (ṢAAS). When the Messenger of God (ṢAAS) arose, Abū Jahl b. Hishām said, "O Quraysh, Muḥammad is persisting, as you know, in criticizing our religion, reviling our forefathers, ridiculing our values and insulting our gods. I swear by God that I'll sit and wait for him tomorrow carrying a rock, and if he prostrates in his prayer, I'll smash his head with it! And let 'Abd Manāf's people do whatever they like about it afterwards."

Next day Abū Jahl, God curse him! took a rock and sat to wait for the Messenger of God (ṢAAS). That morning, the Messenger of God (ṢAAS) came as usual; his direction of prayer at that time was towards Syria. When he prayed he positioned himself between the corner (of the *ka'ba*) with the "black stone" and the Yemeni corner, facing so that the *ka'ba* was between himself and Syria. By the time he came to pray Quraysh were already sitting in their meeting places, waiting. When the Messenger of God (ṢAAS) prostrated in prayer, Abū Jahl did pick up the rock and approached him. When he got near him, he retreated in fear, his colour pale in terror. His hands lost their grip on the rock and it fell.

Quraysh men went up to him and asked, "What's the matter with you, Abū al-Ḥakam?" He answered, "When I got up to do as I told you yesterday I would and got near him, a stallion camel blocked my way to him. And, by God, I never saw a stallion so big as it, with a neck and fangs like it had! It was about to devour me!"

Ibn Isḥāq related, "It was reported to me that the Messenger of God (ṢAAS) said, 'That was Gabriel. And if he had come near me, he would have taken him.'"

Al-Bayhaqī stated that Abū ʿAbd Allāh, the *ḥāfiẓ*, related to him, quoting Abū al-Naḍr, the jurist, quoting ʿUthmān al-Dāramī, quoting ʿAbd Allāh b. Ṣāliḥ, quoting al-Layth b. Saʿd, from Isḥāq b. ʿAbd Allāh b. Abū Farwa, from Abān b. Ṣāliḥ, from ʿAlī b. ʿAbd Allāh b. ʿAbbās, from his father, from ʿAbbās b. ʿAbd al-Muṭṭalib, who said, "One day I was in the mosque when Abū Jahl, God curse him! arrived. He said, 'I swear by God, that if I see Muḥammad prostrating in prayer, I'll stomp on his neck!"

"I then left and went to the Messenger of God (ṢAAS) and told him what Abū Jahl had said. He left home in a rage and went to the mosque. He was in a hurry to enter through the door, but he hit the wall instead. I told myself that this was an evil day; I put on my cloak and followed him. The Messenger of God (ṢAAS) entered then, recited the verse, 'Read in the name of your Lord who created, created man from a clot.' When he reached the passage relating to Abū Jahl: 'No; man is indeed impious, to see himself self-sufficient' (*sūrat al-ʿAlaq*, XCVI, v.1, 2; 6, 7), a man said to Abū Jahl, 'O Abū al-Ḥakam, that's Muḥammad.' Abū Jahl replied, 'Can't you see what I see? By God, the vistas of heaven have been barred to me!' When the Messenger of God (ṢAAS) reached the end of the *sūrat* he prostrated himself in prayer."

Imām Aḥmad stated that ʿAbd al-Razzāq related to him, quoting Maʿmar, from ʿAbd al-Karīm, from ʿIkrima, who said, "Ibn ʿAbbās stated, 'What Abū Jahl said was, "If I see Muḥammad praying at the *kaʿba*, I will tread on his neck!"'

"This comment reached the Messenger of God (ṢAAS) and he said, 'If he does any such thing the angels will take him, in full view!'"

Al-Bukhārī related this in the same way from Yaḥyā, from ʿAbd al-Razzāq.

Dāwūd b. Abū Hind stated from ʿIkrima, from Ibn ʿAbbās, who said, "Abū Jahl passed by the Prophet (ṢAAS) while he was praying and addressed him with the words, 'Hey, Muḥammad, didn't I forbid you to pray? You know there to be no one who can call upon more people in council than I can.'

"The Prophet (ṢAAS) reprimanded him and Gabriel spoke the words, 'Let him call his henchmen; we will summon the angels of punishment! (*sūrat al-ʿAlaq*, XCII, v.17–18). By God, if he does summon his people, the angels of justice will inflict punishment on him.'"

Aḥmad and al-Tirmidhī related this; and al-Nasāʾī authenticated it through Dāwūd.

Imām Aḥmad stated that Ismāʿīl b. Yazīd Abū Zayd related to him, quoting Furāt, from ʿAbd al-Karīm, from ʿIkrima, from Ibn ʿAbbās, who said, "Abū Jahl stated, 'If I see Muḥammad at the *kaʿba* praying, I'll fight him till I tread on his neck!'"

He said that he (the Prophet) also used the words, "If he does so, then the *zabāniyya*, (the angels of punishment) will take him away in full view."

Abū Jaʿfar b. Jarīr stated that Ibn Ḥumayd related to him, quoting Yaḥyā b. Wāḍiḥ, quoting Yūnus b. Abū Isḥāq, from al-Walīd b. al-ʿĪzār, from Ibn ʿAbbās, who said, "Abū Jahl said, 'If Muḥammad ever again prays at the shrine, I will kill him!'

"And so God Almighty sent down the verses, 'Read in the name of your Lord who created' up to the verse 'We will certainly smite his forehead, the lying, sinful forehead; let him summon his henchmen, and we will summon the *zabāniyya*' (*sūrat al-ʿAlaq*, XCVI, v.15–18).

"Then the Prophet (ṢAAS) came and prayed and Abū Jahl was asked, 'Well, what's stopping you?' He replied, '(The space) between myself and him is black with his squadrons.'"

Ibn ʿAbbās stated, "And, by God, if he had so much as moved, the angels would have seized him, while the people looked on."

Ibn Jarīr stated that Ibn ʿAbd al-Aʿlā related to him, quoting al-Muʿtamir, from his father, from Nuʿaym b. Abū Hind, from Abū Ḥāzim, from Abū Hurayra, who said, "Abū Jahl asked, 'Is Muḥammad to place his face down among your backs?' 'Yes', they replied."

The account continues, "So he said, 'By al-Lāt and al-ʿUzzā, if I see him praying like that, I'll stomp on his neck and I'll flatten his face down into the dust!' So he went to the Messenger of God (ṢAAS) while he prayed in order to tread on his neck, but everyone was surprised to see him retreat and put his hands out as if to protect himself."

He went on, "So he was asked what was the matter, and Abū Jahl replied, 'Between him and myself there is a trench of fire, terrifying things, and wings.'"

The account continues, "And the Messenger of God (ṢAAS) commented, 'If he had come near me the angels would have picked him apart limb by limb.'"

He said, "And God Almighty revealed – I don't know whether or not this is in the *ḥadīth* from Abū Hurayra – 'No, man is indeed impious, to see himself self-sufficient' (*sūrat al-ʿAlaq*, XCVI, v.6–7), and so on to the end of the *sūrat*."

Aḥmad, Muslim, al-Nasāʾī, Ibn Abū Ḥātim and al-Bayhaqī related this from a *ḥadīth* of Muʿtamir b. Sulaymān b. Ṭarkhān of Taym.

Imām Aḥmad stated that Wahb b. Jarīr related to him, quoting Shuʿba, from Abū Isḥāq, from ʿAmr b. Maymūn, from ʿAbd Allāh, who said, "I never saw the

Messenger of God (ṢAAS) say a prayer against Quraysh except on one occasion. He was praying while a group of Quraysh sat there; there was the placenta (*salā*) of a sacrificed camel near by him. Quraysh asked, 'Who will pick up that placenta and throw it over his back?' ʿUqba b. Abū Muʿayṭ replied, 'I will.' And he picked it up and threw it over his back. The Messenger of God (ṢAAS) remained there prostrating until Fāṭima came and removed it off his back. The Messenger of God (ṢAAS) then said, 'God take this crowd of Quraysh! O God, take away ʿUtba b. Rabīʿa! O God, take away Shayba b. Rabīʿa! O God, take away Abū Jahl b. Hishām! O God, take away ʿUqba b. Abū Muʿayṭ! O God, take away Ubayy b. Khalaf – or Umayya b. Khalaf – they're like a patch of thorns!'"

ʿAbd Allāh stated, "And I saw all of them killed at the battle of Badr, and they were carried off to al-Qalīb; except for Ubayy, or Umayya b. Khalaf; he was a very large man and so was kept separate."

Al-Bukhārī related this tradition in several places in his *ṣaḥīḥ* collection, and Muslim related it with lines of authority from Ibn Isḥāq.

The man who should rightly be referred to in this tradition is Umayya b. Khalaf. It was he who was killed at the battle of Badr. His brother Ubayy, however, was killed at the battle of Uḥud, as we will explain hereafter. The word *al-salā*, "placenta", used above is what emerges in birth with a baby camel, like the placenta of a woman's baby.

In some versions told in the *ṣaḥīḥ* collection, when Quraysh did this they laughed so hard they fell right over one another; that is, one would collapse onto the one next to him because of the violence of their laughter. God curse them!

Regarding the same incident, when Fāṭima threw it off him, she drew near Quraysh and insulted them. And also it is said that when the Messenger of God (ṢAAS) finished his prayer he held up his hands to curse them. And when they saw him do this their laughter died down, fearing his imprecation. They say he cursed all the Quraysh chiefs, singling out in his prayer seven of them. In most accounts six of these are named, they being ʿUtba and his brother Shayba, the two sons of Rabīʿa, al-Walīd b. ʿUtba, Abū Jahl b. Hishām, ʿUqba b. Abū Muʿayṭ, and Umayya b. Khalaf. Ibn Isḥāq stated, "I forget the seventh." But I state that he was ʿUmāra b. al-Walīd; his name is given in the *ṣaḥīḥ* of al-Bukhārī.

The Story of al-Irāshī, the man from Irāsh.

Yūnus b. Bukayr stated, from Muḥammad b. Isḥāq, who said that ʿAbd al-Malik b. Abū Sufyān al-Thaqafī stated, "A man from Irāsh brought in to Mecca some camels he owned and Abū Jahl b. Hishām bought them from him. But he was slow in paying for them and so the man from Irāsh came to the place where Quraysh met; the Messenger of God (ṢAAS) was also there at the time, sitting near the mosque. The man asked them, 'O Tribe of Quraysh, whic will give me help against Abū al-Ḥakam b. Hishām? I am a strang and he has cheated me.'

"The Quraysh council replied, 'You see that person' – indicating the Messenger of God (ṢAAS) both to mock him and because of the enmity they knew existed between him and Abū Jahl – 'go to him. He will help you against him.'

"So the man from Irāsh went and stood before the Messenger of God (ṢAAS) and related his story to him. The Messenger of God (ṢAAS) got up and left with him. When Quraysh saw him do so they told one of their men to follow and see what he would do.

"The Messenger of God (ṢAAS) then left and went to Abū Jahl's house and knocked on the door. Abū Jahl said, 'Who is there?' He replied, 'It's Muḥammad; come outside!' So Abū Jahl came outside, there being not a drop of blood in his face, his colour having turned pale. The Prophet (ṢAAS) then said to him, 'Give this man his due!' Abū Jahl replied, 'Don't leave before I give him what I owe.' He then went back inside and returned with the money he then paid to him. The Messenger of God (ṢAAS) then left and said to the man from Irāsh, 'Now, go to your destination.' The man then went again before the Quraysh council and said, 'May God reward him well; I have received what was due to me.'

"The man Quraysh had sent to watch came back to them and they asked what he had seen. He replied, 'It was incredible! I swear, when he knocked on Abū Jahl's door and he came out, his spirit was not accompanying him! He told him to give the man his due, and Abū Jahl replied, "Don't leave till I bring it out for him." He then went back inside, then came out and gave it to him.'

"Soon thereafter Abū Jahl arrived and Quraysh asked, 'Well, what's wrong with you? By God, we never saw the like of what you did.' He replied, 'It was terrible! As soon as he knocked on my door and I heard his voice, I was filled with terror. Then when I went outside to him, there on his head was a stallion camel more fearful than any I ever saw before; its neck and teeth were unlike those of any camel. I swear, if I had refused, it would have eaten me!'"

Division

Al-Bukhārī stated that ʿAyyāsh b. al-Walīd related to him, quoting al-Walīd b. Muslim, quoting al-Awzāʿī, from Yaḥyā b. Abū Kathīr, from Muḥammad b. Ibrāhīm al-Taymī (who said) that ʿUrwa b. al-Zubayr related to him that he asked Ibn ʿAmr b. al-ʿĀṣ, "Tell me what the worst thing was the polytheists did to the Messenger of God (ṢAAS)."

He replied, "While the Prophet (ṢAAS) was praying at the *ḥijr* (the outer enclosure of the *kaʿba*) ʿUqba b. Abū Muʿayṭ went up to him, drew his robe around his neck and began choking him hard.

"Abū Bakr, God bless him, approached, took him by the shoulders and pulled him off the Prophet (ṢAAS) saying, 'Would you murder a man for saying, "God is my Lord; He has brought you clear signs from your Lord" to the end of the verse" (*sūrat Ghāfir*, XL, v.28).

Ibn Isḥāq gives the same *ḥadīth* but uses the words "Yaḥyā b. ʿUrwa related to me: I asked ʿAbd Allāh b. ʿAmr . . .".

ʿAbda gives it in the form: "from Hishām, from his father, who said, '"ʿAmr b. al-ʿĀṣ was asked . . .'. And Muḥammad b. ʿAmr said, 'from Abū Salama, who said, "ʿAmr b. al-ʿĀṣ related to me . . .'."

Al-Bayhaqī stated it, and Sulaymān b. Bilāl related it, from Hishām b. ʿUrwa as ʿAbda gave it.

Al-Bukhārī is the sole authority giving this anecdote; he told it in several places in his *ṣaḥīḥ* collection. In one of these he related it to ʿAbd Allāh b. ʿAmr b. al-ʿĀṣ. That account is closest to that of ʿUrwa. The fact that it was related from ʿAmr (rather than from the son of ʿAmr) is more likely, since the incident had occurred so early.

Al-Bayhaqī narrated from al-Ḥākim, from al-Aṣamm, from Aḥmad b. ʿAbd al-Jabbār, from Yūnus, from Muḥammad b. Isḥāq, who said that Yaḥyā b. ʿUrwa related to him, from his father ʿUrwa, who said that he asked ʿAbd Allāh b. ʿAmr b. al-ʿĀṣ, "What is the worst thing you saw Quraysh inflict on the Messenger of God (ṢAAS)?" He replied, "I saw them once when all their chiefs had gathered at the *ḥijr* of the *kaʿba* and they were discussing the Messenger of God (ṢAAS). They said, 'We've been extraordinarily patient in putting up with this man; he has ridiculed our values, reviled our forefathers, criticized our religion, made divisions among us and insulted our gods. We've put up with a lot from him.' They used words such as these."

He went on, "While they were thus engaged, the Messenger of God (ṢAAS) appeared. He approached on foot, kissed the 'black stone', then passed on by them as he circumambulated the *kaʿba*. They, as I recognized from the face of the Messenger of God (ṢAAS) then said some insulting things to him. He went on his path but when he came round past them on his second circuit they again, as I saw from his face, insulted him. When he came round for the third time, they did the same.

"He then spoke, 'Are you listening, O Quraysh? By Him in whose hands is my soul, I'm bringing you slaughter!'

"His words had such great impact on them that they went totally silent. Then those previously most harsh to him addressed him with kindness, saying, 'Why don't you be sensible and leave, Abū al-Qāsim? You've never acted foolishly.' And so the Messenger of God (ṢAAS) left.

"Next day Quraysh met again in the *ḥijr* and I was there with them. They discussed their interactions with him and said to one another, 'You mentioned what he did to you and what you did to him, until he brought out what you didn't like; so you let him go!'

"While they were engaged in this discussion, the Messenger of God (ṢAAS) appeared and they leapt upon him as one man and surrounded him, accusing him, 'Haven't you said so-and-so?' making reference to the negative comments they had heard he had made about their gods and their religion.

"The Messenger of God (ṢAAS) replied, 'Yes; I am the one who said that.'

"Then I saw one man grab him by the top fastening of his robe. At this Abū Bakr put himself between them, weeping, and said, 'Shame on you! Would you murder a man for saying, "My Lord is God?"' At this they let him go.

"That incident was the worst treatment he ever had from Quraysh."

Section: On the uniting of the Quraysh chiefs against the Messenger of God (ṢAAS) and his Companions, and their meeting with his uncle Abū Ṭālib who was protecting and aiding him; their pressure upon Abū Ṭālib to deliver him to them, and how he resisted them in that objective, through the aid and strength of God.

Imām Aḥmad stated that Wakīʿ related to him, from Ḥammad b. Salama, from Thābit, from Anas, who said, "The Messenger of God (ṢAAS) stated, 'I've suffered harm for God, whereas no one should be harmed; I've been frightened for God, whereas no one should be afraid. At one time, 30 days and nights had passed, and neither I nor Bilāl had what any human can eat except what could be concealed by Bilāl's armpit!'"

Al-Tirmidhī and Ibn Māja gave this text from a *ḥadīth* of Ḥammād b. Salama. Al-Tirmidhī stated, "It is a fine, true tradition."

Muḥammad b. Isḥāq stated, "His uncle Abū Ṭālib showed his compassion and gave his protection to the Messenger of God (ṢAAS) and stood in front of him.

"And the Messenger of God (ṢAAS) continued performing God's work by practising his religion openly and allowing nothing to deter him.

"When Quraysh saw that the Messenger of God (ṢAAS) would not give up anything they had complained to him about, neither his separating from them nor his criticism of their gods, and they recognized that his uncle Abū Ṭālib was sympathetic towards him and was standing in front of him and refusing to deliver him to them, some of the Quraysh leaders went to Abū Ṭālib. These men were: ʿUtba and Shayba, two sons of Rabīʿa b. ʿAbd al-Shams b. ʿAbd Manāf b. Quṣayy, Abū Sufyān Sakhr b. Ḥarb b. Umayya, Abū al-Bakhtarī (whose given name was al ʿĀṣ b. Hishām b. al-Ḥārith b. Asad b. ʿAbd al-ʿUzzā b. Quṣayy), al-Aswad b. ʿAbd al-Muṭṭalib b. Asad b. ʿAbd al-ʿUzzā, Abū Jahl (whose real name was ʿAmr b. Hishām b. al-Mughīra b. ʿAbd Allāh b. ʿUmar b. Makhzūm), al-Walīd b. al-Mughīra b. ʿAbd Allāh b. ʿUmar b. Makhzūm b. Yaqaẓa b. Murra b. Kaʿb b. Luʾayy, Nabīh and Munabbih, the two sons of al-Ḥajjāj b. ʿĀmir b. Hudhayfa b. Saʿīd b. Sahm b. ʿAmr b. Husayṣ b. Kaʿb b. Luʾayy, and al-ʿĀṣ b. Wāʾil b. Saʿīd b. Sahm." And Ibn Isḥāq added "or those of these men who did go."

"They said, 'O Abū Ṭālib, your nephew has cursed our gods, criticized our religion, ridiculed our values and said our forefathers erred. Either you interpose yourself between us – you disagree with him just as we do – or we'll take care of him for you!'

"Abū Ṭālib gave them a polite and gracious reply and they then left him.

"Thereafter the Messenger of God (ṢAAS) continued as before, openly practising God's religion and calling upon people to embrace it. But then things between them became more heated until the men were mutually hostile and alienated from one another.

"Quraysh discussed the Messenger of God (ṢAAS) a great deal, complaining to one another and urging one another on to take action against him.

"They then went again to Abū Ṭālib, and told him, 'O Abū Ṭālib, you have seniority, prestige, and position among us, and we have asked you to keep your nephew away from us, but you have not done so. We can't any longer put up with his behaviour in reviling our forefathers, ridiculing our values, and criticizing our gods until such time as you make him desist, or we will battle with him and you in this matter, until one or other side perishes.' They said something of this sort, and then they left.

"It grieved Abū Ṭālib to be alienated from his people, and he was neither sympathetic to the call for Islam by the Messenger of God (ṢAAS) nor to the idea of abandoning him."

Ibn Isḥāq stated that Yaʿqūb b. ʿUtba b. al-Mughīra b. al-Akhnas related to him that he was told that when Quraysh, made these comments to Abū Ṭālib, he sent a message to the Prophet (ṢAAS) in which he said, "O Nephew, your people have come to me and stated various things" – referring to what they had told him – "so protect me and yourself, and don't burden me with more than I can bear." The Messenger of God (ṢAAS) thought that Abū Ṭālib had changed his attitude, and that he had abandoned him and his fellow Muslims, and lacked the strength to help and protect him.

"So the Messenger of God (ṢAAS) told him, 'O Uncle, if they were to place the sun in my right hand and the moon in my left on condition I abandon this course until God decide it or I perish, I would not abandon it.'

"Then the Messenger of God (ṢAAS) broke down in tears and rose to leave.

"As he turned away, Abū Ṭālib called out to him, 'Come close, nephew!' So the Messenger of God (ṢAAS) approached him and Abū Ṭālib told him, 'Go ahead, nephew, and say whatever you wish. I will never give you up for any reason.'"

Ibn Isḥāq stated, "When Quraysh learned that Abū Ṭālib had refused to abandon the Messenger of God (ṢAAS) and was determined to break with them in enmity because of this, they went to him, bringing ʿUmāra b. al-Walīd with them. They told him, as I have heard, 'O Abū Ṭālib, this is ʿUmāra b. al-Walīd, the strongest and best-looking young man of Quraysh. Take him and use his mind and strength and adopt him as your own son; he is yours. And hand over to us this nephew of yours who has opposed your religion and that of your forefathers, broken up the unity of your people and ridiculed our values, so that we may kill him. It will be just one man for another!'

"Abū Ṭālib responded, 'By God, what evil is this you ask of me! Will you give me your son to feed for you, while I give you mine for you to kill? This, by God, will never happen!'

"Al-Muṭʿim b. ʿAdī b. Nawfal b. ʿAbd Manāf b. Quṣayy then said, 'By God, Abū Ṭālib, your people have been fair with you and have done their best to avoid offending you. But I don't see you give them anything in return.'

"Abū Ṭālib replied to al-Muṭʿim, 'I swear by God they have not been fair with me. You have agreed to ostracize me and turn the people against me. So do what you think fit.' Or words to that effect.

"The situation worsened and the conflict became more heated, with the people adopting different sides and expressing mutual hostility.

"Abū Ṭālib spoke verses about all this criticizing al-Muṭʿim b. ʿAdī and those of Banū ʿAbd Manāf and the other Quraysh tribes who were hostile to him. In these verses he made reference to their request to him and to their alienation:

> 'Tell ʿAmr, al-Walīd and Muṭʿim: "Instead of your (worthless) protection I'd rather have a camel calf
>
> That was sickly and ungainly, that moaned a lot, its urine dripping down its legs,
>
> That was left behind the herd and couldn't keep up, one that looked more like a stoat when climbing the dunes."
>
> I see both our brothers, sons of our father and our mother, who reply when asked, "It's someone else's problem."
>
> No, it is their concern, though they disappeared with the speed of a rock dropping from atop Mt. Dhū ʿAlaq.
>
> I single out ʿAbd Shams and Nawfal, both having dropped us like hot coals
>
> They have slandered and insulted their brothers (in front of) the people; their hands now hold nothing for them
>
> They have shared their prestige with men whose fathers are unknown except for being of low repute.

And Taym and Makhzūm and Zuhra are among them, men who had once been allied with us when help was desired.

By God, enmity between us and you will never end, so long as any of our progeny survive.'"

Section: Concerning their use of excessive violence against individual, powerless Muslims.

Ibn Isḥāq stated, "Quraysh then incited each other against those individual tribesmen who were Companions of the Messenger of God (ṢAAS) and had accepted Islam.

"Each tribe persecuted the Muslims among them, using violence and trying to seduce them from their faith.

"God gave protection to the Messenger of God (ṢAAS) against them through his uncle Abū Ṭālib.

"When Abū Ṭālib saw what Quraysh were doing, he called upon Banū Hāshim and Banū ʿAbd al-Muṭṭalib to join him in aiding and defending the Messenger of God (ṢAAS). They did join with him and agreed to his request, except for Abū Lahab, that enemy of God.

"He spoke some verses on this subject, praising them and urging them to fulfil their promises of help and support for the Messenger of God (ṢAAS):

'If Quraysh were to assemble one day to express their pride, the ʿAbd Manāf would be their heart and core

And if the chiefs of ʿAbd Manāf were counted, then in Hishām would be their most noble and ancient of line

If Quraysh do one day express their pride, then Muḥammad will be the one chosen from their core, and their noble one;

Quraysh had their men, both high and low, against us, but they have not succeeded and their hopes are dashed.

In former times we never tolerated evil; if people turned their heads down, we straightened them out.

We defended their sanctuary every evil day, knocking from its walls those attacking it.

Through us the withered stalk is renewed, under our care its roots turn moist and grow.'"

Section: Concerning the objections presented by the polytheists to the Messenger of God (ṢAAS); how they troubled him with their asking of him various kinds of signs and miracles, and how this was due to their obstinacy rather than to their seeking guidance.

They were therefore not granted many of their requests or wishes because The Truth, glory be to Him, knew that if they had seen what they wanted, they would have continued straying in their tyranny, error and sin.

God Almighty stated, "And they swear by God, with their mightiest oaths, that if a sign came to them they would believe in it. Say: 'Signs are with God alone.' And what would make you perceive that if such came, they would still not believe? Supposing we turn their hearts and their vision upside down, they will not believe, as at the first time. So we will leave them straying in their tyranny. Even if we sent down the angels to them, and even if the dead spoke to them, and even if we gathered together all things from before, they would not believe unless God wished it. But most of them are foolish" (*sūrat al-Anʿām*, VI, v.109–11).

And He said, "Even those against whom God's word has proved true will not believe, even if all signs were to come to them until they see the painful punishment" (*sūrat Yūnus*, X, v.96–7).

The Almighty spoke, "Nothing prevented us from sending the signs except the fact that the earlier peoples disbelieved in them; We did give Thamūd the she-camel in full view, but they used it for evil. We do not send signs for any purpose but to warn" (*sūrat al-Isrāʾ*, also known as *sūrat Banū Isrāʾīl*, XVII, v.59).

And the Almighty said, "And they said, 'We will not believe in you until you break forth a spring from the earth for us. Or until you have a garden of date-palms and grapes amidst which you make streams gush forth. Or until you make the sky fall upon us in pieces, as you have claimed you will. Or until you bring God and the angels before us. Or until you have a house of gold cloth. Or until you rise up to heaven. And we will not believe in your ascension until you bring down for us a book we can read.' Say: 'Glory be to God; am I anything but a mortal man, a messenger?'" (*sūrat al-Isrāʾ*, XVII, v.90–3).

We have discussed these verses and those similar to them in their places in the *Tafsīr* (*Exegesis*). And all praise be to God.

Yūnus and Ziyād related, from Ibn Isḥāq, and from a certain scholar, namely a sheikh from Egypt named Muḥammad b. Abū Muḥammad, from Saʿīd b. Jubayr and ʿIkrima, from Ibn ʿAbbās, who said, "Leaders from Quraysh chiefs met – and he enumerated their names – after sunset at the rear of the *kaʿba*. Some said, 'Send for Muḥammad and speak with him and argue with him so you will find excuse for him.'

"So they sent a message to him, saying, 'The chiefs of your people have assembled to speak with you.'

"The Messenger of God (ṢAAS) came to them quickly, believing that there had been a change in their attitude to him. He was eager for them to accept the truth for their error, which was painful to him. He sat down with them.

"They said, 'O Muḥammad, we sent for you to reconcile with you. By God, we know of no Arab man who has ever brought his people as much trouble as you have. You have reviled the forebears, criticized the religion, ridiculed the values, cursed the gods, and divided our community. Every unpleasant thing possible you have done to make a rift between you and us.

"'If you had come to say these things merely to seek wealth, we would have collected money for you from our own until you were the richest among us. If what you wanted was prestige, we would have placed you in leadership over us. If you had wanted sovereignty, we would have made you king over us. If what you were bringing us was because of a spirit that had possessed you (they used the word *raʾī* for *tābiʿ* meaning spirit) and that may be the case, we would expend our resources seeking a potion to free you from him, or we would excuse you.'

"The Messenger of God replied, 'What you have said does not apply to me. I have not brought you my message seeking your money, nor honour among you, nor sovereignty over you. God has sent me to you as a Messenger; He has revealed a document to me and has ordered me to bring you good news and to warn you. I have brought you a message from my Lord and have given you counsel. If you accept what I have brought you, then that is for your good on earth and in the hereafter. If you reject it, I will await God's decision, until He decides between myself and you.' The Messenger of God used some such words.

"They responded, 'O Muḥammad, if you will not accept what we are offering you, then you will realize that there are no people with less land than us, nor any less wealthy, nor any with a more difficult life. So ask for us your Lord who has sent you with whatever he has sent you, to level out for us these mountains that close us in, and spread out our country and give us some rivers here that flow like those in Syria and Iraq. Ask him to resurrect for us some of our dead forefathers, including among them Quṣayy b. Kilāb, since he was a truth-telling sheikh. We will then ask them whether what you say is true or false.

"'If you do what we ask and they believe you, we will believe you and recognize your status with God, and that he has sent you as a messenger, as you say.'

"The Messenger of God (ṢAAS) replied, 'This is not why I have been sent. I have only brought you from God what He has sent me with. I have informed you of what I was sent to convey to you. If you accept it, then that is your good fortune on earth and in the hereafter. If you reject it, I must wait patiently for God's decree and for Him to judge between us.'

"They responded, 'If you won't do this for us, take something for yourself. Ask your Lord to send us down an angel who will verify what you say and make us leave you alone. Ask him to provide for us some gardens, some castles and treasures of gold and silver, and to take care of those needs we see you have, for we see you engage in business and earn your living like us. That way we will know the favour and prestige you have with your Lord – if, that is, you are a messenger as you claim.'

"He replied, 'I'm not going to do so. I'm not one to ask such things of his Lord. That is not why I have been sent to you. God has sent me to announce and to warn. If you accept my message, then that is your good fortune here on earth and in the afterlife. If you reject it, then I must be patient and leave the matter up to God, until He decides between myself and you.'

"They replied, 'Well then, make the sky fall down as you have claimed your Lord can do if He wishes. We'll not believe in you unless you do this.'

"He answered, 'That is up to God. If He wishes, He will do that to you.'

"They commented, 'O Muḥammad, did your Lord not know we would sit with you and ask you questions as we have asked and make requests we have made, and so come forward to you and inform you how to respond to us, and tell you what He would then do about us if we did not accept the message from you?'

"'We have learned that you just receive this instruction from a man in al-Yamāma known as *al-Raḥmān*;[78] we will never, by God, believe in that *al-Raḥmān*! We've made every excuse for you, Muḥammad, but, by God, because of what you've done to us we'll not leave you alone until we destroy you or you destroy us!'

"One of them said, 'We worship the angels who are God's daughters.' Another said, 'We'll not believe in you till you bring us God and the angels beforehand.'

"When they had said this, the Messenger of God (ṢAAS) arose to leave them. ‘Abd Allāh b. Abū Umayya b. al-Mughīra b. ‘Abd Allāh b. ‘Umar b. Makhzūm, who was his cousin, being the son of his aunt ‘Ātika, daughter of ‘Abd al-Muṭṭalib, got up with him and said to him, 'O Muḥammad, your people have made certain offers to you that you have not accepted. Then they made requests for themselves so that they could discover your status with God, but you did nothing. Then they asked you to send promptly some punishment that would scare them. By God, I'll never believe in you until you put up a ladder to heaven then climb it, with me watching, until you reach there, bring back with you a copy of a document accompanied by four angels who testify that you are as you claim! And yet, by God, even if you did that, I think I'd not believe you!'

"He then left the Messenger of God (ṢAAS), who went off home sad and regretful at his failure to achieve what he had expected when his people had summoned him, and at the alienation he had seen them express towards him."

This assembly where those leaders met with him had been one of injustice, antagonism, and stubbornness. Divine wisdom and God's mercy decreed that they not be granted what they had requested, because God knew that they would not have faith thereby, and that it would hasten their punishment.

78. Apparently a reference to the "false prophet" Musaylima.

Imām Aḥmad stated that ʿUthmān b. Muḥammad related to him, quoting Jarīr, from al-Aʿmash, from Jaʿfar b. Iyās, from Saʿīd b. Jubayr, from Ibn ʿAbbās, who said, "The people of Mecca asked the Messenger of God (ṢAAS) to turn Mt. al-Ṣafā into gold for them and to move away the mountains so that they could grow crops. He was told, 'It is up to you whether you give them respite, or what they ask, and then if they disbelieve they will perish as did those nations who came before them.'

"He replied, 'No; I will give them respite.'

"And so God Almighty sent down, 'Nothing prevented us from sending the signs except the fact that the earlier peoples disbelieved in them; We did give Thamūd the she-camel in full view, but they used it for evil. We do not send signs for any purpose but to warn'" (*sūrat al-Isrāʾ*, XVII, v.59).

Al-Nasāʾī related this tradition from Jarīr.

Aḥmad stated that ʿAbd al-Raḥman related to him, quoting Sufyān, from Salama b. Kuhayl, from ʿUmrān b. Ḥakīm, from Ibn ʿAbbās, who said, "Quraysh said to the Prophet (ṢAAS), 'Pray to your Lord for us to turn Mt al-Ṣafā into gold and we will believe in you.' 'You would really do so?' he asked. 'Yes,' they replied.

"So he did pray and Gabriel came to him and spoke, saying, 'Your Lord greets you and tells you, "If you wish, then al-Ṣafā will become gold for them. But all those who disbelieve thereafter I will either punish as I never have any humans before, or, if you wish it, I will open up for them the door of forgiveness and repentance."'

"He replied, 'No, let it be forgiveness and repentance.'"

Both these two chains of authority are excellent and were transmitted by a group of followers of the Prophet (ṢAAS) including Saʿīd b. Jubayr, Qatāda, Ibn Jurayḥ and others.

Imām Aḥmad and al-Tirmidhī recounted from a *ḥadīth* of ʿAbd Allāh b. Mubārak, who said that Yaḥyā b. Ayyūb related to him, from ʿUbayd Allāh b. Zaḥr, from ʿAlī b. Yazīd, from al-Qāsim, from Abū Umāma, from the Prophet (ṢAAS) who said, "My Lord, Almighty and All-glorious is He, proposed to me that he would transform the Mecca valley into gold. But I replied, 'No, O God, one day I am satisfied, the next hungry, or something close thereto; and when I am hungry, I humble myself before you and think of You, and when satisfied I give praise and thanks to You.'"

(Imām) Aḥmad gave this tradition without comment. Al-Tirmidhī stated, "This *ḥadīth* is good." And ʿAlī b. Yazīd considered it weak.

Muḥammad b. Isḥāq stated that an Egyptian sheikh, who came to him some 40 years before, related to him from ʿIkrima, from Ibn ʿAbbās, who said, "Quraysh sent al-Naḍr b. al-Ḥārith and ʿUqba b. Abū Muʿayṭ to the Jewish rabbis at

Medina, telling the two men, 'Ask them about Muḥammad; describe him to them and relate to them what he says. They are the people of the first scriptures. They have knowledge we don't possess about prophets.'

"So al-Naḍr and ʿUqba went off to Medina and asked the rabbis about the Messenger of God (ṢAAS), describing him and what he said to them. The two men told them, 'You are the people of the Torah; we have come for you to tell us about this countryman of ours.'

"The rabbis told them, 'Ask him about three subjects we will inform you about. If he responds, he is a prophet with a mission. If he does not, he is a pretender for you to treat as you will.

"'Ask him about the young warriors who passed away in earlier times and what happened to them. They had a very strange experience.

"'Also ask him about the great traveller who went far out to the east and far to the west, and what became of him. Then ask him what the *rūḥ* (soul or spirit) is.

"'If he answers these questions, then he is a prophet and so follow him. If he does not, then he is a fake and you should do with him what seems right to you.'

"Al Naḍr and ʿUqba returned to Quraysh and told them, 'O Quraysh, we bring you the means to decide the issue between yourselves and Muḥammad. The rabbis told us to ask him certain questions.' They then told Quraysh what these were.

"So Quraysh went to the Messenger of God (ṢAAS) and said to him, 'O Muḥammad, answer us these.' They then questioned him as they had been told. The Messenger of God (ṢAAS) replied, 'I will tomorrow give you the answer to what you have asked.' But in saying this, he omitted the phrase, 'if God wills it'.

"They then left him. The Messenger of God (ṢAAS) thereafter remained for 15 days without revelation or any visitation from Gabriel. And so the Meccans spread rumours, saying, 'Muḥammad promised us it would be the next day, but it's been 15 now without him having answered any one of the matters we asked him.' The cessation of revelation greatly troubled the Messenger of God, and he was hurt by what the Meccans were saying about him.

"Then Gabriel, peace be upon him, brought him from God, the Almighty and All-Glorious, the *sūrat al-Kahf* (XVIII). In this there is reprimand for his sadness about them and information on the matters concerning the ancient warriors and the mighty traveller about whom they had questioned him. God Almighty also stated, 'And they ask you about the *rūḥ* (the soul). Say, the *rūḥ* is by order of my Lord. And you are given but little knowledge' (*sūrat al-Isrāʾ* (or *Banū Isrāʾīl*), XVII, v.85)."

We have spoken about that at length in the *Tafsīr* (*Exegesis*); the reader wishing more information on this will find it there.

Also revealed was God's statement, "or did you think that the men of the cave and the inscription were a wonder from among our signs?" (*sūrat al-Kahf*, XVIII, v.9).

He then proceeded to detail their story. In the course of this God interjected by his commanding the use of "the exception" as a matter of determination, not comment, in His words, "And do not say of anything, 'I will do that tomorrow,' unless God wills it. And remember God when you are forgetful" (*sūrat al-Kahf*, XVIII, v.23–4).

He then made mention of the story of Moses, because it is related to that of *al-Khiḍr*, and then he proceeded to tell about *Dhū al-Qarnayn*. God then said, "They will ask you about *Dhū al-Qarnayn*. Say, I will relate you an account of him" (*sūrat al-Kahf*, XVIII, v.83). He then explained all about him and what happened to him.

God stated in the *sūrat* (beginning with) *Subḥān*: "And they ask you about the *rūḥ* (i.e. soul or spirit). Say: the *rūḥ* is by order of my Lord" (*sūrat al-Isrā'*, XVII, v.85). That is, it, the *rūḥ*, is a strange and marvellous part of His creation, something God ordained; He said "Be" (Let there be *rūḥ*), and so it "was". And it is not up to you to scrutinize all He has created. To represent or portray real nature and essence would be too difficult for you. It is something related to the power and (ultimate) wisdom of the Almighty. This is why He stated: "And you are given but little knowledge" (*sūrat al-Isrā'*, XVII, v.85).

It is well established in both *ṣaḥīḥ* collections that the Jews asked this of the Messenger of God (ṢAAS) when he was in Medina, and so he recited this verse to them.

This verse was either revealed a second time or he made reference to it as a response, even though its revelation came previously. Those who maintain it was revealed only at Medina and exclude it from the *sūra Subḥān* (i.e. *sūrat al-Isrā'*) are wrong. But God knows best.

Ibn Isḥāq stated, "When Abū Ṭālib feared that the crowds of Arabs would overwhelm him and his people, he composed his ode in which he claimed refuge at the Mecca sanctuary because of his position there. In it he expressed his friendship for his people's leaders, but told them and others in his poem that he was not surrendering the Messenger of God (ṢAAS) and that he would never abandon him for any reason, even if it meant dying in his defence. Abū Ṭālib spoke the verses:

'Having seen that the people are without friendship and that they have severed all ties and connections

And have openly expressed their enmity, inflicted harm and obeyed the orders of the implacable enemy

And have allied with a people against us who are suspicious, and bite their fingers in rage at us behind our backs,

I have remained firm towards them, my spear flexible, my sword sharp and of royal provenance.

I assembled my brothers and kin at the *kaʿba* and gripped the ropes of its covering,

Standing together and facing its doors, the place where those having made oaths fulfil them,

The area where pilgrims kneel their mounts and where the flow of blood comes from the gods Isāf and Nāʾil,

Their mounts branded on their shoulder or neck base, prime pampered beasts between seven and nine years old.

On them you see ornaments of cowry shells and marble tied to their necks which are like fronds heavy with dates.

I seek sanctuary with the Lord of men from all aggressors seeking evil and men who persist in lies,

From those who hate and strive to harm us and from those who attach to the religion what we have not attempted.

By Thawr and by Him who set Thabīr in its place and by those who both ascend Ḥirāʾ and descend,

By the *kaʿba*, the true House in Mecca's valley, and by God, I swear, God is never unaware.

By the "black stone" when it is touched by those who move around it at morn and evening,

By Abraham's tread upon the moist rock, both feet bare and wearing no sandals,

By the courses run between al-Marwatayn and al-Ṣafā and by the images and statues at both places.

By all those who ride in to pilgrimage at God's house and all who make vows and all who come on foot.

By the furthest shrine they head for, for Mt. ʿArafāt, and the place where the streams meet and flow

And the places where they halt at evening above the mountains, where they make their mounts stop by placing their hands on their animals' foreparts.

By the night of the assembly at the Minā stations; are there any shrines or stations above them?

And by the crowding when the horses swiftly pass by as if they are escaping a falling rain.

By the great *Jamra*, the mound of stones, when pilgrims approach it, casting their stones at its top.

By Kinda tribe when at evening at al-Ḥisāb and the pilgrims of Banū Bakr b. Wāʾil pass them by.

Both allies who have affirmed the bond between them, and referred back to it all kinds of relationships

And by their breaking down the very tallest of trees and bushes as they race by, like swift-paced ostriches,

Is there after this any better refuge for one seeking it? Does anyone offer refuge who is just and fears God?

Our enemies had the best of us and wished we were used to block the gates to Turk and Kābul.

You have lied, by God's House; we leave Mecca and our land without you being confounded?

You have lied, by God's House; we subdue Muḥammad, not fight and resist in his defence?

We give him up before we are piled up dead around him, and leave behind our children and our wives?

A people will rise up with steel against you, like camels rising when they bear waterskins,

Until we see our enemy stretched out from his wounds, all awry, like a cripple.

We will, by God, if what I see is in earnest, have our swords become mixed with others like them

In the hands of a young fighter like a flame, a brave man, trustworthy, defending the truth, heroic.

And so months, days, a year become inviolate for us, and then will come another season, after the next.

How, curse you, could a people abandon a chief who protects his honour, not some foul-mouthed coward

And a noble for whom the clouds are made to rain, the provider for orphans and supporter of widows?

The most needy of the Hāshim tribe resort to him; with him they find mercy and respect

By my life, Usayd and his first born led us to being hated, and they cut us up for anyone to eat.

Neither ʿUthmān nor Qunfudh had sympathy for us, but obeyed the order of those tribes

They obeyed Ubayy and the son of their ʿAbd Yaghūth, neither of them caring what others said of us

We fared the same from Subayʿ and Nawfal, and all turned away in opposition, not acting kindly.

If they both should be discovered or God take hold of them, we'll take revenge measure for measure

And that Abū ʿAmr insisted on hating us, to drive us out to join herdsmen of sheep and camels

Whispering about us at morning and evening; whisper away, O Abū ʿAmr, and then deceive!

He swears to us by God, he'll not deceive us; but yes, we perceive him obviously untrustworthy.

His hate for us has made all the high ground between Akhshab and Majādil too constrained for him.

Question Abū al-Walīd, "How did you benefit us by coming to us, then turning away, like a deceiver!"

"You used to be a man whose opinion and kindness had influence over us, for you were once no fool.

"And so, ʿUtba, do not listen to those who secretly hate us, envious, mendacious, hate-filled slanderers."

As Abū Sufyān passed by me he looked away, as though he were a royal prince of a great line.

He gets away to high Najd and its cool waters, claiming, "No, I'm not abandoning you."

He tells us, as though a true counsellor, that he is sympathetic but he hides his innate ill-will.

O Muṭ'im, I did not desert you when needing help, nor any critical time needing deeds of valour

Nor on that day of conflict when they attacked you violently, fierce men, implacable enemies.

O Mut'im, the people have entrusted a task to you, and I, when given a task, don't shun it;

May God punish 'Abd Shams and Nawfal for us, soon, not delayed, and harsh.

In proper measure, not a grain-weight less, it being testimony about itself, not that of some miscreant.

Fools are they who would exchange in barter the Banū Khalaf and al-Ghayāṭal for us.

We are the very heart of the essence of Hāshim and the tribe of Quṣayy in all prime regards.

Sahm and Makhzūm have biased and incited against us in enmity every scoundrel and sinner.

O 'Abd Manāf, you men are the best of your people, so do not ally in your affairs with every sponger.

By my life, you have gone weak and ineffectual, failing badly in the view of anyone of good judgement;

Till recently you were the firewood for one pot, but now you're the fuel for various pots and cauldrons.

Let Banū 'Abd Manāf enjoy our plight and abandonment, and our being forsaken in our refuge.

If indeed a tribe, we will have revenge for your acts and you will taste the fruits of indiscriminate warfare.

Tell Quṣayy that news of us will spread, and announce to Quṣayy that after us they will be defeated.

Yet if great misfortune had one day befallen Quṣayy, we would not have stood away, forsaking them;

If they had fought valiantly amidst their homes, we would have helped them with their women and children.

So all we considered friends or relatives we've found, I swear, of no avail

Excepting a group of the Kilāb b. Murra tribe who are innocent of the fault of falseness to us.

The finest of the tribe is our nephew Zuhayr, without dispute, a sharp sword, alone, unsheathed,

The tallest standing of the pride of the chieftains, a fine man, belonging to a line at the very centre of glory.

By my life, I am utterly devoted to Aḥmad and his brethren, with all the constancy of a close admirer.

For who of all is like him, who could be hoped to compete when judges assess him for superiority?

He is mild-tempered, intelligent, just, stable, the ally of a God of whom he is ever aware.

Noble in his work, noble and noble-born, a man with an inheritance of glory, constant and unbroken

And the Lord of men has aided him with victory, and he has brought forth a religion the truth of which shall stay.

By God, were I not thereby to cause disgrace that would be brought out against our sheikhs in the assemblies

We would have followed him regardless of fate, in all seriousness, not mere talk.

They know that our son is not thought a liar by us, nor does he pay attention to silly nonsense.

Among us Aḥmad is so deeply rooted that the best efforts of upstarts fall short of him.

I cared for him myself, protected him, and defended him by our heads and chests."'

Ibn Hishām commented, "These seem to me the verses of this poem that are genuine. But some scholars expert in poetry reject most of them."

I would say that this ode is truly fine and very effective. No one but he to whom it is ascribed could have spoken it; it is more perfect than the seven *muʿallaqat* odes! It is more effective in conveying its meaning than all of them are.

Al-Umawī gave its text in his *maghāzī* history at greater length, with additions. But God knows best.

Division

Ibn Isḥāq stated: "They then became aggressive towards those who had accepted Islam and followed the Messenger of God (ṢAAS).

"Each tribe attacked all the defenceless Muslims in them, imprisoning them or persecuting them by beating them, depriving them of food and drink and by putting them out on the burning hot ground of Mecca when the heat was most extreme. They were trying to deter them from their religion.

"Some, due to the severity of their suffering, were dissuaded from it, while others stood up to them, God giving them His protection.

"Bilāl, who became Abū Bakr's freed-man, at that time belonged to Banū Jumaḥ, being one of their slaves born to a foreign mother. His name was Bilāl b. Rabāḥ and his mother's name was Ḥamāma. He was sincere in Islam, a man pure of heart. Umayya b. Khalaf would place him outside at heat of noon, then order that a huge rock be placed on his chest. He would then tell him, 'By God, you'll stay like this till you die, unless you disavow Muḥammad and pray to al-Lāt and al-‘Uzzā!'

"Bilāl, while in this state, would say only, 'One! One!'"

Ibn Isḥāq stated that Hishām b. ‘Urwa related to him, from his father, who said, "Waraqa b. Nawfal used to pass by Bilāl when he was being persecuted in this way as he was saying, 'One! One!' Waraqa would then say to Bilāl, 'One! One! by God, O Bilāl!'

"Waraqa would then go to Umayya b. Khalaf and the others of the Banū Jumaḥ who were doing this and say, 'I swear by God, that if you murder him I'll use his tomb as a shrine!'"

I observe that some consider this *ḥadīth* as dubious, since Waraqa died directly after the Prophet (ṢAAS) received his mission, during the period of intermission of the revelation. Those who first accepted Islam did so following the revelation of the verse, "O You who are all wrapped up" (*sūrat al-Muddaththir*, LXXIV, v.1). And so how could Waraqa pass by Bilāl as he was being tortured? The tradition is doubtful.

Then Ibn Isḥāq recounted how Abū Bakr passed by Bilāl as he was under torture and bought him from Umayya by exchanging a black slave he owned. Thereafter he manumitted Bilāl and so saved him from persecution.

He then related how Abū Bakr purchased a number of slaves, both male and female, who had accepted Islam. These included, with Bilāl, ‘Āmir b. Fuhayra, Umm ‘Umays and Zinnīra, who lost her sight but had it restored by God Almighty. Also there were al-Nahdiyya and her daughter, both of whom he bought from Banū ‘Abd al-Dār; their mistress had sent them both to mill some flour, and Abū Bakr heard her say to them, "By God, I will never free either of you!" Abū Bakr then told her, "Retract that, Umm so-and-so!" The woman replied, "I retract. Now you have spoiled them, so you free them!" "How much are they?" he asked. She named a price and he agreed, "All right, I'll take them. They are free now. So return her flour to her." They asked, "Shouldn't we finish milling it, and then give it back to her?" "That's fine, if you want to."

He purchased a slave-girl of Banū Mu᾿ammil, a clan of the Banū ‘Adī; ‘Umar used to strike her over Islam.

Ibn Isḥāq continued to say that Muḥammad b. ‘Abd Allāh b. Abū ‘Atīq related to him, from ‘Āmir b. ‘Abd Allāh b. al-Zubayr, from one of his family, who said, "Abū Quḥāfa said to his son Abū Bakr, 'Son, I see you are setting free people who are powerless. If you want to do this, why don't you free some powerful men who could protect and defend you?'

"Abū Bakr replied, 'I'm only doing what it is I want.'"

Ibn Isḥāq went on: "And it is related that the following verses were revealed specifically about him and what his father had said, 'To those who give, are pious and believe in goodness we will provide ease and facilitate' and so on to the end of the *sūrat*" (*sūrat al-Layl*, XCII, v.5–7).

We have previously given the account of Imām Aḥmad and Ibn Māja, from ʿĀsim b. Bahdala, from Zarr, from Ibn Masʿūd, who said that, "The first who openly became Muslims were seven persons: the Messenger of God (ṢAAS), Abū Bakr, ʿAmmār and his mother Sumayya, Ṣuhayb, Bilāl, and al-Miqdād.

"The Messenger of God (ṢAAS) was protected by God through his uncle, and Abū Bakr was protected by his tribe. The others were seized by the polytheists, bound in chains and set in the hot sun. All ultimately complied with their persecutors' wishes except for Bilāl; he subjugated himself to God Almighty. His people did not care for him, they ultimately gave him over to the guards who paraded him in the quarters of Mecca while he repeated, 'One! One!'"

Al-Thawrī related this from Manṣūr, from Mujāhid, but it lacks a complete chain of early authorities.

Ibn Isḥāq stated, "Banū Makhzūm used to set ʿAmmār b. Yāsir and his father and mother, all of whom had become Muslims, outside at heat of noon, torturing them with the hot ground of Mecca. The Messenger of God (ṢAAS) would pass by them and say to them, as I have heard, 'Be patient, O family of Yāsir; you are destined for paradise.'"

Al-Bayhaqī related, from al-Ḥākim, from Ibrāhīm b. ʿIṣmat al-ʿAdl, who said that Al-Sarrī b. Khuzayma related to him, quoting Muslim b. Ibrāhīm, quoting Hishām b. Abū ʿUbayd Allāh, from Abū al-Zubayr, from Jābir, who said that the Messenger of God (ṢAAS) passed by ʿAmmār and his family while they were being tortured. He said, "Be of good cheer, O family of ʿAmmār, O family of Yāsir; you are destined for paradise."

His mother, however, they actually did kill, for she refused anything but Islam.

Imām Aḥmad stated, "Wakīʿ related to us, from Sufyān, from Manṣūr, from Mujāhid, who said, 'The first martyr to meet her death early in Islam was ʿAmmār's mother Sumayya. Abū Jahl thrust a spear into her heart.'"

This account lacks a complete chain of early authorities.

Muḥammad b. Isḥāq stated, "That sinner Abū Jahl was the one who incited the men of Quraysh against them. When he heard of a man of status and influence who had accepted Islam he would upbraid and insult him, saying, 'You have abandoned the religion of your father, a man better than you. We will deprecate your values, deride your opinions, and destroy your reputation.' If the Muslim were a merchant, he would say, 'We will, by God, boycott doing business with you and will ruin you.' If the Muslim were defenceless, Abū Jahl would beat him and incite others against him. May God damn and punish him!"

Ibn Isḥāq also said that Ḥakīm b. Jubayr related to him, from Saʿīd b. Jubayr, who said, "I asked ʿAbd Allāh b. ʿAbbās, 'Did the polytheists so persecute the Companions of the Messenger of God (ṢAAS) that they were forgiven if they gave up the faith?'

"'Oh yes,' he replied. 'They would so beat people and so deprive them of food and water that they would be unable to sit up. Eventually they would do whatever their persecutors incited them to. If they were asked, 'Are al-Lāt and al-ʿUzzā gods in their own right, other than God?' they would reply, 'Yes; they are!' This was just to avoid their torture."

I here observe that it was concerning this that God sent down, "Whoever disavows God after having believed in Him, except for those who are compelled (to do so) while their hearts are content in the faith, but whoever allows himself to accept disbelief shall have God's wrath upon them, and they shall receive terrible punishment" (*sūrat al-Naḥl*, XVI, v.106).

These people were forgiven because of the contempt and extreme pain they suffered; may God, in all his power and strength, preserve us from the like.

Imām Aḥmad stated that Abū Muʿāwiya related to him, quoting al-Aʿmash, from Muslim, from Masrūq, from Khabbāb b. al-Aratt, who said, "I was a chieftain and I was owed money by al-ʿĀṣ b. Wāʾil. So I went to him to get payment but he told me, 'No, by God, I'll not pay you until you express disbelief in Muḥammad!' I replied, 'I will never, by God, express disbelief in Muḥammad until you die and then are resurrected!' He responded, 'Well, if I do die and am resurrected and you come to me and I then have property and sons, then I'll pay you!' And so God Almighty sent down: 'And have you seen him who disbelieves in our signs yet says: "I will certainly be given wealth and sons . . ." and so on, to the verse ending "and he shall come to us alone"'" (*sūrat Maryam*, XIX, v.77–80).

In both *ṣaḥīḥ* collections and elsewhere this tradition is given in various lines of transmission from al-Aʿmash.

According to al-Bukhārī's text, the wording should be "I was a chieftain in Mecca, and I made a sword for al-ʿĀṣ b. Wāʾil and went to him for payment."

Al-Bukhārī stated that Al-Ḥumaydī related to him, quoting Sufyān, quoting Bayān and Ismāʿīl, both of whom said that they heard Qays say that he heard Khabbāb say, "I went to the Prophet (ṢAAS) when he was using his cloak as a pillow in the shadow of the *kaʿba*; we had recently suffered violence from the polytheists. I asked him, 'Aren't you praying to God?'

"He sat up, his face flushed red, and said, 'Those who came before you did would be combed with metal down through their flesh and sinews to the bone, but that would not deter them from their religion. They would have saws put on their hair parting and have their heads split in two, but would not be deterred from their religion. God will certainly so conclude this matter that a person will be able to ride from Yemen to Ḥaḍramawt and fear only God, Almighty and All Glorious is He.'"

Another statement is also added "and wolves attacking his sheep". And in one account there are also the words, "But you are impatient".

Al-Bukhārī alone, and not Muslim, gives this tradition. It was also reported from another line of transmission from Khabbāb, but in a shorter form than this. But God knows best.

Imām Aḥmad stated that ʿAbd al-Raḥmān related to him, from Sufyān and Ibn Jaʿfar, that Shuʿba related to them, from Abū Isḥāq, from Saʿīd b. Wahb, from Khabbāb, who said, "We complained to the Prophet (ṢAAS) at the intensity of the heat of the ground, but he would not make a complaint for us; that is, in prayer." Ibn Jaʿfar said "but he would not listen to our complaint."

He also said that Sulaymān b. Dāwūd related to him, as did Shuʿba, from Abū Isḥāq, who said that he heard Saʿīd b. Wahb say that he heard Khabbāb say, "We made complaint to the Messenger of God (ṢAAS) about the intensely hot ground, but he would not listen to our complaint."

Shuʿba stated, "that is, at the heat of midday".

Muslim related this, quoting al-Nasāʾī and al-Bayhaqī from a *ḥadīth* of Abū Isḥāq al-Sabīʿī, from Saʿīd b. Wahb, from Khabbāb, who said, "We made a complaint to the Messenger of God (ṢAAS) about the intense heat of the ground" – to this al-Bayhaqī added the words "on our faces and palms" – "but he would not listen to our complaint."

Ibn Māja related it, from ʿAlī b. Muḥammad al-Ṭanāfusī, from Wakīʿ, from al-Aʿmash, from Abū Isḥāq, from Ḥāritha b. Maḍrib al-ʿAbdī, from Khabbāb, who said, "We complained to the Messenger of God (ṢAAS) about the intense heat of the ground, but he would not listen to our complaint."

It occurs to me – though God knows best – that this *ḥadīth* is abbreviated from the former one. That is, they complained to him at the treatment they were receiving from the polytheists. They were being tortured on the intensely hot ground and so using their hands to protect themselves while being dragged along on their faces, as well as being given those other forms of torture mentioned by Ibn Isḥāq and others. They therefore requested him to pray on their behalf that God might punish the polytheists, or to seek help against them. He promised to do so, but did not fulfil this for them in the current circumstances, but reminded them of those who had preceded them. Those people had received treatment far worse than they were getting, but this had not deterred them from their religion. He cheered them by assuring them that God would bring this matter to a conclusion, and would do so openly, clearly and decisively over an area far and wide, so that a traveller would be able to go from Ṣanʿāʾ to Ḥaḍramawt and have nothing to fear but God, and nothing to fear for his sheep from wolves. But, he told them, they were being impatient.

For this reason, he stated, "We made complaint to the Messenger of God (ṢAAS) about the intense heat of the ground on our faces and palms, but he would not listen to our complaint", i.e. he would not pray for us at that time.

As for those who see evidence in this for not deferring the midday prayer until it is cooler, or on the need to touch the place of prayer with the palms, as is a judgement reached by al-Shāfiʿī, these views may be debated or considered. But God knows best.

CHAPTER: THE ARGUMENTATION OF THE POLYTHEISTS AGAINST THE MESSENGER OF GOD (ṢAAS), AND THE COGENT ARGUMENTS THAT REFUTED THEM; HOW WITHIN THEMSELVES THEY RECOGNIZED THE TRUTH, EVEN THOUGH THEY EXPRESSED DISAGREEMENT OUT OF STUBBORNNESS, ENVY, MALICE AND DENIAL.

Isḥāq b. Rāhawayh stated that ʿAbd al-Razzāq related to him, from Maʿmar, from Ayyūb al-Sakhtiyānī, from ʿIkrima, from Ibn ʿAbbās, that al-Walīd b. al-Mughīra went to the Messenger of God (ṢAAS) who recited the Qur᾿ān to him. Al-Walīd seemed to be impressed by it, and this fact reached Abū Jahl. He therefore went to al-Walīd and told him, "Uncle, your people want to collect for you some money." Al-Walīd asked why, and he went on, "To give it to you. Because you went to Muḥammad to oppose his influence!"

Al-Walīd replied, "But Quraysh know that I am one of their wealthiest men."

Abū Jahl said, "Well, do make some statement telling your people that you disavow him."

He replied, "What should I say? By God, there's not one man among you with a better knowledge than myself of poetry, of its various metres and odes, or of the verses by spirits. But, I swear, what he speaks is nothing like these; by God, there is a spendour in what he says. There's a gracefulness about him. He is effective and productive at all levels. He achieves greater heights than anyone. He overwhelms all beneath him."

Abū Jahl commented, "Your people will not be pleased with you until you make a statement about him."

"Well", al-Walīd asked, "leave me alone till I can give it some thought."

When he had done so, he said, "This is nothing but sorcery brought him by others." And so God revealed the verses, "Leave Me (to deal with) him whom I created, alone; and I made for him extensive wealth, and sons to be seen" (*sūrat al-Muddaththir*, LXXIV, v.11–13).

Al-Bayhaqī related it thus, from al-Ḥākim, from ʿAbd Allāh b. Muḥammad al-Sanʿānī at Mecca, from Ibn Isḥāq's account. Ḥammad b. Zayd related it from Ayyūb, from ʿIkrima, but with an incomplete chain of early authorities. That account states that the Prophet recited to al-Walīd the verses, "God enjoins justice, kindness and charity to one's kinsfolk, and prohibits immorality, evil and wickedness. He admonishes you, so that you may take heed" (*sūrat al-Naḥl*, XVI, v.90).

Al-Bayhaqī stated, from al-Ḥākim, from al-Aṣamm, from Aḥmad b. ʿAbd al-Jabbār, from Yūnus b. Bukayr, from Muḥammad b. Isḥāq, who said that Muḥammad b. Abū Muḥammad related to him, from Saʿīd b. Jubayr, or ʿIkrima, from Ibn ʿAbbās, that al-Walīd b. al-Mughīra met with a group of men of Quraysh. He was, at that time, one of their respected elders. The time was that of the pilgrimage. He addressed them, saying, "Delegations of Arabs will now be coming to you, and they will have heard of this associate of yours. So unite in one opinion about him, without dissension between you that would make you contradict one another."

He was told, "O Abū ʿAbd Shams, you tell us; you establish a position for us that we can uphold."

He replied, "No; you must speak, and I will listen."

They responded, "We say he is a soothsayer."

He replied, "No; he is no soothsayer. I have seen soothsayers and he doesn't engage in the rhymed mumbling doggerel they use."

They commented, "Well, then we say he is crazy, possessed by spirits."

"No," he replied, "he is not crazy; we have seen and known those who are crazy, and he has none of their choking, erratic movement and mumbling."

"Then we say he is a poet."

"No," he disagreed, "he is no poet. We know poetry in all its metrical forms, and what he speaks is not poetry."

"Then we say he is a sorcerer."

"No," he said, "he is no sorcerer. We've seen sorcerers and their magic and he doesn't do any of their tying and untying."

"What are we to say then, O Abū ʿAbd Shams?"

He replied, "By God, there is a splendour in what he speaks. In essence he is like a palm tree whose branches give much fruit. All you have been saying will be recognized as false. The closest thing is for you to say, 'This man is a sorcerer who comes between a man and his religion, a man and his father, a man and his wife, a man and his brother, and a man and his tribe.'"

They then dispersed and set about taking seats (and waiting) for people when they arrived for the festivities. They would warn them about the Messenger of God (ṢAAS) whenever they passed by, and told them all about him.

And God revealed concerning al-Walīd, "Leave Me (to deal with) him whom I created, alone; and I made for him extensive wealth, and sons to be seen" (*sūrat al-Muddaththir*, LXXIV, v.11–13). And concerning those men who had rendered the Qurʾān into disparate parts, God stated, "And so, by your Lord, we will certainly question all of them concerning what they have been doing" (*sūrat al-Ḥijr*, XV, v.92–3).

And I comment that God Almighty also stated, indicating their ignorance and lack of wisdom, "And they even said, 'A jumble of dreams! He just made it up! He's a poet! So let him bring us a sign, like those that former (prophets) were dispatched with'" (*sūrat al-Anbiyā'*, XXI, v.5). And so they were at a loss what to say of him; everything they did say was false. For he who deviates from the truth is mistaken in all he says. God Almighty stated, "See how they made comparisons to you! They have gone astray, and they will find no path" (*sūrat al-Isrā'*, XVII, v.48).

Imām 'Abd b. Ḥumayd stated in his *musnad* collection of *ḥadīth* that Abū Bakr b. Abū Shayba related to him, quoting 'Alī b. Mishar, from al-Ajlaḥ, the son of 'Abd Allāh al-Kindī, from al-Dhayyāl b. Ḥarmala al-Asadī, from Jābir b. 'Abd Allāh, who said, "Quraysh met one day and agreed to determine who among them was the most knowledgeable in magic, sorcery, and poetry. That person would then approach the man who had caused dissension and division amongst them and had found fault with their religion, talk to him and decide how to respond to him. They agreed that 'Utba b. Rabī'a was the obvious choice, and they approached him and told him, 'It is to be you, O Abū al-Walīd.'

"'Utba then went to the Messenger of God (ṢAAS) and said, 'O Muḥammad, who is better, you or 'Abd Allāh?' The Messenger of God (ṢAAS), remained silent.

"Then he said, 'Who is better, you or 'Abd al-Muṭṭalib?' The Messenger of God (ṢAAS) remained silent.

"'Utba then said, 'If you claim those men to be better than you, the fact is they worshipped the gods you have criticized. If you claim to be better than them, then speak so we can hear what you say. By God, we've never seen any fool more harmful to his people than you; you have caused division and dissension among us, criticized our religion and so disgraced us in the eyes of the Arabs that the rumour is current among them that there is a magician or a sorcerer amidst Quraysh. By God, fellow, it seems all we have to await is the cry of a pregnant woman for us all to be at one another with swords till we wipe ourselves out! If it is need that is your problem, we'll make a collection for you till you're the wealthiest man in Quraysh; if it is status you want, choose any women of Quraysh you like and we'll marry you to ten of them.'

"The Messenger of God (ṢAAS) responded, 'Are you done?' 'Yes,' replied 'Utba. The Messenger of God (ṢAAS) then spoke: 'In the name of God, the Most Merciful and Beneficent. *Ḥā Mīm*. A revelation from the Most Merciful and Beneficent. A book whose verses have been detailed in an Arabic Qur'ān for a people who are aware . . .' and so on until he reached the verse, 'But if they turn aside, say: "I warn you of a terrible punishment like that which destroyed 'Ād and Thamūd"' (*sūrat Ḥā Mīm*, also called *sūrat al-Fuṣṣilat*, XLI, v.1–13).

"ʿUtba said, 'That's sufficient. You've nothing else?'

"'No,' he replied.

"ʿUtba then went back to Quraysh and they asked what had happened. He replied, 'I didn't omit saying to him anything you talked about.'

"'And did he respond?' they asked. 'Yes,' he answered. Then he stated, 'Well, no; by Him who erected it as a building, I didn't understand anything he said, except that he warned you of a terrible punishment like that of ʿĀd and Thamūd.'

"They commented, 'Woe upon you! The man speaks to you in Arabic, but you don't know what he said?'

"He replied, 'I swear, I didn't understand a thing, except for the reference to the terrible punishment.'"

Al-Bayhaqī and others related this from al-Ḥākim, from al-Aṣamm, from ʿAbbās al-Dūrī, from Yaḥyā b. Maʿīn, from Muḥammad b. Fuḍayl, back to al-Ajlaḥ. There is some dispute about it.

This version added "and if all you want is leadership, we'll swear allegiance to you, and you can be our chief for life."

And in that version, when he had finished speaking the verse, "But if they turn aside, say: 'I warn you of a terrible punishment like that which destroyed ʿĀd and Thamūd'", ʿUtba put his hand over the mouth of the Prophet (ṢAAS) and implored him for mercy to stop. ʿUtba, moreover, did not return to his people, but hid himself from them.

And so Abū Jahl said, "By God, O Quraysh, ʿUtba must have been quite taken by Muḥammad, and liked his food. It's just some impulse that has possessed him. Let's go and get him!"

Later Abū Jahl said, "Well, ʿUtba, I swear, we concluded you must have been quite taken by Muḥammad, and enjoyed yourself with him. If you're in need, we'll collect money for you so you can dispense with Muḥammad's food."

"ʿUtba became angry and swore he would never speak to Muḥammad again. He told Abū Jahl, 'You well know I'm one of the wealthiest men of Quraysh. I did go to him and . . .' He then related the story to them and concluded 'and he responded to me with something I swear was not magic, not poetry and not sorcery. He recited, "In the name of God, the Most Merciful and Beneficent. *Ḥā Mīm.* A revelation from the Most Merciful and Beneficent," until he reached, "But if they turn aside, say: 'I warn you of a terrible punishment like that which destroyed ʿAd and Thamūd.'" I then put my hand over his mouth and implored him for mercy to stop. And you all well know that Muḥammad does not lie in whatever he says. I was afraid that punishment would descend upon you.'"

Al-Bayhaqī then stated, from al-Ḥākim, from al-Aṣamm, from Aḥmad b. ʿAbd al-Jabbār, from Yūnus, from Muḥammad b. Isḥāq, who said that Yazīd b.

Abū Ziyād, a freed-man of the Banū Hāshim, told him from Muḥammad b. Kaʿb, who said that it was related to him that ʿUtba b. Rabīʿa, who was a wise leader, said one day while he was sitting in the Quraysh meeting hall and the Messenger of God (ṢAAS) was sitting alone in the mosque, "O Quraysh, should I not go to this fellow and make him offers, some of which he might accept, and then leave us alone?"

"Yes, do that Abū al-Walīd!" they told him.

ʿUtba then arose and sat next to the Messenger of God (ṢAAS) and gave him his speech – as given above – and offered him wealth, leadership and so on.

Ziyād b. Isḥāq stated that ʿUtba said, "O Quraysh, should I not go to Muḥammad and talk to him and make him offers, some of which he might accept, so we give them to him and he would leave us alone?" That occurred when Ḥamza had accepted Islam and Quraysh recognized that the followers of the Messenger of God (ṢAAS) were increasing and expanding. So they said, "Yes, Abū al-Walīd, do go and talk to him."

ʿUtba then arose and sat down near the Messenger of God (ṢAAS) and said, "O nephew, you know the status and respect your people give you, and the nobility of your lineage, but you have caused much trouble to your people. By this, you have destroyed their unity, ridiculed their values, criticized their gods and their religion, and claimed that their forefathers were unbelievers. Listen to me now, as I make you some offers to consider; perhaps you might be able to accept some of these."

The Messenger of God (ṢAAS) replied, "I am listening, Abū al-Walīd."

ʿUtba went on, "O nephew, if all you want by bringing up this matter is wealth, we will collect money from ourselves for you and so you will be the richest of us all. If what you are seeking by it is honour, we will make you our leader and never make decisions without you. If what you want by it is sovereignty, we will make you our king. If whatever comes to you is some spirit you see but can't remove by yourself, we will seek out a potion for you and spend our own money to free you from it. A spirit may well take possession of a person until he is cured of it." His words were similar to these.

When he had finished, the Messenger of God (ṢAAS) asked, "Well, Abū al-Walīd, are you done?"

"Yes," he replied.

"Then listen to me."

"I will," said ʿUtba.

The Messenger of God (ṢAAS) then spoke, "In the name of God, the Most Merciful and Beneficent. *Ḥā Mīm.* A revelation from the Most Merciful and Beneficent. A book whose verses have been detailed in an Arabic book for a people who are aware . . ." He went on reciting it, while ʿUtba listened, placing his hands behind his back and using them as a support as he did so.

"When the Messenger of God (ṢAAS) came to the ending where prostration is sought, he prostrated himself, then asked, "Well, did you hear, Abū al-Walid?"

"Yes, I heard," he replied.

"Now it's up to you," observed the Messenger of God (ṢAAS). ʿUtba then arose and went to his associates who told one another, "By God, Abū al-Walīd looks quite different now from what he did before he left."

When they sat down with him, they asked, "Well, what happened to you, Abū al-Walīd?" "What happened, by God," he replied, "was that I heard speech such as I never did before. I swear, it was not poetry, nor sorcery; obey me and do as I shall. Keep away from him and what he does; avoid him. For, by God, what I heard him speak is going to cause a stir. If the Arabs destroy him, others will have taken care of him for you. But if he betters the Arabs, his dominion will also be yours, his power your power, and you will be most pleased with him."

They replied, "By God, he has bewitched you with his tongue, O Abū al-Walīd."

"Well, that's my advice to you; do with it as you see fit," ʿUtba told them.

Yūnus then related, from Ibn Isḥāq, some poetry Abū Ṭālib spoke in which he praised ʿUtba.

Al-Bayhaqī stated that Abū Muḥammad ʿAbd Allāh b. Yūsuf al-Aṣbahānī informed him, quoting Abū Qutayba Salama b. al-Faḍl al-Adamī of Mecca, quoting Abū Ayyūb Aḥmad b. Bishr al-Ṭayālisī, quoting Dāwūd b. ʿAmr al-Ḍabbī, quoting al-Muthannā b. Zurʿa, from Muḥammad b. Isḥāq, from Nāfiʿ, from Ibn ʿUmar, who said, "When the Messenger of God (ṢAAS) had recited to ʿUtba '*Ḥā Mīm.* A revelation from the Most Merciful and Beneficent', he went to his people and told them, 'O people, obey me now in this matter, though you may oppose me later. For, by God, I heard from this man words the like of which my ears never heard before. I didn't know what to reply to him.'"

This *ḥadīth* is very strange to come from such a source.

Al-Bayhaqī then related, from al-Ḥākim, from al-Aṣamm, from Aḥmad b. ʿAbd al-Jabbār, from Yūnus, from Ibn Isḥāq, who said that al-Zuhrī said to him, "I was told that Abū Jahl, Abū Sufyān and al-Akhnas b. Sharīq went out to overhear the Messenger of God (ṢAAS) as he prayed at night in his home. Each of them sat down to listen to him, none knowing where the others were sitting. They spent the night listening to him until dawn when they left individually. On the way back they met and each criticized the other, saying, 'Don't do that again. For if some foolish person were to see you, he'd have his suspicions about you.' They then parted.

"The next night each of these men returned to where he had sat and they spent the night listening to him. When dawn came they dispersed, but met on the way. They said to one another what they had before and then left.

"The third night each again took his seat and spent the night listening to him. At dawn they dispersed and met on the way home. 'This time', they told one another, 'let's not leave without making a pact not to return.' They made this promise to one another and parted company.

"That morning al-Akhnas b. Sharīq took his stick and went off to see Abū Sufyān at home. He told him, 'Abū Ḥanẓala, give me your views on what you have heard from Muḥammad.' He replied, 'Abū Thaʿlaba, I swear, I've heard certain things I know, and I also know what was implied by them, but others I've heard I don't know, nor what was implied by them.' Al-Akhnas commented, 'Me too, I swear!'

"Al-Akhnas then left and went to see Abū Jahl at home. He asked him, 'Abū al-Ḥakam, what's your view on what you've heard from Muḥammad?' 'You mean what have I heard? We and Banū ʿAbd Manāf have been rivals for status. They feed the poor, and so do we. They help people, and so do we. They give to charity, and so do we. We've kept pace with them like two racehorses. Then they say, one of us will be a prophet who receives revelation from heaven! How can we compete with that? I swear, we will never listen to him, nor believe him.' Having heard this, al-Akhnas b. Sharīq left."

Then al-Bayhaqī stated that Abū ʿAbd Allāh, the *ḥāfiẓ*, related to him, quoting Abū al-ʿAbbās, quoting Aḥmad, quoting Yūnus, from Hishām b. Saʿd, from Zayd b. Aslam, from al-Mughīra b. Shuʿba, who said, "The first day I knew the Messenger of God (ṢAAS) was when I was walking along an alley in Mecca accompanied by Abū Jahl b. Hishām. When we met the Messenger of God (ṢAAS), he said to Abū Jahl, 'Abū al-Ḥakam, come to God and to his Messenger. I invite you to God!'

"Abū Jahl replied, 'Muḥammad, have you stopped cursing our gods? Don't you just want us to testify that you have fulfilled your mission? We testify that you have. And, I swear, if I knew that what you say is the truth, I would follow you.'

"The Messenger of God (ṢAAS) then left, and Abū Jahl came over to me and said, 'By God, I really do know that what he says is true, but something is holding me back. Banū Quṣayy have said, "We want the privilege of the *ḥijāba*" (the placing of the cloth over the *kaʿba*). We agreed. Then they said, "We want the privilege of the *saqāya*" (the provision of drink for the pilgrims). We agreed. Then they said, "We want the privilege of the *nadwa*" (feasting the pilgrims). We agreed. Then they said, "We want the privilege of the *liwā*" (the ceremonial unfurling of the banners). We agreed. They provided food, and we did too. Then, when we were running neck and neck, they said, "We have a prophet among us!" By God, I'll not do it!'"

Al-Bayhaqī stated that Abū ʿAbd Allāh, the *ḥāfiẓ*, informed him that Abū al-ʿAbbās Muḥammad b. Yaʿqūb al-Aṣamm related to him, quoting Muḥammad

b. Khālid, quoting Aḥmad b. Khalaf, quoting Isrā'īl, from Abū Isḥāq, who stated, "The Prophet (ṢAAS) passed by Abū Jahl and Abū Sufyān while they were both seated. Abū Jahl said, 'This is your prophet then, O Banū ʿAbd Shams.' Abū Sufyān replied, 'You're surprised that one of us could be a prophet? A prophet could arise among those fewer in number and lower in status than us!'

"Abū Jahl commented, 'I'm surprised that a young man among sheikhs of age and maturity could be a prophet!'

"The Messenger of God (ṢAAS) overheard them and approached. He addressed them, 'As for you, Abū Sufyān, it's not because you care for God and His Messenger that you became angry; you're just burned for the lineage. As for you, Abū al-Ḥakam, you are going to laugh very little and weep a great deal.' Abū Jahl commented, 'So, nephew, what an evil you promise me coming out of your being a prophet!'"

This *ḥadīth* is lacking early links in its chain of authorities, and it is somewhat strange; equally strange are the comments of Abū Jahl, God curse him! In reference to him and people like him, God Almighty stated, "And when they see you, they take you for a joke, saying, 'Is this fellow he whom God sent as a messenger? He might almost have enticed us away from our gods, if we had not stayed patiently with them.' They will know when they see the punishment who it is who strays furthest from the path" (*sūrat al-Furqān*, XXV, v.41–2).

Imām Aḥmad stated that Hushaym related to him, quoting Abū Bishr, from Saʿīd b. Jubayr, from Ibn ʿAbbās, who said, "This verse was sent down while the Messenger of God (ṢAAS) was in hiding in Mecca, 'and do not speak the prayer loudly, nor speak it too softly'" (*sūrat al-Isrā'*, XVII, v.110).

He went on, "When he prayed with his followers, he would raise his voice as he recited the Qur'ān. On hearing this, the polytheists would curse the Qur'ān, along with him who sent it down and him who conveyed it. And so God Almighty told his Prophet Muḥammad (ṢAAS), 'and do not speak the prayer loudly' that is, when you recite it, lest the polytheists hear it and curse the Qur'ān. And 'nor speak it too softly' lest your followers won't hear the Qur'ān and learn it from you. And so 'seek a path between these'" (*sūrat al-Isrā'*, XVII, v.110).

This tradition is similarly given by both authors of the *ṣaḥīḥ* collections, from a *ḥadīth* of Abū Bishr Jaʿfar b. Abū Ḥayya.

Muḥammad b. Isḥāq stated that Dāwūd b. al-Ḥusayn related to him from ʿIkrima, from Ibn ʿAbbās, who said, "When the Messenger of God (ṢAAS) spoke the Qur'ān loudly as he prayed, people would move away and refuse to listen to him. If anyone did want to hear any of what the Messenger of God was reciting as he prayed, he had to strain his ears away from the rest. And if he knew that they were aware that he was listening he would have to leave, for fear of harm from them. And so he would not listen. But if the Messenger of God (ṢAAS) were to lower his voice, those who were listening would hear nothing. Therefore God Almighty revealed, 'and do not speak the prayer loudly' or they will disperse away from you. And also 'nor speak it too softly' or those trying hard to hear it, believing it may be beneficial to them, will not be able to do so. And so, 'seek a path between these.'"

GLOSSARY

ABBREVIATIONS AND NAME-RELATED TERMS

Abū means father. According to Arabic grammatical rules, this word changes to Abī when governed by a preceding word. While, therefore, Abū Ṭālib would mean Ṭālib's father, when the word Ibn, son, is prefixed to the name, the form changes to Abī, and so Ibn Abī Ṭālib, would mean 'the son of Ṭālib's father'. To avoid confusion in this text, however, the term is left here universally as Abū.

The letters 'al-' before a noun represent in Arabic the definite article, 'the'.

The letter b. when part of a name represents a shortened form of the word 'Ibn', 'son'. Thus, the name 'Yaʿqūb b. 'Utba' means 'Yaʿqūb, son of ʿUtba'. In a composite name, as are often given in this text, such as 'Yaʿqūb b. ʿUtba b. al-Mughīra b. al-Akhnas' the names of Yaʿqūb's father, grandfather, and great grand-father are given.

The letters bt, a shortened form of the Arabic *bint*, indicates 'girl' or 'daughter'. Thus the name ʿĀʾisha bt. Abū Bakr refers to ʿĀʾisha, daughter of Abū Bakr.

The letters ṢAAS are inserted after mention of the Prophet Muḥammad. These letters stand for the Arabic words *ṣallā Allāhu ʿalayhi wa sallam*; this invocation, recited by Muslims after every reference to the Prophet, whether by name or inference, is normally translated as 'May God's peace and blessings be upon him'.

GLOSSARY ITEMS

Words defined in footnotes associated with the text are not generally included in this glossary.

afkhādh: plural of *fakhdh* (q.v.).

aḥādīth: plural of *ḥadīth* (q.v.).

agnatic: related through descent on the father's side.

ʿālim (pl. *ʿulamāʾ*): scholars or theologians of Islam.

anṣār: the plural of *nāṣir*, helper, or victor. Most commonly met, in this text, in the plural form, it refers to the early Medinan allies of the Prophet who officially fraternized with the *muhājirīn*, those Muslims who had initially gone into exile from Mecca to Medina in their support for Islam.

ʿarab al-ʿāriba: the original Arabs, who are assumed to have spoken the language of Yaʿrub b. Qaḥṭān.

ʿarab al-mustaʿriba: 'the arabized Arabs', initially referring to those who spoke the Arabic of Ishmael, the dialects of the Ḥijāz, that is. The term is also applied to those not descended from the Arabs of Arabia, but who have been assimilated into Arab culture and who speak Arabic as their native tongue.

ʿArafāt (also ʿArafa): a plain some 13 miles east of Mecca. Essential parts of the *ḥajj* pilgrimage ceremonies occur there, centered on a small granite hill, also known by the same name.

ʿashīra (pl. *ʿashāʾir*): an agnatic group. The word is commonly translated as tribe. An *ʿashīra* is composed of several *afkhādh* (q.v.), while several *ʿashāʾir* form a single qabīla (q.v.).

badana: an animal, commonly a camel, to be offered for sacrifice by a pilgrim at the *ḥajj* (q.v.).

baraka: blessing, in particular that divine force that enables prosperity and happiness. Persons of great piety or holiness are believe suffused with *baraka*, which radiates from them to those around them.

Bakka: an ancient alternative or original name for Mecca. In legend, the name comes from the Arabic verb *bakā*, he wept, applied to Adam's sadness at descending to the barren environment of Arabia after his expulsion from paradise.

baṭn (pl. *buṭūn*): an agnatic group smaller than a *qabīla* (q.v.) but larger than a *fakhdh* (q.v.).

dafʿ: the word used to denote the act of departure from ʿArafāt during the pilgrimage rites.

fakhdh (pl. *afkhādh*): a group of several families claiming descent from the same ancestor.

al-fajr: the dawn; also the superogatory prayer, recommended but not required, performed immediately after dawn. It consists of two *rakʿāt* (q.v.) to be recited audibly.

faṣīla (pl. *faṣāʾil*): an agnatic group consisting of the nearest members of one's *ʿashīra* (q.v.).

ghazwa (pl. *ghazawāt*): armed engagements in which the Prophet Muḥammad participated personally. Those he initiated but without his own direct participation are known as *sarāyā* (pl. of *sariyya*).

ḥadīth (pl. *aḥādīth*): a saying, reported action or anecdote relating the words or deeds of the Prophet Muḥammad. An *isnād* (q.v.) precedes the *ḥadīth* and lists the persons by whom the reported material was transmitted.

ḥadīth marfūʿ: a *ḥadīth* related by one of the Companions of the Prophet (see *ṣāḥib*) and quoted directly from the latter.

ḥāfiẓ (pl. *ḥufāẓ*): a person who has memorized the entire *Qurʾān*. Also one of the sacred attributes – the Guardian, the Protector – by which God is known.

ḥajj: the pilgrimage to the holy places of Mecca set annually to take place in the first half of the month of *Dhū al-Ḥijja*.

ḥanīf: 1) a devout pre-Islamic monotheis. 2) a person sincerely searching for the ancient religion practised by Abraham, with whom the word is particularly associated.

ḥanīfiyya: the religion of Abraham and the *ḥanīfs*.

ḥaram (or *ḥarām*): a term denoting what is sacred, forbidden or inviolable.

ḥijāba: the office of the custodian of the *kaʿba*; he is known as the *ḥājib*.

ḥijra (or hegira): the emigration of the Prophet Muḥammad and his supporters from Mecca into exile in Medina. The date of this event was later adopted as the commencement of the Muslim era, calculated as 622 AD.

ijāza: 1) rendering something legal or permissible. 2) the act of transmitting a *ḥadīth* and attributing the same to an authority without actually having heard that person recite it.

ifāḍa: the movement or departure or pilgrims from ʿArafāt following their performance of the *wuqūf*, 'the standing'.

iḥrām: 1) the rendering sacred or inviolate. 2) the name given to the clothing donned by Muslims entering the *iḥrām* state prior to their participation in the pilgrimage.

isnād: the prefatory material to a *ḥadīth* (q.v.) that lists the sequence of scholars or witnesses who transmitted the account from the time of the Prophet Muḥammad up to the time when it was written down.

izār: the cloth that covers the pilgrim from waist to knees when he commits himself to the sacred state of *iḥrām*.

jāhiliyya: denoting childlike foolishness or ignorance, the word is commonly applied to the period prior to the advent of Islam.

jamra (pl. *jamrāt*): ancient stone pillars symbolizing Satan at Minā. These are pelted with pebbles during the pilgrimage rites, the stones being known as *jamrāt*.

kaʿba: the ancient cube-like structure within the great mosque in Mecca positioned some feet from the sacred spring *zamzam* (q.v.). It is towards this site that Muslims direct their prayers (see *qibla*).

al-Khalīl: 1) a town, also known as Hebron, some 32 miles south of Jerusalem and the site of the Tomb of the Patriarchs, sacred both to Jews and to Muslims. 2) a name or attribute implying close friend or confidant; the word is particularly associated with Abraham.

liwāʾ: 1) a flag, banner or signpost. 2) the issuance of this to those making the pilgrimage to the *kaʿba*.

maqām Ibrāhīm: the 'station' of Abraham. A sanctuary positioned a few feet from the *kaʿba* where Abraham and his co-religionaries would stand for prayer during the summer months.

maghrib: the west or direction in which the sun sets. Also, the fourth canonical Islamic prayer performed at dusk. It consists of three *rakʿāt*; at the first two of these the prayers are spoken audibly, the third in silence.

masjid: the place where the Muslim prostrates in prayer, usually a mosque.

Minā: a location some four miles east of Mecca on the road to ʿArafāt.

ḥadīth mursal: a *ḥadīth* which is considered by scholars to have a fault or inconsistency in the chain of its transmission.

al-Muzdalifa: a location some half way between Minā and ʿArafāt. It is there that pilgrims returning from ʿArafāt spend the night.

nadwa: the act of presiding over assemblies of pilgrims at the *kaʿba*.

parasang: a Persian term for a unit of length, also known as a *farsakh*. One *parasang* equals approximately one league, some three miles, that is.

qabīla (pl. *qabāʾil*): a large agnatic group whose members trace descent from a single ancestor. Often translated as tribe. A *qabīla* is larger than an *ʿashīra* (q.v.) but smaller than a *shaʿb* (q.v.).

qāḍī: a judge appointed by a Muslim community to administer and adjudicate issues of Islamic law.

qibla: the direction to which a Muslim faces when praying. Initially towards Jerusalem but later changed by the Prophet Muḥammad so that Muslims would face Mecca and the *kaʿba* there.

rakʿa (pl. *rakʿāt*): a unit of prayer consisting of a variety of gestures and postures. These *rakʿāt* total 17 each day, divided between the five canonical prayer periods.

al-raḥīm: The All-Compassionate; one of the sublime epithets applied to God.

al-raḥmān: the All-Merciful; one of the sublime epithets applied to God.

Ramaḍān: the ninth month of the Muslim lunar calendar. The month of fasting, it was during *Ramaḍān* that divine revelation first came to the Prophet Muḥammad, and it is therefore particularly venerated.

ridāʾ: a length of unsewn cloth that is draped over the left shoulder and around the torso of the pilgrim. This garb is donned by the pilgrim when he enters the *iḥrām* state.

rifāda: the provision of pilgrims with wheat and raisins by certain members of Quraysh of Mecca.

al-saʿy: the ritual rapid walk or jog performed during the pilgrimage between al-Ṣafā and al-Marwa.

sabaʾ: the community and kingdom ruling South-West Arabia for centuries prior to the mission of the Prophet Muḥammad.

ṣāḥib (pl. *aṣḥāb, ṣaḥāba*): companion; that community of men who knew and supported the Prophet Muḥammad during his mission.

ṣaḥīḥ: a *ḥadīth* (q.v.) the chain of transmission of which is considered by Muslim scholars to be reliable beyond any reasonable doubt; also, a collection comprised only of such *aḥādīth*.

samʿan: the receipt of a *ḥadīth* (q.v.) from a scholar by listening to him or her recite it and then repeating it back. This method of transmitting and receiving a *ḥadīth* was considered the most trustworthy of all.

shaʿb (pl. *shuʿūb*): a tribal group larger than a *qabīla* (q.v.); a nation, race or people.

shahāda: the profession of faith in Islam by reciting in Arabic the words: 'There is no God but God and Muḥammad is His Messenger'.

shaykh (pl. *shuyūkh*): an elderly man; a tribal or spiritual leader; a distinguished and devout scholar.

shīʿa: the doctrine and its adherent, a *shīʿī*, that considers ʿAlī, son of Abū Ṭālib and husband of the Prophet Muḥammad's daughter Fāṭima, was the legitimate spiritual and political heir to the Caliphate of Islam.

sunna: the body of recorded words, actions, gestures and practices of the Prophet Muḥammad. This material constitutes the second foundation of Islam and its legal system, the holy Qurʾān being the first and prime source. In the plural form, *sunan*, reference is made to the compilation, by various authorities of the reported words and actions of the Prophet.

tafsīr: exegesis and commentary, particularly applied to the Qurʾān.

tasmiyya: the enunciation by a Muslim of the formula: 'In the name of God, the All-Merciful, the All-Compassionate' prior to any act or activity in which he or she might engage.

ṭawāf: ritual circumambulation of a religious site, normally the *kaʿba*.

tubbaʿ (pl. *tabābiʿa*): the title applied to the kings of pre-Islamic Yemen.

wuḍūʾ: the ritual ablution necessarily practiced by Muslims prior to their performance of prayer.

zamzam: the sacred well positioned close to the *kaʿba* (q.v.) within the *ḥarām al-sharīf*, the sacred enclosure encompassing the great mosque in Mecca. Muslims believe the well to have been miraculously opened through the agency of Gabriel to provide water for Abraham's wife Hagar and their son Ishmael.

INDEX

This index gives the names of all persons and places mentioned in the text, except for those to whom only passing and minimal reference is made. In some cases Ibn Kathīr refers to an individual by several different names. For example, Abū ᶜUmar b. ᶜAbd al-Barr is sometimes referred to by that name, and elsewhere by the abbreviation Ibn ᶜAbd al-Barr, or even Abū ᶜUmar. These alternative referents are listed here with cross references where appropriate. In some cases Ibn Kathīr gives an honorific – for example, Abū Ṭālib (Ṭālib's father) – by which that person, usually of great fame, was commonly known, sometimes without further full designation anywhere in the text. Such names are listed in this index as they appear in the body of the work. Place names are listed here in full, with the exceptions of Mecca and Medina, to which cities there are innumerable references throughout.

It has been seen as unnecessarily cumbersome to index certain prime sources for Ibn Kathīr's work – such as Ibn Isḥaq – to whom reference is made on almost every page. Similarly, quotations given from the Qurʾān are cited in full in the text, but without separate listings in this index.

S

CENTER FOR MUSLIM CONTRIBUTION TO CIVILIZATION

The Center for Muslim Contribution to Civilization, a non-government, non-profit making cultural organization, strives to lead Muslims and non-Muslims alike to a better understanding of the Muslim contribution to civilization and to a better knowledge of Islam.

Located in Doha, State of Qatar, the Center has the warm support of its patron, the Emir of Qatar, H.H. Sheikh Hamad Bin Khalifa Al-Thani. Presenting accurate translations of some of the best known works of the most eminent Muslim savants, spanning the 800 years of the classical period of Islamic civilization (*c*. 620 AD to *c*. 1500 AD), since its establishment in 1983 the Center has produced nine volumes covering five major works in different fields of knowledge.

For further information on the work of the Center, all correspondence should be directed to

The General Supervisor
Center for Muslim Contribution to Civilization
P.O. Box 327
Doha
State of Qatar
Arabian Gulf